Functional
Soft Tissue
Examination
and Treatment
by Manual Methods

The Extremities

Warren I. Hammer, DC, MS, DABCO
Chiropractic Center
Norwalk, Connecticut

AN ASPEN PUBLICATION®
Aspen Publishers, Inc.
Gaithersburg, Maryland
1991

Library of Congress Cataloging-in-Publication Data

Hammer, Warren I.
Functional soft tissue examination and treatment by manual methods:
the extremities / Warren I. Hammer.
p. cm.
Includes bibliographical references.
Includes index.
ISBN: 0-8342-0185-2
1. Chiropractic — Diagnosis. 2. Extremities — Diseases — Diagnosis.
I. Title. [DNLM: 1. Biomechanics. 2. Chiropractic — methods.
3. Connective Tissue Diseases — diagnosis.
4. Connective Tissue Diseases — therapy.
5. Extremities. WB 905 H224f]
RZ250.H36   1990
615.5'34 — dc20
DNLM/DLC
for Library of Congress
90-1047
CIP

Aspen Publishers, Inc., grants permission for photocopying for limited personal or
internal use. This consent does not extend to other kinds of copying, such as
copying for general distribution, for advertising or promotional purposes, for
creating new collective works, or for resale. For information, address Aspen
Publishers, Inc., Permissions Department, 200 Orchard Ridge Drive, Suite 200,
Gaithersburg, Maryland 20878.

The authors have made every effort to ensure the accuracy of the information herein,
particularly with regard to technique and procedure. However, appropriate information sources should be consulted, especially for new or unfamiliar procedures. It is the
responsibility of every practitioner to evaluate the appropriateness of a particular opinion in the context of actual clinical situations and with due consideration to new
developments. Authors, editors, and the publisher cannot be held responsible for any
typographical or other errors found in this book.

Editorial Services: Ruth Bloom

Library of Congress Catalog Card Number: 90-1047
ISBN: 0-8342-0185-2

Printed in the United States of America

1 2 3 4 5

To the women in my life:
My wife *Martha*
for her joy, love, and understanding,
and
my daughters *Mel* and *Deb*
for their support and enthusiasm

Table of Contents

Contributors

Mary Kay Campbell, PT
Private Practice
Formerly, Clinical Education Coordinator
Orthopedic Arthroscopic and Sport Injury Specialists
San Diego, California

Joseph A. Cimino, BS, DC
Postgraduate Faculty Member
New York Chiropractic College
Old Brookville, New York
Instructor
Western States Chiropractic College
Portland, Oregon

Ian H. Fraser, BA, MSc, PhD
Associate Professor and Assistant Director
Division of Biological Sciences
Canadian Memorial Chiropractic College
Department of Physiology and Biochemistry
Toronto, Ontario, Canada

Peter A. Gale, DC
Needham Chiropractic Associates P.C.
Needham, Massachusetts

Warren I. Hammer, DC, MS, DABCO
Private Practice
The Chiropractic Center
Norwalk, Connecticut
Formerly, Faculty Member and Postgraduate Faculty
  Member

New York Chiropractic College
Old Brookville, New York
Postgraduate Faculty
Cleveland Chiropractic College
Los Angeles, California

H. Stephen Injeyan, BSc, MSc, PhD, DC
Associate Professor and Director
Division of Biological Science
Department of Physiology and Biochemistry
Canadian Memorial Chiropractic College
Toronto, Ontario, Canada

John C. Lowe, MA, DC
Postgraduate Faculty
Northwestern College of Chiropractic
Bloomington, Minnesota
Cleveland Chiropractic College
Los Angeles, California
Faculty, Motion Palpation Institute
Huntington Beach, California
Private Practice
Houston, Texas

John Mennell, MD
Clinical Professor of Osteopathic Medicine
Michigan State University
East Lansing, Michigan
Retired
Advance, North Carolina

Daniel Mühlemann, PT, DC
Private Practice
Lecturer
College of Physical Therapy
Triemli City Hospital
Zurich, Switzerland

W.D. Peek, BSc, PhD
Formerly, Associate Professor
Canadian Memorial Chiropractic College
Department of Anatomy
Toronto, Ontario, Canada

Andrew H. Rice, DPM, FACFS
Department of Surgery
Norwalk Hospital
Park City Hospital
Norwalk, Connecticut
Bridgeport Surgical Center
VA Medical Center
West Haven, Connecticut

Joseph J. Smolders, BA, DC
Private Practice
Toronto, Ontario, Canada

Preface

Almost every week in my office a patient complains of an extremity problem, stating that her doctor told her that she had a tendinitis, bursitis, arthritis, and so on. Upon questioning as to how the doctor determined that it was a "tendinitis," the patient says that the doctor "just felt" the painful area. Of course patients cannot be relied upon to remember all the physical tests performed by their physicians, but after they receive a functional soft tissue examination on their painful lesion they invariably state that they previously were not examined in such a manner. Often, their entrance diagnosis of "tendinitis," "bursitis," or "arthritis" is based only on their case history and palpation and not on a functional examination that truly differentiates the tissues causing the pain.

Manual treatment of soft tissue lesions is more effective if the practitioner can determine the exact tissue or tissues that are involved. For that matter, medical treatment is certainly more effective if the exact tissue is known. Much too often therapy is automatically applied to the most tender area, which is not necessarily the source of the pain. Ellis[1] performed an experiment comparing the results of injection into shoulder lesions. The first group was injected into the most tender area and the second group was injected in the tissue diagnosed by functional soft tissue examination. The results showed that if tenderness was used as the guide 29% of the cases became asymptomatic after treatment but that when anatomic analysis was used 73% became asymptomatic. Is it not more logical to differentiate a subscapular tendinitis from a biceps tendinitis by comparing the resisted testing of the biceps to that of the subscapularis? Is it not more logical to diagnose a patella

tendinitis by painful resisted leg extension than by only the tenderness found at the inferior pole of the patella? Clearly, any treatment on areas not specifically designated as the source of the pain becomes a generalized approach requiring the "treat and pray" method. Palpation for tenderness, crepitus, swelling, and the like is of course essential, and at times palpation for maximum tenderness must be relied upon (see Chapter 1, Tenderness and Palpation section). Emphasizing functional examination leads us to more reliable treatment of the dysfunction rather than the pain.

Because manual treatment represents a conservative, drugless method of healing, the premise of this book is to explain a functional examination of the extremities and to demonstrate and relate this examination to conditions treatable by manual methods. This is not to imply that drugs, surgery, and sophisticated methods of examination are not necessary. On the contrary, if conservative methods are not applicable, more aggressive methods must be utilized.

The first half of the book begins with an introduction to soft tissue analysis, the pathology of soft tissue, the pertinent anatomy and biomechanics of the extremities, and the functional examination of the extremities. At the end of the extremity chapters are charts that allow the practitioner to relate easily the examination findings to the lesions. The second half of the book is written by experts in particular methods of manual treatment, and there is a final chapter on rehabilitation.

With the explosion of present-day knowledge, no professional reference book or textbook is large enough to include all methods of examination and treatment. This book attempts to explain a logical method of examining soft tissues, including pertinent specific testing procedures and reliable manual treatment methods that have stood the test of time. Most of the lesions discussed are those that may be amenable to manual treatment. All methods of manual treatment and rehabilitation are not included, nor does this text discuss the taking of a detailed case history and its analysis, which is absolutely essential. Neurologic problems are only discussed in relation to the differential diagnosis of the conditions presented.

REFERENCE

1. Ellis RW. Shoulder tendinitis and injection therapy. *J Orthop Med.* 1986;3:2–3.

Warren I. Hammer

Acknowledgments

Many have assisted me in the preparation of this book. I sincerely thank them for their time and participation:

To Evan Rashkoff, MD, for his generous editing of chapters 3 through 7;

To Lino Panetta, DC, and Gary Greenstein, DC, for their countless hours of research that a book such as this requires;

To my models, Andrew Kramer and Deborah Hammer Kramer, DC;

To David Bolinski, medical illustrator, and Rosemarie Stiller, photographer, who have helped enrich this text;

And finally to those who provided me with knowledge, inspiration, and support, such as Marino Passero, DC, Kenneth Passero, DC, Larry Lefkowitz, MD, Sheldon Delman, DC, Keith Overland, DC, Leonard J. Faye, DC, Donald Petersen, DC, Martha Sasser, Loretta Stock, the Chiropractic Knights, and my chiropractic office assistants Olive Duff, Cheryl Tovini, Tiffini Burden, Lauri Ragsdale, Lorraine Derivan, Lynn Maltas, Jennifer Richmond, and Marisa Macchiarulo.

Part **I**

Introduction

Chapter 1

Basics of Soft Tissue Examination

Warren I. Hammer

The prime purpose of examination is to determine the source of pain. To determine the source of pain in human soft tissue, we must assess the function of the tissue. Most books about extremity examination give the reader a list of physical tests and describe particular conditions. There is usually no logical order or explanation of the relationship of these tests to each other, and often many of the tests described are totally nonspecific.

For example, a widely accepted test for the hip is Patrick's test for fabere sign. The hip is stressed after being put into flexion, external rotation, and abduction. This test stresses the sacroiliac joint, the anterior capsule of the hip joint, the adductors, and the iliopsoas muscles, among others. It would be more informative and time-saving to test specifically the sacroiliac joint, hip joint, and related muscles individually.

Finkelstein's test is often directly related to de Quervain's disease, but the passive stretching of the extensor and abductor tissues of the thumb and first metacarpal also stresses the trapeziometacarpal joint, a common area of arthritis, or the radiodorsal aspect of the wrist, where an intersection syndrome may be present. To assess the function of the tissues involved in de Quervain's disease, it is essential to test the extensor pollicis brevis and abductor pollicis longus muscles because these are the musculotendinous areas that are causative, so that isometric muscle testing will elicit the pain. Tendinitis is always tender to palpation and painful on resistive testing. Tenderness may also be elicited with stretching.

There is no question that the contributions of Dr James Cyriax in *Diagnosis of Soft Tissue Lesions*, volume 1 of his *Textbook of Orthopaedic Medicine*, are of tremendous significance in the diagnosis of soft tissue lesions. Anyone familiar

with his *Textbook* will realize that his work has greatly influenced the present book. This book is an updated work that stresses soft tissue analysis and relates it to conservative manual methods of treatment and rehabilitation. Some of Cyriax's important contributions to soft tissue examination include his differential analysis of passive and contractile tissue and his discovery of the capsular pattern.

Nevertheless, Cyriax had a rather biased, rigid viewpoint regarding chiropractic and osteopathy. He accused both professions of accepting only one cause of disease: in the former, the subluxation, and in the latter, the osteopathic lesion. He did not acknowledge that both theories had been repudiated many years earlier by both professions. He never accepted fixation of the spine in relation to the apophyseal joints; in his opinion any fixation was solely an internal derangement (ie, of the disc). He described almost anyone other than a medical doctor who manipulated the spine as a layman who, when lucky, managed to jiggle a disc fragment into place but otherwise misled patients in a most reprehensible way.[1] Interestingly, the manipulations taught by him were general, nonspecific techniques designed to be learned during a weekend. Some of his followers to this day repeat verbatim his pronouncements and refuse to accept change.

PASSIVE AND CONTRACTILE SOFT TISSUE EXAMINATION

Passive Testing

Passive tissue refers to tissue that does not have its own contractile ability, such as joint capsules, bursae, fasciae, or ligaments. By definition, passive testing is neither active nor spontaneous and requires an examiner to perform the movement. After performing the passive motion tests, we cannot definitely incriminate the passive tissue until we test the contractile tissue. Passive movements stretch the muscular component at the end range and may be used to corroborate irritated contractile tissue. Passive motion also measures the range of joint motion and muscle flexibility and is used to evaluate joint play.

Because active motion stresses both the contractile and the passive tissue, active motion is best used as a guide to the status of the patient with regard to range of motion rather than as an assessment of tissue involvement. Although an active and passive motion producing pain in the same direction refers to passive tissue involvement, and although an active and passive motion producing pain in the opposite direction refers to contractile tissue involvement, it is more systematic to perform all the passive motions together and then all the contractile motions together. Normally, active motion is always less than passive motion because of the limitation created by the contracted muscle.

The assessment of passive testing is by evaluation of what is known as end feel or the feeling perceived by the examiner at the final stressed range of passive motion. Cyriax[2] distinguishes among six types of end feel:

1. bone-to-bone: a hard end feel; this is normal in elbow extension and abnormal in elbow flexion
2. soft tissue: normal tissue approximation with, for example, elbow, knee, or hip flexion; this is abnormal if less soft as a result of scar tissue, contracture, or arthrosis
3. spasm or "twang": results when passive movement stresses a fracture, inflamed joint, or metastasis; this is always abnormal
4. capsular: normally the firm end feel of a normal shoulder, hip, or knee at the end of rotation; it is abnormal if the capsular feeling is firmer than usual or associated with a decreased range of motion
5. springy block: indicates an intra-articular pathology such as loss of knee extension due to a torn meniscus or loose body and is always abnormal; a spinal fixation would elicit a springy block; loss of movement due to a muscular spasm may cause a springy bounce
6. empty feeling: occurs when the examiner feels that more movement is possible but the patient demands that the motion stop because of severe pain; may indicate anything from an acute bursitis to cancer and is always abnormal

Contractile Testing

Contractile tissue refers to the muscular component and also to the tendon stressed by its contracting muscle. The muscle belly, the musculotendinous junction, the body of the tendon, and the tendoperiosteal junction are all included. Cyriax developed methods of testing that help pinpoint which particular area is involved. He emphasized testing the muscle to elicit maximum strength while the joint is in its most relaxed, neutral position to reduce joint compression. Testing a muscle in its neutral position (eg, by using shoulder abduction with the arm at the side) eliminates the pain of impingement and instability. It would seem that muscle testing will create some joint stress even if the joint is in its most relaxed position. For this reason, passive testing should always be performed first to help rule out the passive joint structures. If the etiology of the condition is considered primarily contractile, it often pays to test the muscle in several ranges of its motion to determine whether it is involved at different angles.

Muscle testing that responds without pain and normal strength usually indicates a normal muscle. Pain associated with normal strength may indicate minor involvement of a muscle or tendon. Pain and weakness may indicate a more severe muscle or tendon lesion, but the pain may also be responsible for some of the weakness. Finally, weakness without pain may refer to a neurologic problem or a complete muscle or tendon rupture.

The history of a patient may reveal that the pain does not occur immediately after use of the extremity but possibly during or at the end of activity. Often one or two resisted muscle tests may not elicit pain. Repetitive loading (ie, testing 10 to 15 isometric contractions in a row) may be necessary to create the pain of which the patient complains. Sometimes the patient must be examined during or after activity to find the source of the pain, or the muscle may have to be examined in ranges other than the neutral position.

A functional examination attempts to examine the total function of the involved tissue to pinpoint the source of the pain. Stressing just one motion (eg, passive motion without resisted muscle testing) prevents complete differentiation of the tissues involved.

It is probably impossible to test functionally a particular tissue without stressing some adjoining related tissue, but most of the functional tests described are as specific as possible. The correlation of the positive and negative passive, resistive, and other additional tests allows the practitioner to reach a more precise conclusion.

It is difficult to imagine examining soft tissue without first distinguishing whether the passive or contractile tissue (or both) is involved. Nevertheless, in the United States even to this day most practitioners do not consciously attempt to make this distinction. Reports continue to be published that attempt to distinguish, for example, between a "stiff and painful shoulder" and "adhesive capsulitis." The "stiff and painful shoulder" includes conditions such as tendinitis, rotator cuff tears, and arthrosis of the joint. The adhesive capsulitis is described as showing limited motion both actively and passively. All the above could be distinguished simply by relating the examination to the differentiation of passive and contractile tissue.

The adhesive capsulitis of the shoulder would probably show on examination a loss of passive lateral rotation, glenohumeral abduction, and medial rotation with a harder end-feel than normal. Resistive testing of the associated shoulder muscles would probably test strong (unless there was atrophy) and painless. Elimination of the contractile forces by resisted isometric muscle testing and the finding of pain and limitation on the passive testing would automatically point to a capsular shoulder problem. Tendinitis and rotator cuff tears would be evaluated by isometric muscle testing, which would indicate pain and relative strength (tendinitis) or pain and weakness (tears). Of course radiology and other tests may be necessary to confirm the functional examination, but the logical distinction between passive and contractile tissue certainly points the examiner in a more definite direction.

Another obvious example of distinguishing between passive and contractile tissue in arriving at the source of pain is a sprain of the acromioclavicular ligament. This structure is made up completely of passive ligamentous tissue. It is an area not under muscular control. Passive testing such as passive abduction and passive horizontal adduction would create pain, whereas contractile testing of the shoulder cuff or adductor muscles would test painless.

CAPSULAR PATTERN

Another of Cyriax's great contributions to soft tissue analysis is his concept of the capsular and noncapsular pattern.[2] A capsular pattern refers to a particular sequence of passive limitation of motion in a joint controlled by muscles. If the entire capsule is shortened or inflamed, or if the synovial membrane lining the capsule by itself is inflamed, passive testing of the joint will demonstrate a proportional limitation of motion for that particular joint. For example, conditions that shorten the capsule, such as arthrosis or any type of arthritis that affects the capsule and synovium, will express a capsular pattern. Even acute conditions affecting only the synovium (eg, ligamentous knee injury) will cause a capsular limitation of motion due to the muscular spasm protecting the capsule. The capsular pattern in the knee and elbow is more limitation of flexion than extension. Every arthritic shoulder or, more commonly, an adhesive capsulitis will demonstrate more limitation of lateral rotation, less limitation of glenohumeral abduction, and least limitation of medial rotation compared to all the other motions. Every joint has its own particular pattern of capsular limitation; these are discussed separately in later chapters. If only a portion of the capsule is involved (shortened), only movements that stretch that portion of the capsule will be involved instead of a capsular pattern.

Many clinicians who may not be familiar with the capsular pattern confirm Cyriax's concept. Neviaser and Neviaser[3] describe shoulder limitation in adhesive capsulitis as restricted motion, both actively and passively, primarily in three planes: abduction or elevation, internal rotation, and external rotation. Mintz and Fraga[4] found the capsular pattern in the elbow to be more limiting of flexion than extension in foundry workers with osteoarthritis of the elbow. Fareed and Gallivan[5] mention that exquisite pain on external rotation was the most sensitive indicator of the presence of frozen shoulder syndrome. The earliest sign of the shoulder capsular pattern will be limitation of external rotation by itself.

On more than one occasion patients have been seen who are told that they have an "arthritic elbow." The full range of flexion and extension with bone-to-bone end feel on extension and soft tissue end feel on flexion with rare exceptions eliminates the diagnosis of arthritis. Often the same patient will exhibit pain on resisted wrist extension and abduction, which confirms a chronic lateral epicondylitis.

The noncapsular pattern refers to conditions that do not primarily affect the capsule. For example, acute bursitis will show more limitation of abduction than lateral rotation. A loose body in the elbow or knee will usually reveal more limitation of extension than flexion.

TENDERNESS AND PALPATION

The preface to this text discusses the importance of functional testing compared to treating the most tender area in regard to injection of shoulder lesions. Often tissues that are embryologically related will refer to the same area: for example, the shoulder capsule, bursa, supraspinatus, and infraspinatus, which are supplied mainly by C-5, will refer along the same sclerotome or dermatome and can all create similar tenderness at the deltoid tubercle or beyond. Chapter 11, on myofascial pain and dysfunction syndromes, describes how trigger points can give rise to referred pain that is not dermatomal, myotomal, or sclerotomal.

As important as tenderness is, we must rely first on a complete functional extremity examination of all the areas that can create the tenderness before we accept tenderness as the sine qua non. Anterior thigh pain demands at least a functional examination of the lumbar spine, hip, and knee. On particular occasions tenderness may be all that we have. For example, a chronic meniscus problem may not elicit pain on any of the meniscus stress tests, and we may have to rely on the history and localized tenderness at the joint line. Garrick and Webb[6] mention an apparent peroneal tendinitis revealed by pain on isometric testing of the peroneal muscles; but palpation of maximal tenderness just medial to the tendons may indicate a posterior ankle impingement due to an enlarged posterior process of the talus. Besides a functional extremity examination, pressing on an active trigger point or performing a specific intersegmental spinal or extremity joint play examination will all help us be more specific in our therapy. Sometimes friction could be used to anesthetize an area when we are in doubt (see Chapter 12). A functional examination that aggravates the tender spot should be performed before we attach major credence to the tender area.

A common example of an incomplete nonfunctional examination is the use of "shoulder impingement" syndrome as a diagnostic entity. Impingement, like whiplash, represents a mechanism of injury rather than a diagnosis. Various shoulder impingement tests are used to determine that something is impinged upon. Some physicians inject lidocaine into the subacromial area and, on finding less pain on the previously painful impingement signs, decide that there is something being pinched. The patient may even be relieved of symptoms, but a functional examination will help evaluate the specific area of impingement and possible causes of the impingement. While a radiologic examination may incriminate extrinsic causes such as an acromial spur, enlarged coracoid process, an abnormally curved or hooked acromion, acromioclavicular osteophytes, or tendon calcification, a functional examination can incriminate the intrinsic causes. For example, isometric resistive testing might incriminate the tenoperiosteal or musculotendinous portion of the supraspinatus, the infraspinatus, the subscapularis, the long head of the biceps, or the subacromial bursa. The cause of impingement may be discovered by a functional examination for shoulder instability or rotator cuff weakness.

Efficacious manual therapy depends on pinpoint accuracy. A complete functional examination will often give the practitioner a working diagnosis. Of course radiologic studies and tests (magnetic resonance imaging, computed tomography, arthrography, and the like) may be needed if the patient does not show early progress or if the interpretation of the functional examination is uncertain.

SPINAL RELATION TO EXTREMITY SOFT TISSUE LESIONS

The results on soft tissue extremity lesions by only manual adjustment of the spine are often dramatic, but extremity articular and peripheral muscular-fascial tissues also contribute to the source of somatic pain. Most research results have incriminated radicular causation as the reason for spinal manipulative results,[7-9] but empirically restoration of spinal mobility and function in itself is related to improving the homeostasis of the surrounding extremity soft tissue.[10-29] Interestingly, the relation of the spine to the somatoautonomic and somaticosomatic components has recently been "discovered" by the medical profession.[30]

The separation of the healing arts into those using medication and those using conservative, drugless methods has advanced the healing arts more rapidly than otherwise might have been the case. The drugless healers such as the chiropractors, naturopaths, physical therapists, and acupuncturists have been forced to concentrate their research and efforts toward restoring health without the use of drugs and their inevitable side effects. New and improved methods of manual treatment and rehabilitation are continually being developed.

STEROIDS AND SOFT TISSUE

It has been stated that limited controlled studies and extensive clinical experience support the efficacy of corticosteroids in the palliation of rheumatoid arthritis and other inflammatory musculoskeletal conditions.[31] Limited controlled studies and

extensive clinical experience over the last 90 years also support chiropractic and other conservative methods of healing. Nirschl[32(p639)] states "there are no scientific data to indicate that anti-inflammatory medications have a biologic healing stimulus." He separates pain relief from the promotion of healing. Healing of tissue is accomplished by restoring normal biomechanics through rehabilitation and the use of manual techniques as explained in this text. Nirschl[32] mentions three concepts to initiate a healing stimulus: (1) enhancement of peripheral aerobics (oxygenation, nutrition, and collateral circulation); (2) collagen induction, strengthening, and alignment; and (3) enhancement of biochemical changes associated with endurance training.

Some of the side effects of corticosteroids are avascular necrosis, especially of the hip,[33] which results from an adverse effect on lipid metabolism causing fatty emboli; tendon rupture due to the inhibition of the formation of healing adhesions, which results in weakening[34]; alteration of biomechanical ligamentous properties due to inhibition of the formation of granulation and connective tissue[35,36]; arthropathy due to softening of the subchondral bone, delay in chondroitin synthesis, and inhibition of the formation of ground substance in mesenchymal tissue (articular cartilage)[37]; vertebral osteoporosis[38]; infectious arthritis and bursitis[31]; and depressed mental status due to decreased corticoadrenal function.[39] Some of the articular damage has been attributed to steroid analgesia, which results in microtrauma[31] due to painless overuse.

Local injection of corticosteroids has proven to have a systemic effect on remote collagenous structures,[40] as evidenced by diminished joint swelling distant from the injected site, transient eosinopenia, and depression of plasma cortisol levels reflecting hypothalamic-pituitary-adrenal axis suppression.[31] Johnson[41] states that steroid injection at the wrist should be used only in the most select instances at the distal attachments of tendon to bone. Steroid injection into the most tender spot may produce rupture of the tendon or its insertion. Tendinitis is definitely relieved by injection of corticosteroids, but with tendinitis there is microtearing. A high concentration of steroid may relieve the pain and thereby allow an athlete to transform the microtear into a rupture. The achilles and patellar tendons are most often involved.[38]

Because of the adverse effects of corticosteroids on soft tissues and cartilage, it is important to know whether exercise or manipulation will have an adverse effect during or immediately after steroid therapy.[42] Further studies are needed. Medical doctors differ in their opinions about how often joints and soft tissue should receive steroids from a maximum of once every 1 to 3 months to a maximum of no more than once in the course of a treatment program.[32,43] They also state that tendon injection should be in the sheath and never into the tendon.[41]

CHART INTERPRETATION

At the end of the chapters on extremity examination are functional diagnosis charts, which correlate the functional tests with the lesions. Plus (+) means that pain will probably occur from a specific test. For example, lateral epicondylitis cannot be diagnosed without pain on resisted wrist extension, and a diagnosis of supraspinatus tendinitis requires pain on resisted shoulder abduction.

Plus/minus (+ / −), or possible pain, is used to indicate that either related or unrelated tests may or may not aggravate the involved tissue. Other tests not directly related to the source of the pain may aggravate the tissue as well. Of course some of these tests may be related to the source of the pain and also may or may not be painful depending on the severity of the condition. For example, an infraspinatus tendinitis is always painful on resisted lateral rotation (+). Depending on the size of the lesion passive medial rotation (stretching of the infraspinatus) may or may not be painful (+ / −), and stressing the coracoacromial ligament by way of the coracoacromial impingement test may or may not always aggravate the infraspinatus tendon.

Possible limited range of motion on passive testing is indicated by L. The limited movement will have an abnormal end feel. The term *possible* limited range of motion is used because if L refers to a capsular pattern then all the ranges of limitation of the capsular pattern may not be present. In the knee under *meniscus* the top four passive motions may show an L, but depending on the site of the meniscal tear possibly only one, or all, or none of the motions may be limited. If a condition is acute, there will possibly be more limitation (L) than if the condition is chronic.

Possible laxity of ligamentous tissue is indicated by LAX. Again, the term *possible* is used depending on the extent of the ligamentous sprain.

Each chart presupposes that an adequate history was taken and that appropriate laboratory and radiologic studies were utilized. It is also assumed that the area of involvement was inspected and put through active motions to determine the allowable level of motion. It should also be noted that inflammatory conditions (eg, bursitis) affect both passive and contractile elements on testing, which leads to many pluses and minuses in both the passive and contractile sections of the chart. Often, as the inflammation subsides, retesting allows us to pinpoint the specific causative lesion if there is one.

It may help practitioners new to these procedures to hang the charts in their examining room until they have memorized the tests and their significance.

REFERENCES

1. Potter GE. On experts and empire-builders. *J Can Chiropr Assoc.* 1982;26:57–59.

2. Cyriax J. *Textbook of Orthopaedic Medicine.* London: Bailliere-Tindall; 1982;1:52–56.

3. Neviaser RJ, Neviaser TJ. The frozen shoulder, diagnosis and management. *Clin Orthop Relat Res.* 1987;223:61.

4. Mintz G, Fraga A. Severe osteoarthritis of the elbow in foundry workers. *Arch Environ Health.* 1973;27:78.

5. Fareed DO, Gallivan WR. Office management of frozen shoulder syndrome. Treatment with hydraulic distension under local anesthesia. *Clin Orthop Relat Res.* 1989;242:178.

6. Garrick JG, Webb DR. Overuse injuries—assessment and management. In: *Sports Injuries: Diagnosis and Management.* Philadelphia: WB Saunders; 1990:30–31.

7. Jackson R. *The Cervical Syndrome.* 2nd ed. Springfield, Ill: Charles C Thomas; 1958:174.

8. Cinquegrana OD. Chronic cervical radiculitis and its relationship to "chronic bursitis." *Am J Phys Med.* 1968;47:23.

9. Massey EW, Rilely TL, Pleet AB. Coexistent carpal tunnel syndrome and cervical radiculopathy (double crush syndrome). *South Med J.* 1981; 74:957–959.

10. Illi FW. The statics and dynamics of the spine and pelvis in health and disease. *J Natl Chirop Assoc.* 1951;13–15.

11. Wells P. Cervical dysfunction and shoulder problems. *Physiotherapy.* 1982;68:66–73.

12. Illi FW. *Highlights of 45 years of experience and 35 years of research.* Geneva: Institute for the Study of the Statics and Dynamics of the Human Body; 1970.

13. Grice A. A preliminary study of muscle tone, changes pre and post manipulation. *J Can Chirop Assoc.* 1974;18.

14. Janse J, Kissinger RN. The relationship of the mechanical integrity of the feet, lower extremities, pelvis and spine to the proper function of the various structural and visceral systems of the body. *J Natl Coll Chirop.* 1954;26:6–9.

15. Wickes D. Effects of thoracolumbar spinal manipulation on arterial flow in the lower extremity. *J Manip Physiol Ther.* 1980;3:1.

16. Jessen AR. Chiropractic is the treatment of choice for bursitis. *J Chirop.* 1967;4:33–36.

17. Arkuszewski Z. Joint blockage: a disease, a syndrome or a sign? *Man Med.* 1988;3:132–134.

18. Grieve GP. *Common Vertebral Joint Problems.* Edinburgh: Churchill Livingstone; 1981:188.

19. Farrow RC. Shoulder pain and stiffening. *Physiotherapy.* 1961; 47:326.

20. Gunn CC, Milbrandt WE. Tennis elbow and the cervical spine. *Can Med Assoc J.* 1976;114:803–809.

21. Ebbetts J. Autonomic pain in the upper limb. *Physiotherapy.* 1971;57:270.

22. Greenman PE. Manipulative therapy in relation to total health care. In: Korr IM, ed. *The Neurobiologic Mechanisms in Manipulative Therapy.* New York: Plenum; 1977:47.

23. Lewitt K. *Manipulative Therapy in Rehabilitation of the Motor System.* London: Butterworths; 1985:25.

24. Cibulka MT, Rose SJ, Delitto A, et al. Hamstring muscle strain treated by mobilizing the sacroiliac joint. *Phys Ther.* 1989;666:1220–1223.

25. Muckle DS. Associated factors in recurrent groin and hamstring injuries. *Br J Sports Med.* 1982;16:37–39.

26. Gunn CC, Milbrandt WE. Tenderness at motor points: an aid in the diagnosis of pain in the shoulder referred from the cervical spine. *J Am Osteopath Assoc.* 1977;77:196.

27. Kellgren JH. On the distribution of pain arising from deep somatic structures with charts of segmental pain areas. *Clin Sci.* 1939;4:35.

28. Korr IM. Clinical significance of the facilitated state: symposium on the functional implications of segmental facilitation. *J Am Osteopath Assoc.* 1955;54:265–282.

29. Wall P. The mechanisms of pain associated with cervical vertebral disease. In: *Cervical Pain, Proceedings of the International Symposium.* Oxford: Pergamon; 1971.

30. Arkuszewski Z. Editorial. *J Man Med.* 1989;4:42–43.

31. Gray RG, Gottlieb NL. Intra-articular corticosteroids: an updated assessment. *J Orthop Relat Res.* 1983;177:235–263.

32. Nirschl RP. Soft-tissue injuries about the elbow. *Clin Sports Med.* 1986;5:639.

33. Fisher DE, Bickel WH. Corticosteroid-induced avascular necrosis. *J Bone Joint Surg Am.* 1971;53:859.

34. Kapetanos G. The effect of the local corticosteroids on the healing and biomechanical properties of the partially injured tendon. *Clin Orthop Relat Res.* 1982;163:170–179.

35. Barfred T. Achilles tendon rupture. *Acta Orthop Scand.* 1973:152.

36. Behrens F, Shephard N, Mitchell N. Alteration of rabbit articular cartilage by intra-articular injection of glucocorticoids. *J Bone Joint Surg Am.* 1975;57:70.

37. Bentley G, Goodfellow JW. Disorganisation of the knees following intra-articular hydrocortisone injections. *J Bone Joint Surg Br.* 1969;51:498–504.

38. Sweetnam R. Editorial and annotations, corticosteroid arthropathy and tendon rupture. *J Bone Joint Surg Br.* 1969;51:397.

39. Hench PS, Kendall EL, Slocumb CH, et al. Effects of cortisone acetate and pituitary ACTH on rheumatoid arthritis, rheumatic fever and certain other conditions. *Arch Intern Med.* 1950;85:545–666.

40. Melmed EP. Spontaneous bilateral rupture of the calcaneal tendon during steroid therapy. *J Bone Joint Surg Br.* 1965;47:104.

41. Johnson RK. Soft-tissue injuries of the forearm and hand. *Clin Sports Med.* 1986;5:704.

42. McDonough AL. Effects of corticosteroids on articular cartilage. A review of the literature. *Phys Ther.* 1982;62:835–839.

43. Parkes JC. Overuse injuries of the elbow. In: Nicholas JA, Hershman EB, eds. *The Upper Extremity in Sports Medicine.* St Louis, Mo: Mosby; 1990:336.

Chapter 2

Pathology of Musculoskeletal Soft Tissues

H. Stephen Injeyan, Ian H. Fraser, and W.D. Peek

In discussing the pathologic aspects and healing of soft tissue structures associated with the musculoskeletal system, it is important that we first have an overview of their biochemical, anatomic, and histologic organization. Evidently, the repair mechanisms as well as the success of the repair response depend on the nature of the tissue in terms of its biochemistry, structural organization, vascularity, and nervous connections. Further, it is necessary to decide which tissues to include in the discussion because the term *soft tissue* is quite nonspecific. For example, it could include nerve, muscle, vascular structures, tendon, ligament, joint capsule, and generalized space-filling connective tissues. Because the objective of this book is to provide basic information regarding tissues that in case of injury may respond to manipulative therapy, this chapter is limited to discussion of skeletal muscle, tendon, myotendon junction, and ligament.

BIOCHEMISTRY OF SOFT TISSUE COMPONENTS

Connective tissue is composed of a number of specialized protein macromolecules. Collagen is present in largest amounts and acts to maintain shape and to resist stress. Tissues with elastic properties may also contain elastin and microfibrillar proteins. Fibronectin and proteoglycans hold these fibers together in the extracellular matrix. The assembly and properties of these components are discussed separately; muscle components are described in the appropriate microanatomy sections.

Collagen

Structure and Synthesis

Collagen provides an extracellular framework of considerable tensile strength. The basic unit of collagen is made up of three closely intertwined polypeptide chains forming a triple-helical structure 300 nm long and 1.5 nm in diameter. It has been postulated that five of these align in a quarter-staggered fashion to produce a microfibril 3.5 nm thick.[1] End-to-end and lateral aggregation leads to formation of a fibril ranging from 60 to 175 nm in diameter. Several fibrils associate to form fibers. These processes are presented diagramatically in Fig. 2-1.

Single procollagen α-polypeptide chains are synthesized in fibroblasts. Hydroxylation of specific proline and lysine residues occurs in the endoplasmic reticulum.[1] Addition of galactose and glucose to specific hydroxylysine residues by glycosyltransferases then takes place. The extent of these posttranslation modifications depends on the time it takes for the three α chains to align and form a tight triple-helical structure. After secretion, the nonhelical segments at each end, which had served to align the individual chains, are removed by appropriate peptidase action. Then the long, thin, rod-shaped tropocollagen molecules align to form highly ordered

This chapter is dedicated to the memory of *W. Peek*, a dear friend and an excellent teacher, whose untimely death came during the preparation of this manuscript.

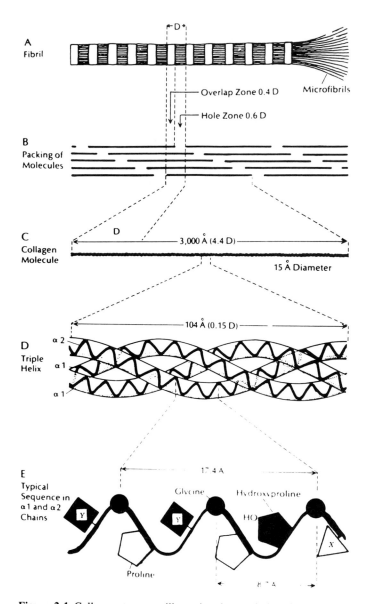

Figure 2-1 Collagen structure, illustrating the regularity of primary sequence, the left-handed α helix, the right-handed triple helix, the 300-nm molecule, and the organization of molecules in a typical fibril, within which the collagen molecules are cross-linked. *Source:* Figure by B. Tagawa. Reprinted with permission from *Hospital Practice* (1977;12:61), Copyright © 1977, HP Publishing Company.

arrays called fibrils, which in turn aggregate to form the larger collagen fibers. Lysyl oxidase converts lysine and hydroxylysine residues to allysine and hydroxyallysine, respectively. These aldehyde groups are chemically reactive and form various covalent linkages.[2] Acid-labile bands are replaced by more stable adducts after a period of time. These covalent cross-links lock the fibrils together and give the collagen mechanical stability.

Types

Distinct fibrillar structures of collagen are found in specific tissues. These variations are due to differences in the subunit α

chains. Only the major forms of the 12 genetic types of collagen so far discovered are discussed.[3]

Type I collagen, the most abundant form, is made up of two α-1(I) chains and an α-2 chain (Fig. 2-1). This type has a low content of hydroxylysine and carbohydrate and forms broad fibrils with diameters as large as 400 to 500 nm. It is the predominant collagen in bone, skin, ligament, and tendon. Type II collagen consists of 3 α-1(II) chains and has a high content of hydroxylysine and carbohydrate. Fibrils formed are thinner than type I and are usually found in cartilage, nucleus pulposus, and the vitreous body.

Type III collagen (three α-1(III) monomers) has a high content of hydroxyproline but is low in hydroxylysine and carbohydrate. Interchain disulfides may occur at the carboxyl end of the helix. It forms reticular fibers that are of small diameter (50 nm). It predominates in pliable organs such as blood vessels, the uterus, and the gastrointestinal tract and is often associated with type I fibers. Its content is not detectable in tendon but may be as high as 9% to 12% in ligaments.[2] It also appears in embryonic development and during the healing process. Type IV collagen consists of α-1(IV) and α-2(IV) chains. There is a high content of hydroxylysine residues, many of which are fully glycosylated. The alanine content is low, and 3-hydroxyproline is also present. The procollagen extension pieces are retained, and monomers are linked by disulfide bonds. This type is the major structural component of basement membranes and forms a scaffolding to which proteins such as laminin and heparan sulfate proteoglycan may bind.[4]

Elastin

Pulled elastin fibers stretch, but when tension is released they return to their original shape. These fibers consist of an elastin core embedded in and coated with microfibrillar proteins. Elastin is synthesized in fibroblasts as proelastin subunits of 72,000 molecular weight (MW). Although the glycine content is the same (33%), the overall amino acid composition is quite different from that of collagen. There are more hydrophobic residues such as valine and alanine, less proline and hydroxyproline, and no hydroxylysine. This hydrophobic molecule is not glycosylated and does not form a triple-helical structure.

After secretion, specific lysyl groups are modified by extracellular lysyl oxidase. The proelastin monomers bind to the microfibrillar network and coalesce, forming the interior of the elastin fiber. Three reactive aldehydes and a lysyl group that are near each other react, forming desmosine and isodesmosine adducts. Each chain is linked to many others by these cross-links, resulting in a complex three-dimensional network. Intervening sequences form helical coils that may be stretched, accounting for the remarkable elastic properties of these fibers.[5,6]

Proteoglycans

Proteoglycans are negatively charged glycoproteins containing as much as 95% carbohydrate. They bind strongly to cations and water, forming a viscous gel. This heterogeneous, hydrophobic, gelatinous matrix, in which other connective tissue components are embedded, gives a tissue elasticity and resistance to compression.

Proteoglycan aggregates contain three major molecules. Hyaluronic acid, a polymer of glucuronic acid and glucosamine, forms the thin central core to which are attached the proteoglycan subunits via specific binding sites, forming a configuration resembling a bottlebrush.[7] The subunits contain keratan sulfate and chondroitin sulfate oligosaccharide chains covalently attached to a polypeptide backbone. The large amount of carbohydrate and the presence of negatively charged sugar and sulfate groups make the aggregates hydrophilic. They bind collagen specifically and may regulate the thickness of collagen fibers. Furthermore they interact with other extracellular matrix components.[4]

Fibronectin

Extracellular matrix fibronectin consists of two different subunits of 200,000 and 250,000 MW. It has specific binding sites for collagen, proteoglycans, and cell gangliosides and hence acts as a glue interacting with cells and the extracellular matrix components.[4]

MICROSCOPIC ANATOMY OF SOFT TISSUES

Skeletal Muscle

Muscular tissues are highly specialized to perform one major function: contraction. As such, these tissues provide motive forces wherever they are required in the body. Individual muscle cells are elongate structures and are often referred to as fibers. The prefixes *sarco-* and *myo-* are used to denote a relationship to muscle. Thus the plasmalemma of muscle fibers is termed *sarcolemma*, the cytoplasm *sarcoplasm*, the endoplasmic reticulum *sarcoplasmic reticulum*, and the mitochondria *sarcosomes*. Individual muscle fibers are often termed *myofibers* and the contractile filaments *myofilaments*. The available literature regarding the structure and function of skeletal muscle is extremely large. This review attempts to outline only major features and is based largely on other, more complete review articles assembled by Engel and Banker.[8]

General Histology and Ultrastructure

Muscles are bound together by connective tissue in a manner that permits some freedom of movement of fibers internally and provides structural continuity with associated structures (eg, tendon and periosteum). The entire muscle is surrounded by the epimysium, a sheath of connective tissue that is continuous with overlying deep fascia (Fig. 2-2). Thin septa of connective tissue extend inwardly from this sheath and subdivide the muscle into bundles (fasciculi), each of which is surrounded by a sheath termed the perimysium. Within bundles, each fiber is invested by the endomysium, a delicate sheath of connective tissue that is composed primarily of collagen fibers and also contains reticular fibers, capillaries, lymphatic vessels, and nerves. There are no intercellular junctions in skeletal muscle, so that the endomysium serves to bind the fibers together. Individual muscle fibers are generally surrounded by an external lamina, which resembles the basal lamina of epithelial tissues. Fibers may or may not run the entire length of whole muscles or bundles. Adult skeletal muscle fibers exhibit satellite cells, which lie external to the sarcolemma but internal to the external lamina. Muscle fibers develop from myotubes that arise by fusion of variable numbers of myoblasts; satellite cells are considered myoblasts that remain undifferentiated and act as a reservoir of cells that can take part in hypertrophy and healing of muscle fibers.

Skeletal muscles are generally richly vascularized, but because of their variable activity patterns there are mechanisms for varying blood supply to the fibers. Blood vessels penetrate via the epimysium and run in the perimysium and endomysium parallel to the long axes of the fibers. Blood entering terminal arterioles may either pass directly into capillary beds surrounding individual fibers or be directed into arteriovenous anastomoses.[9] The pathway taken by the blood depends on the level of activity of the muscle. During periods of intense activity blood is directed through the capillaries, whereas at rest a much greater proportion is shunted directly into venules, bypassing the capillaries.

The basic unit of structure of skeletal muscle is the muscle fiber. Each fiber is a syncytium, that is, a multinucleate mass of cytoplasm enclosed in the sarcolemma. The dimensions of individual fibers are variable and related to the relative size of the muscle of which they are a part. In humans, skeletal muscle fibers vary in length and range from approximately 1 mm to more than 4 cm. Similarly, diameters range from approximately 10 to 100 μm. They are unbranched and cylindric in shape, with remarkably uniform diameter. Nuclei are located peripherally, just inside the sarcolemma. Seen at high magnification in the light microscope as well as in the electron microscope, longitudinal sections of skeletal muscle exhibit a pattern of highly regular, alternating light- and dark-staining bands running across the fiber perpendicular to its long axis (Fig. 2-3). These are the A band, a broad, densely staining band; the I band, a palely staining band between A bands; the H band, a light band located in the middle of the A band; the M line, a thin, dark line bisecting the H band; and the Z line, a thin, dark line bisecting the I band. The interval between two adjacent Z lines is defined as a sarcomere.

Much of the volume of the fiber is occupied by the contractile apparatus, which is composed largely of myofilaments that can be observed in electron micrographs but cannot be distinguished in the light microscope. Myofilaments are organized into the myofibrils, elongate bundles 1 to 2 μm in di-

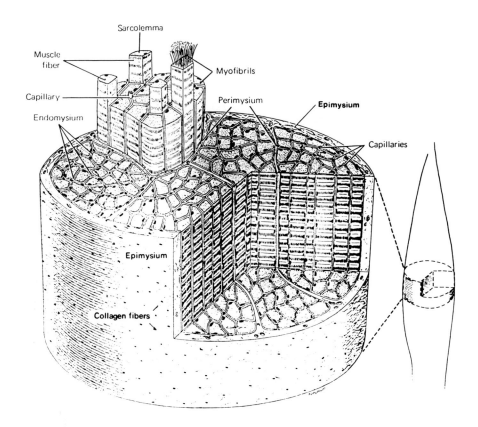

Figure 2-2 Structure of skeletal muscle. To the right is a drawing showing where the enlarged segment was taken from a muscle. *Source:* Reprinted from *Basic Histology*, ed 6 (p 195) by LC Junqueira and J Carneiro with permission of Appleton & Lange, © 1989.

Figure 2-3 Muscle fiber. This electron micrograph shows portions of seven myofibrils of a single muscle fiber of the rabbit psoas muscle. In this longitudinal section of noncontracted, relaxed muscle cross-banding is seen clearly, with the dark A (anisotropic) bands bisected by the lighter H bands with a central thin, dark M line. The I (isotropic) bands are lighter-staining and are bisected by the very dark Z lines or discs, with sarcomeres extending between adjacent Z lines. Between myofibrils are slender slips of nonfibrillar sarcoplasm containing small sarcosomes and vesicular and tubular elements. × 13,000. (Courtesy of Dr. H.E. Huxley.)

ameter that exhibit the same banded appearance as the entire muscle fiber. Further, the banding of adjacent myofibrils is generally in register, leading to the regular arrangement of striations often seen across the entire fiber. Myofibrils generally run the entire length of the fiber, and the spaces between them are occupied by sarcoplasm containing abundant, large mitochondria, ribosomes, and cytoplasmic inclusions, including variable amounts of glycogen and small lipid droplets. Small Golgi complexes, moderate numbers of free ribosomes, abundant mitochondria, and cytoplasmic inclusions are also located in the peripheral sarcoplasm, usually at the ends of nuclei.

Electron micrographs of longitudinal sections of skeletal muscle reveal that there are two types of myofilaments present and that it is the overlapping arrangement of these that is responsible for generating the striated appearance seen in the light microscope (Fig. 2-3). The two types of filament are chemically different and can be distinguished on the basis of thickness. The thick myofilaments are approximately 10 nm thick and 1.5 μm in length; the thin myofilaments are approximately 5 nm thick and 2.0 μm in length. The thick filaments run the width of the A band, and the thin filaments are attached at one end to the Z line and extend at the other end to the edge of the H band. Thus the I band exhibits only thin filaments, the H band only thick filaments, and the remainder of the A band interdigitating thin and thick filaments. High-magnification electron micrographs reveal that the thick filaments possess lateral projections, which can form cross-bridges, in contact with the thin filaments in regions of overlap. In the region of the M line thick filaments are interconnected by transversely oriented filaments approximately 4 nm in diameter. The contraction of skeletal muscle involves a shortening of the fiber due to shortening of individual sarcomeres in myofibrils. This is accomplished by a sliding motion of thin filaments relative to thick filaments involving precisely controlled formation of cross-bridges between them. Z lines, to which the thin filaments are attached, are thus pulled together, resulting in a shortening of the sarcomeres. The lengths of the thick and thin filaments themselves do not change. During this process the width of the A band remains unchanged, and the I and H bands disappear.

A cross-section of a myofibril exactly through a Z line reveals that the latter is disc-shaped and, for this reason, more accurately referred to as a Z disc. The function of the Z disc is to link the thin filaments of adjacent sarcomeres. Its structure is extremely complex, and the precise manner of attachment of the thin filaments to it is still unresolved. Examination of the Z disc at high magnification reveals that it is composed of filaments interwoven into a latticelike arrangement. The most widely accepted model proposes that Z-disc filaments are organized such that each thin filament on one side of the disc is linked to four thin filaments on the opposite side. Although not easily observed in routinely prepared tissue, a cytoskeleton of intermediate (10-nm) filaments that support the myofilaments and link Z discs of adjacent myofibrils together and possibly to the sarcolemma is revealed by special staining techniques. The presence of such a cytoskeleton explains why Z discs of adjacent myofibrils are generally in register across the width of the fiber.

Skeletal muscle exhibits a complex system of membranous organelles. The smooth endoplasmic reticulum is highly specialized, forming a delicate, lacelike sleeve of anastomosing tubules and saccules (the sarcoplasmic reticulum) around each myofibril. This sleeve is interrupted by and closely associated with another system of tubules, the transverse tubules or T tubules (T system). The membrane of each T tubule is an inward extension of the sarcolemma into the fiber, and the enclosed lumen is continuous with the extracellular space. T tubules penetrate into the fiber, branching and encircling the myofibrils at the levels of A–I junctions. On each side of these T tubules dilated portions of sarcoplasmic reticulum form terminal cisternae. Thus each T tubule is associated with two terminal cisternae, the three structures forming a triad. There are two triads per sarcomere. As an inward extension of the sarcolemma the T system serves to conduct action potentials deeply into the fiber, thus initiating contraction. Adjacent terminal cisternae are continuous with longitudinally oriented, tubular components of the sarcoplasmic reticulum. Complex anastomoses of these tubules usually exist at the level of the underlying H band. The sarcoplasmic reticulum stores calcium ions, which plays an important role in the mechanism of contraction.

Heterogeneity of Skeletal Muscle Fibers

Skeletal muscle fibers exhibit structural, biochemical, and functional heterogeneity, and there are several ways of classifying them.[10] Seen in the fresh condition, some muscle fibers exhibit a deep red color due to high sarcoplasmic concentrations of myoglobin, a protein-iron complex similar to hemoglobin. Other fibers exhibit less myoglobin and are lighter in color. The former are termed *red fibers* and the latter *white fibers*. Red fibers are of smaller diameter than white and are more richly vascularized. Ultrastructurally they exhibit larger and more numerous mitochondria, much less glycogen, thicker and less regular Z discs, and less elaborate sarcoplasmic reticulum. Red fibers are capable of sustained contraction, and they tire slowly. This is due to their abundant blood supply and to the capacity of the respiratory pigment myoglobin to facilitate the transfer of oxygen from the capillaries to mitochondria of the muscle. White fibers are capable of generating large amounts of adenosine triphosphate (ATP) rapidly but tire quickly because of depletion of glycogen reserves. Muscle fibers may also be classified according to the principal mechanisms used to generate ATP: oxidative, in which ATP is generated primarily by oxidative phosphorylation, and glycolytic, in which glycolysis serves as the primary means of forming ATP.

The characteristics, and hence the classes, described above are determined by the type of motor neuron innervating the fibers. There is an additional means of classification, one that represents the only method of clearly distinguishing fiber types: speed of contraction.[10] Here fibers may be classified as slow twitch or fast twitch. Speed of contraction depends on which isozymes of myosin ATPase are present in the thick filaments. These isozymes are referred to as *slow myosin, fast red myosin*, and *fast white myosin*.[11] Combinations of the features used to classify the various types of fibers provide a final scheme into which almost all skeletal muscle fibers fall: type I (slow twitch red oxidative), type IIA (fast twitch red oxidative), type IIB (fast twitch white glycolytic), and type IIC (fast twitch intermediate). The last of these exhibit structural features of both red and white fibers. Although single fiber types may make up entire muscles in lower vertebrates, mammalian muscles including those of humans are, with a few specialized exceptions, composites. Slow and fast oxidative fibers usually form the bulk of postural muscles.

Innervation

Skeletal muscles are innervated by axons of α motor neurons located in the ventral horns of the spinal cord. The neurons and the muscle fibers are organized into motor units, a single motor unit consisting of one neuron plus all the fibers that it innervates. The number of muscle fibers in a motor unit is directly related to the relative fineness of movement that is required, the number increasing with decreasing degree of control. All muscle fibers in a motor unit contract simultaneously; graded contractions in muscles are due to recruitment of variable numbers of motor units, the number increasing with increasing degree of contraction. In individual motor units all muscle fibers are of the same type. On the basis of the speed of contraction of the muscle fibers and the conduction velocity of the motor neuron innervating them, motor units may be classified as fast or slow. In general, slow motor units consist of slow muscle fibers innervated by small neurons with a low threshold of stimulation. Fast motor units consist of muscle fibers innervated by larger neurons with a high threshold of stimulation and a fast conduction velocity.[12] Slow motor units generally exhibit significantly fewer muscle fibers than the large ones and, because of the low threshold of stimulation of their motor neurons, are recruited first.

The specialized synapse between a motor axon and a muscle fiber is termed a *motor end plate*, and with few exceptions there is one per fiber, usually located near the midpoint of its long axis. The axon terminal of the motor neuron lies in a depression formed by an invagination of the sarcolemma referred to as the *primary synaptic cleft*. The sarcolemma is further infolded and forms a series of secondary synaptic clefts, a feature that greatly increases postsynaptic surface area, where the sarcolemma is sensitive to neurotransmitter. The external lamina of the muscle fiber is present in the region of the motor end plate and follows all the contours of the secondary synaptic clefts. In the immediate area of the motor end plate the sarcoplasm is devoid of myofibrils and usually contains numerous nuclei and large numbers of mitochondria. Depolarization of the motor axon results in the release of neurotransmitter, which is stored in synaptic vesicles in the axon terminal.

Tendons

Tendons, as the physical links between muscles and bones, are transmitters of mechanical energy. As such, there are several essential requirements that must be met. They must be capable of withstanding large tensile forces, they must be relatively inextensible to minimize transmission loss of energy, they must ensure smooth transfer of energy, they must be flexible, and in many instances they must be capable of yielding absolute freedom of movement between themselves and closely apposed tissues. Because tendons perform similar functions regardless of their location in the body, they generally resemble one another anatomically and histologically. Further, tendons in other mammals are similar to those of humans, thus providing sources of experimental material for investigation. This brief review utilizes both human and nonhuman mammalian studies. Specific references to the source of tissue is made only where necessary. The numerous investigations into tendon structure show little standardization in terminology. Accordingly, the names employed here correspond to those utilized by Strocci et al[13] because they are more consistent with the terminology of *Nomina Histologica* and are in keeping with similar terms applied to muscle and nerve.

Most tendons are cordlike or straplike structures of variable length and cross-sectional profile; their thickness is propor-

tional to the size of the muscles from which they originate and to the degree of tension applied to them. Seen in the light microscope, tendons exhibit several levels of organization. Tendon fibers are oriented longitudinally and appear to be separated by tendon cells (mature fibroblasts). Bundles of tendon fibers are termed *primary fascicles* and are surrounded by the endotendineum, a layer of loose connective tissue. In larger tendons, groups of primary fascicles may themselves be organized into secondary fascicles surrounded by peritendineum. The entire tendon is surrounded by the epitendineum, a layer of connective tissue that is continuous with both endotendineum and peritendineum. In many cases the epitendineum is continuous with surrounding areolar connective tissue, a condition that may result in the imposition of a degree of drag on the tendon in its movements.[14] There are various examples[13,15–17] in which several tendons are grouped together and surrounded by the paratendineum, a common connective tissue sheath. This is continuous with the epitendineum and of similar histologic structure.

The light microscopic appearance of tendon cells in fascicles is variable depending on the plane of section. In longitudinal sections they appear as flattened structures arranged in rows between tendon fibers, whereas in cross-section they exhibit a stellate appearance. These observations are suggestive of close interrelationships among cells and between cells and fibers and are confirmed by three-dimensional studies. Squier and Bausch[18] studied tendons of rat tail by scanning and transmission electron microscopy and observed that tendon cells exhibit thin cytoplasmic sheets that extend up to 3 μm transversely, frequently forming junctional attachments with similar processes from other cells. Longitudinal processes often exceed 20 μm in length and form attachments with other cells in the same column. Further, the cytoplasmic processes often exhibit invaginations containing single fibrils or small groups of fibrils, which are the subunits that make up tendon fibers. Tendon cells exhibit extensive rough endoplasmic reticulum, large numbers of free ribosomes, and a well-developed Golgi complex,[19] features that are characteristic of cells that are active or have the potential to become active in the synthesis and export of protein.

The application of tensile loads to tendon by means of clamps indicates that the tensile strength of tendon is approximately 620 to 1050 kg/cm^2.[20] The absolute tensile strength of tendons is difficult to measure, however, because clamping does not ensure that stress will be uniformly applied across the entire diameter and, further, because clamping probably results in damage to the tissue. Nevertheless, tendons are strong enough to withstand several times the tension that their attached muscles can generate.[21] This and the ability of tendons to resist stretch are due to the fact that approximately 80% of their dry weight is composed of collagen fibers[22] and that of this about 95% is type I collagen,[23] the strongest fiber in the body. Other noncellular components include types III and IV collagen, elastic fibers, and proteoglycans.[16] Tendon fibers are aggregates of collagen fibrils that follow a gently spiraling course parallel to the long axis of the tendon. Individual fibrils of adult human tendon generally range from 60 to 175 nm in diameter, with the larger-diameter fibrils frequently being connected by interfibrillar bridges.[15] Studies on rat tail tendon by freeze-fracture and freeze-etch techniques reveal the presence of similar interconnecting filaments forming networks that are continuous with the collagen fibrils.[24]

Examination of longitudinal sections of unstressed tendon by light microscopy reveals that the fibers exhibit a regular wavy appearance, which is referred to as *crimping* and is a property of the individual collagen fibrils.[25] The distance between wave crests (or troughs) is referred to as the *crimp length*, and the height of the wave is known as its *amplitude*. This varies in different parts of the tendon, for example between fascicles and sheaths and among tendons.[16] Neighboring fascicles usually exhibit crimp registry,[26] but variation in wave pattern both within and among fascicles of individual tendons may exist.[27] The crimping of collagen fibrils in tendon has an important functional significance because the initial application of a tensile force has the effect of reversibly eliminating the crimp. Thus the function of the crimp appears to be to act as a shock absorber, protecting the fibrils against sudden applied loads[28] and ensuring a smooth transfer of energy from muscle to bone.

Although many tendons are relatively linear in form there are many examples in which they are required to bend around joints, passing under ligamentous bands or retinacula or through fascial slings or osseofibrous tunnels.[14] Excellent examples are found in the flexor tendons of the fingers, where a series of retinacular structures form pulleys,[29,30] an important function of which is to prevent bowstringing.[30] In areas such as these, tendons exhibit synovial sheaths that form double-walled, sleevelike structures. The inner or visceral layer is attached to either the epitendineum or the paratendineum by loose connective tissue, and the outer or parietal layer is attached to surrounding tissues. The two layers are continuous at the ends of the sheath, thus enclosing a cavity containing synovial fluid. In addition a mesenterylike mesotendineum often connects the layers, carrying blood vessels, lymphatics, and nerves both to the tendon proper and to the synovial sheath.

Myotendinous Junction

As seen in the light microscope, the connective tissue of the epimysium, perimysium, and endomysium gradually continues into the connective tissue of the tendon. At this level the ends of the muscle fibers appear to be tapered or rounded. The electron microscope, however, reveals that the structure of the myotendinous junction is considerably more complex, having structural specializations of both connective tissue and muscle fibers. The ends of each fiber exhibit deep invaginations lined by external lamina. Electron micrographs of these regions reveal extensive interdigitation between muscle fiber and connective tissue.[31] This greatly increases surface area for adhesive interaction between muscle and tendon.[32] There

does not appear to be any direct attachment of tendon fibers to muscle fibers; rather, collagen fibrils in the tendon intertwine with those of the connective tissue sheaths of the muscle. In addition, reticular fibers of the endomysium, which are anchored in the external lamina, wrap around collagen fibrils from tendon, providing firm attachment.[33] The terminal segments of muscle fibers in the region of interdigitation with tendon exhibit dense accumulations of subsarcolemmal material in the region of the junction with tendon. Thin filaments insert into this material, thus providing structural continuity between sarcolemma and terminal sarcomeres.[34]

Ligament

Diarthrodial joints are enclosed in the joint capsule, a tough connective tissue wrapping that consists of two layers. The inner, synovial layer lines the joint cavity, and the outer, fibrous layer blends with the ligaments and the articulating bones.[35]

Ligaments are specific thickenings of the fibrous capsule. They are usually white cordlike or bandlike structures made of dense collagenous connective tissue.[36] Microscopically, the structure of ligament is similar to that of tendon (see above). It is composed of collagen with intervening rows of fibrocytes. The main collagen is type I collagen. Type III is also a consistent component, probably contributing to the specific structural-functional properties of ligament.[2] Interwoven with the collagen bundles are elastin fibers, which provide this tissue a measure of extensibility. The amount of elastin varies from ligament to ligament. Elastic ligaments, such as ligamentum flavum, are predominantly composed of elastin. These are arranged in parallel bundles and are interwoven by collagen fibers.[37]

As discussed above for tendon, ligaments also exhibit crimping. This provides a shock-absorbing mechanism and contributes to the flexibility of ligament.[2] The periodicity and amplitude of crimp appears to vary from ligament to ligament and may reflect functional adaptation of individual ligaments.[2] The lubrication and gliding properties of ligament are acquired as a result of its proteoglycan component, as discussed above for tendon.

COMMON MECHANISMS OF HEALING: A SYNOPSIS

Tissues respond to injury with a set of genetically programmed mechanisms to replace the damaged components and to restore normal function. These are conveniently discussed under the headings of inflammation, repair, and remodeling and maturation. The details of these processes are discussed in many excellent textbooks of pathology[38-40] and in review articles.[41-43] The following synopsis serves as a background to facilitate further discussions of the pathology and healing of skeletal muscle, tendon, and ligament.

Inflammation

Clinically, inflammation is often characterized by swelling, heat, pain, and the impairment or loss of function. Both clinically and pathologically two major types of inflammation are distinguished: acute and chronic inflammation. The latter may be a sequel to unresolved acute inflammation, or it may develop as such from the beginning.

At the cellular level, the onset of acute inflammation is marked by the release of several chemical mediators by platelets, mast cells, and basophils at the site of injury. Vasoactive mediators regulate the response of the vasculature to injury, and chemotactic factors affect the recruitment of polymorphonuclear leukocytes from the vascular compartment to the tissues. These in turn produce additional chemical mediators that are utilized during the inflammatory process to control the damage and to remove the irritant in preparation for repair. Although some of the details of the inflammatory response may vary according to the site of injury or the stimulus that produces it, most inflammatory responses are remarkably similar.

Acute inflammation gradually leads to the formation of granulation tissue. This is characterized by the replacement of polymorphonuclear leukocytes by monocytes, lymphocytes, and plasma cells and later by the proliferation of endothelial cells and fibroblasts in the area of injury. Ultimately, these would lead to the restoration of the vascular supply and connective tissue matrix, respectively, during the process of repair that would normally follow. Under conditions in which the acute inflammatory response fails to come to a successful resolution, however, chronic inflammation develops. Common causes are persistence of the inflammatory stimulus, which may range from infectious agents to repeated direct trauma, and hypersensitivity reactions.[39] The major cellular components of chronic inflammation are lymphocytes, plasma cells, macrophages, and fibroblasts. The presence of these cells suggests a variable degree of response to antigenic stimuli and is indicative of attempts at both clearing the tissue of cellular debris and laying down fibrous tissue by fibroblasts. The outcome of chronic inflammation often depends on the nature of injury. For example, in some injuries of infectious etiology the inflammatory process often terminates by the formation of granulomatous nodules. If, however, chronic inflammation is the result of repeated trauma, such as in the case of some of the occupational or sports-related injuries, removal of the trauma and successful management of the case may result in a variable degree of reversal of the process and restoration of normal function.

Repair

This phase of healing ideally results in the restoration of normal living tissue. The successful outcome depends on the interplay of accumulated granulation tissue and the cell type of which the affected tissue is composed. Tissues composed of labile cells (eg, mucosa) repair readily, those composed of stable cells (eg, liver) repair well on adequate activation, and those composed of permanent cells (eg, nerve or cardiac muscle) may not be restored to normal structure and function. When the restoration of normal tissue involves differentiation of specific cells into specialized cell types, the process is referred to as *regeneration*.[44] An excellent example of this is skeletal muscle fiber regeneration.

The repair process is characterized by a high level of activity of fibroblasts, which synthesize matrix components and eventually produce a fibrous scar. Repair by fibrous tissue is generally described as occurring by primary or secondary union (intention). The former occurs in injuries in which the damaged surfaces are physically well apposed, and the interplay of component cells and fibroblasts gives rise to a minimal scar. In contrast, healing with secondary union occurs in injuries that result in considerable separation of damaged surfaces. Repair in this case is characterized by contraction of the wound gap by myofibroblasts and the accumulation of a great deal of granulation tissue, ultimately resulting in a healing tissue that is structurally and functionally deficient.

Remodeling and Maturation

During this phase, which usually overlaps repair, the newly accumulated matrix components undergo organizational and orientative changes designed to optimize the structural and functional integrity of the healed tissue. The most striking feature of this process is the high turnover of collagen. Although the absolute quantity of collagen in the wound does not increase, there is a high level of synthetic activity with simultaneous destruction. The balance between these processes is obviously crucial for the eventual net accumulation of collagen and the ultimate outcome of the healing process. The mechanisms involved in the regulation of collagen turnover are not precisely understood. Self-regulatory mechanisms involving cell–cell and cell–matrix interactions, including contact inhibition and negative feedback loops, are probably involved.[45] The role of collagenase in the degradation of old collagen as new collagen is synthesized has been recognized for some time.[46] A direct phagocytic role of fibroblasts in the degradation of collagen during the remodeling phase has also been suggested. Tension across the scar appears to enhance this phagocytic activity.[47]

Mechanically, the hallmark of the remodeling phase is the reorientation of collagen fibers to lines of wound stress accompanied by a marked increase in wound strength. Under experimental conditions immobilization of healing wounds has been shown to compromise wound strength, presumably as a result of a failure of collagen fiber orientation along appropriate stress lines.[48] The mechanisms controlling fiber reorientation are not well understood. McGaw[47] showed that there is a stress-induced activation of fibroblasts that leads to collagen degradation by phagocytosis. Furthermore, considering the piezoelectric properties of collagen, McGaw proposed that rearrangements in fiber orientation may be achieved through a differential breakdown of fibers of certain orientation that may have acquired a characteristic stress-induced piezoelectric charge.[47]

At the molecular level, maturation and strengthening of collagen are achieved as a result of the development of crosslinks. The formation of intermolecular and interfibrillar crosslinks was discussed above. It is of interest that cross-linking may be in two forms—stable and unstable (in dilute acids)—and that the ratio of the two forms differs in different tissues and generally increases in favor of the stable form with maturation and aging.[49]

Timeframe of Healing

Finally, it is important to put the different phases of the healing process into a timeframe. The inflammatory phase is relatively brief and leads to the commencement of the proliferative-synthetic phase 3 to 7 days after injury, provided that the source of injury is removed. The repair phase may last from a few days to weeks depending on the specific tissue, the site, and the extent of injury and may be influenced by local parameters including metabolic and mechanical factors.[50]

During the remodeling phase the turnover of collagen may last several months, and maturation may not be complete 12 months or longer after injury. Ultimately the nature of the repaired tissue depends on the interaction of many factors, including the age of the patient, the type of tissue, the extent of injury, the site and size of the scar, and forces acting on the scar during the healing process.[46]

REPAIR MECHANISMS IN MUSCULOSKELETAL SOFT TISSUE INJURIES

Muscle

The synopsis of the normal histologic-molecular organization of musculoskeletal soft tissues presented above illustrates the relative complexity of skeletal muscle. In terms of both subcellular specialization as well as its dependence on the integrity of vascular and nervous networks, skeletal muscle repair is an exceedingly complex process.

Skeletal muscle has considerable regenerative capabilities. It is generally accepted that mechanisms involved in skeletal muscle healing include both regeneration and repair by scar formation.[40,51] Evidently the more regenerative processes are allowed to predominate and the more repair by secondary union is kept to a minimum, the more successful is the functional restoration of the damaged muscle. The capacity for regeneration is determined genetically, but the success of regeneration is determined primarily by the type and extent of injury.[52]

The nuclei of differentiated muscle cells appear to be arrested in the G0 phase of the mitotic cycle. As such, they do not show any DNA replicative or mitotic activity and are incapable of regeneration.[53] Muscle regeneration is achieved by specific cells called *myosatellite cells*,[54] whose relationship to the myofiber was discussed above. The myosatellite cell gives striated muscle a substantial and specific repair capacity.[55]

The process of regeneration of myofibers forms a continuum with that of degeneration. Caplan et al[52] summarized these changes in muscle fibers injured by local ischemia as follows (Fig. 2-4): Intrinsic mechanisms first cause membrane damage, disruption of sarcomeres at the Z bands, mitochondrial swelling, and pyknosis. This is followed by a cell-mediated assault, primarily by macrophages, which enter the myofiber and remove the necrotic cytoplasm. Coincident with this stage the myogenic satellite cells become activated. They proliferate beneath the basal lamina of the damaged muscle fiber and at some point withdraw from the cell cycle and fuse, forming new myotubes. The details of the process have been observed in vitro.[56] The newly formed myofibers exhibit intense synthetic activity, accumulating contractile proteins and assuming their characteristic structural organization. The basement membrane surrounding the myofiber is also synthesized de novo at this time.[57] The final stage in the regenerative process involves the integration of neural elements of synaptic connections through the newly formed basement membrane, resulting in the formation of a functional neuromuscular junction.[58,59] The differentiated muscle fiber retains a characteristic number of satellite cells, which assume their normal anatomic positions.[60]

The process described above is limited to the regeneration of myofibers whose continuity has not been disrupted, as for example when cell damage is produced by local transient ischemia. When the continuity of a muscle fiber is disrupted, repair occurs by budding.[61] This is characterized by the formation of sarcoplasmic outgrowths at the cut ends of the myofiber, which eventually become embedded in a mass of dense connective tissue. The regeneration of transected muscle is further complicated by disruption of innervation and vascular supply and damage to the extracellular matrix. Healing of these tissues is achieved by scar tissue formation and deterioration or loss of function. Evidently the regeneration of entire muscle involves a much higher level of organizational complexity compared to the events outlined above for a single fiber. Experimentally regeneration of muscle may be accomplished from minced fragments[62] or from grafts of entire muscle.[63] Although successes in this area give impetus for further research, the resulting regenerates are not functionally normal.

In a practical sense, muscle regeneration depends on the type and extent of injury. On the basis of the available literature, some of which was discussed above, it appears that, except for injuries involving muscle fibers in which the continuity of the fiber is not disrupted and the innervation, vascular supply, and extracellular matrix are left intact, muscle will regenerate with loss of normal tissue architecture and function. With this in mind, determination of the specific type

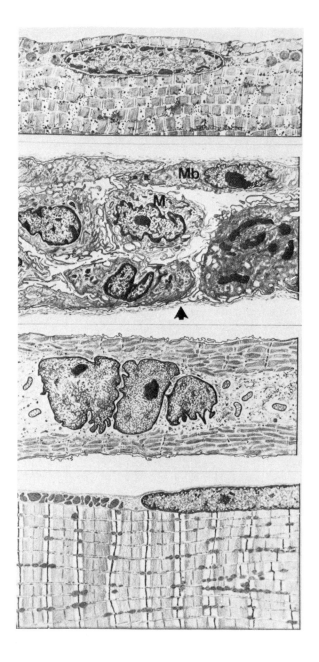

Figure 2-4 Summary drawings of major phases of the degeneration and regeneration of a single muscle fiber. (*Top*) Early ischemic damage. The nucleus is becoming pyknotic, with chromatin clumping inside the nuclear membrane. The mitochondria are swollen, and the bundles of contractile filaments are breaking apart throughout the muscle fiber. (*Top center*) Fragmentation phase. Macrophages (M) associated with ingrowing vasculature enter the degenerating muscle fiber and remove bundles of contractile filaments and other cytoplasmic debris. Beneath the basal lamina (arrow) spindle-shaped myoblasts (Mb) line up in preparation for the formation of new muscle fibers. (*Bottom center*) Myotube. Beneath the original basal lamina, myoblasts have fused to form a multinucleated fiber with bundles of newly forming contractile filaments at the periphery. (*Bottom*) Muscle fiber. The mature regenerated muscle fiber is in most respects indistinguishable from a normal muscle fiber. *Source:* Reprinted from *Injury and Repair of the Musculoskeletal Soft Tissues*, (p 248) by SL-Y Woo and JA Buckwalter with permission of the American Academy of Orthopaedic Surgeons, © 1987.

of muscle injury is essential for the successful management of muscle injury cases.

Injury to muscle may be caused by a wide range of stimuli, including infections and metabolic diseases, trauma, and iatrogenic causes.[52] Nevertheless, muscle injuries most commonly seen in office practice may be discussed under the headings of exercise-induced injuries, muscle strain, and contusions (ischemic injuries).

Exercise-Induced Injuries

Exercise, particularly when performed strenuously and irregularly, causes damage to muscle. Clinically, this is manifested as muscle soreness and is characterized by morphologic and metabolic changes. Several reviews[64,65] provide an excellent account of the changes and discuss the mechanisms of injury.

After exhaustive endurance exercise such as long-distance running, damage is thought to be primarily due to metabolic disturbances and ischemia.[66] Extensive disruption of muscle fiber also occurs after short-term contraction exercises. Eccentric contractions have been shown to produce greater injury by far than concentric or isometric contractions,[67–69] and this appears to be due to the development of greater tension per cross-sectional area in eccentric muscle contraction.[70]

The morphologic changes seen in exhaustive or short-term contraction injuries are identical. The most common ultrastructural finding is abnormalities of the Z disc manifested as broadening, streaming, and, in some cases, total disruption. Other changes include myofibrillar, sarcolemmal, mitochondrial, and cytoskeletal damage.[71–73] These changes are reversible. Time-course ultrastructural studies have shown markedly less disruption and eventually complete repair of exercise-induced muscle damage.[69,72,73] The repair process involves the accumulation of cellular infiltrates and activation of satellite cells, leading to the formation of myotubes via the regenerative processes described above.[41,52] Finally, this type of muscle injury gives rise to an adaptive response. After repeated exercise little or no damage is produced.[68,74] The mechanisms involved in this process are not well understood.

Muscle Strain Injuries

These are indirect injuries to specific muscles produced as a result of sudden stretching or during eccentric activity. The injury consists of a partial or complete tear of muscle fibers at the myotendinous junction.[75] Histologic studies in experimental animal models in which specific muscles were subjected to controlled loading have shown disruption of muscle fiber and hemorrhage with subsequent development of an inflammatory response including granulation tissue and scar formation at the myotendinous junction.[76] When the loading force is sufficiently high to cause a complete tear, the tendon has been shown to avulse from the muscle, often with a few millimeters of muscle still attached.[77] Structurally this appears to coincide with the area of extensive membrane infoldings and junction amplification[78] and suggests a weak link. The precise reasons and mechanisms for the consistent failure of muscle–tendon preparations at the myotendinous junction require further investigation, however. Repair mechanisms have not been investigated either. It is likely that both muscle and tendon repair processes come into play, greater amounts of scar tissue formation being expected with more severe tears.

Ischemia-Induced Muscle Damage

This type of injury may result from damage to specific vessels supplying a muscle or even a muscle fiber or be secondary to a compartment syndrome.[52] Compartment syndrome is a condition in which increased pressure in a closed compartment bounded by bone and fascia diminishes tissue perfusion and leads to ischemic injury.[79] In animal models, ligation experiments have shown a time-dependent progression of damage with morphologic changes resembling those due to exhaustive endurance exercise.[80] Such changes may include disruption of the sarcolemma, contractile apparatus, mitochondria, and sarcotubular system.[66] The extent of injury is proportional to the magnitude and duration of the pressure.[52] Hence prompt diagnosis is crucial, and surgical decompression may be necessary. Furthermore, nerve injury may also result from the increased pressure; this should be kept in perspective.

Muscle damage due to ischemia may heal well if damage is limited to the individual fibers without disruption (see above) and if blood supply is restored without delay. If blood deprivation is long enough to result in extensive cell death and fiber discontinuity, however, healing will proceed with a variable amount of fibrous tissue deposition.

Muscle Contusion

This type of injury results from nonpenetrating blunt trauma. It is characterized by the formation of hematoma and an intense inflammatory reaction within minutes to hours of injury. Muscle damage is due to (1) the crushing injury and (2) the ischemia and cell death that follow. Thus repair involves a variable amount of muscle regeneration and dense connective tissue deposition. The extent of initial vascular damage and subsequent revascularization plays a crucial role in the successful outcome of the repair process.[81] In a series of studies in which the rat gastrocnemius muscle was used as a model, Jarvinen and co-workers[81,82] showed that early mobilization after a crush injury enhanced healing by promoting all parameters studied. These included the speed and intensity of revascularization and the speed of accumulation and quality of repaired tissue in terms of both fiber orientation and tensile properties.

A major complication of contusion injuries is the formation of bone within the muscle, which is known as *myositis ossificans*. The cellular processes as well as the relatively high incidence of this condition seen in sports injuries have been described.[83] The effect of early mobilization on the progress or possible prevention of this condition has not been studied.

Tendon

It has long been recognized that tendon repair proceeds via the three stages of soft tissue healing. Nevertheless, the question of whether an intrinsic fibroblastic response is responsible for driving the repair process has been a matter of some debate.[84–86] Most investigators in the field now agree that both extrinsic and intrinsic cellular responses contribute to the healing process, depending on the type and site of injury. Most tendon injuries are classified either as avulsion injuries (as for example in some of the athletic injuries) or, more frequently, as transection injuries with or without associated crushing injury to the neighboring tissues. Failure of tendon along its length is rare, and most failure secondary to stretching occurs at the myotendinous junction.[75]

In avulsion injuries in which the tendon insertion on bone is separated, repair is by a bony callus formation[87] provided that the avulsed fragment is successfully reinserted. If not, a variable amount of fibrous tissue deposition occurs, predisposing to future injuries.

In response to transection injuries, generally inflammation occurs during the first few days after injury, and fibroblastic and vascular contribution may come from various tissues surrounding the injury site.[86] These may include subcutaneous tissues, deep fascia, the synovial sheath, and the periosteum of any involved bony structures. Healing in this fashion (ie, by an extrinsic cellular response) is characterized by the formation of dense collagen and adhesions and appears to be stimulated by trauma to the tendon sheath and by immobilization.[86–88]

Intrinsically, fibroblasts (tenocytes) from the epitenon and the endotenon may become involved, and in the absence of a synovial sheath they have the capacity for complete repair.[89] The predominance of extrinsic rather than intrinsic fibroblastic recruitment during repair appears to be determined by whether or not the synovial sheath is involved in the injury. When injury is confined to the tendon structure alone, healing is achieved entirely by the proliferation of intrinsic fibroblasts. When the synovial sheath is injured, however, extrinsic mechanisms appear to overwhelm the intrinsic mechanism, resulting potentially in extensive adhesion formation.

After the proliferative phase, there is random accumulation of collagen. This continues for about 8 weeks and is followed by a phase of remodeling and maturation, during which collagen fibers become oriented along the longitudinal axis of the tendon under the influence of the normal loads applied by its muscle. The strength of collagen fibers increases during this time with increasing cross-linking and fiber assembly. Furthermore, there is a gradual shift to type I collagen from type III, which also contributes to the strengthening of the tendon. These changes have been well documented.[16,90]

In view of the structural organization of tendon and the remodeling and maturation phase required for its collagen to develop, rehabilitative care after repair is particularly important. Gelberman and associates[91,92] and others[85] demonstrated that early, controlled mobilization of healing canine flexor tendons influenced the cellular response of the healing process and morphologically resulted in a dramatic reduction of adhesion formation. Furthermore, the strength of healed tendons has been shown to be superior to controls in which mobilization was delayed.[91,93] Similarly, an augmentation of extrasynovial flexor tendon healing by continuous passive motion has been demonstrated by Salter[94] in a rabbit model. The precise mechanisms whereby passive mobilization alters the healing process of injured tendon are not well understood. It has been suggested that mobilization may stimulate the intrinsic tendon healing response, specifically that of the epitenon fibroblasts, thereby resulting in an effective repair with minimal scar formation.[16,93] In addition, it is possible that early passive mobilization may actively reduce adhesion formation and promote the organizational phase of the healing process. After repair controlled mobilization provides intermittent tensile stress, which appears to be highly desirable for the promotion of the remodeling phase.[47,48] Finally, mobilization may play a beneficial role in tendon healing by promoting nutrient transport to the area.[95]

Ligaments

As discussed above, the molecular organization of ligaments affords a higher degree of flexibility compared to that of tendons.[36,96] Nevertheless, large loads are capable of overcoming this tensile resistance and result in injury, which usually manifests as a complete or partial tear or a stretch injury probably associated with multiple microtears.[36] Clinically, these have been classified as grades I, II, and III.[36,97] Grade I is characterized as mild injury with no associated joint laxity, grade II is characterized as moderate injury with mild but clinically insignificant laxity, and grade III is characterized as severe injury with significant laxity resulting from a complete tear of the ligament.

Ligament healing is achieved via the same basic mechanisms involving inflammation, repair, and remodeling as discussed above.[36] Several factors, however, including the severity of injury and the specific ligament involved determine the outcome of the healing process.

Generally, the acute inflammatory phase occurs during the first 72 hours and yields a scar that is rich in monocytes and macrophages. In the next few days fibroblasts increase in number, and by the end of the first week a random array of collagen fibers is present in the scar matrix. As in tendon, initially the predominant collagen is type III with a small proportion of type I.[98] Other matrix components that accumulate at this time are fibronectin,[99] water, and glycosaminoglycans.[100] This proliferative and synthetic activity of fibroblasts continues for about 6 weeks and marks the phase of repair and regeneration. During this time the gap between the torn ligament ends is filled with a vascular granulation tissue.[36] Several weeks into the repair phase, remodeling processes become operational. Gradually the cellularity of the scar is decreased along with an accompanying decrease in synthetic activity.

The collagen matrix becomes better organized and appears histologically to be better aligned with the long axis of the ligament. The biochemical profile approaches that of the normal ligament tissue. This includes a restoration of the normal relative ratio of type III to type I collagen and the establishment of a reducible cross-linking profile characteristic of normal ligaments.[2,96] The phase of maturation continues for months and years. Even then the healed tissue is morphologically less organized, and the original tensile strength is not regained completely.[100]

The ultimate outcome is dependent on the interplay of several factors. Ligament type and associated local conditions have been shown to be important. For example, the anterior cruciate ligament heals poorly[101,102] compared to the medial collateral ligament.[100,103] Another factor that influences the healing process is the stresses acting on the scar. Of particular interest are the effects of training and mobilization-immobilization regimens on the healing of ligaments. It has been shown that in the anterior and posterior cruciate ligaments of the cat knee there is a significant increase in the number of small-diameter fibrils and a concomitant decrease in the number of larger-diameter fibrils after prolonged exercise. In that study, however, the total cross-sectional area of fibrils of the exercised ligaments was smaller than that of the controls, suggesting that exercise did not increase the tensile strength of the ligaments.[104] On the other hand, the increase in small-diameter fibrils may suggest decreased stiffness of these ligaments.[105] In support of this, immobilization of the rat medial collateral ligament has been shown to diminish the number of small-diameter fibers[106] and presumably leads to joint stiffness. The precise mechanism by which immobilization leads to joint stiffness has not been elucidated. It appears that a combination of mechanisms may be involved.[107] These include formation of intra-articular adhesions[108,109] and an active contraction of ligaments by fibroblasts in a process mediated by contractile proteins.[110]

CONCLUSION

Musculoskeletal soft tissues exhibit diverse biochemical and structural characteristics that must be kept in perspective when their injury and healing are being considered. Healing of all these tissues is achieved through the basic mechanisms of inflammation, repair, and remodeling that are common to all other tissues. Assuming an intact vascular and nervous supply, however, the specific tissue structure in terms of cellularity, characteristic molecular components, and organization determines the outcome of the repair process.

One of the most exciting aspects of research in this area concerns the effects of mobilization on the healing of injured musculoskeletal soft tissues. Ample experimental evidence has accumulated demonstrating the beneficial effects of mobilization on the healing of muscle, tendon, and ligament injuries. It appears that mobilization may affect tissue healing by influencing several parameters through various mechanisms that have not been fully elucidated. Studies on the effects of mobilization and other forms of manual therapy offer a challenging area of investigation for those involved in the practice of manual and physical therapy.

REFERENCES

1. Nimni ME, Harkness RD. Molecular structures and functions of collagen. In: Nimni ME, ed. *Collagen*. Boca Raton, Fla: CRC Press; 1988;1:1–78.

2. Amiel D, Kleiner JB. Biochemistry of tendon and ligament. In: Nimni ME, ed. *Collagen*. Boca Raton, Fla: CRC Press; 1988;3:223–251.

3. Burgeson RE. New collagens new concepts. *Annu Rev Cell Biol*. 1988;4:551–577.

4. Yamada KM. Cell surface interactions with extracellular materials. *Annu Rev Biochem*. 1983;52:761–799.

5. Sandberg LB, Soskel NT, Leslie JG. Elastin structure, biosynthesis, and relation to disease states. *N Engl J Med*. 1981;304:566–579.

6. Krstic RV. *General Histology of the Mammal*. Berlin: Springer-Verlag; 1985.

7. Heinegard D, Paulson M. Structure and metabolism of proteoglycans. In: Piez KA, Reddi AH, eds. *Extracellular Matrix Biochemistry*. New York: Elsevier; 1984:277–328.

8. Engel AG, Banker BQ, eds. *Myology*. New York: McGraw-Hill; 1986;1.

9. Jerusalem F. The microcirculation of the muscle. In: Engel AG, Banker BQ, eds. *Myology*. New York: McGraw-Hill; 1986;1:343–356.

10. Fawcett DW. *A Textbook of Histology*. Philadelphia: Saunders; 1986.

11. Gauthier CF. Skeletal muscle fiber types. In: Engel AG, Banker BQ, eds. *Myology*. New York: McGraw-Hill; 1986;1:255–284.

12. Buchthal F, Schmalbruch H. Motor unit of mammalian muscle. *Physiol Rev*. 1980;60:90–142.

13. Strocci R, Leonardi L, Guizzardi S, et al. Ultrastructural aspects of rat tail tendon sheaths. *J Anat*. 1985;140:57–67.

14. Warwick R, Williams PL. *Gray's Anatomy*. Edinburgh: Longman Group; 1973.

15. Dyer RF, Enna CD. Ultrastructural features of adult human tendon. *Cell Tissue Res*. 1976;168:247–259.

16. Gelberman R, Goldberg V, An K-N, et al. Tendon. In: Woo S L-Y, Buckwalter JA, eds. *Injury and Repair of the Musculoskeletal Soft Tissues*. Park Ridge, Ill: American Academy of Orthopaedic Surgeons; 1988:5–44.

17. Rowe RW. The structure of rat tail tendon. *Connect Tissue Res*. 1985; 14:9–20.

18. Squier CA, Bausch WH. Three-dimensional organization of fibroblasts and collagen fibrils in rat tail tendon. *Cell Tissue Res*. 1984;238: 319–327.

19. Jozsa L, Balint JB, Reffa A, et al. Histochemical and ultrastructural study of adult human tendon. *Acta Histochem (Jena)*. 1979;65:250–257.

20. Hildebrand M. *Analysis of Vertebrate Structure*. New York: Wiley; 1974.

21. Davison PF. Tendon. In: Weiss JB, Jayson MIV, eds. *Collagen in Health and Disease*. Edinburgh: Churchill Livingstone; 1982:498–505.

22. Akeson WH, Amiel D, Woo S L-Y. Immobility effects of synovial joints: the pathomechanics of joint contracture. *Biorheology*. 1980;17: 95–110.

23. Cetta G, Tenni R, Zanaboni G, et al. Biochemical and morphological modifications in rabbit achilles tendon during maturation and ageing. *Biochem J*. 1982;204:61–67.

24. Gotoh T, Sugi Y. Electron-microscopic study of the collagen fibrils of rat tail tendon as revealed by freeze-fracture and freeze-etching techniques. *Cell Tissue Res*. 1985;240:529–534.

25. Diamant J, Keller A, Baer E, et al. Collagen: ultrastructure and its relationship to mechanical properties as a function of ageing. *Proc R Soc B*. 1972;180:293.

26. Kastelic J, Galeski A, Baer E. The multicomposite structure of tendon. *Connect Tissue Res*. 1978;6:11–23.

27. Rowe RW. The structure of rat tail tendon fascicles. *Connect Tissue Res*. 1985;14:21–30.

28. Hukins DWL. Biomechanical properties of collagen. In: Weiss JB, Jayson MIV, eds. *Collagen in Health and Disease*. Edinburgh: Churchill Livingstone; 1982:49–72.

29. Doyle JR. Anatomy of the finger flexor tendon sheath and pulley system. *J Hand Surg Am*. 1988;13:473–484.

30. Hoving EW, Hillen B. Functional anatomy of the vagina fibrosa of the flexors of the fingers. *J Hand Surg Br*. 1989;14:99–101.

31. Tidball JG. Myotendinous junction: morphological changes and mechanical failure associated with muscle cell atrophy. *Exp Mol Pathol*. 1984;40:1–12.

32. Trotter JA, Hsi K, Samora A, et al. A morphometric analysis of the muscle-tendon junction. *Anat Rec*. 1985;213:26–32.

33. Trotter JA, Corbett K, Avner BP. Structure and function of the murine muscle-tendon junction. *Anat Rec*. 1981;210:293–302.

34. Mackay B, Harrop TJ, Muir AR. The fine structure of the muscle-tendon junction in the rat. *Acta Anat (Basel)*. 1969;73:588–604.

35. Kelly DE, Wood RL, Enders AC. *Bailey's Textbook of Microscopic Anatomy*. Baltimore: Williams & Wilkins; 1984.

36. Frank C, Amiel D, Woo S L-Y, et al. Normal ligament properties and ligament healing. *Clin Orthop*. 1985;196:15–25.

37. Cormack DH. *Ham's Histology*. Philadelphia: Lippincott; 1987.

38. Cotran RS, Kummar V, Robbins SL. *Pathological Basis of Disease*. Philadelphia: Saunders; 1989.

39. Rubin E, Farber JL. *Pathology*. Philadelphia: Lippincott; 1988.

40. Walter JB. *Pathology of Human Disease*. Philadelphia: Lea & Febiger; 1989.

41. Cullen MJ, Mastalgia FL. Pathological reactions of skeletal muscle. In: Mastalgia FL, Walton J, eds. *Skeletal Muscle Pathology*. New York: Churchill Livingstone; 1982:88–139.

42. Peacock EE Jr, Van Winkle W Jr. The biochemistry and the environment of wounds and their relation to wound strength. In: Peacock EE Jr, Van Winkle W Jr, eds. *Surgery and Biology of Wound Repair*. Philadelphia: Saunders; 1976:81–203.

43. Ross R. The fibroblast and wound repair. *Biol Rev*. 1968;43:51–96.

44. Goss RJ. *Principles of Regeneration*. New York: Academic Press; 1969.

45. Shekhter AB: Connective tissue as an integral system: role of cell–cell and cell–matrix interactions. *Connect Tissue Res*. 1986;15:23–31.

46. Van der Meulen JCH. Present state of knowledge and processes of healing in collagen structures. *Int J Sports Med*. 1982;3:4–8.

47. McGaw WT. The effect of tension on collagen remodelling by fibroblasts: a stereological ultrastructural study. *Connect Tissue Res*. 1986;14: 229–235.

48. Noyes FR, Torvik PJ, Hyde WB, et al. Biomechanics of ligament failure. II. An analysis of immobilization exercise and reconditioning effects in primates. *J Bone Joint Surg Am*. 1974;56:1406–1418.

49. Bailey AJ, Robins SP, Balian G. Biological significance of the intermolecular cross-links of collagen. *Nature (London)*. 1974;251:105.

50. Medoff RJ. Soft tissue healing. *Ann Sports Med*. 1987;3:67–70.

51. Carpenter S, Karpati G. *Pathology of Skeletal Muscle*. New York: Churchill Livingstone; 1984.

52. Caplan A, Carlson B, Faulkner J, et al. Skeletal muscle. In: Woo S L-Y, and Buckwalter JA, eds. *Injury and Repair of the Musculoskeletal Soft Tissues*. Park Ridge, Ill: American Academy of Orthopaedic Surgeons; 1988: 213–291.

53. Stockdale FE, Holtzer H. DNA synthesis and myogenesis. *Exp Cell Res*. 1961;24:508–520.

54. Mauro A. Satellite cell of skeletal muscle fibers. *J Biophys Biochem Cytol*. 1961;9:493–495.

55. Bischoff R. The myogenic stem cell in development of skeletal muscle. In: Mauro A, Shafiq S, Milhorat A, eds. *Regeneration of Striated Muscle and Myogenesis*. Amsterdam: Excerpta Medica; 1970:218–231.

56. Bischoff R. Proliferation of muscle satellite cells on intact myofibers in culture. *Dev Biol*. 1986;115:129–139.

57. Gulati AK, Reddi AH, Zalewski AA. Changes in the basement membrane zone components during skeletal muscle fiber degeneration and regeneration. *J Cell Biol*. 1983;97:957–962.

58. Bayne EK, Anderson MJ, Fambrough DM. Extracellular matrix organization in developing muscle: correlation with acetylcholine receptor aggregates. *J Cell Biol*. 1984;99:1486–1501.

59. Sanes JR, Marshall LM, McMahan UJ. Reinnervation of muscle fiber basal lamina after removal of myofibers: differentiation of regenerating axons at original synaptic sites. *J Cell Biol*. 1978;78:176–198.

60. Schultz E. A quantitative study of satellite cells in regenerating soleus and extensor digitorum longus muscles. *Anat Rec*. 1984;208:501–506.

61. Hall-Craggs ECB. The regeneration of skeletal muscle fibers per continuum. *J Anat*. 1974;117:171–178.

62. Carlson BM. *The Regeneration of Minced Muscles*. Basel: Karger; 1972.

63. Faulkner JA, Carlson BM. Contractile properties of standard and nerve-intact muscle grafts in the rat. *Muscle Nerve*. 1985;8:413–418.

64. Howald H. Training-induced morphological and functional changes in skeletal muscle. *Int J Sports Med*. 1982;3:1–12.

65. Ebbeling CB, Clarkson PM. Exercised-induced muscle damage and adaptation. *Sports Med*. 1989;7:207–234.

66. Hoppeler H. Exercise-induced ultrastructural changes in skeletal muscle. *Int J Sports Med*. 1986;7:187–204.

67. Armstrong RB. Muscle damage and endurance events. *Sports Med*. 1986;3:370–381.

68. McCully KK, Faulkner JA. Injury to skeletal muscle fibers of mice following lengthening contractions. *J Appl Physiol*. 1985;59:119–126.

69. Newham DJ, Jones DA, Clarkson PM. Repeated high force eccentric exercise: effects on muscle pain and damage. *J Appl Physiol*. 1987;63:1381–1386.

70. Rogers KL, Berger RA. Motor unit involvement and tension during maximum, voluntary concentric and isometric contractions of the elbow flexors. *Med Sci Sports*. 1974;6:253–259.

71. Armstrong RB, Ogilvie RW, Schwane JA. Eccentric exercise-induced injury to rat skeletal muscle. *J Appl Physiol*. 1983;54:80–93.

72. Friden J, Sjostrom M, Ekblom B. Myofibrillar damage following intense eccentric exercise in man. *Int J Sports Med*. 1983;4:170–176.

73. Friden J. Muscle soreness after exercise: implications of morphological changes. *Int J Sports Med*. 1984;5:57–66.

74. Clarkson PM, Tremblay I. Rapid adaptation to exercise-induced muscle damage. *J Appl Physiol*. 1988;65:1–6.

75. Garrett W, Tidball J. Myotendinous junction: structure, function and failure. In: Woo S L-Y, Buckwalter JA, eds. *Injury and Repair of Musculoskeletal Soft Tissues*. Park Ridge, Ill: American Academy of Orthopaedic Surgeons; 1988:171–207.

76. Nikolaou PK, Macdonald BL, Glisson RR, et al. Biomechanical and histological evaluation of muscle after controlled strain injury. *Am J Sports Med*. 1987;15:9–14.

77. Almekinders LC, Garrett WE Jr, Seaber AV. Histopathology of muscle tears in stretching injuries. *Trans Orthop Res Soc*. 1984;9:306.

78. Tidball JG, Daniel TL. Myotendinous junctions of tonic muscle cells: structure and loading. *Cell Tissue Res*. 1986;245:315–322.

79. Mubarak S, Hargens AR. *Compartment Syndromes and Volkmann's Contracture*. Philadelphia: Saunders; 1981:106–118.

80. Gordon L, Buncke HJ, Townsend JJ. Histological changes in skeletal muscle after temporary independent occlusion of arterial and venous supply. *Plastic Reconstr Surg*. 1978;61:576–580.

81. Jarvinen M. Healing of a crush injury in rat striated muscle. *Acta Pathol Microbiol Scand*. 1976;142:47–56.

82. Lehto M, Jarvinen M, Nelimarkka O. Scar formation after skeletal muscle injury: a histological and autoradiographical study in rats. *Arch Orthop Trauma Surg*. 1986;104:366–370.

83. Rothwell AG. Quadriceps hematoma: a prospective clinical study. *Clin Orthop*. 1982;171:97–103.

84. Lundborg G, Rank F. Experimental studies on cellular mechanisms involved in healing of animal and human flexor tendon in synovial environment. *Hand*. 1980;12:3–11.

85. Manske PR, Lesker PA. Histologic evidence of intrinsic flexor tendon repair in various experimental animals: an in vitro study. *Clin Orthop*. 1984;182:297–304.

86. Potenza AD. Tendon and ligament healing. In: Owen R, Goodfellow J, Bullough P, eds. *Scientific Foundation of Orthopaedics and Traumatology*. London: Heinemann Medical, 1980:300–305.

87. Sevitt S. *Bone Repair and Fracture Healing in Man*. Edinburgh: Churchill Livingstone; 1981.

88. Munro IR, Lindsay WK, Jackson SH. A synchronous study of collagen and mucopolysaccharide in healing flexor tendons of chickens. *Plast Reconstr Surg*. 1970;45:493–501.

89. Manske PR, Gelberman RH, Van de Berg JS, et al. Intrinsic flexor tendon repair: morphological study in vitro. *J Bone Joint Surg Am*. 1984;66:385–396.

90. Hutton P, Ferris B. Tendons. In: Bucknall TE, Ellis H, eds. *Wound Healing for Surgeons*. London: Bulliere-Tindall; 1984:286–296.

91. Gelberman RH, Woo S L-Y, Lothringer K, et al. Effects of early intermittent passive mobilization on healing canine flexor tendons. *J Hand Surg*. 1982;7:170–175.

92. Gelberman RH, Botte MJ, Spiegelman JJ, et al. The excursion and deformation of repaired flexor tendon treated with protected early motion. *J Hand Surg Am*. 1986;11:106–110.

93. Hitchock TF, Light TR, Bunch WH, et al. The effect of immediate controlled mobilization on the strength of flexor tendon repairs. *Trans Orthop Res Soc*. 1986;11:216.

94. Salter RB. The biologic concept of continuous passive motion of synovial joints. The first 18 years of basic research and its clinical application. *Clin Orthop*. 1989;242:12–25.

95. Manske PR, Lesker PA. Nutrient pathways of flexor tendons in primates. *J Hand Surg*. 1982;7:436–444.

96. Amiel D, Frank C, Harwood F, et al. Tendons and ligaments: a morphological and biochemical comparison. *J Orthop Res*. 1984;1:257–265.

97. Oakes BW. Acute soft tissue injuries: nature and management. *Aust Fam Physician*. 1982;10(suppl):3–16.

98. Williams IF, McCullagh KG, Silver IA. The distribution of types I and III collagen and fibronectin in the healing equine tendon. *Connect Tissue Res*. 1984;12:211–227.

99. Grinnell NF. Fibronectin and wound healing. *J Cell Biochem*. 1984;26:107–116.

100. Frank C, Amiel D, Akeson WH. Healing of the medial collateral ligament of the knee: a morphological and biomechanical assessment in rabbits. *Acta Orthop Scand*. 1983;54:917–923.

101. O'Donoghue DH, Frank GR, Jeter GL, et al. Repair and reconstruction of the anterior cruciate ligament in dogs: factors influencing long-term results. *J Bone Joint Surg Am*. 1971;53:710–718.

102. Noyes FR, McGinniss GH. Controversy about treatment of the knee with anterior cruciate laxity. *Clin Orthop*. 1985;198:61–76.

103. Woo S L-Y, Gomez MA, Inoue M, et al: New experimental procedures to evaluate the biomechanical properties of healing canine medial collateral ligaments. *J Orthop Res*. 1987;5:425–432.

104. Larsen N, Parker AW. Physical activity and its influence on the strength and elastic stiffness of knee ligaments. In: Howel ML, Parker AW, eds. *Sports Medicine: Medical and Scientific Aspects of Elitism in Sports*. Brisbane: Australian Sports Medicine Federation; 1982;8:63–73.

105. Tipton CM, Schild RJ, Tomanek RJ. Influence of physical activity on the strength of knee ligaments in rats. *Am J Physiol*. 1967;212:783–787.

106. Brinkley JM, Peat M. The effects of immobilization on the ultrastructure and mechanical properties of the medial collateral ligament of rats. *Clin Orthop*. 1986;203:301–308.

107. Andriacchi T, Sabiston P, DeHaven K, et al. Ligaments: injury and repair. In: Woo S L-Y, Buckwalter JA, eds. *Repair of the Musculoskeletal Soft Tissues*. Park Ridge, Ill: American Academy of Orthopaedic Surgeons; 1988:103–132.

108. Evans EB, Eggers GWN, Butler JK. Experimental remobilization of rat knee joints. *J Bone Joint Surg Am*. 1960;42:737–758.

109. Woo S L-Y, Matthews JV, Akeson WH, et al. Connective tissue response to immobility: correlative study of biomechanical and biochemical measurements of normal and immobilized rabbit knees. *Arthritis Rheum*. 1975;18:257–264.

110. Dahners LE. Ligament contractions—a correlation with cellularity and actin staining. *Trans Orthop Res Soc*. 1986;11:56.

Part II

The Extremities

Chapter 3

The Shoulder

Warren I. Hammer

To remain the most mobile joint in the body, the shoulder must sacrifice stability. Except for the superior coracohumeral ligament, the shoulder does not have the strong ligaments and capsule that stabilize all other human joints.[1] The muscles therefore have the dual function of providing mobility and stabilization. When we think of the shoulder, we must include besides the glenohumeral joint, the acromioclavicular joint, the sternoclavicular joint, and the scapulothoracic functional joint. Some consider the extracapsular joint between the coracoacromial arch and the greater tuberosity another functional joint.[2] Synchronized movement requires normal capsular and ligamentous flexibility along with the balance of muscles. Our examination must therefore include a differential stress of the associated soft tissues so that we can locate the source or sources of the problem.

PERTINENT FUNCTIONAL ANATOMY AND BIOMECHANICS

Although abduction of the humerus is usually tested in the coronal (frontal) plane, elevation of the humerus is more physiologically efficient in the plane of the scapula (Fig. 3-1). In this type of elevation the arm is raised 30° to 45° anterior to the coronal plane (the normal resting position of the scapula) so that the mechanical axis of the humerus approximates the mechanical axis of the scapula.[3] It has been stated that true abduction of the arm should not be in the coronal plane but in the scapular plane, where the inferior part of the capsule is not twisted and the deltoid and supraspinatus are optimally aligned for elevation of the arm.[4] Patients with painful shoulders due to subacromial lesions (bursitis or lesions of the rotator cuff or biceps) automatically elevate their arms in the scapular plane. For abduction in the scapular plane no appreciable humeral rotation is required. Scapular abduction places most of the muscles near their optimum fiber length.[5,6] According to Kessler and Hertling,[7] full elevation of the humerus in sagittal flexion and coronal abduction is an impure swing. To end up at full elevation for sagittal flexion, the humerus must rotate medially on its long axis. For coronal abduction the humerus rotates laterally on its long axis. For full abduction (in the coronal plane) approximately 90° of external rotation is used.[8] Other possible reasons for lateral rotation during abduction are to clear the greater tuberosity from the acromion and coracoacromial ligament[9] or to prevent impingement of the humeral head on the glenoid rim.[10]

Clinical: Because lateral rotation is necessary before full coronal abduction is attainable, in conditions involving limited abduction due to capsulitis or muscle contracture, stretching procedures should initially be directed toward improving lateral rotation. The infraspinatus and teres minor should be checked for flexibility and strength because they are responsible for producing the necessary external rotation for arm elevation.

SCAPULOTHORACIC MOTION

During the first 30° of humeral abduction or 60° of humeral flexion, motion is localized at the glenohumeral joint. The scapula attempts to stabilize and does not substantially change

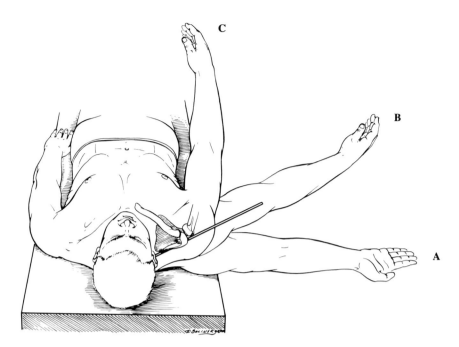

Figure 3-1 Planes of elevation. Abbreviations: **A**, coronal; **B**, scapular; **C**, sagittal. *Source*: Copyright © 1990 by David Bolinsky.

position (setting phase). Then scapulothoracic interaction with glenohumeral movement takes place in a ratio of 2:1 (or other reported ratios of 3:2 or 1.25:1[11,12]). In the overall 3:2 ratio (scapular plane) humeral-scapular movement is described as 4:1 during the first 30° of humeral abduction and 5:4 during the remaining abduction, averaging out to 3:2. This relationship is called the *scapulohumeral rhythm*.[13] Scapular rotation occurs through action at the acromioclavicular and sternoclavicular joints. The upper trapezius, lower trapezius, levator scapulae, and serratus anterior act together as a force couple that rotates and elevates the scapula upward, thus allowing for complete abduction. The scapula during arm elevation moves around anterior, elevates, and rotates upward on the rib cage.

Three advantages of scapular rotation are[8]:

1. it maintains the normal resting length of the deltoid by maintaining the muscle length of the deltoid origin from the approaching insertion
2. it increases joint stability by placing the glenoid fossa under the humeral head
3. it removes the acromion from the path of the elevating humerus

Rowe[14] states that the scapula acts as a shock absorber because of its ability to recoil and absorb the impact when there are direct blows to the shoulder or indirect blows from the humerus (Fig. 3-2).

Clinical: Of the 180° of abduction (the average person does not reach 180°), the scapula moves approximately 60°. In the absence of glenohumeral motion[15] scapulothoracic movement by itself can elevate the humerus approximately 65° by the so-called shrugging mechanism. This mechanism can be

noted on inspection as resulting from lesions (rupture) of the deltoid or rotator cuff or acute inflammatory processes in the area. Often with subacromial impingement and inflammation, asynchronous scapulothoracic motion occurs in an attempt to clear the humeral head away from the inflammation.

The scapula, which is responsible for one-third of shoulder motion, must always be considered in every shoulder problem. Recent electromyographic (EMG) analysis of shoulder function in tennis players showed that in the serve, forehand, and backhand strokes the serratus anterior was essential; because the serve in tennis is similar to the overhand throw, this muscle is especially important for pitchers as well. Ryu and colleagues[16] state that efficient serratus anterior function is essential in stabilizing the scapula against the thoracic wall and in rotating the scapula to form a stable platform against which the humeral head can move. Fatigue of the serratus anterior muscle may endanger scapulothoracic-glenohumeral synchrony and lead to abnormal compensatory biomechanics.

Figure 3-2 Shock-absorbing function of the scapula. The recoil mechanism of the scapula absorbs impacts of blows to the shoulder, a mechanism that the hip joint lacks. *Source*: Reprinted with permission from *Clinical Orthopaedics* (1961;20:41), Copyright © 1961, J.B. Lippincott Company.

The most important upward rotators of the glenoid are the trapezius and the serratus anterior. Perry[17] explains that, although both these muscles are almost of equal size, EMG analysis during swimming shows that the serratus works at 75% of its maximum whereas the trapezius works from 34% to 42% of its maximum. She states that a 75% workload of the serratus during prolonged swimming cannot be maintained. Training and rehabilitation must include increased emphasis on all the scapular muscles.

Swimmers often overdevelop their pectoral and anterior cervical muscles, resulting in slumping posture and weak scapular retractors and adductors (rhomboids, middle trapezius, and upper fibers of latissimus dorsi) and lateral rotators (Figs. 3-3 to 3-7). Weak scapular musculature may result in failure to position the glenoid in time under the humeral head during the recovery phase (abduction and external rotation) of swimming. This may result in acromial impingement of the humeral head structures due to failure of the humeral head to clear the acromion completely. The overdevelopment of internal shoulder rotators compared to external rotators is a possible cause of tendinitis (swimmer's shoulder).

It is essential to consider the relationship between the scapular and the glenohumeral joint in all shoulder problems. Because the rotator cuff muscles originate off the scapular, inharmonious scapular movement due to fatigued scapular muscles must put the cuff muscles at a disadvantage. Rotator cuff muscles, which also function as dynamic stabilizers to the

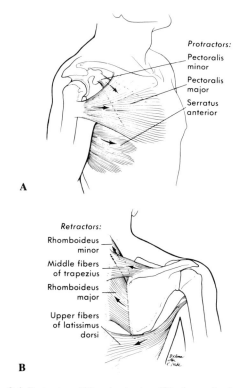

Figure 3-4 Protractors (**A**) and retractors (**B**) of scapula. *Source*: Reprinted with permission from GP Bogumill, ''Functional Anatomy of the Shoulder and Elbow'' in *Symposium on Upper Extremity Injuries in Athletes*, (p 198) by the American Academy of Orthopaedic Surgeons, St. Louis, 1986, The C.V. Mosby Co.

Figure 3-3 Swimmer's posture. Sagittal posture analysis shows that this swimmer has forward shoulders and prominent lordosis. *Source*: Reprinted with permission from *Clinics in Sports Medicine* (1986;5[1]:11), Copyright © 1986, W.B. Saunders Company.

humeral head, when weakened would create added stress for the static shoulder stabilizers (capsule and ligaments). Abnormal scapulothoracic rhythm, by its effect on the levator scapulae and upper trapezius, may also be responsible for cervical spine involvement and myofascial trigger points.

We must always ensure scapula mobility by ensuring flexibility and strength of the involved muscles. Often the rotator cuff and scapular muscles must be strengthened while the pectorals must be stretched. The lateral rotators should be strengthened to balance the excessively strong internal rotators. Subsequent chapters discuss stretching, mobilization, trigger point possibilities, and rehabilitation of scapular muscles.

STERNOCLAVICULAR-ACROMIOCLAVICULAR MOTION

The clavicular joints are synovial joins. The total range available at the clavicular joints must of necessity equal the 60° total range of the scapulothoracic joint.[18] The sternoclavicular joint elevates 4° for every 10° of humeral elevation, up to 90°. It stops elevating at 90°. The acromioclavicular joint moves 20° to 25° during the first 30° of humeral elevation. The acromioclavicular joint becomes close packed between 90° and 120° (ie, locked so that the joint is unable to elevate

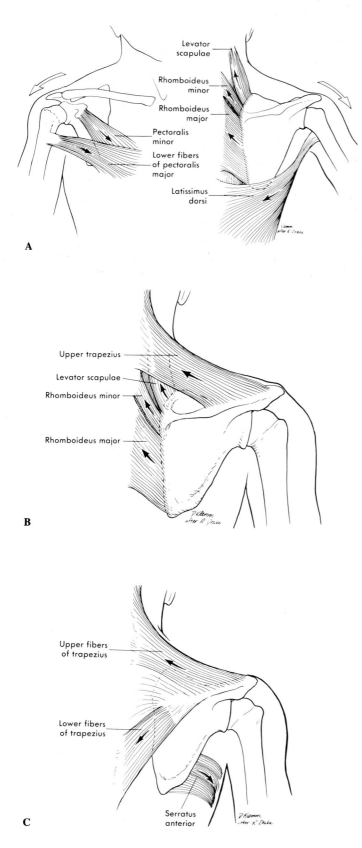

A

B

C

Figure 3-5 Elevators (**A** and **B**) and upward rotators (**C**) of scapula. *Source:* Reprinted with permission from GP Bogumill, "Functional Anatomy of the Shoulder and Elbow" in *Symposium on Upper Extremity Injuries in Athletes*, (p 201) by the American Academy of Orthopaedic Surgeons, St. Louis, 1986, The C.V. Mosby Co.

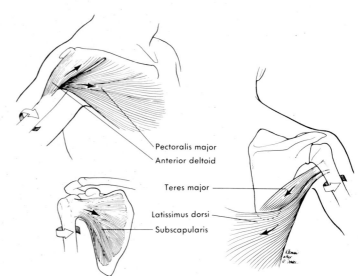

Figure 3-6 Internal rotators of arm. *Source:* Reprinted with permission from GP Bogumill, "Functional Anatomy of the Shoulder and Elbow" in *Symposium on Upper Extremity Injuries in Athletes*, (p 204) by the American Academy of Orthopaedic Surgeons, St. Louis, 1986, The C.V. Mosby Co.

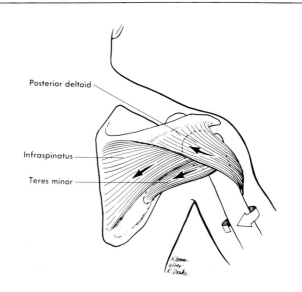

Figure 3-7 External rotators of arm. *Source:* Reprinted with permission from GP Bogumill, "Functional Anatomy of the Shoulder and Elbow" in *Symposium on Upper Extremity Injuries in Athletes*, (p 204) by the American Academy of Orthopaedic Surgeons, St. Louis, 1986, The C.V. Mosby Co.

further). Additional elevation of the scapula after the close-packed acromioclavicular position occurs because as the scapula rotates upward the coracoid process rotates downward, causing the coracoclavicular ligaments to pull the clavicle into long-axis rotation.[7] The acromioclavicular joint is more related to scapular motion and clavicular rotation than the sternoclavicular joint, which acts as a lever arm and stabilizer.

Clinical: Sports that emphasize excessive abduction and external rotation cause repetitive axial clavicle rotation, resulting in abnormal sheer stress at the acromioclavicular joint. Pain appearing at the acromioclavicular joint on active or passive abduction beginning at approximately 90° elevation and continuing to the 180° end range may indicate an acromioclavicular lesion. Pain occurs because acromioclavicular stress is provided by the close-packed position and long-axis rotation. Horizontal adduction is another acromioclavicular close-packed position that creates pain when the joint is involved.

For complete forward flexion and abduction of the shoulder, there is approximately 60° of scapula rotation and 90° to 105° of glenohumeral rotation. The remaining 10° to 15° of shoulder flexion or abduction is produced by spinal extension or spinal lateral flexion. If only one arm is abducted or flexed, lateral displacement of the spinal column produced by the contralateral spinal muscles is necessary. When both arms are abducted or flexed, exaggeration of the lumbar lordosis by the lumbar muscles is necessary.[19] Spinal manipulation may therefore improve the final 10° to 15° of shoulder abduction and flexion by restoring increased upper thoracic spinal extension. It is essential to restore normal joint play to both the acromioclavicular (A-C) and sternoclavicular (S-C) joint (see Chapter 10).

MUSCULAR FORCES

The muscles surrounding the shoulder must create the balance of forces necessary for stability and mobility. The shallow glenoid cannot provide the stability that an acetabulum can provide, nor can the ligaments and capsule provide enough stability as in other joints. Of course, this instability is necessary for mobility. Inferior dislocation while the arm is at one's side with a weight being held in one hand is prevented by the superior capsule, coracohumeral ligament, supraspinatus and infraspinatus (active ligaments), and to a lesser extent the posterior deltoid, which imitates the general direction of the supraspinatus. The concept that the glenoid tilts upward to support the resting humeral head has recently been challenged by roentgenographic analysis showing the mean alignment of the glenoid fossa to be tilting downward 5°.[17] Without a weight in the hand there may not be any EMG activity, the arm being supported by the capsule. Interestingly, with a heavy load in the hand the muscles with a vertical pull, such as the deltoid, triceps, and biceps brachii, are electromyographically silent whereas the horizontally directed supraspinatus and infraspinatus are active.[20,21]

Clinical: People with forward head tilt, slumping shoulder posture, thoracic kyphosis, or hemiplegia, all of which may be related to supraspinatus weakness, lose the support of the glenoid cavity, which now faces increasingly downward. The arm is caused to abduct slightly, which relaxes the superior capsule and results in increased tone to the rotator cuff muscles. The increased stress to the remaining capsule may cause increased collagen production and result in capsular fibrosis.[7]

Overstretching of the scapular muscles and eventual tightening of the anterior (pectoral, subscapular, and scalene) muscles may occur. Facilitation of these muscles may create inhibition and shutting down of the cuff muscles.[22] Perry[8] mentions that slumping posture also causes excessive stretch on the levator scapulae and some stretch on the upper trapezius (Fig. 3-8). Improved ergonomics and posture will help prevent shoulder problems.

SHOULDER MUSCLE ACTIONS

1. *Shoulder flexion* (forward in the sagittal plane): primarily anterior deltoid and the clavicular portion of the pectoralis major; secondarily coracobrachialis and biceps brachii, which act mainly during the first 90° of flexion (Fig. 3-9).
2. *External rotation:* infraspinatus, teres minor, and posterior deltoid (Figs. 3-7 and 3-10).
3. *Internal rotation* (Figs. 3-6 and 3-10): subscapularis, teres major, latissimus dorsi, pectoralis major, and anterior deltoid. The subscapularis is the only one that comes close to being a pure internal rotator. The pectoralis major combines internal rotation with adduction, the anterior deltoid flexes the shoulder as it internally rotates, and the latissimus dorsi and teres major combine internal rotation with adduction and extension.
4. *Adduction and extension* (Fig. 3-11): latissimus dorsi, teres major, the lower portion of the pectoralis major,

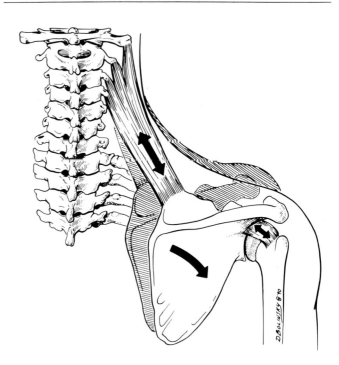

Figure 3-8 Slumping posture causes excessive stress to the levator scapulae, parascapular muscles, capsule, and cuff. Eventual shortening of the pectoral fascia, myofascial trigger points, and fibrosis may occur. *Source:* Copyright © 1990 by David Bolinsky.

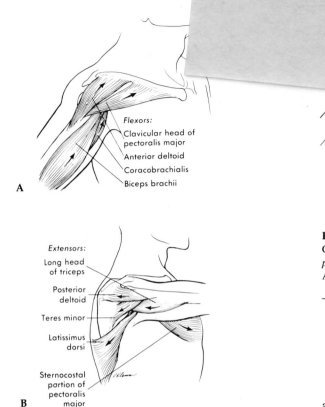

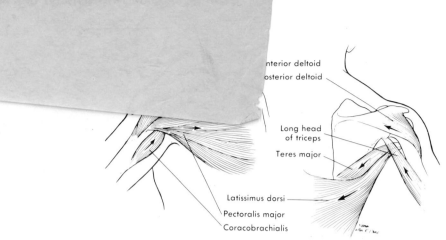

Figure 3-11 Adductors of arm. *Source*: Reprinted with permission from GP Bogumill, ''Functional Anatomy of the Shoulder and Elbow'' in *Symposium on Upper Extremity Injuries in Athletes*, (p 203) by the American Academy of Orthopaedic Surgeons, St. Louis, 1986, The C.V. Mosby Co.

5. *Abduction:* principally the deltoid and supraspinatus (see under Force Couple, below) (Fig. 3-12).

Clinical: Resisted muscle testing is used to determine, among other things, whether the contractile unit elicits pain. Pain and almost normal strength on testing indicates that some part of the muscle is involved. Learning the muscle action allows us to evaluate many muscular problems. Examining a patient in the motion or position that elicits pain will also provide valuable information. People with excellent muscle tone may require repetitive testing to elicit their pain.

Figure 3-9 Flexors and extensors of arm. *Source*: Reprinted with permission from GP Bogumill, ''Functional Anatomy of the Shoulder and Elbow'' in *Symposium on Upper Extremity Injuries in Athletes,* (p 201) by the American Academy of Orthopaedic Surgeons, St. Louis, 1986, The C.V. Mosby Co.

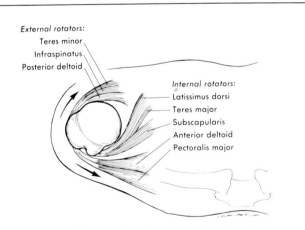

Figure 3-10 Rotators of arm from above. *Source*: Reprinted with permission from GP Bogumill, ''Functional Anatomy of the Shoulder and Elbow'' in *Symposium on Upper Extremity Injuries in Athletes*, (p 203) by the American Academy of Orthopaedic Surgeons, St. Louis, 1986, The C.V. Mosby Co.

FORCE COUPLE

The principal force couple required to rotate (elevate) the arm is made up of the deltoid and rotator cuff muscles. In general, the chief functions of the cuff muscles (supraspinatus, infraspinatus, subscapularis, and teres minor) are to create joint compression and downward depression, creating a fixed fulcrum so that the deltoid can rotate the arm upward. Radiologically a decreased width (5 mm or less) of the humeral acromial space may indicate a cuff rupture. If rotator cuff function is impaired even slightly for any reason the corresponding normal fulcrum of the humeral head will be lost, and abnormal upward displacement (deltoid shear) of the humeral head will be allowed[21] (Fig. 3-13). The compressive force on the glenoid should always be equal to or greater than the vertical shear force caused by the deltoid (a crucial reason why rotator muscle strength should always be assessed). At 90° of abduction the shear and compressive forces should be equal.

The literature regarding the function of the cuff muscles (especially the supraspinatus) and the deltoid has been contradictory. A recent study[23] on 10 normal volunteers was per-

the posterior deltoid, and the long head of the triceps. These are the main muscles that act as the arm is brought down to the side of the body from the overhead position against resistance. The latissimus dorsi and teres major also extend the shoulder while the lower portion of the pectoralis major draws the arm forward as they adduct. The posterior deltoid is important in hyperextension.

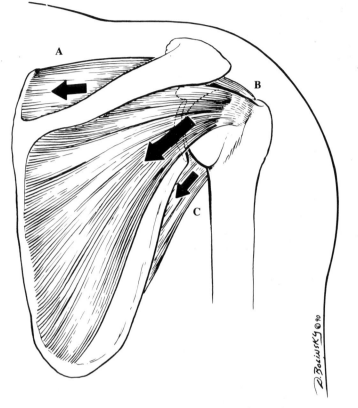

Figure 3-12 Shoulder dynamic stabilizers. The supraspinatus (**A**) acts mainly as a humeral head compressor while the infraspinatus (**B**) and subscapularis (**C**) act as depressors. *Source:* Copyright © 1990 by David Bolinsky.

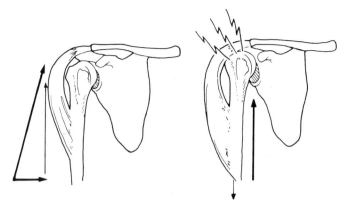

Figure 3-13 Independent deltoid muscle action. Dominant force pattern is vertical shear. Impingement against acromion is induced. *Source:* Reprinted from *The Shoulder*, (p 17) by CR Rowe (Ed) with permission of Churchill Livingstone, © 1988.

Smith[24] showed that the long head of the biceps with the arm in external rotation is able, although with poor leverage, to abduct the humerus. Basmajian and Deluca[20] state that the biceps brachii contributes in maintaining abduction while the arm is laterally rotated and the forearm is supinated. The long head of the biceps stabilizes the humeral head on the glenoid during powerful elbow flexion and forearm supination,[25] acting in effect as a humeral head depressor.

Howell et al[23] showed in one experiment that during both forward flexion and elevation in the scapular plane the subscapularis contributed 12% of the torque at 120° of elevation, where it showed electrical activity and had a 10-mm moment arm. The infraspinatus has no moment arm in the motion arc from 0° to 90° in the plane of the scapula and only a 5-mm moment arm at 120° of elevation. Moment arm may be defined as the length of a line from the center of rotation perpendicular to the force vector of the muscle[14] (Fig. 3-14). The greater the moment arm, the greater the power of rotation. The supraspinatus moment arm is 24 mm. These investigators also showed that in these two planes of motion (forward flexion and scapular) the subscapularis, coracobrachialis, long head of the biceps, and clavicular portion of the pectoralis major, acting in concert, were unable to elevate the arm against the force of gravity.[23]

Clinical: It is apparent that people with either rotator cuff tears or deltoid paralysis could have the ability to elevate their arms 180° but with much less lifting strength than normal. Pain will inhibit the initiation of abduction with fresh rupture of the supraspinatus. Pain creates disuse, which creates weakness and muscular imbalance. Eventual subluxation and impingement may result. The loss of function of either the deltoid or the supraspinatus would therefore account for the drop-arm test (described later).

The loss of strength of any of the rotator cuff muscles decreases the necessary stabilization of the humeral head. Abduction of the arm in any plane would create abnormal upward excursion of the humeral head and a high-riding

formed in which isolated paralysis of the suprascapular and axillary nerves was induced. Some of the conclusions were:

- the supraspinatus and deltoid muscles are equally responsible for producing torque about the shoulder joint in the functional planes of motion (forward flexion and elevation in the plane of the scapula)
- the supraspinatus and deltoid muscles are responsible for essentially all the torque generated at the shoulder in the functional planes of motion
- the deltoid muscle is capable of initiating elevation in the plane of the scapula

Although the deltoid might initiate abduction without the supraspinatus, the initiation of effort would be inefficient because the deltoid has a low angle of pull, which reduces the muscle's leverage and thereby causes upward displacement of the humeral head.

Perry[17] state that the supraspinatus is anatomically too small to lift the arm independently and that 98% maximum effort of the supraspinatus can only elevate the arm 30°. She also states that the supraspinatus does not initiate abduction by itself and that dynamic EMG shows that the middle and anterior deltoids and supraspinatus function synchronously.

It is questionable whether we can abduct our arms without the use of the supraspinatus and deltoid. Lehmkuhl and

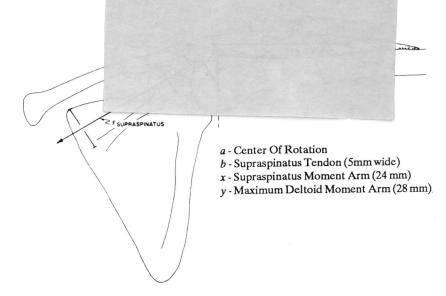

a - Center Of Rotation
b - Supraspinatus Tendon (5mm wide)
x - Supraspinatus Moment Arm (24 mm)
y - Maximum Deltoid Moment Arm (28 mm)

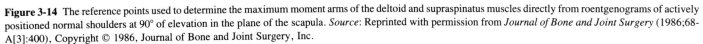

Figure 3-14 The reference points used to determine the maximum moment arms of the deltoid and supraspinatus muscles directly from roentgenograms of actively positioned normal shoulders at 90° of elevation in the plane of the scapula. *Source*: Reprinted with permission from *Journal of Bone and Joint Surgery* (1986;68-A[3]:400), Copyright © 1986, Journal of Bone and Joint Surgery, Inc.

humerus, resulting in impingement. As Noah and Gidumal[26] explain, the deltoid's action, when unopposed, leads to secondary impingement. Garrick and Webb[27] state ''that most cases of impingement syndrome are simply the result of insufficiency of the stabilizing muscles of the shoulder, which permits the humeral head to be displaced when the arm is moved.'' Eventual fatigue of the scapulothoracic muscles also aggravates the impingement because these muscles normally aid in acromial elevation. Inferior impingement is probable because tears tend to occur on the underside of the cuff.[28]

It is therefore important to examine selectively and increase the strength of the rotator cuff and scapulothoracic muscles after pain is relieved to protect against recurrent deltoid shear and instability due to weakness of the dynamic shoulder stabilizers. According to Inman et al,[12] the supraspinatus is not the initiator of abduction but works together with the deltoid progressively throughout the entire range of motion.

PASSIVE STABILITY

The glenoid fossa is anteverted, thereby anatomically providing more stability posteriorly than anteriorly. Although passive stability of the shoulder is thought of as resulting from support by the static passive structures such as the glenoid labrum, capsule, and glenohumeral ligaments, the dynamic stabilizers such as the rotator cuff muscles and scapular rotators must be included.

The shoulder requires considerable capsular laxity to allow its mobile range of motion. It is so loose and lax that the bones may even be separated from each other by 2 or 3 cm by a distractive force. The rotator cuff muscles are intimately blended with the fibrous capsule.[29] Bland[30] states that the

capsule should be thought of as a conjoined tendon containing the insertions of the capsular (cuff) muscles. The inner surface of the capsule is lined with synovium and extends into the lining of biceps tendon sheath, which is considered an extension of the joint cavity. When the arm is resting in neutral the superior portion of the capsule is taut, and the inferior portion lies in lax folds; the inferior part of the capsule is the least supported and is subjected to the greatest strain because it is stretched tightly across the rounded head of the humerus when the arm is fully abducted.[29] Full horizontal flexion tenses the posterior capsule, and external rotation tightens the anterior capsule.

Anterior stability is probably of the most concern because 95% of glenohumeral subluxation or dislocation occurs in an anterior-inferior direction.[31] Up to 45° of abduction important anterior stabilizers are the subscapularis tendon and inferior glenohumeral ligament. As abduction approaches 90° the subscapularis tendon does not cover the anterior-inferior portion of the humeral head, so that the superior band of the inferior glenohumeral ligament provides the main support. At the upper range of abduction anterior stability is provided by the axillary pouch of the inferior glenohumeral ligament, which is the longest and strongest of the three glenohumeral ligaments. The anterior and middle glenohumeral ligaments are mere thickenings of the capsule. The posterior stability of the humeral head is provided by the tendons of the infraspinatus and teres minor tendons.[21]

Bigliani[32] and Turkel[33] state that the inferior glenohumeral ligament is the most important structure in preventing anterior-inferior instability with shoulder elevation. With elevation, tension across the capsule shifts more inferiorly. Bigliani[32] states that with the arm at the side in external rotation the middle glenohumeral ligament is an important anterior stabilizer. Then with abduction, as the humeral head shifts inferior, the inferior glenohumeral ligament becomes the chief stabilizer. The inferior glenohumeral ligament also acts as a posterior stabilizer because it is shaped like a hammock, extending posteriorly behind the humeral head.[34]

Clinical: In the treatment of adhesive capsulitis and especially the early stages of the capsular pattern, our approach must be based on treating both the passive and the contractile tissues. Joint play techniques, stretching techniques, trigger point techniques, and all other treatments must take into account all the viscoelastic elements in the connective tissue of ligamentous joint capsules, tendons, and muscles. Muscle and joint tissues both contribute to total stiffness, and neither is so dominant that alterations in the other are obscured.[35] More discussion is provided under Adhesive Capsulitis (see below, Shoulder Lesions).

FUNCTIONAL EXAMINATION OF THE SHOULDER

Inspection

Anteriorly the symmetry of trapezius and deltoid muscles should be observed and compared bilaterally. The humeral head should appear as a smooth, rounded contour anterior to the acromion. Abnormal protrusion or flattening of the greater tuberosity, indicating dislocation or deltoid atrophy, should be sought. Symmetry of clavicle, acromioclavicular, and sternoclavicular joints is observed. Posteriorly the supraspinatus and infraspinatus fossae are observed for atrophy. Because the infraspinatus muscle is more superficial than the supraspinatus, it is more likely to appear atrophied if both muscles are involved.

The scapulae should be symmetric and not winging. Scapular-glenohumeral rhythm is checked by holding a finger on the inferior-lateral border of the scapula and asking the patient to abduct the arm. The point at which the finger (scapula) moves in relation to glenohumeral motion is noted (see above, Scapulothoracic Motion). If the serratus anterior is involved because of weakness in or trauma to the long thoracic nerve, winging will appear with the tip of the scapula coming up; if the spinal accessory nerve is involved, affecting the trapezius, the whole scapula will rotate out, downward and laterally. Winging can be functionally tested by having the patient push against a wall. Andrews[36] tests for slight weakness of the serratus anterior by observing a patient bearing weight straight-armed between two tables. As the serratus muscle fatigues, the involved scapula rides out. Laterally, the humeral head should appear anterior to the acromion. The dominant side is usually lower and hypertrophied compared to the nondominant side.

Audible and palpable crepitus during shoulder movement usually refers to scarring of the subacromial bursa, a torn glenoid labrum, osteoarthritis of the A-C joint, or loose bodies.

Active Abduction in Coronal Plane to 180°

Only 4% of men and 28% of women actually reach 180°. In one study the mean range for women was 171° and for men 167°.[17] Active tests that combine lateral rotation and abduction (Fig. 3-15A) and medial rotation and adduction (Fig. 3-15B) may also be used.

Because active motions stress both contractile and inert tissue, active testing is used as a baseline to assess the present status of the shoulder against future progress. The examiner should observe an approximate 2:1 scapulohumeral ratio and possible reversal of rhythm where there is shrugging, in which case the scapula moves first and more than the humerus (suggesting adhesive capsulitis, ruptures, or subacromial

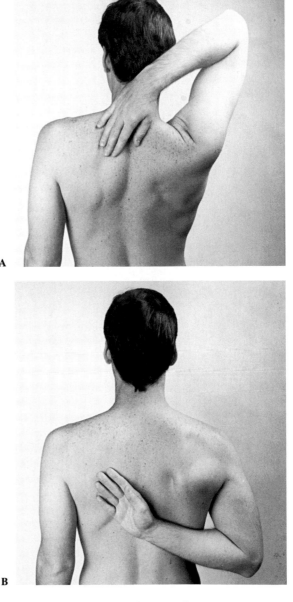

Figure 3-15 (**A**) Active combined lateral rotation and abduction. (**B**) Active combined medial rotation and adduction.

inflammatory conditions). The examiner should also be aware of the area of pain and at what range the pain arises (see below). Abduction may be measured as the angle between the rib cage and the elevated arm.

Passive Abduction

Passive abduction (Table 3-A-1 in Appendix 3-A) in or slightly posterior to the coronal plane allows a more reliable impression of the presence of a painful arc.[37] Range of motion is 180° (Fig. 3-16).

Painful arc (Fig. 3-17) will present with no pain to approximately 60° to 80°, pain to approximately 120° to 130°, and then no pain. During this range the greater tuberosity approaches the acromion. In forward flexion or abduction, a painful arc may represent a pinching in the subacromial space due to inflammation of the superior portion of the tenoperiosteal portion of the supraspinatus and infraspinatus, subscapularis, biceps tendon, and bursa. Pain during arc can also be caused by an osteophyte off the inferior acromioclavicular joint, enlargement of the outer end of the clavicle, a hypertrophied coracoacromial ligament, or an enlarged anterior-inferior surface of the acromion. A painful arc would negate deltoid or adductor muscle involvement because they are not subacromial. Painful arc could occur with active motions, for example in forward flexion or going from an abducted to an adducted position.

Because in the coronal plane the humerus externally rotates to clear the greater tuberosity from the coracoacromial arch, if abduction of the arm with the hand pronated (internal shoulder rotation) causes pain in the 60° to 130° range and abduction with the hand supinated then relieves the pain between 60° and 130°, then there is a strong possibility of pathology in the subacromial area. Pain beginning from 90° of abduction to the end range (180°) may indicate an acromioclavicular involvement (Fig. 3-17). Pain only at the end range of abduction may be due to loss of accessory joint play of the A-C joint. Pain at the end range causing a pinching effect could indicate involvement (degeneration, inflammation or partial tears) of the tenoperiosteal portion of the supraspinatus and infraspinatus and the subacromial bursa. The examiner must be aware of varieties of end feel in all passive testing.

Passive Lateral Rotation

Passive lateral rotation can be tested with the arm at the side, which stretches the subscapularis and middle glenohumeral ligament (average range, 40° to 60°), or with the arm at 90° of abduction with the elbow flexed 90°, pointing forward, and elevated upward (average range, 90°) (Fig. 3-18). This position stresses the inferior glenohumeral ligament and subscapularis muscle. Lateral rotation is the most limited motion of the capsular pattern. It also stresses the acromioclavicular

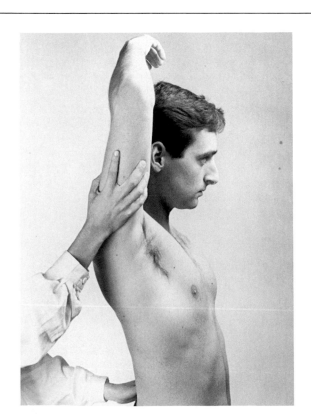

Figure 3-16 Passive coronal abduction.

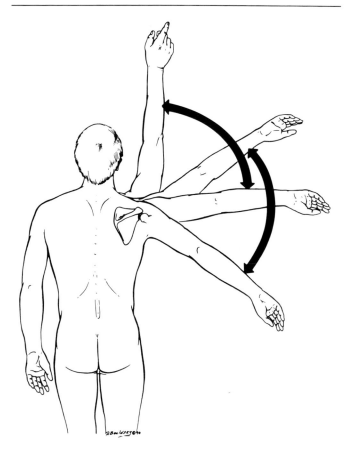

Figure 3-17 Painful arc. Pain occurs approximately between 60° and 130°. Pain beginning about 90° and continuing to end range may indicate an acromioclavicular problem. *Source:* Copyright © 1990 by David Bolinsky.

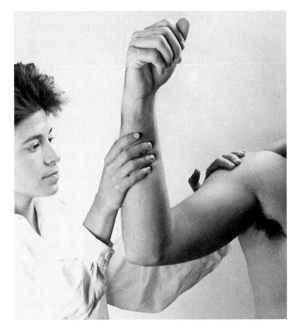

Figure 3-18 Passive shoulder lateral rotation at 90° abduction.

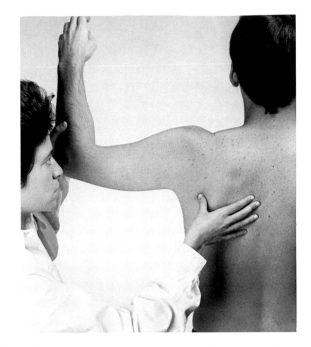

Figure 3-19 Passive glenohumeral abduction with a fixed scapula.

ligament and may be limited by subcoracoid bursitis or contracted pectoral muscles. Hypermobility may indicate capsular or ligamentous disruption (see below, Shoulder Instability). Loss of external rotation in full abduction may be due to anterior subluxation. Posterior pain may be due to impingement irritation of the infraspinatus.

Passive Glenohumeral Abduction with a Fixed Scapula

Scapula movement is eliminated by stabilizing the inferior lateral edge of the scapula while passively abducting the arm until scapula movement is felt (average range, 90° to 105°). The status of the glenohumeral joint and capsule is then assessed. Glenohumeral abduction is the second most limited motion of the capsular pattern (Fig. 3-19).

Passive Medial Rotation

Passive medial rotation (Fig. 3-20) is tested in the following manner. The patient's forearm is placed behind the back and pulled backward while the shoulder is stabilized. Alternatively, with the patient's arm at the side with the elbow flexed 90° and the arm pointing forward, the forearm is moved internally while the shoulder is stabilized (average range, 55° to 80°). A third method is to place the patient's arm in 90° of abduction with the elbow flexed 90° and pointing forward (Fig. 3-21), then internally rotate the shoulder (average range, 70°). The test stretches the infraspinatus and teres minor. Medial rotation is the third most limited motion of the capsular pattern.

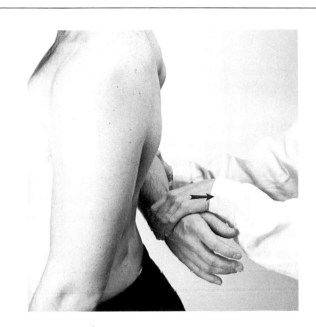

Figure 3-20 Passive shoulder medial rotation.

The usual test for shoulder internal rotation has the patient adducting the shoulder behind the back in an attempt to see how high up the spine he or she can reach with the thumb. This test is not a true test of shoulder internal rotation.

Passive Horizontal Adduction

In testing passive horizontal adduction (Fig. 3-22), the patient's arm is pressed across the chest above the nipple line (average range, 130°). This stretches the posterior deltoid and

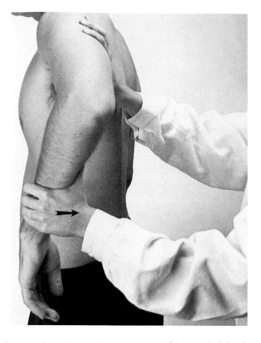

Figure 3-21 Passive shoulder medial rotation at 90° humeral abduction.

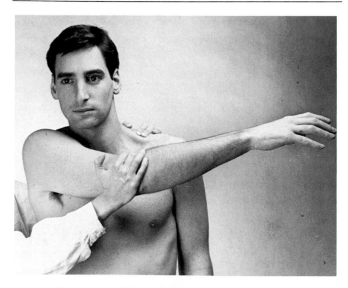

Figure 3-22 Passive shoulder horizontal adduction.

compresses the acromioclavicular joint. It may pinch the subscapularis on the coracoid process and also may pinch the subcoracoid bursa. Motion may be limited because of tightness and pain in the posterior capsular structures or posterior capsulitis. The test may aggravate the anterior labrum and a degenerated sternoclavicular joint.

Resisted Abduction

In testing resisted abduction (Fig. 3-23), the patient's shoulder is stabilized with one of the examiner's hands; the other hand is held against the lateral epicondyle of the patient's

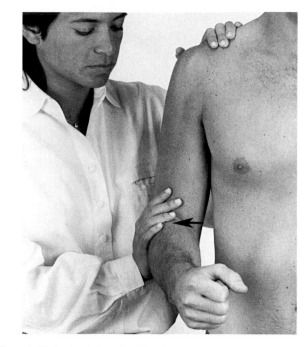

Figure 3-23 Resisted shoulder abduction.

elbow, which is flexed to 90°. This test measures the strength of both the supraspinatus and the middle deltoid. The deltoid is seldom involved. The supraspinatus in the supraspinatus fossa is palpated while testing by having patient extend and ipsilaterally bend the head and neck so that the face is rotated toward the opposite side.[38] This relaxes the overlying trapezius.

To achieve selective isolation of the supraspinatus, the patient abducts the arm to 90° and then forward flexes 30° with the extended arm and hand internally rotated and the thumb down (Fig. 3-24). This test resists only the supraspinatus and a

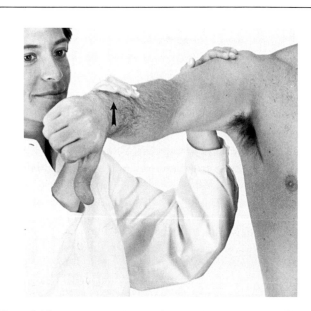

Figure 3-24 Isolated resisted supraspinatus (minimal central deltoid action) tested in scapular plane.

small portion of the middle deltoid.[39] It may aggravate inert tissues (bursa, capsule, or ligament) because they are under stress with the arm abducted, which is a reason why we test muscles in the neutral rested position or test passive structures first to eliminate inert input. Garrick and Webb[27] state that during the above supraspinatus test, if there is weakness of the supraspinatus, anterior deltoid, or even the other cuff muscles due to cuff lesions or shoulder instability, a pectoral substitution pattern may be observed. Upon resistive testing, you would see increased tone and size of the clavicular part of the pectoralis major.

Resisted Adduction

Resisted adduction (Fig. 3-25) tests primarily the pectoralis major and latissimus dorsi and secondarily the teres major and anterior deltoid. With one hand the examiner stabilizes the anterior-inferior acromion (the tone of the pectoralis major on contracting can be palpated) and resists against the medial humeral epicondyle of the elbow in 90° of flexion. Pain results in the axillary or pectoral areas.

Resisted Lateral Rotation

Resisted lateral rotation (Fig. 3-26A) tests the infraspinatus and teres minor. The tester stabilizes the patient's flexed elbow against the patient's waist (to prevent abduction of the elbow) and resists against the distal forearm. Resistance should not be directed against the patient's hand or wrist, which tests the wrist extensors.

It is impossible in muscle testing to distinguish between the teres minor and infraspinatus because both are active in lateral rotation. Testing with the arm at the side may emphasize the teres minor, and testing with the arm elevated 90° and the forearm forward (Fig. 3-26B) may emphasize the infraspinatus. Muscle testing in different ranges of motion may reveal a tendinitis not necessarily found in neutral testing positions. The examiner must be certain that the passive testing clears the joint inert tissue of involvement before the muscle test is accepted as positive when testing through a range of motion.

The infraspinatus is involved much more often than the teres minor. Painful resisted lateral rotation associated with pain on

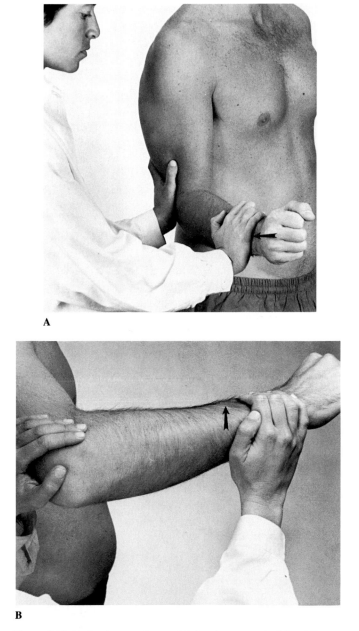

A

B

Figure 3-26 Resisted teres minor and infraspinatus emphasizing (**A**) teres minor and (**B**) infraspinatus.

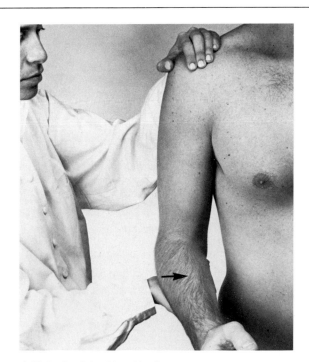

Figure 3-25 Resisted shoulder adduction.

resisted adduction indicates teres minor involvement. Painful resisted abduction associated with painful resisted lateral rotation is usually due to supraspinatus involvement, especially if abduction is more painful, but it could also be due to a double lesion.

Resisted Medial Rotation

Resisted medial rotation (Fig. 3-27) tests primarily the subscapularis but also includes the pectoralis major, latissimus dorsi, and teres major, which would be ruled out by resisted adduction. The tester stabilizes the patient's flexed elbow against the patient's waist (to prevent elbow abduction) and resists medial rotation against the volar side of the distal forearm.

Resisted Elbow Flexion

Speed's test[37] (Fig. 3-28A) is used to assess the biceps brachii. The patient's arm is extended and in 90° of forward flexion; and the hand is supinated. The tester resists against the distal forearm. Janda[40] states that when the elbow is hyperextended the biceps brachii must create immediate activity at full strength. Pain may be localized either at the acromioclavicular joint (if the supraglenoid origin is involved), at the bicipital groove or biceps belly, or at the musculotendinous portion or its insertion at the radial tuberosity.

Resistance against the elbow in 75° of flexion and next to the trunk can also be tested (Fig. 3-28B). The biceps is tested with the hand supinated, the brachialis is tested with the forearm pronated, and the brachioradialis is tested with the forearm in midposition. Resistance can also be applied against the patient's extended forearm with the shoulder extended and the

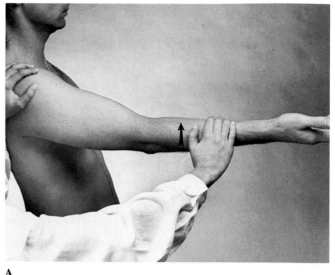

A

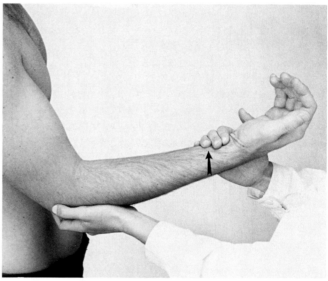

B

Figure 3-28 (**A** and **B**) Resisted elbow flexion.

hand pronated (Fig. 3-29). This position, without resistance, is excellent for palpation of the subacromial bursa. To confirm involvement of the biceps, the examiner should always test resisted supination (Fig. 3-30).

Other Tests of Shoulder Function

Besides the above tests, the following functional stability tests, apprehension tests, the relocation test, and the impingement test to stress the coracoacromial ligament should be used when indicated. Additional tests pertinent to specific lesions are discussed later.

Resisted testing of shoulder flexion, which involves the anterior deltoid, coracobrachialis, pectoralis major, and biceps, and resisted testing of shoulder extension involving the

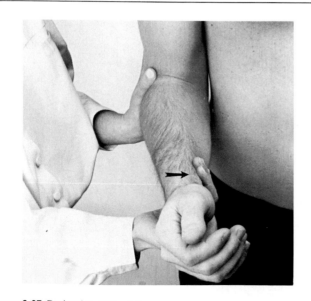

Figure 3-27 Resisted medial rotation.

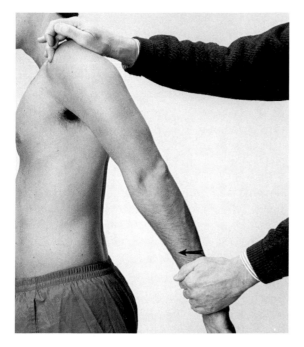

Figure 3-29 Resisted shoulder flexion.

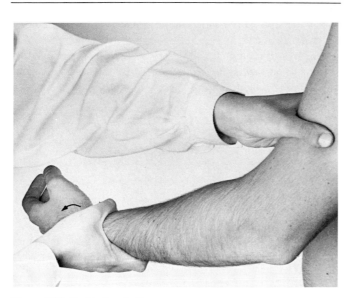

Figure 3-30 Resisted supination.

latissimus dorsi, teres major, posterior deltoid, teres minor, and triceps are not usually performed. These two tests involve such a variety of muscles that specific muscle interpretation is impossible.

Stability Tests

Stability tests are used to test for occult and overt shoulder instabilities due to capsular and glenoid labrum ruptures (Bankart's lesion), excessive capsular laxity, impacted compression fracture of the humeral head (Hill-Sachs lesion), and attenuated and ruptured cuff muscles (especially the subscapularis).[15]

Anterior instability: The patient stands with the arm abducted at 90° and the elbow flexed at 90°. The examiner stands behind the patient and slowly increases external rotation while pushing forward on the posterior humerus (Fig. 3-31). The same test may be performed with the arm elevated 180° in slight extension (Fig. 3-32); this may elicit an apprehension sign, especially in throwers or tennis players. Patients with recurrent anterior dislocation problems will present with immediate apprehension and pain. Patients with mild anterior subluxation will exhibit discomfort rather than severe pain and apprehension.[41]

Patients also can be examined supine with the shoulder slightly off the edge of the table. The examiner holds the

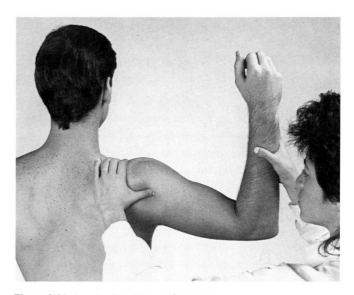

Figure 3-31 Anterior instability, 90° abduction.

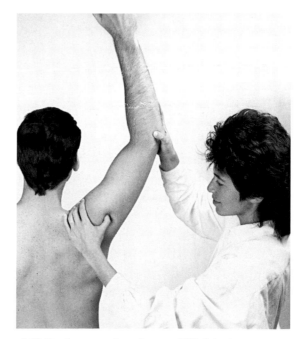

Figure 3-32 Passive external rotation near 180° abduction.

patient's distal forearm under the axilla,[15] leaving both hands free to stabilize the patient's arm and to apply posterior to anterior pressure on the proximal humerus (Fig. 3-33A). Rowe[14] describes a sensitive test in which the patient leans forward 45°. The examiner extends the patient's arm slightly and pushes the humeral head anteriorly (Fig. 3-33B).

Anterior instability of an occult or obvious subluxation can be a factor in the etiology of an impingement syndrome through rotator cuff fatigue and traction stress. Garth et al[42] mention how repetitive throwing, with its increased external rotation, may create capsular laxity and, along with muscular imbalance, may lead to instability. Muscle imbalance such as strong internal rotators and injured external rotators may result in transient anterior humeral head displacement. The cuff muscles (dynamic stabilizers) stabilize the humeral head and maintain the positioning of the humeral head during its movement. It is apparent that overuse of the static stabilizers may aggravate the dynamic stabilizers, just as overuse of the dynamic stabilizers may aggravate the static stabilizers (Fig. 3-34).

It is essential to determine the relationship between shoulder instability (as a potential cause of strain) and tendinitis of the dynamic stabilizers. The discussion of impingement and instability (below) describes the apprehension and relocation test for analysis of this problem.

Posterior instability: The examiner sits behind the patient, holding the patient's 90° flexed, slightly internally rotated, and adducted arm, and slowly pushes the patient's elbow posteriorly (Fig. 3-35A). There will be normal excessive posterior motion in pitchers. Fowler[43] states that posterior translation of the humeral head up to 50% of the glenoid width may be normal whereas greater than 50% would stress the rotator cuff.

The patient can be examined supine with the shoulder slightly off the edge of the table, as in the anterior test, with the distal forearm under the examiner's axilla; pressure is exerted anterior to posterior (Fig. 3-35B). Rowe[14] describes the same test with the patient bending forward 45° and the arm flexed

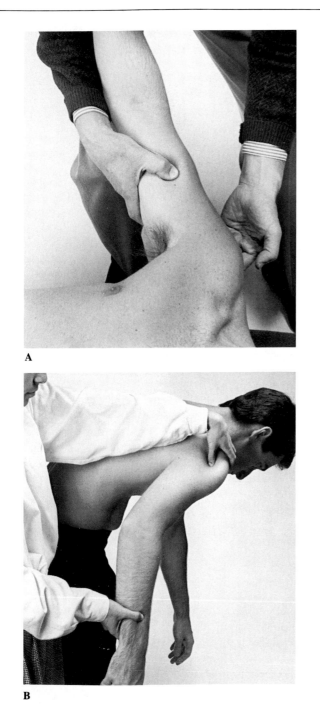

A

B

Figure 3-33 (A and B) Anterior instability test.

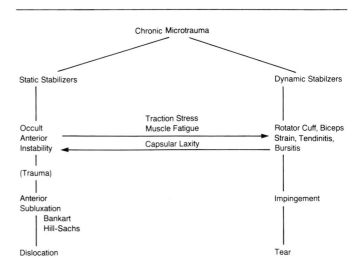

1. STATIC STABILIZERS: Glenoid labrum, joint synovium and capsule, and glenohumeral ligaments (especially glenohumeral inferior ligament).
2. DYNAMIC STABILIZERS: rotator cuff muscles, scapular rotators.
3. Chronic microtrauma and overhead activities can cause attenuation of static restraints. The dynamic stabilizers are then forced to overwork, compensating for the static stabilizers. Overfatigue of the dynamic stabilizers will result in additional stress to the static stabilizers.
4. Overdevelopment of internal rotators and underdevelopment of external rotators may cause excessive anterior displacement.

Figure 3-34 The effect of chronic stress on the shoulder stabilizers.

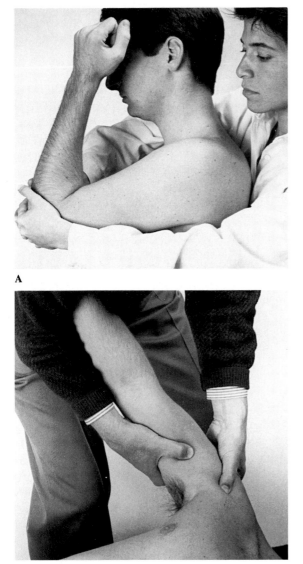

A

B

Figure 3-35 (**A** and **B**) Posterior instability test.

Figure 3-36 Posterior instability test.

Figure 3-37 Inferior instability test. Appearance of sulcus is palpated beneath thumb.

slightly forward while the examiner pushes the humeral head anterior to posterior (Fig. 3-36).

Inferior instability: With the patient leaning forward 45°, the examiner presses down on the humeral head and tractions inferiorly on the patient's wrist (Fig. 3-37). The appearance and palpation of a sulcus indicate inferior instability. Inferior instability is usually associated with multidirectional instability. Multidirectional instability usually includes anterior, posterior, and inferior laxity resulting from a loose redundant inferior pouch (capsule).[32]

Impingement Test for Coracoacromial Ligament

This is a nonspecific test that stresses the supraspinatus, long head of the biceps, and subacromial bursa. The patient's arm is flexed 90° and slightly adducted; the elbow is flexed about 90°. The examiner internally rotates the forearm, caus-

ing irritated tendons and bursal tissue near the greater tuberosity to be compressed by the coracoacromial ligament (Fig. 3-38). The coracoacromial ligament should palpate tender if it is involved (see Chapter 12 for palpation of the ligament and a possible treatment). Andrews[36] describes an impingement test in which the examiner holds the acromial arch down (preventing scapular movement) and abducts the shoulder in different planes of motion. All impingement tests are nonspecific regarding the exact cause of the impingement.

Subacromial Spur Test

Ciullo[44] describes a severe pain, when the patient's arm is forward flexed past 180°, at the anterior-inferior edge of the

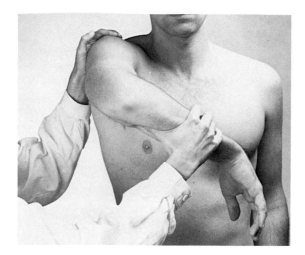

Figure 3-38 Coracoacromial impingement test.

acromion. This test is specifically valid only if roentgenography reveals a spur (a 15° caudad view may be required).

LESIONS

Tendinitis

One of many theories regarding the etiology of tendinitis refers to repetitive intrinsic overload and microtrauma due to repetitive muscle contractile tension.[45] Activity relating to eccentric loading is more likely to stress tendons than concentric activity because eccentric contraction creates more force production and therefore greater tendon stress.[46] A common theory considers the inherent avascularity of the supraspinatus, the infraspinatus near its insertion, and the biceps tendon as it courses over the head of the humerus,[47] which presumably cause a wringing out of the vessels on adduction. Lohr and Uhthoff[48] recently confirmed the hypovascularity of the "critical zone" near the insertion of the supraspinatus tendon, but they found sparse vascular distribution on the articular side of the tendon compared to a well-vascularized bursal side. They state that the articular side is therefore more susceptible to degenerative changes and tearing. They note that in these partial tears on the articular side the lack of circulation may be the reason that there is little or no inflammatory reaction at this site. Ciullo,[44] however, holds that mechanical shoulder irritation occurs in abduction and that the avascularity of the critical zone may have developed as an evolutionary protective mechanism to prevent recurrent hemorrhage in an area that is susceptible to recurrent microtrauma. Ciullo states that nourishment would come by diffusion or by way of bursal adhesions. Other causes of tendinitis are overfatigue and weakening of rotator cuff and scapulothoracic muscles, creating a secondary inferior impingement (upward humeral head migration) caused by deltoid shear and inadequate acromial elevation.[26] Garrick

and Webb[27] state that the impingement syndrome does not necessarily mean that the subacromial space is decreased. They feel that overuse and insufficiency of the shoulder stabilizing muscles allows the humeral head to be continually displaced by the more developed prime movers such as the deltoid and pectoralis major resulting in tendinitis. They use the example of power lifting (bench press) where the weaker stabilizing muscles suffer at the expense of the stronger prime movers (pectoralis major). Insufficiency of shoulder dynamic stabilizers can result in clinical and occult anterior instability, causing increased traction stress and predisposing to rotator cuff injury.[49]

Tendon degeneration associated with aging can result in enthesopathy (insertional tendinopathy) causing tendinitis, spur formation, bursal hypertrophy, fibrosis, and scarring. Extrinsic direct impingement of the cuff against the anterior edge and undersurface of the anterior third of the acromion, coracoacromial ligament, and acromioclavicular joint[50] can be causative. Impingement due to bony narrowing of supraspinatus outlet is possible. Morrison and Bigliani[51] described three types of anterior lateral acromions: Type I (flat), Type II (curved), and Type III (hooked). They found that 80% of their patients' cuff tears on the bursal side were associated with the hooked Type III acromions and none with the flat Type I acromion. Sarkar et al[52] found that thickening of the coracoacromial ligament as a causation of impingement may be secondary to involvement of the subacromial tissues. Swelling and thickening of the bursa and supraspinatus strain the coracoacromial ligament from below so that the impingement process may actually precede the thickening of the ligament. An autoimmune mechanism with antibody produced against denatured collagen and other structural proteins[30]; and overtraining, poor technique, and poor equipment are also factors. As the condition progresses, swelling, fibrosis and thickening of the cuff tissue may hypertrophy to the point of decreasing the subacromial space, creating another type of impingement process, especially with overhead shoulder use. Most of the above etiologies are responsible for creating what is known as an impingement syndrome, which can mechanically cause subacromial bursitis, rotator and biceps tendinitis and eventual tearing. Because of the above etiologies, it is rare not to find thinning and fibrillation of the rotator cuff by the fifth decade.[53]

Clinical: The principal diagnostic key for tendinitis is pain on resisted muscle testing that mimics the patient's complaint. There is usually no weakness except that due to pain inhibition or disuse. Atrophy is seldom present. As more people are involved in recreational sports, problems with the cuff in the 30- to 40-year-old age groups are becoming more frequent. The patient may complain of pain during activity that usually lessens later.

Neer and Welsh[54] divided tendinitis in athletes into three stages. Stage 1 consists of edema and hemorrhage usually up to age 25, stage 2 consists of fibrosis and tendinitis between the ages of 25 and 40, and stage 3 consists of severe degeneration and rupturing in patients older than 40. Patients may complain of night pain, which is due to the inflammation's forming minor, filmy adhesions that are broken as the patient moves.[55]

Depending on the severity of the inflammation pain may be felt anywhere down the C5–6 sclerotome, extending from the shoulder to the wrist. Local tenderness may be palpated over particular cuff muscles, but if at all possible findings should be based on specific resisted muscle testing because the most painful area is not always the source of pain. Roentgenograms are usually negative, showing no calcium deposits. In chronic tendinitis of the cuff there may be areas of sclerosis, erosion, or small cystic changes at the greater tuberosity.[55]

Supraspinatus Tendinitis

The cuff muscle most commonly involved in tendinitis is the supraspinatus. The most common sites of involvement are just before the insertion on the greater tuberosity and at the musculotendinous junction. The superior portion of the tenoperiosteal insertion may elicit a painful arc; the musculotendinous portion, which is not subacromial, does not elicit a painful arc. Pain on full passive abduction to 180° may stress the underside of the tenoperiosteal junction on the roof of the glenoid.[56]

Functional tests

1. Pain and relatively strong on resisted abduction.
2. Possible pain on resisted lateral rotation.
3. Possible painful arc.
4. Possible pain on active and passive abduction to 180°.
5. Possible pain on stretching of the supraspinatus (Fig. 3-39).

Infraspinatus Tendinitis

The patient may feel pain in the posterior shoulder area. Two principal sites of involvement are at the insertion of the infraspinatus in the middle part of the greater tuberosity and the musculotendinous portion. The teres minor is rarely involved.

Functional tests

1. Pain and relatively strong on resisted lateral rotation.
2. Pain on resisted lateral rotation and adduction (may be referred from the teres minor, which is also a weak adductor).
3. Possible painful arc if the superior surface of the insertion is involved.
4. Possible pain on passive medial rotation stretch.
5. After positive resisted test, the most tender area is palpated for treatment.

Subscapularis Tendinitis

Pain is usually located on the anterior shoulder, with localized pain over the lesser tuberosity.

Functional tests

1. Pain and relatively strong on resisted medial rotation.
2. Possible pain on active or passive horizontal adduction.
3. Possible painful arc if the insertion at the upper portion of the lesser tuberosity is involved.[49]

Note: Anterior shoulder muscle pain may also be related to strain of the pectoralis major and latissimus dorsi at their insertions and at the anterior deltoid origin (see Chapter 12). Resisted testing and stretching of these muscles will help localize the problem area. Rarely, the subscapularis may be impinged as it passes beneath the coracoid process (coracoid impingement).

Biceps Tendinitis-Tenosynovitis

The shoulder capsule is lined with synovium, and the sheath of the biceps tendon is an extension of the shoulder joint synovial lining beginning at the glenoid labrum. Therefore, bicipital tendinitis may often be associated with tendinitis of the rotator cuff or the anterior aspect of the shoulder joint (or both). The biceps tendon does not slide in the groove, but the humerus moves on a fixed tendon for a distance of about 1.5 in.[57] Tenosynovitis of the long head of the biceps is invariably found under and just distal to the transverse humeral ligament. Biceps tendinitis usually results from overuse, a direct blow, laxity of the transverse humeral ligament resulting in subluxation, chronic irritation, or anatomic reasons such as a narrow or shallow bicipital groove or rough supratubercular area. Booth and Marvel[58] state that tendinitis resulting from acute trauma is infrequent because of the greater osseous protection afforded this tendon compared to the tendons of the rotator cuff.

Bicipital tendinitis is not a common shoulder problem. Pain in the bicipital area is more often due to and associated with cuff tendinitis, but this area may be involved by itself. Palpat-

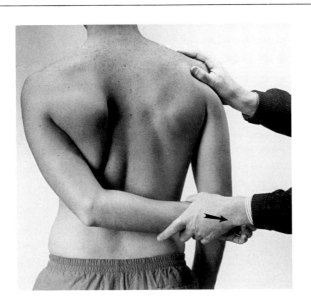

Figure 3-39 Stretching of the supraspinatus.

ing the long head of the biceps for tenderness may be difficult if the anterior and middle deltoid is overdeveloped. It may be necessary for the examiner to palpate the biceps with the patient supine while the arm is held to relax the deltoid.

Functional tests

1. Speed's test: painful and relatively strong on resisted shoulder flexion. Resisted testing of the biceps with the elbow flexed is not as reliable a test as when the elbow is extended.[55]
2. Pain on resisted supination (elbow flexed, pronated forearm supinated against resistance).
3. Straight-arm flexion test: Patient hyperextends a straight pronated arm and attempts flexion against resistance; may be painful on stretch without resistance (see Fig. 3-29).
4. Patient holds arm in 180° of abduction and lateral rotation and slowly brings the arm to the side. Pain may occur as the tendon is forced against the lesser tubercle. An audible or palpable click may indicate an elongated or dislocating biceps tendon (see below).
5. Possible painful arc if the lesion is located at the intracapsular area (rare). A painful arc is not present with the usual bicipital groove lesion.[56]
6. A lesion at the glenoid origin may create pain over the acromioclavicular joint. This pain may be elicited by testing resisted adduction with the arm slightly extended.[56]

Muscle-Tendon Treatment: Treatment consists of ice and various modalities (friction, trigger point, mobilization, and rehabilitation) (see Chapters 10 through 14). Because eccentric muscle overload is a frequent cause of tendinitis, rehabilitation can be directed toward improving eccentric stress. Curwin and Stanish[59] recommend stretching (because it increases the resting length of the tendon), which lessens strain; eccentric progressive muscle strengthening (rubber tubing); and exercises that emphasize increasing the speed of muscle contraction, which may allow the tendon to accept more load. In the early stages of isometric or isotonic exercise, the arms should be near the patient's side to prevent aggravation. As pain subsides, exercises can progress up to 180°. Exercises and stretching may be used that cause slight discomfort, but not pain.

Besides the cuff muscles it is necessary to ensure the strength and flexibility of the serratus, trapezius, levator scapulae, rhomboids, teres major, and latissimus dorsi muscles. In biceps tendinitis, the use of a strap just distal to the long head irritation (similarly used in lateral epicondylitis) may offer relief during use. The strap creates a new origin for the biceps tendon and helps to rest the strained area.

Calcific Tendinitis

Because calcification is seldom seen with degenerative rotator cuff disease, calcific tendinitis may not be patholog-

ically related to rotator cuff degeneration.[60] The observations that this condition occurs in relatively young people (30 to 50 years old) and that calcium deposits are not a problem in the elderly support this thesis. The calcium deposit is usually in the supraspinatus tendon and sometimes in the infraspinatus tendon. Subscapularis deposits are usually asymptomatic. When trauma or overuse creates a hyperemia the symptomless, dry-state calcium develops a toothpastelike consistency, which irritates the overlying bursa and causes a secondary bursitis. The inflammatory process may remain localized, or the calcium may evacuate into the bursa and relieve the condition, or the bursa may just become inflamed from the irritation.

In the acute stage the signs and symptoms are similar to those of an acute bursitis. Excruciating pain is elicited in almost all passive and resisted tests for 1 to 4 days. There is a positive painful arc, producing the "jag and wince" phenomenon described by Codman.[11] The condition is self-limited, and remission occurs in 6 to 14 days.[58] If the deposit ruptures spontaneously the patient will experience immediate relief. Patients can seldom wait, however, and usually require needling or aspiration. Diagnosis is confirmed by the presence of an amorphous calcium deposit on roentgenography.

In the chronic stage the calcium is dehydrated and pinches the subacromial tissue when the shoulder is rotated or elevated. An aching (twingelike) shoulder pain is usually created by one specific motion, such as abduction, flexion, or extension,[61] depending on the location of the deposit. A painful arc may be the only positive functional test.

Functional tests: Functional tests for acute and chronic calcific tendinitis are as described for acute and chronic bursitis (see below).

Treatment: Treatment is conservative and comprises the use of an arm sling, ice, stretching, and various modalities (trigger point, joint mobilization, and rehabilitation). Surgery is rarely necessary.[62]

Bursitis

Of the eight bursae around the shoulder, only the large subacromial bursa has clinical significance.[8] Codman[11] states that such designations as subdeltoid, subcoracoid, and supraspinatus bursae describe extensions of the subacromial bursa or the glenohumeral capsule. The subacromial bursa is bounded superiorly by the coracoacromial ligament and acromion and inferiorly by the rotator cuff and capsule. The bursa extends over the proximal humerus beneath the deltoid and beneath the coracoid process. The bursa is lined with a synovial membrane whose walls are closely connected, creating a "potential space."[1] The bursa allows free, well-lubricated movement of the greater tuberosity beneath the acromion in abduction of 60° to 130° and of the deltoid over the proximal humerus. According to Bland et al[30] and others,[58] virtually all cases of subacromial bursitis have a preceding tendinitis or tenosynovitis in the rotator cuff or the biceps tendon and sheath or some inflammatory process in the bone or joint about the shoulder; the spread of inflammation to the bursa is a secondary event.

By middle age the bursal walls become thickened and the cavity filled with adhesions.[30] Bursal thickening and loss of ability to glide perpetuate increased wearing and fraying of the cuff, also resulting in tendinitis.

Clinical: Acute bursitis may result with or without calcific tendinitis. As with the latter, patient presentation is that of excruciating pain without relief on repositioning; all active movements are painful. Heat or swelling may be palpable.

Functional testing

1. Passive: noncapsular because there is more pain and limitation on passive abduction than on passive lateral rotation (see Chapter 1, Capsular Pattern).
2. Passive: empty end feel (ie, the examiner feels that more movement is present, but the patient's pain prevents further movement).
3. Usually painful resisted testing in acute stage in all directions because of tension on the inflamed bursa. As the condition subsides, resisted cuff testing should be strong and painless or may elicit pain incriminating a particular tendon.

Chronic Subacromial Bursitis

Symptoms are vague; the patient may complain of pain only after excessive overhead use or may complain of a dull, unlocalized ache. Night pain is common.

Functional testing

1. Possible painful arc.
2. All passive tests may or may not aggravate the pain.
3. Depending on acuteness of bursitis, isometric muscle testing of the cuff muscles may incriminate none to most of the muscles.
4. The bursa may be palpated under the anterior acromion with the patient's arm extended.

Subcoracoid Bursitis

Subcoracoid bursitis is an uncommon condition. There is usually localized pain inferior to the tip of the coracoid process. Patte[63] states that impingement may occur in the coracohumeral space between the coracoid process and the lesser tuberosity. Computed tomography studies have shown a decrease in the above space in shoulder flexion and medial rotation.[64] The tissues pinched under the hook of the coracoid are the thickest part of the subscapularis tendon, the superior and middle parts of the glenohumeral ligament and the subcoracoid bursa. Patte states that protuberances of the lesser tuberosity and abnormal structure of the coracoid process can impinge especially when associated with overuse in flexion-

internal rotation as in swimmers and gymnasts. The coracohumeral space can be decreased by an isolated traumatic tear of the subscapularis (usually associated with a dislocation of the long head of the biceps), scarring after a traumatic tear of the coracohumeral ligament, functional disability due to laxity of a partial supraspinatus tear in the anterior part, and calcification of the subscapularis.

Functional testing

1. Pain on passive horizontal flexion.
2. Pain on extreme passive lateral shoulder rotation.
3. Pain on flexion and medial rotation of the arm (coracoacromial impingement test).

Functional Differentiation between Tendinitis and Bursitis

Because tendinitis usually precedes bursitis, they may be present simultaneously. Every tendinitis condition will be accompanied by pain on one or two specific resisted tests, with probable positive passive stretching of the involved tendon. Because the joint is rarely involved, even if active range of movement may be painful and limited, full passive movement in tendinitis should be possible.

When a bursa becomes inflamed, there may be any combination of positive resisted and passive tests that do not specifically identify a particular problem. This explains why the functional diagnostic chart (Appendix 3-A) shows numerous $+/-$'s for bursitis. A chronic subacromial bursitis may present with only a painful arc and no pain or weakness on resisted testing. After the tendons, the main structure left in the painful arc area is the bursa. Bursitis is usually a secondary problem, so that other causes of the painful arc would also have to be considered (eg, chronic tendinitis, degeneration, osteophytes, spurring of the inferior acromioclavicular joint, or enlargement of the outer anterior end of the clavicle and other extrinsic and intrinsic possibilities previously discussed).

Treatment of Bursitis

All the factors causing tendinitis must be addressed in the treatment of chronic bursitis. Frictioning of the underlying tendon and fibrotic bursa often eliminates chronic bursitis problems (see Chapter 12).

Rotator Cuff Ruptures

According to Bland et al,[30] ruptures seldom occur before age 50 but are relatively common after age 60. Full-thickness tears occur most often in persons 70 years or older. It is almost impossible to rupture tendons in a healthy young adult; if rupture does occur, it will be due to avulsion of the greater tuberosity rather than avulsion of the tendon itself. Usually, according to Ellman,[65] "the cuff wears before it tears."

Partial or incomplete tears of the cuff can be on the articular side, the bursal side, or intratendinous. As of this writing, Ellman states that "even the most sophisticated MRI studies report difficulty in imaging small- and partial-thickness cuff tears." He states that the exact location and extent of incomplete tears can be documented with shoulder arthroscopy and that arthroscopic examination cannot reveal an intratendinous disruption until either the articular or bursal side is involved. In the older patient there may be a feeling of a snap. There may also be an insidious process in which the person may have been complaining of shoulder pain and stiffness and comes to realize that he or she can only raise the arm about 45°, after which the shoulder must be shrugged to raise the arm a little higher.

Clinical: It is necessary to distinguish partial or incomplete tears from complete or full-thickness tears because complete tears may require surgery. The most common traumatic cause is falling on an outstretched arm, which creates a destructive impingement. Partial tears may be associated with degenerative tendinitis and will present with findings and symptoms similar to those associated with tendinitis. Sometimes a gradual attrition of the degenerated tendon occurs, creating increased weakness so that rupture "sneaks up" on the patient. The healing process in the rotator cuff tear takes place only when the torn edges are in contact. In a partial tear some bridging of the gap by normal tissue remains, and fibrous tissue may tend to fill this hiatus.[66] Full-thickness tears often occur in tennis players older than 40 years of age.[32]

Painful or painless weakness is the chief complaint, and the amount of weakness on muscle testing and active motion helps distinguish between a partial and a complete tear. "A large rotator cuff tear is frequently associated with weakness in both abduction and external rotation."[37] Muscle atrophy of the infraspinatus or supraspinatus (or both) is usually visible in 2 to 3 weeks. Andrews[36] states that palpating the supraspinatus insertion and feeling crepitus while the shoulder is abducted to 90° and rotated medially and laterally is a sign of a supraspinatus tear.

Subscapularis rupture usually occurs as a complication of anterior capsule stress, especially in hard throwing. The stress on the head of the humerus can loosen the labrum and glenoid anchorage, allowing head luxation. Anterior stability testing will reveal laxness and create painful patient apprehension.

In an analysis of 292 shoulders, Samilson and Binder[67] found that 59% of full-thickness tears managed nonoperatively had excellent to good results. Patients who have had their rotator cuffs injected with cortisone are more prone to tears.[68] Usually a massive tear should be operated on, especially in a young individual, but according to Leach and Schepsis[55] rotator cuff tears do not require emergency surgery, as tears of ligaments around the knee do. Others[69] state that the main indications for surgical treatment are severe, unremitting pain after 3 months of conservative treatment or increasing loss of shoulder function.

A significant radiologic finding of rotator cuff tear is narrowing of the acromiohumeral interval to 5 mm or less as a result of loss of cuff compression and depression of the humeral head. Magnetic resonance imaging and arthrography will pinpoint the tear.

Functional testing

- Partial-thickness tears:
  1. Active range may or may not be complete (depends on the amount of pain and the muscular development of the patient).[70]
  2. Passive range is full and usually painless unless there is associated impingement.
  3. Painful and weak resisted testing.
  4. If the patient is unable to abduct to 90°, injection of a local anesthetic or numbing by friction massage (see Chapter 12) may enable the patient to abduct weakly to about 150°.
  5. Drop-arm test (see below) may be positive.
- Full-thickness tears:
  1. Active range of motion is seldom more than 30° of abduction, but patients may have large tears of the rotator cuff and still retain full elevation as long as some depressor action of the cuff remains.[71]
  2. Passive range is usually full unless the tear bunches up. The tear may be palpable; crackling, popping, and palpable crepitus may be elicited on passive rotation.
  3. Remarkably weak and usually painful resisted testing.
  4. Drop-arm test is positive; this tests mostly the supraspinatus for a significant tear. The examiner passively abducts the patient's arm to 90° and then releases the arm. The patient may be unable to lower the arm with control or may drop the arm to the side (Fig. 3-40).

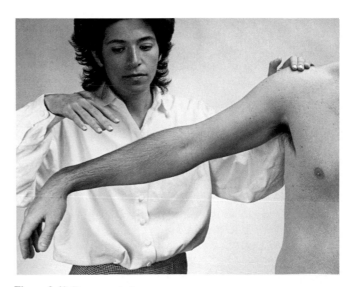

Figure 3-40 Drop-arm test.

Treatment: Ellman recommends double-contrast arthrograms in patients over 40 years of age if their symptoms persist over 3 months. He states that partial-thickness tears are often associated with anterior instability in young athletes. Therefore, especially if the instability exists, the dynamic shoulder stabilizers should be strengthened to compensate for the overstretched static stabilizers. This would still be the primary treatment without the presence of instability. It is important that the rotator cuff musculature be strengthened in the subimpingement range in the early stages so as not to aggravate the lesion.

Bicipital Ruptures

Lippmann[72] states that the long head of the biceps, like the appendix, is an unimportant vestigial structure, useful but not essential to serviceable shoulder function. Perry[8] states that after EMG analysis it is doubtful that the long head is a significant stabilizing force at the glenohumeral joint (as was once thought[50]). The biceps is important in throwing acting as an eccentric decelerator of the forearm. Booth and Marvel[58] distinguish between two types of bicipital ruptures: involvement of the transverse humeral ligament and the intertubercular fibers of the biceps tendon.

Clinical: Older patients, because of degeneration of tissues, may not recall any trauma. The problem is usually related to catching or lifting a weight with the arm held in abduction or external rotation. An abducted and externally rotated arm causes the biceps tendon to displace medially. Neviaser[62] states that the biceps tendon always displaces medially, never laterally. Patients may complain of their shoulder "going out," and they may reduce the tendon themselves.

Transverse humeral test:[62] The examiner subluxates the patient's biceps tendon from the bicipital groove by abducting the arm 90°, flexing the elbow 90°, and bringing the shoulder into external rotation (this moves the tendon medially) (Fig. 3-41A). The examiner palpates the biceps tendon and internally rotates the shoulder, which replaces the biceps tendon in the groove (moves tendon laterally), creating an audible or palpable snap (Fig. 3-41B).

Functional tests

- Rupture of transverse humeral ligament or subluxation of tendon:
  1. Weak and painful resisted biceps test.
  2. Positive transverse humeral test.
  3. Positive Yergason's test: The patient stands with the elbow flexed 90° at the side. The examiner grasps the elbow and distal forearm and externally rotates the shoulder while the patient resists elbow flexion. If positive, the tendon will move out of the groove.

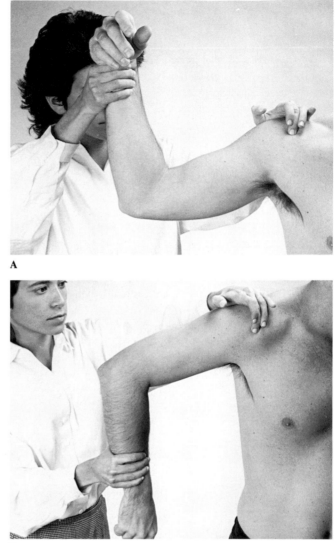

Figure 3-41 Transverse humeral test. (**A**) External rotation. (**B**) Internal rotation.

4. Patient's arm held in 180° abduction and lateral rotation and slowly brought to the side; pain may occur as tendon is forced against the lesser tuberosity. Palpable click may indicate an elongated or dislocating biceps tendon.

- Rupture of long head (possible history of a "snap" and visible biceps lump at distal humerus):
  1. Painful and extremely weak resisted biceps test in the acute condition; there may be minimal pain and weakness in the chronic condition.
  2. The significance of a ruptured proximal biceps is that it almost always means rotator cuff pathology (E Rashkoff, personal communication, 1990).

Treatment: Rehabilitation may be all that is necessary because only 20% of elbow flexion power is lost.[73]

Osteoarthritis

Glenohumeral Joint

Osteoarthritis in the glenohumeral joint is uncommon because this joint is non–weight bearing. Arthritis accounts for only 5% of all shoulder pain.[74] There is a capsular pattern on passive testing. Roentgenography my show sclerosis, cysts, and tear-drop osteophytes on the inferior joint surface. Loose bodies in the inferior capsule are sometimes palpable, causing a painful catch on abduction and rotation.

Acromioclavicular Joint

This joint is more often involved than the glenohumeral joint. Roentgenography helps confirm the diagnosis by showing diminished joint space and osteophytes (the best views are taken in the anteroposterior plane with the arm abducted to 100° and externally rotated or 15° caudad). Osteoarthritis in this location may be related to a degenerative cuff and subsequent humeral head superior subluxation (deltoid shear) because an acromioclavicular osteophyte is usually on the inferior acromioclavicular joint. There is pinpoint pain over the joint and crepitus. The joint may appear bulbous.

Functional tests

1. Passive pain during abduction from 90° to 180°.
2. Pain on passive horizontal adduction.
3. Resisted tests negative.
4. Possible crepitus with passive dorsal-ventral A-C joint gliding.
5. Possible painful arc if an inferior acromioclavicular spur is present.

Treatment: Treatment consists of rest, ice, and mobilization of the acromioclavicular, sternoclavicular, and glenohumeral joints (see Chapters 10 and 14). Because limited glenohumeral motion may create increased compensatory acromioclavicular joint motion and degeneration, acromioclavicular joint arthritis may be relieved by glenohumeral joint mobilization.[75]

Acromioclavicular Sprain

Grades I and II show positive findings on the first three functional tests for acromioclavicular osteoarthritis (see above). These may respond to friction massage and strengthening of the upper trapezius (shoulder shrugs with weights). A sling is used until the pain subsides. Garrick and Webb[27] state that grade II and grade III injuries will elicit tenderness in the coracoclavicular space while grade I injuries will not.

Adhesive Capsulitis

Adhesive capsulitis is rare in patients younger than 40 and more common in sedentary workers than in laborers. The incidence of the condition has decreased in frequency because many more people now participate in active upper extremity exercises.[62] The inferior portion of the capsule (axillary fold) has the largest portion of synovial membrane, and the superior, anterior, and posterior portions of the capsule (rotator cuff) are more musculotendinous. The axillary fold develops adhesions, preventing mostly lateral rotation, abduction, and medial rotation (capsular pattern). Adduction, flexion, and extension in the sagittal plane are the last motions to be compromised.[58] Nobuhara et al [2] discuss the shoulder tissue involved in causing the capsular pattern of adhesive capsulitis. They state that limitation of external rotation is due to contracture of the coracohumeral ligament which prevents the greater tuberosity from further movement. Limitation of abduction is due to adhesion of the subacromial bursa. When restricted abduction becomes chronic, secondary contracture occurs in the long rotators (pectoralis major, latissimus dorsi and teres major muscles). They state that in flexion, the coracohumeral ligament is relatively relaxed.

Uhthoff and Sarkar[76] write of a progressive fibrous proliferation that restricts mostly lateral rotation. They describe a fibrosis of the articular capsule, the rotator cuff tendons, particularly the subscapularis and its extension to the coracohumeral ligament.

The etiology is uncertain, but almost all the previously discussed lesions can, with the spread of inflammation from the tendons, sheaths, bursa, cartilage, bone, synovium, and surrounding muscles, eventually result in an adhesive process. Fareed and Gallivan[77] noted that the area of initial and primary involvement is a triangular anatomic synovial fold between the long head of the biceps and the subscapularis tendons. This bare area of synovial tissue is in contact with the adjacent subscapularis muscle and tendon, long head of the biceps, anterior glenoid, and humerus, and adhesions eventually form between the capsule and these structures.

Clinical: Early recognition of the lesion makes reversal of the problem much easier. Initially, the patient may complain only of a stiff and painful shoulder without any particular cause. Rowe[14] states that a rotator cuff derangement or tear can eventually cause restricted motion and mimic the frozen shoulder.

Early examination usually shows no pain on resisted isometric muscle testing, with minimal to no loss of end feel on passive testing. There may only be slight pain on lateral rotation (the earliest limitation of capsular pattern). Overstretching of the shoulder may create pain and paresthesia down the C-6 dermatome, mimicking a radiculopathy, but the radiation of the pain from the shoulder will be to all the fingers instead of to the C-6 distribution.[15] Cervical stress tests will not create shoulder pain unless there is an accompanying cervical problem.

The condition may progress to an acute "capsulitis" phase, with various resisted tests causing a sharp aching pain but essentially being strong; there may be severe pain in passive testing. The condition may test like an acute or chronic bursitis with a painful capsular pattern. At this stage there may be intense night pain that affects sleep.

The final stage is extreme limitation of motion in the capsular pattern, with pain only when the tissue is stretched. Because of a limited capsular pattern, the patient may present with the arm in internal rotation and adduction. There may be minimal atrophy of the deltoid and supraspinatus muscles. Rowe[14] states that an unrecognized chronic posterior dislocation may present as a frozen shoulder. Arthrography would finalize the diagnosis.

Treatment: Neviaser[62] divides treatment into stages that are based on the amount of abduction. If abduction can take place over 90°, conservative treatment takes 2 to 5 months. The next category includes patients who cannot abduct over 90°; in such cases manipulation under general anesthesia is used, with full recovery taking place in 3 to 6 months. Manipulation under general anesthesia should be reserved for patients who do not make progress with conservative care in 6 months (E Rashkoff, personal communication, 1990).

Rizk et al[78] and Sapega et al[79] explain that the best way permanently to lengthen connective tissue structures without compromising their structural integrity is to use prolonged, low-intensity stretching at elevated tissue temperatures and subsequent cooling of the tissue before releasing the tension. An effective procedure that the patient could do at home is first to warm up the shoulder with moist heat for 10 to 15 minutes and then to lie supine with the shoulder in external rotation while holding a 1- to 2-lb weight and maintaining the stretched position for up to 45 minutes or more with the moist heat on the anterior shoulder. The patient may feel discomfort, but not pain. Moist heat packs may have to be replaced every 10 minutes to maintain heat. During the last 10 to 15 minutes, ice should be applied. The patient should follow this procedure at least 5 days per week (Fig. 3-42). Painless joint mobilization

should also be used for breaking adhesions (see Chapters 10, 13, and 14). Friction over the fibrous cuff may be beneficial.

Instability

It was noted in the section on tendinitis that clinical and occult anterior instability can cause traction stress and be a predisposing factor to rotator cuff involvement.[49] O'Brien et al[80] state that laxity may be normal but is also a predisposition to instability, which is a clinical entity. They further state that instability may occur from a single traumatic incident, from repetitive microtrauma such as swimming or throwing, or in people with no history of trauma.

Rowe[14] states that the most common lesion resulting in recurrent shoulder dislocation and subluxation is loss of stability along the rim of the glenoid due to avulsion of the capsule and labrum from the rim, which is known as *Bankart's lesion* (Fig. 3-43). Tearing of the labrum, which is attached to the glenoid, is an indicator that the capsule is not attached. The labrum itself may not be the primary pathology relating to the instability. Another common lesion is the Hill-Sachs lesion, which is a defect in the posterolateral part of the humeral head that is due to a traumatic impacted compression fracture. Other pathologic findings causing instability may be excessive laxity of the capsule secondary to repeated injury or an increase in the interval between the subscapularis and the supraspinatus, out over the humeral head.[81] Bigliani[32] states that individuals younger than 30 who have anterior shoulder pain probably have instability. Increased weakness of the dynamic stabilizers result in compensatory stress to the static stabilizers (see Fig. 3-34). Muscle lesions are also responsible, although (contrary to current thought) Rowe[14] found that in 158 shoulders operated on for recurrent anterior dislocation the subscapularis muscle was normal in 83%.

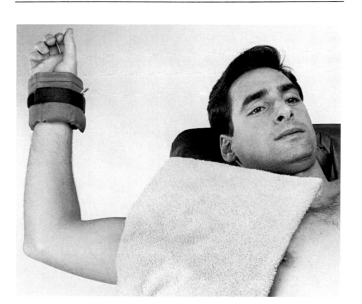

Figure 3-42 Passive prolonged stretch treatment for adhesive capsulitis.

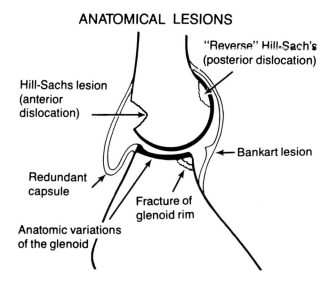

ANATOMICAL LESIONS

Figure 3-43 Outline of the anatomic lesions producing instability of the shoulder. *Source*: Reprinted from *The Shoulder*, (p 165) by CR Rowe (Ed) with permission of Churchill Livingstone, © 1988.

Clinical: Shoulder instability may be a subtle finding and difficult to assess. Posterior subluxation pain may occur during the follow-through of a throw but is rare compared to anterior subluxation (increased anterior humeral head translation in the glenoid). Sports such as throwing, swimming, or tennis, which require abduction and overextension, may cause sudden pain, weakness ("slipping out"), a clicking sensation, or a general ache after use. Even minimal instability can increase the traction stress on the cuff and result in fatigue and injury to the rotator cuff. Anterior instability may cause posterior shoulder pain because as the shoulder moves anteriorly it tractions the posterior capsule. O'Brien et al[80] state that repetitive traction and compression of the rotator cuff during subluxation may cause a patient to present with symptoms and signs of an impingement syndrome (painful arc, tendinitis-bursitis signs, and positive coracoacromial ligament impingement test). Treatment for impingement will probably fail if an underlying cause of instability is not corrected.

Instability and Impingement

Instability, occult or apparent, may be a reason that treatment of, say, a supraspinatus tendinitis may be unsuccessful in the long term.

Jobe and Kvitne[41] showed how the interpretation of an apprehension test and a relocation test can determine whether an impingement syndrome is related to shoulder instability. The apprehension test is performed with the patient supine and the arm abducted, externally rotated, and slightly extended. The examiner increases the external rotation while pushing the head of the humerus posterior to anterior (Fig. 3-44). The patient may complain of pain with or without apprehension. Patients with instabilities that result in recurrent dislocation usually experience apprehension and possible anterior or posterior pain on testing; those with mild anterior subluxation may

experience only anterior pain without apprehension.[39] The relocation test is an apprehension test associated with posterior force on the proximal humerus to test apprehension while the instability is reduced (Fig. 3-45). Reducing an instability during the relocation test should eliminate the pain.

Performing an apprehension test (Table 3-1) on patients with impingement signs and without instability usually will not create pain, but it may create pain if the impingement is severely inflamed. If no pain is created with the apprehension test the relocation test will also be painless, and if there is a painful apprehension test the relocation test will probably create the same pain. In other words, with primary impingement (without instability) the relocation test will not change the symptoms created by the apprehension test. The relocation test is used to confirm the presence of instability.

If instability of an occult or mild subluxation is present and is related to impingement signs, the relocation test will relieve the pain created by the apprehension test. In recurrent dislocations or severe subluxations without impingement, the apprehension test will create apprehension and possible pain and will be relieved by the relocation test.

Unless the movements that cause the instability are eliminated or a strengthening program to compensate for the instability is developed, the secondary tendinitis will not respond to manual methods.

Functional tests

1. Pain or apprehension on testing of supine or standing patient for shoulder anterior, posterior, or inferior stability.
2. Relocation test relieves pain.
3. Resisted testing for loss of strength of rotator muscles (especially external rotators), deltoids, and scapular stabilizers. If there is weakness of the rotator cuff and anterior deltoid muscles, resistive testing of these muscles may reveal pectoral substitution causing excessive

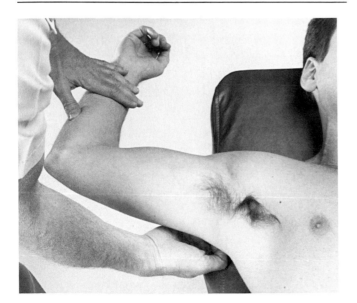

Figure 3-44 Supine apprehension test.

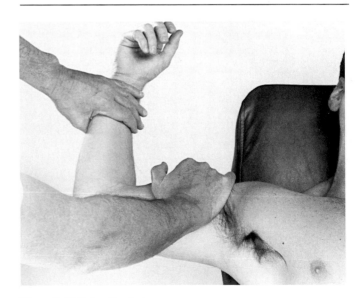

Figure 3-45 Relocation test.

Table 3-1 Impingement and Instability in Anterior Shoulder Pain

	Impingement without Anterior Instability	Instability (Occult to Anterior Subluxation) with Secondary Impingement	Severe Sublux to Recurrent Dislocation without Impingement
Apprehension Test	+/−	+ A	+ B
Relocation Test	NC	R	R
Subacromial Impingement	+	+	−

Key: Painful: +
No Pain: −
Possible Pain: +/−
Relief: R
No Change: NC
A: Apprehension Test Creates Pain without Apprehension.
B: Apprehension Test Creates Pain with Apprehension.

Chart Explanation:

Subacromial Impingement: Refers to any test or lesion that compromises the subacromial space (ie, impingement tests, tendinitis, bursitis, subacromial spur, painful arc).
Occult Anterior Instability: Transient anterior subluxation of the shoulder of which the patient is unaware.
Anterior Subluxation: Glenoid head moves excessively relative to the glenoid fossa but short of actual dislocation.
Apprehension Test: Stressing head of humerus posterior to anterior while arm is abducted, externally rotated, and extended. Patient may complain only of pain or become apprehensive to prevent pain (Fig. 3-44).
Relocation Test: With supine patient in apprehensive position of abduction, extension, and lateral rotation, examiner pushes head of humerus posterior (Fig. 3-45).

shoulder protraction and observable increased pectoral tone on the weak side.[27]

Treatment: If the anterior instability is acute, immobilization in internal rotation for up to 6 weeks may be needed. If it is subacute or chronic, less immobilization is required. (Painless motion is encouraged as soon as possible.) It is extremely important to strengthen the rotator cuff muscles for instability problems, but in the early stages of strengthening for anterior instability there should be no weight work with the shoulder in positions of abduction, external rotation, or extension. In anterior instability the adductors and internal rotators (subscapularis) are especially important. For posterior instability it is essential to strengthen the external rotators and posterior deltoid. If impingement signs are present, exercises should not be done with the shoulder in the 90° abducted position, which causes encroachment of the subacromial space. It is also important to check the scapular rotators for strength and flexibility. The scapular rotators may be strengthened by shoulder shrugs (upper trapezius), push-ups for the serratus anterior, and chin-ups or pull-downs for the latissimus dorsi.[41] All manual methods applicable for stretching, joint play, trigger points, and friction may have to be included.

Glenoid Labrum Tears

The glenoid labrum was thought to be a fibrocartilaginous structure located at the circumference of the glenoid cavity, but recent studies[82] indicate that it is more a redundant fold of capsular tissue than fibrocartilage. It is the attachment point of the capsule, and anchoring the capsule to the glenoid rim is important for glenohumeral stability.[83] The labrum is not as significant as the entire capsule in acting as a barrier against instability.[32,33] According to Leach and Schepsis,[55] a glenoid labrum tear is a difficult condition to diagnose and is usually associated with recurrent shoulder subluxation or dislocation.

Clinical: The patient may present with recurrent pain and "catching" or "snapping" in the anterior or posterior shoulder. Rotation of an abducted shoulder might cause the snapping over the anterior or posterior glenoid rim. Surgery may be needed.

The glenoid clunk test (Fig. 3-46) stresses the head of the humerus against the torn glenoid, producing an audible

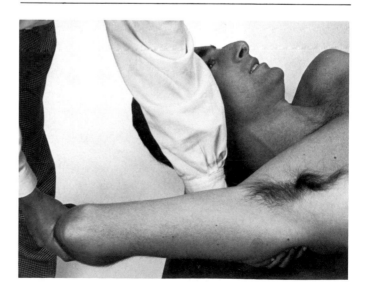

Figure 3-46 Glenoid clunk test.

"clunk" or grinding that is due to anterior-superior or posterior-superior labrum tears. The labrum tear could be isolated or associated with instability. The patient's arm is maximally abducted while the examiner simultaneously pushes the humeral head anteriorly and externally rotates the shoulder. Whenever a shoulder has a torn glenoid labrum, its cause should be assumed to be glenohumeral instability until proven otherwise.[55]

Throwing Shoulder

The analysis of the mechanics of throwing and pitching provides an effective way to understand the causes of shoulder problems. On the basis of the phases of throwing, it is possible to analyze which soft tissues are stressed and the possible lesions that may occur when the tissues are overstressed.

In the "cocking" phase, when the shoulder is externally rotated and abducted, the main muscles involved are the deltoid, supraspinatus, infraspinatus, and teres minor. The subscapularis is eccentrically decelerating the externally rotating humerus. Eventual anterior subluxation may result from the repetitive stress to the anterior capsule. Strain of the above muscles plus impingement of the subacromial space could occur, causing tendinitis and bursitis.

In the acceleration phase the pectoralis major, latissimus dorsi, and long head of the triceps are the most active. This phase could be responsible for lesions to the above muscles plus more subacromial stress (cuff tendinitis, bursitis, and eventual tearing) and biceps tendon subluxation. As the ball is released, the glenoid labrum may tear.

During the follow-through and deceleration phase, eccentric contraction of the lateral rotators is chiefly involved. Lesions such as tendinitis of the posterior cuff and long head of the triceps and posterior subluxations are possible.

Throughout most of the phases the scapular rotators are functioning to position the glenoid for optimum glenohumeral stability and may become overused. The loss of balance between the dynamic and static stabilizers due to repetitive throwing, especially at the estimated 7000° of motion per second performed by professional pitchers, eventually can result in the above lesions. Most of the lesions can be discovered by functional testing.

Adolescent Shoulder

Because of skeletal immaturity, overtraining or injury in an adolescent poses particular problems. Special consideration must be paid to the epiphyseal plate, articular cartilage, and musculotendinous unit.[84] When we examine an adolescent athlete it is normal to find increased range of motion, excessive translation of the glenohumeral joint in all directions, and hypermobility of the acromioclavicular, sternoclavicular, and scapulothoracic joints with winging. At the same time we may also find muscle imbalance and decreased muscle flexibility

due to rapid growth. Adolescents who undertake repetitive activities without constant flexibility training are more prone to injury. With growth there is an uneven increase in strength, which also adds to the joint imbalance. Adolescents with long arms often have underdeveloped muscles that are not capable of protecting tendons and joints.[85] Ireland and Andrews[84] hold that true impingement is not usual in the young athlete and that the underlying cause is probably a muscle imbalance with an instability pattern, resulting in shoulder subluxations that increase the distractive forces on the rotator cuff leading to cuff tendinitis. Stretching programs are needed to lengthen short, strong, tight muscles and to strengthen their antagonists.[76]

A hard throw may disrupt the epiphyseal plate, and with repetitive throwing "Little League shoulder" (microfractures of the proximal humeral growth plate) may develop. These adolescents may reveal a loss of internal rotation at 90° that is due to a tight posterior capsule and an increase in external rotation that is due to an anterior laxity and creates a tendency toward anterior subluxation. Again, anterior instability may lead to secondary impingement.[86]

Whether dealing with adolescents or adults, it is always important to establish muscle flexibility and normal joint play motion before strengthening. But the patient should not be allowed to return to stressful activity until normal strength and endurance are achieved. Garrick and Webb[27] state that when weak muscles are asked to work to their limit, they will tighten and be prone to reinjury.

Weakness and No Pain–Differential Diagnosis

Although the response of weakness and no pain on muscle testing may indicate a chronic rupture, the usual cause is neurologic. The following are some of the more common neurologic conditions that affect the upper extremity. A neuritis may create a deep diffuse pain, but the muscle test usually reveals weakness and no increased pain. Some investigators hold that a positive EMG is essential to confirm the diagnosis.[87]

Suprascapular Nerve Injury

Etiology: Isolated traumatic suprascapular nerve palsy without associated fracture is rare.[88] Direct trauma to the shoulder is the most common cause.[89] Overuse injuries, such as those incurred from the overhead motions of serving and spiking of a volleyball, may result in repeated stretching of the suprascapular nerve[90]; acromioclavicular separation, excessive horizontal adduction, traction lesions, and glenohumeral dislocation, have been incriminated. The etiology may be idiopathic.

Inspection may reveal atrophy of either the supraspinatus or infraspinatus, but because the supraspinatus is covered by the trapezius and the infraspinatus is more superficial infraspinatus atrophy will be more apparent.

Functional tests

1. Resisted test: weakness and no pain of supraspinatus and infraspinatus. According to Turek,[15] if the nerve is compressed at the level of the suprascapular notch or in the supraspinous fossa both the infraspinatus and the supraspinatus will test weak. If the nerve is compressed at a lower level (spinoglenoid fossa), then only the infraspinatus may test weak.
2. Possibly increased pain on passive horizontal adduction (which tenses the nerve).
3. Possible tenderness when pressure is exerted over the suprascapular notch.
4. Black and Lombardo[91] have found a "painful arc" of shoulder abduction from 90° to 160° and a positive impingement sign. This may be due to a branch of the suprascapular nerve coursing in the subacromial bursa.

Long Thoracic Nerve Injury

Etiology: Injury may result from nontraumatic (viral) agents or from trauma (eg, overstretching between the head and shoulder, repetitive arm abduction in the swimmer's backstroke, or trauma to the lateral rib cage). The etiology may also be idiopathic.

Functional tests

1. Resisted test of serratus anterior: weak and no pain.
2. Winging of scapula and inability actively to raise arm above 130° to 140° because rotation of the scapula is deficient. Winging appears as inferior tipping.

Spinal Accessory Nerve Injury

Etiology: Subluxation or dislocation of the sternoclavicular or acromioclavicular joint, cervical lateral traction injuries, and hockey stick injury to the upper trapezius are all possible causes.

Functional tests

1. Reduced active range of motion in flexing or abducting arm above the horizontal. Levator scapulae and rhomboids by themselves cannot keep the glenoid superior for full arm abduction.
2. Resisted test: trapezius is weak and painless.
3. Winging of the whole scapula which moves laterally.

Axillary Nerve Injury

Etiology: Possible causes are trauma to the upper humerus resulting in compression of the nerve and dislocations or fracture-dislocations of the humerus. A direct blow between the coracoid and the head of the humerus may also injure this nerve.

Functional test

1. Resisted testing of deltoid and teres minor muscles: weakness and no pain.

Swimmer's Shoulder

Swimmer's shoulder is a general term for the subacromial impingement syndrome or tendinitis of the biceps and rotator cuff muscles. It represents chronic irritation of the humeral head and rotator cuff on the coracoacromial arch during abduction of the shoulder[92] (Fig. 3-47).

To understand the mechanism of injury, it is important to review the mechanics of the swimming stroke. The stroke mechanics and phases of freestyle, butterfly, and backstroke swimming are similar and differ from those of the breaststroke. The following discussion deals with the freestyle stroke (Table 3-2). There are two basic phases: the pull-through phase and the recovery phase. In the pull-through phase (underwater), beginning with the "catch" or hand entry, the main muscles involved are the pectoralis major and latissimus dorsi, which create the necessary adduction and internal rotation for propulsion. In the recovery phase (hand out of the water, beginning with elbow lift), the main muscles involved are the supraspinatus, infraspinatus, middle deltoid, and serratus anterior.[93] The main shoulder motions are internal rotation and adduction during the pull-through phase and external rotation with abduction during the recovery phase.

The recovery phase is 35% of the stroke cycle. As soon as the elbow rises as the hand leaves the water, external rotation and abduction should begin and be completed by midrecovery.

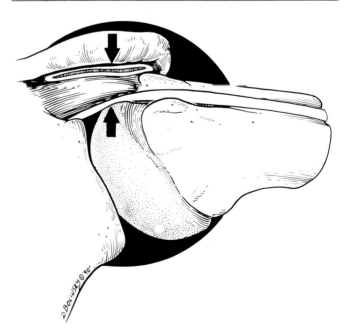

Figure 3-47 Swimmer's shoulder. Abduction stress creates subacromial impingement. *Source*: Copyright © 1990 by David Bolinsky.

Table 3-2 Shoulder Mechanics in Swimming

Stroke and Phases	Description
Freestyle	
Pull-through phase	
Hand entry	Shoulder external rotation and abduction. Body roll begins.
Midpull-through	Shoulder at 90° abduction and neutral internal-external rotation. Body roll is at maximum of 40° to 60° from horizontal.
End of pull-through	Shoulder internally rotated and fully adducted. Body has returned to horizontal.
Recovery phase	
Elbow lift	Shoulder begins abduction and external rotation. Body roll begins in opposite direction from pull-through.
Midrecovery	Shoulder abducted to 90° and externally rotated beyond neutral. Body roll reaches maximum of 40° to 60°. Breathing occurs by turning head to side.
Hand entry	Shoulder externally rotated and maximally abducted. Body has returned to neutral roll.
Backstroke	
Pull-through phase	
Hand entry	Shoulder external rotation and abduction. Body roll begins.
Midpull-through	Shoulder at 90° abduction and neutral internal-external rotation. Body roll maximum.
End of pull-through	Shoulder internally rotated and abducted. Body roll horizontal.
Recovery phase	
Hand lift	Shoulder begins abduction and external rotation. Body roll allows arm to clear water.
Midrecovery	Shoulder at 90° abduction. Body roll maximum.
Hand entry	Shoulder at maximum abduction. Body roll neutral.
Butterfly	
Pull-through phase	Same as freestyle with absence of body roll in all stages. To avoid shoulder flexion or extension, the hands are spread apart at the midpull-through stage.
Recovery phase	Again, similar to freestyle with absence of body roll. Body lift allows both arms to clear water. Shoulder flexion-extension does not occur.

Source: Reprinted with permission from *American Journal of Sports Medicine* (1980;8[3]:160), Copyright © 1980, American Orthopaedic Society for Sports Medicine.

At midrecovery the body roll should be 40° to 60°, which helps clear the humeral head from the acromion. At hand entry, the shoulder is externally rotated and at maximum abduction. If the thumb and index finger enter the water first instead of the middle finger, the possibility of excessive internal rotation exists.[94]

The following are some of the possibilities that may create impingement in a swimmer's shoulder:

- overdevelopment of the pectoral muscles at the expense of the scapular retractors, adductors, and elevators (rhomboids, middle and upper trapezii, levator scapulae, and upper fibers of latissimus dorsi); see discussion (above) of shoulder and scapular muscles
  1. The swimmer may show a winged scapula.
  2. Weak scapular muscles will fatigue, and the scapula will not rotate the glenoid superiorly in time to remove the acromion from the elevating humerus.[85] Eventual impingement will occur.
  3. Asynchronous scapulothoracic motion leads to fatigue of the cuff muscles which all originate off the scapula. Overfatigue of these dynamic shoulder stabilizers strains the static stabilizers resulting in humeral instability, traction stress, and cuff tendinitis.

- overdevelopment of the pectoral muscles at the expense of the external rotators

1. Testing of swimmers with impingement pain will usually reveal relative weakness of the external rotators.[42]
2. Weakened and fatigued external rotators allow the greater tuberosity to impinge during abduction because relative internal rotation is occurring during the recovery phase instead of external rotation. Full external rotation should occur at midrecovery instead of late recovery.[95] The swimmer will demonstrate a low elbow.
3. The force couple imbalance between the internal and external rotators may result in a tendinitis of the external rotators.
4. At early recovery there may be excessive internal rotation associated with abduction, causing impingement.

- poor swimming technique
  1. As mentioned, at hand entry if the thumb and index finger enter the water first instead of the middle finger there may be excessive early internal rotation, causing impingement.[93]
  2. Diminished body roll (less than 40° to 60°) and not enough elbow height during recovery decrease the external rotation necessary for clearing of the humeral head from the acromion.
  3. Prolonged adduction and an excessive midline cross-over pattern during the pull-through phase may cause

wringing out of the crucial vascular zone of the cuff muscles (Fig. 3-48).

4. Dropped elbows during either the recovery or the pull-through phase mean that the shoulders are relatively externally rotated. This may occur if the internal rotators and adductors are not strong enough. Keeping the arm in relative external rotation keeps the muscles of propulsion (internal rotators and adductors) at a disadvantage.[91]

- normal overuse of the shoulder due to excessive training (because in the underwater pull phase the humeral head is normally forced up into the coracoacromial arch)[44]

1. During the catch phase of swimming the arm is in abduction, forward flexion, and external rotation. This position, with overuse, is likely to stress the acromial arch.

2. Overfatigue of the cuff muscles occurs preventing these muscles from performing their function of humeral head stabilization.

3. Cuff fatigue results in superior migration of the humeral head, causing impingement during the recovery phase.

- need in loose-jointed swimmers, during overuse, to overwork the rotator cuff muscles to support the shoulder

The following case history serves as an excellent example of how an understanding of shoulder biomechanics and its relation to the swimming stroke together with the use of a functional examination can enable the examiner to arrive at a diagnosis and treatment.

A 22-year-old woman who had been swimming competitively for 10 years presented with recent anterior lateral right shoulder pain extending to the deltoid tubercle. She competed as a freestyle sprint and middle-distance swimmer. Over the last 2 months she was complaining of pain that began during the first 15 minutes of her workout and continued for several hours. She had no night pain and, except for the above complaint, was only aware of her shoulder pain with excessive use, such as house painting. She had no history of trauma or pain relating to her upper or lower extremities and was in excellent health.

Roentgenograms of the cervical spine and shoulder were unremarkable. Examination of the cervical-thoracic spine and sensory, motor, deep reflex, and vascular surveys of the upper

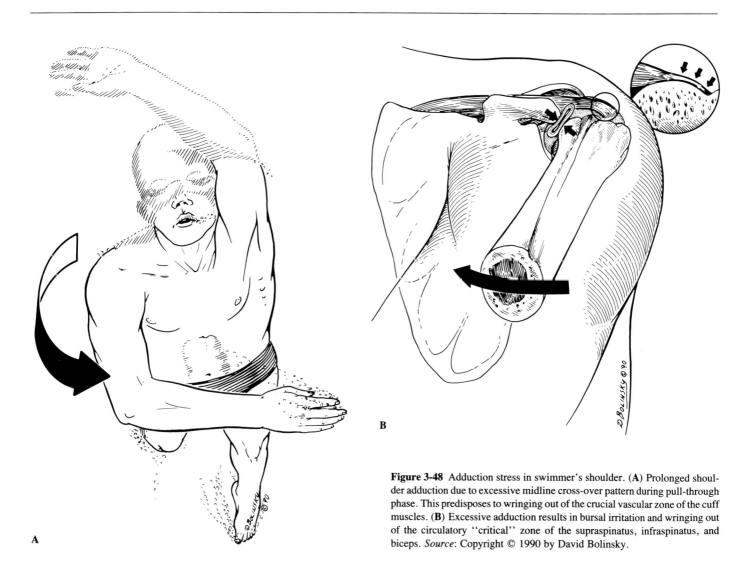

Figure 3-48 Adduction stress in swimmer's shoulder. (**A**) Prolonged shoulder adduction due to excessive midline cross-over pattern during pull-through phase. This predisposes to wringing out of the crucial vascular zone of the cuff muscles. (**B**) Excessive adduction results in bursal irritation and wringing out of the circulatory "critical" zone of the supraspinatus, infraspinatus, and biceps. *Source*: Copyright © 1990 by David Bolinsky.

extremities were negative. The significant findings of the postural examination were a forward head position, rounded shoulders, and a lumbar lordosis. Inspection of the shoulders and related muscles and joints revealed normal contour and no atrophy.

Functional shoulder examination: The left shoulder tested normal. The following findings refer to the right shoulder.

1. Active coronal abduction was painful between 70° and 110° (painful arc) and again at 180°. Active combined lateral rotation with abduction and medial rotation with adduction were equal bilaterally and minimally painful.
2. Passive coronal abduction was pain free to 70°, painful to 110°, and pain free (painful arc) until the end range, which was painful.
3. Passive lateral rotation was pain free and limited to 75°.
4. Passive medial rotation was slightly painful.
5. Passive glenohumeral abduction reached 105° and was painless.
6. Passive horizontal adduction was painless.
7. Resisted abduction was strong and not painful until the eighth repetition of the test.*
8. Resisted lateral rotation was not painful until the seventh repetition of the test* and revealed weakness.
9. Resisted medial rotation was strong and painless.
10. Resisted adduction was strong and painless.
11. Resisted shoulder flexion was strong and painless (Speed's test).
12. Stability tests of the capsule and labrum clunk test were normal.
13. The relocation test revealed no change in symptoms.
14. The coracoacromial ligament impingement test was minimally painful.
15. Active trigger points were located in both the infraspinatus and the supraspinatus.
16. Joint play examination revealed loss of humeral inferior glide.

Palpation: Palpation of the areas that testing incriminated (ie, the tenoperiosteal portion of the supraspinatus and infraspinatus) revealed sensitivity. Palpation of the subacromial bursa at the anterior acromion was not tender. Palpation of the coracoacromial ligament was minimally painful.

Discussion: The asterisks (*) indicate that one resisted test of the particular muscle may be painless. In athletes, especially when they do not experience pain until later in their activity, repetitive loading is often necessary. Sometimes they should be functionally tested immediately after their pain begins during their workout. Because this patient did not experience symptoms until 15 minutes into her workout, resisted testing one or two times was not sufficient to aggravate her problem. She obviously had excellent muscle tone, and her condition had not progressed to the point that pain occurred early on. After repeated resisted testing the patient stated that

the pain she felt was similar to her swimming pain. Usually, when the patient has the pain at examination time, resisted muscle testing plus the other tests are painful on the first attempt.

After the passive structures are eliminated as sources of pain, resisted muscle testing could also be done at different ranges of motion. Muscles could be tested at the angle of the patient's complaint.

Test interpretation: The most tender point to palpation was at the area where the supraspinatus inserts into the greater tuberosity. Friction anesthesia (see Chapter 12) was applied to the area for approximately 2 to 3 minutes until the patient reported numbness. Resisted testing of the infraspinatus and supraspinatus was significantly less painful, as were tests 1, 2, 4, and 14.

Abduction pain at 180° represented possible impingement at the undersurface of the involved supraspinatus tendon. The painful arc represented compression of tendon insertions in the subacromial area. Decreased range on passive lateral rotation revealed pectoral shortening. Pain on medial passive rotation represented a stretch pain to the inflamed infraspinatus. Pain on resisted muscle testing without the loss of significant strength at the supraspinatus and infraspinatus represented a probable tendinitis of one or both of these tendons. The weakness detected on testing the right lateral rotator indicated probable weakness due to underdevelopment (which is common in swimmers) rather than a neurologic problem. The negative passive tests plus the two painful resisted tests indicated a tendinitis rather than a bursal involvement because bursal involvement usually creates a combination of resisted and passive tests resulting in a nonspecific picture, whereas in this case palpation of the bursa was pain free. The relocation test, stability tests, and labrum clunk test eliminated the possibility of subluxation or labral tears. The painful impingement test may indicate an irritated or hypertrophied coracoacromial ligament or pressure on an irritated supraspinatus or biceps; Speed's test, however, was strong and painless, thereby eliminating biceps involvement.

The functional examination pinpointed the insertion areas of the supraspinatus and infraspinatus muscles as the source of the pain. In manual treatment it is necessary to know the exact source of pain to obtain the best results. Simply injecting an anesthetic or steroid into the area and calling it an impingement syndrome cannot be considered treating the underlying cause of pain.

Treatment: Office treatment would consist of the following:

1. Friction massage of involved tendons (supraspinatus and infraspinatus) and the coracoacromial ligament. Friction is applied at each visit until the involved tendons can be tested with resisted isometric testing at least 10 times in a row without pain before treatment (see Chapter 12).
2. Joint play correction of the shoulder (for loss of inferior glide) (see Chapter 10).

3. Evaluation and removal of involved trigger point areas in the supraspinatus and infraspinatus (see Chapter 11).
4. Therapeutic muscle stretching of possible shortened muscles (pectorals, latissimus dorsi, and teres major) (see Chapter 13) and strengthening of possible weak scapular adductors, retractors, and lateral rotators (see Chapter 14). All the shoulder girdle muscles and even the lower extremity musculature should be tested for flexibility and strength. In swimmers it is essential to create a balance between the internal and external rotators, which usually means stretching the internal rotators and strengthening the external rotators. Griep[96] proved that swimmers who maintain flexibility by way of a stretching program have less tendinitis. Faulty swimming stroke patterns must be corrected.

REFERENCES

1. Simkin PA. Tendinitis and bursitis of the shoulder: anatomy and therapy. *Postgrad Med.* 1983;73:177.
2. Nobuhara K, Sugiyama D, Ikeda H, et al. Contracture of the shoulder. *Clin Orthop.* 1990;254:105–110.
3. Poppen NK, Walker PS. Normal and abnormal motion of the shoulder. *J Bone Joint Surg Am.* 1976;58:195–201.
4. Johnston TB. Movements of the shoulder joint—plea for use of "plane of the scapula" as a plane of reference for movements occurring at humeroscapula joint. *Br J Surg.* 1937;25:252.
5. Bechtol CO. Biomechanics of the shoulder. *Clin Orthop.* 1980;146:39.
6. Mountcastle VB, ed. *Medical Physiology.* 13th ed. St Louis, Mo: Mosby; 1974;1:86–87.
7. Kessler RM, Hertling D. *Management of Common Musculoskeletal Disorders: Physical Therapy Principles and Methods.* Philadelphia: Harper & Row; 1983:534–535.
8. Perry J. Anatomy and biomechanics of the shoulder in throwing, swimming, gymnastics and tennis. *Clin Sports Med.* 1983;2:254–255.
9. Kent BE. Functional anatomy of the shoulder complex: a review. *Phys Ther.* 1971;51:867–868.
10. Saha AK. *Theory of Shoulder Mechanism: Descriptive and Applied.* Springfield, Ill: Thomas; 1961.
11. Codman EA. *The Shoulder.* New York: Todd; 1934.
12. Inman VT, Saunders JB de CM, Abbot LC. Observations on the function of the shoulder joint. *J Bone Joint Surg.* 1944,26:1–30.
13. Jobe FW, Moynes DR, Brewster CE. Rehabilitation of shoulder joint instabilities. *Orthop Clin North Am.* 1987;18:473.
14. Rowe CR. *The Shoulder.* New York: Churchill Livingstone; 1988.
15. Turek SL. *Orthopaedics: Principles and Their Application.* 4th ed. Philadelphia: Lippincott; 1984;2.
16. Ryu RK, McCormick J, Jobe FW, et al. An electromyographic analysis of shoulder function in tennis players. *Am J Sports Med.* 1988;16:481–485.
17. Perry J. Biomechanics of the shoulder. In: Rowe CR, ed. *The Shoulder.* New York: Churchill Livingstone; 1988:17–33.
18. Cochran GVB. *A Primer of Orthopaedic Biomechanics.* New York: Churchill Livingstone; 1982.
19. Kapandji IA. *The Physiology of the Joints.* 2nd ed. New York: Churchill Livingstone; 1970;1:72.
20. Basmajian JV, Deluca CJ. *Muscles Alive: Their Functions Revealed by Electromyography.* 5th ed. Baltimore: Williams & Wilkins; 1985.
21. Sarrafian SK. Gross and functional anatomy of the shoulder. *Clin Orthop Relat Res.* 1983;173:11.

22. Wilk KE. Shoulder examination. Presented at Symposium, Advances in Knee and Shoulder; April 2–4, 1990; Cincinatti Sports Medicine and Deaconess Hospital.
23. Howell SM, Imobersteg MA, Segar DH, et al. Clarification of the role of the supraspinatus muscle in shoulder function. *J Bone Joint Surg Am.* 1986;68:398–404.
24. Lehmkuhl DL, Smith LK. *Brunnstrom's Clinical Kinesiology.* 4th ed. Philadelphia: Davis; 1984.
25. Kumar VP, Satku K, Balasubramaniam P. The role of the long head of biceps brachii in the stabilization of the head of the humerus. *Clin Sports Med.* 1989;244:172–175.
26. Noah J, Gidumal R. Rotator cuff injuries in the throwing athlete. *Orthop Rev.* 1988;17:1093.
27. Garrick JG, Webb DR. *Shoulder Injuries in Sports Injuries: Diagnosis and Management.* Philadelphia: WB Saunders; 1990:55–97.
28. Andrews JR, Angelo RL. Arthroscopy in the diagnosis and treatment of rotator cuff injuries. Presented at the American Orthopedics Society Conference on Sports Medicine; February 1986; New Orleans.
29. Williams PL, Warwick R. *Gray's Anatomy.* 36th ed. Philadelphia: Saunders; 1980.
30. Bland JH, Merrit JA, Boushey DR. The painful shoulder. *Semin Arthritis Rheum.* 1977;7.
31. Gordon EJ. Diagnosis and treatment of common shoulder disorders. *Med Trial Tech Q.* 1981;28:25–73.
32. Bigliani LU. Multi-directional instability. Presented at symposium, Advances in Knee and Shoulder; April 2–4, 1990; Cincinatti Sports Medicine and Deaconess Hospital.
33. Turkel SJ. Stabilizing mechanisms preventing anterior dislocation of the glenohumeral joint. *J Bone Joint Surg Am.* 1981;63:1208–1217.
34. Lindenfeld TN. Surgical indications, treatment of anterior instability. Presented at symposium, Advances in Knee and Shoulder; April 2–4, 1990; Cincinatti Sports Medicine and Deaconess Hospital.
35. Johns RJ, Wright V. Relative importance of various tissues in joint stiffness. *J Appl Physiol.* 1962;17:824.
36. Andrews JR. Shoulder examination. Presented at Symposium, Advances in Knee and Shoulder; April 2–4, 1990; Cincinatti Sports Medicine and Deaconess Hospital.
37. Hawkins RJ, Hobeika P. Physical examination of the shoulder. *Orthopedics.* 1983;6:1275.
38. Kendall HO, Kendall FP, Wadsworth GE. *Muscles: Testing and Function.* 2nd ed. Baltimore: Williams & Wilkins; 1971.
39. Yocum LA. Assessing the shoulder: history, physical examination, differential diagnosis and special tests used. *Clin Sports Med.* 1983;2:285.
40. Janda V. *Muscle Function Testing.* London: Butterworths; 1983.
41. Jobe FW, Kvitne RS. Shoulder pain in the overhand or throwing athlete: the relationship of anterior instability and rotator cuff impingement. *Orthop Rev.* 1989;18:963–975.
42. Garth WP, Allman FL, Armstrong WS. Occult anterior subluxations of the shoulder in noncontact sports. *Am J Sports Med.* 1987;15:579–585.
43. Fowler PJ. Upper extremity swimming injuries. In: Nicholas JA, Hershman EB, eds. *The Upper Extremity in Sports Medicine.* St. Louis, Mo: Mosby; 1990:891–902.
44. Ciullo JV. Swimmer's shoulder. *Clin Sports Med.* 1968;5:115–127.
45. Nirschl RP. Prevention and treatment of elbow and shoulder injuries in the tennis player. *Clin Sports Med.* 1988;7:291.
46. Teitz CC, ed. *Scientific Foundations of Sports Medicine.* Toronto: Decker; 1989.
47. Rathbun JB, Macnab I. The microvascular pattern of the rotator cuff. *J Bone Joint Surg Br.* 1970;52.
48. Lohr JF, Uhthoff HK. The microvascular pattern of the supraspinatus tendon. *Clin Orthop.* 1990;254:35–38.

49. Glousman R. The relationship of instability to rotator cuff damage—conservative and surgical repair. Presented at the American Academy of Orthopedic Surgeons annual meeting; February 1988; Atlanta.

50. Neer CS. Impingement lesions. *Clin Orthop*. 1983;173:1.

51. Morrison DS, Bigliani LU. The clinical significance of variations in acromial morphology. *Orthop Trans*. 1987;11:234.

52. Sarkar K, Taine W, Uhthoff HK. The ultrastructure of the coracoacromial ligament in patients with chronic impingment syndrome. *Clin Orthop*. 1990;254:49–54.

53. DePalma AF. *Surgery of the Shoulder*. 2nd ed. Philadelphia: Lippincott; 1973.

54. Neer CS, Welsh RP. The shoulder in sports. *Orthop Clin North Am*. 1977;8:585.

55. Leach RE, Schepsis AA. Shoulder pain. *Clin Sports Med*. 1983;1:127.

56. Cyriax J. *Textbook of Orthopaedic Medicine: Diagnosis of Soft Tissue Lesions*. 8th ed. London: Bailliere-Tindall; 1982.

57. Meyer AW. Spontaneous dislocation and destruction of the tendon of long head of biceps brachii: 59 instances. *Arch Surg*. 1928;17:493.

58. Booth RE, Marvel JP. Differential diagnosis of shoulder pain. *Orthop Clin North Am*. 1975;6.

59. Curwin S, Stanish WD. Tendinitis: its etiology and treatment. In: Teitz CC, ed. *Scientific Foundations of Sports Medicine*. Toronto: Decker; 1989:25–44.

60. Uhthoff HK, Sarkar K, Gomez J. Presented at the annual meeting of the Canadian Orthopedic Association; June 1977; Toronto.

61. Simon WH. Soft tissue disorders of the shoulder: frozen shoulder, calcific tendinitis and bicipital tendinitis. *Orthop Clin North Am*. 1975;6.

62. Neviaser RJ. Painful conditions affecting the shoulder. *Clin Orthop*. 1983;173:65.

63. Patte D. The subcoracoid impingement. *Clin Orthop*. 1990;254:55–59.

64. Gerber C, Terrier F, Ganz R. The role of the coracoid process in the chronic impingement syndrome. *J Bone Joint Surg*. 1985;67B:703.

65. Ellman H. Diagnosis and treatment of incomplete rotator cuff tears. *Clin Orthop*. 1990;254:64–74.

66. Bateman JE. Cuff tears in athletes. *Orthop Clin North Am*. 1973;4:722–733.

67. Samilson RL, Binder WF. Symptomatic full thickness tears of the rotator cuff: an analysis of 292 shoulders in 276 patients. *Orthop Clin North Am*. 1975;6:725.

68. Sweetnam R. Corticosteroid arthropathy and tendon rupture. *J Bone Joint Surg Br*. 1969;51:397.

69. Post M, Silver R, Singh M. Rotator cuff tear: diagnosis and treatment. *Clin Orthop Relat Res*. 1983;173:81.

70. Shevlin MG, Lehmann JF, Lucci JA. Electromyographic study of the function of some muscles crossing the glenohumeral joint. *Arch Phys Med Rehabil*. 1969;50:264–270.

71. Warren RF, O'Brien SJ. Shoulder pain in the geriatric patient: part I, evaluation and pathophysiology. *Orthop Rev*. 1989;28:130.

72. Lippmann RK. Frozen shoulder, periarthritis, bicipital tenosynovitis. *Arch Surg*. 1943;47:283–296.

73. Kulund DN. *The Injured Athlete*. 2nd ed. Philadelphia: Lippincott; 1988.

74. Bennett RM. The painful shoulder. *Postgrad Med*. 1983;73:153.

75. Cibulka MT, Hunter HC. Acromioclavicular joint arthritis treated by mobilizing the glenohumeral joint: a case report. *Phys Ther*. 1985;65:1514.

76. Uhthoff HK, Sarkar K. An algorithm for shoulder pain caused by soft-tissue disorders. *Clin Orthop*. 1990;254:121–127.

77. Fareed DO, Gallivan WR. Office management of frozen shoulder syndrome: treatment with hydraulic distension under local anesthesia. *Clin Orthop Relat Res*. 1989;242:177–183.

78. Rizk TE, Christopher RP, Pinals RS, et al. Adhesive capsulitis (frozen shoulder): a new approach to its management. *Arch Phys Med Rehabil*. 1983;64:29–33.

79. Sapega AA, Quedenfeld TC, Moyer RA, et al. Biophysical factors in range of motion exercise. *Phys Sports Med*. 1981;93:57–65.

80. O'Brien SJ, Warren RF, Schwartz E. Anterior shoulder instability. *Orthop Clin North Am*. 1987:395–407.

81. Rowe CR. Recurrent transient anterior subluxation of the shoulder: the "dead arm syndrome." *Clin Orthop*. 1987;223:18.

82. Moseley HF, Overgaard B. The anterior capsular mechanism in recurrent anterior dislocation of the shoulder. *J Bone Joint Surg Br*. 1962;44:913.

83. Jackson DW. *Shoulder Surgery in the Athlete*. Rockville, Md: Aspen; 1985.

84. Ireland ML, Andrews JR. Shoulder and elbow injuries in the young athlete. *Clin Sports Med*. 1988;7:473–483.

85. Becker TJ. The athletic trainer in swimming. *Clin Sports Med*. 1986;5:9–24.

86. O'Neill DB, Micheli LJ. Overuse injuries in the young athlete. *Clin Sports Med*. 1988;7:591–601.

87. Solheim LF, Roaas A. Compression of the suprascapular nerve after fracture of the scapular notch. *Acta Orthop Scand*. 1978;43:338.

88. Moskowitz E, Rashkoff ES. Suprascapular nerve palsy. *Conn Med*. 1989;53:639.

89. Ringel SP, Treihaft M, Carry M, et al. Suprascapular neuropathy in pitchers. *Am J Sports Med*. 1990;18:84.

90. Ferretti A, Cerullo G, Russo G. Suprascapular neuropathy in volleyball players. *J Bone Joint Surg Am*. 1987;69:260–263.

91. Black KP, Lombardo JA. Suprascapular nerve injuries with isolated paralysis of the infraspinatus. *Am J Sports Med*. 1990;18(13):225–228.

92. Richardson AB, Jobe FW, Collins HR. The shoulder in competitive swimming. *Am J Sports Med*. 1980;8:159–163.

93. Nuber GW, Jobe FW, Perry J, et al. Fine wire electromyography analysis of muscles of the shoulder during swimming. *Am J Sports Med*. 1986;14:7–11.

94. Zarins B, Andrews JR, Carson WG. *Injuries to the Throwing Arm*. Philadelphia: Saunders; 1985.

95. Malone TR, Falkel JE, Murphy TC. *Shoulder Injuries: Sports Injury Management*. Baltimore: Williams & Wilkins; 1988.

96. Griep JF. Swimmer's shoulder: the influence of flexibility and weight training. *Phys Sports Med*. 1985;8:92.

Appendix 3-A

Shoulder Functional Diagnosis Chart

Table 3-A-1 Shoulder, Functional Diagnosis

Key
+ Pain
+/− Possible pain
L Possible Limited ROM
W Weak

Tests	Acute Bursitis	Chronic Bursitis	Subcoracoid Bursitis	Capsular Lesion	Supraspinatus Musculotend.	Supraspinatus Tenoperiost.	Infraspinatus Tendinitis	Subscapularis Tendinitis	Biceps Tendinitis	Acromioclavicular Sprain	Ruptures (1)	Suprascapular Neuritis	Long Thoracic Neuritis (2)	Axillary Neuritis (3)	Spinal Accessory Neuritis (4)
Passive Abduction (180°)	+L	+/−		+/−	+/−	+/−				+ Over 90°		+/−			
Painful arc (60°–130°)		+/−					+/−	+/−	+/−	+/−		90°–160°			
Passive Lateral Rot. (90°)	+L	+/−	+/−	+ L Most				+/− Stretch				+/−			
Passive Glenohum. Abd. Scapula fixed (90°–105°)	+L	+/−		+/− L Less											
Passive Medial Rot. (70°)	+L	+/−		+/− L Least			+/− Stretch					+/−			
Passive Horiz. Add. (130°)	+L	+/−	+				+/− Stretch	+/−		+		+/−			
Resisted Abduction	+/−	+/−			+	+					W	W +/−			
Resisted Adduction	+/−	+/−						+/−			W				
Resisted Lat. Rot.	+/−	+/−			+/−	+/−	+				W	W +/−		W +/−	
Resisted Med. Rot.	+/−	+/−						+			W				
Resisted Elbow Flex. (If + test supination)	+/−	+/−	+/−						+ +		W				
Coracoacromial Impingmt.	+	+/−				+/−	+/−		+/−			+/−			

Additional tests
Instability: anterior, posterior, inferior.
Relocation
Glenoid Labrum,
Transverse Humeral,
Drop Arm,
Joint Play

1. Resisted testing of muscle: W & pain.
2. Resisted testing of serratus anterior: W & no pain.
3. Resisted testing of teres minor and deltoid: W & no pain.
4. Resisted testing of trapezius: W & no pain.

Chapter 4

The Elbow and Forearm

Warren I. Hammer

A principal function of the main joints of the upper extremity (shoulder, elbow, and wrist) is to position the hand at the mouth.[1] An elbow locked in near extension would limit us more than an immobile shoulder because shoulder movement can be compensated by scapulothoracic movement. The importance of the elbow is expressed in impairment ratings of the upper extremity; the elbow is given 70% and the shoulder and wrist are given 60% each of the total extremity.[2] With full extension considered 0° of flexion, most elbow activities[3] are performed in an arc of elbow flexion between 30° and 130° and forearm rotation of 100° divided equally between pronation and supination.

The forearm is often affected by muscle, tendon, and nerve problems originating at the elbow area. The major wrist flexors and extensors originate from the distal humerus. Use of the wrist alone for power, without the use of the rest of the upper extremity and body, can adversely affect the forearm and elbow. Of course, as with all problems of the upper extremity, conditions such as cervical nerve root involvement, double crush syndrome, thoracic outlet syndrome, and cardiogenic pain must be ruled out. Total functional examination of the cervical spine and shoulder must be included because deficits in these areas relating to flexibility, strength, and proprioception create compensatory stress in the distal areas.

Pain and limitation of motion due to trauma and overuse often respond to the healing effect of manual therapy and rehabilitation. A word of caution regarding manipulation of elbow: Intra-articular problems should not be manipulated in early stages until the joint can be fully extended and the inflammation is markedly reduced.

FUNCTIONAL ANATOMY AND PERTINENT BIOMECHANICS

The elbow has two main joints, a flexion-extension joint (olecranon-trochlear) and a rotatory joint (radiocapitellar), and a third, lesser joint, the proximal radioulnar. The presence of two main joints results in less bony stability and a greater range of motion compared to the more stable knee joint.[4] Therefore, the elbow is subject to dislocation and a large variety of strains, sprains, and compression neuropathies.

Ranges of Motion

Active flexion from 0° extension is 145° to 150°, and passive flexion is about 160°. Active pronation measured with the elbow flexed 90° and resting along the trunk is 85°, and active supination is 90°. According to Kapandji,[1] active flexion is more limited than passive flexion because of the contracted muscles of the arm and forearm. Passive flexion is limited by bony structures (the head of the radius against the radial fossa and the coronoid process against the coronoid fossa), tension of the posterior capsular ligament, and passive tension in the triceps. Active and passive elbow extension is limited by the impact of the olecranon process on the olecranon fossa, tension of the medial anterior oblique ligament and anterior capsule, and resistance of the anterior muscles (biceps, brachialis, and supinator).

Clinical: The capsular pattern is more limitation of flexion than of extension (both are limited). The elbow provides a clear example of differentiating passive inert tissue from contractile tissue. After resisted testing is found to be normal, passive testing, when limited (in flexion or extension), would incriminate the remaining inert tissue: capsule, ligament, or bone. An irritated contracted flexor muscle might limit passive extension but will usually test painful or weaker than normal on resisted testing.

Carrying Angle

In the anatomic position with the arm extended and the forearm supinated, there is a normal valgus of the forearm of 10° to 15° in men and 20° to 25° in women. Deviations from normal may occur from past trauma or epiphyseal growth disturbances.

Muscular Component

Elbow Flexion

Primary movers are the biceps brachii, brachialis, and brachioradialis. The secondary flexors are the flexor carpi radialis and pronator teres. The biceps is continuously active during elbow flexion with the forearm supinated, but with the forearm in the pronated position the biceps plays little if any role in flexion, maintaining elbow flexion, or acting as an antagonist during elbow extension.[5] The brachialis is a strong flexor of the forearm regardless of the amount of pronation or supination; it is the "workhorse" of flexion.[6,7]

Elbow Extension

The medial head of the triceps is the prime extensor, and the lateral and long heads are considered accessory muscles. The anconeus is another accessory extender.

Forearm Pronation

Prime movers are the pronator teres and pronator quadratus. During pronation the proximal head of the radius does not move in space, but the distal end of the radius does.[8]

Forearm Supination

Prime movers are the biceps and supinator. The biceps does not act as a supinator if the forearm is extended unless there is resistance to supination; otherwise, unopposed supination with the arm extended would result in flexion of the forearm. In strong resisted supination with the arm extended there usually is some elbow flexion. Therefore, whenever we test the supinator against resistance the biceps is activated.

Clinical: Because elbow flexion in any position always involves the brachialis, which is not a supinator, if there is pain on resisted elbow flexion painful testing of supination may incriminate the biceps brachii. Painful palpation of the radial

head with active or passive pronation and supination in different degrees of flexion may indicate radial head fracture.

Strength

Extension strength is 70% that of flexion strength. Supination strength is normally about 15% greater than pronation strength. The dominant extremity is 5% to 10% stronger than the nondominant side.[3]

Elbow Stability

Instability of the elbow occurs primarily with valgus stress; varus instability is not common.[9] Nature has apparently recognized this fact because the lateral ligaments are not as supportive as the medial collateral ligaments. The medial collaterals consist of an anterior and posterior oblique portion and a transverse portion (Fig. 4-1). The anterior oblique portion offers medial stability through almost total flexion and extension, and the posterior oblique offers medial stability in the range of 60° to 135° of flexion and extension. The transverse ligament contributes little to stability. Valgus stability is maintained more by the anterior oblique liagment than by the olecranon because excision of a large portion of the olecranon does not result in instability whereas excision of the anterior oblique produces massive instability.[10] The lateral collateral ligament originates from the lateral condyle and inserts on the annular ligament of the radius rather than into bone. The elbow does not have a functional lateral collateral ligament.[10]

Clinical: Elbow instability is not a common problem. Ligaments may be injured with fractures or dislocations. All elbow dislocations are posterior. Healing of elbow ligaments appears to be adequate because only 1% to 2% of elbow dislocations result in recurrent instability.[11] Repetitive throwing, tennis, and hammering can cause chronic valgus insufficiency, and a single stress from a fall on an outstretched hand can cause an acute rupture. The flexor pronator muscles are more commonly involved than the ligaments and capsule.

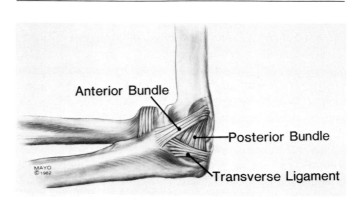

Figure 4-1 The classic orientation of the medial collateral ligament, including the anterior and posterior bundles as well as the transverse ligament. This last structure contributes relatively little to elbow stability. *Source:* Reprinted by permission of Mayo Foundation, © 1982.

Baseball pitching is the best example of repetitive elbow valgus stress, especially during the early acceleration phase (from the end of maximal external rotation of the shoulder until the release of the ball (Fig. 4-2).)[12] During early acceleration the trunk and shoulder are brought forward with the arm and forearm behind in external rotation. Repetitive valgus stress creates microtears, which if carried to extremes can lead to the formation of scar tissue, calcific densities, and finally ossification. From then on even a trivial trauma could lead to rupture.[12] During valgus stress, as the elbow becomes less efficient it creates tensile forces on the medial ligament, tendons, and flexor muscles; compressive forces then occur on the lateral radiocapitellar area (osteochondritis dissecans and osteocartilaginous loose bodies) along with shear forces caused by the medial tip of the olecranon impinging on the medial wall of the olecranon fossa, resulting in osteophytes, loose bodies, and an incongruous joint space. Valgus stress may eventually result in stretch neuropraxia of the ulnar nerve, causing hypermobility of the nerve (see below, Ulnar Entrapment Neuropathy).

Schwab et al[10] state that in valgus stress, while the flexor muscle mass is the first line of defense, medial collateral ligament rupture is more common than forearm flexor muscle rupture. These investigators point out that flexor muscle rupture would be due to sudden massive wrist flexion (eg, in throwing or tennis serve).

Elbow functional testing (see below) is performed to differentiate ligamentous, muscular, and loose body sources of pain due to valgus stress.

FUNCTIONAL EXAMINATION OF THE ELBOW

Inspection will easily reveal swellings or dislocations because the joint is subcutaneous. Most swelling appears beneath the lateral epicondyle, there being more synovial tissue on the lateral side. The carrying angle should be noted. The patient is asked to flex, extend, pronate, and supinate the elbow actively to determine limitations of movement. The following functional tests are listed in Appendix 4-A.

Passive flexion gives a normal soft tissue end feel up to 160° (Fig. 4-3). There is a capsular pattern if passive flexion is limited more than passive extension. A springy block end feel may be a loose body (rare in flexion). A bone-to-bone limited end feel may be osteoarthrosis. Passive flexion may aggravate an ulnar neuropathy (see below, Ulnar Entrapment Neuropathy) and is limited and painful in injury to the brachialis. It may also be painful because of stretch of a triceps lesion.

Figure 4-2 Repetitive elbow valgus stress, which occurs at the early and late stages of the acceleration phase in pitching. Maintaining the shoulder at 90° abduction, and therefore in minimal scapular rotation, compromises the subacromial space. *Source:* Copyright © 1990 by David Bolinsky.

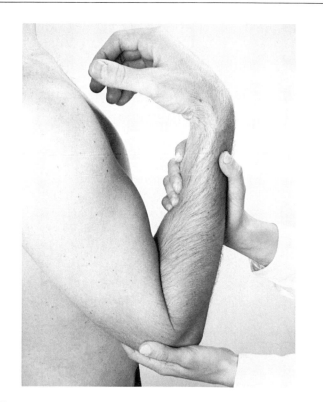

Figure 4-3 Passive elbow flexion.

Passive extension should have a normal bone-to-bone end feel (Fig. 4-4). A springy block end feel may be due to loose bodies. Elbow extension is usually the first motion to be limited and the last to be restored with intrinsic joint problems.[13]

Passive pronation is tested with the patient's elbow flexed at 90°. The examiner grasps the proximal forearm with both hands and pronates for end feel (Fig. 4-5). There may be pain if compression involves the biceps brachii insertion. There is limited hard end feel in advanced arthritis (associated with a capsular pattern) and pain and limitation in involvement of the proximal radioulnar articulation, radiocapitellar incongruity, or a radial head fracture (which will cause "twang" end feel). The test may compress the median nerve in the presence of pronator syndrome (see below).

Passive supination is tested with the patient's elbow flexed at 90°. The examiner grasps the proximal forearm with both hands and supinates for end feel (Fig. 4-6). There is pain and limitation in involvement of the radioulnar articulation, radial head fracture (twang), or advanced arthritis (associated with a capsular pattern).

Valgus stress (elbow abduction stress test) is applied by flexing the elbow 15° to 20° to relax the anterior capsule and to remove the olecranon from the fossa. The forearm and hand are supinated as the elbow is stressed valgus (Figs. 4-7 and 4-9B). This test stresses primarily the anterior oblique medial collateral ligament plus associated ligaments. Any valgus movement elicited while testing in full extension would indicate massive disruption of the joint. Maintaining a valgus stress while flexing and extending the elbow causes compression of the

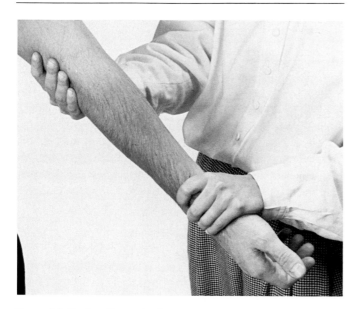

Figure 4-4 Passive elbow extension.

Figure 4-6 Passive elbow supination.

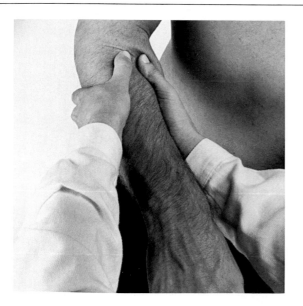

Figure 4-5 Passive elbow pronation.

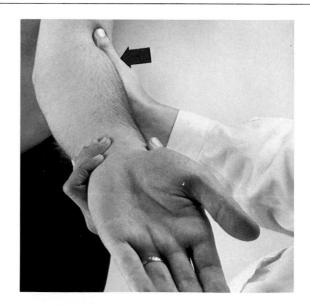

Figure 4-7 Valgus stress.

radiocapitellar joint. Problems related to lateral compression such as osteochondritis dissecans (loose bodies), incongruous joint (overgrowth of radial head), and degeneration may be indicated.

Varus stress (elbow adduction stress test) is applied by flexing the elbow 15° to 20° to relax the anterior capsule and to remove the olecranon from the fossa. The humerus is fully internally rotated, and the forearm is pronated. Stress is applied in the varus direction (Figs. 4-8 and 4-9A). This test is useful because it eliminates the compensatory shoulder rotation that is present in typical varus elbow testing.

Anteroposterior instability is usually obvious. Anterior laxity could be due to cartilage loss from rheumatoid arthritis.[13] Anterior instability can be tested in an anteroposterior or posteroanterior direction on the forearm with the elbow at 90° flexion. Degrees of instability are defined as follows: 5° opening (less than 5 mm), mild; 10° opening (less than 10 mm), moderate; and greater than 10° (10 mm), severe.[14]

Resisted flexion is tested as for the shoulder (Speed's test) or with the elbow flexed 75° to 90° and the hand supinated (Fig. 4-10). In testing the biceps, pain at the biceps belly, the musculotendinous area, or the insertion at the radial tuberosity of the radius should be considered (see Chapter 3 for testing for involvement of the upper level of the biceps long head). Because all flexor bellies are stressed with biceps testing, it is necessary to differentiate among them. Pain on resisted supination incriminates the biceps, and pain with the forearm pronated incriminates the brachialis; the brachioradialis is tested with the forearm in neutral. Resisted elbow flexion with the forearm supinated rarely may tense the lacertus fibrosus (a continuation of the anterior, medial, and distal bicipital mus-

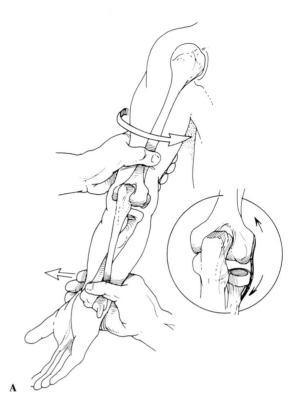

A

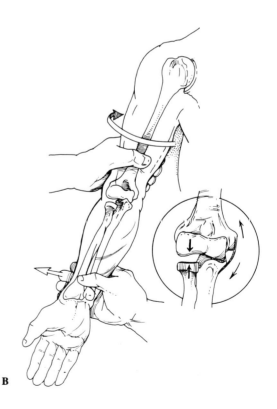

B

Figure 4-9 Elbow instability. **(A)** Varus instability of the elbow is measured with the humerus in full internal rotation and a varus stress applied to the slightly flexed joint. **(B)** Valgus instability is evaluated with the humerus in full external rotation while a valgus stress is applied to the slightly flexed joint. *Source:* Reprinted from *The Elbow and Its Disorders*, (p 71) by BF Morrey with permission of W.B. Saunders Company, © 1985.

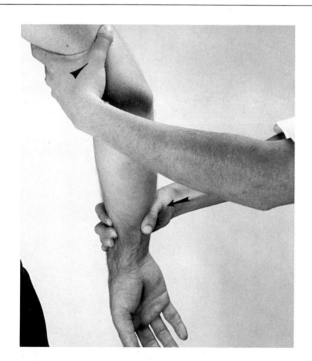

Figure 4-8 Varus stress.

cular fibers and aponeuroses), compressing the median nerve (see below, Median Nerve Entrapment).

Resisted extension (Fig. 4-11) is tested as follows. The patient stands with the elbow flexed at 45° and the arm abducted 90°. The examiner resists against the forearm toward flexion. Testing at 90° of shoulder abduction prevents the inferior-superior compression of the subacromial area, which occurs in testing at lower ranges. This test assesses the triceps muscle and creates tension and pain in an inflamed brachialis muscle.[15]

Resisted pronation is tested by having the patient flex the elbow to 90° with the arm against the trunk with the forearm in the neutral position. The examiner resists against the volar surface of the distal radius and applies counterpressure against the dorsal surface of the ulna (Fig. 4-12). This tests both the pronator teres and the distal pronator quadratus. It also stresses

the common tendon of the humeral medial epicondyle (medial epicondylitis is much more common than involvement of the pronator teres). Resisted pronation for 60 seconds may aggravate the median nerve (see below, Median Nerve Entrapment) by contracting the flexor pronator muscles.[16]

In resisted supination, according to Basmajian and Deluca,[5] all forceful movements of supination require the cooperation of the biceps to some degree. To put the synergistic biceps brachii in a disadvantageous position when testing the supinator,[17] supination is resisted with the shoulder and arm in almost maximum extension. The upper arm is stabilized to prevent humeral rotation (Fig. 4-13). This tests the supinator primarily and the biceps secondarily. It also stresses the common tendon of the humeral lateral epicondyle (lateral epicondylitis). It may create median nerve symptoms by tensing the lacertus fibrosus.

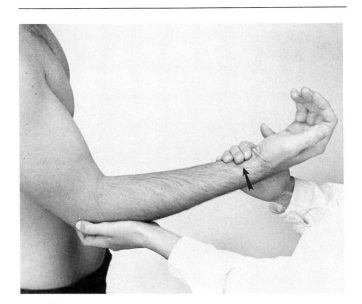

Figure 4-10 Resisted elbow flexion.

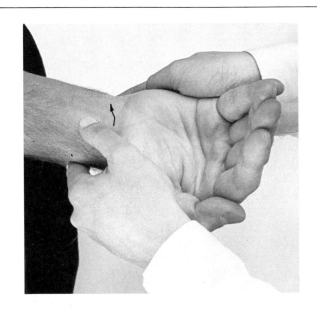

Figure 4-12 Resisted pronation.

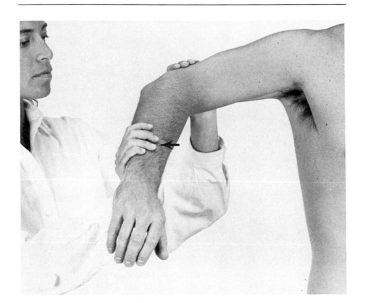

Figure 4-11 Resisted elbow extension.

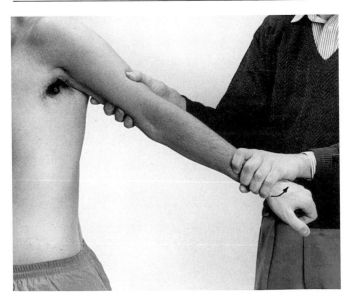

Figure 4-13 Resisted supination.

Resisted wrist flexion is tested with the elbow in full extension and the muscles of the thumb and fingers relaxed in flexion to prevent substitution by the finger flexors. The examiner resists against the palm (Fig. 4-14). This tests the common flexor tendon at the medial epicondyle, the origin of the flexor carpi ulnaris at the medial margin of the olecranon process and the upper two-thirds of the dorsal border of the ulna, all of which represent possible areas of treatment in medial epicondylitis. If the above tests are positive and if resisted pronation is also painful, medial epicondylitis should be considered the source of the pain before the pronator teres.

Resisted wrist extension is tested with the elbow in full extension for maximum extensor stress and with the fingers relaxed in flexion to prevent substitution by the finger extensors (Fig. 4-15). This tests the common extensor tendons from the lateral epicondyle (brevis and carpi ulnaris) and the extensor carpi radialis longus from the distal third of the lateral supracondylar ridge of the humerus. The extensor ulnaris also has origins from the aponeurosis on the dorsal border of the ulna. Different locations of origins may explain different sites of tenderness on palpation, although the anterior border of the

lateral epicondyle is the most frequent site of pain in lateral epicondylitis.

LESIONS OF THE ELBOW

Lesions of the soft tissues of the elbow (Appendix 4-A) that benefit most from conservative treatment are caused by stress overuse, such as repetitive wrist flexion-extension, forearm rotation, and exposure to vibrating machinery. All these factors can result in strain, myofascial, trigger point, and tendinitis lesions. Cooney[18] further mentions prolonged postural positions that require continuous wrist flexion or intermittent pinching or grasping as potential etiologies. He states that stress-overuse injuries in athletes and workers usually cause symptoms of pain after rather than during the work or play. Pain during activity usually indicates increased severity of the lesion. Poor technique, training, and equipment are other common causes of soft tissue irritation. Jobe and Nuber[12] define overuse as when the body's physiologic ability to heal itself lags behind the microtrauma that develops with repetitive action. Besides affecting the contractile tissue, overuse trauma may also damage the noncontractile ligament, bone, and cartilage or create peripheral neural entrapment.

Bicipital Tendinitis (Distal Biceps)

Besides lifting, repetitive hyperextension of the elbow with pronation due to throwing (Fig. 4-16) or repetitive stressful

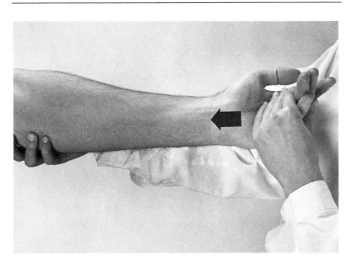
Figure 4-14 Resisted wrist flexion (with extended elbow).

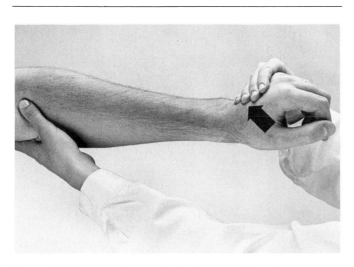
Figure 4-15 Resisted wrist extension (with extended elbow).

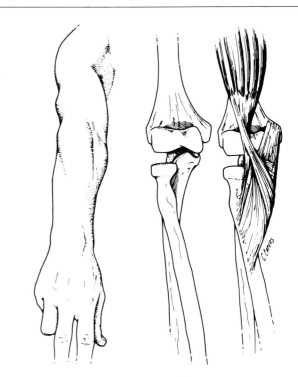
Figure 4-16 Bicipital tendinitis. Repetitive hyperextension with pronation of the elbow can stress the distal biceps and lacertus fibrosus in the antecubital fossa. *Source:* Reprinted with permission from *Clinics in Sports Medicine* (1987;6[2]:375), Copyright © 1987, W.B. Saunders Company.

pronation-supination movements can cause a chronic strain of the distal biceps and lacertus fibrosus in the antecubital fossa of the elbow.[14] Functional testing will cause pain in the area, and palpation will reveal where the most sensitive lesion is located. Usual areas of involvement are the distal biceps belly, the musculotendinous portion of the biceps, or the bicipital insertion of the radial tuberosity. The last two locations are rarely involved.

Functional tests

1. Definite pain on resisted elbow flexion.
2. Probable pain on resisted elbow supination. Weakness and pain in 1 and 2 may indicate a distal biceps tendon avulsion. The defect may be palpable.
3. Possible pain on passive proximal elbow pronation at the biceps insertion.
4. Possible pain on passive elbow flexion.
5. Possible pain on passive wrist extension with the elbow fully extended.

Treatment: Treatment includes friction massage to the involved site, trigger point assessment, therapeutic muscle stretching (TMS), elbow mobilization, and rehabilitation.

Brachialis Strain

Because the brachialis crosses the elbow as muscle, not as tendinous tissue, it is prone to hemorrhage when injured and has a high potential for significant scar formation and, rarely, myositis ossificans. According to O'Donoghue,[19] myositis ossificans is a frequent complication of the combination of contusion and hematoma involving the muscle near its origin on bone. There is ossification of infiltrated blood along the muscle origin on the bone. Cooney[20] states that ankylosis, with or without myositis ossificans, is the most frequent complication after elbow injury. He describes soft tissue contracture after trauma (tear, contusion, or rupture) to the periarticular muscle, capsule, and periosteum. The elbow joint flexes to accommodate the hemarthrosis and hemorrhage into the muscles, resulting in hematoma, fibrous degeneration, and possible calcification in the muscle. All the above preclude early mobilization of a lesioned elbow.

Functional tests

1. Definite pain on resisted flexion (with forearm pronated which reduces biceps involvement).
2. Mild to no pain on resisted supination.
3. Possible pain on resisted elbow extension.
4. Possible pain on passive flexion.
5. Possible pain on passive wrist extension with elbow fully extended.

Clinical: Because of the danger of myositis ossificans, if the contused muscle and hematoma do not heal promptly

roentgenograms taken in 2 to 3 weeks may reveal an osseous mass. A brachialis injury should not be manipulated or massaged until it is certain that myositis ossificans is not present. Ideally a bone scan should be used to determine that the osseous mass has fully matured and ceases to be active. Cyriax and Cyriax[21] recommend immobilizing the elbow in painless flexion with a collar-and-cuff bandage with a slow increase over time to full extension. Only heat and painless motion should be used. Cyriax[22] states that the muscle should not be massaged until full extension is reached.

Treatment: For the typical strain, rest, painless activity, friction massage, trigger point therapy, stretching, and rehabilitation will heal the problem.

Triceps Tendinitis (Posterior Tennis Elbow)

Hunter and Poole illustrate that movements requiring excessive elbow extension and supination of the forearm (eg, the tennis backhand stroke) can create an inflammation near or at the triceps insertion (Fig. 4-17). The serve and overhead shot can also involve the triceps. This is a rare lesion, however.

Functional tests

1. Definite pain on resisted elbow extension.
2. Possible pain on passive elbow flexion.

Treatment: This lesion responds well to manual methods (friction, trigger point, joint mobilization, and rehabilitation).

Supinator Strain

Before supinator involvement is considered, functional tests should be done for lateral epicondylitis, which may be the primary source of the pain.

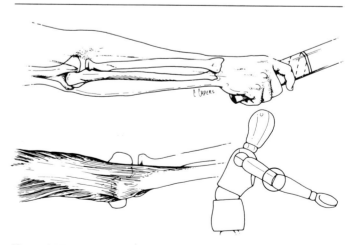

Figure 4-17 Triceps tendinitis. Excessive elbow extension with supination of the forearm can cause tendinitis of the triceps at its insertion on the olecranon. *Source:* Reprinted with permission from *Clinics in Sports Medicine* (1987;6[2]:375), Copyright © 1987, W.B. Saunders Company.

Functional tests

1. Definite pain on resisted supination.
2. Possible pain on passive pronation.
3. Possible pain on resisted biceps test.

Treatment: This lesion responds well to manual methods (friction, trigger point, joint mobilization, and rehabilitation).

Pronator Teres Strain

Before pronator muscle involvement is considered, functional tests should be performed for medial epicondylitis, which may be the primary source of the pain. Cabrera and McCue[23] state that the flexor pronator muscles are repetitively valgus stressed in throwing at the end of the cocking phase and during the early acceleration phase. At the release and deceleration phase of throwing, the flexor pronator muscles contract to pronate and flex the wrist. Repetitive stress and muscle fatigue can eventually lead to tears, eventual myostatic contractures, and loss of elbow extension. Legwold[24] mentions that during the tennis serve the racket head travels at 300 to 350 miles/hour until impact, when it slows to 150 miles/hour, stressing the forearm pronators.

Functional tests

1. Definite pain on resisted pronation.
2. Possible pain on passive supination.

Lateral Epicondylitis (Tennis Elbow)

Paraepicondylitis is perhaps a more suitable name for this lesion because the epicondyle itself is not inflamed. The lesion is a tendinitis mainly of the extensor carpi radialis brevis and is usually associated with actions that stress the wrist extensors (eg, the tennis backhand stroke). Numerous tissues about the lateral elbow have been blamed for epicondylitis, among them the radial humeral bursa; numerous conditions are also blamed, such as chondromalacia of the radiocapitellar joint, annular ligament tears, periosteal avulsion, radial nerve entrapment,[25] and others.

Morrey et al[14] state that the radiohumeral bursa is an uncommon primary site of involvement in tennis elbow. Nirschl[26] holds that the principal lesion is at the origin of the extensor carpi radialis brevis. Leach and Miller[25] mention that the brevis is intimately related to the annular and lateral ligaments, the capsule, and covering fascia. When these particular tissues are operated on the extensor brevis is also released, which is the reason for the relief of symptoms. Other muscles that might be involved are the extensor digitorum communis, extensor carpi radialis longus, and, rarely, the extensor carpi ulnaris. Cyriax[22] stated that the extensor carpi radialis brevis is involved at the tenoperiosteal insertion at the

humeral lateral epicondyle (the most common site), at the body of the tendon (over the radial head), or at the muscle belly (1 to 2 in distal to the radial head). He stated that the least common site is the supracondylar ridge of the humerus where the extensor carpi radialis longus originates. Karg (personal communication, 1990) reported involvement of the longus muscle in a tennis player learning to "cut" the ball by excessive wrist extension and radial deviation. Nirschl[27] blames intrinsic tendon overuse (repetitive microtrauma), especially among patients in the 35- to 55-year age group, inadequate conditioning (lower and upper extremities), and constitutional factors (mesenchymal syndrome, gout, estrogen deficiency, or hereditary mechanical issues) as the chief factors resulting in injury. Microtears result in eventual fibrous angiofibroblastic degeneration and rupture. Nirschl[27] finds the angioblastic tissue primarily in the extensor brevis origin.

Clinical: A frequent cause of tennis elbow is poor technique: leading with the elbow during the backhand stroke instead of leading with the lower body and shoulder, and failure to relax the wrist extensors after the backhand stroke. The most tender area is usually on the anterior portion of the lateral epicondyle or slightly distal. Origins and insertions of muscles vary, and asymmetry in the human body is the norm. Often, the most tender area is not quite where we expect it to be. Muscles have more than one origin that may be involved. For example, the extensor carpi radialis brevis also originates from the radial collateral ligament, and the extensor carpi ulnaris also originates from the posterior border of the ulna. These unexpected areas may have to be considered as friction massage sites. Of course, the whole basis of functional testing is first to discover the pathologic tissue and only then to palpate for tenderness.

In chronic lateral elbow tendinitis due to fibrosis and loss of tissue extensibility, there may be a loss of passive wrist flexion.

Functional tests

1. Definite painful resisted wrist extension.
2. Possible painful resisted wrist abduction.
3. Possible painful resisted supination.
4. Possible pain and limited wrist flexion when stretching a fully flexed wrist with an extended elbow and pronated forearm.
5. Possible pain on resisted finger extension (the extensor digitorum originates from the common tendon of the lateral epicondyle).

Treatment: Treatment comprises friction massage, trigger point, and joint mobilization. Patients may be allowed to work or play during treatment if the pain does not increase. Exercise is introduced as tolerated, beginning with isometric wrist extension (five sets of 10 repetitions twice a day). Patients should ice the area after exercise. Eventually rubber tubing and free weights are used as the pain lessens. Rubber tubing exercises in the early stages should stress endurance by minimal resistance (discomfort, not pain), rapid contraction stretching during wrist flexion and extension. After being able to complete 3 sets of 10 repetitions, less rapid greater resistance tubing exercises may be incorporated. After exercise and during the day, the patient should stretch the flexed wrist on an extended arm. A counterforce brace at the proximal forearm or wrist extensor brace may relieve the elbow during use.

The examiner may use Mills' manipulation as long as there is full elbow extension. Because the extensor carpi radialis muscle spans two joints, it is important for the examiner to maintain the patient's wrist in full flexion with the elbow flexed about 45°. While the wrist flexion is maintained, the elbow is thrust into extension (Fig. 4-18). The purpose of this manipulation is to separate the scar to create a permanent lengthening. Evaluation and improvement of playing or working technique are essential.

Medial Epicondylitis (Golfer's Elbow)

Medial epicondylitis is a tendinitis usually associated with activities that stress wrist flexion and pronation, such as the tennis serve, baseball pitching (end of acceleration phase[28]), overhead tennis strokes, pull-through swimming strokes, and hammering. In the tennis serve there is wrist flexion and ulnar deviation, both of which stress the flexor carpi ulnaris (which originates from the medial epicondyle and the medial margin of the olecranon process). Other muscles that are affected on the medial side are the pronator teres, flexor carpi radialis, palmaris longus, and flexor digitorum sublimis.[24]

Clinical: After functional testing, localized tenderness is usually found[29] at the anterior tip of the medial epicondyle and distally about 1 in along the track of the pronator teres and the flexor carpi radialis. Professional tennis players have medial epicondylitis more often than lateral epicondylitis because of their aggressive wrist flexion serve.

Functional tests

1. Definite pain on resisted wrist flexion.
2. Possible pain on resisted wrist adduction.
3. Possible pain on resisted pronation.
4. Possible pain by stretching a dorsiflexed wrist and fully extended elbow with a supinated forearm.
5. Possible pain on resisted finger flexion of the proximal interphalangeal joints (the flexor digitorum superficialis originates from the medial epicondyle by the common flexor tendon).

Treatment: Treatment is similar to that for lateral epicondylitis except that exercise and stretching are directed toward the wrist flexors. Stretching should be done with arm extended and the hand supinated, with pressure being directed by the patient on the dorsiflexed hand. Evaluation of working or playing technique is essential. A manipulation the opposite of Mills' may also be effective. The examiner holds the patient's dorsiflexed wrist with a 45° flexed elbow. While maintaining the wrist in maximum dorsiflexion and supination, the examiner thrusts the elbow into extension (Fig. 4-19). It should also be realized that both the above wrist flexors and extensors can be stressed by eccentric overloading. For example, forced

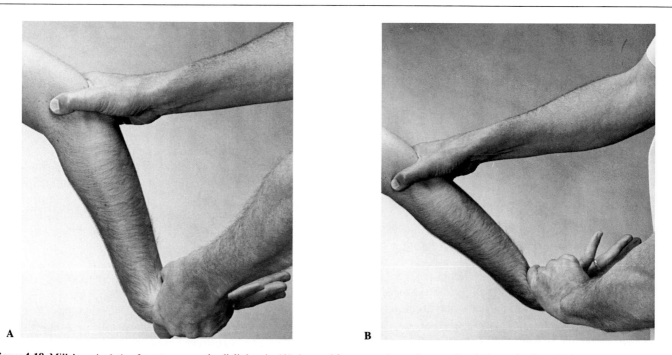

A   **B**

Figure 4-18 Mills' manipulation for extensor carpi radialis brevis. **(A)** Arm and forearm are internally rotated, wrist is maximally volar flexed. Elbow is contacted on olecranon and flexed 45°. **(B)** Elbow is brought into extension while wrist is maintained in volar flexion.

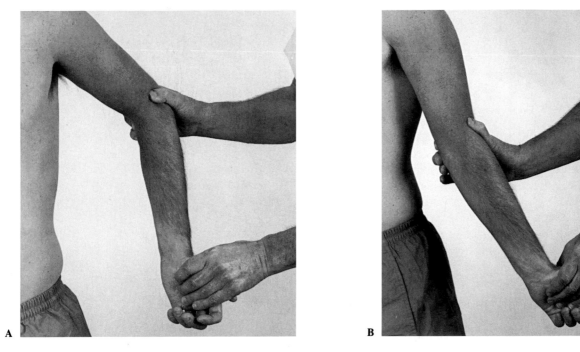

Figure 4-19 Supination manipulation for medial epicondylitis. (**A**) Wrist is maximally dorsiflexed and supinated, elbow is flexed to 45°; examiner grasps olecranon. (**B**) While maintaining wrist dorsiflexion and supination, examiner thrusts elbow into extension.

wrist extension (concentric) may aggravate and stress the wrist flexors (eccentric).

Ligamentous Sprain

Functional tests

1. Varus stress for lateral ligaments.
2. Valgus stress for medial ligaments.

An excellent example of functional testing is distinguishing between involvement of the flexor-pronator muscles (contractile) or medial ligamentous sprain (inert). Resisted testing of the wrist flexors and pronator teres would be more painful than valgus stress testing if the contractile tissue was the principal source of pain. Valgus stress may also evoke instability compared to the normal elbow.

"Little League Elbow"

O'Neill and Micheli[30] describe "Little League elbow" as a generic term referring to several overuse injuries in young throwers. They mention osteochondritis dissecans of the capitellum with or without loose bodies, injury and premature closure of the proximal radial epiphysis, overgrowth of the radial head, and medially stressed valgus overuse. Bennett and Tullos[9] state that the repetitive valgus stress of throwing causes microtrauma of the medial anterior oblique ligament and compression of the radiocapitellar joint.

Any adolescent engaged in an activity with repetitive stress to the elbows should be told to report elbow pain immediately to prevent progressive involvement. Rest and strengthening and stretching of the entire arm along with training techniques to lessen valgus are necessary. Because there has not been complete fusion of the secondary ossification center, an x-ray examination may show a medial epicondylar epiphyseal growth plate fatigue fracture. This area is a weak attachment for the flexor pronator muscles, so that a strong muscular contraction could result in avulsion of the medial epicondyle. In loss of varus or valgus stability, we must consider both the medial and lateral sides of the joint.[9] For example, when one side is unstable there may be excessive compression of the bony structures on the opposite side.

King et al[31] state that elbow flexion contracture may be a physiologic attempt at repair or stabilization. Jobe and Nuber[12] point out that people not involved in throwing sports can function quite well with a ruptured ulnar collateral ligament but that disruption in a throwing athlete may require prompt surgical attention.

Functional tests

1. Possible lateral elbow pain by flexing and extending the elbow while maintaining a valgus stress.
2. Possible pain and increased range on valgus stress test.
3. Possible loss of passive elbow extension due to early flexion contracture. Elbow flexion contracture, which is common in professional pitchers, may represent serious damage in a child or adolescent.[32]

Treatment: Treatment consists of rest, cryotherapy, and intensive rehabilitation to increase the strength and flexibility of the surrounding musculature.

Loose Bodies

Milgram[33] classifies loose bodies into three groups: osteochondral fractures, degenerative disease of the articular surface, and proliferative disorders of the synovium. In the young, elbow stress can cause the exfoliation of cartilage, resulting in loose bodies usually in the medial and lateral compartments or the posterior olecranon fossa. Osteochondritis dissecans usually affects the anterolateral surface of the capitellum. The follow-through phase of pitching results in elbow extension and forearm pronation, causing shear stress of the radiocapitellar joint. Youngsters up to age 13 seldom need surgery, but those 13 and older may eventually develop joint incongruity and involvement of the articular cartilage. Degenerative osteophytes may be an end result and may become loose bodies. Usually a 20-year-old will complain of loss of extension, swelling, and "catching." Similar complaints of a twingelike painful catching or chronic ache may be present in the elderly. Most loose bodies are trapped by synovium and never cause a problem, however (E Rashkoff, personal communication, 1990).

Functional tests

1. Passive extension may be limited; springy block rather than the normal bone-to-bone end feel may be noted.
2. Passive flexion may be limited; springy block rather than the normal soft end feel may (rarely) be noted.

Treatment: This lesion may respond to joint mobilization, which moves the fragment from the stressed location. One to three treatments may be effective for weeks, months, or years. Depending on the location and size of the fragment, surgery may be necessary.

Cyriax and Cyriax[21] use a technique that emphasizes (1) maintaining 90° flexion of the elbow to stretch the ligaments and to open the joint and (2) a long-axis intermittent rotational thrust of the forearm ending in elbow extension. The procedure is first carried out four or five times with rotation in one direction. If the same springy block is felt on passive elbow extension, then the same procedure is carried out with rotation in the opposite direction. Figure 4-20 demonstrates the technique by a single practitioner. It is important to hold the 90° elbow flexion traction for about 10 seconds (Figure 4-20A). Figure 4-20B shows the long-axis rotatory thrust ending in external rotation, and Figure 4-20C shows the long-axis final rotational thrust ending in internal rotation. Before the final thrust is reached at 0° (extension), two or three rotatory long-axis thrusts are given.

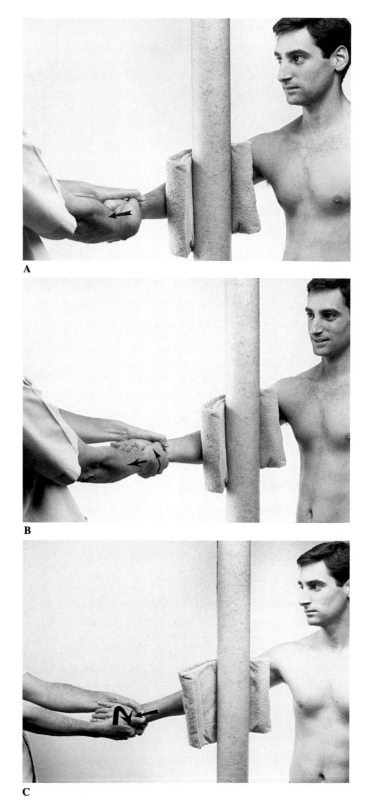

Figure 4-20 Elbow loose body manipulation. **(A)** Long-axis traction is maintained with elbow flexed 90° for 10 seconds. **(B)** While traction is maintained, forearm is alternately brought into supination and neutral position until full supination and elbow extension are reached. A final long-axis supination-extension jerk is given at end. **(C)** Final position of long-axis extension-pronation jerk, which began as in **(A)** except forearm was alternately brought into pronation and neutral.

Osteoarthritis

According to Tompkins,[34] primary degenerative arthritis of the elbow is conspicuously rare as a primary form of involvement. Tompkins also states that the most common x-ray finding is osteophyte formation of the medial ulnohumeral joint. The patient may show a mild flexion contracture. Localization only in the elbow is usually found in patients who experience chronic microtrauma due to pneumatic tools or after fractures.[35] Pain and limitation of motion are the most common symptoms.

Because there is more synovial tissue on the lateral portion of the elbow compared to the medial portion, conditions that cause synovial tissue effusion will cause swelling beneath the lateral epicondyle. Synovitis may be caused by trauma, infection, tumor, or conditions causing chronic inflammatory arthritis. It is essential to find the primary cause of the synovitis through laboratory procedures.

Functional tests

1. Capsular pattern of more limitation of passive flexion than extension (depending on the location of an osteophyte sometimes extension could be more limited).
2. Limitation of passive pronation and passive supination in severe cases.

Treatment: May relieve with joint play and electrical modalities.

Bursitis

Of the various bursae of the elbow, only the olecranon bursa has been found to have any clinical significance in bursitis.[36] The traumatic type is usually pain free and treated symptomatically with hourly warm soaks, a splint, and compressive dressing. Aspiration of the sac does not usually prevent recurrence of swelling because of continued flexion and extension. There usually is pain if there is a septic or crystalline inflammatory process.[36] In acute bursitis there is diffuse swelling at the proximal forearm, and in chronic bursitis the swelling is more localized.[6]

Functional test

1. Noncapsular finding of limited passive flexion with normal passive extension.

ELBOW ENTRAPMENT NEUROPATHIES

Manual methods are not as successful with entrapment neuropathies as with localized muscle, tendon, and ligamentous lesions, but joint mobilization, friction massage, trigger point therapy, and stretching procedures should not be dis-

counted. Manually altering the local tissue relationships can at times reduce the entrapment.

The main reason for discussing the functional testing of elbow neuropathy is to enable differential diagnosis with the preceding lesions. Often the clinical findings of entrapment are similar to those of the epicondylitis lesions. The epicondylitis may be caused by intermittent entrapment compression. Electromyographic (EMG) and nerve conduction studies are not necessarily confirmatory. The specific etiology may be as simple as a crush injury or as complex as repetitive motion resulting in chronic irritation from muscular hypertrophy, fascial thickenings, aberrant muscles, bony or vascular anomalies, and hypermobile nerves.[23]

Entrapment symptoms depend on the type of nerve affected and the amount of compression. Entrapment of a sensory nerve usually causes cutaneous sensory loss, pain, and paresthesia, and motor nerve entrapment may cause paralysis or a diffusely localized, dull aching pain because the motor nerve may contain nociceptive afferent fibers of muscular and extramuscular origin.[35]

Radial Nerve Entrapment (Radial Tunnel Syndrome, Posterior Interosseous Syndrome)

Persistent pain around the lateral epicondyle that does not respond to manual therapy could be due to radial nerve entrapment. The radial nerve, on reaching the front of the lateral epicondyle, divides into the posterior interosseous and superficial sensory nerves. The posterior interosseous nerve, a pure motor nerve, passes between the two heads of the supinator muscle. The most frequent site of compression is the arcade of Frohse, which is an arch formed by the proximal edge of the supinator. This arcade is fibrous about one-third of the time and can compress the nerve. Compression proximal to the arcade or at the division of the radial nerve may only cause sensory paresthesia, because of compression of the superficial sensory nerve, or may involve the radial recurrent nerve, which mimics lateral epicondylitis.[23] Compression at the arcade or distally on the posterior interosseous nerve can affect the forearm and hand extensor muscles but usually does not affect the brachioradialis or the extensor carpi radialis brevis and longus, which are innervated proximal to the arcade (Fig. 4-21). The reason a motor nerve such as the posterior interosseous nerve or the deep motor branch of the ulnar nerve will, when compressed, create an aching pain during activity is that these motor nerves carry sensory fibers from the joint and muscles and even from some skin receptors.[37]

According to Spinner and Linscheid,[16] if the entire nerve is compressed there would be weakness on resisted extension of the fingers and thumb at the metacarpophalangeal level and on wrist extension. With partial compression paralysis, there may be weakness only at the fourth and fifth fingers at the metacarpophalangeal joints on extension. EMG would determine whether the compression is occurring at the proximal arcade of

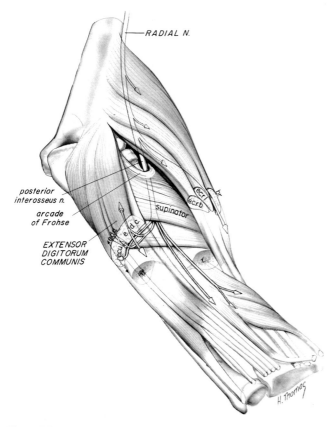

Figure 4-21 Details of the innervation provided by the posterior interosseous nerve. The nerve may be traced to the supinator. The terminal branches are shown (br = brachioradialis; ecrl = extensor carpi radialis longus; ecu = extensor carpi ulnaris; r = radius; u = ulna). *Source:* Reprinted from *Injuries to the Major Branches of the Forearm*, ed 2 by M Spinner with permission of W.B. Saunders Company, © 1978.

the supinator or more distally. It may take 7 to 9 months before an EMG is positive.

We must be aware of the possibility of lateral epicondylitis and entrapment occurring together. In the typical case in which there is no paralysis, the symptoms will be similar to those of lateral epicondylitis. Numbness and weakness of the wrist, finger, and thumb seldom occur.[37]

Functional tests (similar to those for lateral epicondylitis except for possible differences in location of tenderness and weakness if entrapment is severe)

1. Possible pain on resisted supination with the elbow extended (causes constriction at the arcade of Frohse by supinator muscle) or on resisted wrist extension.
2. Possible pain and weakness on resisted finger extension (there will be weakness of the wrist extensors if compression is occurring above the arcade of Frohse).
3. Passive pronation of proximal forearm with wrist flexion may compress the nerve.
4. Probable positive Tinel's sign at compression area.

Lister[38] states that a differential test for lateral epicondylitis and radial tunnel syndrome is resisted middle finger extension

with the elbow, wrist, and hand extended. This stresses the extensor carpi radialis brevis' fibrous medial edge, which presses on the posterior interosseous nerve. If a radial tunnel syndrome is present this test will be the most painful compared to passively flexing the fingers and wrist of an extended elbow, which would be more painful in a lateral epicondylitis.

Clinical: The lateral epicondyle may or may not be tender; the lateral epicondyle is almost always tender in the typical tennis elbow. The usual point of tenderness in radial entrapment is anterior, four finger breadths distal to the lateral epicondyle over the supinator muscle (the entrapment site).[23] There may be exquisite tenderness.

Ulnar Entrapment Neuropathy

The superficial location of the ulnar nerve at the cubital tunnel presents a strong possibility of involvement, especially because it has been shown that the ulnar nerve is larger at the entrance to the cubital tunnel than anywhere else along its course.[39] The nerve can become compressed about ⅓ in proximal to the medial epicondyle at the arcade of Struthers, posterior to the medial epicondyle (the cubital tunnel), and at the proximal flexor of the forearm.[16,40]

With elbow flexion the cubital tunnel narrows, and the ulnar nerve can be compressed by the arcuate (epicondylar olecranon) ligament, between the tendinous heads of the ulnar and humeral origins of the flexor carpi ulnaris, or as a result of bulging of the medial collateral ligament. Valgus stress or deformities, repetitive trauma, and repetitive elbow flexion all may create the overuse inflammatory-fibrosis-adhesion situation, which results in compression. Increased physiologic muscle hypertrophy (at the medial head of the triceps) and a hypermobile ulnar nerve due to a ligamentous laxity or recurrent nerve subluxation causing traction and friction on the nerve have been blamed.[12,41] Sometimes a healed elbow fracture or injury may develop a ''tardy ulnar palsy'' 1 to 15 years later, which usually requires surgery. Symptomatically a patient may feel intermittent tingling and paresthesias in the ring and little finger and pain in the elbow radiating to the ulnar aspect of the forearm and hand. Abnormal anastomosis of the median and ulnar nerves in the forearm (Martin-Gruber anastomosis) is common, so that ulnar motor function may be normal in an advanced case.[23]

Functional tests

1. Positive Tinel's sign in the ulnar groove or just below the epicondyle (a subluxating ulnar nerve may present a positive Tinel's sign proximal to the medial epicondyle).[42]
2. Pain aggravated by elbow flexion.[16] Patients who sleep with their elbows flexed may complain of a ''sleep paralysis.''[43]
3. Rarely, motor weakness (because the motor nerve is deeper than the sensory nerve in the tunnel[41]).

4. Sensory loss in the dorsoulnar aspect of the hand (classic localizing sign).[16] Compression of the ulnar nerve at the wrist (Guyon's canal) affects the volar sensory nerve, so that the dorsal sensory branch is usually unaffected.[44]
5. Nerve conduction studies not always positive.[12]

Differential diagnosis: The differential diagnosis includes thoracic outlet syndrome, cervical nerve root compression, and wrist compression (at Guyon's canal).

Treatment: Treatment consists of rest in a wrist and elbow splint in mild flexion for 2 weeks, trigger point therapy of involved muscles, and possible friction of adhesions. The patient may need rehabilitation therapy if there is a moderate degree of motor deficit. Eisen and Danon[39] state that 90% of patients with a mild or early lesion, as judged by fairly specific electrodiagnostic criteria, recover spontaneously.

Median Nerve Entrapment (Forearm)

There are two types of median nerve entrapment: a pronator syndrome, which causes pain without sensory or motor deficits, and an anterior interosseous syndrome, which causes motor weakness without a sensory deficit and is rare.[44]

Pronator Syndrome

Compression may occur under the lacertus fibrosus (Fig. 4-22), between the two heads of the pronator teres, at the origin of the flexor digitorum sublimis, or, rarely, at the level of the distal humerus. It may result from repetitive upper extremity exertion (forceful repetitive forearm pronation) or direct trauma in the proximal forearm.[23] There is usually a vague, fatiguelike complaint of pain and numbness on the proximal volar forearm (median distribution). Pronator syndrome must be differentiated from carpal tunnel syndrome, which can also refer pain in the forearm and wrist (see test 6 below). EMG might rule out carpal tunnel syndrome.

Functional tests

1. Direct pressure over the pronator teres 4 cm distal to the cubital crease with concurrent resistance against pronation (this is the most reliable test).[16]
2. Probable pain on resisted pronation for 60 seconds or on holding of resisted pronation of the flexed elbow to full extension, both of which tighten the pronator.
3. Resisted elbow flexion and supination of the forearm (may tighten the lacertus fibrosus) (Fig. 4-23).
4. Resisted flexion of the long finger proximal interphalangeal joint, which creates compression under the arch of the flexor digitorum sublimis (Fig. 4-23).
5. Possible Tinel's sign over the median nerve in the proximal forearm.
6. Compression in the proximal forearm can affect the palmar cutaneous nerve, which supplies the palm of the hand which does not go through the carpal tunnel.

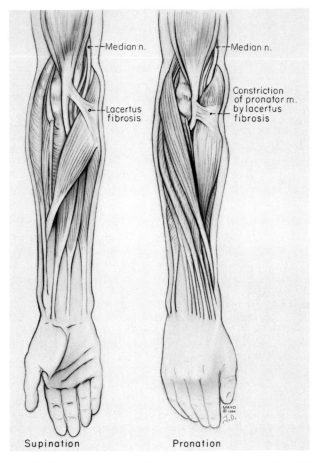

Figure 4-22 Pronator syndrome. When the arm pronates, contraction of the pronator muscle may result in indentation of this structure by the lacertus fibrosus. Such a process may give rise to entrapment of the median nerve and the so-called pronator syndrome. *Source:* Reprinted by permission of Mayo Foundation, © 1984.

Therefore, loss of sensation in the central palm indicates median nerve involvement distal to the carpal tunnel.[32]

Anterior Interosseous Syndrome

The anterior interosseous portion of the median nerve supplies only the motor fibers to the flexor pollicis longus, the flexor digitorum profundus of the second and third fingers, and the pronator quadratus. It may be injured in crush trauma or overuse in throwing, racket sports, or weight lifting. The nerve may be compressed at its origin some 5 to 8 cm distal to the lateral epicondyle or farther distally.[45] There is usually a severe pain in the proximal forearm that subsides in 8 to 12 hours, leaving a weakness of pinch between the thumb and forefinger and loss of dexterity.[16] If the onset was insidious, previous diagnoses of tendinous rupture to multiple sclerosis may have been considered.[16]

Double Crush Neuropathy

A localized lesion in the upper extremity may be associated with or triggered by another lesion along the same axon. A

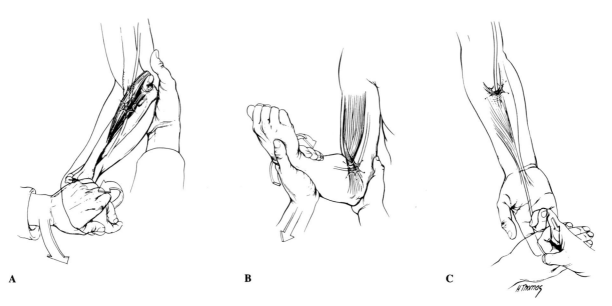

A   B   C

Figure 4-23 Features of the physical examination that help to demonstrate the so-called pronator syndrome. (**A**) Proximal forearm pain is increased by resistance to pronation and elbow flexion as well as to flexion of the wrist. (**B**) Pain in the proximal forearm that is increased by resistance to supination is also suggestive of compression by the lacertus fibrosus. (**C**) Resistance of the long finger flexor produces pain in the proximal forearm when compression of the median nerve occurs at the flexor digitorum superficialis arch. *Source:* Reprinted from *Injuries to the Major Branches of the Forearm,* ed 2 by M Spinner with permission of W.B. Saunders Company, © 1978.

cervical spondylosis affecting the median nerve may not be symptomatic, but it may exacerbate a carpal tunnel syndrome. Treatment of the cervical spine may alleviate the carpal tunnel syndrome, or treatment of the syndrome might possibly alleviate the cervical problem. Jones[40] gives the example of the ulnar nerve, which may be affected by the combination of a cervical disc protrusion or thoracic outlet problem with a cubital tunnel involvement or by a cubital tunnel involvement associated with a compression at Guyon's canal. Upton and McComas[46] blame the double crush problem on serial lesions along an axon stressing the axoplasmic flow and causing distal axons to be susceptible to irritation. Both proximal and distal levels of a nerve should be evaluated and treated. For example, the cervical spine should always be evaluated when dealing with what appears to be a local neuropathy at the shoulder, elbow, or wrist.

REFERENCES

1. Kapandji IA. *The Physiology of the Joints.* New York: Churchill Livingstone; 1979:1.

2. Swanson AB, Goran-Hagert C, Swanson G. Evaluation of impairment in the upper extremity. *J Hand Surg Am.* 1987;12:919.

3. Morrey BF, Askew LJ, An KN, et al. A biomechanical study of normal elbow motion. *J Bone Joint Surg Am.* 1981;63:872.

4. Radin EL. Biomechanical applications in the upper extremity. In: Pettrone FA, ed. *Symposium on Upper Extremity Injuries in Athletes.* St Louis, Mo: Mosby; 1986:3–10.

5. Basmajian JV, Deluca CJ. *Muscles Alive: Their Functions Revealed by Electromyography.* 5th ed. Baltimore: Williams & Wilkins; 1985.

6. Morrey BF, ed. *The Elbow and Its Disorders.* Philadelphia: Saunders; 1985.

7. Frankel VH, Nordin M. *Basic Biomechanics of the Skeletal System.* Philadelphia: Lea & Febiger; 1980.

8. Bogumill GP. Functional anatomy of the shoulder and elbow. In: Pettrone FA, ed. *Symposium on Upper Extremity Injuries in Athletes.* St Louis, Mo: Mosby; 1986:206–210.

9. Bennett JB, Tullos HS. Ligamentous and articular injuries in the athlete. In: Morrey BF, ed. *The Elbow and Its Disorders.* Philadelphia: Saunders; 1985:502–522.

10. Schwab GH, Bennett JB, Woods GW, et al. Biomechanics of elbow instability: the role of the medial collateral ligament. *Clin Orthop Relat Res.* 1980;146:44.

11. Linscheid RL, Wheeler DK. Elbow dislocations. *JAMA.* 1965; 194:1171.

12. Jobe FW, Nuber G. Throwing injuries of the elbow. *Clin Sports Med.* 1986;5:621–623.

13. Morrey BF, Volz RG. The physical examination of the elbow. In: Morrey BF, ed. *The Elbow and Its Disorders.* Philadelphia: Saunders; 1985:62–72.

14. Morrey BF, An KN, Chao EYS. Functional evaluation of the elbow. In: Morrey BF, ed. *The Elbow and Its Disorders.* Philadelphia: Saunders; 1985:73–91.

15. Cailliet R. *Soft Tissue Pain and Disability.* Philadelphia: Davis; 1979.

16. Spinner M, Linscheid RL. Nerve entrapment syndromes. In: Morrey BF, ed. *The Elbow and Its Disorders.* Philadelphia: Saunders; 1985:691–712.

17. Walther DS. *Applied Kinesiology.* Pueblo, Colo: Systems DC; 1981;1.

18. Cooney WP III. Bursitis and tendinitis in the hand, wrist and elbow: an approach to treatment. *Minn Med.* 1983;66(8):491–494.

19. O'Donoghue DH. *Treatment of Injuries to Athletes.* 3rd ed. Philadelphia: Saunders; 1976.

20. Cooney WP III. Contractures and burns. In: Morrey BF, ed. *The Elbow and Its Disorders.* Philadelphia: Saunders; 1985;433–451.

21. Cyriax J, Cyriax P. *Illustrated Manual of Orthopaedic Medicine.* London: Butterworths; 1985.

22. Cyriax J. *Textbook of Orthopaedic Medicine.* 8th ed. London: Bailliere-Tindall; 1989:2.

23. Cabrera JM, McCue FC. Nonosseous athletic injuries of the elbow, forearm and hand. *Clin Sports Med.* 1986;5:682.

24. Legwold G. Tennis elbow: joint resolution by conservative treatment and improved technique. *Phys Sports Med.* 1984;12:172.

25. Leach RE, Miller JK. Lateral and medial epicondylitis of the elbow. *Clin Sports Med.* 1987;6:263.

26. Nirschl RP. Tennis elbow. *Orthop Clin North Am.* 1973;4:787–800.

27. Nirschl RP. Prevention and treatment of elbow and shoulder injuries in the tennis player. *Clin Sports Med.* 1988;7:289–308.

28. Roy S, Irvin R. *Sports Medicine: Prevention, Evaluation, Management, and Rehabilitation.* Englewood Cliffs, NJ: Prentice-Hall; 1983.

29. Nirschl RP. Soft tissue injuries about the elbow. *Clin Sports Med.* 1986;5:638.

30. O'Neill DB, Micheli LJ. Overuse injuries in the young athlete. *Clin Sports Med.* 1988;7:602.

31. King JW, Brelsford HJ, Tullos HS. Analysis of the pitching arm of the professional baseball pitcher. *Clin Orthop.* 1969;67:116.

32. Post M. *Physical Examination of the Musculoskeletal System.* Chicago: Year Book Medical; 1987.

33. Milgram JW. The classification of loose bodies in human joints. *Clin Orthop.* 1977;124:282.

34. Tompkins RB. Nonrheumatoid inflammatory arthritis. In: Morrey BF, ed. *The Elbow and Its Disorders.* Philadelphia: Saunders; 1985:656–663.

35. Werner CO. Lateral elbow pain and posterior interosseous nerve entrapment. *Acta Orthop Scand.* 1979;174(suppl):18.

36. Reilly JP, Nicholas JA. The chronically inflamed bursa. *Clin Sports Med.* 1987;6:351.

37. Mosher JF. Peripheral nerve injuries and entrapments of the forearm and wrist. In: Pettrone FA, ed. *Symposium on Upper Extremity Injuries in Athletes.* St Louis, Mo: Mosby; 1986:179.

38. Lister G. *The Hand: Diagnosis and Indications.* New York: Churchill Livingstone; 1984.

39. Eisen A, Danon J. The mild cubital tunnel syndrome: its natural history and indications for surgical intervention. *Neurology.* 1974;24:612.

40. Jones JA. Pitfalls in the management of cubital tunnel syndrome. *Orthop Rev.* 1989;14:36–38.

41. Jobe FW, Fanton GS. Nerve injuries. In: Morrey BF, ed. *The Elbow and Its Disorders.* Philadelphia: Saunders; 1985:497–501.

42. Zarins B, Andrews JR, Carson WG. *Injuries to the Throwing Arm.* Philadelphia: Saunders; 1985.

43. Adelaar RS, Foster WC, McDowell C. The treatment of the cubital tunnel syndrome. *J Hand Surg Am.* 1984;9:92.

44. Morgan RE, Terranova W, Nichter LS, et al. Entrapment neuropathies of the upper extremity. *Am Fam Physician.* 1985;31:131.

45. McCue FC III, Miller GA. Soft-tissue injuries to the hand. In: Pettrone FA, ed. *Symposium on Upper Extremity Injuries in Athletes.* St Louis, Mo: Mosby; 1986:84.

46. Upton AR. Differentiation between lesions in the primary and secondary divisions of the nerve roots. In: Buerger AA, Tobis JS, eds. *Approaches to the Validation of Manipulation Therapy.* Springfield, Ill: Thomas; 1975:118–119.

Elbow Functional Diagnosis Chart

Table 4-A-1 Elbow, Functional Diagnosis

Key
+ Pain
+/− Possible Pain
L Possible Limited ROM
LAX Possible Laxity

TESTS	Osteoarthritis	Tenoperiosteal	Musculotendinous	Brachialis Strain	Triceps Tendinitis	Supinator Strain	Pronator Teres Strain	Lateral Epicondylitis	Medial Epicondylitis	Medial Ligament Sprain	Lateral Ligament Sprain	Loose Bodies
		Lower Biceps Strain										
Passive Flexion (160°)	+/− L MOST	+/−	+/−	+/−	+/−					L+/−	L+/−	Springy Block
Passive Extension (0°)	+/− L LESS			+/−						L+/−	L+/−	Springy Block
Passive Pronation (85°)	L	+				+/−						
Passive Supination (90°)	L						+/−					
Valgus Stress										+ LAX		
Varus Stress											+ LAX	
Resisted Flexion		+	+	+		+						
Resisted Extension				+/−	+							
Resisted Pronation							+		+/−			
Resisted Supination	+/−	+/−				+		+/−				
Resisted Wrist Flexion									+ (2)			
Resisted Wrist Extension								+ (1)				
Joint Play Evaluation												

(1) + with elbow extended and passive volar wrist flexion.
(2) + with elbow extended and passive wrist dorsiflexion.

Chapter **5**

The Wrist and Hand

Warren I. Hammer

THE WRIST

Mechanically, the wrist is one of the most complex joints in the body[1] (Fig. 5-1). Passive functional testing for ligamentous injury cannot be as specific as for most knee injuries, for example, and palpation must receive greater attention. Because of the complex nature of the wrist, the evaluation of acute injuries often requires specialized knowledge and sophisticated testing such as bone scan, arthroscopy, and magnetic resonance imaging (MRI). The diagnosis of "sprain" is abused, and patients may be condemned to chronic instability and prolonged impairment if a sprain is wrongly diagnosed. Wilgis and Yates[2] state that wrist sprain should be a diagnosis of exclusion and used less often now that wrist evaluation is more sophisticated. As in all the joints described in this book, the history of the injury is of paramount importance in evaluating the source of the pain.

Patients with wrist and hand lesions usually complain of localized pain, but we must remember the possibility of distal referral. The C-6 dermatome and sclerotome may extend to the wrist and first two fingers. Pain and paresthesia in the wrist and hand may be discogenic or a possible carpal tunnel syndrome. Less often, pain may refer in a distal to proximal direction as in a retrograde carpal tunnel, causing cervical pain without hand or wrist symptoms. As with the shoulder and elbow, we must always scan the total upper extremity and be aware of neuropathies, arthritides, and visceral possibilities.

Most injuries to the wrist are due to compressive loading of the joints, excessive muscular overuse, or peculiarities of a sport.[3] In the tennis stroke a stiff wrist is recommended, which refers stress to the stronger elbow and shoulder. Striking the ball with a loose wrist (snapping motion), as in racquetball and squash, is more likely to stress the wrist.[4] Culver[5] states that concepts of how the wrist functions normally and after injury are constantly changing and that the seriousness of many wrist injuries is underestimated, many times leading to chronic instability.

FUNCTIONAL ANATOMY AND PERTINENT BIOMECHANICS

Detailed anatomy and biomechanics of the hand and wrist are subjects beyond the scope of this text. The information presented about these subjects is primarily for understanding the functional examination and its relation to manual therapy.

A functional definition of the wrist is the region between and including the distal ends of the radius and ulna and the bases of the metacarpals, which includes the carpals and their ligaments (both intracapsular and interosseous) and the triangular fibrocartilage complex (TFCC).[5] This definition includes three degrees of freedom: flexion-extension, abduction-adduction, and pronation and supination; in the last of these the main movement[6] is a rotational displacement of the lower end of the radius about the ulna, with gliding of the ulnar head in the sigmoid notch of the radius occurring as the forearm moves during pronation and supination.[7] The distal ulnar head is not immobile during forearm rotation. During pronation the distal ulnar moves posteriorly and distally in relation to the radius, and during supination it moves anteriorly and proximally in relation to the radius. During forearm rotation the radius, with its fixed hand, rotates around the distal ulna.[7]

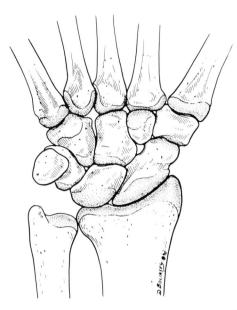

Figure 5-1 The wrist (volar surface). *Source:* Copyright © 1990 by David Bolinsky.

Mennell[8] holds that any joint in the wrist may be primarily involved in the movements of supination and pronation of the hand and forearm. He shows how loss of joint play (anterior-posterior glide) of the ulnotriquetral joint could be responsible for pain and limitation during wrist supination.

Range of Motion

The range of motion in the wrist[9] comprises the following:

1. abduction (radial deviation): average, 19° with a range of 11° to 39°
2. adduction (ulnar deviation): average, 29° with a range of 19° to 35°
3. flexion: average, 75° with a range of 52° to 93°
4. extension: average, 64° with a range of 42° to 79°

According to Kapandji,[6] in abduction and adduction the movements at the radiocarpal and midcarpal joints are almost equal (slightly more midcarpal in abduction and more radiocarpal in adduction). Wrist flexion occurs mostly at the radiocarpal joint (50°) and less at the midcarpal joint (35°), and extension has the reverse pattern (35° at the radiocarpal and 50° at the midcarpals).

As a result of the tension of opposing muscles and the synergistic relation between wrist and finger motion, full range of wrist flexion should be measured with the fist slightly open and full wrist extension with the fingers flexed. The optimal position for measuring hand function and finger power is slight extension (20°) with ulnar deviation. Because of tension of the long extensors during wrist flexion the fingers are forced open, and therefore grip strength is weaker. Wrist movements with wrist extension reinforce finger movements.

Flexor and Extensor Retinacula

The location and functions of these structures are often overlooked. The flexor retinaculum (transverse carpal ligament) is over the carpals, originating from the tubercle of the trapezium and scaphoid on the lateral side and coursing to the hook of the hamate and pisiform on the medial side. Its proximal border is the distal skin crease of the wrist. It lies over the carpal tunnel and is the location of the origin of the thenar and hypothenar muscles.[10] The extensor retinaculum is more posterior than the flexor retinaculum, attaching laterally to the anterior border of the radius and medially to the triquetral and pisiform bones. The main function of both retinacula is to prevent bowstringing of the tendons that cross the wrist during flexion and extension.[11] Either retinaculum may require friction massage.

Wrist Muscles

The only muscle that inserts into the wrist carpal bones is the flexor carpi ulnaris. Most of the remaining wrist flexors and extensors insert into the metacarpals. In essence, all the long powerful wrist flexors and extensors bypass the carpus, with the result that the carpus functions as an intercalated segment that is acted on by muscles not attached to it. The carpal bones assume positions depending on the relative stresses that are applied around them.[11]

Muscles that extend, abduct, and adduct the hand at the wrist include the extensor carpi radialis longus (extends and abducts the wrist; inserts into the base of the second metacarpal), the extensor carpi radialis brevis (extends and abducts the wrist; inserts into the base of the third metacarpal), and the extensor carpi ulnaris (extends and adducts the wrist; inserts into the base of the fifth metacarpal).

The extensor carpi radialis longus and brevis can be specifically tested with the wrist in simultaneous extension and abduction (see below, Functional Examination of the Wrist). Because of its insertion on the third metacarpal, the extensor carpi radialis brevis is more concerned with wrist extension than abduction. The extensor carpi ulnaris can be specifically tested with the wrist in simultaneous extension and adduction. The ulnaris stabilizes the wrist and prevents radial deviation during pronation.[9] The insertions of these muscles into the metacarpals are irritated sites that often respond to friction massage (see Chapter 12).

Muscles that flex, abduct, and adduct the hand at the wrist include the flexor carpi ulnaris (inserts into the pisiform, hook of the hamate, and base of the fifth metacarpal; flexes and adducts the wrist), the flexor carpi radialis (inserts into the base of second metacarpal; flexes and abducts the wrist), and the palmaris longus (flexes the wrist; rarely involved and absent in 13% of normal individuals[12]).

The flexor carpi ulnaris and radialis may also be tested by combining their functions of flexion-adduction and flexion-abduction (see below, Functional Examination of the Wrist).

Like the extensors, they may develop insertional tendinitis, which is aided by friction massage.

Clinical—wrist flexors and extensors: Resisted wrist flexion and extension with abduction or adduction may stress the origin or insertion of the above muscles, but we must be aware of the synergistic effects of these muscles. Resisted ulnar deviation requires the synergistic contraction of both the flexor and extensor carpi ulnaris, and resisted radial deviation requires the extensor and flexor carpi radialis aided by the abductor pollicis longus and extensor pollicis brevis.[13] If we test wrist flexion or extension without the accompanying radial or ulnar deviation, we might have to retest resisted abduction or adduction to localize the side of the wrist lesion. Clenching the fist in a neutral position might create wrist or elbow pain on either the medial or the lateral side because both flexors and extensors are synergistically contracting. It is important to test the particular flexor or extensor with simultaneous abduction and adduction to determine the pain source and then to palpate for the most tender site.

WRIST STABILITY (CARPALS AND LIGAMENTS)

There is no particular motor control of the carpals because the flexor carpi ulnaris is the only muscle that inserts into the carpals. All the tendons that bypass the wrist are responsible for carpal movement, and the carpals require their own stability. This stability is provided by the joint contact surfaces of the individual bones and the ligaments that bind the carpals to the distal radius and ulna.[5]

Culver[5] mentions two groups of ligaments: the intracapsular ligaments, which bind the distal radius and ulna to the proximal and distal carpals, and the interosseous ligaments, which bind the carpals to each other. The volar intracapsular ligaments (Fig. 5-2), especially the three originating from the radius and inserting into the capitate, triquetral, and scaphoid, are the main wrist stabilizers; the major dorsal intracapsular ligament is the dorsal radiocarpal ligament.[5] The dorsal wrist ligaments are more slack than the volar ligaments, allowing more wrist flexion than extension.[10] The dorsal wrist ligaments are much weaker than the volar ligaments. Because of the shape of the carpals, most carpals dislocate dorsally; the lunate tends to dislocate volarly.

The TFCC represents the ligamentous and cartilaginous tissues consisting of the radioulnar ligament, ulnar collateral ligament, meniscus homolog, articular disc, and extensor carpi ulnaris sheath, all making up the triangular area at the distal ulna[7] (Fig. 5-3). The TFCC acts as a cushion between the ulna and the carpus, preventing ulna-lunate abutment and the consequent development of chondromalacia.[14] It also stabilizes the ulnar head in the sigmoid notch of the radius.[2]

The term *ulnar variance* refers to the relative length of the ulna with respect to the radius: If the ulna is short relative to the radius, it is an ulnar minus variant; it is an ulnar positive variant if the ulna is relatively longer. When the distal articular

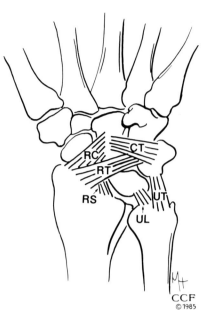

Figure 5-2 Palmar intracapsular ligaments. Radiocapitate ligament (RC), which originates from the radial styloid, extends across the palmar waist of the scaphoid, and inserts into the capitate. Radiotriquetral ligament (RT), which is the strongest palmar ligament, extends from the radius across the palmar pole of the lunate, to which it attaches, and inserts into the triquetrum. Radioscaphoid ligament (RS) is deep to and ulnar to the radiotriquetral ligament and directed onto the palmar aspect of the scaphoid and the scapholunate ligament. Ulnolunate (UL) and ulnotriquetral (UT) ligaments run from the triangular fibrocartilage to the lunate and triquetrum, respectively. Capitotriquetral ligament (CT) connects the capitate and triquetrum, bridging the midcarpal joint. *Source:* Courtesy of Cleveland Clinic Foundation, Cleveland, Ohio.

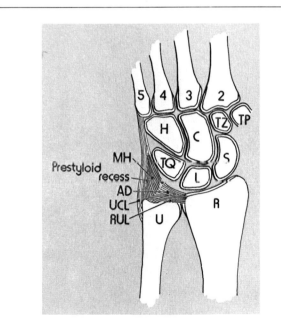

Figure 5-3 The component parts of the TFCC: the meniscus homolog (MH), prestyloid recess, articular disc (AD), ulnar collateral ligament (UCL), and radioulnar ligaments (RUL). H = hamate; C = capitate; TZ = trapezoid; TP = trapezium; S = scaphoid; L = lunate; TQ = triquetrum; R = radius; U = ulna. *Source:* Reprinted with permission from AK Palmer et. al., "The Triangular Fibrocartilage Complex of the Wrist—Anatomy and Function" in *Journal of Hand Surgery* (1981;6:153), St. Louis, 1981, The C.V. Mosby Co.

surface of the radius extends beyond that of the ulna (minus), there is more stress exerted on the lunate bone in ulnar deviation because a shortened ulna increases the shear and compression on the lunate, increasing the possibility of lunate compression fracture and avascular necrosis.[15] This is a common finding in Kienböck's disease, which is surgically treated by lengthening the ulna. With an ulnar minus variant the TFCC is thick, and with an ulnar positive variant the TFCC is thin. Repetitive or traumatic ulnar deviation on a thin TFCC would stress the TFCC and surrounding tissues.

Clinical: Linscheid and Dobyns[3] state that in activities and sports in which ulnar deviation is required, such as baseball batting and carpentry (hammering), perforations or ligamentous tears may occur in the TFCC or lunotriquetral interosseous ligament. In this situation positive ulnar variance (thin TFCC) would be a problem. Roentgenography may show the positive ulnar variance. Passive ulnar deviation would be painful (compresses the TFCC) with associated pain at the ulnar styloid, possible clicking, crepitus, and pinpoint tenderness over the TFCC. There may be pain on volar-dorsal translation of the distal ulna. Arthrography, arthroscopy, or MRI may be required to assess the extent of the tear.[4]

FUNCTIONAL EXAMINATION OF THE WRIST

Because of the complexity of the wrist area, passive functional tests are nonspecific. In comparison to the resisted tests the passive tests help determine the probable type of tissue involved, but palpation of point tenderness and knowledge of local anatomy are essential. These help the examiner develop a procedure of palpation that encompasses all the wrist structures and enables simultaneous comparison with the opposite wrist. A painful click on palpation may indicate instability. Often a bone scan, computed tomography, cineradiography, wrist arthrography, or MRI is necessary to arrive at a final diagnosis.

The following tests assess wrist function (see Table 5-A-1 in Appendix 5-A):

1. active wrist flexion, extension, radial deviation, ulnar deviation, pronation, and supination: These assess the allowable range of motion as limited by pain.
2. passive distal radioulnar pronation (Fig. 5-4): The patient's elbow is flexed to 90° against the trunk. The examiner grasps the lower forearm just proximal to the radioulnar styloids and pronates for end feel. This test stresses the radioulnar ligament and the joint capsule. If the ulnar head is more prominent than on the normal side, there may be involvement of the TFCC or the dorsal radioulnar ligament or fracture of the base of the ulnar styloid (passive "twang" reaction) and a painful click.[16]
3. passive distal radioulnar supination (Fig. 5-5): The test is performed as above except that the examiner supi-

nates for end feel. This stresses the radioulnar ligament and joint capsule and may aggravate a tenosynovitis of the extensor carpi ulnaris.[17] The capsular pattern of the radioulnar joint is present if there is pain and limitation on both extreme passive pronation and supination.[18] There may be limited bone-to-bone passive sensation in the presence of a previous fracture or osteoarthrosis.[18]
4. passive pronation of the carpals (Fig. 5-6): The examiner grasps the metacarpals of the hand and passively pronates to end range. The patient's elbow is flexed at 90° against the trunk. This stresses the dorsal intracapsular (radiocarpal) and interosseous ligaments. Elicitation of point tenderness is necessary to determine the

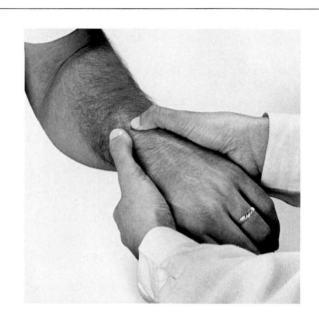

Figure 5-4 Passive distal radioulnar pronation.

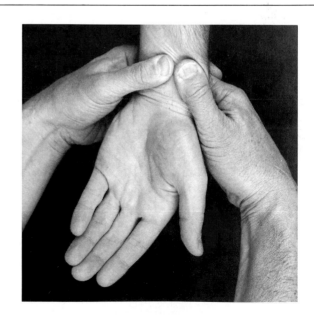

Figure 5-5 Passive distal radioulnar supination.

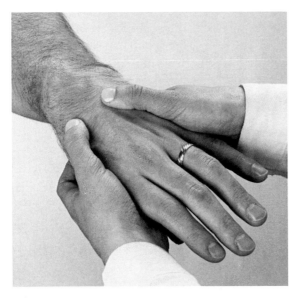

Figure 5-6 Passive pronation of carpals.

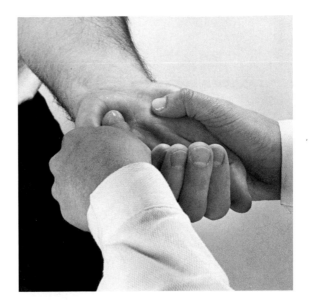

Figure 5-7 Passive supination of carpals.

involved ligament. The test may also stress insertional tendinitis areas.

5. passive supination of the carpals (Fig. 5-7): The examiner grasps the metacarpals of the hand and passively supinates to end range. The patient's elbow is flexed to 90° against the trunk. This stresses the palmar intracapsular (radiocarpal) and interosseous ligaments. Elicitation of point tenderness is necessary to determine the involved ligament. The test may also stress insertional tendinitis areas (eg, the extensor ulnaris). *Note:* A wrist x-ray instability series and individual examination of the carpals is necessary to determine acute or chronic carpal instability.

6. passive wrist palmar flexion (Fig. 5-8): The examiner presses against the dorsal metacarpals of the patient's relaxed, open hand. This tenses the dorsal wrist ligaments and carpals and may determine a possible perilunar dislocation injury and also compresses volar wrist ligaments and carpals. Palmar flexion associated with radial deviation causing a painful click may indicate a subluxing proximal pole of the scaphoid dorsally over the rim of the radius. This may represent a scapholunate instability.[2] There may also be a subluxated capitate bulge on the dorsum of the wrist. The test also may stress an extensor insertion tenosynovitis.

7. passive wrist extension (Fig. 5-9): The examiner presses against the patient's open palm. Most wrist injuries occur in dorsiflexion, causing compression and impaction of the scaphoid, triquetrohamate, and surrounding areas. The test tenses volar wrist ligaments and carpals and compresses dorsal wrist ligaments and carpals (especially the scaphoid). Movement may be limited in capitate subluxation. Wrist extension in ulnar deviation stresses the triquetrohamate area. The test also may stress a flexor insertion tenosynovitis.

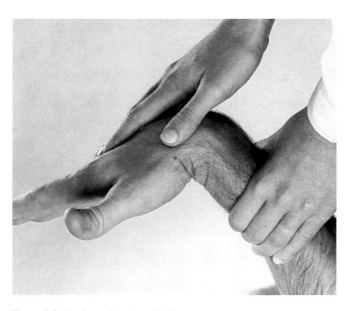

Figure 5-8 Passive wrist palmar flexion

Figure 5-9 Passive wrist extension.

8. passive radial deviation (Fig. 5-10): The examiner grasps the proximal second to fifth metacarpals and stresses them in a radial direction. This tenses the ulnar collateral ligament and compresses the radioscaphoid area (creating impingement pressure on the scaphoid tuberosity from the radial styloid). Golfers may compress this area in decelerating the golf club during the backswing.[2] The test also compresses the scaphoid (which is the most common wrist fracture site) and tenses the flexor and extensor carpi ulnaris muscles.

9. passive ulnar deviation (Fig. 5-11): The examiner grasps the proximal hand and stresses it in an ulnar direction. This stretches the radial collateral ligament, compresses the TFCC, and tenses the flexor and extensor carpi radialis muscles.

10. resisted wrist extension with simultaneous radial deviation (Fig. 5-12):[18] The patient's elbow is flexed, the forearm pronated with the fingers relaxed in slight flexion, and the hand slightly radially deviated. The examiner resists against the dorsal distal metacarpophalangeal joint of the index finger. This tests insertion areas and distal tendons of the extensor carpi radialis longus and brevis. There is simultaneously minimal stress to associated agonists (abductor pollicis longus, extensor pollicis longus, and extensor pollicis brevis).

11. resisted wrist extension with simultaneous ulnar deviation (Fig. 5-13):[18] The patient's elbow is flexed, the forearm pronated with the fingers in relaxed flexion, and the hand slightly ulnar deviated. The examiner resists against the dorsum of the fifth metacarpal. This tests the extensor carpi ulnaris insertion area and the distal tendon.

12. resisted wrist flexion with simultaneous radial deviation (Fig. 5-14):[18] The patient's elbow is flexed with the forearm between supination and midposition and the fingers relaxed. The examiner resists against the thenar eminence. This tests the insertion area of the

flexor carpi radialis and creates minimal stress on the extrinsic flexors of the fingers and thumb.

13. resisted wrist flexion with simultaneous ulnar deviation (Fig. 5-15):[18] The patient's elbow is flexed, the forearm supinated, the fingers relaxed, and the hand slightly ulnar deviated. The examiner resists against the hypothenar eminence. This tests the insertion area of the flexor carpi ulnaris.

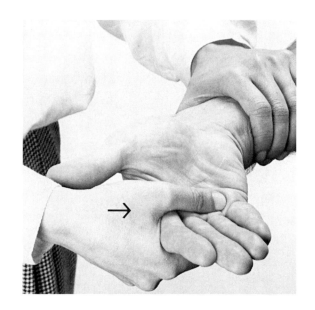

Figure 5-11 Passive ulnar deviation.

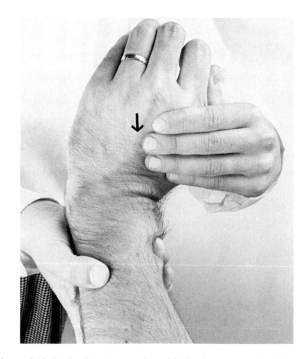

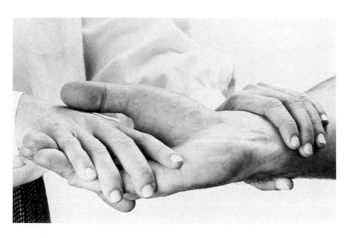

Figure 5-10 Passive radial deviation.

Figure 5-12 Resisted wrist extension with simultaneous radial deviation.

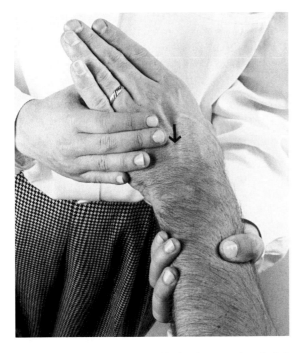

Figure 5-13 Resisted wrist extension with simultaneous ulnar deviation.

Figure 5-14 Resisted wrist flexion with simultaneous radial deviation.

WRIST LESIONS

Degenerative Arthritis

Degenerative arthritis (see Table 5-A-1 in Appendix 5-A) is not a common condition in the wrist (it is more common in the phalanges and the thumb carpometacarpal joint). Watson and Ryu,[19] after analyzing 4000 wrist roentgenograms, found that 95% of all wrist degenerative arthritis is located at the scaphoid and periscaphoid areas. They stated that the area of sclerosis is the most significant pain source and that, if there is only narrowing without sclerosis, there is probably enough cartilage in the joint for continued function.

Capsular pattern: There is about the same amount of limitation of flexion as of extension at first; the end stage results in fixation in midposition.[16]

Treatment: The condition is helped by joint play technique and reduction of manipulatable persistent carpal subluxations (eg, of the capitate) with subsequent friction massage to the involved area.

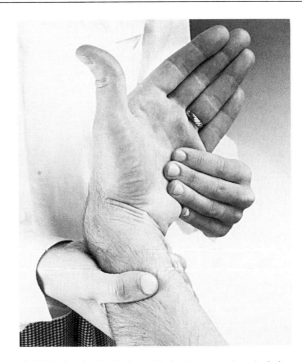

Figure 5-15 Resisted wrist flexion with simultaneous ulnar deviation.

Ligamentous Lesions

Except for cases of obvious fracture or dislocation, in the initial examination of all the extremity joints the examiner must first consider the ligamentous support structure, especially if the condition is acute. This is a main reason that passive testing is applied before resistive testing. Examination of motion of the normal extremity is essential for comparison.

It is important to determine the degree of sprain because failure to recognize a second- or third-degree sprain (see below) may result in chronic instability and posttraumatic arthritis. Ordinary roentgenograms may reveal abnormal gaps between carpals if a static instability exists. Sometimes wrist stress films, cineradiography, or fluoroscopy may be needed.

O'Donoghue[20] distinguishes among three categories of ligamentous sprain. In first-degree (mild) sprain the ligament remains strong and functional; there are few torn fibers and minimal hemorrhage into the ligament. First-degree sprains are treated by friction, muscle rehabilitation, and support if needed. In second-degree (moderate) sprains at least half the fibers remain intact; the ligamentous ends are close enough to heal. Healing may require 6 to 10 weeks, and up to 4 months may be needed for complete return of stability. Swelling should subside in 2 to 3 weeks. Immobilization is always necessary. In third-degree (severe) sprains there is a complete tear through the ligament with separation of the ends. The ligamentous ends must be brought together to allow normal healing.

Most acute wrist injuries result from a fall on the thenar region of an outstretched hand with the forearm pronated, forcing the wrist into hyperextension.[21] Swelling of the wrist is proportional to the extent of the injury. Because swelling is not common with mild ligamentous lesions, increased swelling should indicate the probability of fracture or dislocation. A normal ligament is never tender to palpation. If there is no suspicion that the ligament is injured, then with tenderness there is something wrong in the joint that the ligament supports. Kessler and Hertling[22] state that sometimes normal passive testing will not reveal ligamentous pain; in such cases only specific joint play movement or having the patient lean forward on the forearm and extended hand can reveal ligamentous pain. These investigators hold that this would create pain arising from a palmar radiolunate or a dorsal radiocarpal ligament.

In chronic ligamentous instabilities of the wrist, patients usually complain of a painful click (joint incongruity) and intermittent pain with particular activities. They usually can localize the area of pain.[5] Patients may also complain of weakness (diminished grip strength).

Posner[23] states that the most common fracture of the carpus occurs at the navicular (8% of all fractures in organized sports). He holds that any wrist injury with tenderness in the anatomic snuffbox should be considered a fracture of the navicular. Because weeks may intervene before enough resorption takes place at the fracture line, initial roentgenograms may appear negative. A bone scan would be positive within the first few days.

Joint play examination of individual carpals can be used to test for instability patterns. Osterman et al[4] mention a radial stress test for scapholunate instability. With the patient's hand supinated, the examiner stabilizes the lunate with the index finger on the dorsal side and the thumb on the volar side and presses the opposite thumb on the volar distal pole of the scaphoid. The examiner then passively deviates the patient's wrist in radial and ulnar positions, which will create a click and pain. Basically, fixing any two carpals with the thumb and index finger of both hands and passively deviating the hand in radial and ulnar deviation may create the painful click and the patient's symptom.

Treatment: Most second- and all third-degree sprains should be referred to orthopedic specialists for complete evaluation and treatment. Many patients with chronic ligamentous wrist pain often are greatly relieved by joint play mobilization and friction massage to hypomobile carpals that are due to fibrous adhesions. Often with first- and mild second-degree sprains, splinting and physical therapy are all that is required.

Insertional Wrist Tendinitis and Tenosynovitis

Chronic overuse causing tissue overload, sudden trauma (as in gripping the steering wheel in a head-on automobile collision), improper sport technique, inadequate equipment, too rapid retraining after a layoff, improper warm-up, and poor body mechanics are all possible causes of irritation to the insertional areas of the extrinsic forearm muscles. The primary symptom may be a vague deep ache that is either localized or referred proximally or distally. In the early stages symptoms usually occur after the activity. In the later stages pain occurs during activity, and finally the pain may become continuous. According to Wood and Dobyns,[24] of the six dorsal wrist compartments (Fig. 5-16) the most common site of tendinitis is the first (the abductor pollicis longus and extensor pollicis brevis; see below, The Hand); the sixth compartment (the extensor carpi ulnaris) and the second compartment (the radialis brevis and longus) are the next most commonly involved. Involvement of the remaining dorsal extensors is uncommon.

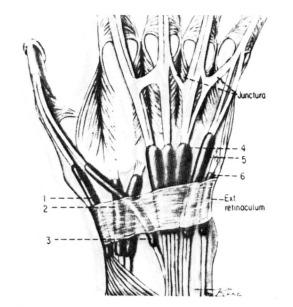

Figure 5-16 The six dorsal compartments of the extensor tendons at the wrist. Symptomatic tenosynovitis can involve any of these tendon compartments but is most common in (1) the abductor pollicis longus and the extensor pollicis brevis, (2) the extensor carpi radialis longus and brevis, (3) the extensor pollicis longus, and (6) the extensor carpi ulnaris. It is less common in (4) the extensor digitorum communis and (5) the extensor digiti minimi. *Source:* Reprinted with permission from *Orthopedic Clinics of North America* (1982;13[3]:484), Copyright © 1982, W.B. Saunders Company.

These investigators also state that flexor carpi ulnaris tendinitis is more common than flexor carpi radialis tendinitis.

Osterman et al [4] distinguish between primary and secondary wrist tendinitis. Primary tendinitis may be due to simple overuse, and secondary tendinitis may have an underlying cause such as wrist instability that prevents normal healing.

Johnson[25] holds that most patients with insertional tendinitis feel pain only with specific motions and that most daily activities do not cause pain.

Extensor Carpi Ulnaris

The patient complains of pain on the dorsal ulnar part of the wrist. Because the sheath is more superficial than the radial wrist extensors,[25] swelling of the sheath or synovitis may be more evident. Cyriax and Cyriax[26] describe the lesion at three main areas: at the ulnar groove, between the ulna and the triquetral, and at the base of the fifth metacarpal.

Functional tests

1. Definite pain on resisted wrist extension with ulnar deviation.
2. Possible pain on passive supination of the carpals.
3. Possible pain on passive flexion.
4. Possible pain on passive radial deviation.

Treatment: Treatment includes friction massage to involved sites. Temporary wrist immobilization in slight extension may be necessary (see Chapters 10, 12, and 14).

Extensor Carpi Radialis Longus and Brevis

The lesion is usually located on or near the insertion on the base of the second or third metacarpal.

Functional tests

1. Definite pain on resisted wrist extension with radial deviation.
2. Possible pain on passive flexion.
3. Possible pain on passive ulnar deviation.

Treatment: Treatment is the same as for extensor carpi ulnaris tendinitis.

Flexor Carpi Ulnaris

This is the most involved of the flexor tendons.[24] There is usually a localized pain, but because of the broad area of insertion into the pisiform and hypothenar fascia pain may be referred to the medial and posterior elbow.[25] Moving the pisiform may create pain, and calcific densities may appear on roentgenograms as the cause of ulnar paresthesias.[25]

Functional tests

1. Definite pain on resisted wrist flexion with ulnar deviation.
2. Possible pain on passive wrist extension.

Treatment: Friction massage to the involved site (the pisiform area) and temporary wrist immobilization in slight flexion are helpful (see Chapters 10, 12, and 14).

Flexor Carpi Radialis

According to Johnson,[25] because this tendon inserts deep, close to the scaphotrapezial and metacarpotrapezial joints, before it inserts into the base of the volar second metacarpal, inflammation of this tendon may involve the surrounding joints. Painful joint play testing of these joints may indicate either a joint problem or a combination joint and tendon problem. Positive resisted testing by itself would incriminate only the tendon.

Functional tests

1. Definite pain on resisted wrist flexion with radial deviation.
2. Possible pain on passive wrist extension.

Treatment: Treatment is the same as that for flexor carpi ulnaris tendinitis.

Tenosynovitis

Ulnar tendon tenosynovitis (possibly bilateral) may be the first sign of rheumatoid arthritis.[27] On the dorsal wrist the tendon sheaths extend about 1 in above and below the dorsal retinaculum, and on the volar side the sheaths extend from the proximal wrist to the palm and may be continuous with the digital tendon sheaths of the thumb and little finger.[28]

Clinical: As a result of thickening of the sheaths with inflammatory exudate, the wrists must be in a flexed or extended position when friction is applied to roll the sheath on the taut tendon. Synovitis of the extensor tendons is usually more obvious than of the flexor tendons, which are deep to the palmar fascia and may not be noticed. Synovitis of the extensor tendons may present as an elongated swelling on the dorsum of the hand and lower forearm.[9] Rheumatoid arthritis must be ruled out. All the separate fibro-osseous tunnels of the dorsal extensors can become inflamed, resulting in stenosing tenosynovitis and "squeaking" tendons (see below). Eventual triggering may occur on the flexor tendons at the metacarpophalangeal joints.

Subluxation of the Extensor Carpi Ulnaris Tendon

This lesion may result from minimal trauma and is due to a disruption of the tendon's fibro-osseous sheath by wrist hyper-supination and ulnar deviation, which is accompanied by the sensation of tearing and/or an audible snap. The tendon may be restored to position with pronation. The lesion is conservatively treated with the forearm immobilized in pronation and the wrist in radial deviation.[24]

Intersection Syndrome

Intersection syndrome occurs proximally to the de Quervain location, where the abductor pollicis longus and extensor pollicis brevis muscle bellies obliquely cross the underlying radial wrist extensor tendons. It occurs in people who use the wrist repetitively.[24] A swelling may appear 4 to 8 cm proximal to Lister's tubercle (one-third of the way across the dorsum of the wrist from the radial styloid process[29]). The pathology has been blamed on myositis, adventitial bursitis, stenosing tenosynovitis, and other conditions.[24] Muscle testing results may be similar to de Quervain testing (see section on de Quervain's tenovaginitis). The location of pain and possible swelling proximal to the radial styloid process on the proximal dorsal forearm help differentiate from de Quervain. Movement of the wrist may create a squeaky crepitus sensation (squeaker's wrist; Fig. 5-17).

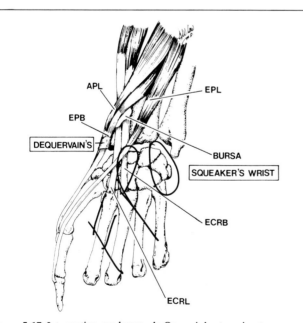

Figure 5-17 Intersection syndrome. de Quervain's stenosing tenosynovitis occurs at the level of the radial styloid, where the abductor pollicis longus (APL) and extensor pollicis brevis (EPB) pass through a fibro-osseous canal. The abductor pollicis longus tendon is often multiple. The intersection syndrome occurs where the musculotendinous junction of these first extensor compartment muscles overlaps the second extensor compartment muscles, the extensor carpi radialis brevis (ECRB) and longus (ECRL). There is a potential bursa in this area that may get irritated, and extension and radial deviation of the wrist will produce a crepitant sound, hence the term "squeaker's wrist." *Source:* Reprinted with permission from *Clinics in Sports Medicine* (1988;7[2]:331), Copyright © 1988, W.B. Saunders Company.

Treatment: Treatment comprises splint immobilization,[25] friction, physical therapy modalities, and therapeutic muscle stretching (TMS).

Acute Calcific Tenosynovitis

Osterman et al[4] compare this condition to an acute shoulder calcific tendinitis. The patient may be in severe pain, and there may be marked erythema and swelling that look like an infection. Roentgenograms will show calcification. The condition responds dramatically to steroids and immobilization and less dramatically to immobilization, manual therapy, and modalities.

Carpal Tunnel Syndrome

The carpal tunnel is surrounded by bone on three sides with the flexor retinaculum on top. It can be related to sports activity or any repetitive wrist or hand activity that might create a digit flexor tenosynovitis.[24] In athletes nonspecific synovitis is the most common cause; hypertrophied or abnormal flexor superficialis or lumbrical muscles are other possible causes.[30] Space-occupying lesions such as Colles' fracture, Smith's fracture, dislocated carpal bone, tumor, and rheumatoid arthritis must be considered along with the mechanical etiology of prolonged wrist dorsiflexion with gripping during the day.[10] Other causes may include thyroid and collagen disease and fluid retention.

Clinical: Examination will reveal a positive Tinel's sign over the flexor retinaculum, positive Phalen's sign, and nocturnal paresthesia of three and a half radial fingers that is relieved with movement. Wood and Dobyns[24] mention that direct compression over the median nerve in the distal forearm causes symptoms. Paresthesias are usually a more predominant symptom than pain. Later signs include thenar atrophy, diminished two-point discrimination, and weakness of the muscles of the median nerve distribution. EMG and nerve conduction studies may be necessary if the diagnosis is in doubt.

Treatment: The wrist is splinted in neutral (or 10° dorsiflexion) night and day.[10] Friction massage helps if there is pain on resisted wrist and finger flexion due to a flexor digitorum superficialis tenosynovitis. Carpal joint mobilization and passive stretching also help. Motor signs may be an indication for surgery.

Guyon's Ulnar Tunnel Syndrome (Handlebar Palsy)

Guyon's tunnel is a distal area of compression of the ulnar nerve and artery as they pass between the medial pisiform and the lateral hook of the hamate. The syndrome involves the sensory supply to the ulnar palm and one and a half ulnar fingers, and the motor supply to all the interossei, the adductor pollicis, and the lumbrical muscles to the ring and little fingers as well as the hypothenar muscles. Because the ulnar nerve originates from C-8 and T-1, examination should always include the cervicothoracic spine and elbow area. The cause may be trauma, ganglion, lipoma, ulnar artery thrombosis, or aneurysm.[30] There may be a positive Tinel's sign at the pisiform affecting one and a half ulnar digits. Typically there are motor and sensory deficits in later stages. Involvement of the ulnar artery may cause vascular symptoms or only paresthesia. Doppler ultrasonography may be needed if a vascular examination does not reveal the problem.

Treatment: Conservatively a splint, therapy modalities, and rest may help. If the nerve is compressed by a chronic tendinitis of the insertion of the flexor carpi ulnaris, friction may be a possibility.

Carpal Subluxation

After wrist sprains, a carpal bone may be fixed in a position that restricts its normal movement. Joint play examination and treatment often resolve the problem. Cyriax[17] states that when this problem exists there will be limitation of motion in only one direction. For example, if the capitate is involved there will be limited active and passive wrist extension, and the capitate may bulge slightly on wrist flexion. Treatment consists of setting the capitate in a dorsal to volar direction while the wrist is under traction. Several treatments with friction massage of the surrounding carpal ligaments will then alleviate the problem, although recurrence is possible.

THE HAND

The human has a greater degree of thumb opposition than any other species. Because of its inherent differences, the thumb is discussed separately from the fingers.

FINGERS: FUNCTIONAL ANATOMY AND PERTINENT BIOMECHANICS

Planes of Finger Abduction and Adduction

The middle finger represents the median plane, so that movement of the fingers away from the middle finger represents abduction and movement toward the middle finger represents adduction. The middle finger therefore abducts to either side since it has no adductors.

Range of Motion

The range of motion in the hand comprises the following[9,29,31]:

1. Metacarpophalangeal joints: flexion, 85°; passive extension, 0° to 45°. The metacarpophalangeal joints have a few degrees of lateral motion in neutral or extension, but because of the tautness of the collateral ligaments during flexion they have only slight motion in flexion. Thus metacarpophalangeal ligament lateral integrity should be tested in 90° of flexion.
2. Proximal interphalangeal joints: flexion, 115°; extension, 0°.
3. Distal interphalangeal joints: flexion, 80°; passive extension, 20°.
4. Whole fingers: abduction, 20°; adduction, a few degrees. These movements are a function of the metacarpophalangeal joint. Increased thickness of the fingers decreases their range of motion.

Clinical: All the articulations of the phalanges are stable through most of the ranges of motion except the metacarpophalangeal joint, which is less stable in extension or hyperextension because the collateral ligaments are slack. The joint may be immobilized in flexion but never in extension or hyperextension because slack ligaments and muscles (interossei) are more likely to develop contractures and cause joint locking than when they are under tension.[9,29]

Muscles

The fingers do not contain muscle bellies and are moved in flexion and extension solely by flexor and extensor tendons.[29]

Extrinsic Flexors

Extrinsic muscles that flex the digits originate in the proximal arm and forearm and insert in the hand. The flexor digitorum superficialis inserts into the volar shafts of the middle phalanges of the second to fifth digits. It flexes the middle phalanges of these digits and aids in flexion of metacarpophalangeal and wrist joints. The flexor digitorum profundus inserts into the volar base of the distal phalanges of the second to fifth digits and flexes the distal phalanges of these digits.

The intrinsic muscles originate and insert in the hand. The lumbricals originate from the radial side of the four flexor digitorum profundus tendons and insert on the radial side of the extensor expansions distal to the metacarpophalangeal joints. They flex the second to fifth proximal phalangeal joints and extend the interphalangeal joints.

The volar interossei originate on the palmar surface and radial side of fifth and fourth metacarpals, on the ulnar side of the second metacarpal, and from the palmar surface of the ulnar side of the base of the first metacarpal. The dorsal interossei originate between the adjacent sides of all the metacarpals. Both the volars and the dorsals have dual insertions into the bases of the proximal phalanges and the extensor expansions of the digits. The volars adduct the fingers, and the dorsals abduct the fingers. The dorsal interosseous insertions into the second and third phalanges cause abduction to resist the thumb during pinch. The interossei, like the lumbricals, flex the metacarpophalangeal joint and extend the interphalangeal joints. According to Kapandji,[6] when the metacarpophalangeal joint is flexed 90° the interphalangeal joints are extended entirely by the extensor digitorum without the interossei, but when the metacarpophalangeal joint is extended the interphalangeal joints are extended solely by the interossei. The movements of the phalanges can be independent of the position of the wrist by virtue of the interosseous muscles.[9] The lumbricals are active in all phases of metacarpophalangeal flexion; they are known as the *flexor starters* of this joint.

Bunnell's test for interossei and lumbrical contracture: If the interossei and lumbricals are tight or contracted, passive flexion of the proximal interphalangeal joint is difficult if the proximal phalanx (metacarpophalangeal joint) is held in extension. This is corroborated if the metacarpophalangeal joint is flexed (relaxing the interossei) and the proximal interphalangeal joint can be passively flexed.[9,29,32] With the metacarpophalangeal joint flexed, if the proximal interphalangeal joint will not fully flex there may be a tight capsule (Fig. 5-18).

Clinical: The remaining intrinsic muscles associated with the four medial digits are the hypothenar muscles, which abduct and flex the little finger. Pain on resisted testing of any of the finger muscles may point to a muscular lesion that may require manual therapy. The flexor muscles become tendons in the lower distal forearm where they are prone to tendinitis and tenosynovitis. Rarely, if the flexor digitorum superficialis under the transverse carpal ligament develops a tenosynovitis hypertrophy, it may be a cause of a carpal tunnel syndrome that may respond to manual therapy. See Chapter 12 for treatment of interosseous hand problems.

Extrinsic Extensors

Extrinsic muscles that extend the digits[12] include the following. The extensor digitorum divides into four tendons proximal to the wrist through a synovial sheath to insert into the extensor expansions of the fingers into the proximal dorsal part of the middle and distal phalanges. It extends the fingers at the metacarpophalangeal and interphalangeal joints and aids in wrist extension.

The extensor digiti minimi has its own compartment and sheath in the extensor retinaculum and inserts into the extensor expansion of the little finger. It is the main extensor of the little finger at the metacarpophalangeal and interphalangeal joints. The extensor digitorum tendon to the little finger is not well developed.

The extensor indicis passes through the same synovial sheath as the digitorum tendons and inserts into the extensor expansion of the second finger. It extends the index finger.

Extrinsic extensor tightness test: Tightness is usually due to adherence of extensor tendons over the dorsum of the hand or wrist[32] because there are no transverse ligaments on the dorsal surface of the metacarpophalangeal joints. Normally, with the wrist in neutral and the metacarpophalangeal joint passively extended, the proximal interphalangeal joint should be able to flex. If the metacarpophalangeal joint is passively flexed and if the proximal interphalangeal joint is restricted from flexing, then the extrinsic extensors are check-reining the flexion of these joints, or a possible joint capsule contracture exists that would probably be alleviated by joint play mobilization.[29]

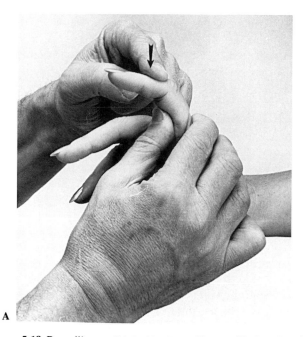

Figure 5-18 Bunnell's test. **(A)** Positive Bunnell's test. **(B)** Corroboration of positive Bunnell's test.

Clinical: Because the extensor digitorum and extensor digiti minimi originate off the lateral epicondyle from the common extensor tendon, resisted finger extension may test positive (painful) in a lateral epicondylitis.

THUMB: FUNCTIONAL ANATOMY AND PERTINENT BIOMECHANICS

Kapandji[6] states that most movements of the thumb occur at the carpometacarpal joint, allowing the thumb to take up most positions with respect to the hand with additional movements at the metacarpophalangeal joint. He states that movements of both joints occur at two degrees of freedom, flexion-extension and adduction-abduction, and a third degree of freedom attributable to the play provided by the elasticity of the ligaments. A combination of the above movements is responsible for opposition, rotation, and circumduction.

Planes of Motion

The following planes of motion[33] refer to the hand in the anatomic position. Flexion-extension occurs in a plane parallel to the plane of the palm. It refers to combined movement at the carpometacarpal, metacarpophalangeal, and interphalangeal joints. Abduction-adduction is primarily a function of the carpometacarpal joint, although slight abduction-adduction occurs at the metacarpophalangeal joint. Movement occurs in a plane at right angles to the flexion-extension plane (ie, perpendicular to the plane of the palm with abduction away from the palm and adduction toward the palm).

Range of Motion

The range of motion in the thumb comprises the following[31]:

1. Flexion: interphalangeal joint, 80°; metacarpophalangeal joint, 55°; carpometacarpal joint, 35°.
2. Passive hyperextension: interphalangeal joint, 15°; metacarpophalangeal joint, 10°.
3. Abduction: 60°.

Opposition, which is based on a composite movement of abduction, rotation, and flexion of the tip of the thumb to the proximal digital crease of the small finger,[31] is difficult to measure and may require radiologic analysis.

Muscles

An important reason for thumb mobility is that the nine muscles that move the thumb can combine their actions in numerous ways in finely graduated movement combinations.[12,13]

Extrinsic Thumb Flexor

The flexor pollicis longus inserts into the base of the distal phalanx; it has its own synovial sheath and is a deep muscle originating from the anterior surface of the radius distal to the oblique line. It flexes the tip of the thumb.

Extrinsic Thumb Extensors and Abductors

The abductor pollicis longus lies just distal to the supinator and inserts into the base of the first metacarpal. It abducts and extends the thumb at the carpometacarpal joint.

The extensor pollicis brevis inserts into the base of the proximal phalanx of the thumb. Its tendon lies with the abductor pollicis longus above the styloid process of the radius and the lateral collateral ligament of the wrist joint, with which it forms the anterior border of the snuffbox. It extends the thumb at the carpometacarpal and metacarpophalangeal joints.

The extensor pollicis longus forms the posterior border of the snuffbox. It inserts into the base of the distal phalanx of the thumb and extends the thumb at the metacarpophalangeal and interphalangeal joints.

Clinical: The above three muscles may be involved in localized tendinitis, de Quervain's disease (see lesions below), and extensor intersection syndrome.

Intrinsic Muscles of the Thumb

The abductor pollicis brevis, opponens pollicis, and flexor pollicis brevis insert into the metacarpal and proximal interphalangeal joints, resulting in abduction and flexion (opposition) of the thumb. Together these muscles make up the thenar group.

The adductor pollicis inserts into the medial side of the base of the proximal phalanx of the thumb. It adducts the thumb and assists in opposition.

The first palmar interosseous flexes and adducts the proximal phalanx of the thumb.

Both the flexors and extensors have sheaths surrounding their tendons as they approach the wrist. The flexor digitorum superficialis and profundus have a common sheath, and the dorsum contains six osseofibrous tunnels each with their own synovial sheaths.[12]

Clinical: Synovitis of the sheaths may present as elongated swelling on the dorsum of the hand and lower forearm and on the volar surface of the forearm. Swelling is usually lessened at the extensor retinaculum and the transverse carpal ligament.[9] With sheath inflammation there is usually crepitus. In synovitis of the extensor tendons passive testing may be painless.[31] Friction massage at sheath locations must be done with the sheath stretched (ie, in wrist flexion or extension or with radial or ulnar deviation, depending on the side of involvement). Synovitis in the hand is usually related to a rheumatoid condition. Joint synovitis is usually evident dorsally by the resistance of the palmar plate and is usually felt as a boggy swelling. Intractable cases may require splinting, injections, or surgery (tenosynovectomy).

FUNCTIONAL EXAMINATION OF THE FINGERS

1. Active fist clench and then extension of the fingers: This assesses limitation of the range of motion due to pain or structure. In closing of the fingers it is important to see a proper sequence of metacarpophalangeal, proximal interphalangeal, and distal interphalangeal joint flexing in turn[9] because grasping is difficult if the proximal or distal interphalangeal joint flexes first. Fingers should extend together beyond neutral. In complete flexion the fingers should converge toward the scaphoid tubercle.[9] Finger abduction and adduction should also be checked. *Note:* Passive joint motion depends not only on articular freedom but also on limitation by contractures of the skin and soft tissues and obstruction to tendon movement.[9] Individual joints are passively tested by stabilizing (contacting) the proximal and distal interphalangeal joints and performing gradual joint play mobilization movements. Excessive motion due to collateral ligamentous rupture or dislocation may be present. It may also occur in a chronic condition that the patient describes as a "weak joint."[31]

2. Passive flexion of metacarpophalangeal, proximal interphalangeal, and distal interphalangeal joints: The examiner may test all these joints together or individually. The wrist is held in neutral or a slightly extended position to test full finger flexion range. There may be pain and limitation in osteoarthritis and in extensor tenosynovitis if passive finger flexion is tested with a fully flexed wrist.

3. Passive extension of metacarpophalangeal and proximal and distal interphalangeal joints individually or together: Testing in the neutral wrist position tenses the phalangeal and palmar tendons. Extension is limited in palmar contractures and trigger nodules and is limited with possible pain in osteoarthritis. There may also be pain in flexor tenosynovitis.

4. Passive finger abduction: This test may stress the volar interossei.

5. Passive finger adduction: This test may stress the dorsal interossei. *Note:* Passive abduction and adduction stresses the metacarpophalangeal joint. To achieve these motions the joint must be extended. Testing a 90° flexed joint passively should allow no movement because of taut collateral ligaments (tests the stability of the metacarpophalangeal collaterals).

6. Resisted finger flexion: The examiner can resist all fingers together or individually. To test the digitorum profundus, with the patient's wrist slightly extended the examiner stabilizes the proximal and middle phalanges and resists against the anterior distal phalanx (Fig. 5-19). To test the digitorum superficialis, again with the wrist slightly extended the examiner stabilizes the proximal phalanx and resists against the anterior middle phalanx (Fig. 5-20). The lumbricals and volar and dorsal interossei are tested by fixing the metacar-

pophalangeal joints and resisting against the anterior proximal phalanges (second through fifth). Bunnell's test for intrinsic muscle tightness can be performed. The examiner may resist the fingers in flexion as a group by resisting against all distal and then middle phalanges; this tests for flexor tenosynovitis. The examiner can test the flexor digiti minimi by resisting against the anterior proximal phalanx with the interphalangeal joint of the little finger extended. The patient attempts to flex the metacarpophalangeal joint of the little finger (Fig. 5-21). There may be pain in osteoarthritis of the fingers. Weakness and no pain indicates a probable C-8 nerve root lesion. *Note:* as in other areas, partial rupture of tendons in the hand would test as weakness and pain on resisted testing.

7. Resisted finger extension: The examiner can test the fingers as a group (by resisting the pronated and flexed metacarpophalangeal joints at the dorsal surfaces of the proximal phalanges) or individually (Fig. 5-22). The examiner can also test individually the extensor digiti minimi (little finger) and extensor indicis (second finger) by resisting the proximal phalanx of each of these fingers while the patient clenches the other three fingers (Fig. 5-23). This tests individual extensor compartments for tenosynovitis. There may be pain in osteoarthritis. Weakness and no pain indicates a probable C-7 nerve root lesion.

8. Resisted finger abduction: To test the dorsal interossei, the examiner resists abduction on the radial side of the proximal phalanges of the index and middle fingers and on the ulnar side of the proximal phalanges of the middle and fourth fingers (Fig. 5-24). To test the abductor digiti minimi, the examiner resists abduction of the little finger on the ulnar side of the proximal phalanx (Fig. 5-25). There is definite pain in dorsal

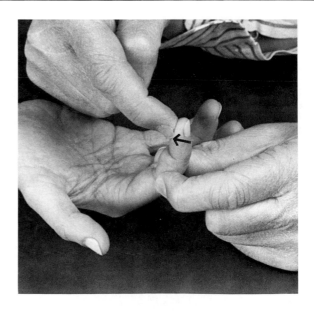

Figure 5-19 Resisted digitorum profundus flexion of single phalanx.

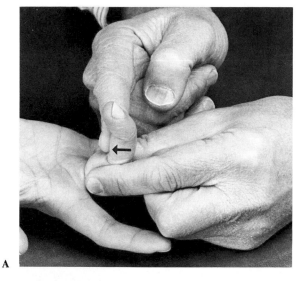

Figure 5-20 Resisted digitorum superficialis flexion. **(A)** Single phalanx. **(B)** Four phalanges.

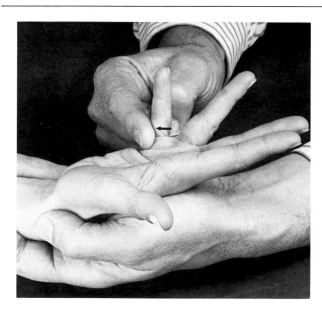

Figure 5-21 Resisted flexor digiti minimi flexion.

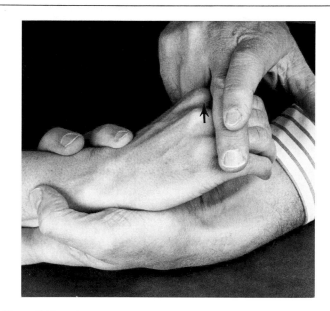

Figure 5-22 Resisted finger extension (all fingers).

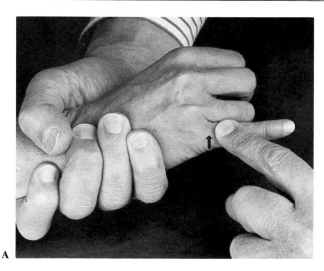

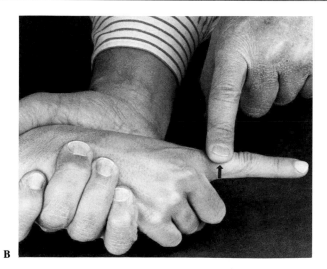

Figure 5-23 **(A)** Resisted extensor digiti minimi extension. **(B)** Resisted extensor indicis extension.

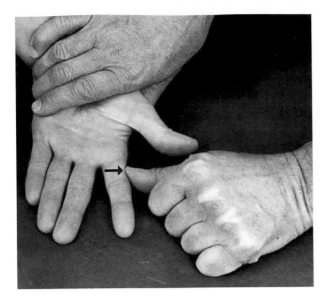

Figure 5-24 Restricted abduction of index finger (dorsal interossei).

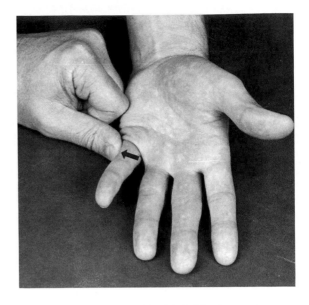

Figure 5-25 Resisted abductor digiti minimi abduction.

interossei tendinitis. Weakness and no pain indicate a probable T-1 nerve root lesion.

9. Resisted finger adduction (Fig. 5-26): To test the volar interossei, the examiner resists adduction on the ulnar side of the proximal phalanges of the thumb and index finger and on the radial side of the proximal phalanges of the ring and little fingers. The middle phalanx is not supplied with adductors. There is definite pain in volar interossei tendinitis. Weakness and no pain indicate a probable T-1 nerve root lesion.

10. Thumb passive movement: Flexion (transpalmar adduction) stresses the thumb proximal interphalangeal and metacarpophalangeal joints, extensors, and adductors (this becomes Finkelstein's test with the addition of wrist ulnar deviation, which may indicate de Quervain's disease) (Fig. 5-27). Extension (radial abduc-

tion) tenses the thumb flexors and may stress the thumb proximal interphalangeal, metacarpophalangeal, and trapeziometacarpal joints. There may be pain in flexor pollicis longus tenosynovitis. Retroposition (a combination of extension and backward stretch) stresses the thenar muscles, the anterior trapeziometacarpal joint, and the radial collateral ligament of the thumb metacarpophalangeal joint. There may be pain in flexor pollicis tendinitis (Fig. 5-28). Abduction (palmar) stresses the trapeziometacarpal joint and the ulnar collateral ligament of the thumb metacarpophalangeal joint (Fig. 5-29). All the above may be painful in trapeziometacarpal arthritis.

11. Thumb resisted extension: This test involves movement of the interphalangeal joint by the extensor pollicis longus and the metacarpophalangeal joint by the exten-

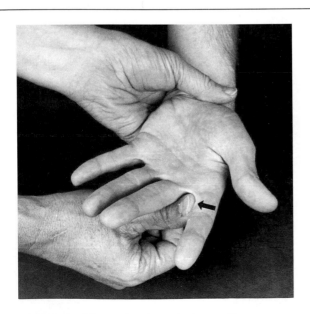

Figure 5-26 Resisted finger adduction (volar interossei).

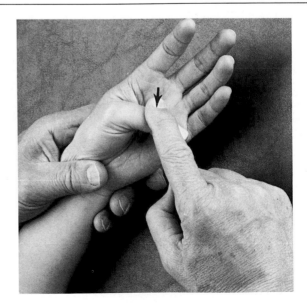

Figure 5-27 Thumb passive flexion.

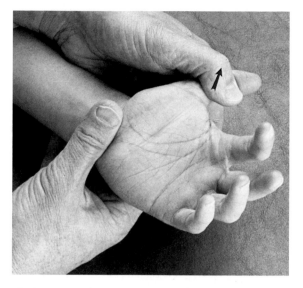

Figure 5-28 Thumb passive retroposition.

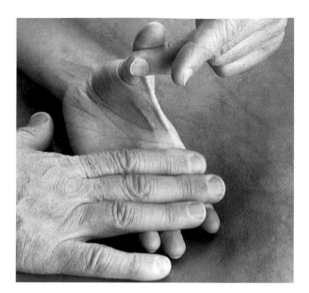

Figure 5-29 Thumb palmar abduction.

sor pollicis brevis. In testing the extensor pollicis longus, the patient's thumb is extended at the metacarpophalangeal joint and flexed at the interphalangeal joint. The examiner resists against the thumbnail while stabilizing the proximal phalanx from both sides[16] (Fig. 5-30). In testing the extensor pollicis brevis, the patient's thumb is flexed at the metacarpophalangeal joint. The examiner resists against the dorsal proximal phalanx of the thumb while stabilizing the metacarpal[16] (Fig. 5-31). The abductor pollicis longus also aids in thumb extension (also known as radial abduction). To test this muscle, the examiner resists against the lateral surface of the distal end of the first metacarpal in the direction of adduction and flexion[34] (Fig. 5-32). There is definite pain in de Quervain's disease and possible pain in trapeziometacarpal osteoarthritis. Weakness and no pain indicate a probable C-7 nerve root lesion.

12. Thumb resisted flexion: This test involves movement of the interphalangeal (flexor pollicis longus) and metacarpophalangeal (flexor pollicis brevis) joints. In testing the flexor pollicis longus, the patient's thumb is extended and abducted. The examiner resists against the palmar surface of the distal phalanx while stabilizing the proximal thumb phalanx from both sides[16] (Fig. 5-33). In testing the flexor pollicis brevis, the patient's thumb is extended and abducted. The examiner resists against the palmar surface of the proximal phalanx while stabilizing the first metacarpal (Fig. 5-34). There is definite pain in flexor pollicis longus tenosynovitis. Weakness and no pain indicate a probable C-7 or C-8 nerve root lesion.

13. Thumb resisted abduction (palmar; ie, perpendicular to the plane of the palm): This movement is mainly due to the abductor pollicis brevis,[16] which inserts into the

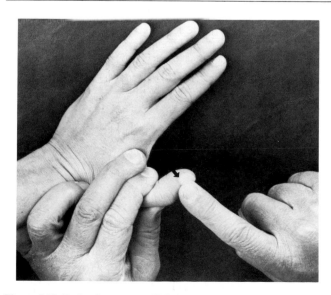

Figure 5-30 Resisted extensor pollicis longus extension.

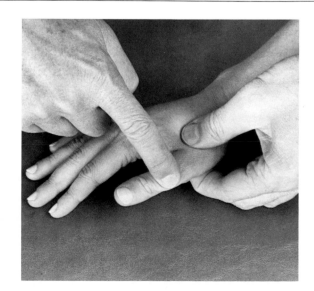

Figure 5-31 Resisted extensor pollicis brevis extension.

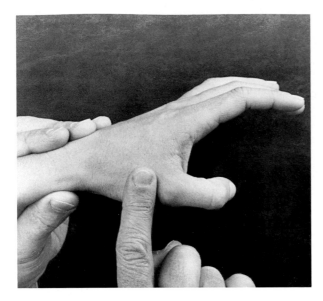

Figure 5-32 Resisted abductor pollicis longus extension.

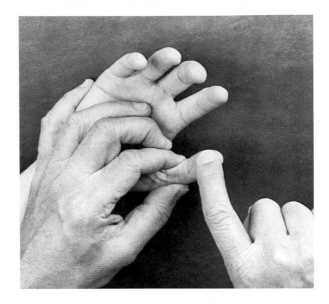

Figure 5-33 Resisted flexor pollicis longus flexion.

radial side of the base of the thumb's proximal phalanx. The abductor pollicis longus, which inserts into the radial side of the base of the first metacarpal bone, aids the abductor pollicis brevis in palmar abduction but is principally an extensor of the carpometacarpal joint. Extension of the thumb is also considered radial abduction (see above, thumb resisted extension). In testing the abductor pollicis brevis, the patient's thumb is held at a right angle to the palm. The examiner resists against the proximal phalanx in the direction of adduction toward the palm while stabilizing the wrist (Fig. 5-35). There is definite pain in de Quervain's disease and

possible pain in trapeziometacarpal osteoarthritis. Weakness and no pain indicate a probable C-7 nerve root lesion.

14. Thumb resisted adduction: Janda[16] states that palmar adduction (90° to the palm) is mostly due to the first dorsal interosseous rather than the adductor pollicis. The test involves resisted adduction against the ulnar and palmar portion of the thumb, with most of the pressure being exerted on the distal first metacarpal bone (Fig. 5-36). This assesses both the first dorsal interosseous and the adductor pollicis. Weakness and no pain indicates a probable C-8 nerve root lesion.

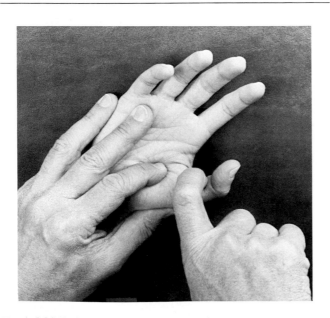

Figure 5-34 Resisted flexor pollicis brevis flexion.

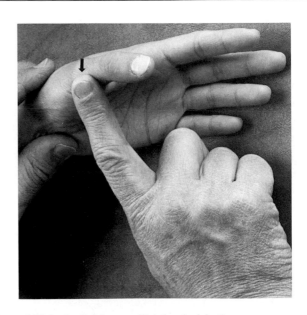

Figure 5-35 Resisted abductor pollicis brevis abduction.

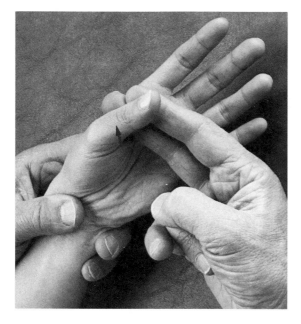

Figure 5-36 Thumb resisted adduction.

HAND LESIONS TREATED BY MANUAL METHODS

Osteoarthritis

The greatest incidence of osteoarthritis is in individuals 45 years of age in the interphalangeals and the first carpometacarpal.[35] Heberden's nodes of the distal phalanges appear to be related to a hereditary problem that increases with age, and Bouchard's nodes of the proximal interphalangeal joints are related to an inflammatory factor. Bouchard's nodes may end up with a severely deformed joint that stops progressing. The Heberden distal node may continue to progress but may not appear as deformed as Bouchard's.[35]

Osteoarthritis of the trapeziometacarpal joint is often related to generalized osteoarthritis, although the shape of its saddle joint has also been related to the degeneration[36] (Table 5-A-2 in Appendix 5-A). Once the trapeziometacarpal joint becomes hypermobile a painful synovitis occurs, and the possibility of accelerated articular attrition is increased.[37]

Functional tests (trapeziometacarpal osteoarthritis)

1. Definite pain on passive thumb retroposition or palmar flexion (transpalmar adduction).
2. Development of a capsular pattern[26] of limited and possibly painful thumb abduction.
3. Pinpoint tenderness on anterior or posterior (or both) sides of the joint.

Lister[31] describes a pathognomonic maneuver in which, with the metacarpophalangeal joint slightly flexed, axial rotation is applied to the first metacarpal alternately distracting and compressing the trapeziometacarpal joint, creating pain.

Treatment: Cyriax[17] states that deep massage to the capsule will relieve traumatic arthritis of this joint. Joint play mobilization can be attempted; joint play mobilization also often relieves chronic arthritic pain of the phalanges.

Flexor Tendon Tenosynovitis

Lister[31] states that synovitis of the flexor tendons most frequently occurs in rheumatoid patients and also in diabetics. Chronic overuse (eg, overstretching) can aggravate the tendons, causing pain 2 to 5 inches proximal to the wrist. Sometimes a nodule may form on the tendon over the A1 metacarpophalangeal joint pulley, which may be palpable and cause a locking of the finger in flexion; when the patient attempts to extend the finger, the encroached nodule may suddenly free up or "trigger." The examiner can palpate the pulley and feel a tender nodule while passively flexing and extending the patient's fingers. This triggering may create a traumatic tenosynovitis in the flexor tendon and even affect the extensor tendons, causing dorsal extensor pain and tendinitis. There may be diffuse swelling proximal to the transverse carpal ligament, which may even be a cause of carpal tunnel syndrome. Swelling in the palm is difficult to detect except at the base of the index finger, where it may be more evident.[9] Synovial disease should be suspected when finger flexion is painful or limited but the joints appear normal.[9]

Functional tests

1. Definite pain on resisted finger flexion, as a group or individually (especially the little finger or thumb).
2. Possible pain on passive finger extension.
3. Pain and crepitus on compression of the tendon and sheath while the patient actively moves the hand.[27]

Treatment: A painful lesion proximal to the wrist may respond to friction, stretching, trigger point, and rehabilitation (see Chapters 12 through 14). Cyriax[17] states that friction on the long tendon flexors of the palm is of no benefit.

Extensor Tendon Synovitis

There may be swelling on the dorsum of the hand and wrist associated with overuse (Fig. 5-37). Synovitis involves the extensor retinaculum and separate extensor compartments. In the extensors, synovial disease should always be suspected, as is true for the flexors. Swelling is usually not visible at the retinaculum and may be made more prominent during resisted finger extension.

Functional tests

1. Definite pain on resisted finger extension, as a group or individually (especially the little and index fingers and the thumb).

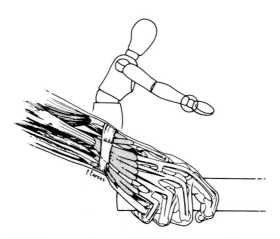

Figure 5-37 Extensor tendon synovitis. Stress generated by the backhand technique may result in dorsal tenosynovitis. *Source:* Reprinted with permission from *Clinics in Sports Medicine* (1987;6[2]:376), Copyright © 1987, W.B. Saunders Company.

2. Possible pain on passive finger flexion with the wrist flexed.

Treatment: Treatment is similar to that used for the flexors. Figure 5-38 illustrates therapeutic splinting.

Interossei Tendinitis

Interossei tendinitis is common in musicians as a result of finger overuse, a sudden stretching of a finger at the metacarpophalangeal joint in abduction, or adduction stressing the insertional portion of the interossei into the base of the proximal phalanx. The lesion may be located in the muscle belly or the insertion (or both).

Functional tests, dorsal interossei

1. Definite pain on resisted finger abduction.
2. Possible pain on passive metacarpophalangeal adduction.

If there is pain on passive abduction and a capsular pattern of equal limitation of flexion and extension at the metacarpophalangeal joint, the condition may represent a joint problem.

Functional tests, volar interossei

1. Definite pain on resisted finger adduction.
2. Possible pain on passive metacarpophalangeal abduction.

As above, the condition must be differentiated from a joint problem.

Treatment: Cyriax[18] states that the primary cure for interossei tendinitis is friction massage and that steroids are ineffective (see Chapter 12).

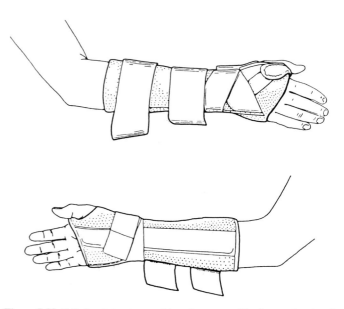

Figure 5-38 Splinting in treatment of dorsal tenosynovitis. *Source:* Reprinted with permission from *Clinics in Sports Medicine* (1987;6[2]:376), Copyright © 1987, W.B. Saunders Company.

de Quervain's Tenovaginitis

Synovitis refers to inflammation of the sheath, whereas *vaginitis* refers to inflammation of the tendon and sheath. de Quervain's tenovaginitis (see Fig. 5-17) is more common in middle-aged women as a result of overuse of the thumb in pinching or excessive ulnar deviation. The inflammation usually involves the abductor pollicis longus and extensor pollicis brevis as they pass through a fibro-osseous tunnel near the radial styloid. These tendons are forced to angulate around the wrist to reach their insertion, which may be stressed by ulnar deviation. There may be localized swelling and radiation of pain either proximally or distally. The usual test for this condition is Finkelstein's test, which involves a passive thumb flexion and wrist ulnar deviation movement. Although this test is considered pathognomonic,[24] it is not completely adequate because the stretching may elicit pain due to an arthritic trapeziometacarpal or scaphotrapeziotrapezoidal joint, an intersection syndrome, or a possible distal thumb extensor tendon involvement. A functional muscle test combined with the passive test will more adequately specify the cause.

Functional tests

1. Definite pain on resisted thumb extension or abduction (or both).
2. Probable pain on passive thumb flexion and ulnar deviation (Finkelstein's test).

Treatment: Splinting, friction, stretching, trigger point, and rehabilitation are all effective therapies. Surgery may be needed in the final stage of the disease, when thickening of the fibro-osseous canal may become stenotic.[24]

REFERENCES

1. Linscheid RL. Kinematic considerations of the wrist. *Clin Orthop Relat Res*. 1986;202:27.

2. Wilgis EF, Yates AY. Wrist pain. In: Nicholas JA, Hershman EB, eds. *The Upper Extremity in Sports Medicine*. St Louis, Mo: Mosby; 1990:483–493.

3. Linscheid RL, Dobyns JH. Athletic injuries of the wrist. *Clin Orthop Relat Res*. 1985;198:141–150.

4. Osterman AL, Moskow L, Low DW. Soft-tissue injuries of the hand and wrist in racquet sports. *Clin Sports Med*. 1988;7:329–348.

5. Culver JE. Instabilities of the wrist. *Clin Sports Med*. 1986;5:725–739.

6. Kapandji IA. *The Physiology of the Joints*. New York: Churchill Livingstone; 1970;1.

7. Palmer AK, Werner FW. Biomechanics of the distal radioulnar joint. *Clin Orthop Relat Res*. 1984;187:26–42.

8. Mennell JM. Manipulation of the joints of the wrist. *Physiotherapy*. 1971:248.

9. Tubiana R. *Examination of the Hand and Upper Limb*. Philadelphia: Saunders; 1984.

10. Cailliet R. *Hand Pain and Impairment*. 3rd ed. Philadelphia: Davis; 1984.

11. Bogumill GP. Functional anatomy of the forearm and hand. In: Pettrone FA, ed. *Symposium on Upper Extremity Injuries in Athletes*. St Louis, Mo: Mosby; 1986:71–72.

12. Moore KL. *Clinically Oriented Anatomy*. Baltimore: Williams & Wilkins; 1983.

13. Lehmkuhl LD, Smith LK. *Brunnstrom's Clinical Kinesiology*. 4th ed. Philadelphia: Davis; 1984.

14. Mandelbaum BG, Bartolozzi Ar, Davis CA, et al. Wrist pain syndrome in the gymnast—pathogenetic, diagnostic and therapeutic considerations. *Am J Sports Med*. 1989;17.

15. Sundberg SB, Linscheid RL. Kienböck's disease: results of treatment with ulnar lengthening. *Clin Orthop Relat Res*. 1984;187.

16. Linscheid RL, Dobyns JH. Physical examination of the wrist. In Post M, ed. *Physical Examination of the Musculoskeletal System*. Chicago: Year Book Medical; 1986.

17. Cyriax J. *Textbook of Orthopaedic Medicine*. 8th ed. London: Bailliere Tindall; 1982;1.

18. Janda V. *Muscle Function Testing*. London: Butterworths; 1983.

19. Watson HK, Ryu J. Evolution of arthritis of the wrist. *Clin Orthop Relat Res*. 1986;202:57–67.

20. O'Donoghue DH. *Treatment of Injuries to Athletes*. Philadelphia: Saunders; 1976.

21. Mayfield JK. Mechanism of carpal injuries. *Clin Orthop Relat Res*. 1980;149:45–54.

22. Kessler RM, Hertling D. *Management of Common Musculoskeletal Disorders*. New York: Harper & Row; 1983.

23. Posner MA. Injuries to the hand and wrist in athletes. *Orthop Clin North Am*. 1977;8:593–617.

24. Wood MB, Dobyns JH. Sports-related extraarticular wrist syndromes. *Clin Orthop Relat Res*. 1986;202:93–95.

25. Johnson RK. Soft-tissue injuries of the forearm and hand. *Clin Sports Med*. 1986;5:701–707.

26. Cyriax JH, Cyriax PJ. *Illustrated Manual of Orthopaedic Medicine*. London: Butterworths; 1985:67.

27. Maitland GD, Corrigan B. *Practical Orthopaedic Medicine*. London: Butterworths; 1985.

28. Nalebuff EA, Potter TA. Rheumatoid involvement of tendon and tendon sheaths in the hand. *Clin Orthop Relat Res*. 1968;59:149.

29. Hoppenfeld S. *Physical Examination of the Spine and Extremities*. New York: Appleton-Century-Crofts; 1976.

30. Mosher JF. Peripheral nerve injuries and entrapments of the forearm and wrist. In: Pettrone F, ed. *Symposium on Upper Extremity Injuries in Athletes*. St Louis, Mo: Mosby; 1986:174–175.

31. Lister G, ed. *The Hand: Diagnosis and Indications*. 2nd ed. New York: Churchill Livingstone; 1984.

32. American Society for Surgery of the Hand. *The Hand: Examination and Diagnosis*. 2nd ed. New York: Churchill Livingstone; 1983.

33. Williams PL, Warwick R. *Gray's Anatomy*. 36th ed. Philadelphia: Saunders; 1980.

34. Kendall HO, Kendall FP, Wadsworth GE. *Muscle Testing and Function*. 2nd ed. Baltimore: Williams & Wilkins; 1971.

35. Peyron JG. Osteoarthritis: the epidemiologic viewpoint. *Clin Orthop Relat Res*. 1986;213:117–123.

36. North ER, Rutledge WM. The trapezium-thumb metacarpal joint: the relationship of joint shape and degenerative joint disease. *Hand*. 1983;15:201.

37. Eaton RG, Littler JW. Inflammation. In: Lister G, ed. *The Hand: Diagnosis and Indications*. 2nd ed. New York: Churchill Livingstone; 1984:234.

Appendix 5-A

Wrist, Fingers, and Thumb Functional Diagnosis Charts

Table 5-A-1 Wrist Functional Diagnosis

Key
+   Pain
+/−   Possible Pain
L   Possible Limited ROM
LAX   Possible Laxity

TESTS	Arthritis	Extensor Carpi Ulnaris Tendon	Extensor Carpi Radialis Tendon	Flexor Carpi Ulnaris Tendon	Flexor Carpi Radialis Tendon	Intersection Syndrome	Dorsal Ligament Sprain	Palmar Ligament Sprain	Ulnar Collateral Ligament Sprain	Radial Collateral Ligament Sprain	Radioulnar Ligament Sprain	Triangular Fibrocartilage	Capitate Subluxation
Passive Radioulnar Pronation	+/− L										+		
Passive Radioulnar Supination	+/− L										+		
Passive Carpal Pronation							+ L					+/−	
Passive Carpal Supination		+/−						+ L				+/−	
Passive Wrist Flexion (75°)	+ L	+/−	+/−			+/−	LAX +L	+/−					
Passive Wrist Extension (65°)	+ L			+/−	+/−		+/−	+ L LAX					+ L
Passive Radial Deviation (20°)		+/−		+/−					+ LAX			+/−	
Passive Ulnar Deviation (30°)			+/−		+/−					+ LAX		+ L	
Resisted Extension Radial Deviation			+			+							
Resisted Extension Ulnar Deviation		+											
Resisted Flexion Radial Deviation					+								
Resisted Flexion Ulnar Deviation				+									
Joint Play Evaluation													

Table 5-A-2 Fingers and Thumb Functional Diagnosis

Key
+   Pain
+/-   Possible Pain
L   Possible Limited ROM

TESTS	Lesions / Osteoarthritis: Trapeziometacarpal	Osteoarthritis: Fingers	de Quervain	Volar Interossei	Dorsal Interossei	Extensor Tenosynovitis	Flexor Tenosynovitis	Flexor Pollicis Longus Tenosynovitis
Fingers								
Passive Flexion		L +/-				-/+		
Passive Extension		L +/-					-/+	
Passive Abduction				+/-				
Passive Adduction					+/-			
Resisted Flexion		+/-					+	
Resisted Extension		+/-				+		
Resisted Abduction					+			
Resisted Adduction				+				
Thumb Passive Flexion	+/-		+ (1)					
Passive Extension	+/-							+/-
Passive Retroposition	+/-							
Passive Abduction	L +/-							
Resisted Extension	+/-		+					
Resisted Flexion	+/-							+
Resisted Abduction	+/-		+					
Resisted Adduction	+/-							
Joint Play Evaluation								

(1) Passive Flexion and Ulnar Wrist Deviation

Chapter **6**

The Hip and Thigh

Warren I. Hammer

A diffuse pain over the anterior thigh to the knee or shin and pain in the midinguinal area, lateral thigh, medial thigh, medial knee, buttock, or posterior ilium may all be referred pain from the hip joint and bursae. The hip is often overlooked as a source of pain because attention is mistakenly directed to the lumbar spine or sacroiliac joint. Posterior and lateral buttock pain on lumbar extension is usually due to spinal disease, but we must be aware that hip extension also occurs with lumbar extension, so that the hip must not be overlooked. When the foot hits the ground the structures of the lower extremity all become part of a closed kinetic chain; this chain constitutes a linkage system imparting stress to all the structures in it. Therefore, it is essential to examine all the related structures (feet, knees, hips, sacroiliac joints, and spine) to determine the primary lesion or lesions. Hip pain often reveals itself during walking, whereas disc pain might reveal itself with standing.

FUNCTIONAL ANATOMY AND PERTINENT BIOMECHANICS

Like the shoulder joint, the hip joint possesses three degrees of freedom: sagittal (flexion-extension), frontal (abduction-adduction), and transverse (medial and lateral rotation).

There are two important angles between the neck of the femur and the shaft of the femur. The neck-shaft angle or femoral neck angle, a frontal plane angle, is normally 125°; more than 125° is coxa valga, and less than 125° is coxa vara (Fig. 6-1). Many clinicians today consider 135° normal, more

than 140° coxa valga, and less than 130° coxa vara (E. Rashkoff, personal communication, 1990).

Clinical: Roentgenography is necessary for a definite diagnosis of coxa valga or coxa vara. Ipsilateral coxa valga may cause an ipsilateral high ilium and an anatomic long leg (pelvic obliquity). This may result in hip adduction and eventual tight adductors. Saudek[1] states that the ipsilateral abductors may become weak. Treatment consists of balancing the leg length deficiency with inserts. It is questionable whether stretching the adductors and strengthening the abductors will help. Coxa vara causes an ipsilateral low ilium and an anatomic short leg.

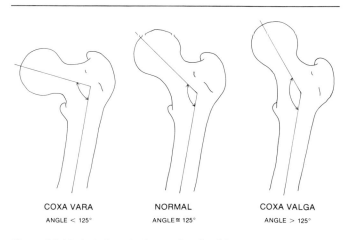

Figure 6-1 Neck-shaft angle. *Source:* Reprinted from *Basic Biomechanics of the Skeletal System* (p 151) by VH Frankel and M Nordin with permission of Lea & Febiger, © 1980.

The greater trochanter may be closer to the ilium and restrict hip abduction if the coxa vara is less than 120°. Both coxa valga and coxa vara always present with a positive Trendelenburg's sign (see below). Because of the pelvic obliquity and leg length deficiency, lumbar and sacroiliac problems usually arise.

The femoral neck anteversion or retroversion angle, which is the angle of torsion or declination, measures the anterior-posterior position of the neck of the femur with respect to the long axis of the shaft of the femur and the femoral condyles (or the increased internal or external rotation of the femur in relation to the femoral neck). This angle of torsion may be measured radiographically. In abnormal femoral anteversion (Fig. 6-2), the femoral condyles are internally rotated with respect to the femoral neck. The average angle in adults is about 12° to 25°.[2-4] Therefore some anteversion is normal and provides the gluteus maximus with a longer lever arm, allowing the muscle to act more efficiently in maintaining upright posture over the hip joint. If the angle is more than 25° (excessive femoral neck anteversion) the femur during gait internally rotates, causing a potential valgus knee and a toe-in

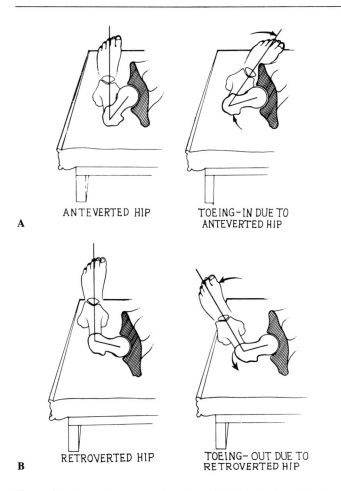

A   ANTEVERTED HIP   TOEING-IN DUE TO ANTEVERTED HIP

B   RETROVERTED HIP   TOEING-OUT DUE TO RETROVERTED HIP

Figure 6-2 Abnormal femoral anteversion. (**A**) Excessive femoral anteversion. (**B**) Femoral retroversion. *Source:* Reprinted from *Physical Examination of the Spine and Extremities* (p 159) by S Hoppenfeld with permission of Appleton & Lange, © 1976.

or hyperpronation of the foot. If the angle is less than 12° (femoral neck retroversion), there may be a toe-out or hypersupination gait.

Kessler and Hertling[3] state that in an excessively anteverted hip incongruity of the hip joint can occur, causing weight bearing on a smaller area of the hip joint surface. This may result in increased wear. Congenital and excessive anteversion may over time lead to osteoarthritis.[5]

Clinical: Anteversion can easily be seen with the patient in the standing position and the feet placed in the normal 30° toe-out position or in a parallel position to exaggerate the problem. In what has been called the "miserable malalignment syndrome,"[6] there are often internally rotated femurs with a compensatory anteriorly rotated pelvis, inward-facing kneecaps, and an increased Q angle (the angle between the direction of the rectus femoris and the patellar tendon; see Chapter 7) associated with external tibial torsion compensated by foot subtalar pronation (see Fig. 7-14A). Examination of the supine patient may reveal the feet to be parallel instead of in the normal 30° to 45° toe-out position. In standing retroversion there may be external femoral torsion and compensatory internal tibial torsion with supinated feet. Comparison of supine or prone internal and external hip range of motion is another indication. If internal rotation is 30° greater than external rotation or more, increased femoral anteversion is probable.

Treatment: A symptomatic manual approach to anteversion would include hip mobilization, stretching of tight internal rotators (see Chapter 13), strengthening of external rotators, and removal of any myofascial aberrations. Abnormal femoral anteversion represents a causative factor in patellofemoral problems (see Chapter 7). Attempted treatment of retroversion would include stretching of external rotators and strengthening of internal rotators along with hip mobilization.

Range of Motion

The hip range of motion comprises the following:

1. *flexion:* active, 120°; passive, 140°. The amount of hip flexion depends on knee flexion because hip flexion with the knee extended is limited by the hamstrings. There is maximum hip flexion with both knees flexed as a result of flattening of the lumbar curve and posterior tilting of the pelvis.[7]

2. *extension:* active, 15° to 20°; passive, up to 30°. The range of active extension is increased when the knee is extended because flexion of the knee shortens the biceps and decreases extension ability. It is important to hold down the crest of the ilium during examination because a lumbar lordosis as well as the anterior pelvis increases the range of extension.

3. *abduction:* active, 45°; passive, 50° or slightly more. The 180° abduction split is really a combination of

abduction, lateral rotation, and flexion because the pelvis must tilt anteriorly and the lumbar spine must hyperextend to slacken the iliofemoral ligaments.[7]

4. *adduction:* 20° to 40° active and passive. Because of the opposite extremity pure adduction is 0°, so that we are really testing a combination of adduction-flexion or adduction-extension.
5. *medial (internal) rotation:* 30° to 40° active and passive.
6. *lateral (external) rotation:* 45° to 60° active and passive. Measurement of rotation is usually done with the patient prone and the knee flexed 90°. Rotation with the extremity extended is less than with the knee flexed, and lateral rotation with the hip flexed 90° (the patient is supine or sitting) may be greater because the flexed hip relaxes the iliofemoral and pubofemoral ligaments, which restrict lateral rotation.[2,7] Extension tightens the capsule.

The estimated minimum necessary range of hip motion necessary for common daily activities (eg, tying shoes) is hip flexion of at least 100°, abduction at least 20°, and external rotation of at least 20°.[2]

Hip Stability

The capsule of the hip surrounds the neck of the femur and is strengthened by two anterior and one posterior ligaments (Fig. 6-3). Anteriorly the inverted Y ligament, known as the iliofemoral ligament (the strongest in the body), tightens, especially in hip extension as the head of the femur presses forward, in extension with medial rotation, and in flexion with combined lateral rotation.[8] The pubofemoral ligament is the

second anterior ligament, and the ischiofemoral ligament is the only posterior ligament. All the ligaments are relaxed during hip flexion. During lateral rotation all the anterior ligaments are taut, and during medial rotation the anterior ligaments are slack while the ischiofemoral ligament tenses.[7] Sitting with the legs crossed in slight adduction is therefore an unstable position because the ligaments are lax and trauma against the long axis of the femur could create a hip dislocation.

Other important reasons for hip stability are related to the inherent structure of the acetabulum and femoral head, the strong vacuum in the acetabulum itself, and Kapandji's[7] idea of the short rotators (piriformis, obturator externus, and gluteus medius and minimus) assisting in coaptation.

Muscles

The following muscles for hip movements are the primary movers for the three degrees of hip joint motion. It must be remembered, however, that the position of the hip (flexion, extension, and so forth) alters the function and efficiency of the muscle and that these primary muscles have secondary actions. For example, the adductor longus also functions as a flexor up to 50° of hip flexion because the femur lies inferior to the muscle origin, but at 70° of hip flexion, when the femur lies superior to the muscle origin, the adductor longus acts as a hip extensor. Most of the hip flexors can also abduct-adduct or laterally and medially rotate; the extensors can abduct or adduct, and the abductors can produce abduction–flexion–medial rotation or abduction–extension–lateral rotation.[7]

Prime Movers of the Hip

The hip primary musculature constitutes the following (Figs. 6-4 through 6-7):

1. *flexors:* psoas major and minor, iliacus
2. *extensors:* gluteus maximus, hamstrings
3. *abductors:* gluteus medius
4. *adductors:* adductor magnus, longus, and brevis; gracilis
5. *lateral rotators:* piriformis, obturator externus and internus, gemellus superior and inferior, gluteus maximus
6. *medial rotators:* gluteus minimus, tensor fasciae latae.

Accessory Hip Movers

The hip accessory muscles are as follows:

1. *flexors:* sartorius, rectus femoris, tensor fasciae latae, pectineus, adductor brevis and longus, adductor magnus (oblique fibers), gracilis, anterior portion of gluteus minimus and medius
2. *extensors:* posterior portion of gluteus medius and minimus, adductor magnus (ischiofemoral portion)
3. *abductors:* tensor fasciae latae, gluteus minimus and maximus, piriformis, sartorius

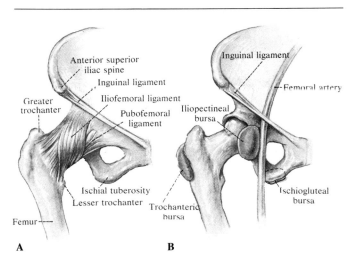

A   **B**

Figure 6-3 Hip capsule. (**A**) Anterior aspect of the hip joint and adjacent bony structures. The fibers of the iliofemoral and pubofemoral ligaments fuse with those of the underlying articular capsule. The synovial membrane lines the inner surface of the articular capsule. (**B**) Relationship of distended iliopectineal, trochanteric, and ischiogluteal bursae to the hip joint and adjacent structures. *Source:* Reprinted from *Rheumatologic Interviewing and Physical Examination of the Joints*, ed 2, by HF Polley and GG Hunder with permission of W.B. Saunders Company, © 1978.

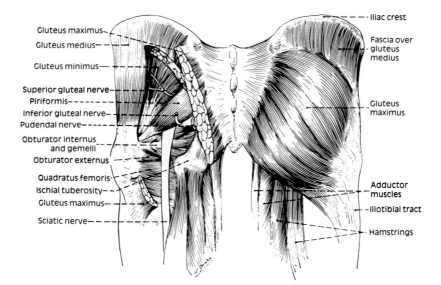

Figure 6-4 Musculature of the buttocks. *Source:* Reprinted from *Functional Anatomy of the Limbs and Back*, ed 5 (p 17-2) by WH Hollinshead with permission of W.B. Saunders Company, © 1981.

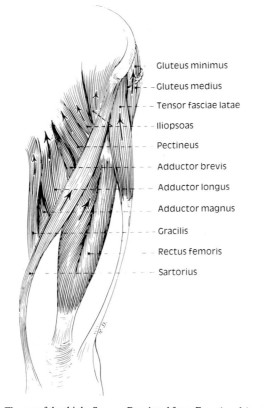

Figure 6-5 Flexors of the thigh. *Source:* Reprinted from *Functional Anatomy of the Limbs and Back*, ed 5 (p 18-6) by WH Hollinshead with permission of W.B. Saunders Company, © 1981.

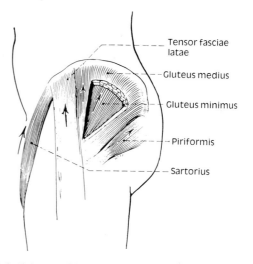

Figure 6-6 Abductors of the thigh. *Source:* Reprinted from *Functional Anatomy of the Limbs and Back*, ed 5 (p 18-2) by WH Hollinshead with permission of W.B. Saunders Company, © 1981.

   6. *medial rotators:* anterior portion of gluteus medius and minimus, gracilis, semitendinosus, semimembranosus, pectineus

Clinical: Medial rotation of the hip is not done specifically by a particular muscle group (eg, flexors or lateral rotators) but as a secondary action of muscles belonging to other groups. The hip extensors are three times stronger than the flexors as a result of their functions in maintaining upright posture and walking[9] because they are bulkier and more efficiently positioned. The medial rotators are one-third as strong as the external rotators.[7] Patients with a hip that is fixed in slight flexion or in flexion contracture or with ankylosis causing an inability to extend the leg freely may compensate while walking by an increased anterior pelvic tilt and lumbar lordosis (to

   4. *adductors:* pectineus, gluteus maximus, obturator internus and externus, quadratus femoris, hamstrings, psoas major
   5. *lateral rotators:* adductor brevis, longus, and magnus; posterior portion of gluteus medius and minimus; pectineus; biceps femoris

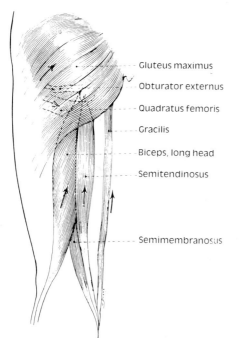

Gluteus maximus

Obturator externus

Quadratus femoris

Gracilis

Biceps, long head

Semitendinosus

Semimembranosus

Figure 6-7 Posteriorly placed adductors of the thigh. *Source:* Reprinted from *Functional Anatomy of the Limbs and Back*, ed 5 (p 17-4) by WH Hollinshead with permission of W.B. Saunders Company, © 1981.

Table 6-1 Pelvic Motion

Motion	Muscles	Action
Anteroposterior pelvic tilt		
Anterior tilt	Hip flexors	Pull pelvis anteriorly and inferiorly
Posterior tilt	Lumbar spine extensors	Pull posterior pelvis superiorly
	Hip extensors	Pull posterior pelvis inferiorly
	Trunk flexors	Pull symphysis pubis anteriorly
Lateral pelvic tilt	Hip abductors	Coupled pelvic motion by contralateral eccentric and concentric contractions

Source: Reprinted with permission from FH Sim and SG Scott, "Injuries of the Pelvis and Hip in Athletes: Anatomy and Function" in *The Lower Extremity and Spine in Sports Medicine*, (p 1130) by JA Nicholas and EB Hershman, St. Louis, 1986, The C.V. Mosby Co.

increase hip extension) and by increased transverse rotation of the pelvis and increased knee flexion (to lengthen the step on the fixed side).[1,8]

It is important to evaluate the flexibility and strength of the adductors in relation to the abductors because of their effect on the pelvis. Adduction contracture could cause a high ipsilateral ilium and apparent short leg (possible equinus) and abduction of the opposite hip; an abduction contracture could cause a low ipsilateral ilium, apparent long leg, and adduction of the opposite hip. Abduction and adduction contracture of the hip usually take place in advanced osteoarthritis (Fig. 6-8).[8] Contracture or shortening of the hip flexors and extensors can affect leg length and pelvic and lumbar curves. Medial and lateral rotators can affect pelvic transverse rotation, which in turn affects lower extremity rotation (Table 6-1).

Relation of Leg Length to Pelvic and Hip Distortion

Patients without leg length deficiency, level iliac crests, and normal posture usually do not have significant spinal or hip deformations or severe joint contractures, but in any leg length deficiency the hip and sacroiliac areas (among other areas, such as the feet, knees, or femur) and the balance of related musculature must be evaluated.

Just as a short leg can cause a change in pelvic mechanics, so pelvic, sacroiliac, and hip distortion can result in either functional or anatomic leg length deficiency. Anatomically the vertical dimension of the ilium on one side could be short, or a past problem such as Perthes' disease or intertrochanteric or femoral neck fracture may create a limb length discrepancy. Functional (apparent) limb deficiency could be caused by contracted hip abductors (apparent long leg) or contracted hip adductors (apparent short leg). A hip that is low, extended, or externally rotated could cause a functional lengthening, and a hip that is elevated, flexed, or internally rotated could cause a functional shortening.[10] An iliac bone that is rotated anteriorly can cause a functional lengthening, and one that is rotated posteriorly can cause a functional shortening. An osteoarthritic hip (Fig. 6-8) could cause an apparent (functional) short leg that on standing would demonstrate a compensatory high iliac crest due to contracted hip adductors. Contracted hip abductors might show a low iliac crest and a functional long leg.

Obviously, comparison of iliac crests by itself is not enough to reveal a limb deficiency. Sacroiliac rotation and muscle imbalance and their effect on the hip joint must be considered in functional pelvic hip sacroiliac causes. A weak gluteus medius may cause functional shortening in an athlete or heavy patient.[10] Rarely, a weak piriformis allowing hip internal rotation may cause a functional shortening. Short hip flexors also would cause functional shortening.

Capsular Pattern

Investigators seem to differ as to the exact sequence of the hip's capsular pattern. They disagree as to whether flexion, medial rotation, or abduction is the most restricted, but the limitation is usually most in medial rotation, less in flexion and extension, and least in abduction, with lateral rotation being the last movement to be restricted.

The most common site of hip degeneration is the superolateral joint space.[9] The coxalgic gait is usually performed with the hip in external rotation and minimal flexion and

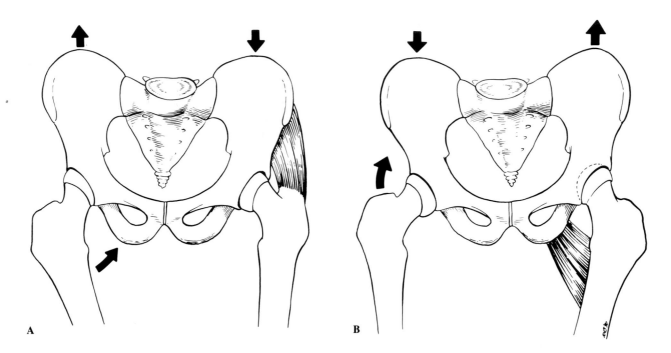

A   B

Figure 6-8 Osteoarthritis of the hip. Pelvic obliquity due to contracted abductors (**A**) causes a functional long leg and lowering of the pelvis; the opposite side shows an adduction of the hip and raised pelvis. In an adduction contracture (**B**) the leg becomes functionally shorter, with raising of the pelvis; the opposite hip abducts and lowers the pelvis. *Source:* Reprinted from A Steindler, *Kinesiology of the Human Body*, 1977. Courtesy of Charles C Thomas, Publisher, Springfield, Illinois.

abduction, which is the least irritating position for an inflamed hip because it decompresses the joint and capsule.

FUNCTIONAL EXAMINATION

The examiner should inspect for quadriceps and gluteal wasting, adductor or abductor spasm, pelvic obliquity, and leg length. Abnormal gait may appear as a sudden leaning on the stance side with a lowering of the pelvis on the opposite side because of a painful hip or weak abductors (see below, Trendelenburg's test). The sudden appearance of a lumbar lordosis in the stance phase may indicate flexion contracture on the stance side. A backward lurch of the trunk during the stance phase may suggest hip extensor weakness on the side of the stance leg or hip flexor weakness on the side of the swing leg.[3] Joint effusion is rarely seen or palpated because of overlying muscles.

In the following passive tests the ilium should be level, and the examiner should use counterpressure on the opposite anterior superior iliac spine (ASIS) when applicable (see Table 6-A-1 in Appendix 6-A).

1. *Active tests:* The standing patient actively abducts by spreading the legs apart (45°), adducts each leg across the standing leg (20°), flexes each knee to the chest (120°), and extends each leg (20°). Sitting or lying, the patient rotates the leg with the hip flexed 90° (internal rotation, 40°; external rotation, 60°).

2. *Passive flexion* (Fig. 6-9): The examiner flexes the supine patient's knee against the chest (140°). Knee flexion relaxes the hamstrings to allow increased hip

flexion. There should be a soft end feel. The examiner can put one hand under the patient's lumbar spine to feel the spine touching the hand (flattening of the lumbar curve) while flexing the hip. If the opposite knee flexes, there is probable shortening of hip flexors (Thomas' test). If, when the patient's opposite knee is flexed 90° off the end of the table, ipsilateral hip flexion causes the opposite leg to rise, there is probably rectus femoris shortening. There is a limited or hard end feel

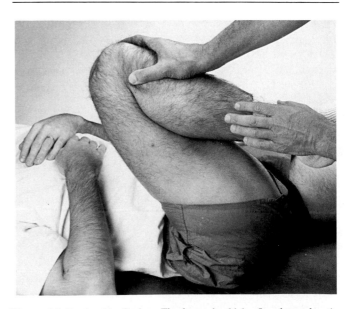

Figure 6-9 Passive hip flexion. The knee should be flexed to relax the hamstrings.

in osteoarthrosis (part of the capsular pattern). There is definite pain in psoas or iliopectineal bursitis and possible pain in trochanteric bursitis; a combination of passive flexion, adduction, and internal rotation may be painful in these cases. There may be pain in upper rectus tendinitis and springy block in hip loose body (rare in flexion).

3. *Passive extension* (Fig. 6-10): With the patient prone, the examiner stabilizes the posterior ilium to prevent lumbopelvic motion. The examiner grasps and raises either a flexed or extended knee (30°). There is limited or hard end feel in osteoarthrosis (part of the capsular pattern). There may be pain in psoas or iliopectineal bursitis, psoas tendinitis, and upper rectus tendinitis. There may also be limitation due to flexion contracture.

4. *Passive abduction* (Fig. 6-11): With the patient supine, the examiner stabilizes the level pelvis and brings the distal leg outward (to 50° or more) without externally rotating the leg. Hip pathology limits abduction more often than adduction.[11] Passive abduction also tests the flexibility of adductors. Abducting with the knee flexed eliminates testing of the gracilis. The test is usually painful in adductor tendinitis. There is possible limitation in osteoarthrosis (capsular pattern) and possible pain in trochanteric bursitis. If at the end range of abduction bending the knee allows increased range of motion, there may be gracilis shortening.[1]

5. *Passive adduction* (Fig. 6-12): With the patient supine, the examiner stabilizes the level pelvis and brings the slightly flexed hip and leg over the opposite leg or adducts with the opposite leg off the table (30°). There may be pain in gluteus medius tendinitis. There will probably be pain, especially if the test is coupled with flexion and internal rotation, in iliopectineal, psoas, and trochanteric bursitis.

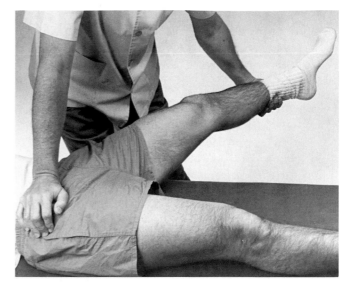

Figure 6-11 Passive hip abduction.

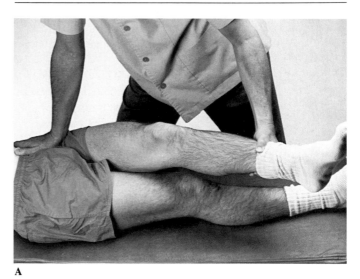

A

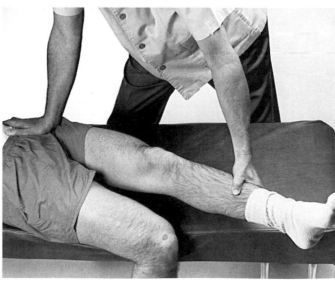

B

Figure 6-12 Passive hip adduction.

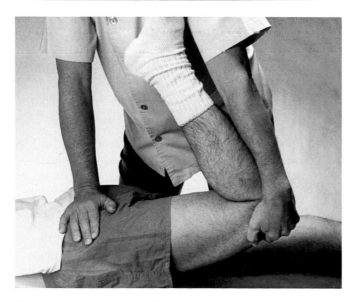

Figure 6-10 Passive hip extension.

6. *Passive medial rotation* (Fig. 6-13): The patient is prone, supine, or sitting. The knee is flexed 90°, and the leg is rotated outward. There should be a normal capsular end feel. If the patient is supine the extended leg may be rotated internally (40°). Loss of the normal rubbery end feel may be the earliest sign of osteoarthrosis or osteoarthritis. There may be pain in hip bursitis and upper rectus tendinitis. This test checks for shortness of external rotators. Femoral retroversion presents as limited medial rotation and increased lateral rotation. Femoral anteversion is abnormal if internal rotation exceeds external rotation by more than 30°.

7. *Passive lateral rotation* (Fig. 6-14): The patient is prone, supine, or sitting. The knee is flexed 90°, and the leg is rotated inward. With the patient supine the extended leg is rotated internally (60°). Motion is seldom severely limited in osteoarthritis. There may be pain in hip bursitis, a springy block end feel with loose bodies, and pain in gluteus medius tendinitis. This test checks for shortness of internal rotators. *Note:* Measuring medial and lateral rotation in the prone (extended) position is more functional because the hip is extended as in walking.[3]

8. *Resisted flexion* (Fig. 6-15): The patient is supine with the hip flexed approximately 30°. The examiner must stabilize the ASIS to prevent compensatory abdominal muscle use by the creation of a lumbar kyphosis.[9] The examiner resists against the anterior distal femur. If the femur tends to rotate laterally and to abduct, the sartorius may be substituting; if the femur medially rotates, the tensor fasciae latae may be substituting.[12] There is definite pain in psoas tendinitis, possible pain in psoas or iliopectineal bursitis, and possible pain in upper rectus tendinitis. There may be weakness in psoas abscess; intra-abdominal inflammation; L-1,

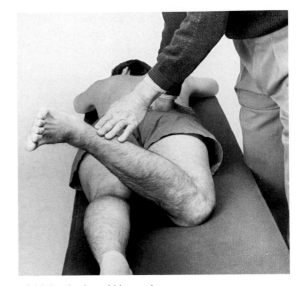

Figure 6-14 Passive lateral hip rotation.

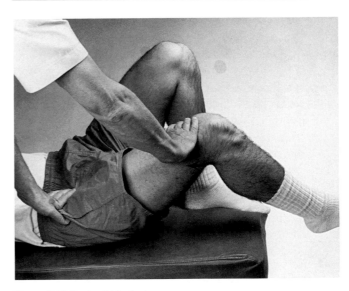

Figure 6-15 Resisted hip flexion.

L-2, or L-3 nerve root involvement; or psoas rupture. There is possible pain and weakness in avulsion fracture of the ASIS from the sartorius and possible pain and weakness in avulsion fracture of the lesser trochanter off the iliopsoas.

9. *Resisted extension* (Fig. 6-16): The patient is supine with the leg extended. The examiner flexes the hip 20° and resists against the posterior ankle while the patient pushes the extended leg toward the table. This test puts more extensor stress on the hamstring origin than the prone test for the gluteus maximus with the knee flexed. Tendinitis of the gluteus maximus is extremely rare. There is definite pain in hamstring ischial tendinitis and possible pain in ischial bursitis. Weakness without pain indicates possible L-4, L-5, or S-1 nerve root involvement.

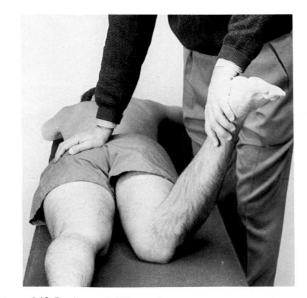

Figure 6-13 Passive medial hip rotation.

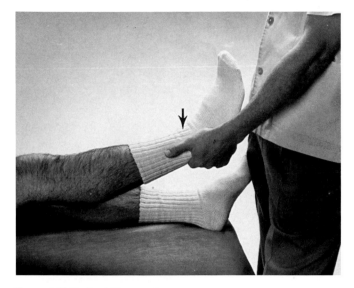

Figure 6-16 Resisted hip extension.

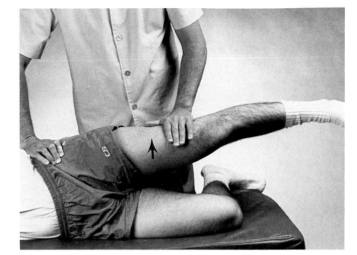

Figure 6-18 Resisted hip abduction.

10. *Resisted adduction* (Fig. 6-17): In the sidelying position, the patient holds the side of the table for stabilization. The examiner abducts the upper leg about 30° and holds it there, resisting against the medial lower thigh. There will be pain in adductor tendinitis. Weakness without pain indicates possible L-2, L-3, or L-4 nerve root involvement.

11. *Resisted abduction* (Fig. 6-18): In the sidelying position, the patient flexes the lower leg and hip to help in stabilizing the pelvis. The examiner places one hand on the greater trochanter to feel hip movement; the other hand resists against the distal lateral femur. It is important not to allow any backward or forward movement of the pelvis; the hip should be slightly extended. The test is definitely painful in trochanteric bursitis and gluteus

medius tendinitis (a rare condition). There may be weakness in gluteus medius rupture. Weakness without pain indicates L-4, L-5, S-1 (the predominant neurologic level[13] is L-5).

12. *Resisted medial rotation* (Fig. 6-19): To eliminate compensatory hyperextension of the lumbar spine and tilting of the pelvis, Janda[9] recommends that the supine patient lie with the untested leg flexed and the tested leg resting with a bent knee over the edge of the table. The examiner holds the lower third of the femur and resists against the lateral malleolus. The test may be painful in trochanteric bursitis.

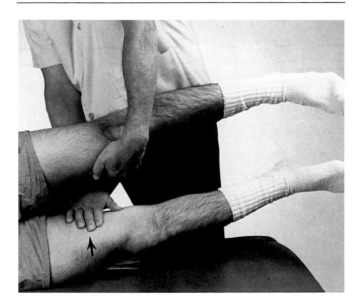

Figure 6-17 Resisted hip adduction.

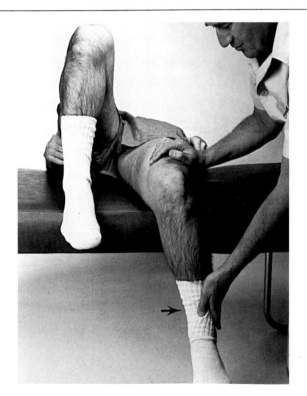

Figure 6-19 Resisted hip medial rotation.

13. *Resisted lateral rotation* (Fig. 6-20): Testing is similar to that for medial rotation except that the examiner resists against the medial malleolus. The test may be painful in trochanteric bursitis and piriformis syndrome.

14. *Resisted knee extension* (Fig. 6-21): Janda[9] states that testing with the hip flexed prevents the rectus femoris from working at full strength (hip flexion shortens the distance between the origin and the insertion of the rectus, whereas a neutral or extended hip stretches the rectus, thereby increasing its efficiency). The patient should be lying supine with the nontested leg flexed on the table and the tested leg hanging over the edge of the table. The examiner resists against the distal tibia with the other hand under the posterior distal thigh. The test is definitely painful in upper rectus, muscle belly, and patellar tendinitis (see Chapter 7). Testing knee extension in the prone position may elicit pain when supine testing does not. There may be pain and weakness due to avulsion at the anterior inferior iliac spine (AIIS). Weakness without pain indicates L-2, L-3, or L-4 nerve root involvement.

15. *Resisted knee flexion* (Fig. 6-22): The patient is prone with the knee flexed less than 90° (knee extension is 0°). The examiner must hold down the posterior ilium and resist proximal to the ankle. Two separate tests are applied: (1) with the hip rotated medially (tests the medial hamstrings) and (2) with the hip rotated later-

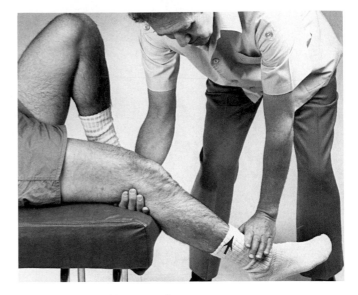

Figure 6-21 Resisted knee extension.

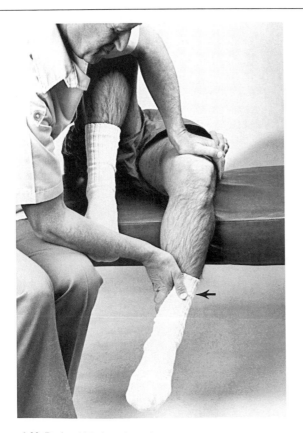

Figure 6-20 Resisted hip lateral rotation.

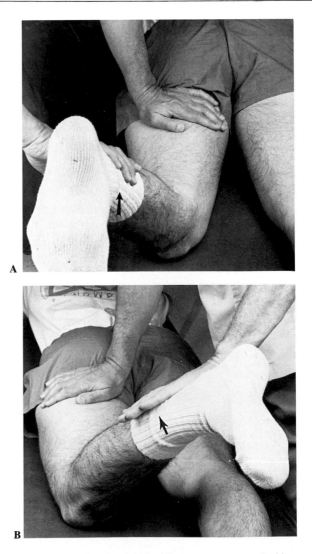

Figure 6-22 Resisted knee flexion. (**A**) Medially rotating the hip tests the medial hamstrings. (**B**) Laterally rotating the hip tests the lateral hamstrings.

ally (tests the biceps femoris). The test is definitely painful in hamstring ischial tendinitis and strain of muscle belly and hamstring insertions (see Chapter 7). Weakness without pain in medial hamstring testing indicates L-4, L-5 (the predominant neurologic level[13]), or S-1 nerve root involvement. Weakness without pain in lateral hamstring testing indicates L-5, S-1 (the predominant neurologic level[13]), or S-2 nerve root involvement.

16. *Additional hip tests*:

- *Trendelenburg's sign:* The patient stands on the involved leg and raises the uninvolved knee to the chest. If positive, the pelvis on the uninvolved side drops; this represents weakness of the gluteus medius on the standing leg side. During this sign, the body shifts to the standing side and shifts the line of gravity lateral to the hip joint center to make gravity an auxiliary force in abduction.[8] If there is pain in the right hip, for example, the patient may lurch to the right during gait to distribute the center of gravity over the femoral head and thereby to reduce the stress on the gluteus medius. If the patient has a hip abduction contracture and a painful hip there would be limited adduction, which may result in a negative Trendelenburg's sign because it is necessary to be able to adduct an involved hip to demonstrate a positive sign. It is unusual for a patient with hip pain to have a negative Trendelenburg's sign.[14] The test may be positive in osteoarthritis and neurologic diseases.

- *Ober's test:* (Fig. 6-23): Ober's test can determine tightness or contracture of the tensor fasciae latae, iliotibial band, and even the gluteus medius and maximus. The test also reproduces pain resulting

from hip flexor muscle contractures.[15] The test is performed by having the patient lie on the uninvolved side with the knee flexed to help reduce the lumbar lordosis. The examiner lifts the involved flexed or extended leg at the ankle while stabilizing the pelvis with the other hand and then abducts and extends the hip in line with the body, allowing the iliotibial band to move posteriorly over the greater trochanter. The examiner then slowly lowers the upper leg; if the leg drops to the table, the test is negative; if it remains abducted, the test is positive. Turek[16] states that when the tensor is tight the thigh will be sustained momentarily in the abducted position before falling toward the table. Ober[17] described the test with the upper limb knee flexed. The iliotibial tract originates from the lateral iliac crest and receives tendinous extensions of the fascia from the gluteus maximus and tensor fasciae latae muscles proximally and inserts into Gerdy's tubercle on the proximal portion of the lateral tibial metaphysis.[18] The tensor fasciae latae also functions in knee extension[19] (see below, trochanteric bursitis, and Chapter 7, iliotibial band friction syndrome).

LESIONS

Osteoarthritis

Primary osteoarthritis of the hip (Table 6-A-1 in Appendix 6-A) is presently considered extraordinarily rare. In one report, 90% of all cases of so-called primary osteoarthritis in which there was enough information to assess the normality of the hip joint at the cessation of growth showed pre-existing subtle or gross abnormalities in the configuration of the acetabulum or femoral head (or both) on x-ray studies.[20]

Clinical: Patients are usually middle-aged or older. In the early stage, pain may be felt at the end of the day; eventually there is morning stiffness due to low-grade inflammation. The patient also may experience stiffness after resting. Pain may be felt in the groin, buttock, lateral thigh, or medial knee, among other areas. Eventually the pain causes sleep disturbance. As the capsule becomes fibrosed and inflamed, the typical pain and capsular pattern develop with restriction in activities; restriction due to pain limits hip medial rotation, extension, flexion, and abduction, causing the hip to be positioned more in lateral rotation, flexion, and adduction. The patient typically walks with the thigh in external rotation. There may be abductor lurch, and pain is usually on the long leg side. Cyriax[21] mentions loss of hip extension as a cause of backache due to compensatory hyperextension of the lumbar joints during gait.

Treatment: Treatment includes weight loss and evaluation of the kinetic chain; strengthening of abductors and improvement of flexibility of the hip muscles; prolonged stretching

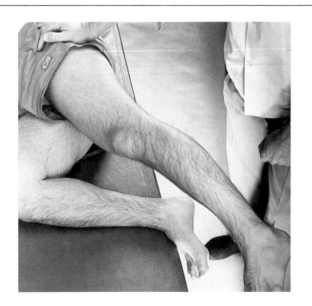

Figure 6-23 Positive Ober's test.

techniques to increase limited ranges; joint play mobilization of the hip, knees, and feet; use of a cane; trigger point therapy; and manipulation of the spine and sacroiliac joints.

Functional tests

1. Definite capsular pattern.
2. Usually negative resisted testing unless an intense inflammatory component creates painful testing in almost all nonassociated directions.

Soft Tissue Injuries

Medoff[22] classifies athletic soft tissue hip injuries into two groups: the friction type, caused by repetitive friction of the iliotibial band on the superficial trochanteric bursa; and the failure type, caused by stressing of collagen fibers of tendons and muscles beyond their ultimate yield strength and resulting in a range of lesions (from mild tendinitis with minor microscopic failure of collagen fibers to a frank muscle or tendon rupture with hemorrhage, marked inflammation, and loss of function).

Bursitis

As with the shoulder, on functional testing bursitis presents a variable appearance. The bursae are passive structures that normally elicit pain on passive stretching or compression, and they may also be irritated by resisted muscle testing. Cyriax[21] states that diagnosis at the buttock is extremely difficult. Bursitis usually presents a nonspecific picture compared to tendinitis, but in the buttock we can be fooled. Often a tendinitis and a bursitis may be associated, as in the gluteus medius area, where it is almost impossible to distinguish between the two. In general, a combination of various nonspecific resisted and passive tests should make us think of acute or subacute bursitis.

A noncapsular pattern of more pain on lateral rotation is usually common, as is a softer end feel than the usual (hard) end feel of the capsular pattern (although a pre-existing capsular pattern may be present). Often night pain and disturbed sleep as well as localized point tenderness over the bursa help in diagnosing. Chronic bursitis often responds to friction but may be painful after the first two or three visits (see Chapter 12).

Hip bursitis is often secondary to structural (rare) or functional deviations. It is extremely important to evaluate the total patient in both dynamic and static states (spine, pelvis, gait, posture, muscle strength and flexibility, joint motion, leg length, feet, work habits, and environment).

Trochanteric Bursitis

The trochanter is the hip bursa most commonly involved in bursitis, which is a relatively frequent but often overlooked cause of pain in the thigh and the pelvic region.[23] The trochanteric bursae comprise two major and one minor bursae. One major bursa is below the gluteus medius muscle, somewhat posterior and superior to the proximal edge of the greater trochanter and the subgluteus maximus. The other major bursa is beneath the tensor fasciae latae and gluteus maximus as they converge to form the iliotibial tract over the greater trochanter. This bursa is localized to palpation on the lateral aspect of the thigh at the junction of the lower edge of the greater trochanter with the lateral proximal femur.[24] Trochanteric bursitis may be associated with ipsilateral hip joint pathology, lumbosacral strain, and obesity. Schapira et al[23] state that abnormal gait patterns associated with lumbosacral strain and hip pathology are related to limited internal hip rotation (early capsular pattern) and reflex tightening of the hip external rotators, the latter of which causes tension of the gluteus maximus fibers on the iliotibial tract.

Iliotibial band tightening (positive Ober's test) is often related to irritation of the bursa because the band moves forward with hip flexion and backward with hip extension. During hip flexion the tensor fasciae latae pulls the iliotibial band anteriorly, and during hip extension the gluteus maximus shifts the band posteriorly.[25] Persistent lifting from a flexed lumbar position back to extension with the knees straight has been blamed as a cause for trochanteric bursitis due to increased lever action of the glutei.[15] This may occur especially in female runners who have a broad pelvis and an excessive Q angle or in runners who have a crossing gait, which causes an adduction pull on the greater trochanter.[26]

Clinical: The patient may describe symptoms similar to L-5 radiculopathy, or the pain could radiate along an L-2 distribution to the knee. There may be an aching pain after running due to overuse.[27] Straight-leg raise or femoral nerve stretch could be painful. Trochanteric bursitis must be differentiated from spinal nerve root pathology, abductor strain, and abductor tendinitis (see below, Tendinitis). Swelling over the trochanteric bursa may be the main complaint.

Treatment: Treatment includes cryotherapy physical therapy modalities and friction massage (only for chronic bursitis) (see Chapter 7 (iliotibial band friction syndrome) and Chapters 12 through 14).

Functional tests

1. Possible pain on passive hip flexion with adduction, passive medial or lateral rotation, and passive abduction.
2. Possible pain on resisted hip extension, abduction, and medial and lateral rotation.
3. Possible positive Ober's test.
4. Possible pain on resisted testing of the tensor fasciae latae.

Iliopectineal and Iliopsoas Bursitis

The iliopectineal bursa is located between the iliopsoas muscle and the hip joint at the iliopectineal eminence (point of union between the ilium and pubis) over the capsule of the hip.[15,28] The iliopsoas bursa lies medially near the insertion of the iliopsoas in the femoral triangle (bounded superiorly by the inguinal ligament, medially by the adductor longus, and laterally by the sartorius).[28]

Clinically the iliopectineal bursa is often mistaken for the psoas bursa. It may be palpated near the head of the femur, which is 1 to 2 cm below the middle third of the inguinal ligament and is found on a horizontal line running halfway between the pubic tubercle and the greater trochanter.[29] Because the iliopectineal bursa may communicate with the hip joint, osteoarthritis of the hip may be a causative factor, so that the examiner should look for a capsular pattern. Swelling may be present.

In iliopsoas bursitis or tendinitis (it is difficult to differentiate between the two), the area may be palpated[30] with the patient supine and the hip flexed 90°; the examiner palpates over the lesser trochanter for tenderness just below the inguinal ligament while passively abducting the hip with the other hand.

Clinical: Both types of bursitis present with pain in the groin and anterior thigh (sometimes down to the knee).

Treatment: Treatment is similar to that for trochanteric bursitis but should include therapy for possible associated osteoarthritis and therapeutic muscle stretching to the psoas. Steroid injection or surgical excision may be needed if the pain persists.

Functional tests

1. Definite pain on passive hip flexion.
2. Probable pain on passive hip extension.
3. Possible pain on passive hip lateral and medial rotation and flexion with adduction.
4. Definite pain on resisted hip flexion.

Ischiogluteal Bursitis

The ischiogluteal bursa is located over the ischial tuberosity and may irritate the sciatic nerve.[16]

Clinical: Swartout and Compere's classic paper on the subject[31] states that an exquisite pain usually occurs suddenly. A sitting job is not necessarily related, but sitting definitely aggravates the condition (sitting on a soft surface more so than on a hard surface). Sleep is painful, and there may be thigh pain on coughing. A radicular pain distribution is not typical. The patient may list toward the side of pain and use a short walking stride. Lumbar extension is painful. Palpation of the ischial tuberosity may reveal a doughy texture. In men pain may be due to a silent prostatitis.[15]

Treatment: Treatment is as above; a foam rubber cut-out cushion should be recommended for use during extended periods of sitting.[15]

Functional tests

1. Probable pain on passive hip flexion.
2. Probable pain on resisted hip extension.

3. Possible pain on resisted knee flexion.
4. Possible pain on straight leg raise.

Tendinitis and Muscle Strains

Strains usually occur from excessive tension (force overload) on eccentrically contracted muscle fibers resulting in muscle tearing.[32] The end result is scar tissue and contractures that, if not eliminated, result in recidivism. When the tendinous or tendoperiosteal portion becomes involved because of repetitive overload, tendinitis results. In the lower extremity, muscles spanning two or more joints are the most frequently injured muscles (ie, hamstrings, triceps surae, and rectus femoris).[33]

Adductors

Clinical: "Groin strain" or "rider's strain" often involves the muscles arising at the pubis, such as the adductor longus, adductor brevis, and gracilis. The musculotendinous area of the adductor longus and the upper area of the adductor magnus may also be involved. The condition tends to result in chronic injury especially if adequate strengthening and stretching of the adductors are neglected. It may be associated with a periostitis, and it may take 6 months to 1 year to heal. The condition is sometimes confused with osteitis pubis (see below).

Treatment: The patient may need a thigh strap. Stretching plus active resistance exercise is necessary; friction massage is essential (see Chapters 10 and 12 through 14).

Functional tests

1. Definite pain on resisted hip adduction.
2. Probable pain on passive hip abduction.

Abductors

Tendinitis involves primarily the insertion, but also the origin, of the gluteus medius muscle. This muscle originates from the outer surface of the ilium between the iliac crest and the posterior glutcal line dorsally and the anterior gluteal line ventrally and inserts into the lateral surface of the greater trochanter.[28]

Clinical: The patient may present with pain similar to that of trochanteric bursitis. Palpation may elicit pain over the greater trochanter insertion or along the belly of the muscle to its origin. Brody[34] states that in runners a broad pelvis, an increased Q angle, leg length deficiency, and a gait in which the feet cross over the midline as well as running on and off sidewalks or on a banked surface can all stress the gluteus medius muscle origin or insertion. He further states that a short leg may cause a pelvic tilt that stresses the abductors on the long leg side. All the above stresses may weaken the gluteus medius (and minimus), eventually allowing the opposite hip to drop (Trendelenburg's sign) and creating an ipsilateral high pelvis and lumbar curve on the opposite side. If the condition persists the ipsilateral gluteus medius may shorten, and an abduction contracture will create an apparent long leg.

Treatment: Depending on the degree of strain, cryotherapy (20 minutes every 2 hours), support, elevation, friction massage, therapeutic muscle stretching (TMS), trigger point, and isometric to isotonic to isokinetic exercises are helpful.

Functional tests

1. Definite pain on resisted abduction.
2. Possible pain on passive adduction with medial rotation.
3. Possible pain on passive medial rotation.
4. Possible pain on passive lateral rotation.

Flexors: Upper Rectus Femoris and Iliopsoas

The anterior groin muscles, which are composed of the adductors, iliopsoas, and rectus femoris, can be irritated by any activity that stretches and strains the area. Teitz[35] mentions how a dancer may develop rectus femoris tendinitis if he or she uses the rectus femoris to flex the hip instead of the iliopsoas. She states that a dancer will be able to raise the leg higher with the use of the iliopsoas because the rectus femoris will be more relaxed and therefore will fold into the groin crease.

The rectus femoris is a weak hip flexor and a strong knee extender and can be overstressed in any sport or action requiring the normal action of hip flexion and knee extension. The usual site of the lesion is the muscle origin at the anterior-inferior iliac spine approximately 3 in inferior to the ASIS. The subcutaneous rectus may exhibit swelling. Pain may be felt in the groin area. Another frequent area is the middle muscle belly. Rupture of the muscle belly similar to the biceps brachii seldom creates serious disability.

Functional tests

1. Definite pain on resisted knee extension.
2. Probable pain (pinch) on passive flexion, extension, or rotation.
3. Inability of the prone patient to flex the knee more than 120° possibly indicating a tight quadriceps.

O'Donoghue[36] states that the most frequent site of iliopsoas strain is the insertion at the lesser trochanter or the musculotendinous junction. Strain is usually due to overactive contraction of the muscle when the thigh is flexed and then forced into extension. He states that the patient complains of groin pain and holds the thigh in a flexed, adducted, and externally rotated position (see above, iliopsoas bursitis for clinical; see also below, avulsion fractures).

Functional tests

1. Definite pain on resisted flexion.
2. Probable pain on passive hip extension.
3. Aggravation on passive flexion and adduction.

Extensors: Hamstring Origin and Belly

The etiology of hamstring strain is as complex as hamstring function. The actions of the hamstrings are directly related to the variable positions and stability of the hip and knee joints. During gait by acting on the hip (ischium) and knee simultaneously[37] during hip flexion with knee flexion or hip extension with knee extension, there is concentric contraction at one end and eccentric contraction at the other end. Knee-hip action may also work with hip flexion and knee extension or hip extension and knee flexion. With increasing contraction from walking to running, the hamstrings eccentrically decelerate hip flexion and knee extension late in the swing phase and then concentrically contract to flex the hip and knee (leading to heel strike) and concentrically extend the hip and flex the knee (in the early stance phase). During this period the hamstrings are also acting as knee stabilizers. Just before toe-off concentric contraction increases, especially for the biceps femoris.

Two phases of the running gait may be the principal moments of stress. First, during the late forward swing phase of recovery, when the muscles are eccentrically contracting to decelerate thigh flexion and knee extension, a deficiency in coordination between the contracting hamstrings and relaxing quadriceps could result in a tear.[38] Second, when the hamstrings rapidly switch from knee stabilization (midsupport phase) to hip extension and knee flexion at the toe-off phase, muscle damage may occur.[37] Because the biceps femoris is most active in the toe-off phase and the medial hamstrings are most active in the late forward swing phase, analysis of the mechanism of injury may help determine the particular muscle involvement.

Fox[39] lists the following factors related to hamstring strain: inadequate hamstring flexibility, hamstring strength imbalance between the lower extremities, quadriceps-hamstring ratio imbalance, external mechanical factors causing inappropriate knee extension and hip flexion (eg, collision), previous injury, muscle weakness, and electrolyte depletion. Other theories of causation point to failure to warm up, improper training, leg deficiency, and even the fact that the short head of the biceps (knee flexor) and the long head of the biceps may not function together because the short head is supplied by the peroneal nerve whereas the long head is supplied by the tibial nerve.[40]

Clinical: It is important to determine whether the strain is mild, moderate, or severe and then to determine the exact location of the tear. The patient after injury should be placed prone with the leg flexed to 15°, at which time the examiner palpates for the tender area or defect. To aid palpation, patient is asked to flex against resistance and also to point with one finger to where he or she feels the pain.[41] The examiner palpates the musculature: A grade 2 or moderate strain usually does not have a palpable defect and manifests a larger area of pain than a grade 1 strain. A third-degree strain is a definite rupture, usually requiring crutches.

When the supine patient's limb is lifted by the heels, the hamstrings are considered tight if the knee flexes at less than

60° of hip flexion.[39] Common areas of hamstring tears are the proximal semitendinosus, about ½ in inferior to the pelvis, or the lateral side of the posterior thigh next to the lateral intermuscular septum. Sometimes a diagnostic problem arises in differentiating a lumbar sciatic posterior thigh involvement from a hamstring sciaticlike problem.

Puranen and Orava[42] discuss a hamstring syndrome that originated at the ischial tuberosity and referred pain to the posterior thigh. In most of their cases the pain began without trauma. There was pain during sitting, stretching of the posterior thigh, and fast running. Pain was seldom felt while the patient was running slowly or lying down. Of the 59 patients in the study, 23 had a history of previous hamstring tears. The investigators often found tautness of the hamstring muscle and tenderness at the ischial tuberosity. They differentiated this condition from ischiogluteal bursitis, which is painful at night and during rest. Although localized tautness and tenderness of the hamstrings might indicate the hamstring syndrome, a functional examination would be even clearer. Repetitive loading of resisted hamstring flexion or repetitive hip extension (see above, hip functional tests) with the leg extended 20° off the table would probably exacerbate the symptoms, as would passive hip flexion and attempted straightening of the leg at the knee. In the findings summarized above, there was positive straight leg raising in only two cases.[42]

Treatment: Grades 1 and 2 strains are treated alike[41]: Ice (applied for only up to 20 minutes; otherwise it may cause tissue damage), compression support, and elevation are the usual first conservative actions. Deep ice massage with the prone patient's leg off the table in muscle eccentric contraction is recommended. Modalities and high-speed isokinetic exercise are also helpful. Increasing painless stretching and strengthening exercise, especially to the particular hamstrings involved, is appropriate. Stretching should be done with the leg in internal rotation, external rotation, and neutral to stretch completely all the hamstring muscles. It is imperative to increase hamstring strength as well as stretching. Light friction massage may be done immediately but deep friction may be contraindicated over an organizing hematoma. The use of transverse friction massage is extremely important in the alignment of scar tissue along normal lines of force to prevent abnormal cross-linkage (see Chapter 12).

It is always important to examine all the related extremity and abdominal muscles for flexibility and strength. Cibulka et al[43] showed that manipulation of patients with sacroiliac dysfunction increased the peak torque in injured hamstring muscles compared to injured patients who were not manipulated. Muckle[44] states that hypomobility of the lower lumbar spinal segments is a cause of repetitive hamstring strains. Anterior pelvic tilt causing increased stretching of the hamstrings has been incriminated as a cause.[45]

Functional tests

1. Probable pain on resisted hip extension.

2. Probable pain on resisted knee flexion. Check all 3 positions: neutral, lateral and medial rotation.
3. Possible pain on passive straight leg raise or hip flexion.

Piriformis Syndrome

This is a rare condition in which a tightened or spastic piriformis muscle stresses the sciatic nerve, causing possible coccygeal, buttock, groin, low back, hip, and leg pain. Pace and Nagle[46] state that the belly of the muscle usually crosses over the sciatic nerve but that in 15% of the population the muscle has two bellies, with the nerve running through both or having two trunks interdigitating with the two bellies. These investigators state that the condition may be responsible for a female complaint of dyspareunia. They use a functional test for the piriformis by placing the hands on the lateral aspects of the patient's flexed knees and asking the patient to push the hands apart. They treat the condition by injecting the piriformis trigger point. There is usually tenderness in the sciatic notch between the greater trochanter and the ischium or superiorly a few inches below the posterior-superior iliac spine.

Treatment: Trigger point technique and TMS are helpful. Figure 6-24 demonstrates a stretching technique for the piriformis. The practitioner stretches the piriformis by flexing, adducting, and internally rotating the patient's hip by using the contract-and-relax technique.

Functional tests

1. Definite pain on resisted lateral hip rotation.
2. Probable pain on passive hip medial rotation and passive hip medial rotation with adduction.

Abdominal Muscle Strains

Almost all the muscles that originate or insert into the pelvis may be strained, including the rectus abdominis, the external

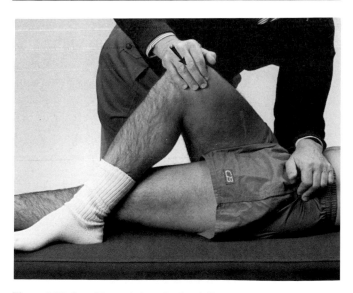

Figure 6-24 Stretching technique for the piriformis.

oblique, and the latissimus dorsi, the latter two of which attach to the iliac crest. There would be pain on bending to the opposite side of the pain. For example, a tennis player hitting an overhead stroke with the ball slightly behind him or her reaches back and snaps the body forward, thereby contracting the rectus and possibly tearing the muscle.[47] There would be abdominal pain on extension: The patient may present in a painful flexed position. Strain and contusion of the muscles attached to the iliac crest are referred to as a *hip pointer*. There may be swelling and ecchymosis at the iliac crest. Other causes may be contusions of the bone or periosteum of the crest.[48]

Treatment: Treatment is rest, support, and eventual abdominal muscle strengthening. Extension exercises to stretch the rectus abdominus are important. Friction to involved areas may aid a chronic problem. A ruptured muscle may require 4 to 6 weeks to heal because chronicity is common.

Abdominal Fascial Injuries

The patient may present with groin pain above the inguinal ligament due to chronic fascial strain.[34] This injury is usually seen in runners and may end up as a chronic problem that is difficult to treat.[34] Friction may be helpful.

Loose Bodies

Cyriax[21] describes this rather common condition, which may simulate a lumbar spinal condition, as a twingelike pain that may occur during walking and is felt on the anterior thigh from the groin to the knee. The pain may cause the leg to weaken suddenly and may last for several steps and recur weeks later. Often the patient is left with a chronic ache until the loose body is manipulated.

Treatment: Treatment consists of manipulation under traction (see Chapter 10).

Functional tests

1. Springy-block end feel instead of normal capsular feel on passive lateral rotation.
2. Rarely, similar end feel on passive flexion.

Osteitis Pubis

The etiology of this lesion is not always certain. It is considered an overuse phenomenon. Pubic pain may occur in athletes from overstressing of the rectus abdominis or adductors. The pain may be localized to the groin, lower abdomen, or pubes; there is usually localized tenderness over the pubes, adductors, or rectus abdominis. If the lesion is severe an adductor spasm may cause a waddling gait, or a clicking may

indicate instability.[19] Radiography may show bone resorption at the pubes and a widening of the pubes.[49] The condition is usually self-limited in a few months.

Treatment: Painless stretching and strengthening are performed as soon as the patient can tolerate it.

Functional tests

1. Definite pain on resisted hip adduction.
2. Definite pain on passive hip abduction.
3. Definite pain on passive hip flexion.

Avulsion Fractures

Although manual methods are not applicable to fractures we must be aware of the possibility of avulsion fractures, especially in hip and pelvic problems of adolescents. In the skeletally immature individual, growth plate injuries are more common than ligamentous or musculotendinous injuries.[50] A similar stress in an adult would probably result in a muscle strain rather than an avulsion.

Avulsion fractures are most common between the ages of 14 and 17 years. Severe muscle contraction or stretch is more common than actual trauma. Usually the bone is avulsed rather than the substance of the tendon. The most common areas of involvement are the anterior-superior spine (sartorius), anterior-inferior spine (rectus femoris), ischium (hamstrings), and iliac crest (abdominal muscles). Avulsion is rare at the abductor insertion of the greater trochanter.[50] Avulsion of the lesser trochanter may occur, creating acute hip or groin pain. Untreated patients may end up with flexion contractures, chronic pain, and extremity weakness.[51] Radiographs are usually positive, and comparison radiographs are advised. Patients may return to competition only after the fracture is completely healed with return of full strength and flexibility. In adolescents we must always rule out the possibilities of stress fractures, a slipped capital femoral epiphysis, and Legg-Calvé-Perthes disease.

According to Garrick and Webb[52] tendinitis type pain is relatively localized while stress fractures may refer to a variety of areas. For example, femoral stress fracture may refer to the adductor area one day and to the buttock the next day.

Treatment: Treatment consists of rest, ice, and eventual rehabilitation by means of friction, trigger point, TMS of shortened muscles, and strengthening of all associated muscles. Most avulsion fractures heal spontaneously with osseous union, and most of the occasional fibrous unions that occur are functional and asymptomatic. Surgical treatment is rarely indicated.[22]

Functional tests

1. Acute pain and weakness on resisted testing depending on the particular muscle.
2. Localized point tenderness.

REFERENCES

1. Saudek CE. In: Gould JA, Davies GJ, eds. *Orthopaedic and Sports Physical Therapy*. St Louis, Mo: Mosby; 1985:365–406.

2. Frankel VH, Nordin M. Biomechanics of the Hip. In: *Basic Biomechanics of the Skeletal System*. Philadelphia: Lea & Febiger; 1980.

3. Kessler RM, Hertling D. *Management of Common Musculoskeletal Disorders*. New York: Harper & Row; 1983.

4. Cailliet R. *Foot and Ankle Pain*. Philadelphia: Davis; 1968.

5. Halpern A, Tanner J, Rinsky L. Does persistent femoral anteversion contribute to osteoarthritis? *Clin Orthop*. 1979;145:213.

6. Mellion MB. *Sports Injuries and Athletic Problems*. St Louis, Mo: Mosby; 1988.

7. Kapandji IA. *The Physiology of the Joints*. New York: Churchill Livingstone; 1970;2.

8. Steindler A. *Kinesiology of the Human Body*. Springfield, Ill: Thomas; 1964.

9. Janda V. *Muscle Function Testing*. London: Butterworths; 1983.

10. Wallace LA. Limb length difference and back pain. In: Grieve GP, ed. *Modern Manual Therapy of the Vertebral Column*. New York: Churchill Livingstone; 1986.

11. Hoppenfeld S. *Physical Examination of the Spine and Extremities*. Norwalk, Conn: Appleton-Century-Crofts; 1976.

12. Kendall HO, Kendall FP, Wadsworth GE. *Muscle Testing and Function*. Baltimore: Williams & Wilkins; 1971.

13. Hoppenfeld S. *Orthopaedic Neurology, A Diagnostic Guide to Neurologic Levels*. Philadelphia: JB Lippincott; 1947.

14. Lippert FG, Teitz CC. *Diagnosing Musculoskeletal Problems*. Baltimore: Williams & Wilkins; 1987.

15. Sheon RP, Moskowitz RW, Goldberg VM. *Soft Tissue Rheumatic Pain: Recognition, Management, Prevention*. Philadelphia: Lea & Febiger; 1982.

16. Turek SL. *Orthopaedics: Principles and Their Application*. Philadelphia: Lippincott; 1984.

17. Ober FR. The role of the iliotibial band and fascia lata as a factor in the causation of low back disabilities and sciatica. *J Bone Joint Surg Am*. 1986;18:105.

18. Hungerford DS, Lennox DW. Rehabilitation of the knee and disorders of the patellofemoral joint: relevant biomechanics. *Orthop Clin North Am*. 1983;14:397.

19. Sim FH, Scott SG. Injuries of the pelvis and hip in athletes: anatomy and function. In: Nicholas JA, Hershman EB, eds. *The Lower Extremity and Spine in Sports Medicine*. St Louis, Mo: Mosby; 1986;2:1130–1131.

20. Harris WH. Etiology of osteoarthritis of the hip. *Clin Orthop Relat Res*. 1988;213:20–38.

21. Cyriax J. *Textbook of Orthopaedic Medicine*. 8th ed. London: Bailliere Tindall; 1982;1.

22. Medoff RJ. Injuries to the hip in athletes. *Ann Sports Med*. 1987;3:73–76.

23. Schapira D, Nahir M, Scharf Y. Trochanteric bursitis: a common clinical problem. *Arch Phys Med Rehabil*. 1986;67:815.

24. Swezey RL. Pseudo-radiculopathy in subacute trochanteric bursitis of the subgluteus maximus bursa. *Arch Phys Med Rehabil*. 1976;57:387.

25. Lindenberg G, Pinshaw R, Noakes TD. Iliotibial band friction syndrome in runners. *Phys Sports Med*. 1984;12:118–130.

26. Kulund DN. *The Injured Athlete*. 2nd ed. Philadelphia: Lippincott; 1988.

27. American Academy of Orthopaedic Surgeons. *Athletic Training and Sports Medicine*. Chicago: American Academy of Orthopaedic Surgeons; 1985.

28. Gray H, Goss CM. *Anatomy of the Human Body*. Philadelphia: Lea & Febiger; 1954.

29. Magee DJ. *Orthopedic Physical Assessment*. Philadelphia: Saunders; 1987.

30. Corrigan B, Maitland GD. *Practical Orthopaedic Medicine*. Stoneham, Mass: Butterworth; 1983.

31. Swartout R, Compere EL. Ischiogluteal bursitis, the pain in the arse. *JAMA*. 1974;227:551–552.

32. Zarins B, Ciullo JV. Acute muscle and tendon injuries in athletes. *Clin Sports Med*. 1983;2:167.

33. Garrett WE. Basic science of musculotendinous injuries. In: Nicholas JA, Hershman EB, eds. *The Lower Extremity and Spine in Sports Medicine*. St Louis, Mo: Mosby; 1986;2:52–53.

34. Brody DM. Running injuries. In: Nicholas JA, Hershman EB, eds. *The Lower Extremity and Spine in Sports Medicine*. St Louis, Mo: Mosby; 1986;2:1534–1579.

35. Teitz CC. *Scientific Foundations of Sports Medicine*. Philadelphia: Decker; 1989.

36. O'Donoghue DH. *Treatment of Injuries to Athletes*. 3rd ed. Philadelphia: Saunders; 1976.

37. Coole WG, Gieck JH. An analysis of hamstring strains and their rehabilitation. *J Orthop Sports Phys Ther*. 1987;9:77–85.

38. Klafs CE, Arnheim DD. *Modern Principles of Athletic Training*. 4th ed. Baltimore: Williams & Wilkins; 1971.

39. Fox JM. Injuries to the thigh. In: Nicholas JA, Hershman EB, eds. *The Lower Extremity and Spine in Sports Medicine*. St Louis, Mo: Mosby; 1986;2:1087–1117.

40. Burkett LN. Causative factors in hamstring strains. *Med Sci Sports*. 1970;2:39–42.

41. Reese RC, Burruss TP. Athletic training techniques and protective equipment. In: Nicholas JA, Hershman EB, eds. *The Lower Extremity and Spine in Sports Medicine*. St Louis, Mo: Mosby; 1986;2:319–320.

42. Puranen J, Orava S. The hamstring syndrome: a new diagnosis of gluteal sciatic pain. *Am J Sports Med*. 1988;16:517–521.

43. Cibulka MT, Rose SJ, Delitto A, et al. Hamstring muscle strain treated by mobilizing the sacroiliac joint. *Phys Ther*. 1986;66:1220–1223.

44. Muckle DS. Associated factors in recurrent groin and hamstring injuries. *Br J Sports Med*. 1982;16:37–39.

45. Klein KK, Roberts CA. Mechanical problems of marathoners and joggers and solution. In: Landry F, et al, eds. *Sports Medicine*. Miami, Fla: Symposia Specialists; 1976:210.

46. Pace JB, Nagle D. Piriform syndrome. *West J Med*. 1976;124:435–439.

47. Schneider RC, Kennedy JC, Plant ML, et al. *Sports Injuries: Mechanisms, Prevention, and Treatment*. Baltimore: Williams & Wilkins; 1985.

48. Xethalis JL, Boliardo RA. Soccer injuries. In: Nicholas JA, Hershman EB, eds. *The Lower Extremity and Spine in Sports Medicine*. St Louis, Mo: Mosby; 1986;2:1590.

49. Harris NH, Murray RO. Lesions of the symphysis in athletes. *Br Med J*. 1974;4:211.

50. Waters PM, Millis MB. Hip and pelvic injuries in the young athlete. *Clin Sports Med*. 1988;7:513–517.

51. Nicholas JA. Football injuries. In: Nicholas JA, Hershman EB, eds. *The Lower Extremity and Spine in Sports Medicine*. St Louis, Mo: Mosby; 1986;2:1493.

52. Garrick JG, Webb DR. *Sports Injuries and Diagnosis and Management*. Philadelphia: WB Saunders; 1990:175–196.

Appendix 6-A

Hip Functional Diagnosis Chart

Table 6-A-1 Hip Functional Diagnosis

KEY + Pain +/− Possible Pain L Possible Limited ROM TESTS	Osteoarthritis	Trochanteric Bursitis	Iliopectineal & Iliopsoas Bursitis	Ischiogluteal Bursitis	Adductor Tendinitis	Gluteus Medius Tendinitis	Upper Rectus Tendinitis	Iliopsoas Tendinitis	Upper Hamstring Tendinitis	Piriformis Syndrome	Loose Bodies	Osteitis Pubis
Passive Flexion (140°)	L+/−	+/−(1)	+	+/−			+/−	+/−(1)	+/−L		Springy Block +/−	+
Passive Extension (30°)	L+/−	+/−	+/−				+/−	+/−				
Passive Abduction (50°)	L+/−	+/−			+/−							+
Passive Adduction (30°)	+/−	+/−				+/−						
Passive Medial Rotation (40°)	L+/−	+/−	+/−			+/−	+/−			+/−		
Passive Lateral Rotation (60°)		+/−	+/−			+/−	+/−				Springy Block +/−	
Resisted Flexion			+					+				
Resisted Extension		+/−		+					+			
Resisted Adduction					+							+
Resisted Abduction		+/−				+						
Resisted Medial Rotation		+/−										
Resisted Lateral Rotation		+/−								+		
Resisted Knee Extension							+					
Resisted Knee Flexion				+/−					+			

Joint Play Evaluation
(1) passive flexion with adduction.

Chapter 7

The Knee

Warren I. Hammer

Injuries involving the knee receive more attention than any other injuries associated with athletics,[1] and pathology related to the patella is the most frequent single cause of knee pain seen in orthopedic offices.[2] Diffuse anterior thigh and knee pain may be referred from the hip or spine, but patients with knee problems usually localize the knee itself as the source. Posterior knee pain is often related to patellofemoral pathology. Specific knee pain coupled with diffuse thigh pain may also be due to Legg-Calvé-Perthes disease (ages 3 to 12 years; peak age, 6 years) or a slipped capital femoral epiphysis (ages 10 to 15 years), an occult hip fracture, neoplasm, an arthritic hip, or a herniated lumbar disc. Because of the knee's location all structural and functional abnormalities above and below it must be considered, such as spinal mechanics, foot mechanics, leg length, tibial rotation, femoral rotation, genu varum and valgum, patella alta, patella baja, muscle balance, and flexibility, to name a few.

FUNCTIONAL ANATOMY AND PERTINENT BIOMECHANICS

The knee is composed of two joints: the tibiofemoral and the patellofemoral. Kapandji[3] mentions two degrees of freedom for the tibiofemoral joint: flexion and extension in the sagittal plane and rotation in the transverse plane. Grood and Noyes[4] describe the knee as having, in three dimensions, six degrees of freedom, like the human spine: three rotations expressed as flexion-extension, abduction-adduction, and internal-external, and three translations expressed as compression-distraction, medial-lateral, and anterior-posterior. They use this

system to be more specific in their manual stress tests for single or coupled motions when testing for ligamentous laxity (see functional tests).

Tibiofemoral Joint

Knee Flexion

The range of motion in flexion varies greatly among people and is usually greater in women and children (active, to 140°; passive, to 160°). The range of knee flexion is related to the position of the hip. With a flexed hip the hamstrings are stretched, and their efficiency as knee flexors increases; active knee flexion decreases to 120° if the hip is extended, although with a powerful hamstring flexion during hip extension a "follow-through" effect occurs that results in increased range because of passive knee flexion at the end of the active knee flexion.[3] Passive knee flexion should allow the heel to reach the buttock unless there is shortening of the quadriceps or knee capsular ligaments. Flexion is mostly limited by the anterior and posterior cruciates and also by the posterior horns of the menisci and the passive quadriceps.[5] During the middle of the swing phase of gait, maximum knee flexion (75°) occurs.[6]

Knee Extension

Full extension is 0°, but passive extension may be considered normal at a positive extension of 5° to 10°. As the hip extends, the rectus femoris becomes more efficient in knee extension.[3] Extension is limited by the anterior and posterior cruciates, the posterior joint capsule, the anterior horns of the menisci, and the passive hamstrings.[5] The knee never fully extends during gait; full extension (5° flexion) occurs at the beginning of the stance phase at heel strike and just before toe-off.[6]

The screw-home mechanism (Fig. 7-1) must be included with knee extension. Normally the tibia externally rotates 20° on a fixed femur during the last 20° of both passive and active knee extension. It is an involuntary mechanical event. As a person rises from a chair, the femur internally rotates on the fixed tibia.[7] The main reason for this mechanism is that the medial femoral condyle is about 1.7 cm longer than the lateral condyle, so that during knee extension the tibia descends and then ascends along the curves of the medial femoral condyle and simultaneously rotates externally. This motion reverses in early knee flexion. This spiral or helicoid motion gives more stability than a simple hinge joint would; the knee is not considered a simple hinge joint.[6] This stability of terminal rotation allows us to stand erect without quadriceps contraction and to withstand anterior-posterior forces on an extended knee.[7] Of course, associated with the length change of the condyles is muscular rotation and ligamentous guidance (of the cruciates), which are also necessary for the terminal external rotation.

Helfet's test (seldom used) can be employed to analyze this important mechanism. The patient is seated with the knee flexed 90°. A line is drawn on the middle of the patella and over the tibial tuberosity. With full knee extension the tibial tuberosity should externally rotate to about the lateral half of the patella. Failure to do so may indicate abnormal

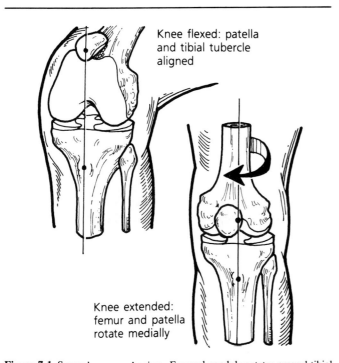

Figure 7-1 Screw-home mechanism. Femoral condyle rotates around tibial spine. *Source*: Reprinted from *Athletic Training and Sports Medicine* (p 281) by AE Ellison et al. (Eds) with permission of the American Academy of Orthopaedic Surgeons, © 1984.

tibiofemoral compression due to a loose body, possible chronic anterior cruciate ligament injury, or degenerative menisci tear creating limitation of movement with catching, grinding, and pain over the medial joint line.[5]

Medial and Lateral Rotation

Both medial and lateral rotation are almost completely limited in knee extension. Both gradually increase up to 90° of knee flexion and then progressively decrease. External rotation at 90° knee flexion reaches 40° to 45°, and internal rotation at 90° knee flexion reaches 30°. Tibial internal rotation is restricted by the anterior cruciates' rotating on the posterior cruciates, the lateral collateral ligament, the posterolateral joint capsule, the arcuate complex, and the menisci.[5] Tibial external rotation is limited mostly by the medial collateral ligament, the posteromedial joint capsule, and the menisci.[5]

Abduction-Adduction

Abduction-adduction is 0° at extension. Both increase a few degrees, with a maximum movement at 30° knee flexion, and then progressively decrease,[6] which is why varus and valgus testing is performed at 30°. The posterior cruciate ligament is the major stabilizer of the tibiofemoral joint in full extension and is most relaxed at 30° flexion. Adduction is limited mostly by the lateral collateral ligament, posterolateral joint capsule, and arcuate complex and secondarily by the anterior and posterior cruciate ligaments and the medial meniscus.[5] Abduction is limited mostly by the medial collateral ligament and the posteromedial joint capsule and secondarily by the anterior and posterior cruciate ligaments and lateral meniscus.[5] These limiting tissues are the ones usually traumatized either singly or in combination when the above motions are overstressed.

Patellofemoral Joint

During knee flexion (ie, as the tibia moves on the femur), the patella moves downward over a distance equal to twice its length, 8 cm,[3] on the femoral condyles. Over 90° of knee flexion the patella also rotates externally.[6] If the femur moves on a fixed tibia the femoral condyles slide on the patella.[7] At full flexion the patella lies in the intercondylar groove. During knee extension only the lower part of the patella is in contact with the femur, and with knee flexion the upper part of the patella comes into greater contact with the femur. This increased contact helps compensate for the increase in patellofemoral compression during flexion[6] and helps distribute patella compressive force more uniformly.

The patella is the largest sesamoid bone in the body and is located in the tendon of the quadriceps. It has two important biomechanical functions[6]:

1. It lengthens the lever arm of the quadriceps muscle force by displacing the quadriceps anteriorly throughout the

range of motion. By increasing the quadriceps angle of pull on the tibia, the lever arm extension force is increased by about 30% (Fig. 7-2).

2. It increases the area of contact between the patella tendon and the femur, thereby allowing a wider distribution of compressive stress on the femur as it transmits the quadriceps force to the tibia.

As extension increases past 45° the lever arm decreases, and the quadriceps muscle must increase its force by about 60% for the last 15° of extension. At full knee extension the patella is above the femoral condyles over the fat pad of the suprapatellar pouch.

Important features maintaining the patella in the femoral groove during movement are the height of the medial and lateral femoral condyles, the muscular balance between the transverse and oblique fibers of the vastus medialis and lateralis muscles, the medial and lateral patella retinacula, and the iliotibial tract.[8] Knee flexion (90°) increases the patellofemoral joint reaction force (compression of the patella against the femur) to 2.5 to 3 times body weight or to 3.3 times body weight in climbing and descending steps, even though the quadriceps tendon force remains constant.[6,9] From 30° to extension (0°) the patellofemoral joint reaction force decreases. Therefore, in terminal knee extension the quadriceps force increases while there is a decrease in patellofemoral contact area and force, but throughout the knee bend the patellofemoral joint reaction force remains higher than the quadriceps muscle force up to 90°.[6]

Clinical: This explains why deep knee bends and maximal full range of motion knee flexion to extension exercises, especially in anterior cruciate ligament and patellofemoral problems, should be used with caution. During normal use, compression of the patella on the femur occurs with the knee loaded from above, but in exercise programs the knee is loaded distally. Extending a flexed knee between 60° and 20° with

free weights below the knee creates maximum patellofemoral forces (especially at 40° to 30°) and is not recommended.[10]

If patellofemoral problems exist, exercise for the quadriceps should be performed either as isometric quadriceps sets, as straight leg raises, or with the knee in terminal extension from 20° to 0° ("short-arc quad exercise"). Another reason for terminal exercises is that degeneration (arthritis) of the patella often occurs in the midpatellar region that contacts the femur between 30° to 45° of knee flexion. Hughston[11] states that a good physiologic exercise for increasing quadriceps strength (as long as the patellofemoral joint is normal and nonpainful) is climbing hills or stairs because the extensor mechanism is an extensor of the femur on the fixed tibia. He feels that increasing extensor mechanism strength by extending the tibia on the fixed femur is erroneous.

Anterior Knee

The anterior knee (Figs. 7-3 and 7-4) is composed primarily of the quadriceps insertions, the medial and lateral fibrous patellar retinacula, and the patella and patellar tendon. The main functions of the extensor mechanism are both to stabilize and to effect a momentum change (deceleration) on the tibiofemoral joint in various knee-joint positions[12] and to decompress the patellofemoral joint (E Rashkoff, personal communication, 1989). During gait the main function of the quadriceps is to prevent collapse of the flexing knee from heel-strike to midstance.[13] Of the four quadriceps, only the rectus femoris affects two joints. It acts as a weak hip flexor and

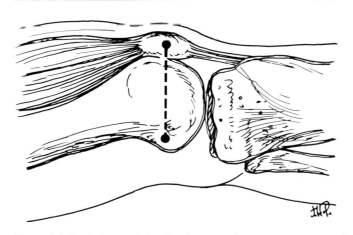

Figure 7-2 Patellofemoral joint. Patella acts to increase moment arm of quadriceps tendon by displacing tendon away from center of knee rotation. *Source:* Reprinted with permission from M Post, *Physical Examination of the Musculoskeletal System* (p 244), Chicago, Year Book Medical Publishers, 1987.

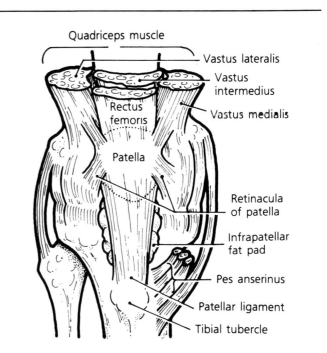

Figure 7-3 Anterior knee musculature. *Source:* Reprinted from *Athletic Training and Sports Medicine* (p 237) by AE Ellison et al. (Eds) with permission of the American Academy of Orthopaedic Surgeons, © 1984.

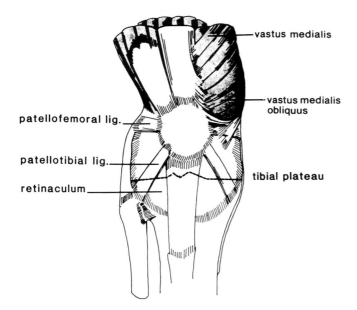

Figure 7-4 Anterior aspect of the knee. The medial and lateral patellotibial ligaments are oblique condensations of the retinacula. *Source*: Reprinted from *Patellar Subluxation and Dislocation* by JC Hughston, WM Walsh, and G Puddu with permission of W.B. Saunders Company, © 1984.

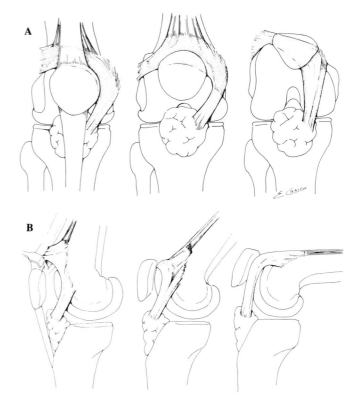

Figure 7-5 Anatomy and location of the suprapatellar plica. Note the articularis genu muscle, which inserts on the superior portion of the plica. *Source*: Reprinted with permission from *Clinics in Sports Medicine* (1989;8[2]:188), Copyright © 1989, W.B. Saunders Company.

cannot by itself produce full extension of the knee.[3] Overall the quadriceps work in concert.

The quadriceps femoris is three times stronger than the flexors because it must counteract the effect of gravity.[3] The vastus medialis and lateralis help form the fibrous retinaculum, which can extend the knee joint when the patellar tendon is ruptured.[2] The rectus intermedius forms the deep layer of the quadriceps, inserting into the proximal patella, and this deep layer is continued where the patellar tendon originates at the distal patella. In the deep layer are medial and lateral patellofemoral and patellotibial ligaments, which appear to be transverse condensations of the medial and lateral retinacula. The intermediate layer is formed by the vastus medialis, vastus lateralis, and rectus femoris; it inserts on the proximal patella and continues distally as tendinous expansions over the anterior patella, becoming part of the patellar tendon and inserting on the tibial tuberosity.[12]

An extension of the vastus medialis (not a separate muscle) is the vastus medialis obliquus (VMO), which inserts into the medial patella at a 55° angle. This muscle functions as the primary medial stabilizer of the patella (it does not function as an extensor) and is often incriminated as a cause of patellofemoral malalignment when it is dysplastic or atrophied. This is revealed when a large dimple appears along the proximal medial patella as the sitting patient extends the knee 45°. Rehabilitation for patellofemoral pain is often directed toward the VMO. Normally the VMO inserts a third or half the way down the medial patella. The lower it inserts, the more stability it provides; the higher it inserts, the less stability it provides.

The plica (Fig. 7-5) represents a vestigial redundant fold of the synovial lining of the knee joint that did not normally resorb during fetal development. It may be normally palpable from the medial infrapatellar fat pad around the medial femoral condyle. It then extends under the quadriceps tendon to the lateral retinaculum.[14] It may become inflamed and fibrotic if injured. Of the three plicae (folds) of the knee, the mediopatellar plica is the most significant. (See below, Plica Syndrome and Chapter 12.)

Medial Knee

In the medial knee (Figs. 7-6 and 7-7) the superficial medial collateral ligament, known as the tibial collateral ligament,[15] originates from the medial epicondyle of the femur just below the adductor tubercle and inserts on the medial tibia 3 to 4 in below the joint line, posterior and deep to the pes anserinus. The ligament lies slightly posterior to the midline (this is important for friction positioning). The ligament itself is not distinctly palpable,[16] although in a thin individual with a normal medial collateral ligament the anterior fibers might be palpable at the joint line.[17] The anterior parallel fibers of the ligament tighten on flexion and relax on extension; the posterior oblique fibers do the opposite (Fig. 7-8). Three functions of the superficial medial collateral ligament are [13]:

1. it is the chief restraint against valgus deformity;
2. it prevents external rotation of the tibia on the femur; and

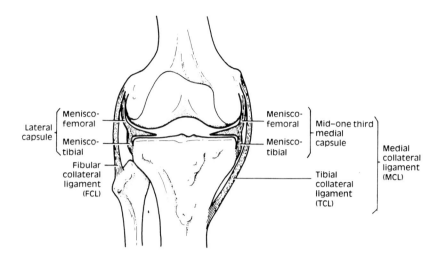

Figure 7-6 Medial aspect of the knee. The tibial collateral ligament originates on the medial epicondyle and inserts on the medial tibia 8 cm below the joint line. The mid–one-third medial capsule originates on the medial epicondyle and inserts on the tibia near the joint line. Functionally (but not anatomically) they are referred to collectively as the medial collateral ligament. The fibular collateral ligament originates on the lateral epicondyle and inserts on the head of the fibula. It overlies the posterior third lateral capsule. *Source*: Reprinted with permission from JA Nicholas and EB Hershman, *The Lower Extremity and Spine in Sports Medicine* (p 935), St. Louis, 1986, The C.V. Mosby Co.

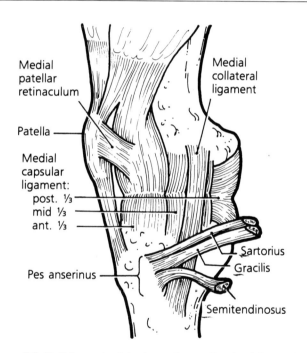

Figure 7-7 Medial aspect of the knee. *Source*: Reprinted from *Athletic Training and Sports Medicine*, (p 238) by AE Ellison et al. (Eds) with permission of the American Academy of Orthopaedic Surgeons, © 1984.

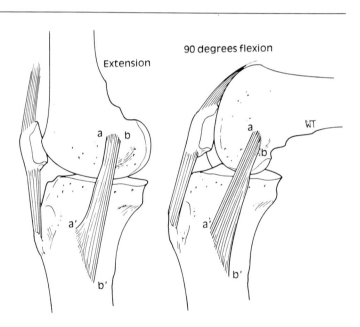

Figure 7-8 Effect of joint motion on superficial medial collateral ligament. During flexion, knee tightens a-a'; conversely, during extension b-b' tightens. *Source*: Reprinted with permission from JA Nicholas and EB Hershman, *The Lower Extremity and Spine in Sports Medicine* (p 663), St. Louis, 1986, The C.V. Mosby Co.

3. it helps as a secondary restraint to anterior tibial translation if the anterior cruciate ligament is absent.

The deep portion of the medial collateral ligament, also known as the mid–one-third medial capsule,[15] is a thickening of the joint capsule and blends with the medial meniscus. It originates on the medial epicondyle and inserts on the tibia near the joint line. Because the lateral knee is more exposed and more often struck, the medial ligament is injured more often than any other ligament of the knee.[18] The lateral meniscus moves more than the medial meniscus, and the lateral collateral ligament is not firmly attached to the lateral meniscus; both result in the ability to withstand more movement stress than the medial side.

Pes Anserinus

The pes anserinus represents the insertion area of three important medial muscles that make up the medial wall of the popliteal fossa and resist valgus stress. The most posterior and lateral is the firm tendon of the semitendinosus, which lies over the semimembranosus. Next is the gracilis, which is anterior and medial to the semitendinosus. Finally, the sartorius is more superficial and has a broader insertion site compared to the other two muscles. The gracilis and semitendinosus are distinct tendons passing over the anterior medial collateral ligament to insert into the anteromedial tibia 2 in

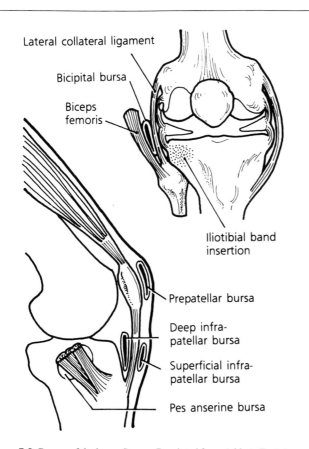

Figure 7-9 Bursae of the knee. *Source:* Reprinted from *Athletic Training and Sports Medicine,* (p 286) by AE Ellison et al. (Eds) with permission of the American Academy of Orthopaedic Surgeons, © 1984.

below the knee joint, medial to the tibial tuberosity. These muscles become more obvious if the patient flexes and internally rotates the tibia against resistance. There is a bursa located at the insertion site of the pes anserinus (Fig. 7-9).

Menisci

The menisci are attached to the tibia, and the periphery of the menisci is attached by the meniscotibial or coronary (deep capsular tissue) ligaments to the tibial plateau. The menisci move posteriorly during flexion and anteriorly during extension. During rotation the menisci follow exactly the displacements of the femoral condyles[3]; that is, they move with the femur (Fig. 7-10). Therefore, when the tibia is internally rotated the medial meniscus moves anteriorly as a result of tautness of the meniscopatellar fibers while the lateral meniscus recedes. The meniscopatellar fibers become taut because during the internal rotation, the femur rotates laterally relative to the tibia dragging the patella laterally. The medial edge of the meniscus can become palpable and it will only palpate painful if it is injured. With the knee flexed 90° and the tibia rotated medially without any accompanying muscle spasm, a torn medial meniscus might be palpated. If on lateral tibial rotation the medial meniscus can still be palpated, the torn meniscus may be preventing the tibia from laterally rotating. Although this test demonstrates the mechanics of meniscal motion, it cannot be considered reliable for assessing meniscal integrity.

The fact that the menisci move anteriorly with extension and posteriorly with flexion is the basis for Steinmann's test to differentiate a meniscus from a collateral ligament lesion. The patient is supine with the knee flexed. The examiner pinpoints the area of localized joint line tenderness and flexes and extends the knee. If a meniscus lesion exists the localized tenderness will disappear, but if a collateral ligament is involved the pinpoint tenderness will remain localized during flexion and extension. The medial coronary ligaments are made taut and therefore are best palpated on the tibial plateau when the tibia is externally rotated.

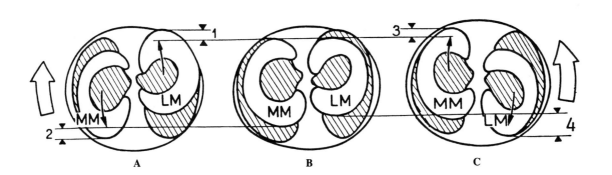

Figure 7-10 Knee menisci. The medial meniscus (MM) and the lateral meniscus (LM) follow exactly the displacements of the femoral condyles. The shaded areas represent the tibia. (**A**) represents lateral tibial rotation causing lateral meniscus to be pulled anteriorly (1) and the medial meniscus to recede (2). (**B**) represents the neutral position. (**C**) represents medial tibial rotation causing the medial meniscus to move forward while the lateral meniscus recedes. *Source:* Reprinted from *The Physiology of the Joints, Vol. 2* (p 101) by IA Kapandji with permission of Churchill Livingstone, © 1970.

Lateral Knee

Iliotibial Band

The iliotibial band (Fig. 7-11) is a stretched ligament,[19] that is to say a thick fascial band of tissue that originates as part of the insertion of the tensor fasciae latae and gluteus maximus (see Chapter 6, Ober's Sign and Trochanteric Bursitis) to insert into the lateral tubercle of the tibia (Gerdy's tubercle), supracondylar tubercle, patella, and patellar tendon. This band provides anterolateral stability to the tibia and provides a restraint to medial subluxation of the patella.[20] The iliotibial band moves posteriorly with knee flexion and anteriorly with knee extension, shifting over the lateral femoral epicondyle at about 30° of knee flexion (see below, Iliotibial Band Friction Syndrome and Pivot-Shift Test). It is free of bone attachments between the lateral femoral condyle and the tibial tuberosity.[21] It can be palpated with the knee extended and the leg raised, against resistance with the knee flexed and the heel pressing into the floor,[16] or by adducting the hip and flexing the knee 20°.

Lateral Collateral Ligament

The lateral collateral ligament (Figs. 7-6, 7-12, and 7-13) attaches from the femoral epicondyle to the head of the fibula, lying in the posterior third of the joint. It is a hard cord that is easily palpable in the figure-four (leg crossed over the thigh) position. It is not attached to the lateral meniscus or capsule. In selective cutting experiments the popliteus muscle prevents more varus opening than the lateral collateral ligament.[13]

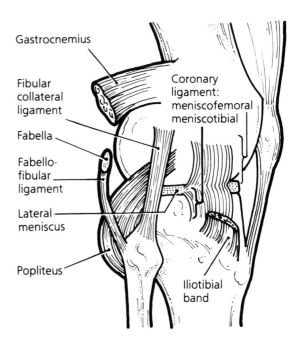

Figure 7-12 Lateral ligament complex. *Source*: Reprinted from *Athletic Training and Sports Medicine* (p 240) by AE Ellison et al. (Eds) with permission of the American Academy of Orthopaedic Surgeons, © 1984.

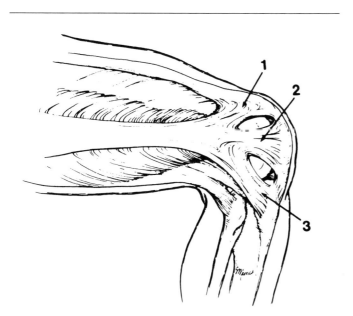

Figure 7-11 Illustration of the insertion areas of the iliotibial band: fibers blending with intermuscular septum and onto the supracondylar tubercle (1), patella and patellar tendon (2), and Gerdy's tubercle (3). *Source*: Reprinted with permission from *Journal of Orthopaedic and Sports Physical Therapy* (1989;11[1]:12), Copyright © 1989, American Orthopaedic Foot Society.

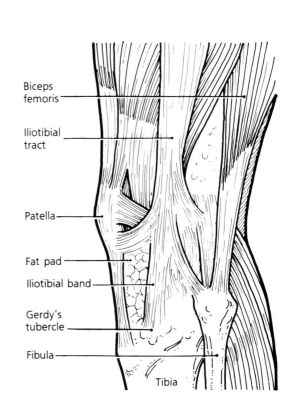

Figure 7-13 Lateral knee musculature. *Source*: Reprinted from *Athletic Training and Sports Medicine* (p 239) by AE Ellison et al. (Eds) with permission of the American Academy of Orthopaedic Surgeons, © 1984.

Popliteus Muscle

The popliteus arises on the lateral surface of the femoral condyle and passes beneath the lateral collateral ligament, attaching to the lateral meniscus and inserting on the posterior surface of the tibia. It flexes and rotates the leg medially. During weight bearing, early in knee flexion it may rotate the femur and lateral meniscus laterally[22] and stabilizes the femur against internal rotation. At the beginning of knee flexion from full knee extension, it unlocks the knee joint by rotating the tibia medially on the femur. In a crouched position with the knees bent it is continuously active.[22] It helps, along with the posterior cruciate ligament, to retard forward displacement of the femur on the flexed tibia during the stance phase of gait and prevents the posterior horn of the lateral meniscus from moving forward. A bursa separates it from the lateral collateral ligament[23] (see below, Popliteus Tendon Tenosynovitis).

Biceps Femoris

The biceps femoris can also be considered a posterior structure, but its insertional area usually presents lateral knee pain. The long head joins the short head, forming a conjoined tendon 3 to 4 in proximal to the fibula head. A theory of excessive hamstring pull (strain) is based on the dual innervation of the biceps: The long head is innervated by the tibial nerve, and the short head is innervated by the peroneal nerve; therefore the short head of the biceps may contract at the same time as the quadriceps.[24]

The conjoined tendon inserts into the styloid of the fibula and then on to Gerdy's tubercle, courses over the proximal tibia, and encircles the distal lateral collateral ligament.[13] Its function is to aid in knee flexion while at the same time keeping the lateral collateral ligament tight. It also externally rotates the tibia.[13]

Lateral Meniscus

Because the lateral meniscus is attached to the popliteus and is more mobile than the medial meniscus, and because the lateral coronary ligaments are more lax than the medial coronary ligaments, injury to the lateral meniscus and lateral coronary ligaments is less common.

Posterior Knee

The popliteal area is surrounded superiorly and medially by the semimembranosus and semitendinosus muscle-tendon, superiorly and laterally by the biceps femoris, and inferiorly by the two heads of the gastrocnemius muscle. The semimembranosus muscle has four tendinous insertions[25]: a major insertion into the posterior medial tibial condyle and fibers to the medial capsule, popliteal capsule, and posterior horn of the medial meniscus. Its function is to perform knee flexion and tibial internal rotation while pulling the meniscus backward

and stabilizing the posterior capsule and posteromedial corner.[13]

The triceps surae is composed of the gastrocnemius and soleus, which both insert into a common tendon that inserts into the calcaneus. The gastrocnemius originates from the posterior condyles and the capsule of the femur, and the soleus originates from the head and upper third of the body of the fibula and the soleus popliteal line on the tibia.[22] The medial head of the gastrocnemius is more frequently injured than the lateral. Waller[26] states that the gastrocnemius-soleus complex functions during 20% to 50% of the stance phase of gait. The calf muscles stop activity before roll-off and are not used for push-off during walking or running. The ankle is the major joint affected by the complex, which acts eccentrically during the first phase of stance and then isometrically as the heel rises off the floor and the toes undergo passive dorsiflexion. Because the triceps surae works mainly by eccentric contraction, prestretching is essential before use. Waller[26] further states that the main function of the gastrocnemius-soleus complex is to stabilize the leg by restraining forward motion of the tibia during the stance phase of gait. This allows the leg to act as a solid support for the body as it propels itself forward (see below, Gastrocnemius-Soleus Strain).

Cruciate Ligaments

Anterior Cruciate Ligament

The anterior cruciate ligament prevents excessive anterior movement of the tibia on the femur and abnormal tibial internal and external rotation,[27] although recent studies in vitro indicate that under clinically applied loads rotation of the tibia is not constrained by the anterior cruciate ligament[28,29] and that the excess rotation may be due to deficiencies of the collateral ligaments, iliotibial band, and capsular restraints instead of this ligament. A recent study[29] showed no increase in tibial internal rotation after sectioning of the anterior cruciate ligament in intact cadaver knees. This ligament limits hyperextension because it is forced against the intercondylar shelf. It also guides the knee through its arc of motion, allowing other ligaments of the knee to tighten and thereby protecting the menisci from excessive force[27]; this is a reason why the menisci are vulnerable after a tear of this ligament.

The anterior cruciate ligament not only acts as a static check-rein and guide to knee motion but is considered an important proprioceptive sensor in the knee.[30] One of its main functions is to perform the screw-home mechanism; any force against this mechanism will tear the ligament, as in internal femoral rotation on a flexed knee or, less commonly, external tibial rotation associated with a valgus force.[14]

The ligament acts as a secondary stabilizer to varus and valgus stress. It was thought to be divided into anteromedial, intermediate, and posterolateral fascicles, with a different portion of the ligament being taut throughout the range of motion,[31] but transverse microscopic sections of the ligament have shown no evidence of separate anatomic bundles.[32] It is thought, however, that a functional arrangement of anteromedial and larger posterolateral bundles does exist.[33] The anteromedial fibers are more taut in flexion, resisting anterior translation of the tibia, and the posterolateral and intermediate fascicles are more taut in knee extension, probably resisting hyperextension.[34]

Posterior Cruciate Ligament

The main function of the posterior cruciate ligament is to prevent excessive posterior displacement of the tibia on the femur or forward displacement of the femur on the tibia; it also prevents hyperflexion. This ligament is responsible for 90% of the resistance to posterior (tibial) displacement with the knee in 90° of flexion. It is maximally taut in full flexion[35] and extension. Hyperflexion of the knee is the most common mechanism of injury; this is also known as "dashboard injury."

KNEE EXAMINATION

Inspection

While performing a knee examination, we must be aware of both the tibiofemoral and the patellofemoral joints. Some functional tests are specific for one joint, and some may overlap. Patients with patellofemoral disorders may present with tibiofemoral symptoms of ligamentous laxity, meniscal problems, loose bodies, and plica involvement, so that a separate examination of the patellofemoral joint must be included. After a case history is taken, inspection and observation of the knees should include the following:

1. *Skin surface:* Scarring (previous operations), amount of hair (vascular status), mottling associated with pain and decreased skin temperature (reflex sympathetic dystrophy), skin atrophy due to use of systemic steroids should also be sought.[36]
2. *Swelling:* There may be loss of normal concavity adjacent to the medial patella tendon with the patient sitting, or a prone patient may exhibit popliteal cyst or aneurysm. The examination must distinguish between a joint (intra-articular) effusion and extra-articular soft tissue swelling, the latter of which includes overuse syndromes. Knee joint (intra-articular) effusion is usually diffuse, symmetric, and associated with a loss of knee contour, although the joint effusion may be minimal and may be distinguished by pushing the suprapatellar pouch. The patella is usually palpable. A major joint effusion will allow the patella to rebound after the patella is pushed anterior to posterior on an extended knee, and a minor joint effusion will show up if the examiner pushes the suprapatellar pouch inferiorly and then presses medially on the lateral side of the patella on an extended knee; this will cause swelling to

appear on the medial side.[16] If the intra-articular swelling is due to a synovitis, it will feel soft and will not elicit a fluid wave (as will a moderate to large intra-articular effusion).

Extra-articular swelling is usually localized, as in a prepatellar bursitis, a septic prepatellar bursitis, or a meniscal cyst.[37] Extra-articular swelling due to medial collateral ligament sprain is localized to the medial side of the knee; early ecchymosis may indicate lateral collateral sprain which seldom presents with swelling (E Rashkoff, personal communication, 1989). Periarticular prominences and associated fullness may be osteophytes.[36] The semimembranosus bursa between the semimembranosus and gastrocnemius tendon is extra-articular; when swollen, it is called Baker's cyst. Because this bursa often communicates with the knee joint, if it is swollen there may be intra-articular pathology such as a torn meniscus or arthritis (E Rashkoff, personal communication, 1989).

A tense effusion that occurs within 4 to 24 hours of a significant injury (hemarthrosis) is 80% of the time an anterior cruciate ligament tear. A patellar dislocation is also a significant cause of an acute knee effusion.[38,39] Severe patellar subluxations or osteochondral fractures are also causes of early effusion. Swelling that occurs 24 hours after injury or later is usually due to inflammatory fluid rather than blood.[40] In the adolescent swelling may be due to an epiphyseal fracture.[38] The cruciates are highly vascular and bleed profusely when injured.[2] An isolated collateral ligament sprain (grade 1 to 2) usually shows slight to sometimes moderate swelling, whereas a torn meniscus, even though it is supposed to have a poor blood supply, may present with substantial swelling.

The amount of swelling in a knee is not necessarily related to the severity of the injury because associated tearing of the joint capsule will allow drainage of the fluid from the joint into surrounding extra-articular soft tissues. With intracapsular swelling the knee usually assumes the resting position of about 25° flexion, which allows the synovial cavity to hold the maximum amount of fluid.[41] This flexed position may lead the examiner to believe that the knee is truly locked when it is really only a pseudolock.

3. *Neurovascular status:* Femoral, popliteal, posterior tibial, and dorsalis pedis pulses are palpated. Excessive calf pressure is also sought.

Patellofemoral Examination

Examination of the patellofemoral joint is aimed at discovering the cause of chronic pain and instability resulting from structural and functional abnormalities relating to this joint. Carson et al[42] examine the patellofemoral joint with the patient standing, sitting, supine, and prone by means of observation, palpation, and specific testing (Tables 7-1 and 7-2).

Table 7-1 Summary of Physical Examination: Extremity Measurements Frequently Associated with Patellofemoral Disorders

Description of Test or Measurement, Comments	Normal	Patient Position	Degree of Knee Flexion	Patellofemoral Disorder or Malalignment
Quadriceps or Q angle—angle formed between line from anterior iliac spine to center of patella and line from center of patella to tibial tubercle	Men, 10° Women, 15°	Supine	0	Increased Q angle with excessive femoral anteversion, genu valgum, external tibial torsion, chondromalacia; may have decreased Q angle with chronic subluxation of patella
Quadriceps mass—circumference 10 cm proximal to patella with active straight leg raising	Equal bilaterally	Supine	0	Associated with VMO dysplasia, congenital hypoplasia, generalized atrophy
Hip range of motion; internal and external rotation	Usually greater external rotation; abnormal if internal exceeds external rotation by more than 30°	Prone	90	Abnormal femoral anteversion or retroversion (may have increased Q angle with excessive femoral anteversion)
Leg-ground angle—evaluation of tibia vara	Less than 10°	Standing	0	Genu varum tibia vara → / Triceps surae contracture ↓ / Hindfoot varus ↓ / Forefoot supination /
Neutral position of subtalar joint; patient lifts medial edge of heel—palpate talar head medially and laterally and check for hyperpronated foot	Subtalar joint should be close to neutral while standing	Standing	0	Compensatory subtalar joint pronation ↓
Ankle dorsiflexion	More than 10°	Supine	0	Primary subtalar joint pronation → Obligatory internal tibial rotation (may be increased or prolonged)
Leg-heel alignment—longitudinal axis of leg to heel (with foot in neutral position)	2°–3° of varus	Prone (feet hanging from table edge)	0	↓
Hindfoot-forefoot alignment—long axis of heel to transverse axis of forefoot (with foot in neutral position)	Long axis of heel normally 90° perpendicular to transverse axis of forefoot	Prone (feet hanging from table edge)	0	Abnormal rotational stress absorbed by soft tissues at knee joint ↓ Peripatellar and anterior knee pain

Source: Reprinted with permission from *Clinical Orthopaedics and Related Research* (1984;185:167), Copyright © 1984, Philadelphia, J.B. Lippincott/Harper & Row.

Standing

The patient is standing with the feet slightly apart and pointing outward 5° to 10°. The knees should be oriented about 7° valgus because the medial femoral condyle extends distally farther than the lateral condyle (Fig. 7-14). The examiner must check the pelvic level (see Chapter 6) and the overall alignment of the femur and tibia and observe the lower extremity for excessive femoral anteversion (ie, femoral shaft inwardly rotating relative to the hip), which will cause the femoral sulcus to be medial to the tibial tubercle. The patellar tendon is then lateral to the patella and exerts an abnormal lateral force during quadriceps contraction,[43] adversely affecting patellofemoral mechanics.

The examiner determines whether the patellae are normally centered. Femoral anteversion can be responsible for "squinting" patellae and associated with genu valgum. An increase in genu valgum during flexion would adversely affect patellar tracking. Laterally placed patellae ("grasshopper eyes") can

be caused by a retroverted hip or weakness of the VMO. Retroversion (see Chapter 6) can be associated with genu varum. Genu varum (except in the newborn to 1-year-old child) is considered abnormal, especially if it begins immediately at the proximal tibia and is associated with a tibia vara, both of which are usually associated with internal tibial rotation. Genu varum is a normal progressive phenomenon in men over the years (E Rashkoff, personal communication, 1989). Genu valgum is usually associated with lateral tibial torsion. Femoral anteversion, hyperpronation of the foot, and a tight iliotibial band can be associated with genu valgum. The above factors may stress a valgus or varus deformity but cannot cause a varus or valgus deformity because these are independent structural configurations of the knee (E Rashkoff, personal communication, 1989). Abnormal genu valgum can be determined by bringing the medial femoral condyles together. Abnormal genu varum may be measured by bringing the medial malleoli together and measuring the distance between the femoral condyles.

Table 7-2 Summary of Physical Examination: Inspection

Physical Findings	Description of Test or Measurement, Comments	Normal	Patient Position	Degree of Knee Flexion	Patellofemoral Disorder or Malalignment
"Squinting" patellae	Patellae medially directed	Midline patellae	Standing, feet straight	0	Increased femoral anteversion or femoral torsion
Genu valgum	Measure intermalleolar distance	Neutral or slight valgus	Standing, feet straight	0	Probable increased Q angle (genu valgum)
Genu varum	Measure distance between knees				Possible compensatory subtalar joint pronation
Genu recurvatum	Observe standing alignment laterally	Neutral	Standing	0	Physiologic generalized laxity or patella alta
Toe-in, toe-out gait	Angle of gait; observe while walking or running	Less than 10° midline deviation	Walking or running	Variable	May have abnormal femoral anteversion, internal tibial torsion, femoral retroversion, external tibial torsion
"Grasshopper-eye" patella	Patella points laterally	Midline	Sitting	90	Recurrent subluxation or dislocation
Wandering patella	Evaluation of patellar tracking; abrupt patellar deviation with active flexion-extension	Smooth midline trajectory	Sitting	0–90	Recurrent subluxation or dislocation, lateral patellar compression syndrome, chondromalacia
Popping or snapping patella	Audible or visual pop of patella with active flexion-extension	Smooth midline trajectory	Sitting	0–90	Plica syndrome, chondral or osteochondral defect
High-riding patellae	Patella points to ceiling	Patella sinks into femoral sulcus	Sitting	90	Patella alta
	Patella proximally located, may be hypoplastic	Inferior pole near lateral femoral condyle	Supine	0	Patellar instability
Prominent anterior fat pad	Bulge beneath distal aspect of femoral condyle	Smooth contour	Supine	0	Patella alta
Low-riding patella	Patella inferiorly displaced	Smooth rounded contour	Sitting	90	Patella infera
Lateral tilt of patella	Patella points laterally	Midline without tilt	Supine	0 and 30	Recurrent subluxation or dislocation, lateral patellar compression syndrome
Prominent medial femoral condyle with patella prominent laterally	Distal femur uncovered; may have severe hamstring spasm	Midline patella	Supine	30 or more	Acute patellar dislocation
Atrophy of VMO, high insertion of VMO	Observe VMO muscle bulk, strength, level of insertion as patient extends against forced resistance	VMO stands out medially; normally inserts a third to half the way down medial edge of patella	Supine	30	VMO deficiency (congenital, atrophic); recurrent subluxation or dislocation; lateral patellar compression syndrome
Effusion	Patellar outline obliterated when marked, usually mild with chronic syndromes	No effusion	Supine	0	Acute subluxation or dislocation, osteochondral fracture Chondromalacia, chronic subluxation

Source: Reprinted with permission from *Clinical Orthopaedics and Related Research* (1984;185:172), Copyright © 1984, Philadelphia, J.B. Lippincott/Harper & Row.

The examiner determines whether there is external or internal tibial torsion (uncommon). If with the feet parallel the patellae face inward, external rotation of the feet to bring the patellae to center would indicate external tibial torsion (Fig. 7-14). External tibial torsion may be evident if the patient is standing with the feet directed outward and the patellae face forward. Internal tibial torsion is present if the feet are adducted and the patellae are facing forward. Tibial torsion can be determined by measuring the malleoli of the feet as they hang over the side of a bench. Normally the lateral malleolus is 15° posterolateral to the medial malleolus. By placing one finger anterior to the lateral malleolus and another

KNEE ALIGNMENT

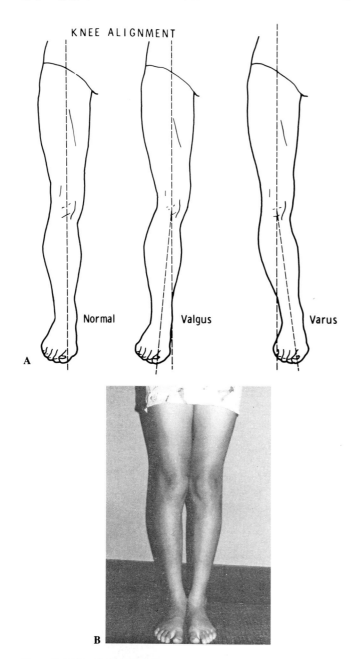

Figure 7-14 Patellofemoral joint examination, standing position. (**A**) Valgus alignment and varus alignment. Normally, knee is oriented about 7° valgus. *Source*: Reprinted with permission from M Post, *Physical Examination of the Musculoskeletal System*, Chicago, Year Book Medical Publishers, 1987. (**B**) "Miserable malignment syndrome." Patient demonstrates femoral anteversion and external tibial torsion. When feet are parallel, kneecaps "squint" toward one another. When patellae point straight ahead, feet are markedly externally rotated. *Source*: Reprinted from *Office Management of Sports Injuries and Athletic Problems* (p 233) by M B Mellon (Ed) with permission of Hanley & Belfus, Inc., © 1988.

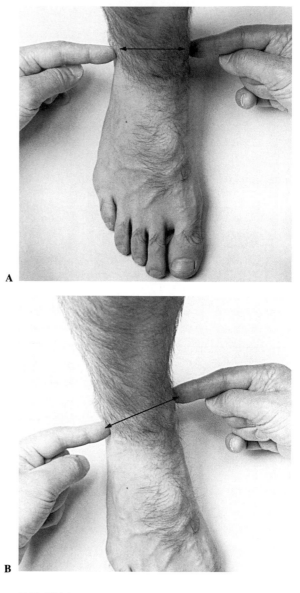

Figure 7-15 Tibial torsion. (**A**) Measuring the malleoli (see text). (**B**) With internal tibial torsion the lateral malleolus is anterior to the medial malleolus.

finger on the apex of the medial malleolus, the examiner should note a straight transverse line; otherwise internal or external torsion may be evident (Fig. 7-15). Tibial torsion may be due to past trauma, congenital reasons, or poor perpetual floor posture, as with a seated child resting on the medial thighs with the legs externally rotated while watching television ("tailor's position"). Carson et al[42] state that if the tibia angulates 10° or more laterally, there is probably a primary or compensatory subtalar pronation causing a compensatory tibial internal rotation, which will stress the knee joint and peripatellar soft tissues. They also state that in gait a deviation of more than 10° from the normal walking or running progression may indicate excessive femoral retroversion or anteversion or tibial internal or external torsion.

The examiner observes the standing patient laterally or the prone patient's legs as they hang off edge of table for genu recurvatum (hyperextension). Bilateral genu recurvatum may refer to generalized ligament laxity (more than 10°) causing hypermobile patellae. The examiner checks other joints for increased laxity by measuring the degree of hyperextension of digits (thumb to distal forearm), elbows, and knees and when the patient is touching the floor with knees extended. This type of patient may not heal properly after ligamentous trauma because of the lack of supporting ligamentous tissue.[2] Loose-jointed individuals experience knee sprains, whereas tight-jointed individuals experience muscle tears. Unilateral genu recurvatum may be due to posterior cruciate or posterolateral capsular injury[14] or a lax anterior cruciate ligament. Alternatively, the patient may be compensating for a lumbar lordosis. Genu recurvatum is often associated with patella alta.

Sitting

The patient sits with the knees flexed 90° and the legs hanging free.

Patellar level: Normal patellae are within the patellofemoral sulcus at 90°. A high-riding patella (patella alta) may point toward the ceiling. With patella alta the higher lateral femoral sulcus can no longer protect against lateral patellar subluxation. Micheli et al[44] state that patella alta may be not only inherited but acquired as a result of adolescent bony overgrowth causing overstretching of the patellar tendon. Inferior patella baja (rarer) adversely affects patellofemoral contact, especially in a knee flexion position, and is related to poor patellofemoral stability and function.[12] With the shortened patellar ligament in patella baja there is an increase in patellofemoral compression.[43] In patella baja with the knee flexed the patella is much closer to the tibial plateau. Insall and Salvati[45] have a radiologic method for distinguishing between patella baja and patella alta. Patella alta can be diagnosed in a lateral knee radiograph with the knee flexed at 30°. The length of the normal patella is about equal to the length of the patellar tendon (with a 20% variation); in patella alta the length of the patella is shorter than the length of the patellar tendon. The examiner also evaluates whether the patella is excessively medial or lateral and relates this to femoral or tibial torsion. Osgood-Schlatter disease (enlarged tender tibial tubercle) should also be sought radiographically.

Patellar tracking: As the tibia flexes on the femur, the patella slides distally a total of about 8 cm. The inferior margin of the patella first makes contact with the femur at 20° of flexion. As flexion increases, the contact area of the patella moves superiorly. At 45° the middle portion is in contact, and at 90° of flexion the superior portion of the patella is in contact with the trochlea. After 90° the quadriceps also makes contact with the trochlea.[13] The tibia externally rotates (screw-home mechanism) on the femur during the last 15° to 20° of terminal knee extension and internally rotates on the femur during the first 15° to 20° of flexion. The examiner should observe and palpate the patella as the patient gently flexes and extends the knee. There should be a smooth, longitudinal trajectory with only minimal (15° to 20°) rotation. Any abrupt movement, particularly between 20° and 35° of flexion as the patella enters and exits the femoral trochlea, is abnormal.[42] The patella should tilt laterally at extreme flexion. In the last 10° of extension the patella should deviate slightly laterally as it leaves the trochlear groove. Extreme terminal lateral movement may indicate patellar subluxation.

Patellofemoral grind and compression: Crepitation and pain may occur while the patella is compressed during flexion between 30° and 60°. If pain occurs, the examiner shifts the patella medially to see whether the patient is relieved during grinding; this indicates tight lateral parapatellar tissue.

Patellar inhibition test: The supine patient first strongly contracts the quadriceps while performing a straight-leg raise. Then with the lower extremity extended, the patient attempts another quadriceps contraction while the examiner exerts fingertip pressure on the superior patellar pole. If the test is positive, pain will prevent the patient from contracting the quadriceps again.

Supine

The examiner's thigh can be placed under the patient's knee to create about 30° to 45° of flexion. The patella can be displaced both medially and laterally by the examiner to determine the degree of retinacular laxity,[46] pain, and apprehension (Fairbank's sign). Carson et al[42] recommend applying a small amount of passive flexion to the knee during the test (Fig. 7-16). Testing for laxity with the knee in full extension is not diagnostic because the patella is proximal to the intercondylar groove and is normally hypermobile.[11] Pain and apprehension are much more common on medial to lateral stress when there is excessive movement and possible lateral tilt of the patella. The medial retinaculum should have a firm end point.[39] During testing, palpation of the tension of the medial or lateral retinaculum adjacent to the patella is important because a defect at the attachment of the VMO on the medial side may be palpable after an acute dislocation, or

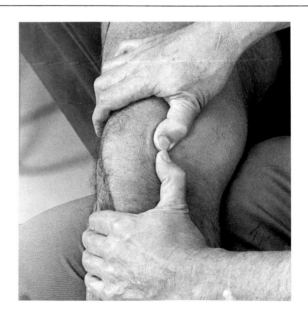

Figure 7-16 Knee examination, patient supine. Patellar apprehension is best tested with knee flexed 30° to 45°.

tightness of the lateral patellar retinaculum may be a cause of patellar pain.[39] Failure of the patella to displace medially more than 1 cm represents a tight lateral retinaculum. If a patient complains of the patella "going out" and if the stability tests are normal, synovial entrapment or a plica involvement should be suspected instead of subluxation-dislocation.[46] Limited motion may be due to local adhesions. Abnormal patellar mobility may be associated with patella alta, increased Q angle (see below: quadriceps angle), genu valgum, loose medial retinaculum,[39] and an atrophic VMO.

At this point, the examiner tilts the patella at one end and palpates the undersurface of the patella facets for tenderness and osteophytes. Carson et al[42] state that the medial patellar facet is usually the most tender and is more often involved in patellofemoral conditions (chondromalacia). These investigators hold that the best way to palpate this facet is to keep the patient's knee supported in 30° of flexion, which tilts the patella laterally. Pushing the patella in a lateral to medial direction will then expose the facet. To palpate the soft tissues (retinacular fibers around the patella) and to eliminate the possibility of palpating the facet or femoral trochlea, the examiner should push and tilt the patella either medially or laterally[44] to feel soft tissues.

Prone

The prone position can also be useful for palpating the patellar facets.

Quadriceps Angle

The Q angle is the angle between the direction of the rectus femoris pull and the alignment of the patellar tendon (Fig. 7-17). It represents a functional angle between the physiologic and anatomic axes of the extensor mechanism. Normally the quadriceps is directed medially and the patella ligament is directed laterally, creating a normal genu valgus. If this genu valgus is increased and associated with medial knee weakness (VMO atrophy), femoral sulcus abnormalities, and any of the other medial or lateral structural weaknesses of the knee, hip, or foot, then the Q angle is significant but by itself is not necessarily diagnostic.

The normal Q angle ranges are controversial, with the average range in women being up to 20° (because of the wider pelvis) and in men up to 15°. It should be measured in the standing (or supine) neutral position with a line drawn from the ASIS to the middle of the patella and another line drawn from the tibial tuberosity through the middle of the patella. An increased angle may be due to femoral anteversion, external tibial torsion, genu valgum, a laterally inserted patellar tendon, pes planus, foot pronation, or (in a woman) a broad pelvis. The woman with a broad pelvis may complain of hip pain that is due to possible tensile stress on the hip abductors. In a patient with a chronic lateral patellar subluxation, the Q angle would be reduced.

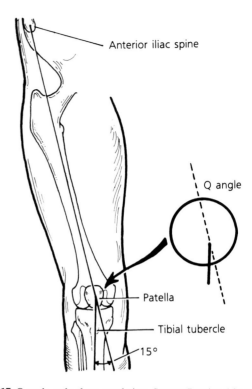

Figure 7-17 Q angle and valgus angulation. *Source*: Reprinted from *Athletic Training and Sports Medicine* (p 273) by AE Ellison et al. (Eds) with permission of the American Academy of Orthopaedic Surgeons, © 1984.

Hughston[11] states that the Q angle should be measured with the quadriceps contracted, which would give a normal angle of 8° to 10°. Contraction of the quadriceps could reduce the Q angle if it caused a lateral shift of the patella or increase the Q angle if it reduced a laterally subluxed patella. Alternatively, the Q angle may measure normal because the patella is laterally placed or because the tibial tubercle is more medial than usual. This indicates that the Q angle measurement by itself may be misleading.[47] A flexed knee should give a Q angle of 0° because the femur rotates externally on the fixed tibia.[12] By flexing the knee 30° and rotating the tibia externally the examiner would be measuring a dynamic Q angle, such as might be occurring when an athlete suddenly turns.[24] A dynamic Q angle could also be measured during gait evaluation with stop-action photography.[48] A dynamically measured Q angle may indicate abnormal possibilities not apparent from a normal statically measured Q angle. The Q angle represents a potential dynamic force that might act to sublux or dislocate the patella.[42]

FUNCTIONAL EXAMINATION

The type of examination performed on a knee differs according to whether the condition is a chronic overuse degenerative problem or an acute traumatic problem. A chronic problem allows us the luxury of using various tests and examinations of the knee in different postures, whereas in an acute involvement the patient may only be in a supine position and our first concern must be with the passive examination of the ligaments. Although all the functional tests in this text begin with a passive examination, the first passive test to be performed with a traumatic knee is Lachman's test because it is less likely to be limited by hamstring spasm, is a less stressful ligamentous stability test, and is the most reliable test for detecting anterior cruciate ligament insufficiency.[38]

Clancy,[38] in increasing order of painful ligamentous stress testing, lists the following tests that should be performed in acute trauma: Lachman's test,[39] the anterior-posterior drawer test, the varus-valgus tests at 30° and 0°, the pivot-shift test, the jerk test (or Slocum's test), and finally the reverse pivot-shift test; these are all described below. Depending on the acuteness of the injury, often the examiner will only have one chance to perform a test because of pain and spasm. The examiner must determine whether there is a mushy end feel compared to the normal firm end feel; this should always be examined first. Noyes and Mangine[49] state that in an acute knee injury the clinical observation of laxity is inhibited by pain, swelling, and hemarthrosis. Therefore, "a little laxity is a lot" and should be considered serious. One of their investigations showed that of 104 injured knees only 4% were correctly diagnosed at the time of original injury. They recommend diagnostic arthroscopy in the early stage of injury in an active athletic patient. When dealing with a chronic overuse syndrome in an athlete, the history should include previous injuries, the type of training program, and the equipment used[39] because the training program may have to be modified.

Grading Sprains

Zarins and Boyle[15] describe the following grading system for sprains (Table 7-3):

Grade 1: up to 5 mm of motion due to microscopic ligament tearing; no loss of function; definite end point

Grade 2: 6 to 10 mm of motion due to partial disruption or stretching of ligament; some loss of function; definite end point

Grade 3: 11 to 15 mm of motion due to complete tearing of ligament; complete loss of function; mushy end point

Grade 4: more than 15 mm of motion

Each joint has primary and secondary joint stabilizers (Table 7-4). For example, the superficial tibial collateral ligament is the primary stabilizer for valgus of the knee, and the deep capsular collateral ligament, posterior oblique ligament, and anterior and posterior cruciate ligaments are the secondary restraints. Clinically, if the primary stabilizer is torn and the secondary stabilizers are tight a low-force valgus test may show mild laxity, and the examiner might not realize that the primary stabilizer is severely injured. Therefore, minimally detectable joint laxity may be more severe than realized. If the secondary restraints are also torn, then low-force valgus test-

ing would show greater laxity.[15] Passive stability testing should be done with initial small loads that are gradually increased in relation to the patient's pain threshold. An acute anterior cruciate sprain may not express excessive anterior motion if the secondary restraints are tight, but in the chronic stage, after the secondary restraints become more stretched, an anterior drawer or Lachman's test would show greater laxity.

Functional Tests

In the following functional tests (Appendix 7-A) the normal side is always tested first.

1. *Active tests:* The patient performs the following active motions to reveal the amount of voluntary restriction. Flexion (0° to 135°) is tested with deep knee bends (squat test); the examiner evaluates the amount of flexion and how the patient arises from the bend. During these actions, the examiner evaluates quadriceps strength and the possible location of pain; pain is localized to the patellofemoral joint if the retropatellar or popliteal fossa is involved, and pain is lateral or medial if the meniscus is involved. Extension is tested with the patient seated and extending a 90° flexed knee. Extensor lag is present if the knee cannot be extended actively to 0° but can be extended passively to 0°. The degree of passive extension is the amount of extension lag. If passive extension is limited, it may be due to pain and weakness resulting from quadriceps or patellar tendon rupture, fracture of the patella, avulsion of the tibial tubercle, intra-articular pathology, hamstring spasm, or just general quadriceps weakness. Helfet's test is done to assess for a normal screw-home mechanism, and patellar tracking is observed. The level of the insertion of the VMO is also checked because the lower it inserts into the patella the more effective it is in stabilizing the patella.[50] Medial and lateral rotation is tested actively with the patient seated and the knee flexed 90°, legs dangling (or prone with the knee flexed). Medial rotation should be 30°, and lateral rotation should be 40° to 45°.

2. *Passive flexion* (Fig. 7-18): The patient is supine. The examiner first flexes the hip to its end range (which shortens the quadriceps) and then flexes the knee. Ideally the heel should reach the buttock (0° to 160°). The capsular pattern includes a loss of extension of 15° to 25° and a loss of flexion of 85° to 95°[51] and may indicate osteoarthritis. Flexion may be limited if there is contracture of the quadriceps or as a result of an effusion causing a pseudolocking from a first- or second-degree tear of the medial collateral or anterior cruciate ligament or patellar tendinitis, Osgood-Schlatter's disease and patellofemoral dysfunction (see below). Flexion also may be limited by true locking from a loose body, meniscal bucket-handle tear, syn-

Table 7-3 Functional Capacity of Injured Ligaments

Extent of Failure	Sprain	Damage*	Amount of Joint Laxity†	Residual Strength	Residual Functional Length	Residual Functional Capacity	Treatment
Minimal	First degree	Less than one-third of fibers failed; includes most sprains with few to some fibers failed; microtears also exist	None	Retained or slightly decreased	Normal	Retained	Rest until acute symptoms subside; active rehabilitation; early return to activity
Partial	Second degree	One- to two-thirds ligament damage; significant damage but parts of the ligaments are still functional	0–5 mm increased opening; fibers in ligament resist opening	Marked decrease	Increased; still within functional range but may act as a check-rein	Marked compromise; requires healing to regain function	When laxitiy is minimal, risk to complete the tear is minimal; treated by early rehabilitation and no plaster immobilization
		Microtears may exist	5–10 mm opening when damage is more considerable	At risk for complete failure			When laxity approaches higher values (5–10 mm) treated by plaster immobilization to allow healing; rehabilitation; delayed return to activity
Complete	Third degree	More than two-thirds to complete failure; continuity remains in part between fibers	If 10 mm opening, remaining fibers are torn; incontinuity and complete failure exist	Little to none	Severely compromised but may provide late check-rein function	Severely compromised or lost	Plaster immobilization; protection for healing when laxity increased 10 mm; continuity of ligament is assumed
		Continuity lost and gross separation between fibers	Depends on secondary restraints to limit amount of laxity, but they later stretch out	None	Lost	Lost	Surgical repair required when continuity of ligament is functionally lost; usually exists when medial or lateral opening increased 10–12 mm

*Estimate of damage is often very difficult. The different types listed can usually be distinguished, however.

†Anterior and posterior cruciate tears are included with the exception that acute tears commonly exist with little to no laxity. Thus the clinical laxity examination is less accurate. In the medial and lateral examination the grading is more accurate for collateral tears.

Source: Reprinted from *Athletic Training and Sports Medicine* (p 268) by AE Ellison et al. (Eds) with permission of the American Academy of Orthopaedic Surgeons, © 1984.

Table 7-4 Primary and Secondary Knee Ligament Restraints

Type of Motion	Primary Restraint	Secondary Restraint
Medial joint opening	Tibial collateral ligament	Mid–one-third medial capsule
		Posterior oblique ligament
		Anterior and posterior cruciates
Lateral joint opening	Fibular collateral ligament	Iliotibial band
		Mid–one-third lateral capsule
		Popliteus
		Biceps femoris
		Anterior and posterior cruciates
Anterior displacement*	Anterior cruciate ligament	Iliotibial band
		Mid–one-third medial/lateral capsule
		Tibial and fibular collaterals
Posterior displacement*	Posterior cruciate ligament	Posterolateral capsule
		Fibular and tibial collaterals
		Popliteus

*Tibia with respect to femur.

Source: Reprinted with permission from JA Nicholas and EB Hershman, *The Lower Extremity and Spine in Sports Medicine* (p 931), St. Louis, 1986, The C.V. Mosby Co.

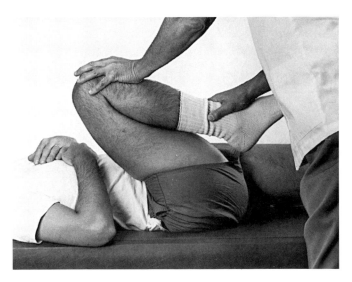

Figure 7-18 Passive knee flexion (hip should be maximally flexed).

ovioma, or other intra-articular disorder. Hamstring shortening can be determined by flexing a level hip 90° and extending the leg. (Tightness of the hamstrings may cause increased quadriceps force on the patellofemoral joint.) Passive knee flexion with the patient prone can indicate a shortened quadriceps. To determine whether the shortening is due to possible intra-articular reasons instead of a shortened quadriceps, the examiner should examine the supine patient with a flexed hip to relax the quadriceps and compare the range of motion. Decreased range of motion with the patient supine may indicate reasons other than quadriceps shortening.

In testing the medial plica, the patient is supine. The examiner flexes the patient's knee about 45° and internally rotates the foot and tibia with one hand and then presses the lateral patella medially with the other hand. While exerting a lateral to medial pressure with the palm of the hand on the patella, the examiner is palpating the medial plica with the fingers. The examiner then flexes and extends the knee, feeling for popping of the plical band[41] or possible abrupt jumping of the patella between 30° and 60° of flexion (Fig. 7-19). The plica is under increased tension with knee flexion. As the knee is passively flexed from 30° to 60°, the medial patellar plica can be seen arthroscopically to glide over the medial femoral condyle, beneath the patella.[52]

3. *Passive extension:* The patient is supine. Two maneuvers are performed. First (Fig. 7-20), the examiner lifts the posterior ankle off the table and presses down on the anterior knee (0° to + 10° is the normal range). Second (Fig. 7-21), while holding the posterior ankle off the table the examiner flexes the knee and performs a bounce-home test by pressing down on the knee while extending the leg. These maneuvers may reveal a genu recurvatum (ie, possible rupture of the anterior or posterior cruciates). If on the first maneuver the tibia rotates posterolaterally, there may be a posterolateral rotatory instability; if there is 5° to 10° of hyperextension compared to the other knee, a posterior or anterior cruciate rupture is possible. Loss of extension may be due to hamstring spasm (pseudolock) or increased pain from a lesion to the knee soft tissue (capsule or ligament), especially in acute posterior cruciate injuries. If the bounce-home test reveals a springy block loss of

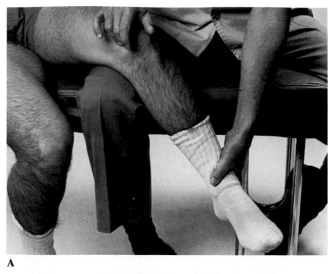

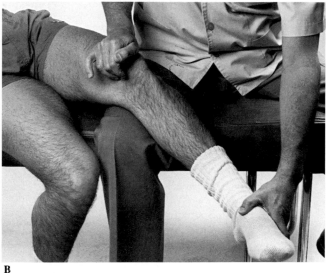

Figure 7-19 Passive testing of medial plica. (**A**) Flexion. (**B**) Extension.

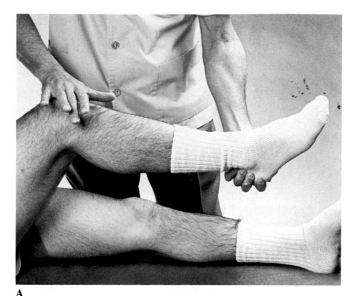

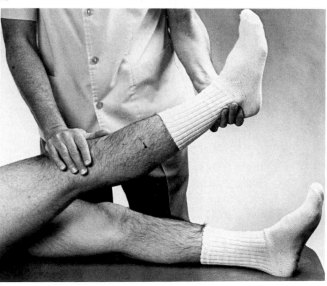

Figure 7-21 Passive knee extension: (**A**) Beginning of bounce-home test. (**B**) End of bounce-home test.

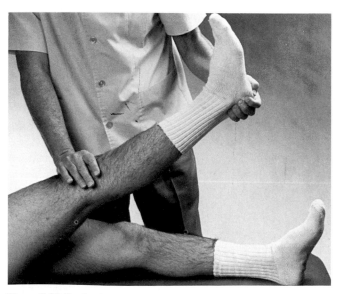

Figure 7-20 Passive knee extension.

complete extension, there may be true locking due to a loose body, a displaced meniscal tear, or entrapment of a torn anterior cruciate ligament (true lock).

4. *Passive lateral rotation* (Fig. 7-22): The patient is supine with the knee flexed 90° and the heel on the table. The examiner grasps the foot and laterally rotates it to its end range while palpating the tibial tubercle to ascertain that there is tibial movement. The test stresses the medial coronary ligaments, medial meniscus, and medial collateral ligament. If meniscus tests and valgus stress tests are normal, there is a probability of coronary ligament sprain (see below, Meniscotibial (Coronary) Ligament Sprain). The test may also stress the pes anserinus insertion. Gersoff and Clancy[53] state that external tibial rotation should be tested with the tibia first flexed at 30° and then flexed at 90°. If the posterior

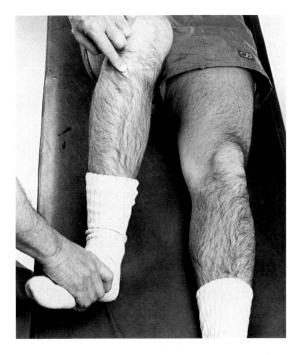

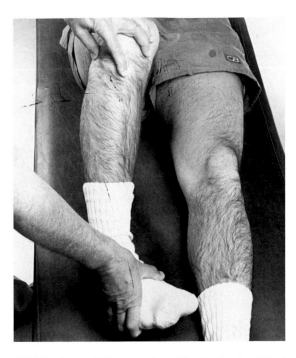

Figure 7-22 Passive knee lateral rotation while palpating tibial tubercle. Knee is flexed 90°.

Figure 7-23 Passive medial knee rotation while palpating the tibial tubercle. Knee is flexed 90°.

cruciate is intact and if the anterior cruciate and posterolateral structures are involved, then greater abnormal external rotation will occur at 30° flexion than at 90° flexion. If the posterior cruciate is also involved, external rotation will be increased at both 30° and 90° of knee flexion. Finally, the test may stress the popliteal muscle (see below, Popliteus Tendon Tenosynovitis).

5. *Passive medial rotation* (Fig. 7-23): Testing is similar to that described above except that the lateral structures (lateral coronary ligaments, lateral meniscus, and fibular collateral ligaments) are stressed.

6. *Passive valgus (abduction) at 30° flexion* (Fig. 7-24A): The patient is supine (head on table); the thigh rests on the table (relative hip extension) to relax and help prevent hamstring spasm while the leg is off the table. The examiner cups the lateral knee joint and holds the foot and tibia in a neutral position to stress specifically the medial collateral ligament. Holding the tibia in external rotation during valgus stress at 30° flexion would also stress the posterior oblique ligament, posteromedial capsule, fibular collateral ligament, popliteus, and posterolateral capsule.[17] In a chronic situation when spasm is not a factor, the foot could be straddled against the examiner's side so that one hand can be used to palpate the opening and integrity of the medial collateral ligament (Fig. 7-24B). Testing valgus or varus at 30° relaxes the medial or lateral posterior capsule and posterior cruciate, allowing more specificity in testing of the collateral ligaments. The examiner observes the joint space for an opening and feels for the end point. The tibial collateral ligament is the primary restraint, and with 30° of flexion the cruciates and posterior capsular ligaments are more relaxed. The first tissue to be involved on the medial side from a lateral or posterolateral stress would be the superficial tibial collateral; with greater force the secondary deep capsule becomes involved. Usually next in order of injury are the posterior oblique ligament, the anterior cruciate, and the posterior cruciate. Rarely, isolated injury to the anterior cruciate ligament can occur without injury to the medial collateral or posterior cruciate ligament (F. Rashkoff, personal communication, 1989). Pain on the lateral side may indicate a loose body, meniscus lesion, or patellofemoral pathology.

7. *Passive valgus at full extension* (Fig. 7-25): Passive valgus at full extension is supported essentially by the anterior and posterior cruciates; therefore, a tibial collateral sprain may be painful but will not show laxity. Testing that exhibits laxity in flexion and stability in extension indicates collateral ligament rupture. The finding of laxity in varus or valgus at full extension relating to anterior or posterior cruciate ligament rupture is more reliable in acute cases than in chronic cases.[53,54] Any opening, especially more than 10 mm, indicates damage to anterior and posterior cruciate structures.[2] Opening also indicates a severe ligamentous disruption that may include the collateral ligaments, posterior medial capsule, and medial quadriceps muscles.

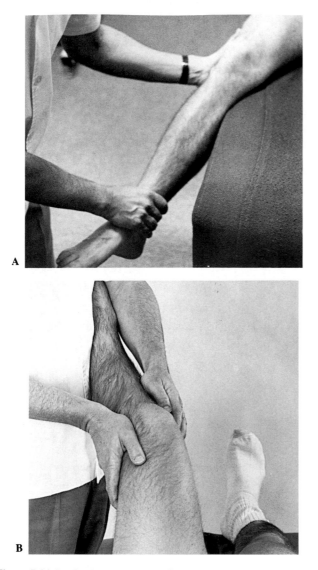

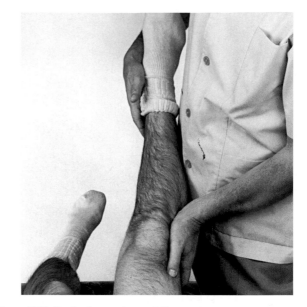

Figure 7-25 Passive knee valgus at full extension.

Figure 7-24 Passive knee valgus at 30° flexion. (A) With thigh resting on table to reduce hamstring spasm. Tibia is held in a neutral position. (B) With foot straddled against examiner's side. Opening of medial collateral ligament can be palpated.

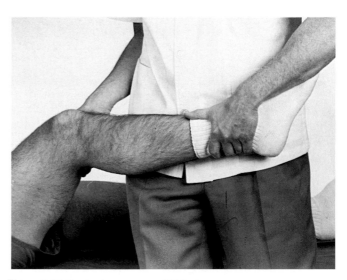

Figure 7-26 Passive knee varus at 30° flexion.

8. *Passive varus (adduction) at 30° flexion* (Fig. 7-26): Although the fibular collateral ligament is the primary restraint to lateral joint opening with varus stress,[55] in selective cutting experiments incising only the popliteus caused greater varus than incising the fibular collateral ligament. It is suggested that the upper popliteus functions as a ligament whereas the distal popliteus functions as a muscle.[13] In order of injury, depending on the amount of varus, the structures involved are first the lateral collateral ligament, posterolateral capsule, arcuate-popliteus complex, iliotibial band, and biceps femoris tendon.[41] There is usually more motion in varus than valgus at 30° flexion; therefore the test must be compared with the opposite side (as usual). Pain on the opposite compressed side indicates a possible loose body or meniscus.

9. *Passive varus at full extension* (Fig. 7-27): Laxity involves especially the posterior cruciate and possibly the anterior cruciate plus the above supporting tissues that are stressed at 30° flexion.[56] Excess movement indicates a severe disruption. No matter the degree of flexion in which varus is tested, increased opening of 1 cm or more over the opposite side should alert us to the possibility of cruciate rupture.[2]

10. *Lachman's and anterior drawer test* (for the anterior cruciate ligament): Lachman's test[39] is best performed with the patient seated and leaning back with the knee hanging over the table (Fig. 7-28). The examiner holds the patient's ankle between his or her legs and cups the posterior proximal tibia with the fingers to exert a posterior to anterior pull while the thumbs palpate the

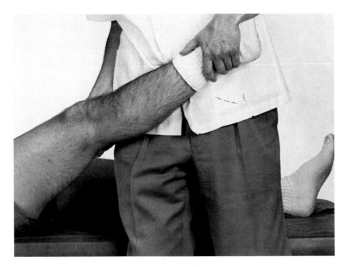

Figure 7-27 Passive knee varus at full extension.

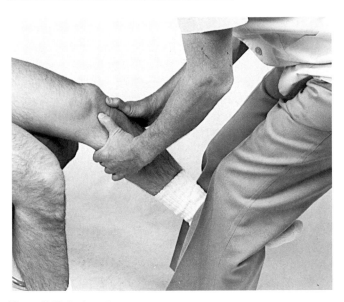

Figure 7-28 Lachman's test.

joint space for movement. The tibia must be held perfectly straight because pulling the tibia anteriorly with either internal or external rotation torque will increase the normal knee intrinsic coupled motion. This would limit the true anterior translation because of increased tautness of the extra-articular restraints.[17] The patient's knee should be flexed only 15° to 20°. This version of Lachman's test is easier than the test in which the examiner must hold the proximal femur with one hand and pull on the distal tibia with the other hand, especially when dealing with a large thigh. The test could also be done with the patient supine; a second examiner could stabilize the femur while the first examiner uses the same contact as above. It is important to palpate the hamstrings before testing because minimal hamstring spasm can negate the test.[38] The anterior drawer test is the same test with the patient's knee

flexed 90°. It is accepted that in acute conditions Lachman's test is less painful, more accurate, and easier to perform. Injured knees often cannot be flexed to 90°, and at 15° to 20° of flexion a tense hemarthrosis, blockage by the posterior medial meniscus,[57] the secondary ligamentous restraints, and spastic hamstring muscles are less effective in restricting anterior tibial motion. The anterior drawer test also requires more force to produce anterior tibial translation than Lachman's test if the secondary restraints are intact.[53] Before attempting the anterior drawer test, the examiner should palpate the medial and lateral femoral condyles and the medial and lateral tibial plateaus. If there is not an 8- to 10-mm step-off on the tibial plateaus (as in the opposite knee), posterior cruciate ligament involvement should be suspected and a false-positive anterior cruciate test will occur.[53] A negative Lachman's test, in association with a positive anterior drawer sign, points toward a posterior cruciate injury.[58] Laxity should be interpreted not only by increased joint motion but also by palpating the final abnormal joint position (subluxation).[17] Jackson[59] states that in partial tears of the anterior cruciate the drawer test would be positive if the anteromedial band alone was torn and that Lachman's test would be positive if the posterolateral band alone was torn. Rosenberg and Rasmussen[60] disagree, stating that they proved Lachman's to be superior to the anterior drawer test because the former creates more maximal tension in all parts of the anterior cruciate ligament whereas the drawer test does not produce maximal tension in any portion of this ligament. False-negative interpretations of Lachman's test may occur if there is sufficient spasm of the hamstrings or a displaced bucket-handle tear of the meniscus. A third-degree medial collateral tear extending to the posteromedial capsule may create a false-positive Lachman's test (pseudo-Lachman). The palpable end point must be absent for Lachman's and the anterior drawer tests to be considered positive. Noyes and Grood[17] state that intact secondary ligamentous restraints or a nonfunctional and elongated anterior cruciate ligament may occasionally give the false sensation of the hard end point.

11. *Resisted knee flexion:* The patient is prone. The examiner flexes the patient's knee to less than 90°. To test the medial hamstrings (semitendinosus and semimembranosus), the examiner resists knee flexion while the patient's hip joint is medially rotated (Fig. 7-29A). To test the lateral hamstrings (biceps femoris), the patient's hip joint is laterally rotated (Fig. 7-29B) while flexion is resisted. The examiner holds the belly of the hamstrings while testing because they tend to cramp. The test is definitely painful in strain and tendinitis of the hamstring muscles, including the origin, belly (see Chapter 6), and medial and lateral insertions. Pain and weakness may result from avulsion

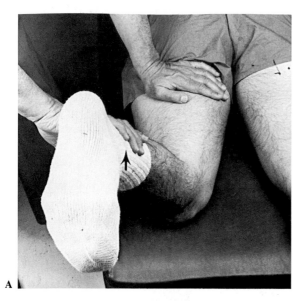

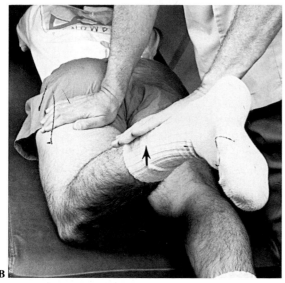

Figure 7-29 Resisted knee flexion. (**A**) More stress is placed on medial hamstrings by medially rotating the hip. (**B**) More stress is placed on lateral hamstrings by laterally rotating the hip.

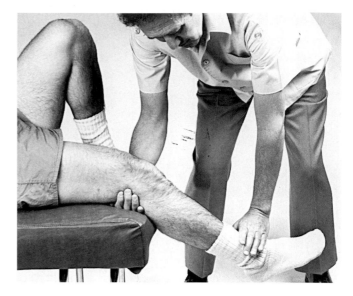

Figure 7-30 Resisted knee extension.

fracture of the fibula head (there may be peroneal nerve damage) or hamstring rupture. Weakness without pain in the medial hamstrings indicates L-5 nerve root involvement and in the lateral hamstrings indicates S-1 nerve root involvement.

12. *Resisted knee extension* (Fig. 7-30): Testing with a flexed hip prevents the rectus femoris from working at full strength. Therefore the patient should be lying supine with the nontested leg flexed on the table and the tested leg hanging over the edge of the table. The examiner resists against the distal tibia with the other hand under the posterior distal thigh. The test is definitely painful in patellar tendinitis. Of course, resisted knee extension could create pain in chondromalacia, patellofemoral arthritis, or effusions secondary to a

torn anterior cruciate ligament or a torn meniscus. Previous passive examination of the knee and patellofemoral joint would have ruled out these lesions, allowing the contractile tests to be specific for contractile structures (see Chapter 1). There may be pain in patellar fracture, patellar tendon involvement, Osgood-Schlatter disease, fracture of the tibial tuberosity, and bursitis. Weakness without pain indicates L-2, L-3, or L-4 nerve root involvement.

Additional Tests

Pivot-Shift Test

This test recreates the ''giving way'' that occurs when an athlete cuts or changes direction. In the acute case this test is almost impossible to perform, and anesthesia is usually necessary. The anterior cruciate is the prime stabilizer of anterolateral rotatory stability (anterior internal rotational movement of the lateral tibial condyle on the femur), which is the most common rotatory instability found in the knee,[2] although recent evidence indicates that clinical testing of rotational instability probably involves more of the collaterals and iliotibial band than the anterior cruciate ligament. Zarins and Boyle[15] state that this type of instability is more of an excessive anterior translation than a rotation. Anterolateral instability may lead to pathology of the articular cartilage and menisci and eventual knee osteoarthritis.[61]

The pivot-shift test may not become positive until 6 weeks after an anterior cruciate tear,[39] although in acute anterior cruciate injuries the test is consistently positive under anesthesia.[62] Crepitation in the flexion phase of the pivot-shift test occurring in the lateral joint line may be a tear of the lateral meniscus[39] (see below, meniscus tests). The importance of a positive pivot-shift test is that it correlates with future development of knee functional instability. Lachman's test examines the present integrity of the anterior cruciate ligament but cannot be depended on for predicting functional instability.[38,52]

The test is performed as follows (Figs. 7-31 through 7-33). The patient is supine. The examiner lifts the foot of an extended leg (about 45°) and puts the palm of the other hand on the lateral tibia and fibular head. In full extension, the lateral tibial plateau will sublux anteriorly if the anterior cruciate or other lateral structures are damaged. Ordinarily the anterior cruciate aids in the normal screw-home mechanism, in which the tibia rotates laterally on extension. If the anterior cruciate is torn, during extension the tibia rotates internally on the anterolateral side and subluxes anteriorly.

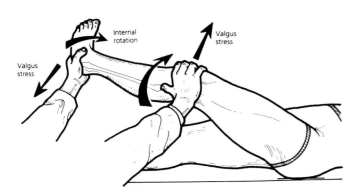

Figure 7-31 Lateral pivot-shift test. *Source:* Reprinted from *Athletic Training and Sports Medicine*, (p 258) by AE Ellison et. al. (Eds) with permission of the American Academy of Orthopaedic Surgeons, © 1984.

The examiner then flexes the knee 5° and internally rotates the foot and tibia. The tibia should not be maximally internally rotated because tightening of the iliotibial band may prevent full anterior tibial translation.[53] The examiner uses the hand on the proximal tibia to exert a strong valgus and anterior force, which helps maintain the anterior tibial subluxation. This force impinges the subluxed tibial plateau against the lateral femoral condyle, jamming the two joint surfaces together and preventing easy reduction as the tibia is flexed on the femur.[62] The hand on the foot pulls laterally to add to the valgus, helping compress the lateral compartment.

The examiner then flexes the knee. If the anterior cruciate ligament is torn, between 20° and 40° flexion, the anteriorly displaced tibial plateau will reduce itself with a possible visible, audible, palpable, and painful clunk. It is thought that the posterior movement of the iliotibial band during flexion (around 30°) aids in reducing the tibia posteriorly.

A false-negative result may be due to a complete tear of the medial collateral complex, elimination of the medial buttress, insufficient valgus force, or excessive maximal internal rotation during testing.[53] A false-positive result can occur with a displaced bucket-handle tear of the medial meniscus (E Rashkoff, personal communication, 1989).

Modified Pivot-Shift Test

Gersoff and Clancy[53] state that the modified pivot-shift test (Fig. 7-34) is more accurate than the pivot-shift for assessing anterior cruciate instability. They hold that internal tibial rotation tightens the iliotibial band, which acts as an extra-articular tenodesis to prevent full anterior tibial translation. The modified test is similar to the pivot-shift test except that the tibia should be held in external rotation rather than internal

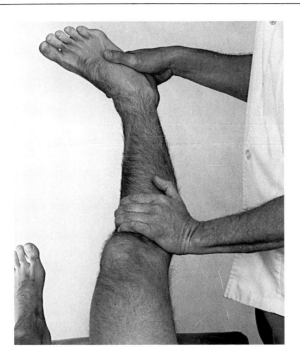

Figure 7-32 Pivot-shift test. Practitioner's left hand is subluxating lateral tibial plateau anteriorly by exerting strong valgus and anterior force. Right hand internally rotates tibia.

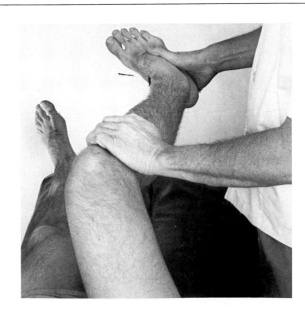

Figure 7-33 Pivot-shift test. Examiner slowly flexes knee. If anterior cruciate ligament is torn, between 20° and 40° knee flexion the anteriorly displaced tibial plateau will reduce itself with possible visible, audible, palpable, and painful clunk.

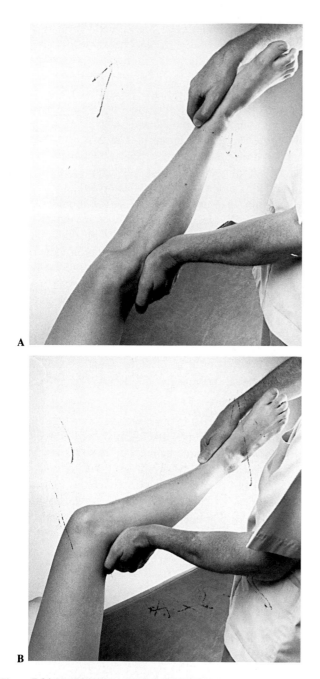

Figure 7-34 Modified pivot-shift test. (**A**) Practitioner externally rotates tibia while using left hand to exert strong valgus and anterior force. This test eliminates possibility of iliotibial band's preventing full anterior tibial translation. (**B**) Examiner flexes knee. If anterior cruciate ligament is torn, between 20° and 40° knee flexion anteriorly displaced tibial plateau will reduce itself with possible visible, audible, palpable, and painful clunk.

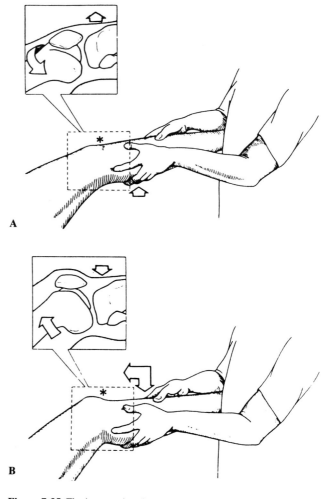

Figure 7-35 Flexion-rotation drawer test. (**A**) In subluxation. (**B**) In reduction. *Source:* Reprinted with permission from FR Noyes, RW Basset, ES Grood, et al, Arthroscopy in Acute Traumatic Hemarthrosis of the Knee in *Journal of Bone and Joint Surgery* (1980;62A:687–695), Copyright © 1980, Journal of Bone and Joint Surgery, Inc.

rotation, thereby allowing increased anterior tibial translation. This modified test expresses more anterior translation than the standard pivot-shift test.

Flexion-Rotation Drawer Test

Noyes and Grood[17] recommend the flexion-rotation drawer test (Fig. 7-35) for examining the status of the anterior cruciate ligament. This test avoids the possible pain of the pivot-

shift test by eliminating any joint compression or valgus force. The supine patient's knee is held in 20° of flexion and neutral position. The weight of the thigh causes the femur to translate posteriorly and to rotate externally, resulting in anterior subluxation of the lateral tibial plateau. The anterior translation of the tibia is detected by observing the forward motion of the tibial plateau, and the rotation is observed by watching the patella rotate externally during the subluxation and internally during the reduction.[17] The examiner then slowly flexes the knee while applying a posterior force on the tibia. As the knee reaches about 40° of flexion, the tibia will reduce itself.

Rotational Instability Tests

In an acute knee injury, straight-plane testing (varus and valgus in the coronal plane and anterior and posterior in the sagittal plane) are all that is really necessary. Rotational instability testing is often too difficult in the acute phase.[63] Noyes and Grood[17] state that rotational instabilities or subluxations must be examined at 20° and 90° of knee flexion. Examination at different angles of flexion will eliminate particular secondary ligamentous restraints, thereby allowing the examiner to be more specific in laxity rotational tests (Table 7-5).

These investigators[17] as well as others[64] state that examining only at 90° and sitting on the patient's foot, as is usually done during testing, limits the amount of allowable rotation and thus the interpretation of laxity of secondary restraining ligaments. After testing for straight anterior laxity at 90° and 20°, the next step is again to apply an anterior load and then internally or externally rotate the tibia, palpating the increase in anterior displacement of each tibiofemoral compartment. An increase in anterior tibial translation refers to laxity of the anterior cruciate ligament; a further increase to the medial or lateral compartment is due to involvement of the secondary medial and lateral constraints (Table 7-5).

Reverse Pivot-Shift Test

Jakob[65] uses this test for assessing posterolateral rotatory instability. The examiner externally rotates the tibia with the knee fully flexed. The examiner then applies a valgus stress to the proximal tibia (Fig 7-36A); this creates the posterolateral subluxation. While maintaining the valgus stress, the examiner slowly extends the externally rotated tibia. At about 40°

knee flexion there is a clunk, indicating reduction of the posterolateral subluxation (Fig. 7-36B).

Clancy[38] states that, if the patient has both a severe posterolateral rotatory instability and an anterior cruciate instability, during the reverse pivot-shift a clunk will occur at 40° flexion (indicating reduction of the posterolateral tibia) and at about 30° to 20° flexion a second clunk will occur. The second clunk represents a forward subluxation of the tibia as a result of an anterior cruciate instability (positive jerk test).

Posterior Instability Tests

Posterior sag sign: If the tibia is posterior because of a posterior cruciate tear and an anterior drawer test is performed, it may be falsely positive. A posterior sag or drop-back test is used instead. The patient is supine with the knees flexed 90° and the feet on the table or the examiner supporting the feet. The examiner observes both knee tibial tuberosities; the involved tibia should drop posteriorly. Palpation will reveal a diminished tibial plateau.

Dynamic posterior shift test (Shelbourne et al)[66]: The examiner is standing lateral to the extremity. He or she flexes the patient's hip and knee to 90° and supports the anterolateral thigh with the inferior forearm, keeping the femur in the neutral position (Fig. 7-37A). With the other hand holding the

Table 7-5 Primary and Secondary Ligamentous Restraints to Laxity Tests

Laxity Test	Primary Restraint				Secondary Restraint		
	Medial	Central	Lateral		Medial	Central	Lateral
Anterior drawer		ACL		20°/90°	TCL + MM		ALS
Anterior drawer + internal rotation		ACL	ALS	20°/90°			FCL + PLS
Anterior drawer + exterior rotation	TCL + MM	ACL		20°/90°	PMS		
Flexion-rotation drawer + pivot-shift		ACL		15°	MM + TCL + PMS		ALS + FCL
Posterior drawer		PCL		20°/90°	PMS + TCL		FCL + PLS
Posterior drawer + external rotation			FCL + PLS	30°		PCL	
		PCL	FCL + PLS	90°			
Posterior drawer + internal rotation	TCL + PMS			20°		ACL + PCL	
	TCL + POL	PCL		90°		ACL	
Valgus	TCL + PMS		Bone	5°		PCL + ACL	
	TCL		Bone	20°	PMS	PCL	
Varus	Bone		FCL + PLS	5°		ACL + PCL	
	Bone		FCL	20°		ACL	PLS
External rotation	PMS + TCL		FCL + PLS	30°	MM	PCL	
	MM + TCL	PCL	FCL + PLS	90°	PMS		
Internal rotation	TCL + PMS	ACL	ALS	20°		PCL	FCL
	TCL + POL	ACL + PCL	ALS	90°			FCL

Abbreviations: ALS, iliotibial band plus anterior plus midlateral capsule; PLS, popliteus, posterolateral capsule; PMS, posterior oblique ligament plus posteromedial capsule; MM, medial meniscus; POL, posterior oblique ligament; TCL, tibial collateral ligament; FCL, fibular collateral ligament.

Source: Reproduced with permission from Noyes FR, Grood ES, Classification of ligament injuries: Why an anterolateral laxity of anteromedial laxity is not a diagnosis entity. In Griffin PP (ed): *American Academy of Orthopaedic Surgeons Instructional Course Lectures XXXVI.* Park Ridge, IL, American Academy of Orthopaedic Surgeons, 1987, p. 194.

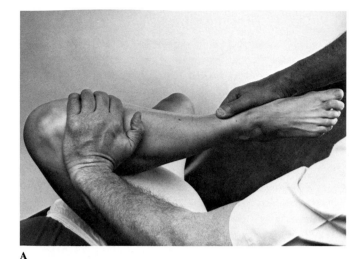

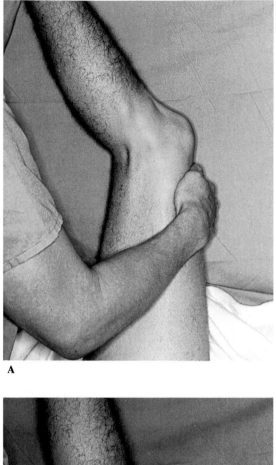

A

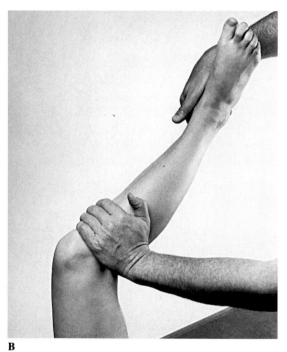

B

Figure 7-36 Reverse pivot-shift test for posterolateal rotatory instability. (**A**) Practitioner externally rotates tibia on fully flexed knee and applies valgus stress to proximal tibia. This will create posterolateral subluxation. (**B**) As practitioner slowly extends leg, at about 40° knee flexion a clunk indicates reduction of posterolateral subluxation.

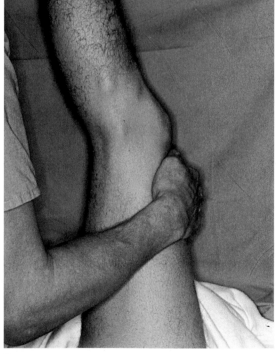

B

distal calf or heel, the examiner slowly passively extends the knee (Fig. 7-37B). If there is posterior instability of the tibia then increasing extension of the knee will stretch and tighten the hamstrings, which will assist gravity in causing posterior subluxation of the tibia. As the knee is brought to full extension, the posterior subluxation will reduce itself and create a visible and palpable jerk or clunk. If the patient's hamstrings are already shortened, the examiner may have to decrease hip flexion as the knee reaches full extension. With straight posterior instability both tibial plateaus will move forward (reduce) equally during knee extension. If there is a post-

Figure 7-37 Dynamic posterior shift test (for posterior tibia instability). (**A**) Practitioner flexes patient's hip and knee to 90°. Initially as leg is passively extended, tightened hamstring will posteriorly subluxate tibia. (**B**) As knee is brought into extension, posterior subluxation will reduce itself, creating a visible and palpable clunk. *Source*: Reprinted with permission from *American Journal of Sports Medicine* (1989;17[2]:76), Copyright © 1989, American Orthopaedic Society for Sports Medicine.

erolateral instability the lateral plateau will be pulled posteriorly during the initial stretch, and tibial anterior rotation will be seen with terminal knee extension.

Meniscus Tests

McMurray's Test[67]: The patient is supine with the knee flexed completely on the fully flexed hip and the heel as near the buttock as the patient can reach. The examiner externally rotates the foot, thereby putting pressure on the medial meniscus tear from the medial femoral condyle (Fig. 7-38A). The examiner then slowly extends the knee while palpating the posterior medial joint line and at the same time exerting a slight varus force at the knee (Fig. 7-38B), attempting to elicit a painful snap that the patient states is characteristic of what he or she feels. The same procedure is followed starting from the flexed knee position with the foot medially rotated and a slight valgus force exerted to stress the lateral meniscus.

A modification of the first test is for the examiner to bring the completely flexed tibia into valgus, externally rotate the foot, and perform a half-moon rotation (Fig. 7-39A). Then, while the tibia is in valgus, the examiner internally rotates the foot and again performs a half-moon rotation (Fig. 7-39B). During the half-moon rotation the knee flexion must be maintained. The examiner then moves the tibia into varus and performs the same procedure: a half-moon rotation with the foot again internally and externally rotated. The examiner should be palpating the posterior joint line during this procedure, checking for pain, apprehension, and a click. A click or snap without pain is not necessarily significant. A click could be due to flexion-extension clicks due to synovial fold (plica), patellar lesions, osteochondral loose bodies, or even the knee reducing from a subluxation as a result of an anterior cruciate tear. The above tests are checking for a posterior horn tear. The tests do not definitely define the location or side of the tear. After testing is completed in full flexion, the same procedure can be carried out in decreasing degrees of flexion to stress the middle third of the meniscus. McMurray's test may be more positive with a response of pain than with an audible or palpable meniscal click.[68] The tests should be repeated if they are not positive on the first try. In a chronic meniscus problem, the above tests may be negative. The examiner may have to rely on the history and joint line tenderness.

Additional meniscus tests: To test for a tear of the anterior horn,[2] the standing patient internally and externally rotates on an extended knee.

In Apley's test, the patient is prone with the knee flexed 90°. The examiner compresses the knee by pressing on the patient's foot. A modification of this test[2,37] to compress the medial meniscus is to move the tibia into slight varus and internally rotate the tibia (Fig. 7-40A) while maintaining foot compression and then to flex and extend the knee, attempting to elicit a painful click (Fig. 7-40B). The same procedure can be done by applying compression to a valgus-directed, externally rotated tibia to compress the lateral meniscus. If clicking is heard around 45° to 60°, the middle meniscus may be

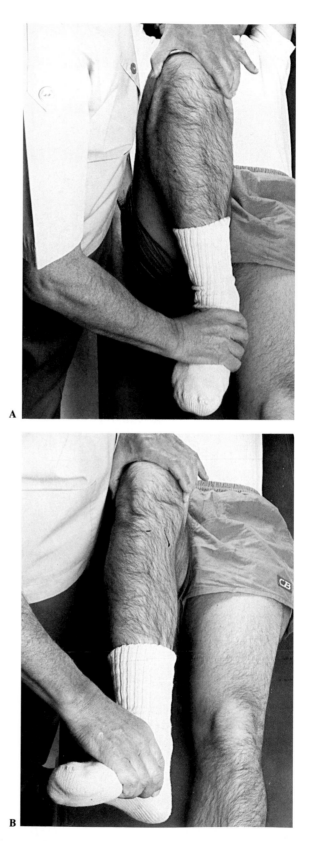

Figure 7-38 McMurray test for trapping displaced posterior horn to middle medial meniscus. Knee is fully flexed, and tibia is externally rotated. **(A)** Beginning of test. **(B)** Examiner slowly extends externally rotated leg to 90° while exerting a slight varus force with left hand. Patient must complain of painful snap if positive. Opposite procedure is used for lateral meniscus testing.

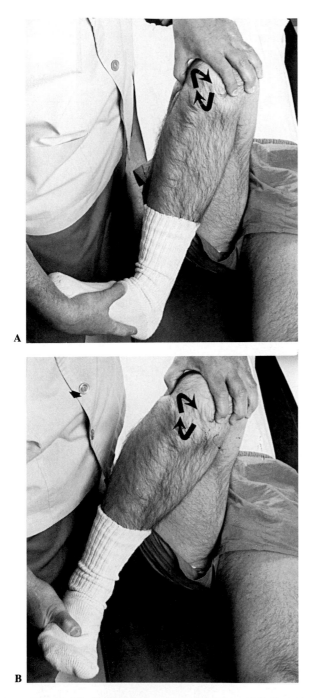

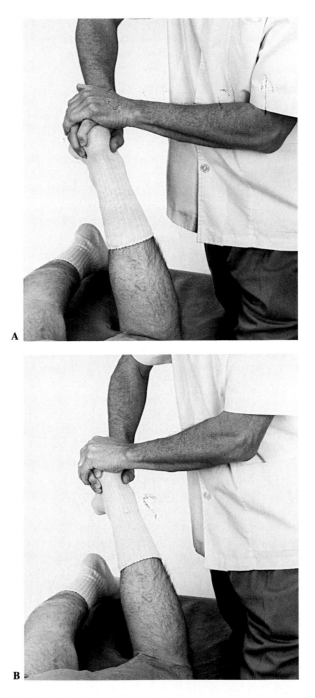

Figure 7-39 Modified McMurray's test. **(A)** Practitioner fully flexes knee, puts leg into valgus, externally rotates tibia, and performs half-moon rotation of knee while keeping knee flexed. **(B)** Same position and procedure as in Figure 7-38B is used except foot is internally rotated.

Figure 7-40 Modified Apley's test. **(A)** To compress medial meniscus practitioner exerts downward pressure, moves tibia into slight varus, and internally rotates foot. **(B)** While maintaining position shown in (A), practitioner slowly flexes and extends knee, attempting to elicit a painful clunk.

involved. Crepitus throughout the grind instead of a click may be due to degenerative joint disease. Compression also may aggravate a patellar problem that is unrelated to the meniscus.

Comments: McMurray's and Apley's tests may elicit pain if the lateral ligaments are involved because rotational loading will aggravate the ligaments, thereby giving a false-positive meniscus test.[38] Varus, valgus, and medial and lateral rotation

testing should therefore be done first. Garrick and Webb[69] feel that the use of the McMurray and Apley grind test in the acute case may further trap the meniscus and increase the injury. They describe a more ''gentle'' test for a meniscal impingement: For a medial meniscus lesion, the knee is flexed 90° and allowed to flop medially thereby opening the medial joint space. The examiner puts his or her fingertip into the joint space to exert pressure against the meniscus. The hip is then abducted and the knee extended. If the meniscus is not torn, there will be no pain. If there is pain or catching, then a medial meniscus lesion is a possibility. The lateral meniscus may be tested in an opposite manner. All the above meniscus tests may be unreliable in the face of degenerative disease from arthritis, which can elicit positive meniscal tests (E Rashkoff, personal communication, 1989) (see below, Meniscus Lesions and Degenerative Joint Disease).

LESIONS

The soft tissue lesions of the knee that can be diagnosed through functional examination and testing are listed in Appendix 7-A.

Tendinitis

In the typical tendinitis overuse-type syndromes there may be local extra-articular swelling rather than the diffuse, symmetric intra-articular swelling. Pain usually diminishes with rest.

Extensor Patellar Tendinitis (Jumper's Knee)

This is a traction overuse syndrome that can be divided into either quadriceps tendinitis or patellar tendinitis depending on whether the quadriceps bone-tendon junction of the superior patella or the bone-tendon junction of the inferior patella is primarily involved. Quadriceps tendinitis is more common in the age group older than 30 years compared to patellar tendinitis, which is more common in the adolescent population. Involvement of the quadriceps in an adolescent is probably an avulsion of the proximal patellar epiphysis rather than actual quadriceps tendinitis.[70]

The most common area of involvement is the inferior pole of the patella. Other areas of involvement include the lateral and medial patella (insertional tendinitis of the vastus medialis or lateralis); the superior pole of the patella, and sometimes near the tibial insertion of the patellar tendon.[71–73] Involvement near the tibial insertion might be Osgood-Schlatter disease, which can be considered another overuse type lesion of the insertion of the tendon into a growth center or traction apophysis.[69] The condition is common in sports, especially basketball[74] and volleyball,[75] and any occupation involving excessive climbing or kneeling.

This is a typical overuse pathology.[76] Most of the pathology consists of fibroblastic proliferation, necrosis, myxomatous degeneration, and increased thickness of the insertional fibrocartilage at the bone-tendon junction. Pure tendon pathology has been noted only in cases treated with steroid injection.[75] Patients so treated at the patellar tendon are prone to developing ruptures.[77] Because no one has seen the pathology of acute inflammation, there has been confusion regarding the use of the term *patellar tendinitis*.[78]

Symptoms may include burning pain with use or after prolonged sitting with the knee flexed. There may be localized swelling and erythema along the patellar tendon depending on the amount of inflammation. In chronic cases, a nodule of scar tissue that is often tender can be palpated in the tendon or near its insertion site into the patella.[2] Subtle lateral subluxation may be a cause of overloading of the patellar tendon.[2] Tight hamstrings may create abnormal extensor stress, but Ferretti et al[79] found that the only correlating factors between tight hamstrings and jumper's knee were hard playing surfaces and overtraining, not malalignment of the extensor mechanism.

Other conditions that must be considered with jumper's knee are Osgood-Schlatter disease (involvement of the tibial apophysis) and inflammation of the fat pad below the patellar tendon, which may become fibrosed (usually as a result of multiple surgeries or trauma). If the fibrosis increases there may be scarring of the retropatellar tendon bursa and patellar tendon down to the proximal tibia,[46] causing a patella baja. Retropatellar bursitis may cause pain on active terminal knee extension, which compresses the bursa.[46] There may be fibrosis of the plica or lateral patellotibial ligament, which may mimic patellar tendinitis.

Blazina[80] describes four stages of jumper's knee. Stage 1 is pain only after activity. Stage 2 is pain at the beginning of activity that disappears after warm-up and returns after activity. Stage 3 is constant pain at rest and inability of the patient to participate in sports. Stage 4 is complete rupture of the patellar tendon.

Functional tests

1. Probable pain on resisted knee extension. A lesion located at the inferior pole may not be revealed by testing. The examiner should tip open the inferior pole by pressing down on the superior pole of the patella and pressing in with a finger. Local tenderness will be present. Findings should always be compared with those for the opposite knee.
2. Possible pain on passive knee flexion.

Treatment: The condition responds extremely well to friction massage. The examiner should assess for the necessity of hamstring stretching and quadriceps strengthening. Use of a Palumbo brace may diminish the tensile stress at the bone-tendon junction.[78]

This condition is not self-limiting. Without proper treatment and with continued overuse, it may progress through the different stages described above. Stage 3 may sometimes be irreversible and require surgery.[73] During the acute phase the standard methods for treating overuse syndromes may be used: rest (while symptomatic); warm-up before use; stretching; ice after use; patella-restraining brace; and eventual strengthening of the quadriceps, hamstrings, hip abductors and adductors. Colosimo and Basset[78] do not operate until after 6 months of conservative treatment.

Black and Alten[76] describe an exercise that relieves pain in both acute and chronic conditions and gets athletes back to competition quickly. They also use it as a preactivity stretching routine or even during competition. First, the patient completely plantar flexes the foot with the knee extended while the examiner puts pressure over the toes and dorsal foot to stretch the anterior crural muscles. A set of 10 stretches is done for 30 seconds each. Next, a concentric-eccentric exercise is performed. The supine patient's knee is flexed 30° while resting on a pillow. The examiner holds the proximal tibia and with the other hand holds the dorsal phalanges and metatarsals. The examiner resists against foot dorsiflexion and maintains resistance, allowing the patient to dorsiflex to 90° and then to plantar flex against resistance. Black and Alten[76] recommend three sets of 10 to 15 repetitions. They state that the active shortening and lengthening of the anterior compartment muscles under tension reduce infrapatellar pain (see Chapter 10). Rehabilitation of the VMO isometrically (quadriceps sets) and isotonically is essential.

Hamstring Insertional Tendinitis

When dealing with the medial hamstring insertion differentiation must be made with a pes anserinus bursitis, which may refer pain to the distal medial hamstrings. Differentiation between these two conditions is not always clear (see below, Pes Anserinus Bursitis; see also Chapter 6). Long-distance runners are prone to tendinitis of the insertion of the semimembranosus on the posterior medial capsule of the knee.[71] Foot pronation may affect the semimembranosus insertion (Fig. 7-41). The semimembranosus and popliteus syner-

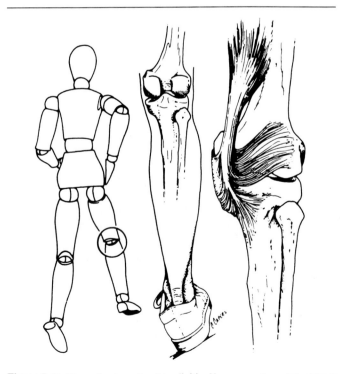

Figure 7-41 Hamstring insertional tendinitis. Hyperpronation of the foot or internal torsion of the hip and femur can stress the insertion of the semimembranosus at the knee. *Source*: Reprinted with permission from *Clinics in Sports Medicine* (1987;6[2]:385), Copyright © 1987, W.B. Saunders Company.

gistically prevent excessive external rotation of the tibia. Internal torsion or anteversion of the hip and femur may stress the semimembranosus insertion.[71] There is usually pain in activities involving active knee flexion. In palpating for involvement of the distal biceps, to reduce any stress from an irritated iliotibial band (which may confuse the palpatory localization of pain) the examiner could abduct the thigh with the patient prone to relax the iliotibial band.

Functional tests

1. Pain on resisted testing of knee flexion of medial and/or lateral sides.
2. Possible pain on passive internal or external rotation of the tibia on the femur when the patient is supine with the knee extended.

Treatment: Along with all the established methods of treating hamstring strains (see Chapters 6, 10, and 12), friction is a primary treatment for chronic hamstring strains. Hamstring injury is repaired only by scar formation; there is no muscle repair.[81] Along with stretching and examination of the running technique, Hunter and Poole[71] recommend resisted toe curls and posterior tibialis strengthening. Besides stretching, strengthening of the hamstrings is necessary before returning to full activities.

Popliteus Tendon Tenosynovitis

The patient usually complains of pain on downhill running or walking but no pain on uphill running because a function of the popliteus muscle is to retard forward displacement of the femur on the flexed tibia during the stance phase of gait (see Popliteus Muscle). Pain occurs on the lateral aspect of the knee on weight bearing with the knee flexed 15° to 20°.[82] There may be pain on sitting cross-legged. Pain may begin within a few minutes to 24 hours after extensive activity, and symptoms may disappear immediately or within 24 hours.[82] An easy way to palpate the popliteus muscle for tenderness after functional testing is to have the patient sit in a figure-four position (ankle over the opposite knee), palpate the fibular collateral ligament, and then to feel the popliteal muscle anterior to the fibular collateral ligament over the lateral femoral condyle.

A synovial bursa separates the muscle from the collateral ligament, and another bursa separates it from the femoral condyle[23] inside the joint. Both a tenosynovitis and a bursitis therefore may be present; these are clinically difficult to distinguish.

Functional tests

1. Definite pain on resisted testing of popliteus (patient is prone with the knee flexed 20°). Basmajian and Deluca[22] state that the most activity of the popliteus muscle with the patient prone occurs at 20° flexion. The patient rotates the tibia medially on the femur while the examiner resists against the distal medial foot with counterpressure against the lateral calcaneus (Fig. 7-42).

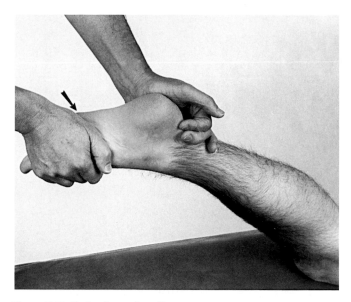

Figure 7-42 Resisted test of popliteus.

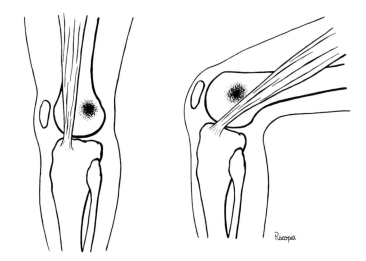

Figure 7-43 Iliotibial band friction syndrome. With motion of the knee the iliotibial band passes over the prominent lateral femoral condyle, and pain can arise at the condyle. *Source*: Reprinted with permission from JA Nicholas and EB Hershman, *The Lower Extremity and Spine in Sports Medicine* (p 1003), St. Louis, 1986, The C.V. Mosby Co.

2. Possible pain on passive external rotation of the tibia on a fixed femur while the patient is supine.
3. Possible pain on standing on the affected leg with the knee flexed 30° and actively rotating the femur internally on a fixed tibia.[82]

Treatment: Friction, knee and foot joint play mobilization, cryotherapy, trigger point, and therapeutic muscle stretching (TMS) are all helpful. The patient should run only on level surfaces until the lesion is healed (10 days to 6 weeks).[71] The feet (pronation), knee mechanics, and running gait should all be evaluated. Garrick and Webb[69] feel that excessive quadriceps fatigue will predispose to popliteus involvement.

Iliotibial Band Friction Syndrome

This syndrome presents as lateral knee pain due to tightness of the iliotibial band and hip abductors (see above, Iliotibial Band; see also Chapter 6). The condition is usually associated with runners. As a result of movement of the band during flexion and extension of the knee (Fig. 7-43) and hip, a tight band could be responsible for inflammation of the bursae (greater trochanter), along the iliotibial tract, and at the periosteum of the lateral femoral condyle. The patient may feel pain on walking or running either uphill or downhill. The pain is usually felt over the lateral femoral condyle about 1 in above the joint line and may radiate inferiorly to the muscle's insertion on Gerdy's tubercle.[83] Pain is usually most evident at the end of the swing phase, when the decelerating leg reaches heel strike.[84]

Possible causes for this syndrome are leg length deficiencies, cross-over gait, hip abduction contractures, tensor fasciae latae and gluteus maximus contractures, loss of flexibility in the hamstrings and quadriceps, weakness of the quadriceps, varus

knee alignment, internal tibial torsion, tight heel cords, a tight posterior tibialis tendon, and pronation of the feet causing tibial internal rotation, the last of which may stress the band between its insertion and the lateral epicondyle.[23] Boland[23] states that if there is a varus knee alignment a lateral heel wedge may be needed instead of a medial wedge, which may aggravate the condition.

Mennell[85] relates a taut iliotibial band as a cause of a posterior sacroiliac subluxation. He states that the subluxation will not clear up or will continue to recur until the taut band is released. If the band contains sensitive fibrositic deposits, there will be a generalized ache in the thigh.

Functional tests

1. Probable positive Ober's test (see Chapter 6).
2. Probable positive Ober's test performed with flexion and extension of the knee. If Ober's test is positive, the upper thigh and leg will remain passively abducted. The examiner can then increase the tension on the leg by adducting the leg further and, while palpating the lateral condyle, flexing and extending the knee within the 30° to 40° range. This movement should create the patient's pain[14] (Fig. 7-44).
3. Possible pain if supine patient flexes the knee 20° and adducts the hip. This position creates maximal tension on the iliotibial band. The test will probably be painful in severe cases.[39]
4. Possible pain on standing on the affected leg with the knee held in 30° to 40° of flexion.[21]
5. No pain on varus knee stress test.[21]

Treatment: Biomechanical problems relating to the hip, knee, and feet should be evaluated. Stretching of the band

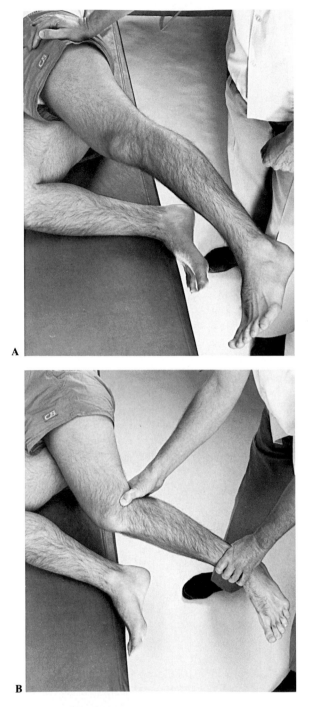

Figure 7-44 Iliotibial band friction syndrome. (**A**) Demonstration of positive Ober's test before testing knee for pain over lateral epicondyle. (**B**) After positive Ober's test reveals tight iliotibial band, examiner contacts lateral epicondyle. Examiner holds contact and flexes knee. At 30° to 40° range of knee flexion, knee pain may occur as iliotibial band passes over lateral femoral condyle.

(Fig. 7-45; see also Chapter 14) and friction massage are helpful. Mennell[85] has developed techniques for manual stretching of the band distal to the greater trochanter, overlying the greater trochanter, and proximal to the greater trochanter (see Chapters 10 and 12).

Figure 7-45 Iliotibial band stretch for left lower extremity. Left buttock is externally rotated; both knees are flexed and left foot is adducted. Based on tensor fasciae latae and band acting as medial hip rotator, lateral knee rotator, and knee extensor.

Gastrocnemius-Soleus Strain

The term *tennis leg* has been used to describe strains and partial tears of the medial head of the gastrocnemius muscle. Rupture or strain can occur at the origin near the popliteal space, within the muscle belly, at the musculotendinous junction, or at the tendinous insertion. Injury usually occurs in slow side-to-side sports[86] or in sudden moves involving a dorsiflexed ankle and extended knee. Patient may present with a plantar flexed foot. Significant swelling and ecchymosis may not occur until several days later.

Functional tests

1. Definite pain on standing toe rise.
2. Definite pain on resisted foot plantar flexion with the knee extended. The soleus muscle is involved if there is pain on resisted foot plantar flexion with the knee flexed 90°.
3. Probable pain and restriction on passive foot dorsiflexion.
4. Possible pain and limitation of active and passive knee flexion.
5. Possible pain and limitation of passive knee extension.

Treatment: Millar's[86] treatment (720 patients over 12 years, with recurrence in only 0.7% of the patients) is as follows:

1. For the first 3 days, two or three times a day; ice for 20 minutes and then passive nonpainful stretching. The patient uses a foot strap, pulling the dorsiflexed foot for 10 seconds and relaxing for 10 seconds for a total of 10 minutes.
2. Ultrasound for 5 minutes to relieve soreness.
3. Isotonic exercises for 10 minutes for the antagonists and then the injured muscle.

Unlike most authorities, who recommend a ¼- to ½-in heel lift to allow more painless early walking, Millar[86] recommends a flat heel, which will allow more correct walking. He recommends interferential therapy for extensive swelling and bruising and eventually standing gastrocnemius stretching and strengthening of the quadriceps (because they will weaken from the accompanying limp). Crutches may be needed in early stages. A compression strap over the whole leg or a posterior leg splint may be needed to maintain the foot in neutral.

Light friction is useful in early stages (see Chapters 10, 13, and 14). A severe strain or partial rupture may cause a muscle retraction and a gap in the muscle, and a complete rupture will prevent the patient from standing on the toes.[24] It may take 2 to 3 months to heal if there is a significant partial tear of the medial head.[87] Swelling at the posteromedial knee can be due to inflammation of the bursae near the medial head of the gastrocnemius and semimembranosus. Acute posterior knee pain is usually due to strain of one of the gastrocnemius muscles, mild sprain of the posterior capsule or a posterior cruciate ligament sprain,[38] or rupture of the plantaris muscle.

The gastrocnemius muscle is stretched by leaning against the wall with the front knee bent, the back leg (shortened muscle) extended, the heel on the ground, and the foot slightly turned in. The soleus is stretched by putting the front foot (shortened muscle) forward with the knee bent and the heel on the ground and leaning forward. Stretch should be felt in the lower calf of the front foot.

Bursitis

Baker's Cyst

According to Henning et al,[39] Baker's cyst is due to swelling of the semimembranosus bursa between the semimembranosus and the gastrocnemius tendon. These investigators state that this bursitis may be due to poor flexibility of the gastrocnemius and hamstrings, resulting in tendinitis. Treatment of the tendinitis usually resolves the cyst. They further state that degenerative joint disease or a torn meniscus are other possible causes (see below).

Pes Anserinus Bursitis

This bursa lies about 2 in below the medial joint line[88] between the pes anserinus (gracilis, sartorius, and semitendinosus muscles) above and the medial collateral ligament and anterior medial proximal tibia below. Larsson and Baum[88] found most of their cases in 50- to 80-year old patients, especially obese women. Of their patients with degenerative joint disease, 75% had associated pes anserinus bursitis. Others[89,90] have found the problem in runners and soccer players.

Pain may occur on walking up stairs, in the early stages of training, or after prolonged use (distance running). There is usually pinpoint tenderness 2 in below the medial joint line, and there may be moderate swelling. Pain may radiate into the medial joint and posteromedially along the medial hamstrings. Possible etiologies are overtraining (excessive miles, excessive hills, and improper or inadequate stretching[90]); shortened medial hamstrings, which may compress the bursa with overuse; knee valgus; heel valgus; external tibial torsion; femoral anteversion; and a broad pelvis (in women) with increased Q angle.

Functional tests

1. Probable pain on resisted medial hamstring testing.
2. Probable pain during resisted knee flexion and extension while the tibia is internally rotated.
3. Possible associated hamstring tendinitis. Pinpoint sensitivity and localized swelling over the pes anserinus may help distinguish between the two.

Treatment: Biomechanical evaluation of the lower extremity regarding torsion and angulation is necessary. Flexibility and strengthening of the hamstrings and gastrocnemius-soleus are important. Orthotics for heel and knee valgus may be necessary. Boland[23] states that although cortisone may reduce the inflammation it does not address the biomechanical problems (see Chapters 10 and 14).

Degenerative Joint Disease

Peyron,[91] in his epidemiologic studies, confirms that osteoarthritis is influenced by age (arithmetic up to 50 to 55 years and geometric thereafter); it is more frequent in men younger than 45 years of age and much more frequent in women after 55 years of age. He states that evidence points to both mechanical overuse and a possible systemic factor of cartilage vulnerability. Turek[92] states that factors such as injury (torn menisci, fractures, dislocating or subluxating patella), loose bodies, obesity (valgus and varus), infection, central nervous system diseases, gouty and rheumatoid arthritis, and subchondral necrosis (osteonecrosis and osteochondritis dissecans) may be related to knee osteoarthritis. He states that the patellofemoral articulation is the site of maximum damage, eroding and damaging the femoral condyle, which in turn damages the tibia and causes painful creaking and grating on active motion even before roent-genograms demonstrate a problem. He further states that chondromalacia of the patella may cause the condition.

A prominent symptom in the early stages is a dull ache that may increase with activity. A possible differentiation from rheumatoid arthritis is that in osteoarthritis the morning stiffness is milder and does not last as long.[93] Post[37] describes a particular gait that may occur in osteoarthritis of the knee depending on whether there is a collapse of the medial or lateral knee compartment due to degeneration. Medial degeneration would result in a varus knee, causing the knee to thrust laterally during gait. With lateral knee degeneration, resulting in a valgus knee, there is a medial thrust during gait.

Idiopathic knee arthritis may occur in the tibiofemoral or patellofemoral joint. Barrett et al[94] describe changes such as joint space narrowing, sclerosis, osteophytes, and cysts as presenting predominantly as varus degenerative joint disease when they occur in the medial compartment, as valgus degenerative joint disease when they occur in the lateral compartment, and as primary patellofemoral arthritis when they occur in the patellofemoral joint. These investigators found that valgus degenerative joint disease was twice as common in women than men and that patellofemoral arthritis was 7 times more common in women than men. They found at surgery that valgus degenerative joint disease occurred more posteriorly on the femoral condyle than varus disease.

Therefore, for the clinician to evaluate degenerative joint disease of the knee on roentgenograms it is important to examine the patient in the weight-bearing position. Rosenberg et al[95] found that posteroanterior weight-bearing studies with the knees in 45° of flexion and the beam centered at the level of the inferior pole of the patella and directed 10° caudad were important for estimating the severity of knee osteoarthritis (Fig. 7-46). The normal cartilage space is usually 4 mm or more medially and 5 mm or more laterally, so that narrowing of the medial space to 1 to 2 mm would indicate major degeneration. Skyline views are used to diagnose patellofemoral arthritis.

Functional tests

1. Capsular pattern of more limitation of flexion than extension.
2. Loss of joint play.

Treatment: Restoration of joint play movements often relieves pain by restoring the lost involuntary accessory movement. Loss of abduction or adduction accessory movement is common. The crepitus of arthritis often refers to the breakdown of collagen. Because one function of collagen is to resist shear stress, exercises that create shear stress such as the progressive resistive type (for the quadriceps) may be detrimental to the arthritic knee. Exercises that generate compression forces such as straight-leg raises, Nordic track, and swimming are more beneficial.[96] Depending on the stage of the condition, the patient may require crutches temporarily to reduce weight bearing. Cryotherapy (20 to 30 minutes three

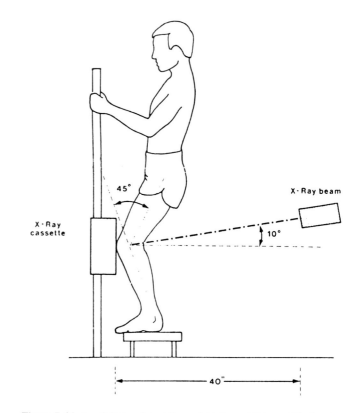

Figure 7-46 A weight-bearing radiograph to document accurately the severity of knee osteoarthritis. Narrowing of the medial space to 1 to 2 mm indicates major degeneration. *Source:* Reprinted with permission from TD Rosenberg, LE Paulos, RD Parker, et al, ''The Forty-five Degree Posteroanterior Flexion Weight-bearing Radiograph of the Knee'' in *Journal of Bone and Joint Surgery* (1988;70A[10]:1479), Copyright © 1988, Journal of Bone and Joint Surgery, Inc.

times per day) and modalities such as ultrasound, and acupuncture may relieve the pain. Biomechanical evaluation of the lower extremity is necessary, including angulation of the extremities and feet, which may benefit from orthoses. Muscle strength and flexibility are important, especially for the quadriceps.

Ligamentous Sprains

A recent hypothesis regarding ligament function[58] states that ligaments have a high and low load function. The high load relies on the strength of the ligament to stabilize the joint against loads that the muscles can no longer support. High load may be related to trauma, which occurs too rapidly for the muscles to equilibrate. Therefore, the ligaments are stressed in a sudden injury when the neuromuscular component is unable to compensate. In situations in which the muscles can compensate, the muscles are stimulated to contract by a ligamentomuscular reflex caused by the tension created in the ligaments. Receptors in the ligament therefore stimulate the muscles to contract, thereby stabilizing the joint. The low load function of ligaments is to maintain normal joint kinematics so that normal joint lubrication and muscle function can occur. Determining the mechanism of injury is important in knee diagnosis; Table 7-6 lists the common mechanisms of knee injury (see also above, Grading Sprains).

Ligamentous injuries usually create localized pinpoint tenderness at the area of injury. Pain does not necessarily have to occur immediately, and if the ligament is completely torn (grade 3) there may be minimal pain and more of a complaint of instability. Partially injured fibers can still be stressed and create more pain than complete tears.[40]

In the description and examination of ligamentous injuries the following discussions are based on involvement of isolated ligaments. It must be realized that depending on the force and nature of the trauma more than one ligament may be involved. For example, a valgus stress associated with external rotation may create a tibial collateral ligament tear, medial capsule tear, and eventual anterior cruciate ligament tear.

Collateral Ligament Sprain

One of the reasons for more injuries occuring at the medial compartment of the knee compared to the lateral compartment is that the soft tissues on the medial side offer more stability than the lateral side. Dye and Cannon[30] showed that rollback of the femur on the tibia is 10 mm on the medial side compared to 24 mm on the lateral side. These investigators state that the medial side is designed for stability whereas the lateral side is designed for mobility; therefore, the lateral compartment will withstand greater increases in laxity and respond better to movement stress (see above, Medial Knee).

Table 7-6 Common Mechanisms of Knee Injury

Mechanism of Injury (Knee Position*)	Ligament Injury
Valgus (straight medial opening)	Medial collateral plus capsular ligaments†
Valgus external rotation	Medial structures, medial meniscus, anterior cruciate, "terrible triad"
Varus (straight lateral opening)	Lateral collateral plus capsular ligaments†
Varus internal rotation	Lateral ligaments plus anterior cruciate
Varus external rotation	Lateral ligaments plus posterior cruciate
Hyperextension	Posterior capsule and posterior cruciate‡
Direct blow driving tibia backward	Posterior cruciate
Direct blow driving tibia forward	Anterior cruciate

*Tibia moving with femur fixed.
†Severe opening implies injury to either one or both cruciates.
‡Severe hyperextension may also injure the anterior cruciate ligament.

Source: Reprinted from *Athletic Training and Sports Medicine*, (p 265) by AE Ellison et al. (Eds) with permission of the American Academy of Orthopaedic Surgeons, © 1984.

The deep portion of the medial collateral ligament, especially the mid–one-third capsule, blends with the medial meniscus. Depending on the amount of force, the outer tibial collateral ligament will tear before the deeper medial capsule. Sprains of the medial collateral ligament are more easily associated with peripheral meniscus tears than the fibular collateral ligament. The latter is separated from the meniscus by the popliteus tendon, tenosynovium, and fat pad.

Medial Collateral Ligament Sprain

This lesion may be due to a contact injury, such as "clipping" from the lateral side in football, or from noncontact involvement, such as in skiing when the inside edge of the ski catches and causes forced valgus in external rotation or in the whip-kick in the breast stroke when tension in the ligament increases as the knee moves from flexion to extension.[97] The most common noncontact injury is a combination of deceleration, valgus, and external rotation of the leg.[40] Usually with a valgus force the menisci are not torn because it takes compression and shear forces to tear a meniscus. It is possible for the meniscus to be detached if the meniscotibial ligament tears, so that a detached rather than a torn meniscus could occur.[15] A clip to the outside of the knee may initially only create pain on the lateral knee; it may be hours before the medial knee becomes bothersome.[53]

The age of the patient is significant when a ligament tears. In a clipping-type trauma to the lateral or posterolateral portion of a flexed knee, a 10- to 16-year-old patient may have separation of the distal femoral epiphysis because the ligaments are stronger than the growth plate; someone between 16 and 40 years may have a tear of the medial collateral and anterior cruciate ligaments.[40]

Depending on the site of medial collateral injury, the maximum pain may occur at its origin, at the joint line, or at the insertion three to four fingerbreadths below the joint line. There may be local extra-articular swelling. Because the tibial collateral ligament is extracapsular, any large effusion is indicative of intra-articular lesions such as meniscal pathology. If a meniscus tear is associated with a medial collateral sprain, there is probably other associated ligamentous damage.[98] The chronic medial collateral lesion usually shows a limited range of motion in the end range flexion or extension. There may or may not be pain on valgus stress unless the patient is examined after use.

Functional tests

1. Definite pain on valgus stress at 30° flexion (examiner must determine the grade of the sprain).
2. No pain on valgus stress in extension.
3. Pain on passive tibial lateral rotation if the ligament is sprained; anterior displacement on the medial side if the ligament is ruptured.

Treatment: Grade 1 and 2 sprains can be successfully treated nonoperatively; complete tears may need surgery because of accompanying cruciate and meniscus lesions.[99] Complete tears of the ligament may be treated nonoperatively if there is clinical (negative Lachman's and pivot-shift tests) or arthroscopic confirmation of a normal anterior cruciate ligament.[100] Light friction massage is recommended for acute grade 1 and 2 sprains, with firmer friction being applied within 2 weeks (see Chapter 12). Table 7-7 summarizes test results and diagnoses of ligamentous injuries, and Table 7-8 gives Clancy's[38] treatment protocol for isolated collateral ligament injuries.

Zarins and Nemeth[40] state that a grade 2 sprain should not be immobilized in a cast because a long cast does not significantly restrict medial opening and because ligaments lose tensile strength with immobilization. They state that as long as the anterior cruciate is not injured treatment should consist of protected weight bearing, splinting for relief of pain, early range of motion, and isometric exercises. With this regime players can return to sports in 3 to 6 weeks.

Some of the criteria suggested by Ellsasser et al[101] for nonoperative treatment of collateral ligament injuries are as follows:

1. In varus-valgus 0° extension the knee should be stable.
2. Valgus-varus range at 30° flexion should not be more than 10° greater than the preinjury range (if known or as judged from the other knee).
3. Significant rotatory or sagittal instability should not be present.
4. Tenderness at the medial collateral ligament should be localized and not diffuse.

These investigators state that patients with well-developed muscles to support their knees usually do not need external support. They also stress early motion.

Mulawka and Jensen[98] stress aggressive reduction of any swelling, which usually tends to inhibit quadriceps contraction. They use a simple hinged brace with a varus strap locked in 30° flexion in the early stages. The brace is unlocked in grade 1 sprains in 7 to 10 days; in grade 2 sprains in 7 to 18 days; and in grade 3 sprains in 10 to 21 days. They state that the diagnosis should be re-evaluated if there is persistent pain and diffusion, lack of return to motion, catching or locking, or "giving way" of the knee.

Indelicato[100] recommends a three-phase nonoperative treatment protocol for third-degree sprains. The first phase consists of an orthosis and 30° of flexion, partial weight bearing with crutches, and strengthening exercises. The second phase allows knee motion from 30° to 90° with subsequent addition of isotonic and isokinetic exercises and full weight bearing without crutches, if tolerable. The third phase includes removal of the orthosis, continuation of the exercise regimen, and institution of a running program. Garrick and Webb[69] state that a temporary subluxation of the knee must occur in a grade 3 sprain; therefore, radiographs are necessary to rule out intra-articular fractures or bony avulsions.

It is essential to obtain as much painless mobility as possible to prevent chronicity resulting from scar tissue adherence of the medial collateral to bone and capsule. For chronic collateral ligamentous lesions, deep friction and knee joint mobilization are recommended to break up chronic scar tissue.

Lateral (Fibular) Collateral Sprain

This lesion is usually caused by a varus stress during hyperextension. The fibular collateral ligament is involved not nearly as often as the medial collateral ligament. When it is involved, it is often associated with involvement of surrounding tissues such as the lateral capsule, biceps tendon, iliotibial tract, and arcuate complex (the capsular ligament between the popliteus muscle and the fibula). The fibular collateral is extra-articular, and if it is torn by itself there will not be an intra-articular effusion unless deeper structures are involved. The ligament can be easily palpated in the figure-four knee position.

Functional tests

1. Definite pain on 30° varus stress test.
2. No significant pain on varus extension.
3. Pain on passive tibial medial rotation if the ligament is sprained; anterior displacement on the lateral side if the ligament is ruptured.

Treatment: Treatment is similar to that used for medial collateral ligament sprains.

Meniscotibial (Coronary) Ligament Sprain

In the deeper portion of the medial collateral ligament the medial portions of the meniscofemoral and meniscotibial ligaments blend in with the joint capsule and tibial collateral ligament. These ligaments originate from the periphery of the femur or tibial plateau and attach to the periphery of the whole menisci. They probably play a role in maintaining the stability of the menisci. The meniscofemoral ligaments are rarely involved compared to the meniscotibial ligaments. The meniscotibial ligaments are usually sprained during knee rotation or flexion and most often on the medial side. In a review of more than 2000 knee arthrograms performed over 8 years, Khoury and associates[102] never encountered a meniscotibial ligament tear over the lateral aspect of the joint.

Hughston et al[103] stated that a positive anterior drawer test was more consistently positive with a tear of the meniscotibial ligament than a tear of the anterior cruciate ligament. The coronary ligament sprain is often overlooked when the primary injury is a meniscus or collateral ligament problem. Often a patient will complain of an achy knee after tennis or of a knee that has never "felt right" since a meniscus operation or after a knee sprain years ago. In this chronic situation, the coronary findings will be pain on extreme passive rotation of the tibia on the femur and possible pain on forced passive flexion or extension.[104] If the coronaries are neglected, scar-

Table 7-7 Summary of Test Results and Diagnosis

Test and Findings	Diagnosis
Valgus at 30°	
No laxity, medial pain.	Grade I superficial medial ligament sprain does not rule out injuries to anterior, posterior, and lateral structures.
Slight to moderate laxity, distinguishable end point, medial pain.	Grade II superficial medial ligament sprain does not rule out other injuries.
Moderate to severe laxity, soft or indistinguishable end point, variable pain.	Grade III superficial medial ligament; other structures at risk because prime stabilizer absent—check in extension.
Valgus at 0°	
No laxity, medial pain.	Grade I superficial medial ligament sprain does not rule out other injuries.
Slight to moderate laxity, distinguishable end point, medial pain.	Grade II superficial medial ligament sprain does not rule out other injuries.
Moderate to severe laxity, soft or indistinguishable end point, variable pain.	Grade III superficial medial ligament sprain, posteromedial and posterior capsular tears. Almost always Grade III anterior cruciate ligament tear (check anterior displacement). More severe injuries will involve posterior cruciate ligament (check posterior displacement).
Varus at 30°	
Stable, lateral pain.	Grade I lateral collateral ligament sprain.
Mild to moderate instability, distinguishable end point, lateral pain.	Grade II lateral collateral ligament sprain, popliteus-arcuate complex.
Moderate to severe instability, soft end point, variable pain.	Grade III lateral collateral ligament sprain, popliteus-arcuate complex. Iliotibial band inconsistently involved. Other structures (biceps) may be involved—check in extension.
Varus at 0°	
Stable, lateral pain.	Grade I lateral collateral ligament sprain.
Mild to moderate instability, solid end point, variable pain.	Grade II lateral collateral ligament sprain, popliteus-arcuate complex.
Moderate to severe instability, soft end point, variable pain.	Grade III lateral collateral ligament sprain, popliteus-arcuate complex. Anterior cruciate ligament almost always involved. Posterior cruciate frequently involved. Other structures commonly injured (eg, biceps and iliotibial band). A severe injury. Be sure to check status of peroneal nerve and circulation.
Anterior tibial displacement at or near 0° (Lachman's test)	
Stable, good end point.	Anterior cruciate intact (does not rule out damage to medial or lateral structures).
Insignificant to slight increase in excursion, soft indistinguishable end point.	Grade III tear of anterior cruciate; medial and lateral sides may be clinically intact.
Significant increase in excursion, soft end point.	Grade III tear of anterior cruciate; high probability of damage to medial, lateral, or both sides.
Anterior tibial displacement at 90°, neutral rotation (anterior drawer test)	
No significant increase in displacement, distinguishable end point.	Does not rule out anterior cruciate injury. Quality of end point is the critical factor. Displacement and end point often difficult to assess; examination in extension is the more sensitive test and thus is the best criterion for diagnosis.
Slight to moderate displacement, variable pain, indistinguishable end point.	Anterior cruciate injury possibly clinically isolated (check in extension and respective sides).
Moderate to severe displacement, soft or absent end point.	Grade III anterior cruciate tear. Involvement of medial, lateral, or both sides.
Posterior tibial displacement	
Soft end point, minimal to mild instability.	Grade III posterior cruciate ligament tear.
Soft end point, moderate to severe instability.	Grade III posterior cruciate ligament tear. Other structures involved (posterior capsule, popliteus-arcuate complex, lateral collateral ligament, medial collateral ligament).

Table 7-8 Treatment Protocol for Isolated Collateral Ligament Injuries: Rehabilitation of First-, Second-, and Third-Degree Isolated Medial and Lateral Collateral Ligament Injuries

---

Day 1 to day 3:
1. Crutches with partial weight bearing
2. Compression dressing—loosen if ankle becomes swollen
3. Ice three to four times a day for 10 minutes
4. Quad sets—three sets of 20 repetitions, three times per day
5. Straight-leg lifts—three sets of 20 repetitions, three times per day
6. Wear knee immobilizer at night

Day 3 to approximately day 7:
1. Whirlpool for range of motion (biking motion), cold water for first 3 to 4 days, then warm water
2. May use swimming pool instead, 30 to 45 minutes straight-ahead flutter kick trying to bend knee
3. Straight-leg raises with maximum weight that can be done 12 times; do three sets of 12 repetitions:
   a. Hip extension
   b. Hip flexion
   c. Hip abduction
      1. Knee kept straight
      2. No hip adduction
4. Continue with crutches and knee immobilizers and can bear weight as tolerated
5. Continue quad set exercises
6. Can discard knee immobilizer after seventh day

Day 7 to day 14 (if 90 degrees of knee flexion present):
1. Whirlpool or swimming for range of motion
2. Exercise bike for 15 minutes, if Fitron 60 rpm
3. Quad sets continued
4. Orthotron, speed 5—3 sets of 10 repetitions or Universal or Nautilus weight program
   a. Quadriceps—3 sets of 12 repetitions with maximum weight tolerated
   b. Hamstrings—3 sets of 12 repetitions with maximum weight tolerated
5. Crutches to be continued until patient can walk without a limp

Day 14 to completion (if full range of flexion and extension):
1. Whirlpool
2. Bike 15 minutes
3. Orthotron—three sets of 10 repetitions at speed 3; three sets of 10 repetitions at speed 5 when equal to opposite side; then three sets of 10 repetitions at speed 7
   Nautilus or Universal—three sets of 12 repetitions of maximum weights for quadriceps and hamstrings
4. Start running program—
   Jog 1 mile then:
   6 × 80 yards at ½ speed
   6 × 80 yards at ¾ speed
   6 × 80 yards at full speed
   6 × 80 yards at ½ speed cutting
   6 × 80 yards at full speed cutting
   Stop at any point when there is pain or a limp. Each day patient must start the entire running program over until it can be completed in 1 day.

To return to practice patient:
1. Must have full range of motion
2. Must have no pain
3. Must have quadriceps and hamstring strength within 90% of the normal leg
4. Must be able to complete the entire running program
5. Should be checked by a physician when he or she completes the entire program if there has been a second- or third-degree ligament injury

---

Source: Reprinted with permission from WG Clancy, "Conservative Treatment of Acute Knee Ligamentous Injuries" in *Symposium on Sports Medicine: The Knee* (pp 195–196) by the American Academy of Orthopaedic Surgeons, St. Louis, 1985, The C.V. Mosby Co.

---

ring may occur and result in diminished movement of the meniscus during rotation, flexion, and extension.[104] Rashkoff holds that there will be scarring of the capsule as well (personal communication, 1989).

Functional tests

1. Pain at the medial plateau on passive lateral knee rotation. Lateral coronary problems are rare.

2. Possible pain on extreme passive knee flexion or extension.
3. Negative passive valgus and meniscus testing (this points to an isolated coronary ligament problem).
4. Possible pain with normal end feel on anterior drawer test.

Treatment: The lesion responds extremely well to friction massage (see Chapter 12).

Anterior Cruciate Ligament

Contact (clipping) and, more often, noncontact injuries may disrupt this ligament. Anterior cruciate involvement may occur in activities related to sudden deceleration and cutting. Noncontact injuries such as landing from a jump (causing a hyperextension of the knee), cutting (causing extension and external rotation of the femur on a fixed tibia), and internal rotation of the tibia on a flexed knee are all possible mechanisms of injury. Sudden deceleration to change direction, especially on artificial turf, may cause a massive quadriceps contraction that results in severe anterior tibial translation. Attempting to prevent falling backward during skiing might produce a severe quadriceps contraction, causing an anterior drawer force on the proximal tibia.[53]

A history of the above mechanisms of injury, an audible "pop," and an acute hemarthrosis within a few hours should raise the suspicion of an anterior cruciate injury. The patient will walk with a painful limp. Of course if the capsule is torn blood may extravasate into the extra-articular soft tissues, so that a lack of swelling is not necessarily related to the mildness of a knee condition. If the anterior cruciate is injured in isolation, varus, valgus, and posterior cruciate testing will be negative. Pain is often posterolateral, representing an avulsion of the ligament from the lateral femoral condyle.[38] DeHaven[105] found 65% of patients with a torn anterior cruciate to have a meniscal tear. Lachman's test will be positive and the pivot-shift test will probably be too painful to administer.

Warren[106] states that in acute injury the pivot-shift test is positive only 38% of the time but that under anesthesia it is positive nearly 100% of the time. He holds that a thorough clinical examination will often decrease the need for arthroscopy, which tends to be overused. Depending on the age of the patient (eg, in a young athlete), the possibility of additional involvement such as the menisci and articular surface as well as equivocal examination findings lead some orthopedists to use arthroscopy routinely. Clancy[38] recommends an arthrogram for suspected anterior cruciate injuries because accompanying posterior horn medial meniscus lesions can be determined 95% of the time. He states that he would not operate if an absent or minimal pivot-shift test was present unless he saw a repairable meniscus on the arthrogram, although if Lachman's test was positive and the pivot-shift was absent or minimal he would use arthroscopy.

Lateral roentgenography of the knee may reveal an avulsion anterior and superior to the tibial spine, where the anterior cruciate inserts. A pathognomonic sign on an anteroposterior roentgenogram is the lateral capsular sign,[107] which depicts an avulsion fracture at the lateral tibial plateau that is due to avulsion of the inferior meniscocapsular area of the lateral meniscus (Fig. 7-47). Increased laxity or suspicion of ACL injury warrants referral to an orthopedist. Is the tear acute or chronic, partial or complete? Is the individual a young active athlete? Is the tear isolated or combined with other lesions? It is important to distinguish between laxity based on functional testing and functional instability based on the patient's inter-

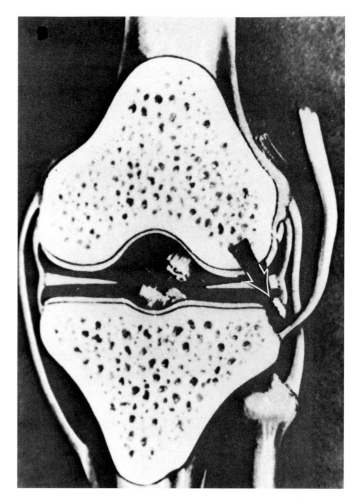

Figure 7-47 The lateral capsular sign: an avulsion fracture (Segond's fracture) of the inferior meniscocapsular area of the lateral meniscus. It is common in anterior cruciate injuries. *Source*: Reprinted with permission from *American Journal of Sports Medicine* (1979;7:27), Copyright © 1979, Williams & Wilkins Company.

pretation. Usually increased laxity correlates with instability, but patients with increased laxity may not experience instability ("giving way").

Functional tests

1. Probable positive Lachman's test.
2. Possible positive pivot-shift test.
3. Negative varus and valgus tests.
4. Possible anterolateral rotational instability.
5. Possible 5° to 10° hyperextension compared to the opposite knee on passive extension. If recurvatum of more than 15° is found, the posterior cruciate is probably also torn.[40]

It is entirely possible for a cruciate lesion not to reveal any laxity. Diagnosis may have to depend on the mechanism of injury and symptomatology.

Treatment (does not refer to postoperative knee): Treatment of anterior cruciate ligament lesions, as with all lesions, must be individualized. Buckley et al[108] successfully treated partial ligament tears by conservative methods. They found that partial tears did not significantly deteriorate after being followed for an average of 49 months. Their conservative treatment consisted of early hamstring strengthening, delayed weight bearing, and eventual quadriceps strengthening.

Initially soft tissue swelling must be decreased, and increased range of motion must be instituted. Tension in the anterior cruciate is least between full flexion and 40° flexion but increases with increased extension.[109] Special knee braces can be prescribed that limit knee extension to 45° and can be worn while resistive knee flexion and extension exercises are used.[108] Terminal knee extension should be instituted slowly to allow protective scarring of secondary restraints and therefore to allow increased joint stability to occur.[110]

The most important muscles to rehabilitate in anterior cruciate injury are the hamstrings because they prevent excessive tibial rotation and anterior tibial glide on the femur. The hamstrings should be strengthened until they are of equal strength compared to the quadriceps on the uninvolved side.[27] Shields et al[27] state that straight-leg raises should not be permitted because they increase anterior subluxation of the tibia on the femur. Progressive exercises from isometric to isotonic (especially eccentric contraction) to isokinetic are recommended. The hamstring muscle can be functionally exercised to compensate for giving way sensation characteristic of anterior cruciate rupture. Examiner extends supine patient's flexed knee attempting to create an anterior-lateral subluxation of tibia (pivot-shift). The patient contracts the hamstring first before the giving way sensation at about 20° to 30° flexion. Partial knee squats (never past 90° to protect the patellofemoral joint) cause cocontraction of the soleus and hamstrings along with the quadriceps and hamstrings.[110] A good order for rehabilitation is crutch walking, cycling, walking, slow running, and fast running.[108]

Posterior Cruciate Ligament

The most common mechanism of posterior cruciate injury is hyperflexion (Fig. 7-48), or the "dashboard injury." Conservative treatment applies only to an isolated injury without bony avulsion. Most injuries are related to other serious knee ligamentous injuries.[111] Fowler and Messieh[35] established their clinical diagnosis of isolated posterior cruciate tear on the history of the injury, a positive posterior sag and drawer test (up to 5 mm anterior-posterior translation), a negative anterior drawer or Lachman's test, a negative varus and valgus test at 30° and in extension, and absence of recurvatum. They confirmed their findings arthroscopically; roentgenograms were taken to rule out bony avulsions. There was definite posterior knee pain.

Functional tests

1. Positive posterior sag and dynamic posterior shift tests.

A

B

Figure 7-48 Hyperflexed knee resulting in posterior cruciate ligament injury. **(A)** Pretibial trauma in hyperflexed knee leading to isolated posterior cruciate ligament injury. **(B)** Hyperflexion of knee is the most common mechanism of injury leading to isolated posterior cruciate ligament tear. *Source*: Reprinted with permission from *American Journal of Sports Medicine* (1987;15[6]:554), Copyright © 1987, Williams & Wilkins Company.

2. Passive knee extension usually limited in acute phase due to spasm of hamstrings and/or gastrocnemius.
3. Negative varus and valgus tests in 30° flexion and extension if an isolated PCL tear.
4. Palpation of 90° flexed knee may not reveal the tibial plateau ridge, as it will in the opposite knee.

Treatment: According to Shields et al,[27] the main emphasis of treatment is strengthening of the quadriceps because the hamstrings may accentuate posterior subluxation. These investigators omit hamstring exercise and start eccentric quadriceps exercises as soon as possible. They also use step-ups, straight-leg raises, and short-arc quadriceps exercises in the early stages. Internal and external rotation exercises are not emphasized initially because they also increase posterior tibial subluxation.

Meniscus Lesions

As with the collateral ligaments, the inherent stability of the medial meniscus compared to the lateral meniscus predisposes the medial meniscus to an increased rate of injury. The lateral meniscotibial ligaments are more elongated and loose than the medial, and the popliteus tendon separates the lateral collateral ligament from the lateral meniscus. The lateral meniscus is also more mobile because the attachments of its anterior and posterior horns are closer together compared to those of the medial meniscus, which are attached at a wider interval.[2]

The mechanism of injury could be a contact-type collision, such as a clip on the lateral side creating a valgus loading associated with a flexion rotation. The most usual mechanism is the noncontact-type, involving rotation in combination with valgus or varus loading. Corrigan and Maitland[112] describe a typical mechanism in which an externally rotated, fixed tibia with a flexed knee causes the medial meniscus to be drawn toward the center, where it is stressed between the condyles of the femur and tibia. The patient then straightens up and extends the knee, causing the femur to internally rotate which entraps and thereby tears the meniscus. The above mechanisms are similar to the mechanisms that cause collateral ligament and cruciate injuries, which is a reason for combination lesions.

Simonsen et al[113] state that it is difficult to diagnose menisci lesions in an acute injury. Only 7% of menisci lesions could be diagnosed clinically in their study. This may be due to the acute patient not being able to tolerate meniscus tests. An acute injury in young patients (usually in their 20s) should always make one suspect more than just the isolated meniscus lesion; a degenerative tear in the meniscus in an older patient (40 years or older) is more likely to be an isolated lesion.

In general, an acute meniscus lesion prevents the individual from walking off the field unaided compared to an isolated ligamentous injury. The pain in a medial meniscus injury is more often in the posterior medial or medial joint line and is rarely localized anteromedially.[38] Lateral meniscus pain is more often midlateral than posterolateral.[38] An isolated meniscus lesion will develop mild effusion gradually over a few days compared to the almost immediate swelling of an anterior cruciate lesion. Only the peripheral 10% to 20% of the meniscus has a blood supply, so that swelling from a meniscal lesion is due to injury to the synovium, peripheral meniscus, and capsule.[114] Immediate locking (loss of knee extension) may occur, especially if a bucket-handle tear (longitudinal type) occurs. DeHaven[115] states that failure to extend the knee may be due to eventual effusion (hamstring spasm and pseudolocking), so that it is important to question the patient to find out whether it was possible to extend the knee fully

immediately after the injury. Rarely, a posterior vertical tear of the lateral meniscus will cause a locking in full flexion.[14] The majority of the time, knee locking occurs in extension.

A patient with a chronic meniscus problem may present with mild to moderate swelling after spending time in a prolonged squat position or for no apparent reason. The swelling may appear with use and disappear with rest. The patient may complain of the knee "giving way," grinding, feeling weak, locking (catching), and unlocking. Prolonged kneeling causes the condyles to compress the degenerative posterior meniscal horn, resulting in tearing.[14] A patient with this lesion, on squatting, may complain of medial knee pain, which indicates a possible tear of the medial meniscus (positive squat test). McMurray's and Apley's tests would probably create grinding and medial pain if the medial meniscus was involved. A positive "bed" sign (pain when the knees touch in bed) could be due to degenerative meniscal tears.

Rashkoff states that the functional tests for meniscus lesions are not completely reliable. For example, even if most of the functional tests are negative he would strongly suspect a medial meniscal lesion if there is effusion, loss of terminal knee extension, and tenderness to palpation at the joint line between the medial collateral and posterior oblique ligaments. He would suspect a lateral meniscus lesion if tenderness to palpation is revealed on the lateral joint line associated with no pain on internal rotation with varus to eliminate involvement of the arcuate ligament (personal communication, 1989).

Sometimes positive meniscal tests may be masking a degenerative knee joint. Roentgenograms taken at 45° of flexion in weight bearing may help differentiate these conditions (see above, Degenerative Joint Disease).

Functional tests

1. Probable positive McMurray's test.
2. Probable positive Apley's test.
3. Possible positive Helfet's test.
4. Possible positive Steinmann's test (see section, Menisci).
5. Possible loss of full passive terminal extension or flexion (or both).
6. Possible loss of passive internal tibial rotation (lesion of the posterior meniscus) or external tibial rotation (lesion of the anterior half of either meniscus).[112]
7. Crepitation at the lateral joint line during the pivot-shift test if there is a lateral meniscus tear.[39]
8. Possible medial or lateral joint pain on squat testing.

Treatment: Manipulation may be performed within the first 24 hours of acute locking (swelling may prevent manipulation) or in chronic locking. Mennell describes a manipulation for a medial locked torn meniscus (Fig. 7-49). He states that in all his years of treating meniscal locking by manipulation he has never had to treat a lateral lock. His procedure for manipulating a left medial meniscus tear is as follows (personal communication, 1989):

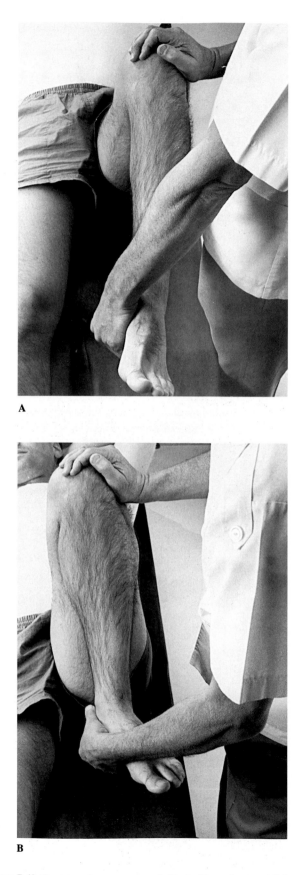

A

B

Figure 7-49 Treatment for an acute medial locked knee due to medial meniscus tear.

1. The examiner, standing on the patient's left side, flexes the patient's left knee approximately 110°.
2. The examiner puts his or her left forearm over the patient's lower tibia and medial malleolus to grasp the calcaneus and then externally rotates the foot (entire procedure may also be attempted with foot internally rotated).
3. With the right hand the examiner steadies the knee with a minor valgus stress. It is important that the tibia remain in a sagittal neutral position (no varus or valgus) during the entire manipulation.
4. The examiner then fully flexes the knee, literally kicking the knee into the buttock.

If locking is not immediately reduced, patient should be referred to an orthopedist.

Estimation of the severity of the lesion, the age of the patient, the degree of knee instability, and the patient's occupation all have significance in determining whether conservative treatment may be attempted. Prolonged loss of knee extension, chronic severe pain, locking, and swelling are definite indicators for possible surgery. An important function of the menisci is to act as load bearers, and it is thought that complete meniscectomy may lead to degenerative arthrosis due to stress on the articular cartilage.[116] Partial meniscectomy is the recommended surgical choice.

Conservative care would be concerned first with reducing the pain and swelling, then with putting the patient on a rehabilitation program that restores full range of motion (stretching), and then with restoration of strength to all associated muscles. Joint play mobilization often helps restore and maintain the meniscus in proper position.

Loose Bodies

Loose bodies in the knee may have various causes. Intra-articular loose bodies may be due to osteochondritis dissecans, osteophytes, or synoviomas; a loose body may be located retropatella that is due to chondromalacia or dislocation. The principal problem that arises is locking of the joint or sudden twinges that are relieved by shaking the knee. Sometimes the loose body may shift position, causing pain on different sides of the same knee.

The first thing that we must determine is whether the locking is true locking or pseudolocking because manipulation is only effective for true locking. Cross and Crichton[14] distinguish between true locking due to meniscal bucket-handle tear, loose bodies, and synovioma and pseudolocking due to hamstring spasm in first- and second-degree collateral ligament and anterior cruciate sprains, effusion in the knee preventing flexion, and medial plica syndrome (which may prevent full knee extension). Onset often occurs for no apparent reason, i.e., rolling over in bed or simply getting out of bed.

Functional tests

1. Loss of passive extension (there is rarely a loss of flexion).
2. Springy block on passive bounce-home knee extension. A springy bounce feeling is probably a pseudolock.

Treatment: Manipulation is the treatment of choice in most people older than 40 years. Teenagers may need surgery to prevent eventual osteoarthrosis. Roentgenography may only distinguish a nidus of bone that may be larger because of surrounding cartilage. Loose bodies are radio-opaque 80% of the time.[14]

The principle of manipulating a loose body is adapted from Cyriax[117] (Fig. 7-50). The joint should be flexed at about 90° and tractioned for about 10 seconds to relax the ligaments and to open up the joint. The examiner, while maintaining the traction, simultaneously rotates the flexed knee in either internal or external rotation while bringing the leg into extension. As the leg is brought into extension, the examiner is rotating the leg repeatedly from the neutral position to external rotation, finally ending up with a long-axis thrust while the leg is in external rotation and allowable extension. If after five external rotations the passive bounce-home test does not lose the blocked feeling, the examiner proceeds the same way with the leg in internal rotation. One or two visits may be all that is needed. There is a tendency for this condition to recur. Mennell's technique for unlocking the meniscus (see above) may also be attempted.

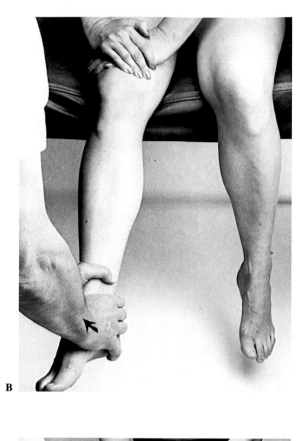

B

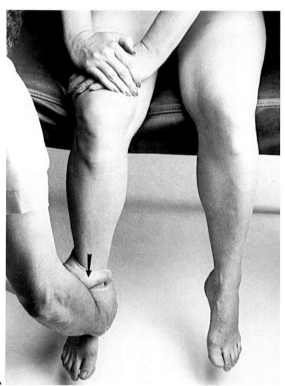

A

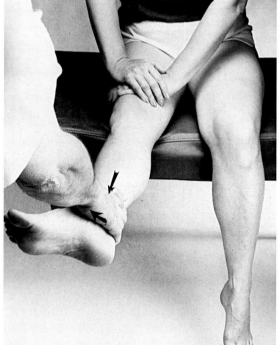

C

Figure 7-50 Loose body manipulation. (**A**) The knee is held flexed in traction for 10 seconds to open the joint. (**B**), Examiner while maintaining traction, begins to extend the knee all the while rotating the tibia lateral and back to neutral. (**C**), Examiner ends the manipulation with a final long axis externally rotated thrust. If springy block on passive extension is still present, repeat above with internal rotation.

Plica Syndrome

The plica is normally present in 60% of the population[118]; plica syndrome is most common in adolescence but may be seen at any age.[52] The mediopatellar plica may become involved as a result of trauma ("dashboard injury" or a severe fall on the knee), giving rise to the usual inflammatory process and fibrosis with consequent reduction in normal extensibility. Alternatively, the problem may develop insidiously from anteromedial femoral stress due to minor repetitive overuse trauma as in jogging, bike riding, or overstretching.

Jacobson and Flandry[46] describe as symptoms pain while sitting with the knee flexed that increases when the patient arises and walks and eventually improves as walking continues. Pain in flexion is due to a shortened plica dropping over the medial femoral condyle (bowstring effect). These investigators state that if the plica gets entrapped in the patellofemoral joint as the quadriceps contracts a pain reflex may give the feeling of the knee "giving way" (this may be confused with patellar subluxation). Pain may occur after a quadriceps strengthening program. Usually pain is localized one fingerbreadth proximal to the inferior pole of the patella medially.[52]

The plica may be normally palpable but will palpate thicker and tender superior and medial to the patella beneath the medial retinaculum. There may be minimal effusion, a complaint of catching, pseudolocking, a snapping sensation, and a popping noise (crepitus). The crepitus of chondromalacia is differentiated from that of plica syndrome because it will be directly under the patella[46] rather than medial. Tight hamstrings may be a predisposing cause. A contracted plica may affect normal patellofemoral mechanics by preventing normal excursion of the quadriceps.[23] It is possible for hypertrophy of the fat pad and synovium to occur, so that these structures become pinched between the patella and femur, causing pain and crepitus similar to that in plica syndrome.

Functional tests

1. Probable positive medial plica test.
2. Probable positive patellar grind or compression test due to trapping of the medial plica between the patella and medial femoral condyle.[52]
3. False-positive McMurray's test (click) with the leg externally rotated. External rotation of the tibia can cause tight wedging of the medial plica between the medial patellar facet and the medial femoral condyle.[51]
4. Possible positive Apley's test with distraction rather than compression.[51]
5. Possible pain in the end range of passive knee flexion.

Arthroscopy is the final word because plica syndrome is often confused with chondromalacia or a medial meniscal tear.

Treatment: Friction massage is used to break down the scar tissue; a T bar may be needed to obtain the necessary pressure. Plica syndrome may present like fibrosis of the fat pad or retinaculum, both of which may respond to a trial of friction. It is important to stretch the hamstrings if necessary and to strengthen the quadriceps, especially the VMO. Full-range exercises of the quadriceps are not recommended because these create excessive patellar compression at 90°; instead, straight-leg raises, short-arc quadriceps exercises (last 5° to 10°), and hip adductor strengthening should be done.

Patellofemoral Dysfunction

Patellofemoral dysfunction is a general term referring to knee extensor overuse lesions or arthralgias leading to degenerative joint disease. Conservative care of patellofemoral dysfunction necessitates a thorough inspection and examination of the total lower extremity from the hip to the feet. The pertinent positive tests for the patella usually consist of abnormal patellar tracking, compression testing, resistive knee extension at 30°, squat testing, and apprehension. Important findings (previously discussed) that we must be aware of in the analysis of patellofemoral problems are:

1. the causative factors creating an abnormal Q angle (some of which are listed below)
2. femoral anteversion or retroversion
3. aplasia, atrophy, or hypertrophy of the medial (VMO) and lateral quadriceps
4. tight hamstrings, vastus lateralis, and iliotibial tract
5. valgus and varus knee alignment
6. height and location of the patella (alta, baja, "squinting," "grasshopper-eye")
7. anatomic abnormalities such as an increased sulcus angle resulting in loss of the lateral buttress effect of the lateral femoral condyle (which predisposes to lateral tilt of the patella and subluxation[119]) and a poorly developed lateral femoral condyle (seen on tangential x-ray views)
8. tightness or laxness of the parapatellar tissues (retinacula, plica, patellar ligaments)
9. loss of accessory patellar joint play (see Chapter 10)
10. tibial torsion
11. subtalar pronation or secondary pronation caused by triceps surae contracture, genu varum, tibia vara, heel valgus, or forefoot supination (see Chapter 8)

It is apparent that determining the underlying cause of patellofemoral dysfunction is not an easy task. Often, however, conservative care consisting of restoring to function as much as possible, especially the VMO, resolves the problem. Listed below are some specific patellofemoral problems that the above analysis should be able to distinguish and that often benefit from conservative care. Symptoms that might raise the suspicion of patellar problems are patellar stiffness, retropatella and peripatellar pain (especially at the medial facet), crepitation, pain on going up or down stairs (or both), a feeling of the knee "giving way," locking, swelling, and pain after prolonged sitting.

Patellofemoral Arthralgias

After the overuse inflammatory conditions (tendinitis and bursitis) another spectrum of patellofemoral conditions comprises patellofemoral arthralgias, which is a general term for conditions that are due to abnormal patellar pressures, abnormal patellar tracking, and malfunctions of the extensor mechanism. These types of conditions fall under the general headings of patellar malalignment syndrome, lateral compression syndrome, and patellofemoral pain syndromes. All these syndromes may eventually result in degenerative cartilage conditions with osteophytes, synovial entrapment, and patellar subluxation.

Treatment for patellofemoral conditions must take into account that normal balance between the medial and lateral knee structures is essential for normal patellar function and tracking. The "law of valgus"[2] explains the normal increased lateral forces of the knee that result from the normal valgus Q angle and the stronger and more fibrous lateral patellar stabilizers. The resisting medial forces (distal VMO and medial retinaculum) and the more prominent lateral femoral condyle balance the stronger distal vastus lateralis, iliotibial tract, and lateral retinaculum. All the factors that increase the Q angle associated with weakness of the medial structures and tightness of the lateral structures cause the patella to move laterally during knee flexion. This causes a painful contraction of the quadriceps. If a pronated foot exists with its associated internal rotation of the tibia, at heel strike the contracting quadriceps causes a bowstring effect that results in lateral stress and instability.[45]

All the above can lead to degeneration. Hughston[11] states that the breaking up of the patellar articular cartilage causing chondromalacia is due to repetitious shear stress and loss of nutrition to the cartilage because of the lack of proper forceful compression on the medial femoral condyle, which is why the medial facet is involved in chondromalacia so much more often than the lateral facet. Suboptimal loading of the cartilage may therefore cause decreased diffusion of nutrition.[46] It is also possible for too much compression to occur, causing chondromalacia of the lateral facet.[46] There is still an argument as to whether chrondromalacia can be considered a primary disease or secondary to malalignment or instability (subluxation).[47] It appears that many of the varieties of patellofemoral diagnoses are simply stages of the same overall etiology but that chondromalacia is really a pathologic diagnosis and often must be distinguished from patellofemoral arthritis. Rashkoff (personal communication, 1989) has created a chart to help differentially diagnose these two conditions (Table 7-9).

Functional tests

1. Probable abnormal patellar tracking.
2. Probable patellar pain on resisted knee extension.
3. Probable pain on patellar compression test.
4. Probable retropatellar or popliteal fossa pain on knee squat test.

Table 7-9 Differentiation between Chondromalacia of Patella and Patellofemoral Arthritis

Disease Entity	Etiology	Location	Age (years)	Sex	Knee Alignment
Chondromalacia	Usually overuse	Medial facet	<40	Mostly female	Varus or valgus
Patellofemoral arthritis	Usually idiopathic	Lateral facet	>60	Both (equal)	Mostly valgus

Source: Rashkoff E, Personal Communication, 1989.

5. Possible pain or apprehension on medial-to-lateral or lateral-to-medial displacement test.
6. Possible loss of passive knee extension because of tight hamstrings.

Treatment: Kramer[120] describes an empiric manual treatment for patellar conditions that are related to excessive lateral pressure or tightness. In the early phases of treatment he stretches the lateral retinaculum by pushing the patella medially and holding it for 1 minute at a time (Fig. 7-51, A and B). As the patient improves, he uses a compression-tracking procedure to facilitate cartilage metabolism. The technique involves the examiner maintaining pressure on the surface of the patella to compress the patellofemoral articulation while tracking the patella medially. The compression begins while the knee is flexed 90° and is maintained until extension (Fig. 7-51C).

Kramer states that adding the stretch and compression-tracking techniques to the usual patellar rehabilitation routines speeds recovery and improves results in the patella malalignment syndrome. He emphasizes that it is important for the patient to do compression tracking at home on a daily basis. He also recommends progressive quadriceps exercises (sets, isometric, and isotonic short arc), use of a soft patellar brace, modalities, and quadriceps stretching (personal communication, 1989).

Baycroft[121] describes a self-treatment method for patellofemoral dysfunction that he considers another type of joint dysfunction and therefore will respond to mobilization as other joints do. The patient is first taught to glide the patella passively in all four directions until pain and restriction diminish (usually 2 to 5 days or longer). Next, the patient is taught to use the web of the hand against the superior patellar pole and to contract the quadriceps. It is important for the patient to stop the contraction as soon as pain is felt. The patient is told to perform this contraction three to six times per day for 2 to 3 days. Baycroft states that the technique should not be used too vigorously and that the range of painless movement will increase rapidly. After a full range of painless active patellar gliding is achieved, the sequence of medial and distal gliding, resisted quadriceps contraction to the painful barrier, and rapid relaxation is repeated with increasing compression until the patient is asymptomatic. Baycroft holds that this technique

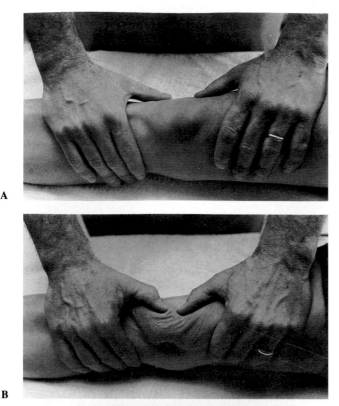

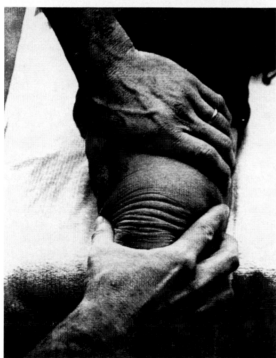

Figure 7-51 Technique for stretching lateral retinaculum. (**A**) The patella is in the midline position; (**B**) medial displacement stretching the lateral retinaculum. (**C**) As the knee is actively extended, the patella is compressed against the patellofemoral surface with medial drift. *Source*: Reprinted with permission from PG Kramer, Patella Malalignment Syndrome: Rationale to Reduce Excessive Lateral Pressure, *Journal of Orthopaedic and Sports Physical Therapy* (1986;8[6]:307–308), Copyright © 1986, the Orthopaedic and Sports Physical Therapy Sections of the American Physical Therapy Association.

stretches tight soft tissues and rehabilitates the quadriceps along with mobilizing the patella.

Again, all the biomechanical possibilities from the hip to the feet should always be considered (see Chapter 10).

Patellar Subluxation

The "law of valgus" emphasizes that the normal excess lateral forces that affect the patella and any congenital deficiency in structure or function of the extensor mechanism would increase the possibility of subluxation. Trauma or noncontact external rotation of the tibia while the quadriceps is contracting can result in subluxation. Lateral subluxation usually occurs with irritation of the medial structures. The patient may complain of knee pain and the sensation of instability or "giving way." There may be synovial swelling and associated patellar tendinitis and retinaculitis (Tables 7-10 and 7-11).

Functional tests

1. Probable positive apprehension sign.
2. Probable pain on resisted knee extension.
3. Possible loss of passive knee extension because of tight hamstrings.
4. Possible general joint laxity.

Treatment: Henry[119] emphasizes that, while some investigators have recommended knee extension exercises in the last 15° to 30°, an arc greater than 45° of flexion will reproduce symptoms. He completely eliminates any flexion to extension component or advanced exercises that stress squatting or running up stairs. Briefly, Henry's regimen consists of:

1. quadriceps isometric setting: Patient sits with the knee flexed (or extended) and dorsiflexes the foot and toes. Patient then pushes his or her heel into the ground away from the body and holds for 10 seconds and relaxes for 5

Table 7-10 Patellofemoral Subluxation*

Symptoms (465 Patients)	Percent
Pain going down stairs	76
Pain on flexion	75
Weakness	73
Giving way	61
Swelling	60
Pain going up stairs	54
Locking	50
Swelling	50

*In a series of approximately 500 knees with patellofemoral subluxation as a primary diagnosis, the symptoms of which the patients complain are noted in their order of decreasing frequency. Obviously not all patients have the same complaints, and not all patients complain of all the symptoms.

Source: Reprinted with permission from *Clinics in Sports Medicine* (1989; 8[2]:263), Copyright © 1989, W.B. Saunders Company.

Table 7-11 Signs of Patellofemoral Subluxation*

Signs (465 Patients)	Percent
Dysplastic VMO	91
High patella	68
Tight patellofemoral ligaments	68
Fairbank's sign†	66
Hypertrophied lateralis	65
Tenderness	60
Loose retinaculum	49
Small patella	45
Genu recurvatum	38
Genu valgum	29
Q angle	21
Femoral neck anteversion	17
Pronated feet	2

*More than 500 patients were examined with a primary diagnosis of patellofemoral subluxation. This table reveals the signs found by the examiners in order of decreasing frequency. Again, it is noted that all the patients with patellofemoral subluxation do not have all the same signs.

†Patella apprehension sign.

Source: Reprinted with permission from *Clinics in Sports Medicine* (1989; 8[2]:263), Copyright © 1989, W.B. Saunders Company.

seconds (begin with one set of 10 repetitions and eventually increase to three sets of 10 repetitions)

2. straight-leg raises (12 in above the table, held for a count of 10)
3. hip abduction, adduction, and flexion with light weights, eventually increasing weights 2.5 lb every 3 to 4 days as tolerated to a maximum weight of one-third body weight
4. stretching of hamstrings, hip abductors, and heel cords
5. use of modalities and a Palumbo brace

REFERENCES

1. Garrick JG. The epidemiology of knee injuries in sports. In: Finerman G, ed. *Symposium on Sports Medicine: The Knee.* St. Louis, Mo: Mosby; 1985.

2. Ellison AE. *Athletic Training and Sports Medicine.* Chicago: American Academy of Orthopedic Surgeons; 1985.

3. Kapandji IA. *The Physiology of the Joints.* New York: Churchill Livingstone; 1970;2.

4. Grood ES, Noyes FR. Diagnosis of knee ligament injuries: biomechanical precepts. In: Feagin J, ed. *The Crucial Ligaments.* New York: Churchill Livingstone; 1987.

5. Peterson L, Frankel VH. Biomechanics of the knee in athletes. In: Nicholas JA, Hershman EB, eds. *The Lower Extremity and Spine in Sports Medicine.* St. Louis, Mo: Mosby; 1986;1:697–709.

6. Nordin M, Frankel VH. *Basic Biomechanics of the Musculoskeletal System.* 2nd ed. Philadelphia: Lea & Febiger; 1989.

7. Lehmkuhl DL, Smith LK. *Brunnstrom's Clinical Kinesiology.* Philadelphia: Davis; 1984.

8. Brody DM. Running injuries. In: Nicholas JA, Hershman EB, eds. *The Lower Extremity and Spine in Sports Medicine.* St Louis, Mo: Mosby; 1986:1534–1579.

9. Reilly DT, Martens M. Experimental analysis of quadriceps muscle force and patellofemoral joint reaction force for various activities. *Acta Orthop Scand.* 1972;43:16–37.

10. Brunet ME, Stewart GW. Patellofemoral rehabilitation. *Clin Sports Med.* 1989;8:323.

11. Hughston JC. Patellar subluxation. *Clin Sports Med.* 1989;8: 153–161.

12. Terry GC. The anatomy of the extensor mechanism. *Clin Sports Med.* 1989;8:163–176.

13. Warren R, Arnoczky SP, Wickiewicz TL. Anatomy of the knee. In: Nicholas JA, Hershman EB, eds. *The Lower Extremity and Spine in Sports Medicine.* St Louis, Mo: Mosby; 1986;1:674–676.

14. Cross MJ, Crichton KJ. *Clinical Examination of the Injured Knee.* Baltimore: Williams & Wilkins; 1987.

15. Zarins B, Boyle J. Knee ligament injuries. In: Nicholas JA, Hershman EB, eds. *The Lower Extremity and Spine in Sports Medicine.* St Louis, Mo: Mosby; 1986;1:929–982.

16. Hoppenfeld S. *Physical Examination of the Spine and Extremities.* Norwalk, Conn: Appleton-Century-Crofts; 1976.

17. Noyes FR, Grood ES. Diagnosis of knee ligament injuries: clinical concepts. In: Feagin J, ed. *The Crucial Ligaments.* New York: Churchill Livingstone; 1987.

18. Salter RB. *Textbook of Disorders and Injuries of the Musculoskeletal System.* 2nd ed. Baltimore: Williams & Wilkins; 1983.

19. Williams PL, Warwick R. *Gray's Anatomy.* 36th ed. New York: Saunders; 1980.

20. Terry GC, Hughston JC, Norwood LA. The anatomy of the iliopatellar band and iliotibial tract. *Am J Sports Med.* 1986;14:39–45.

21. Renne JW. The iliotibial band friction syndrome. *J Bone Joint Surg Am.* 1975;57:1111.

22. Basmajian JV, Deluca CJ. *Muscles Alive.* 5th ed. Baltimore: Williams & Wilkins; 1985.

23. Boland AL. Soft tissue injuries of the knee. In: Nicholas JA, Hershman EB, eds. *The Lower Extremity and Spine in Sports Medicine.* St Louis, Mo: Mosby; 1986;1:983–1012.

24. Kulund DN. *The Injured Athlete.* Philadelphia: Lippincott; 1988.

25. Cailliet R. *Knee Pain and Disability.* Philadelphia: Davis; 1984.

26. Waller JF Jr. Biomechanics and rehabilitation of the gastroc-soleus complex. In: *Symposium on the Foot and Leg in Running Sports.* St Louis, Mo: Mosby; 1982:86–91.

27. Shields CL, Brewster CE, Morrissey MC. Rehabilitation of the knee in athletes. In: Nicholas JA, Hershman EJB, eds. *The Lower Extremity and Spine in Sports Medicine.* St Louis, Mo: Mosby; 1986;1:1055–1085.

28. McQuade KJ, Crutcher JP, et al. Tibial rotation in anterior cruciate deficient knees: an in vitro study. *J Orthop Sports Phys Ther.* 1989;11: 146–149.

29. Gollehon DL, Torzilli PA, Warren RF. The role of posterolateral and cruciate ligaments in the stability of the human knee: a biomechanical study. *J Bone Joint Surg Am.* 1987;69:233–242.

30. Dye SF, Cannon WD. Anatomy and biomechanics of the anterior cruciate ligament. *Clin Sports Med.* 1988;7:715–725.

31. Welsh RP. Knee joint structure and function. *Clin Orthop.* 1980; 147.

32. Odensten M, Gillquist J. Functional anatomy of the anterior cruciate ligament and a rationale for reconstruction. *J Bone Joint Surg Am.* 1985;67:257–262.

33. Arnoczky SP. Anatomy of the anterior cruciate ligament and supporting structures. *Orthop Clin North Am.* 1985;16:15–28.

34. Cabaud HE. Biomechanics of the anterior cruciate ligament. *Clin Orthop.* 1983;172:26–31.

35. Fowler PJ, Messieh SS. Isolated posterior cruciate ligament injuries in athletes. *Am J Sports Med.* 1987;15:555.

36. Shybut GT, McGinty JB. The office evaluation of the knee. *Orthop Clin North Am*. 1982;497–509.

37. Post M. *Physical Examination of the Musculoskeletal System*. Chicago: Year Book Medical; 1987.

38. Clancy WG Jr. Evaluation of acute knee injuries. In: Finerman G, ed. *Symposium on Sports Medicine: The Knee*. St Louis, Mo: Mosby; 1985:185–193.

39. Henning CE, Lynch MA, Glick KR. Physical examination of the knee. In: Nicholas JA, Hershman EJB, eds. *The Lower Extremity and Spine in Sports Medicine*. St Louis, Mo: Mosby; 1986.

40. Zarins B, Nemeth VA. Acute knee injuries in athletes. *Clin Sports Med*. 1983;2:149–165.

41. Magee DJ. *Orthopedic Physical Assessment*. Philadelphia: Saunders; 1987.

42. Carson WG, James SL, Larson RL, et al. Patellofemoral disorders; physical and radiographic evaluation, part I. *Clin Orthop Relat Res*. 1984(185):165–177.

43. Rusche K, Mangine RE. Pathomechanics of injury to the patellofemoral and tibiofemoral joint. In: Mangine RE, ed. *Physical Therapy of the Knee*. New York: Churchill Livingstone; 1988;35–37.

44. Micheli LJ, Slater JH, Woods BS, et al. Patella alta and the adolescent growth spurt. *Clin Orthop Relat Res*. 1980;213:159.

45. Insall J, Salvati E. Patella position in the normal knee joint. *Radiology*. 1971;101:101.

46. Jacobson KE, Flandry FC. Diagnosis of anterior knee pain. *Clin Sports Med*. 1989;8:179–195.

47. Minkoff J, Fein L. The role of radiography in the evaluation and treatment of common anarthrotic disorders of the patellofemoral joint. *Clin Sports Med*. 1989;8:203–232.

48. Hunt GC. Examination of lower extremity dysfunction. In: Gould JA, Davies GJ, eds. *Orthopaedic and Sports Physical Therapy*. St Louis, Mo: Mosby; 1985:428–429.

49. Noyes FR, Mangine RE. *ACL and Meniscal Injury: Arthroscopically Aided ACL Allograft and Meniscal Repair*. City: ProClinica; 1990.

50. Outerbridge RE, Dunlop J. The problem of chondromalacia patella. *Clin Orthop*. 1975;110:177.

51. Kessler RM, Hertling D. *Management of Common Musculoskeletal Disorders*. New York: Harper & Row; 1983.

52. Nottage WM, Sprague NF, Auerbach BJ, et al. The medial patellar plica syndrome. *Am J Sports Med*. 1983;11:211.

53. Gersoff WK, Clancy WG. Diagnosis of acute and chronic anterior cruciate ligament tears. *Clin Sports Med*. 1988;7:727–737.

54. Mellion MB. *Sports Injuries and Athletic Problems*. St Louis, Mo: Mosby; 1988.

55. Grood ES, Noyes FR, Butler DL. Ligamentous and capsular restraints preventing straight medial and lateral laxity in intact human cadaver knees. *J Bone Joint Surg Am*. 1981;63.

56. Hughston JC, Andrews JR, Cross MJ, et al. Classification of knee ligament instability, part II: the lateral compartment. *J Bone Joint Surg Am*. 1976;58:173.

57. Torg JS, Conrad W, Kalen V. Clinical diagnosis of anterior cruciate ligament instability in the athlete. *J Sports Med*. 1976;4:84–93.

58. Sherman MF, Bonamo JR. Primary repair of the anterior cruciate ligament. *Clin Sports Med*. 1988;7:739–749.

59. Jackson RW. The function of the anterior cruciate ligament during anterior drawer and Lachman's testing, an in vivo analysis in normal knees. *Am J Sports Med*. 1984;12:322.

60. Rosenberg TD, Rasmussen GL. The function of the anterior cruciate ligament during anterior drawer and Lachman's testing, an in vivo analysis in normal knees. *Am J Sports Med*. 84;12:322.

61. Cabaud HE, Slocum DB. The diagnosis of chronic anterolateral instability of the knee. *Am J Sports Med*. 1977;5:99–105.

62. Galway HR, MacIntosh DL. The lateral pivot shift: a symptom and sign of anterior cruciate ligament insufficiency. *Clin Orthop Relat Res*. 1980;147:45–50.

63. Marshall JL, Baugher WH. Stability examination of the knee: a simple anatomic approach. *Clin Orthop Relat Res*. 1980;146:78.

64. Butler DL, Noyes FR, Grood ES. Ligamentous restraints to anterior-posterior drawer in the human knee. A biomechanical study. *J Bone Joint Surg Am*. 1980;62:259–270.

65. Jakob RP. Observations on rotatory instability of the lateral compartment of the knee. *Acta Orthop Scand*. 1981;52:191.

66. Shelbourne DK, Benedict F, McCaroll JR, Rettig AC. Dynamic posterior shift test, an adjunct in evaluation of posterior tibial subluxation. *Am J Sports Med*. 1989;17(2).

67. McMurray TP. The semilunar cartilages. *Br J Surg*. 1942;29:407.

68. Ray JM. A proposed natural history of symptomatic anterior cruciate ligament injuries of the knee. *Clin Sports Med*. 1988;7:697–711.

69. Garrick SG, Webb DR. *Sports Injuries: Diagnosis and Management*. Philadelphia: WB Saunders; 1990.

70. Carson WG, James SL, Larson RL, et al. Patellofemoral disorders: physical and radiographic evaluation, part II: radiographic examination. *Clin Orthop Relat Res*. 1984;185:181.

71. Hunter SC, Poole RM. The chronically inflamed tendon. *Clin Sports Med*. 1987;6:371–387.

72. Welsh P, Hutton C. Knee extensor mechanism derangements in sportsmen. *Orthop Rev*. 1983;12:25–30.

73. Martens M, Wouters P, Burssens A, Mulier JC. Patellar tendinitis: pathology and results of treatment. *Acta Orthop Scand*. 1982;53:445–450.

74. Yost JG, Ellfeldt HJ. Basketball injuries. In: Nicholas JA, Hershman EB, eds. *The Lower Extremity and Spine in Sports Medicine*. St Louis, Mo: Mosby; 1986;2.

75. Ferretti A, Ippolito E, Puddu G. Jumper's knee. *Am J Sports Med*. 1983;11:58–62.

76. Black JE, Alten SR. How I manage infrapatellar tendinitis. *Phys Sports Med*. 1984;12:86–92.

77. Kapetanos G. The effect of the local corticosteroids on the healing and biomechanical properties of the partially injured tendon. *Clin Orthop Relat Res*. 1982;63:170–179.

78. Colosimo AJ, Basset FH. Jumper's knee, diagnosis and treatment. *Orthop Rev*. 1990;19:139–149.

79. Ferretti A, Puddu G, Mariani PP, et al. The natural history of jumper's knee. *Int Orthop*. 1985;8:239–242.

80. Blazina M. Jumper's knee. *Orthop Clin North Am*. 1973;4:665–668.

81. Garrett WE, Mumma M, Lucaveche CL. Ultrastructural differences in skeletal muscle fiber types. *Orthop Clin North Am*. 1983;14:413.

82. Mayfield GW. Popliteus tendon tenosynovitis. *Am J Sports Med*. 1977;5:31–36.

83. Lindenberg G, Pinshaw R, Noakes TD. Iliotibial band friction syndrome in runners. *Phys Sports Med*. 1984;12:118–130.

84. Noble CB. Iliotibial band friction syndrome in runners. *Am J Sports Med*. 1980;8:232–234.

85. Mennell JM. *Back Pain: Diagnosis and Treatment Using Manipulative Techniques*. Boston: Little, Brown; 1960.

86. Millar AP. Strains of the posterior calf musculature ("tennis leg"). *Am J Sports Med*. 1979;7:172–174.

87. Friedman MJ. Injuries to the leg in athletes. In: Nicholas JA, Hershman EB, eds. *The Lower Extremity and Spine in Sports Medicine*. St Louis, Mo: Mosby; 1986.

88. Larsson L, Baum J. The syndrome of anserina bursitis: an overlooked diagnosis. *Arthritis Rheum*. 1985;28:1062–1065.

89. Helfet AJ. *Disorders of the Knee*. 2nd ed. Philadelphia: Lippincott; 1982.

90. Reilly JP, Nicholas JA. The chronically inflamed bursa. *Clin Sports Med.* 1987;6:356.

91. Peyron JG. Osteoarthritis, the epidemiologic viewpoint. *Clin Orthop Relat Res.* 1986;213:13–17.

92. Turek S. *Orthopaedics: Principles and Their Application.* 4th ed. Philadelphia: Lippincott; 1984.

93. DiStefano VJ. Skeletal injuries of the knee. In: Nicholas JA, Hershman EB, eds. *The Lower Extremity and Spine in Sports Medicine.* St Louis, Mo: Mosby; 1986;1.

94. Barrett JP, Rashkoff E, Sirna E, Wilson A. Correlations of roentgenographic patterns and clinical behavior in symptomatic idiopathic osteoarthritis of the knee. *Clin Orthop Relat Res.* 1990.

95. Rosenberg T, Paulos LE, Parker RD, et al. The forty-five degree posteroanterior flexion weight-bearing radiograph of the knee. *J Bone Joint Surg Am.* 1988;70:1479–1482.

96. Mangine RE. Rehabilitation considerations in arthritis, exercise vs. immobilization. Presented at Symposium, 1990 Advances in the Knee and Shoulder; April 4, 1990; Cincinnati Sports Medicine and Deaconess Hospital.

97. Schneider RC, Kennedy JC, Plant ML. *Sports Injuries: Mechanisms, Prevention, and Treatment.* Baltimore: Williams & Wilkins; 1985.

98. Mulawka SM, Jensen T. *Medial Collateral Ligament, Isolated Injury to MCL.* ProClinica; 1989.

99. Holden DL, Eggert AW, Butler JE. The nonoperative treatment of grade 1 and 2 medial collateral ligament injuries to the knee. *Am J Sports Med.* 1983;11:340–344.

100. Indelicato PA. Nonoperative management of complete tears of the medial collateral ligament. *Orthop Rev.* 1989;18:947–952.

101. Ellsasser JC, Reynolds FC, Omohundro JR. The nonoperative treatment of collateral ligament injuries of the knee in professional football players. *J Bone Joint Surg Am.* 1974;56:1185–1190.

102. Khoury GY, Usta HY, Berger RA. Meniscotibial ligament tears. *Skeletal Radiol.* 1984;11:192.

103. Hughston JC, Andrews JR, Cross MJ, Moschi A. Classification of knee ligament instabilities, part I: the medial compartment and cruciate ligaments. *J Bone Joint Surg Am.* 1976;58:159.

104. Hammer W. Meniscotibial (coronary) ligament sprain: diagnosis and treatment. *Chirop Sports Med.* 1988;2(2):48–50.

105. DeHaven KE. Diagnosis of acute knee injuries with hemarthrosis. *Am J Sports Med.* 1980;8:9–14.

106. Warren RF. Initial evaluation and management of acute anterior cruciate ligament ruptures. In: Finerman G, ed. *Symposium on Sports Medicine: The Knee.* St Louis, Mo: Mosby; 1985:212–221.

107. Woods GW, Stanley RF, Tullos HS. Lateral capsular sign: x-ray clue to a significant knee instability. *Am J Sports Med.* 1979;7:27.

108. Buckley SL, Barrack RL, Alexander HA. The natural history of conservatively treated partial anterior cruciate ligament tears. *Am J Sports Med.* 1989;17:221–225.

109. Kennedy JC, Weinberg JW, Wilson AS. The anatomy and function of the anterior cruciate ligament as determined by clinical and morphological studies. *J Bone Joint Surg Am.* 1974;56:223–235.

110. Antich TJ, Brewster CE. Rehabilitation of the nonreconstructed anterior cruciate ligament–deficient knee. *Clin Sports Med.* 1988;7:813–826.

111. McMaster WC. Isolated posterior cruciate ligament injury: literature review and case reports. *J Trauma.* 1975;15:1025–1029.

112. Corrigan B, Maitland GD. *Practical Orthopaedic Medicine.* London: Butterworth; 1985.

113. Simonsen O, Jensen J, Mouritsen P, Lauritzen J. The accuracy of clinical examination of injury of the knee joint. *Injury Br J Accident Surg.* 1984;16:100.

114. Arnoczky PS. The blood supply of the meniscus and its role in healing and repair. In: Finerman G, ed. *Symposium on Sports Medicine: The Knee.* St Louis, Mo: Mosby; 1985:109.

115. DeHaven KE. Injuries to the menisci of the knee. In: Nicholas JA, Hershman EB, eds. *The Lower Extremity and Spine in Sports Medicine.* St Louis, Mo: Mosby; 1986:905–928.

116. Dandy DJ, Jackson RW. The diagnosis of problems after meniscectomy. *J Bone Joint Surg Br.* 1975;57:349.

117. Cyriax J. *Textbook of Orthopaedic Medicine.* 8th ed. London: Bailliere Tindall; 1982;1.

118. Jackson RW. The pathologic medial shelf. *Orthop Clin North Am.* 1982;13:307.

119. Henry JH. Conservative treatment of patellofemoral subluxation. *Clin Sports Med.* 1989;8:261–277.

120. Kramer PG. Patella malalignment syndrome: rationale to reduce excessive lateral pressure. *J Orthop Sports Phys Ther.* 1986;8:301–309.

121. Baycroft CM. A self treatment method for patello-femoral dysfunction. *J Man Med.* 1990;5:25–26.

Appendix 7-A

Knee Functional Diagnosis Chart

Table 7-A-1 Knee Functional Diagnosis

Key
+ Pain
+/− Possible Pain
L Possible Limited ROM
LAX Possible Laxity

TESTS	Quadriceps Patellar Tendinitis	Hamstrings (Distal)	Popliteus	Iliotibial	Osteoarthritis	MCL (opposite for LCL)	Meniscotibial	ACL	PCL	Meniscus	Loose Bodies	Plica	Patellofemoral
Passive Flexion (160°)	+/−				L Most		+/−L	+/−	+/−	L	L	+/−	L
Passive Extension (0°)–(+10°)		+/− L			L Less		+/− L	+/−	+/− LAX	L	L		
Passive Lateral Rotation (45°)		+/−	+/−		L	+/−	+	+/−	+/−	L	+/−		
Passive Medial Rotation (30°)		+/−			L		+/−	+/−	+/−	L	+/−		
Valgus 30° Flexion						+ LAX					+/−		
Valgus 0° Extension								+/− LAX	+/− LAX				
Varus 30° Flexion											+/−		
Varus 0° Extension								+/− LAX	+/− LAX				
Lachman–Anterior Drawer							+/−	+ LAX					
Pivot-Shift Tests								+ LAX					
Dynamic Posterior Shift Posterior Sag									+ LAX				
Meniscus Tests										+			
Resisted Knee Flexion		+											
Resisted Knee Extension	+												+/−
ADDITIONAL TESTS													
Resisted Medial Rotation			+										
Ober–Flexion-Extension				+ L									
Rotational Drawer								+/− LAX	+/− LAX				
Medial Plica												+	
Patella Tracking												+/−	+/−
Patella Compression												+/−	+/−
Patella Apprehension													+/− LAX
Joint Play Evaluation													

172

Chapter 8

The Ankle and Foot

Andrew H. Rice

Gait or bipedal locomotion is a spectacular combination of coordinated muscular actions that propels the body from one point to another. Normal and abnormal function of the foot can be observed through careful and critical analysis of the walking or gait cycle.

GAIT ANALYSIS—OBSERVATIONAL GAIT EXAMINATION

Foot pain most frequently arises during the walking cycle; therefore, as diagnosticians we must train ourselves to recognize gait pathomechanics. First we must understand the normal walking cycle. *Gait* is defined as the coordinated muscular actions involved in moving from one place to another. During the walking cycle the examiner should pay careful attention to the leg and rear foot, that is, the calcaneal position. The calcaneal position should be noted at heel strike and midstance. The gross appearance of the medial arch and Achilles tendon should also be noted.

The observed walking cycle comprises two phases: a stance phase and a swing phase. The stance phase is when the foot remains in full contact with the supporting surface and all weight is born on this extremity. This phase represents approximately 65% of the gait cycle. The swing phase is when the foot is non–weight bearing. This phase represents approximately 35% of the walking cycle.

The stance phase can be broken down further into three subphases (Fig. 8-1):

1. *contact subphase:* 25% of stance phase or 15% of complete walking cycle
2. *midstance subphase:* 50% of stance phase or 35% of complete gait cycle
3. *propulsive subphase:* 25% of stance phase or 15% of complete gait cycle

At heel strike the heel is 2° to 4° inverted with respect to the ground. The leg now begins to internally rotate, and the knee flexes. As full weight is carried onto the midfoot, the extremity (femur and tibia) rotates internally 5° to 7°. This internal rotation is then translated to the subtalar joint via a fixed talar position in the ankle mortise. Therefore, internal tibial rotation is translated to the foot as subtalar joint pronation. It is mentioned by several investigators that there is a 1:1 relationship between internal tibial rotation and subtalar pronation.[1,2] Internal rotation of the leg has two effects: subtalar joint pronation and knee flexion. Therefore, the converse must also be true: External leg rotation yields subtalar joint supination and knee extension.

Heel contact is considered 0% of the gait cycle. At heel contact, pressure 10% to 15% in excess of body weight is driven into the lateral heel. This is called the vertical force. This vertical force is dissipated longitudinally along the lateral column and forward to the level of the fifth metatarsal head. It is then transferred medially to the first metatarsal and finally to the hallux at toe-off.

The foot has four functions in the gait cycle. (1) It is a pronating mobile adapter during heel strike and midstance.

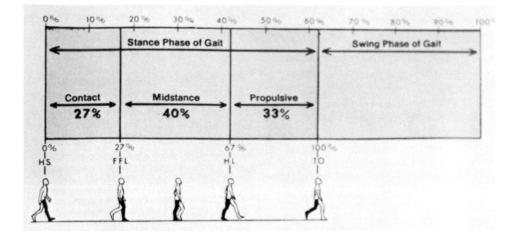

Figure 8-1 Subphases of stance phase of gait. The contact subphase starts at heel strike (HS) and terminates with forefoot loading (FFL). At the end of the contact period, all metatarsals are bearing weight. The midstance subphase is that period of stance in which the entire foot is making ground contact and is bearing the full weight of the body. The midstance subphase starts with forefoot loading and terminates with heel lift (HL). The propulsive subphase is initiated with heel lift and terminates with toe-off (TO). *Source:* Reprinted from *Clinical Biomechanics, Vol. II* (p 128), by ML Root et al. with permission of Clinical Biomechanics Corp., © 1977.

(2) It provides shock absorption. (3) It is a supinating rigid lever late midstance through toe-off. (4) It allows for transverse-plane motion of the leg (internal and external tibial motion and subtalar pronation and supination). The pronating mobile adapter function of the foot allows for subtalar adaptation to terrain and maintenance of balance. Shock absorption is effected by the cancellous bone of the calcaneus and by internal rotation of the tibia and unlocking of the knee. Supinating rigid lever function is attained via external leg rota-

tion, creating a rigid foot architecture. This supports the vertical component during the propulsive phase of gait.

On the basis of the motion of the bisection of the calcaneus on the frontal plane, the normal range of subtalar motion is approximately 30° (Figs. 8-2 and 8-3). Subtalar motion is measured by first bisecting the lower leg and calcaneus posteriorly, then fully inverting the heel or supinating the subtalar joint, and then fully everting the heel or subtalar joint. Normally there is twice the amount of supination as pronation. The

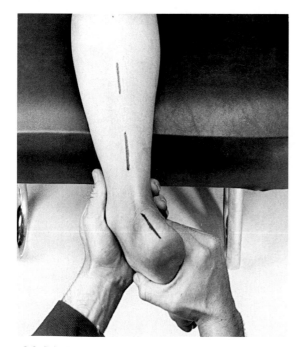

Figure 8-2 Subtalar joint supination.

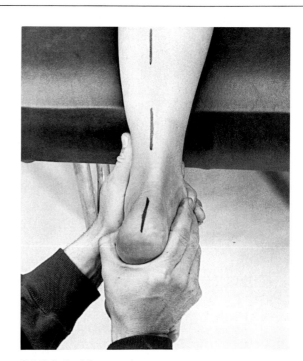

Figure 8-3 Subtalar joint pronation.

neutral position of the subtalar joint is when there is congruence between the calcaneus and the talus. This position can be palpated by feeling for conformity between the talar neck and medial navicular (Fig. 8-4). The subtalar joint axis is oriented 42° from the transverse plane and 16° from the sagittal plane (Fig. 8-5). Figures 8-6 through 8-8 illustrate the talocalcaneal relationship with subtalar supination, subtalar neutral position, and subtalar pronation, respectively. Two axes exist in the midtarsal joint: oblique and longitudinal (Figs. 8-9 and 8-10).

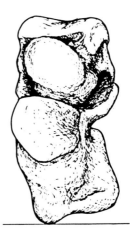

Figure 8-6 Talocalcaneal position in subtalar joint supination. Note calcaneal inversion. *Source:* Reprinted from *Clinical Biomechanics, Vol. II* (p 32) by ML Root et al. with permission of Clinical Biomechanics Corp., © 1977.

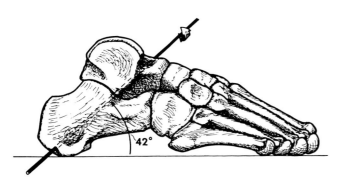

Figure 8-4 Palpating subtalar joint neutral position. The examiner's thumb is placed on the medial navicular and talar neck, and the index and middle fingers are placed on the sinus and neck of the talus. When palpating weight-bearing subtalar joint neutral position, one should note the bisection of the calcaneus posteriorly and its relation to the ground. Note that the position of the calcaneus in this patient is inverted or supinated while the subtalar joint is neutral. This is also known as the neutral calcaneal stance position.

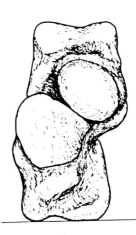

Figure 8-7 Talocalcaneal position in subtalar joint neutral position. In this position the talus is locked against the calcaneus, a stable subtalar position. *Source:* Reprinted from *Clinical Biomechanics, Vol. II* (p 32) by ML Root et. al. with permission of Clinical Biomechanics Corp., © 1977.

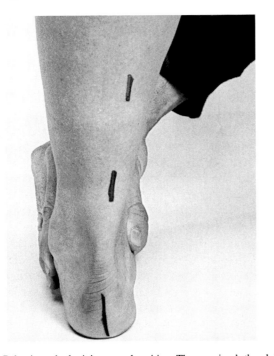

Figure 8-5 Position of the average axis of motion of the subtalar joint as viewed from the lateral side of the foot. The axis forms an average inclination angle of 42° with the transverse plane. *Source:* Reprinted from *Clinical Biomechanics, Vol. II* (p 28) by ML Root et al. with permission of Clinical Biomechanics Corp., © 1977.

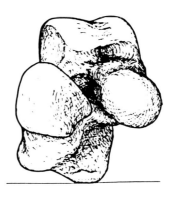

Figure 8-8 Talocalcaneal position in subtalar pronation. Note that the talus appears to have "fallen off" the calcaneus. Also note calcaneal eversion. *Source:* Reprinted from *Clinical Biomechanics, Vol. II* (p 32) by ML Root et al. with permission of Clinical Biomechanics Corp., © 1977.

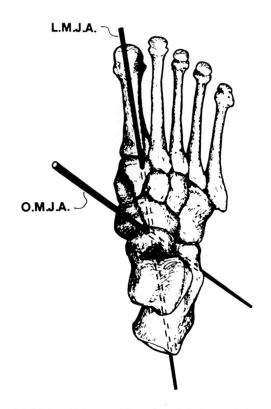

Figure 8-9 Midtarsal joint axes. The midtarsal joint has two independent axes of motion, both providing for motion in the direction of supination and pronation. The oblique midtarsal joint axis (OMJA) primarily provides inversion and eversion of the forefoot, with clinically insignificant motion in the other two body planes. LMJA, longitudinal midtarsal joint axis. *Source:* Reprinted from *Clinical Biomechanics, Vol. II* (p 42) by ML Root et al. with permission of Clinical Biomechanics Corp., © 1977.

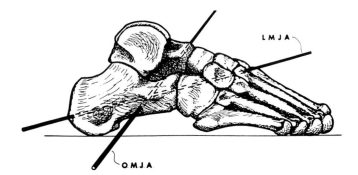

Figure 8-10 Lateral view of the two axes of motion for the midtarsal joint. *Source:* Reprinted from *Clinical Biomechanics, Vol. II* (p 42) by ML Root et al. with permission of Clinical Biomechanics Corp., © 1977.

FUNCTION OF MUSCLES IN GAIT

The extremity musculature has numerous functions in gait (Fig. 8-11). The triceps surae initiates flexion of the knee at heel-off, is a decelerator of pronation and internal rotation of the leg, and helps initiate subtalar joint supination and external rotation of the femur.[2] The gastrocnemius tendon joins alongside the soleus to form the Achilles tendon, which attaches to the middle third of the posterior surface of the calcaneus. The tendons function separately, although they share a common tendon sheath.

The gastrocnemius passes three joints: the knee, the ankle, and the subtalar joint. It functions to maintain flexion-contraction of the knee and prevents hyperextension. Its function begins near the end of the contact subphase and continues into late midstance, ending at toe-off.[2] This muscle assists in deceleration of internal tibial rotation toward the end of the contact subphase and helps initiate subtalar resupination and external rotation of the femur before toe-off.[2] Finally, the gastrocnemius aids in plantar flexion of the foot.

The soleus passes two joints: the ankle and the subtalar joint. It functions to stabilize the lateral foot near the end of the contact subphase through midstance. It decelerates subtalar joint pronation together with other posterior leg group muscles (ie, the tibialis posterior and gastrocnemius).[2] This muscle is responsible for deceleration of knee flexion at the end of the contact subphase and aids in heel lift during the propulsive subphase. Finally, the soleus extends the knee before heel-off by driving the tibia posteriorly.

The tibialis posterior functions to supinate the subtalar and midtarsal joints. This muscle decelerates pronation of the subtalar joint at heel contact and initiates subtalar joint supination.[2] It assists the soleus in re-extension of the knee and stabilization of the midtarsal joint during midstance and midpropulsion. It also stabilizes the lesser tarsus and metatarsal bases (because of its wide insertion). The distal tibialis posterior tendon passes posterior to the medial malleolus, functioning as the muscle pulley and turning anterior to its attachments.

The flexor hallucis longus functions with the soleus and flexor digitorum longus to decelerate forward momentum of the tibia during midstance. It functions with the tibialis posterior, soleus, flexor digitorum longus, and gastrocnemius to increase subtalar joint supination and tibial external rotation during midstance.[2] It assists in stabilizing the hallux against ground-reactive forces during propulsion. The flexor hallucis longus and extensor hallucis longus muscles contract posteriorly on the distal and proximal phalanx, thereby stabilizing the great toe as a rigid beam on the head of the first metatarsal. In propulsion the flexor hallucis longus functions with the gastrocnemius, peroneus longus, and flexor digitorum longus in plantar flexion of the ankle joint and with the abductor hallucis longus and flexor digitorum longus in supination of the oblique midtarsal joint.[2]

The flexor digitorum longus functions with the tibialis posterior, soleus, and gastrocnemius to assist in deceleration of subtalar joint pronation and internal rotation of the leg. During contact it functions with the tibialis posterior, soleus, and peroneus longus to decelerate forward momentum of the tibia in midstance. It functions with the tibialis posterior,

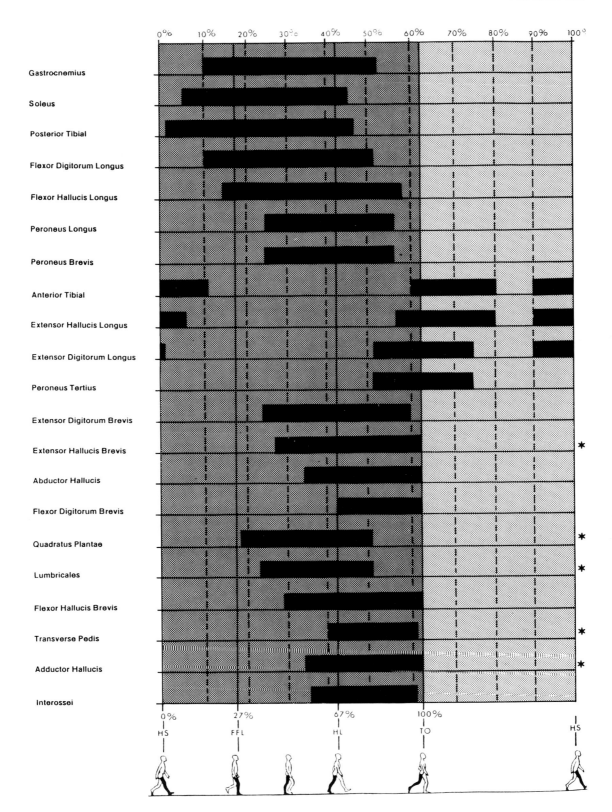

Figure 8-11 Phasic muscular activity: graphic representation of muscular activity related to gait cycle. *Source:* Reprinted from *Clinical Biomechanics, Vol. II* (pp 183–84) by ML Root et al. with permission of Clinical Biomechanics Corp., © 1977.

soleus, gastrocnemius, and flexor hallucis longus to enhance subtalar joint supination and external rotation of the leg during midstance.[2] Finally, it functions to maintain stability of the digits against the reactive forces of the ground at propulsion.

The peroneus longus stabilizes the first ray or medial column of the foot against the lesser tarsal bones and the ground plantarly through the end of the midstance subphase and propulsion. Its abductory force at the midfoot is resisted by the tibialis posterior. The peroneus longus tendon passes posterior to the lateral malleolus and plantar to the peroneal tubercle of the calcaneus, where it is bound by the peroneal retinaculum. It then passes anterior, where at the level of the cuboid it turns plantar to and in the sulcus of the cuboid or peroneal groove. The short plantar ligament covers the peroneal groove. The tendon then courses plantar and anterior to insert into the plantar lateral medial cuneiform and first metatarsal.

The peroneus brevis functions to pronate the subtalar joint and the midtarsal joint. It stabilizes the fifth metatarsal posteriorly against the cuboid and the cuboid against the calcaneus in midstance and early propulsion.[2] The peroneus brevis tendon courses posterior to the medial malleolus and is bound to the peroneal trochlea by the peroneal retinaculum. It then inserts into the styloid process of the fifth metatarsal.

The tibialis anterior assists in dorsiflexion of the foot at toe-off, dorsiflexes the first ray in the early swing phase, assists in toe clearance in midswing, and slightly supinates the foot before heel strike.[2] It resists plantar flexion of the foot at heel strike, which allows smooth loading of the forefoot from lateral to medial during the contact subphase.

The extensor hallucis longus functions to stabilize the first metatarsalphalangeal and interphalangeal joints during propulsion. During swing it aids in dorsiflexion of the ankle joint. It assists in toe clearance and decelerates the foot at heel strike.

The extensor digitorum longus assists the intrinsic muscles in maintaining extensor rigidity of the interphalangeal joints against each other and the head of the first metatarsal during propulsion. It assists in dorsiflexion of the foot and toes for clearance and prevents an excessive supination of the foot during the swing phase. The peroneus tertius runs along the lateral side of the extensor digitorum longus and also assists in dorsiflexion, it inserts into the proximal shaft of the fifth metatarsal.

LESIONS

This section discusses common tendon inflammatory situations and tenosynovitis as well as their common causes, locations, and functional testing (Appendix 8-A, Table 8-A-1).

Achilles Tendon Complex (Gastrocnemius and Solcus)

Achilles tendinitis is probably the most common tendinitis of the foot and ankle. The most common causes of inflam-

matory tendinitis of the gastrocnemius-soleus complex are equinus, abnormal tendon insertion, overuse syndromes, and direct trauma.[3] Achilles tendinitis represents 11% of all running injuries.[4]

Common locations in which tendinitis occurs are the insertion of the tendon on the posterior superior calcaneus and 1 to 2 cm proximal to the insertion.

Functional tests

1. Passive tests
   • Passive ankle dorsiflexion with the knee extended; this tests both the gastrocnemius and the soleus (Fig. 8-12).
   • Passive ankle dorsiflexion with the knee flexed; this specifically tests the soleus contribution to the Achilles tendon complex.
   • The calf-squeeze (Thompson's) test; this assesses for rupture of the Achilles tendon. With the patient lying prone the examiner squeezes the calf and observes for ankle joint plantar flexion. If flexion is absent, Achilles tendon rupture is diagnosed.
2. Resistance test: Involves resisting ankle joint plantar flexion while contracting the gastrocnemius-soleus complex (Fig. 8-13).
3. Palpation by grasping the Achilles tendon medial to lateral while the patient is walking on a treadmill or lying prone.

Treatment: Treatment is aimed at relieving the cause by modifying training techniques, changing shoe gear to avoid direct trauma, using heel lifts or orthotics, and undertaking physical therapy.[5,6] Differential diagnosis may include Achilles bursitis, sciatic neuritis, and posterior-superior fracture of the calcaneus.

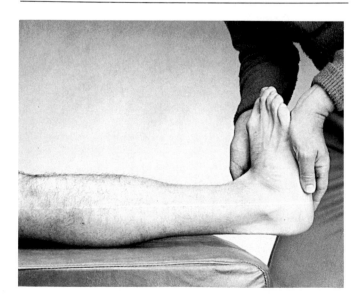

Figure 8-12 Functional testing: passive ankle dorsiflexion with knee extended for soleus and gastrocnemius muscles.

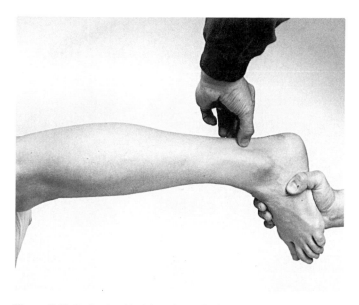

Figure 8-13 Resisted ankle joint plantar flexion with knee extended and palpation of distal Achilles tendon. This tests both gastrocnemius and soleus muscles.

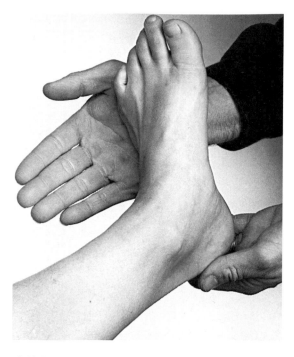

Figure 8-14 Passive ankle dorsiflexion and foot eversion testing tibialis posterior muscle.

Tibialis Posterior

Common causes of tibialis posterior tendinitis and tenosynovitis include previous medial malleolar fracture causing stenosis or synovial adhesions where the tendon courses through the posterior medial and plantar medial malleolar sulci, abnormal insertion, accessory ossicles (ostibiale externum), and an enlarged medial navicular tuberosity. Idiopathic tendinitis and tendinitis due to obesity occur in postmenopausal women. The most common locations of tendinitis are 1 to 2 cm proximal or distal to the medial malleolus, where the tendon overlies the medial navicular, and plantar to the navicular. The location of tenosynovitis is 1 to 2 cm proximal to the medial malleolus and may also be found as the tendon courses around the medial malleolus.

Differential diagnosis includes stress fracture of the medial malleolus, capsulitis of the medial navicular or accessory navicular articulation with the navicular, and fracture of the medial navicular tuberosity.

Functional tests

1. Passive test: Passive ankle dorsiflexion and eversion of the foot (Fig. 8-14).
2. Resistance test: Resisted ankle plantar flexion and foot inversion (Fig. 8-15).
3. Heel raise inversion test: The patient is asked to invert the foot and to raise the heel while standing. The test is positive if the patient is unable to raise the heel.

Treatment: Treatment of acute cases includes rest, ice, nonsteroidal anti-inflammatory medication, a semiflexible orthotic, and a Malleotrain. Severe cases may require immo-

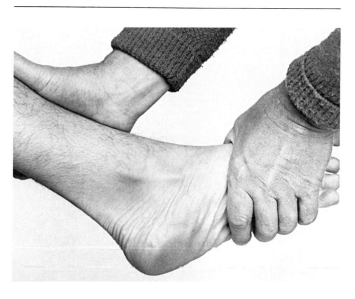

Figure 8-15 Resisted ankle joint plantar flexion and foot inversion testing tibialis posterior muscle.

bilization in a short leg cast or non–weight bearing on crutches. Chronic cases may respond to surgical intervention.

Peroneus Brevis and Longus

Tendinitis is usually related to the pulley action of the lateral malleolus on the tendons. Causes of tendinitis and tenosynovitis include the following: inversion ankle sprains, cuboid fracture (peroneus longus tenosynovitis), an old lateral malleolar fracture, an ineffective peroneal tubercle of the calcaneus, an old styloid injury at the base of the fifth metatarsal, and tarsal coalition (congenital fusion of the tarsal bones). A common location of peroneus brevis or longus tendinitis or tenosynovitis is the retromalleolar area. Peroneus longus tenosynovitis can occur near the peroneal sulcus of the cuboid and near the peroneal tubercle of the calcaneus. Peroneus longus tendinitis can extend from the peroneal sulcus of the cuboid plantarly and then anterior and medial to the peroneus longus insertion. Differential diagnosis includes sural neuritis and stress fracture of the cuboid or lateral malleolus.

Functional tests

1. Passive test (Fig. 8-16): Passive ankle dorsiflexion and inversion of the foot.
2. Resistance tests
   - Resist plantar flexion eversion of the foot while resisting first metatarsal plantar flexion; this is a peroneus longus test.
   - Resist pronation or eversion and plantar flexion; this tests both longus and brevis (Fig. 8-17).

Treatment: Treatment is short leg casting in resistant cases. In those that are less resistant, a semiflexible orthotic with rearfoot posting can be used so that the heel remains perpendicular or slightly everted in midstance. Extrinsic forefoot posting (see below, Orthotics) is not recommended. Surgical intervention must be considered in nonresponsive cases.

Tibialis Anterior

Causes of tendinitis and tenosynovitis are tight laces of high-top athletic shoes, ice skates, and ski boots and downhill

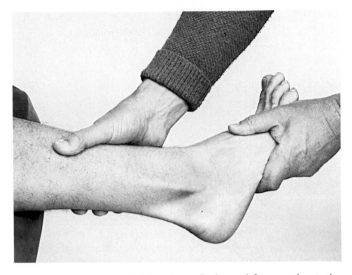

Figure 8-17 Resisted ankle joint plantar flexion and foot eversion testing peroneus longus and brevis muscles.

running and hiking. Tenosynovitis usually occurs below the superior extensor retinaculum and also at the tendon insertion near the medial cuneiform.

Functional tests

1. Passive test: Ankle plantar flexion and foot eversion.
2. Resistance test (Fig. 8-18): Resisted ankle dorsiflexion and foot inversion.
3. Heel walking (patient walks on the heels); this tests for all anterior muscle group problems but most specifically tibialis anterior weakness.

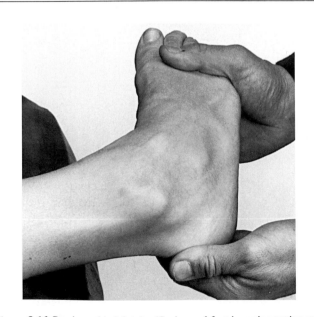

Figure 8-16 Passive ankle joint dorsiflexion and foot inversion testing peroneus longus and brevis muscles.

Figure 8-18 Resisted ankle joint dorsiflexion and foot inversion testing tibialis anterior muscle.

Treatment: Treatment is rest, ice, a semiflexible or rigid orthotic with moderate control, and friction massage.

Extensor Hallucis Longus

Causes of extensor hallucis longus tendinitis are an exostosis corresponding to a hallux limitus, in which a hypertrophic change is seen at the dorsal head of the first metatarsal and an exostosis of the medial cuneiform and the metatarsal joint, which is seen in dancers who exercise en pointes or do grand pliés.

Functional tests

1. Passive test (Fig. 8-19): Passive hallux plantar flexion.
2. Resistance test (Fig. 8-20): Resisted hallux dorsiflexion.

Treatment: Treatment includes rest, ice, nonsteroidal anti-inflammatory medication, and semiflexible orthotics with forefoot extension. In severe cases surgical release may be indicated.

Extensor Digitorum Longus

Causes of tendinitis range from shoe or lace pressure in the vamp area of the shoes, dorsal metatarsal–cuneiform exostosis, metatarsal fractures producing bone callus formation and subsequent tendon irritation, and hammer-digit deformities of toes 2, 3, 4, and 5.

Functional tests

1. Passive test (Fig. 8-19): Digital plantar flexion.
2. Resistance test (Fig. 8-21): Resistance to digital dorsiflexion.

Figure 8-19 Passive hallux and digital plantar flexion testing extensor hallucis longus and extensor digitorum longus.

Figure 8-20 Resisted hallux dorsiflexion testing extensor hallucis longus muscle.

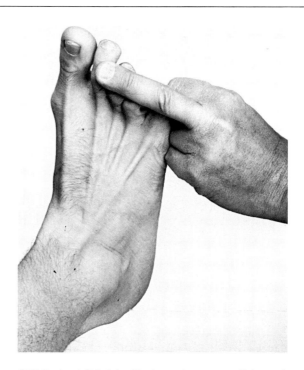

Figure 8-21 Resisted digital dorsiflexion testing extensor digitorum longus.

Treatment: Treatment is rest, ice, anti-inflammatory medication, padding between offending areas of the shoe and the foot, and surgical hammer-toe repair.

Flexor Hallucis Longus

Causes of tendinitis may be injury to the posterior groove of the talus, which the tendon passes (this is seen in inversion ankle sprains, in which the posterior talofibular ligament may rupture and an avulsion of the posterior tubercle of the talus occurs), and a cavus foot. In the cavus foot mechanical advantage is to the flexor hallucis longus muscle and yields overactivity and tendinitis.

Functional tests

1. Passive test (Fig. 8-22): Hallux dorsiflexion.
2. Resistance test (Fig. 8-23): Resisted hallux plantar flexion.

Treatment: Recommended treatment is the same as the initial treatment for extensor digitorum longus tendinitis. With posterior talar injuries surgical repair or excision of the posterior talar process may be necessary.

Flexor Digitorum Longus

Causes of tendinitis are hammer-toes, cavus foot, and direct trauma.

Functional tests

1. Passive test (Fig. 8-22): Digital dorsiflexion.
2. Resistance test (Fig. 8-23): Resisted digital plantar flexion.

Treatment: Recommended treatment is the same as the initial treatment for extensor digitorum longus tendinitis.

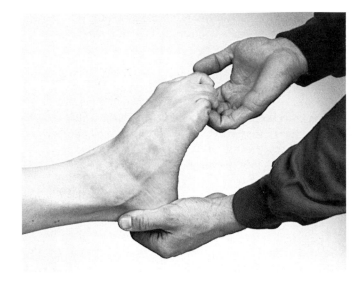

Figure 8-23 Resistance to hallux and digital plantar flexion testing flexor hallucis longus and flexor digitorum longus muscles.

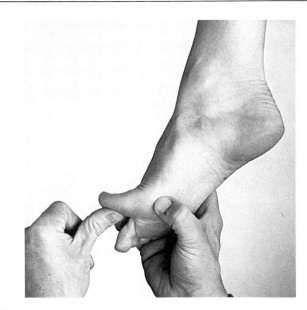

Figure 8-24 Passive test for sesamoiditis.

Sesamoiditis

Sesamoiditis is a condition in which the capsule surrounding the ossicles becomes inflamed. Common causes are cavus or high-arched foot, bunion deformity forcing the sesamoid to drift laterally,[7] and direct trauma (dancing or running injuries).

Functional test

1. Passive sesamoid test: Hallux passive dorsiflexion. Palpate for pain by pressing on plantar medial aspect of first metatarsal phalangeal joint in order to push the tibial and fibular sesamoids laterally (Fig. 8-24).

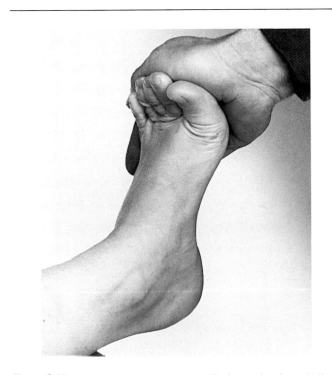

Figure 8-22 Passive hallux and digital dorsiflexion testing flexor hallucis longus and flexor digitorum longus muscles.

"Shin Splints"

Anterior or medial leg pain associated with the shaft of the tibia or fibula may be classified as "shin splints," which is periosteal inflammation associated with an overuse injury and pulling of the muscle from its myotendinous origin. The pain usually begins as a myositis or tendinitis that is left untreated. The onset of pain frequently is several minutes into an athletic activity, or it may begin immediately afterward.

Many causes of shin splints have been proposed, including hyperpronation, improper athletic shoe gear allowing excessive foot motion, and external femoral or tibial torsion. Frequently shin splints are categorized according to their location (ie, anterior compartment, lateral compartment, and medial or posterior compartment).[8]

Anterior Compartment

The tibialis anterior is responsible for 80% of the dorsiflexion power of the foot. It also acts as a strong decelerator of plantar flexion. Frequently anterior compartment shin splints arise in runners overtraining on hills because both uphill and downhill running requires repetitive firing of the tibialis anterior muscle. Most frequently symptoms are worse while running downhill.

Treatments include rest, ice, stretching techniques for the posterior muscle group to allow better ankle joint dorsiflexion, and reduction of ankle equinus. Semiflexible orthotic inlays with conformity to the medial longitudinal arch and rearfoot posting enable the heel to remain perpendicular to the ground at midstance.

Lateral Compartment Shin Splints

Lateral compartment shin splints occur in athletes with hyperpronation where there is overactivity of the peroneal muscle group.

Treatments include rest, ice, and orthotics to control pronation.

Medial Compartment

Tibialis posterior shin splints are the most common shin splints seen in runners and aerobic dancers. The area of pain is usually 1 to 3 cm proximal to the medial malleolus and may be associated with posterior tibial tendinitis, which occurs at the malleolar sulcus or distally near the tendon insertion. Pain is palpated at the junction of the tibialis posterior muscle and tendon and proximally along the course of the muscle belly.

Treatment again includes rest and ice. The patient should be encouraged to wear running and aerobic shoes that are supportive and warned to avoid pronation (medial column) motion. Again, semiflexible orthotic devices with extrinsic rearfoot posting and good medial longitudinal arch conformity can be applied to decrease midstance pronation, and a Malleotran can be used for support. Overall treatments include physical therapy modalities such as ultrasound, friction massage, low-dose aspirin, or oral anti-inflammatories.

Plantar Fasciitis (Heel Pain Syndrome)

Plantar fasciitis is a potentially serious injury characterized by pain primarily at the plantar medial calcaneus or origin of the plantar fascia and running along the course of the medial band of the plantar fascia, sometimes as distal as the first metatarsal head.

The plantar fascia is a thick band of fibrous tissue that arises from the medial and lateral calcaneal tubercles and runs to the plantar metatarsal heads, where it connects with the transverse metatarsal ligament (Fig. 8-25). The plantar fascia provides extensive support to both the longitudinal arch and the transverse metatarsal arch.

Plantar fasciitis is best classified as overuse injuries, that is, microtears and microruptures of the plantar fascia. The overuse injury usually occurs during walking, running, tennis, gymnastics, or basketball. These activities stretch the plantar fascia. The combination of a stretching activity with an underlying biomechanical fault predisposes to the development of fasciitis. In hyperpronation one sees increased tension along the medial longitudinal arch, and the scenario of inflammation due to overuse becomes prevalent. The supinated or cavus foot also shows a predisposition toward the development of fasciitis because of the constant tension on the plantar fascia. Fasciitis may also be associated with equinus.

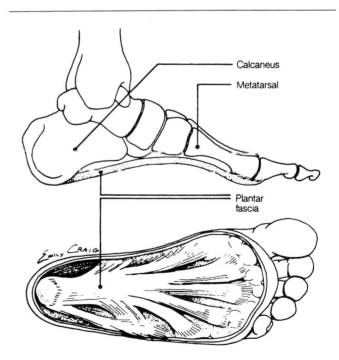

Figure 8-25 The plantar fascia, a dense, fibrous band of connective tissue that extends from the calcaneus to the metatarsals. *Source:* Reprinted with permission from *The Physician and Sports Medicine* (1988; 16[8]: 40), Copyright © 1988, McGraw-Hill Book Company.

No discussion of plantar fasciitis or heel pain should fail to stress the importance of differential diagnosis. The work-up should include lateral foot weight-bearing radiographs. Blood tests to rule out systemic inflammatory arthritis should be considered in cases of bilateral heel pain.

Plantar fasciitis can be diagnosed in the supine patient by extending the knee and maximally dorsiflexing the ankle while simultaneously dorsiflexing all the digits, especially the hallux (Fig. 8-26). Treatments include fascial strapping (Fig. 8-27), warm whirlpool bathing, ultrasound, and orthotic devices.

Equinus

Equinus is a lack of necessary dorsiflexion (8° to 10°) of the ankle (Fig. 8-28). There are two types of equinus: gastroc-soleal and soleal. To test for gastroc-soleal equinus, the examiner extends the knee, dorsiflexes the ankle while maintaining the subtalar joint in neutral position. If there is a lack of normal dorsiflexion this is termed a gastrocnemius-soleus equinus. It is then necessary to test the soleus contribution of the Achilles tendon by flexing the knee and attempting dorsiflexion of the

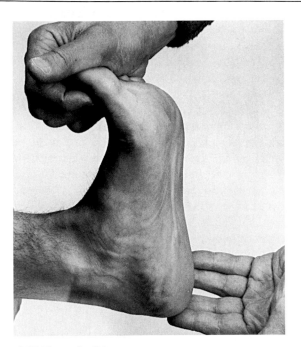

Figure 8-26 Plantar fasciitis test.

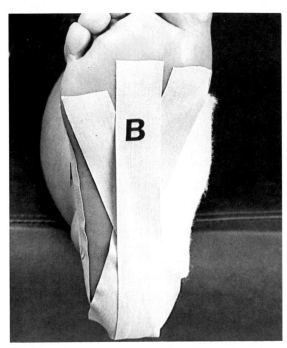

B

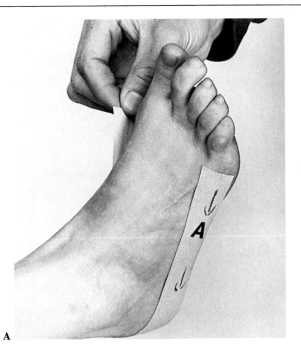

Figure 8-27 Plantar fascial strapping.

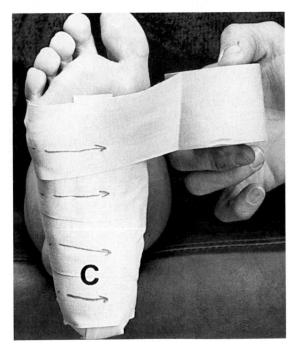

C

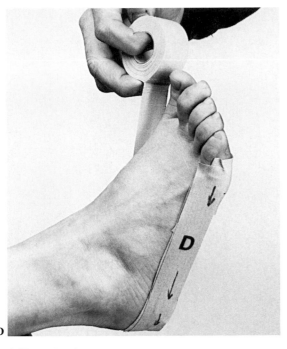

Figure 8-27 continued

ankle joint. If there is a continued lack of dorsiflexion, a soleus equinus is diagnosed.

Rigid bony equinus can be diagnosed by the following test: With the subtalar joint in neutral position, the patient is asked to dorsiflex the ankle with the knee flexed. The anterior distal tibia will meet bony resistance with the talar neck in rigid bony equinus. This type can also be diagnosed on plain weight-bearing lateral roentgenograms.

Spastic equinus is an equinus condition relating to motor neuron lesions affecting the posterior muscle group of the leg.

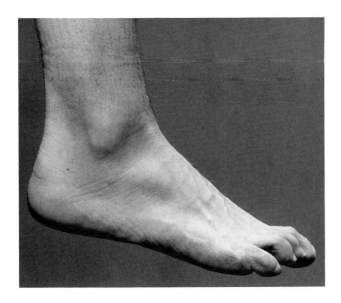

Figure 8-28 Equinus: less than 10° of dorsiflexion to the leg is available with the knee extended and the subtalar joint in neutral.

Ankle Joint Trauma (Distal Tibia, Fibula, and Talus)

A complete discussion of ankle joint trauma is beyond the scope of this chapter. The following section describes a few of the most common trauma-related ankle joint lesions.

Probably of utmost importance when discussing trauma to the ankle is an appreciation of the ligamentous anatomy surrounding the ankle joint. The distal tibiofibular joint, although a nonsynovial joint, is an articulation that is attached by five structures[9]: the anterior inferior tibiofibular ligament, the posterior inferior tibiofibular ligament, the inferior transverse tibiofibular ligament, the interosseous tibiofibular ligament, and the capsule. The tibiofibular talar joint or ankle joint is stabilized medially by the medial collateral ligament complex and laterally by the lateral collateral ligament complex.

The medial collateral ligament or deltoid ligament is composed of superficial and deep portions. The superficial portion has three distinct bands: naviculotibial, calcaneotibial, and superficial talotibial. The deep portion has two distinct bands: deep anterior talotibial and deep posterior talotibial. Deltoid ligament injuries are rarely seen as isolated injuries (ie, without an accompanying ankle fracture). Injuries to the medial collateral ligament complex are tested passively by everting the foot slightly plantar flexed (Fig. 8-29). An anterior drawer test is positive only when the anterior talofibular ligament is also ruptured and there is no medial shift of the talus during the test (see below).

The lateral collateral ligament complex has three distinct bands: the anterior talofibular ligament, the posterior talofibular ligament, and the calcaneofibular ligament. The anterior talofibular ligament is tested passively by ankle plantar

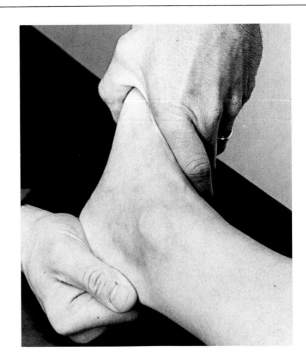

Figure 8-29 Medial collateral ligament test.

flexion and foot inversion (Fig. 8-30) and the anterior drawer test (Figs. 8-31 and 8-32). The latter is positive with ligament rupture, but with intact resistance of the deltoid ligament a medial shift of the talus occurs. Isolated passive testing of the posterior talofibular and calcaneofibular ligaments is difficult because these ligaments rarely rupture individually; they usually rupture together with the anterior talofibular ligament. Rupture of both posterior and anterior ligaments will produce a greater positive anterior drawer test. Rupture of anterior tibiofibular and calcaneofibular ligaments together will perhaps

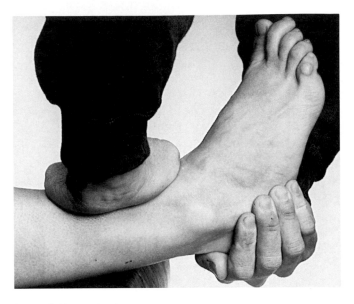

Figure 8-32 Anterior drawer test.

produce a greater inversion component of lateral ligament instability.

ORTHOTICS

Orthotics for the foot are not a cure-all vehicle of foot care. They are removable inlays that act to control or reduce abnormal motion of the foot. Generally they are fabricated from materials of different densities, such as rhohadur, polypropylene, graphite, plastizote, leather, and even steel. The devices are classified by their flexibility or rigidity.

Flexible orthotics are useful when mild to moderate control (rebalancing or realignment) is required. These orthotics are indicated in treating pressure lesions or providing resilient cushioning and are best suited for the geriatric foot. The function of these devices depends on the support of the shoe utilized. Semiflexible orthoses are best utilized for control by athletes during sporting activities and can be used for flat and cavus foot conditions when absolute control of all motion is not indicated. Rigid orthoses are necessary in flexible pediatric and adolescent flat-foot conditions when absolute control of most motion is indicated. Intrinsic posting is when the tilts or posts to the orthotic rear portion (rearfoot) or front portion (forefoot) are built into the mold. Extrinsic posting is when the posts are added onto the exterior of the orthotic.

The four important functions of foot orthoses according to Whitney[10] are as follows:

1. Protection or regional cushioning of the sole of the foot against hard surfaces. These devices often have built-in accommodation or seats for protection of focal points of pressure due to plantigrade metatarsals, preulcerous

Figure 8-30 Anterior talofibular ligament test.

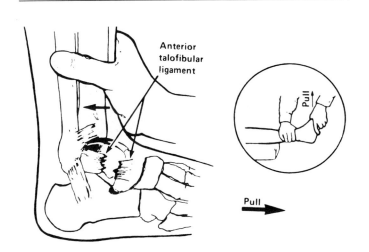

Figure 8-31 Anterior drawer test. *Source:* Reprinted from *Office Management of Sports Injuries and Athletic Problems*, (p 249) by MB Mellon (Ed) with permission of Hanley & Belfus, Inc, © 1988.

conditions of the foot, malalignments, and osseous deformities.

2. Adaptation to changing foot contours. With aging and decreased flexibility, the feet may become poorly adapted to the inner sole of a shoe or sneaker. The orthosis provides an excellent interface between the ground and the sole of the foot, especially in elderly patients or those with a rigid cavus foot.

3. Realignment of flexible foot deformities. The orthotic is used as a brace to reposition a traumatized, paralyzed, or postoperative foot. Orthotic realignment of the pediatric foot will also provide an external stabilizing force during maturation. In this way an orthotic may be a correction inducer in faulty foot alignment and may provide muscle re-education in childhood.

4. Control of the gait cycle. One can control rearfoot position with longitudinal arch conformity and forefoot posting.

REFERENCES

1. Schoenhaus H. Pathomechanic lecture notes.

2. Root ML, Orien WP, Weed JH. *Normal and Abnormal Function of the Foot*. Los Angeles: Clinical Biomechanics; 1977.

3. Gordon GM. Podiatric sports medicine. *Clin Podiatry*. 1984;1: 401–414.

4. Brody DM. Running injuries. *Clin Symp*. 1980;32:2–36.

5. Frey CC, Shereff MJ. Tendon injuries about the ankle in athletes. *Clin Sports Med*. 1988;103:178.

6. Clement DB, Taunton JE, Smart GW. Achilles tendinitis and peritendinitis; etiology and treatment. *Am J Sports Med*. 1984;12:179–184.

7. Pressman MM, Rice AH. Correction of hallux valgus: tendoligamentous sling procedure. In: *Current Therapy in Podiatric Surgery*. Philadelphia: Decker; 1989.

8. Rzonca EC, Baylis WJ. Common sports injuries to the foot and leg. *Clin Podiatric Med Surg*. 1988;5:591–612.

9. Hamilton WC. *Traumatic Disorders of the Ankle*. New York: Springer-Verlag; 1983.

10. Whitney AK. Personal communication, 1982.

Appendix 8-A

Foot and Ankle Functional Diagnosis Chart

Table 8-A-1 Foot and Ankle Functional Diagnosis

Key
Pain +
No Pain −
Possible Pain +/−
Possible Laxity LAX

	Lesions	Deltoid Lig.	Calcan. Fib. Lig.	Post. Talofib. Lig.	Ant. Talofib. Lig.	Sesamoiditis	Plantar Fasciitis	Peroneus Longus	Peroneus Brevis	Ext. Hal. Longus	Ext. Digit. Longus	Tibialis Posterior	Tibialis Anterior	Flex. Hal. Long.	Flex. Digit. Long.	Soleus	Gastrocnemius
PASSIVE TESTS																	
Ankle Dorsiflexion																	
Knee Flexed																+	−
Knee Extended																+	+
Foot Eversion												+					
Foot Inversion								+	+/−								
Ankle Plantar Flexion																	
Foot Eversion													+				
Foot Inversion				+/−	+												
Hallux Dorsiflexion														+			
Hallux Plantar Flexion										+							
Digital Dorsiflexion															+		
Digital Plantar Flexion											+						
Plantar Fascia Test							+										
Sesamoid Test						+											
Heel Inversion			+														
Heel Eversion		+															
Anterior Drawer				+Lax	+Lax												
Resisted Plantar Flexion																	
Neutral																+	+
Inversion												+					
Eversion								+	+								
Hallux														+			
Digits															+		
Resisted Dorsiflexion																	
Inversion													+				
Eversion																	
Peroneus Longus Test								+									
Hallux										+							
Digits											+						
Additional Tests																	
Heel Raise												+/−					
Thompson																	rupture

Part **III**

Manual Treatment

Chapter 9

The Manipulatable Lesion: Joint Play, Joint Dysfunction, and Joint Manipulation

John Mennell

In the past quarter of a century, articles in the field of bodily aches and pains seem to be accepted for publication in the medical literature in an incredibly uncritical manner. The symptoms are those seen in patients who, under normal circumstances, would not be considered sick or ill. The most usual topics that are written about are low back pain, tennis elbow, bursitis (shoulder pain), and the whiplash injury (neck pain).

There seems to be no major disagreement among investigators who write about joint diseases that the pain in the joints of these patients is part and parcel of some causative disease. To name but a few, these are the collagen vascular diseases, rheumatic fever, gout, ankylosing spondylitis, and joint pain from systemic diseases that affect joints such as gonorrhea, tuberculosis, brucellosis, hemophilia, parasites, serum sickness, hemorrhagic villonodular synovitis, tumors, bone diseases, some endocrine and deficiency diseases, and so on; the list seems to be endless.

For the most part the word *pain* is the operative word, yet those who most loudly denigrate the work done in this field do so because of the lack of research papers concerning the structures of the musculoskeletal system. There is a lack of such research papers because the musculoskeletal system is not recognized as a system. Common aches and pains are not life threatening or even terribly interesting to anyone other than those who experience them. Yet no one denies that the loss to society and industry because of them is enormous, often resulting in devastating socioeconomic difficulties for the patients and their families.

It seems strange that it has never been made clear in medical education that those who are interested in pains and especially in chronic pain patients are, in fact, interested in yet another body system. For the convenience of the professional, patients have become fragmented. The cardiologist is interested in the cardiovascular system; the urologist is interested in the genitourinary system; the neurologist is interested in the nervous system; the gastroenterologist is interested in the stomach and intestinal system; the hematologist is interested in the circulatory system; the oncologist is interested in tumors, which seem to be considered a system; the orthopedist is interested in the bony system, in which trauma plays a large part. Again the list seems endless, but where is the person who is interested in the musculoskeletal system as a body system, in fact the largest of all the body systems, that reflects all the changes that may occur in all the other body systems?

Those who demand research findings before they can accept clinical observations and who decry anecdotal evidence forget that the specialties in the healing arts all started with anecdotal witness. Further, all medical research, and the tools that are used in conducting it, are designed, except for biopsies, to study diseased parts after death. One cannot research the musculoskeletal system after death because then there is no function left to study. Therefore, before credible research can be developed protocols for research must be developed around the living and moving subject. At the present time all one can do is report clinical research that for the most part has to be based on anecdotes, which the "scientist" decries.

The difference between this book and others devoted to fragmented parts of the musculoskeletal system is that it is presented by practitioners of the healing arts who, up to now, have not had the "advantages" of studying cadavers or of prescribing any form of medication in their endeavors to bring comfort to their patients. They have had to confine their studies and experiences to pain attributable directly to mechanical faults initially arising from the spine but more lately involving any synovial joint in the musculoskeletal system.

In science one may start a project of study with a theorem. The theorem in our work is that there is a musculoskeletal system. When the system is studied it becomes apparent that it is a hierarchic system, and in such a system one can neither project nor accept the possibility that there are any exceptions to the system. A hierarchic system is either all right or it is wrong, but it must have a foundation acceptable to one of the basic sciences, which in this case is the basic science of mechanics. In this we have to rely on logic and common sense until a better research model is developed. Nevertheless, few would challenge the hypothesis that all the advances in the art of medicine have been postulated to the researchers by the clinicians and that it is then commonplace for the researcher to confirm the observations of the clinician. Therefore, in this musculoskeletal system we are still having to rely on the art rather than the science of medicine, and in this system science has so far failed the art.

In mechanics everything that humans make move has in its design play between the moving parts, which allows for efficiency and economy of function. In mechanics, when this play is lost inefficiency of the moving thing results, and this inefficiency is often associated with some strange noise that may well direct one's attention to the cause of the inefficiency. When play is restored the efficiency of the moving thing returns to normal, and the noise disappears.

The theorem on which the musculoskeletal system is built is exactly that. In every synovial joint in the body without exception there is play between the moving parts of the joint; being a biomechanical norm, a range of play movements is demonstrable in every synovial joint in the body. By definition these play movements can be neither performed nor altered in any way by voluntary muscle action, yet their presence is prerequisite to normal function of each joint. The range of play movements is the same in every joint of the same kind in everybody. It is logical to designate these movements as the movements of joint play.

Loss of play in mechanics impairs function, and it is logical to suppose that loss of joint play in a synovial joint is going to impair function in that joint until play is restored. Thus joint dysfunction becomes a mechanical diagnosis because of impaired function associated with pain. The next logical step is to look for something to relieve these symptoms by restoring normal play. Because play is not under the control of the muscles of the system, exercise cannot be expected to achieve this; it is necessary to find a mechanical means of restoring play. This is joint manipulation performed by a second party. In simple joint dysfunction, function is impaired while structure remains unchanged, e.g. in other pathologic states structure is changed and this impairs function.

Orthodox medicine cannot accept a theorem unless there are acceptable etiologic factors. There are predictable etiologic factors in dysfunction in any synovial joint; thus the system fits the concept of a theorem. The etiologic factors are (1) intrinsic trauma; (2) immobilization, with which must be included disuse and aging; and (3) resolution of some more serious injury or disease process that is identifiable, which includes the results of gross extrinsic trauma (see below).

It is an elementary fact that one should be able universally to accept that a system is made up of specific structures. In the musculoskeletal system these are bone, with its periosteum and endosteum; hyaline cartilage; synovial capsule; ligaments; muscles, with their tendons and in some instances tendon sheaths; fibrocartilage; and bursae. There are structures common to other systems that may have to be considered with the musculoskeletal system; these are fascia, skin, blood vessels, components of the neurologic system, and the lymphatic system. The fascia plays a special part in problems of the feet and the hands; the iliotibial bands in the legs, and the thoracolumbar region in the back.

Having recognized the primary structures of the system, one then has to consider the pathologic conditions that may affect each structure. Generically the pathologic conditions are trauma, inflammation, metabolic disease, tumors, and congenital anomalies. Trauma to most people means that some considerable force has been applied to the system from without; this we designate extrinsic trauma. In the musculoskeletal system one has to accept the concept of intrinsic trauma, which seldom if ever results from direct injury and is not associated with physical signs of inflammation such as swelling, discoloration, or increased local heat.

In assisting the clinician in a diagnostic exercise, there are three primary *nevers*. It is never possible to palpate fluid in a normal joint; it is never possible to palpate a normal synovial capsule; and it is never possible to elicit tenderness on palpation of normal ligaments. If palpation over a ligament produces tenderness, and if by history there is no evidence that it has sustained injury itself, then there is something wrong in the joint that the ligament supports or, in the back, at the intervertebral junction that the ligament supports. Throughout the system there is at least one palpable ligament for every joint (or in the back, every junction). There are two additional but rather special *nevers*: When symptoms of pain are due to metabolic disease of bone, simple osteoporosis never affects the skull or the lamina dura (propria); and primary joint dysfunction is never associated with increased local heat, swelling, or discoloration.

As far as the musculoskeletal system goes, intra-articular menisci and intervertebral discs are the same. There are only five extremity joints in which there are menisci, and not every intervertebral junction has a disc. Any injury to one of these menisci or discs produces in common the history of locking (or blocking) of the joint that is involved. In the back this would mean blocking of a facet joint at the level of meniscal injury. It is logical to unlock a joint that is locked in this manner by manipulative means, and the sooner the better.

In the diagnostic assessment of pain in the musculoskeletal system, the terms *acute* and *chronic* are often used in misleading ways. Either word can be used in relation to time or in relation to the state of a pathologic condition. The term *chronic pain syndrome* usually relates to time and has little bearing on the state of pathology when used in thinking about the musculoskeletal system. For instance, it is commonplace for a patient who has undergone a laminectomy for *a disc lesion* or *a pinched nerve* and still has intractable back pain to be labeled with the diagnosis of chronic pain syndrome. Very often these patients are experiencing mechanical joint dysfunction, which is diagnosable and treatable months or even years after the initial symptoms were noted. These symptoms are caused by blocking of the joints as a result of joint dysfunction, which is associated with the original damage of the disc or the meniscus.

At this time one has to consider another structure of the system that undergoes pathophysiologic changes as a result of a trauma in the system itself or from symptoms that are referred to the system and cannot be differentiated one from the other by the patient. Just as mechanical joint dysfunction as a cause of musculoskeletal pain is commonly overlooked, so is the irritable trigger point, as described by Travell and Rinzler,[1] commonly overlooked. To make a differential diagnosis more difficult, each of these conditions may mimic another, or they may coexist. There is no way to differentiate among them except by clinical means.

Any patient presenting with symptoms that are apparently arising from some structure in the musculoskeletal system and have not been relieved, sometimes for a very long time, merits a fresh history and clinical examination before further treatment is prescribed. When clinicians become acquainted with the potential mechanical problems in the system and with the clinical manifestations of irritable trigger points, they will be amazed at how much chronic pain can be relieved.

Yet another decision has to be made when faced by a so-called chronic pain patient or, for that matter, by any patient with a complaint arising in the musculoskeletal system. The question is whether the primary pathologic change that is causing the symptom is occurring in the *healing* phase or in the *healed* phase. There are principles of treatment for each phase that, if ignored, may have the opposite of the desired effect.

The principle of prescribing treatment for any acute pathologic condition in any structure of the musculoskeletal system is rest from function (use) of the structure in which the primary pathologic condition is situated while maintaining as normal a physiologic state as possible in all the other structures not primarily involved. *Rest from function* does not mean immobilization. Put in another way, this principle says move but do not use. *Movement* means passive movement and the recognition that there is such a thing as the proper "dosage" of movement. This involves well-developed clinical judgment and may vary from day to day. If something should be moved through an arc of 15° but is not moved, morbid changes occur. If that thing should be moved through an arc of 15° and is moved through a greater arc, pathologic changes may occur.

A simple example to emphasize these principles is the patient who has some acute problem in a joint. The joint is rested from function but should be moved passively many times a day within the limit of pain. The muscles must be exercised to maintain their pumping action. This is achieved by the use of isometric exercises or by electrical stimulation with a source of alternating current that mimics the normal cycle of physiologic action. This continued muscle action maintains the tone of the vascular tree, which maintains the nourishment of the injured structure and elements of the nervous system, all of which promote healing and prevent morbidity. It also maintains lymph circulation in as normal a state as possible; this avoids lymph stagnation, which is the most difficult morbid condition to reverse in the healed phase. It becomes a logical conclusion that there is no place for manipulative therapy in the healing phase of any musculoskeletal condition unless the diagnosis of the mechanical pathologic condition is joint dysfunction caused by intrinsic trauma, in which case joint manipulation is the treatment of choice.

From the above it should become clear that injuries to structures in the musculoskeletal system should be treated under the guidance of these principles whether the structures are in the extremities or in the back, and it must be understood that by *back* is meant the occiput to the sacrum, the joints of the pelvis, the joints of the rib cage, and the joints of the sacrococcygeal complex (and let us not forget the temporomandibular joint). It is illogical, for instance, to prescribe rest for something wrong in an extremity and to prescribe an exercise program for what must be the same condition in the back!

When there is evidence that the patient has arrived in the healed (restorative) phase of the disability, the choice of modalities drastically changes from the choice during the healing phase. This changeover point can be determined only on clinical grounds. The most telling feature is that the nature of the patient's pain changes in one important, characteristic manner. During the healing phase, when patients awaken in the morning their symptoms are stiffness and sometimes increased pain. When they move into the healed phase stiffness is not characteristic, and patients state that on waking they feel wonderful until they start to move to get up. In other words morning stiffness is highly suggestive that patients are healing, and freedom from morning stiffness suggests that they have progressed to the healed phase. During the healed phase, exercise programs that follow a warm-up period and are followed by a relaxation period at the end of each session are the keystones of a successful restoration program.

There are some features about exercise that are too often overlooked by therapists. In the healed phase we talk of assistive exercise, free exercise, and resistive exercise. In addition we have to remember that exercises may be concentric and accelerating or excentric and decelerating. The choice between these two forms of exercise is governed by Starling's law of muscle action, which states that a long muscle shortens when it is weakened and can be strengthened only by lengthening decelerating exercises. Under such circumstances if shortening accelerating exercise programs are prescribed they are likely to fail. The rate at which the restorative exercise program progresses is a matter of skilled clinical judgment. A patient is being overloaded by an exercise if breathing ceases during its performance in a free exercise program. The patient must be assisted in such exercise until there is no interference with breathing.

Because almost all prescribed physical therapy may be irritating in one way or another, all treatment sessions should finish with a relaxation period. Patients should be taught Jacobson's[2] relaxation exercise routine for use during the cool-down period. Jacobson's exercises are excellent in promoting sleep at night; sleep deprivation is one of the main causes of delayed physical restoration.

During the restorative phase there is scarcely ever a patient who does not need manipulative attention to synovial joints somewhere or other. A rather gross example of this is that patients who have had their chests opened during a surgical procedure all have back pain resulting from disuse of the costovertebral and interlaminar facet joints somewhere in the thoracic spine. During healing after the surgical procedure breathing is shallow because it hurts the patient. Recollect that one of the etiologic factors of joint dysfunction is disuse. The pain associated with healing from a surgical procedure produces disuse of these joints, often over a long period postoperatively. Most surgeons' reactions to this intractable pain, which often leads to a diagnosis of chronic pain syndrome, are that of course patients hurt and may do so for a very long time, and they must learn to live with it. The fact is that postoperatively joint dysfunction, which is described here, is readily and completely relievable by the restoration of joint play in the involved joints by the use of joint manipulation.

From the foregoing it should not be difficult to understand that stress and tension may produce musculoskeletal pain, especially from joint dysfunction and irritable muscle trigger points. Most practitioners treat such patients with tranquilizers accompanied sometimes by psychologic treatment. It is self-defeating to treat a patient chemically and psychologically if the patient has a correctable musculoskeletal condition. It is sometimes difficult to determine which is the cart and which the horse. It remains a clinical truism that patients cannot respond to psychologic treatment so long as they have an untreated physical cause of symptoms.

JOINT MANIPULATION

The term *joint manipulation* has always been fraught with misunderstanding, and most authors use some variation of the following statements given by Burger and Tobis[3]:

> Objective criteria for *manipulable* back pain can be very difficult to define, given the available diagnostic techniques. . . . This discussion therefore returns to the studies of Dr Newell and Dr Fisk. Dr Newell and his associate found that a small group of individuals might be helped by manipulation but that those individuals could not be selected in advance. Dr Fisk also pointed out that

manipulation was valuable because it helped many individuals whom he could not select in advance, and that it was advantageous to have successfully treated those individuals before considering other forms of treatment. . . . In addition, just as it is not clear what clinical signs characterize a group which would be aided by manipulation, it is not clear what clinical signs should be used for ceasing manipulation. . . . Finally, these two problems are probably consequences of the last difficulty: No one has a definitive or even widely accepted anatomic, physiologic, or biochemical explanation for the mechanisms which underlie the type of back pain for which manipulation is commonly prescribed, and through which patients state they have found relief.

> Allopathic medicine has put in considerable research efforts to solve the back problem, contrary to chiropractic and osteopathic medicine which have based their therapeutic procedures on theories that have mostly been disproven. This, in the author's view, is reason enough not to manipulate patients. Why use methods whose theoretical background has been disproven and whose results are not superior to any form of treatment?

The weaknesses of these conclusions must be self-evident. First, one cannot research a therapeutic endeavor if one has any doubt as to what one is treating; second, no reference is made to any proscribed protocol of any clinical examining procedure; third, there is no definition of the therapeutic maneuver being validated; and fourth, these statements refer to a small topographic area of the system. There is even some doubt as to what structure in the system is being treated by an allegedly specific method.

Normal joint play is postulated as being the normal mechanical prerequisite of normal synovial joint function. Normal joint play movements can be demonstrated only by the use of clinical manipulative examining procedures. The clinical examination is designed to detect impairment or loss of normal joint play, which in terms of mechanics results in impairment or loss of function associated with pain. Thus we arrive at a clinical diagnosis of a cause of pain in the musculoskeletal system local to a structure in the system: mechanical joint dysfunction. To relieve a mechanical fault, it is logical to seek a mechanical means of doing so; this is joint manipulation. The therapy is confined to restoring lost play movements to normal and has nothing to do with the use of any movement under the control of voluntary muscles or the use of any forceful endeavor.

The extent of any joint play movement in any synovial joint is less than ⅛ inch in any plane. Ideally joint dysfunction affects one joint on one side of the body or, in the back, one intervertebral junction, one costovertebral junction, or one sacroiliac joint. The loss of joint play in one joint does not necessarily impair all the functions associated with the area of that joint. Consider the radiocarpal joint as an example. There are two play movements at this joint; loss of one or both results in the impairment or loss of the function of flexion of the wrist with pain when the voluntary movement is attempted by the use of the voluntary muscles or on clinical examination. All the other movements at the wrist are normal and pain free. If more than one joint at the wrist is involved or if there is but one joint clinically involved (resulting in loss of more than one function), then the cause cannot be mechanical. This principle is true throughout the musculoskeletal system. Thus in the back a pain symptom that on examination can be localized to one intervertebral junction on one side of the spine at one level with impairment of one function of the back can confidently be diagnosed as arising from synovial joint dysfunction. If all functional movements of the back are impaired by a lesion that can be clearly demonstrated as arising from one junction of the back, then the cause is not mechanical.

It should be clear, then, that there are rules for examining the musculoskeletal system using manipulative examination techniques. There are also rules for using manipulative therapeutic techniques which, though similar, are not identical to the rules for examination. The rules for using manipulative examining techniques[4] are as follows:

1. The patient must be relaxed and supported in such a way to protect the joint being examined from unguarded movements. Unguarded movements produce pain; this causes the supporting muscles of the joint to go into guarding spasm, which prevents the performance of the examining movement for joint play.
2. The examiner must be relaxed. The examining grip used must not be painful to the patient; it must be firm and protective but not restrictive.
3. One joint must be examined at a time. For instance, the wrist is not examined as such; each joint of the wrist must be examined individually. In the back each joint at each junction on each side must be examined in turn.
4. One movement at each joint is examined at a time. Technically sometimes this is not possible. Under those conditions it is understood that specific adjustment of technique has to be made.
5. In the performance of any one movement, one articulating surface of the joint being examined is moved on the other articulating facet of the joint, which is stabilized. Thus there should always be one mobilizing force and one stabilizing force exerted by the examiner when a joint is being examined. For technical reasons that are clearly defined, again adjustments to this technique have to be made.
6. The extent of a normal joint play movement in the capsule of any synovial joint is never more than ⅛ inch in any plane. Its normal extent in a patient in whom it is impaired can be assessed by examining the same joint either in the contralateral limb or on the other side of the back at the same junction.
7. No forceful movement and no abnormal movement should ever be used. No unguarded movement should be used, and every movement must be controlled.
8. Any examining manipulative movement must be stopped at any point at which pain is elicited. This is in contradistinction to rule 8 in the rules concerning therapeutic techniques involving manipulative maneuvers, which follow.
9. In performing an examining movement of a joint, it is important to take up the slack of the tissues around it before attempting the joint movement.
10. In the presence of obvious clinical signs of inflammation or disease in the part under scrutiny, no examining manipulative movements need or should be undertaken.

For the most part the rules governing therapeutic manipulation[4] are the same as those described above for examining techniques:

1. The patient must be relaxed.
2. The therapist must be relaxed.
3. One joint play movement is restored to normal at one time in any one plane. In joints in which there is a wide range of voluntary movement (eg, the shoulder, the hip, the knee, and each finger and thumb), fractional manipulation has to be used. Fractional manipulation means just going through each pain point and stopping without worrying about restoring more than a fraction of the voluntary movement that is lost.
4. One joint is addressed at one time.
5. One aspect of the joint is stabilized while the other aspect of it is mobilized.
6. The extent of a normal play movement in a joint is less than ⅛ inch in any one plane. In assessing the amount of impairment of play, the joint on the unaffected side is available for comparison. This knowledge controls the extent of the therapeutic movement of the affected side.
7. No forceful movement and no abnormal movement should ever be used.
8. The manipulative movement used is a sharp, springing thrust, push, or pull, which one must differentiate from a forceful movement that lacks control. An uncontrolled movement is an abnormal movement. Should a patient be under an anesthetic, the therapeutic movement should be more gentle and better directed than if the patient were conscious.
9. The springing movement of a therapeutic maneuver requires speed and accuracy, not to be confused with high velocity and low amplitude.
10. Before imparting the therapeutic movement, it is essential to take up the slack as much as possible of all soft tissues surrounding the joint.

The mobilizing movement starts at the point of pain (this has already been elicited by examination) and goes through the point at which pain is elicited to normal (which has been determined by examining the unaffected joint on the opposite side). In the presence of evidence of inflammation or disease, therapeutic manipulation is contraindicated.

It is commonplace to blame stress and tension as causes of musculoskeletal pain in patients who do not respond to therapeutic endeavors. It would be more logical to recognize that patients whose pains do not respond to treatment naturally develop stress and tension as a result of therapeutic failure. One must accept that stress and tension may produce symptoms from morbid changes in muscles, from lack of relaxation, and even from sleep deprivation, but the source of these symptoms is seldom a synovial joint unless there is sufficient disuse of a joint to produce joint dysfunction. On these occasions four therapeutic approaches (physical therapy, rehabilitation therapy, psychological therapy if indicated, or medication) are open to the therapist, and such a patient is going to be unresponsive to treatment unless all of these approaches are addressed. As noted earlier, most psychologists agree that they cannot successfully treat a patient's psychologic needs if there is an underlying physical cause of pain that either has been overlooked or has not responded to the prescribed therapy. The perpetuation of physical pain from trigger points and joint dysfunction is one of the most common causes of this situation. This is a two-way street, meaning that physical causes may not respond to the treatment as one might expect if psychologic factors are ignored.

When studying the ills of the musculoskeletal system, students should not be instructed in manipulative diagnostic or therapeutic techniques for application to the spinal joints until they have gained competence in handling the joints of the extremities. The structures of the musculoskeletal system act and react in the same way in normal function and under abnormal stresses and strains and disease wherever they are situated. Because the spinal synovial joints cannot individually be directly palpated or comfortably handled and moved, one has to infer by logic and common sense that the symptoms and signs that are the results of various etiologic factors in the back are the same as those that are easily appreciated in the extremities.

Because there are no radiographic changes characteristic of joint dysfunction (*chiropractic subluxation* and *osteopathic lesion* are both synonymous) and because no laboratory data are available to suggest this diagnosis, one has to rely on the patients' histories of their complaints and the clinical signs that we elicit by our physical examinations; often, listening to the history is more important than some details of the examination.

REFERENCES

1. Travell J, Rinzler SH. The myofascial genesis of pain. *Postgrad Med.* 1952;11:425–434.

2. Jacobson E. *Self Operations Control.* 3rd ed. Philadelphia: Lippincott; 1964.

3. Burger AA, Tobis JS. *Approaches to Validation of Manipulative Therapy.* Springfield, Ill: Thomas; 1977.

4. Mennell JM. *Joint Pain: Diagnosis and Treatment Using Manipulative Techniques.* Boston: Little, Brown; 1964:754–756.

Chapter 10

Joint Mobilization

Peter A. Gale

Mobilization and manipulation of the extravertebral structures have long been used to treat musculoskeletal pain syndromes. In the evolution of the clinical chiropractic practice, manual therapy of the extravertebral joints has become more of a staple in the chiropractor's armamentarium. The demands of a more athletic society have created overuse syndromes, with joint dysfunction being a primary or secondary component of the overall clinical picture. Therefore, the skill of restoring mobility to the extremities has become of increasing interest to practitioners of manual therapy.

The foundation for this work of restoring peripheral joint function is documented by Mennell.[1] He describes the etiology of joint dysfunction as being a loss of mechanical play in the synovial joint. He compares the human joints with those of machines and explains that play movements are built into all mechanical devices. In the human joints this play is less than 0.125 in.[1] Examination or treatment extending beyond this distance increases the possibility of periarticular damage.

Sandoz[2] describes the ranges of movement in a joint adjustment or manipulation, drawing distinctions among the ranges of movement in exercise, mobilization (physiotherapy), and adjustment. Figure 10-1 is a graphic representation of these three ranges. Exercise of joints is usually confined to the active range. Mobilization of joints and related tissues occurs in the passive range. This range brings the joint just up to the elastic barrier and not beyond. The chiropractic adjustment or manipulation passes through this elastic barrier and into the third range, known as the paraphysiologic space. Going beyond the paraphysiologic space stresses the limits of anatomic integrity, and adverse effects can occur. This is why Mennell[1] stresses

the point of applying an impulse into a joint no farther than 0.125 in.

Mennell, it seems, would concur with Sandoz' graph (Fig. 10-1). He states that joint play cannot be produced by voluntary action of muscle. A loss of voluntary range of motion is apparent, however, when joint play is restricted. Mennell also states that exercise cannot restore joint play; this

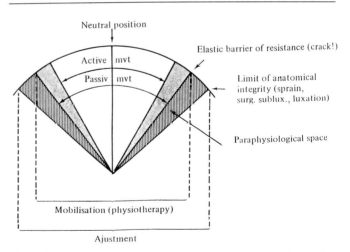

Figure 10-1 Schematic representation of the range of movement in mobilization and adjustment of a normal diarthrodial joint. In passive mobilization, the range of movement is limited by the elastic barrier of resistance. When the movement is forced beyond this barrier, one enters into the paraphysiologic space. At the end of this space, one encounters the barrier of anatomic integrity of the joint. *Source:* Reprinted with permission from R Sandoz, "Some Physical Mechanisms and Effects of Spinal Adjustments" in *Annals of the Swiss Chiropractic Association VI*, pp 91–141, © 1975.

also is apparent in Sandoz' graph. Mennell goes on to state that exercises with a loss of joint play can produce further pain and dysfunction through structural compensation.[1]

A clinical example of this is a patient treated for pain of about 1 year's duration in the lateral aspect of his lower limb. With physical therapy, which consisted mostly of exercise, he began experiencing numbness and tingling of the dorsal and lateral aspects of the foot. His condition went on to include pain at the posterior aspect of the thigh. The orthopedic diagnosis was sciatic neuritis. On examination a restricted superior tibiofibular joint was found. Manipulation of the restricted joint gave almost immediate improvement; several weeks of myofascial treatment were necessary, however, to alleviate the muscular constrictions due to muscular compensation for the now chronically restricted joint.

Exercise rarely restores mobility to an articulation that has a loss of joint play. With time the surrounding tissues and synovial joints that are put under abnormal stress break down. This is the compensation that Mennell[1] also writes about.

A most important concept in the approach of peripheral joint mobilization and manipulation is to think not of treating a joint but of treating its component parts. An example of this is the patient complaining of pain in the shoulder joint. The physician must learn to think of the component parts that make up the shoulder joint because any one of these synovial joints or surrounding soft tissues can be causing the patient's pain. Once the physician becomes proficient at movement palpation, the investigative thought processes evolve to a more finite level.

Many of the following techniques are described by Mennell[1] and other manipulative physicians. At this point a distinction should be made between mobilizing joint structures where no true synovial joint exists and joint manipulation for loss of joint play. An important difference exists between mobilization and manipulation. Manipulation has been shown to increase overall joint mobility above that obtained by mobilization when both were used to treat a synovial joint.[3] Manipulation is the treatment of choice for synovial joint dysfunction. Both procedures are at times necessary to bring full function to a patient's disability. For example, there is no true joint between the scapula and the chest wall. Nevertheless, mobilization of a restricted scapula can be as important as manipulation of a component of the glenohumeral joint in restoring shoulder function.

There are two fundamental rules that apply to all manipulative techniques discussed in this chapter. The first is that palpation of the patient is always performed with light touch. The word *palpation* comes from the Latin word *palpare*, which means "to caress or touch with care." This is essential to the healing process. The second rule is that the examining procedures described that use movement palpation can become treatment merely by adding a short, high-velocity impulse in the direction of restricted mobility. Examination plus impulse (less than 0.125 in) equals treatment. There are alternative treatment procedures shown with certain joints that make manipulation or mobilization more efficient.

THE ANKLE AND FOOT COMPLEX

The component parts of the ankle and foot are the mortise joint, the subtalar joint, the midfoot articulations, and the metatarsophalangeal joints.

Mortise Joint

The mortise joint is formed by the distal malleoli of the tibia and fibula, into which the superior aspect of the talus fits. This joint structure is a major source of stability for the ankle.

The patient complaining of pain in the ankle while walking uphill or up a flight of stairs most often has hypomobility of the mortise joint. Put simply, pain on dorsiflexion should tip the clinician off to mortise joint pathomechanics.

Long-Axis Extension (Fig. 10-2)

Patient: Supine with knee and hip flexed at 90°.

Examiner: Seated with his or her lower back against the patient's posterior upper leg. The examiner cradles the ankle with both hands. The lateral hand contacts the dorsal surface of the foot at the talus. The indifferent (medial) thumb web contacts the posterior aspect of the ankle joint just above the insertion of the Achilles tendon. The foot should be everted to lock the subtalar joint.

Action: The examiner pushes away from his or her body while producing slight counterpressure against the patient's upper leg.

Anteroposterior (AP) Glide of Mortise on Talus (Fig. 10-3)

Patient: Supine; the knee is flexed at 90°. The ankle also is flexed at 90°.

Examiner: Contact hand grasping above the mortise joint. The stabilization hand holds the plantar surface of the foot until the ankle is flexed at 90°.

Action: Push-pull mobilization.

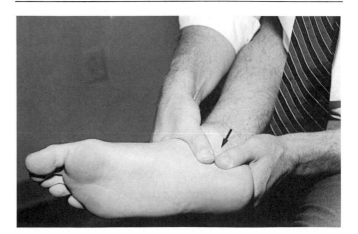

Figure 10-2 Mortise joint: long-axis extension.

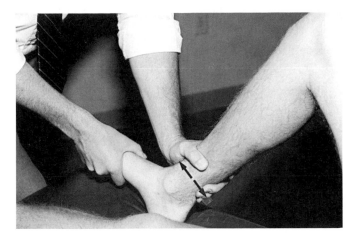

Figure 10-3 Mortise joint: AP glide.

Subtalar Joint

The subtalar joint is located between the talus and calcaneus. The talus has no muscular attachments and literally sits on the calcaneus. There are three play movements palpable.

The patient with subtalar dysfunction will usually complain of pain while walking downstairs or down a hill. Thus pain on plantar flexion should signal the examiner to evert the subtalar joint.

Long-Axis Extension

Patient: Supine as in mortise joint distraction.

Examiner: Contacting the navicular on the dorsal surface with the thumb web and just above the insertion of the Achilles tendon with the indifferent thumb web.

Action: Distraction without eversion.

Subtalar Rock (Fig. 10-4)

Patient: Supine as in position 1.

Examiner: Same hand contact as in long-axis extension.

Action: The joint must first be distracted; then the thumb web contacting the calcaneus pushes with slight wrist flexion. The other thumb web contact pushes in the reverse direction with the same force. This rocks the calcaneus on the talus.

Medial and Lateral Tilt of Subtalar Joint (Fig. 10-5)

Patient: Supine as in position 1.

Examiner: Same hand contact as in long-axis extension of the subtalar joint.

Action: (1) Long-axis extension. (2) The examiner throws the foot down toward the floor without twisting; this opens (tilts) the joint medially. (3) The examiner throws the leg down toward the floor while supporting the foot. The foot should not be everted.

Midfoot Articulations

AP Glide of Metatarsals on Cuneiforms (Fig. 10-6)

Patient: Supine; the knee is flexed at 90°.

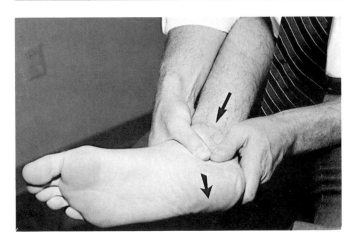

Figure 10-5 Subtalar joint: medial tilt.

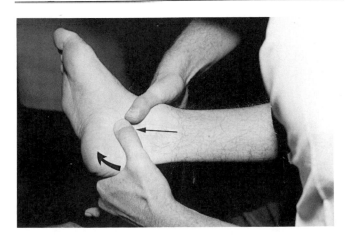

Figure 10-4 Subtalar rock.

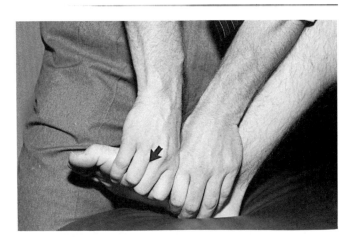

Figure 10-6 AP glide of metatarsals on cuneiforms.

Examiner: Standing laterally to the patient. The examiner finds the base of the first metatarsal bone. The examiner's superior hand is over the cuneiform, and the inferior hand is over the first metatarsal bone.

Action: The inferior hand moves so that the index fingers and knuckles of both hands rub on one another as the metatarsals are moved in AP glide on the cuneiforms.

AP Glide of Cuneiforms on Navicular

Patient: Same as above.

Examiner: Hand position moved approximately one finger width proximally from the position described above so that the superior hand is on the navicular. The inferior hand is on the cuneiforms.

Action: Same as above.

AP Glide of Navicular on Talus

Patient: Supine.

Examiner: Superior hand moved one finger width proximally and onto the calcaneus laterally and the talus medially. The inferior (mobilizing) hand is on the navicular medially and the cuboid laterally.

Action: Same as above.

Metatarsal-Tarsal Mobilization (Fig. 10-7): Rotation of Metatarsal Bases on Cuneiform and Cuboid

Patient: Supine.

Examiner: Stabilizing the dorsal aspect of the cuneiforms and cuboid with the index finger and thumb web. The mobilizing hand makes contact with the metatarsal hand with the index finger.

Action: The metatarsal heads are lifted slightly, and a clockwise and then a counterclockwise mobilizing force is applied.

Intermetatarsal Mobilization (Not a True Joint) (Fig. 10-8)

Patient: Supine.

Examiner: Seated at the foot of the patient. The examiner makes contact with the shaft of the fifth and fourth metatarsals. The index finger is on the dorsal aspect and the thumb on the plantar aspect of the forefoot proximal to the metatarsal heads.

Action: Mobilization of the fifth metatarsal while stabilizing the fourth metatarsal in the AP plane. A rotational mobilization is then performed in a clockwise and then a counterclockwise direction. The third metatarsal is stabilized while the fourth metatarsal is mobilized on it. The second metatarsal is the axis of the foot, and the third and first metatarsals are mobilized on it.

Metatarsophalangeal Joint Manipulation

Long-Axis Extension (Fig. 10-9)

Patient: Supine.

Examiner: Contacting the phalanx with a platform contact. This is a fully flexed index finger acting as the platform with the thumb holding the phalanx bone in place.

Action: While stabilizing the metatarsal head, the examiner contacts the proximal base of the phalanx and pulls.

Medial and Lateral Tilt

Patient: Same as above.

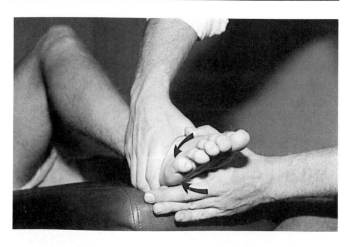

Figure 10-7 Metatarsal-tarsal mobilization.

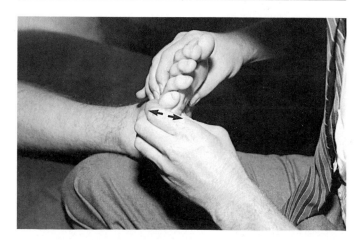

Figure 10-8 Intermetatarsal mobilization.

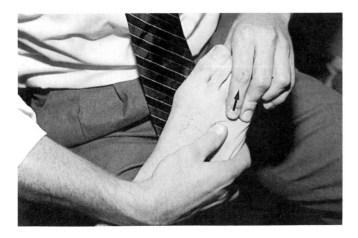

Figure 10-9 Metatarsophalangeal joint: long-axis extension.

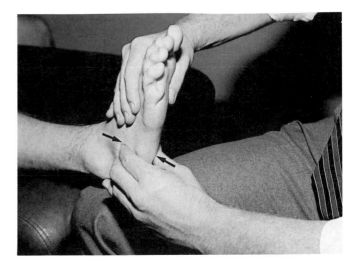

Figure 10-10 Cuboid: AP glide.

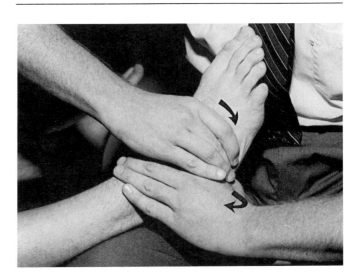

Figure 10-11 Cuboid: AP glide.

Examiner: Same as above.

Action: Same as above except directed in a medial direction and then a lateral direction to tilt the phalanx on the metatarsal head.

AP Glide (Not Shear)

Patient: Same as above.

Examiner: Platform contact on the phalanx while stabilizing the metatarsal head.

Action: Tilt in the plantar direction and then in the dorsal direction.

Rotation

Patient: Same as above.

Examiner: Contacting the phalanx with the index and middle fingers on the dorsal aspect of the bone and on the plantar surface with the thumb (as if picking a flower). While the metatarsal is stabilized, a rotational force is applied clockwise and then counterclockwise.

Cuboid: AP Glide (Figs. 10-10 and 10-11)

Patient: Supine.

Examiner: Contacting the dorsal and plantar surfaces of the cuboid with the index finger and thumb, respectively. The indifferent hand makes contact on the dorsal proximal aspect of the fifth metatarsal shaft.

Action: Joint play is elicited in a plantar-to-dorsal, dorsal-to-plantar motion. The manipulative action approximates that of wringing out a towel, with both hands moving in a rotational manner.

THE SHOULDER

For the sake of discussion the shoulder region is broken down into four component parts: the sternoclavicular joint, the acromioclavicular joint, the scapulothoracic articulation; and the glenohumeral joint.

Glenohumeral joint mobility is supplemented with scapulothoracic, sternoclavicular, and acromioclavicular joint motion. There is great economy built into the glenohumeral joint. The glenoid fossa is a small, pear-shaped cartilaginous socket that is only one-third to one-fourth the size of the humeral head.[4] Approximately 50% of the head of the humerus is covered by hyaline cartilage. At 90° abduction of the glenohumeral joint, almost all the articular cartilage has been used. Within the first 90° the humeral ball moves upward on the glenoid fossa in a rolling and gliding motion. After 90°

the motion is essentially rotation about a fixed point in the fossa.[4] The scapula on the chest wall will make a 40° to 60° arc with full abduction of the glenohumeral joint. Glenohumeral function is dependent on a clavicular rotation around its long axis of approximately 60°, 40° at the meniscal end of the sternoclavicular joint and 20° at the acromial end.

Sternoclavicular Joint (Fig. 10-12)

Patient: Supine with the palm on the umbilicus.

Examiner: Palpating the medial third of the clavicle with the index finger and thumb of each hand.

Action: Joint play is elicited with a superior-to-inferior movement (head to foot). Manipulation is performed with the patient in a sitting posture or with exaggerated motion of the examination.

Acromioclavicular Joint (Figs. 10-13 and 10-14)

Patient: Supine with the palm on the umbilicus.

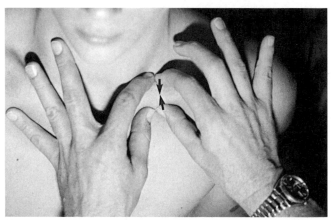

A

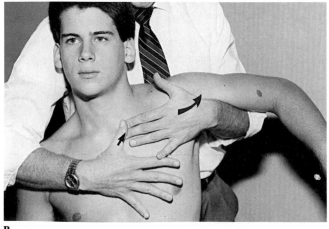

B

Figure 10-12 Sternoclavicular joint examination and manipulation. (**A**) Patient supine. (**B**) Patient sitting.

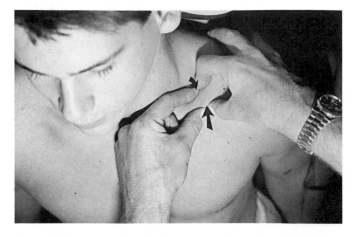

Figure 10-13 Acromioclavicular joint: examination and manipulation.

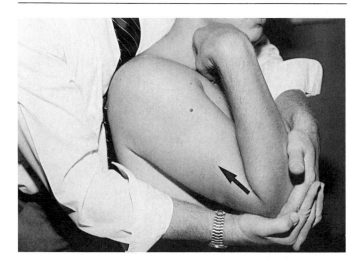

Figure 10-14 Acromioclavicular joint: manipulation in the sitting position.

Examiner: Palpating the outer third of the clavicle with the index finger and thumb.

Action: Alternate pressures anterior to posterior and then posterior to anterior. Manipulation is performed with the patient sitting or with exaggerated motion of the examination.

Scapulothoracic Articulation (Fig. 10-15)

This is a bone-muscle-bone articulation between the thoracic wall and the scapula. Although it is not a true joint, without freedom of movement glenohumeral motion is compromised.

Examination

Patient: Prone.

Examiner: Stabilizing the cap of the shoulder and contacting the scapulothoracic region with the fleshy ulnar portion of the indifferent hand.

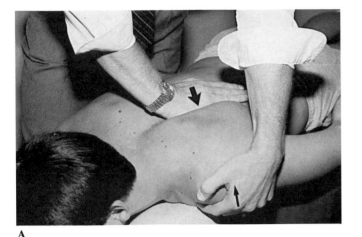

A

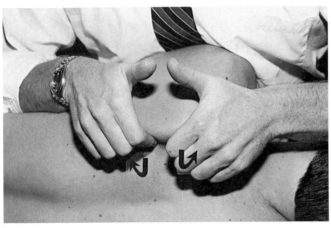

B

Figure 10-15 Scapulothoracic joint. (**A**) Prone. (**B**) Side-lying.

Lateral Deviation of Head of Humerus in Glenoid Cavity (Fig. 10-16)

Patient: Elbow bent at 90° with the palm on the umbilicus.

Examiner: Sitting parallel to the patient. The hand closest to the patient is placed in the axilla, palm facing outward. The indifferent hand supports the patient's elbow.

Action: The examiner pushes the head of the humerus away from the glenoid laterally.

Anterior Movement of Head of Humerus in Glenoid Cavity (Fig. 10-17)

Patient: Elbow extended posterior to take up the slack.

Examiner: Using the profundus muscle to cause the digits and thumb to approximate each other.

Action: The humerus is carried posterior to anterior on the glenoid.

Posterior Shear of Head of Humerus in Glenoid Cavity (Fig. 10-18)

Patient: No extension of the elbow.

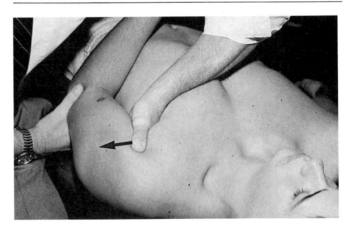

Figure 10-16 Glenohumeral joint: lateral deviation.

Action: Pressure is applied to the scapulothoracic region. The examiner will note whether there is freedom or restriction of movement.

Mobilization

Patient: Side-lying with the involved side up.

Examiner: Same as above.

Action: Protraction of the scapula and rotation along the thoracic wall.

Glenohumeral Joint

There are eight joint play movements of the glenohumeral joint. In all eight motions there is a rotatory movement because of the nature of the glenohumeral articulation. In all eight movements the patient is examined in the supine position. The elbow must be slightly raised so that the glenohumeral joint is in physiologic rest. Manipulation uses an impulse of no more than 0.125 in.

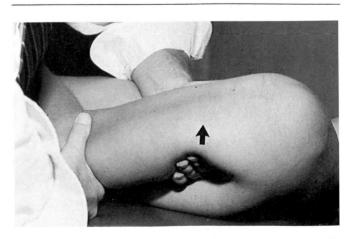

Figure 10-17 Glenohumeral joint: anterior movement of head of humerus in glenoid cavity.

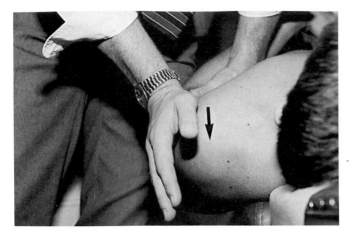

Figure 10-18 Glenohumeral joint: posterior shear of humeral head.

Examiner: Sitting parallel to the patient. The examiner stabilizes the medial aspect of the patient's elbow. The indifferent hand is placed on the greater tuberosity.

Action: The elbow is slightly raised while the contact hand thrusts posteriorly and toward the table.

Posterior-Inferior Glide of Head of Humerus in Glenoid Cavity (Fig. 10-19)

If the greater tuberosity of the humerus does not simultaneously depress and rotate in a gliding motion during abduction, impingement may occur.[2]

Patient: Elbow bent at 90° with the hand resting on the chest.

Examiner: Grasping the patient's humerus as proximal as possible with interconnecting fingers. The examiner's shoulder closest to the patient supports the patient's humerus.

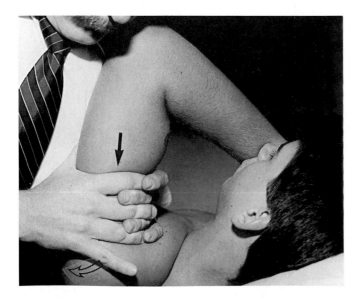

Figure 10-19 Glenohumeral joint: posterior-inferior glide.

Action: Posterior-inferior scooping motion.

Lateral-Posterior Deviation of Head of Humerus in Glenoid Cavity (Fig. 10-20)

Patient: Same as for posterior-inferior glide.

Examiner: Sitting perpendicular to the patient. Both hands grasp the proximal aspect of the humerus. The patient's elbow is supported by the examiner's shoulder.

Action: Lateral-posterior scooping motion.

External Rotation of Head of Humerus in Glenoid Cavity (Fig. 10-21)

Patient: Elbow flexed at 90° with the arm abducted and externally rotated to a comfortable range.

Examiner: Grasping the humeral shafts, with the finger pads on the posterior shaft and the thumb on the anterior shaft.

Action: External rotation.

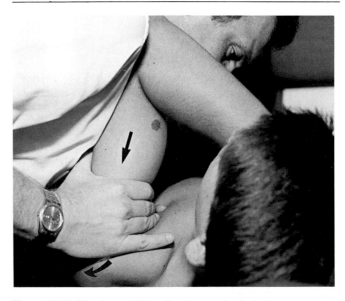

Figure 10-20 Glenohumeral joint: lateral-posterior deviation.

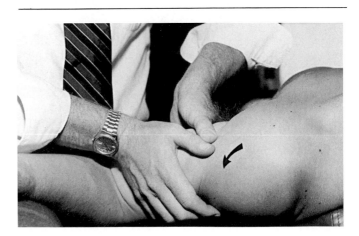

Figure 10-21 Glenohumeral joint: external rotation.

Posterior Shear at 90° (Fig. 10-22)

Patient: Elbow fully flexed and shoulder flexed at 90°.

Examiner: Cupping the posterior aspect of the shoulder joint. The opposite hand contacts the patient's elbow.

Action: Posterior impulse, which stretches the back of the capsule.

Long-Axis Extension of Head of Humerus in Glenoid Cavity (Fig. 10-23)

Patient: Arm resting by the side.

Examiner: Stabilizing the patient's chest wall just medial to the axilla. The indifferent hand grasps proximal to the wrist on the radius and ulna.

Action: Abduction of the arm to just before the point of pain. Manipulation uses decompression in long-axis extension

to take up the slack and then a pull. As long as there is sufficient joint play in the wrist and elbow the manipulative force will be imparted to the glenohumeral joint.

THE ELBOW

Component parts of the elbow are the superior radioulnar joint, the ulnohumeral joint, and the radiohumeral joint.

Superior Radioulnar Joint

Upward Glide of the Head of the Radius on the Ulna (Pulled Elbow) (Fig. 10-24)

This dysfunction of the superior radioulnar joint is classically seen in children. The history is a sudden pull on the child's arm without warning. Stabilizing the patient's distal humerus while pulling on the distal forearm produces no increase in pain. Pushing on the extended wrist through the long axis of the radius produces acute increase of symptoms. There is usually no swelling, redness, or heat at the elbow.

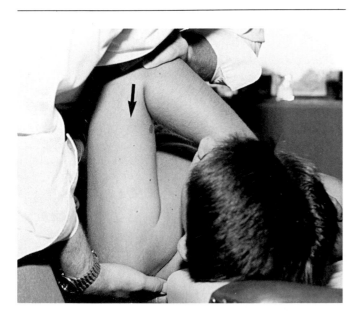

Figure 10-22 Glenohumeral joint: posterior shear at 90°.

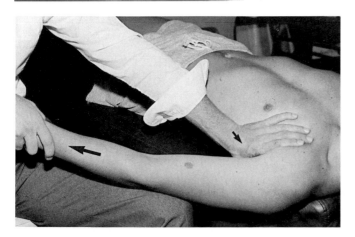

Figure 10-23 Glenohumeral joint: long-axis extension.

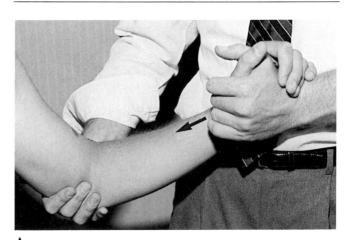

A

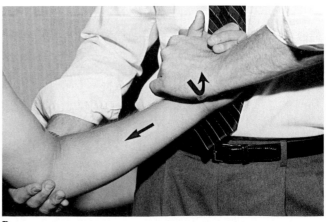

B

Figure 10-24 Superior radioulnar joint. (**A**) Upward glide. (**B**) Upward impulse with supination.

Patient: Standing with the elbow flexed 90° and the wrist fully extended.

Examiner: Standing laterally beside the patient. The examiner with an extended wrist contacts the patient's thenar eminence. The examiner stabilizes the posterior aspect of the subject's elbow. The action is a high-velocity impulse upward through the long axis of the radius with supination. The patient should then be re-examined for pain with the initial procedure.

Downward Glide of Head of Radius on Ulna (Pushed Elbow) (Fig. 10-25)

This dysfunction is often seen in association with a fall. The history is often stumbling and falling on an outstretched hand. The superior radioulnar joint absorbs much of the force, thereby creating dysfunction. During examination the practitioner pushes the radius up into the superior radioulnar joint; there will be no increase in pain. If the examiner stabilizes the arm at the elbow joint while pulling the distal radius and ulnar toward himself or herself, there is usually acute pain. As with the pulled elbow there is no heat, redness, or swelling.

Patient: Standing with the elbow flexed at 90°.

Examiner: Standing medially and in front of the patient. The volar surface of the elbow joint is stabilized. The distal radius and ulna are grasped above the wrist with the other hand.

Action: Pull in long axis with pronation (the head of the radius rotates on the ulna normally).

Rotation of Head of Radius on Ulna (Fig. 10-26)

This dysfunction usually presents with a history of forceful pronation-supination of the elbow and forearm. The examination procedure usually produces acute pain; thus derotating the ulna on the radius improves function.

Patient: Supine with the elbow in full supination.

Examiner: Sitting facing the patient. The most lateral hand rests on the head of the patient's radius.

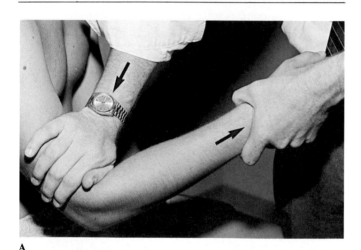

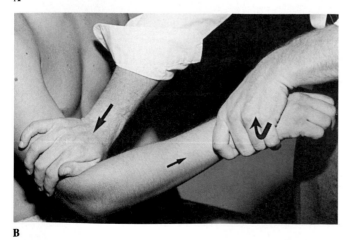

Figure 10-25 Superior radioulnar joint: downward glide of radial head.

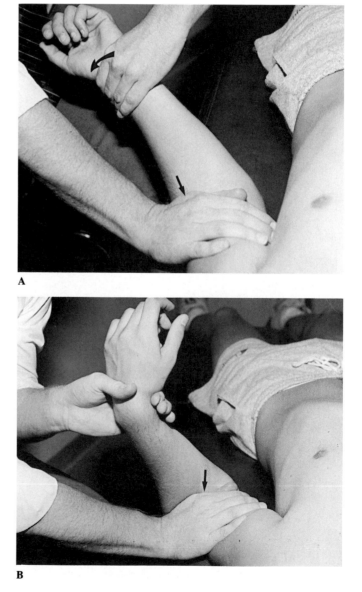

Figure 10-26 Superior radioulnar joint: rotation of head of radius on ulna.

Action: The forearm is brought through a range of motion laterally by the examiner's indifferent hand (increasing the carrying angle) while the elbow is kept in supination. The examiner stops at the point where the head of the radius pinches the examiner's thumb against the metacarpal bone. At this point the forearm is brought into pronation. With dysfunction this maneuver is acutely painful; normally it is pain free. The manipulation then is to pronate the forearm quickly while maintaining stabilization of the radial bone.

Ulnohumeral Joint (Ulna-Olecranon Block) (Fig. 10-27)

This cause of elbow pain is not a true dysfunction. The ulna-olecranon fits into the olecranon fossa. Abnormal movement in extension can cause the synovial fringe to become pinched. Swelling occurs, and there is a pathology in which there is too much synovial swelling to allow the olecranon peck to fit into its fossa. There is boggy palpation with acute pain at the olecranon fossa.

Patient: Supine; the elbow is in approximately 10° of flexion.

Examiner: Contacting the humeral condyles with the cupped palm of the superior hand. The examiner's thumb runs along the humerus laterally and the finger pads medially. The indifferent hand grasps the wrist, keeping the elbow in flexion.

Action: The examiner, with the superior hand at a right angle with the humerus, tilts the humerus laterally and medially. This sweeps the olecranon fossa over the olecranon peck while slowly bringing the elbow into extension.

Radiohumeral Joint (Intra-Articular Meniscus Block) (Fig. 10-28)

Patient: Standing.

Examiner: Thumb on the radial head. The examiner brings the elbow into full flexion. The patient's wrist is brought into full flexion and the forearm into full pronation.

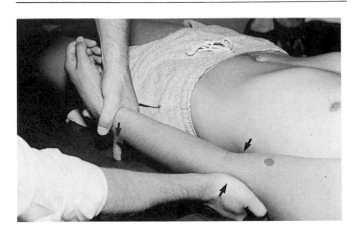

Figure 10-27 Ulnohumeral joint.

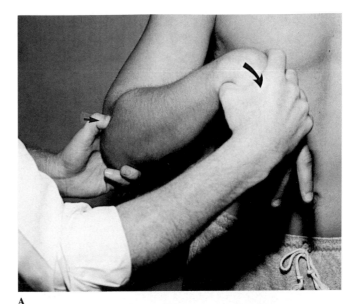
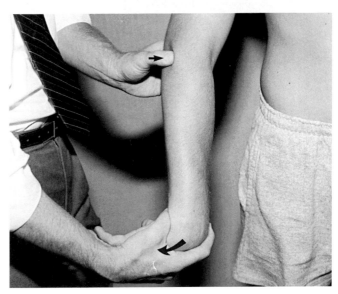

Figure 10-28 Radiohumeral joint (intra-articular meniscus block).

Action: The examiner sweeps the patient's arm into extension while holding the head of the radius with the thumb. With meniscal pathology there will be a block in motion as the examiner approaches extension. At that point of pain a thrust into extension (less than 0.125 in) is applied without losing flexion and pronation of the wrist. The manipulative thrust comes from the radial contact and not the indifferent hand.

Common Extensor Tendon Scar (Fig. 10-29)

Common extensor tendon tears cause a scar that picks up sensory nerve fibers. This creates a painful condition. The therapeutic goal in this lesion is to create an injury, thereby tearing the scar.

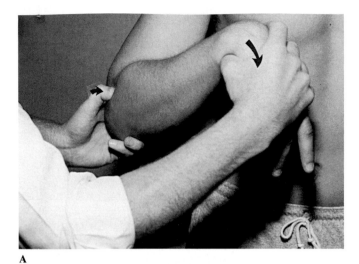

A

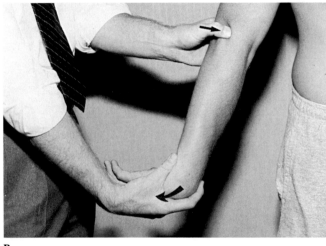

B

Figure 10-29 Manipulation for tearing common extensor scar.

Patient: Standing.

Examiner: Palpating the tender point on the common extensor tendon with the thumb.

Action: The examiner flexes the patient's elbow and wrist and pronates the forearm as in the meniscal manipulation (above). As the examiner brings the elbow into extension, the extensor tendon is stretched. A thrust is delivered at that point, stressing the scar and causing a slight tear.

The tendon is then treated with rest (tennis elbow brace) and contrast bathing with heat and cold for 10 days. This should be followed by decelerating exercises to lengthen the muscle and tendon.

THE WRIST

Assessment of the wrist is broken down into four component parts: the radiocarpal joint, the distal radioulnar joint, the ulnomeniscotriquetral joint, and the midcarpal joint.

Radiocarpal Joint

A loss of joint play at this joint complex most often inhibits flexion of the wrist. The distal end of the radius and the proximal surface of the scaphoid and lunate articulate with the lateral and medial facet of the radius, respectively.

Long-Axis Extension of Radiocarpal Joint (Fig. 10-30)

Patient: Standing with the elbow in 90° of flexion (handshake position).

Examiner: Grasping the styloid process of the ulna and radius with the thumb and index finger. Counterpressure is applied on the volar surface of the elbow joint.

Action: The slack is taken up, and a quick pull of less than 0.125 in is administered toward the examiner.

Posterior Tilt of Scaphoid and Lunate on Radius

Scaphoid (Fig. 10-31)

Patient: Standing with the palm pronated.

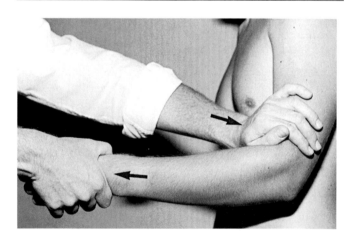

Figure 10-30 Radiocarpal joint: long-axis extension.

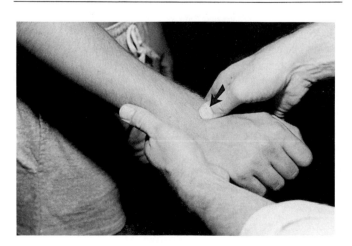

Figure 10-31 Radiocarpal joint: posterior tilt of scaphoid on radius.

Examiner: Palpating down the radius (at the radiocarpal region there is a slight drop-off or depression; this is the scaphoid bone). The examiner uses a two-hand contact; one hand stabilizes and the other palpates. With the palpation hand the examiner places the index finger on the volar surface of the patient's wrist and the thumb on the dorsal surface of the scaphoid.

Action: The manipulative action is to throw the wrist inferiorly; this tilts the scaphoid on the radius.

Lunate

Patient: Same as above.

Examiner: Same as above (the lunate is the next carpal laterally).

Action: The radius is thrown down.

Distal Radioulnar Joint

A loss of joint play at this articulation will restrict pronation of the forearm. The distal radioulnar joint connects by means of the convex radial aspect of the ulnar head to the ulnar notch of the radius.

AP Glide of Ulna on Radius

Patient: Wrist and elbow in neutral.

Examiner: Holding the patient's hand while stabilizing the radius.

Action: The examiner, with the thumb and index finger, moves the patient's ulna in an AP plane of motion.

Rotation of Ulna on Its Axis (Fig. 10-32)

Patient: Same as above.

Examiner: Palpating the flattened surface of the shaft of the ulna.

Action: Rotation of the ulna on its axis.

Ulnomeniscotriquetral Joint

The distal end of the ulna joints with the triquetral bone via an articular meniscus. Dysfunction of this region generally restricts supination of the forearm and wrist.

AP Glide (Fig. 10-33)

Patient: Forearm, wrist, and hand in neutral position.

Examiner: Using the index finger and thumb for palpation and manipulation. The index finger, with a bent phalangeal joint, is on the triquetrum and pisiform. The thumb is on the dorsal surface of the distal ulna.

Action: The examiner squeezes by approximating the index finger and thumb.

Midcarpal Joint

There exists a small degree of motion between the proximal and distal row of carpal bones. For this reason we find articular cartilage on their surfaces. The functional loss with insufficient play in the midcarpal joints causes a functional loss in extension.

Long-Axis Extension

Patient: Elbow flexed at 90° with the forearm in neutral position.

Examiner: Stabilizing the volar surface of the patient's elbow joint at the antecubital fossa. The examiner's contact hand is just distal to the radial and ulnostyloid processes.

Action: Gentle pulling of the wrist with a counteraction of stabilization with the indifferent hand.

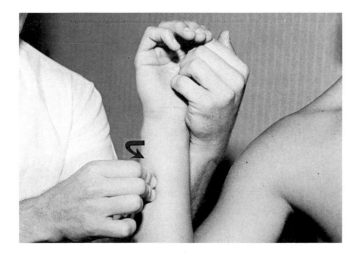

Figure 10-32 Distal radioulnar joint: rotation of ulna on its axis.

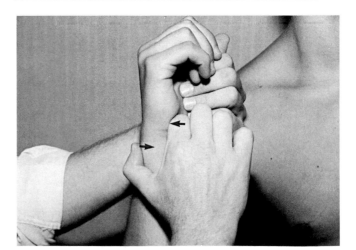

Figure 10-33 Ulnomeniscotriquetral joint: AP glide.

AP Glide of Midcarpal Joint (Fig. 10-34)

This maneuver manipulates the capitate and hamate on the scaphoid and lunate.

Patient: Forearm and wrist in neutral position.

Examiner: Stabilizing the proximal row of carpals, the scaphoid, and the lunate. The index finger and thumb of the distal hand curl around the volar surface of the wrist. The index finger and web of the contact hand are placed over the distal row of carpals (capitate and hamate bones); the thumb curls around the volar surface of the wrist.

Action: The examiner stabilizes the proximal row while gliding the distal row and then allowing the distal row to rebound.

Backward Tilt of Capitate on Scaphoid and Lunate (Fig. 10-35)

Patient: Elbow flexed, forearm and wrist in neutral position.

Examiner: Palpating the middle metacarpal bone to its base. Just lateral to the base of the metacarpal bone is a depression where the posterior surface of the capitate lies. The examiner places the proximal aspect of his or her thenar eminence on the trapezium bone in the depression. For stabilization the examiner palpates the middle crease on the volar aspect of the patient's wrist and lays the thenar eminence of his or her indifferent hand on this crease and perpendicular to the radius.

Action: The patient's hand is flopped over, and the examiner's two hands squeeze the patient's middle carpal joint. If done properly, the patient's fingers should extend.

THE HIP

The hip joint is a stable ball-and-socket joint with the ability to move in flexion and extension, internal and external rota-

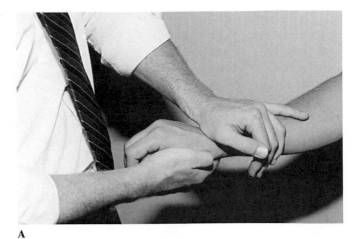

A

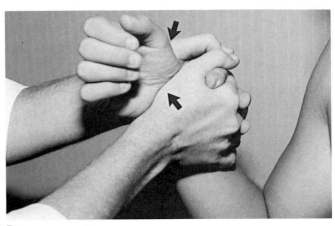

B

Figure 10-35 Capitate adjustment.

tion, and abduction and adduction. Tests of the component parts of the hip joint include long-axis extension, the flexion-contraction sign, the flexion-adduction arc test,[5] and lateral distraction in flexion.

Long-Axis Extension (Fig. 10-36)

Long-axis extension of the hip produces more consistent mobility changes in the hip than any other maneuver.

Patient: Supine with the leg in neutral abduction and neutral external rotation.

Examiner: Contacting the patient's calcaneus and the dorsum of the foot.

Action: Manipulation by impulse and body weight inferiorly. The examiner must remember not to internally rotate the leg; doing so may jam the femur head into the acetabulum. Internal rotation also may transmit the manipulative force through the hip and into the sacroiliac or lumbar facet joints.

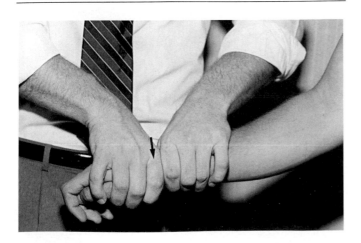

Figure 10-34 Midcarpal joint: AP glide.

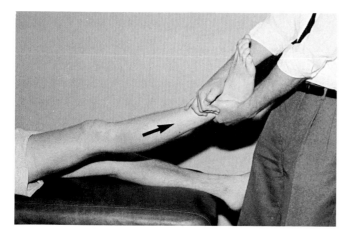

Figure 10-36 Hip joint: long-axis extension.

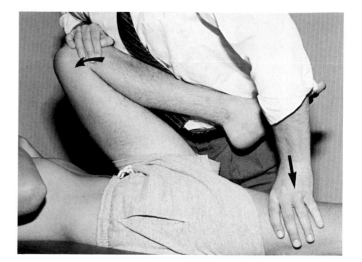

Figure 10-37 Hip joint: flexion-contraction sign.

Flexion-Contraction Sign (Fig. 10-37)

Patient: Supine.

Examiner: Raising the patient's contralateral knee and hip in flexion.

Action: Hip contracture causes the knee on that side to bend and come off the table; this is a positive flexion-contraction sign. The therapeutic goal of manipulation is to restore extension to the affected hip. The examiner stabilizes the femur on the table while at the same time exaggerating the contralateral hip into flexion. This rotates the pelvis (acetabulum) on the head of the femur.

Flexion-Adduction Arc Test (Fig. 10-38)

Patient: Supine with the knee in flexion.

Examiner: Standing perpendicular to the patient. The examiner interlocks his or her fingers over the patient's flexed knee and holds it snugly against the examiner's chest.

Action: Downward pressure is exerted through the femur shaft into the hip joint. The examiner moves through an arc from 90° of hip flexion to full adduction and then from 140° of hip flexion to full adduction. It is common to feel a local sticking point within this arc. Movement can be restored with a sharp, short impulse.

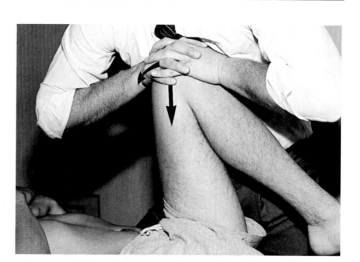

Figure 10-38 Hip joint: flexion-adduction arc test.

Lateral Distraction of Femur Head in Acetabulum (Fig. 10-39)

Patient: Supine; the affected hip is flexed 10°.

Examiner: Standing medial to the affected leg. The thumb web of the superior hand is placed on the proximal aspect of the medial femur. The examiner's stabilizing hand contacts the lateral aspect of the lower leg.

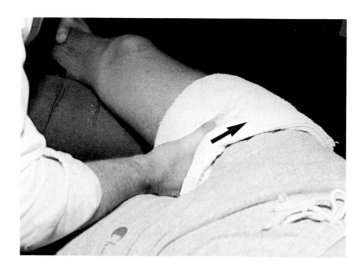

Figure 10-39 Hip joint: lateral distraction.

Action: Force is exerted in lateral deviation. Mobilization can be performed with therapy straps.

THE KNEE

The knee can be thought of as a two-joint structure composed of the tibiofemoral joint and the patellofemoral joint.

Patellofemoral Joint

Injury to the knee joint is most often followed by atrophy of the quadriceps group. With this the patella moves superiorly and slightly laterally because of weakness of the vastus medialis. There are four motions to be examined with reference to the patellofemoral joint.

Superior-to-Inferior Excursion (Fig. 10-40)

Patient: Supine with 5° of knee flexion and support.

Examiner: Holding the superior and inferior aspects of the patella with the thumbs and index fingers of both hands.

Action: The examiner pushes the patella superior to inferior without downward pressure. The patella will glide normally approximately 1 to 2 in. For mobilization several stretching-type pushes into fixation can be done.

Medial-to-Lateral Excursion (Fig. 10-41)

Patient: Same as above.

Examiner: Same as above except the lateral aspects of the patella are held.

Action: The examiner pushes medial to lateral, gliding the patella on the femur. Fixation is thought to be a fibrotic restriction.

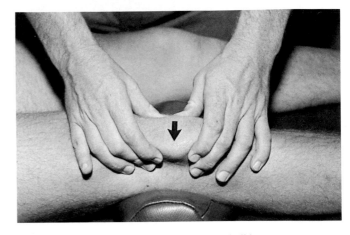

Figure 10-41 Patellofemoral joint: medial-lateral glide.

Lateral-to-Medial Excursion

Patient: Same as above.

Examiner: Same as above.

Action: Lateral-to-medial glide.

AP Rock (Fig. 10-42)

Patient: Same as above.

Examiner: Holding one thumb on the superior aspect of the patella and the other thumb on the inferior aspect of the patella.

Action: The examiner first pushes AP on the superior aspect of the patella and then on the inferior aspect of the patella. This causes a rocking motion.

Tibiofemoral Joint

Varus Tilt (Fig. 10-43)

Patient: Supine with the legs extended.

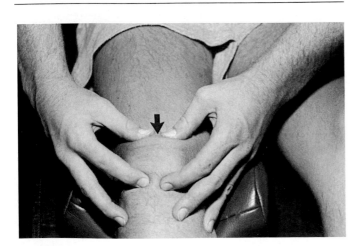

Figure 10-40 Patellofemoral joint: superior-inferior glide.

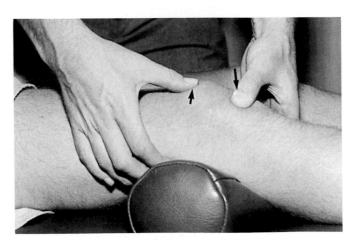

Figure 10-42 Patellofemoral joint: AP rock.

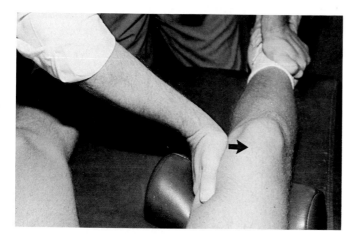

Figure 10-43 Tibiofemoral joint: varus tilt.

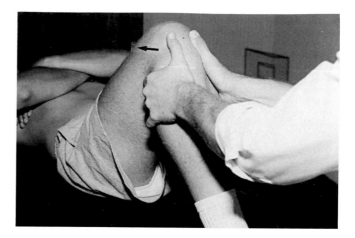

Figure 10-45 Tibiofemoral joint: AP glide.

Examiner: Standing on the medial aspect of the lower extremity. The superior hand is placed on the medial femoral condyles. The inferior hand grasps the ankle.

Action: The examiner brings the knee just off lock and tilts it medial to lateral. Manipulation uses a short, quick impulse directed medial to lateral.

Valgus Tilt (Fig. 10-44)

Patient: Same as above.

Examiner: Same as above.

Action: The examiner brings the knee just off lock and tilts it lateral to medial.

AP Glide (Fig. 10-45)

Patient: Supine with the knee flexed 90°.

Examiner: Seated on the distal aspect of patient's foot for stabilization. The examiner grasps the posterior aspect of the proximal tibia with the fingers. The thumbs are placed on either side of the tibial tuberosity.

Action: A short thrust is delivered posterior to anterior and then anterior to posterior.

Rotation of Tibial Condyles on Femoral Condyles (Fig. 10-46)

Patient: Supine with the knee flexed 90° and supported by the examiner's thighs.

Examiner: Contacting the femoral condyles with the thumb and middle finger on opposite sides with the superior hand. The indifferent hand grasps the patient's calcaneus with the thumb and index finger behind the malleoli.

Action: Medial rotational joint play and lateral rotational joint play.

Long-Axis Extension of Tibial Condyles on Femoral Condyles (Fig. 10-47)

There is no palpable play movement that can give the examiner specific palpatory awareness of loss of play in long-axis extension. Nevertheless, there are times when a clinical decision is made to manipulate this component of the knee joint.

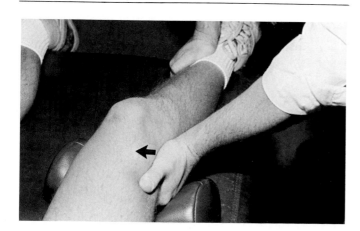

Figure 10-44 Tibiofemoral joint: valgus tilt.

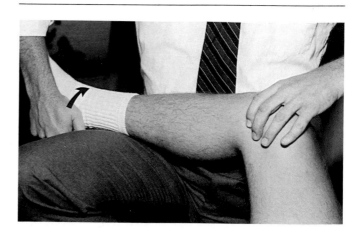

Figure 10-46 Tibiofemoral joint: tibial (lateral) rotation.

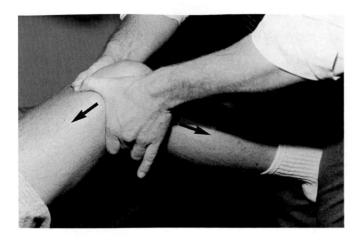

Figure 10-47 Tibiofemoral joint: long-axis extension.

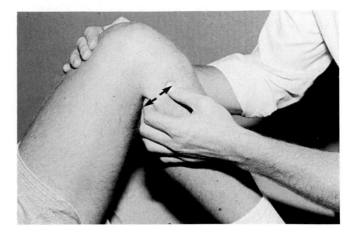

Figure 10-48 Superior tibiofibular joint: AP shear.

Patient: Supine with the leg abducted 45° and off the table.

Examiner: Stabilizing the patient's tibia with his or her inner thighs. Contact is made with both hands on either side of and just proximal to the femoral condyles.

Action: Both of the examiner's knees extend while the examiner simultaneously pushes cephalad with both hands.

Superior Tibiofibular Joint: AP Shear (Fig. 10-48)

Patient: Supine with the knee flexed at 90°.

Examiner: Contacting the superior fibular head with the thumb on the anterior surface and the index finger bent at 45° on the posterior surface.

Action: Anterior-to-posterior and posterior-to-anterior shear.

REFERENCES

1. Mennell JM. *Joint Pain: Diagnosis and Treatment Using Manipulative Techniques.* Boston: Little, Brown; 1964.

2. Sandoz R. *Some Physical Mechanisms and Effects of Spinal Adjustments. Swiss Annals.* 1976;6:91–141.

3. Mierau D, Cassidy JD, Bowen V, Dupuis P, Noftall F. *Manipulation/mobilization of the third metacarpophalangeal joint. Man Med.* 1988;3:135–140.

4. Nordin M, Frankel VH. *Basic Biomechanics of the Musculoskeletal System,* 2nd ed. Philadelphia: Lea & Febiger; 1986.

5. Grieve GP, Dip TP. The hip. *Physiotherapy.* 1983;69:xx–xx.

Chapter 11

Myofascial Pain and Dysfunction Syndromes

Joseph J. Smolders

MYOFASCIAL TRIGGER POINTS

Joseph J. Smolders

Myofascial pain and dysfunction syndromes are intimately associated with what have come to be known as myofascial trigger points (TPs), a term that Travell and Rinzler[1] originally coined to describe these tender spots.

This chapter describes only myofascial-type TPs because these are by far the most prevalent and symptomatic. TPs are also found in tissues other than myofascial; they can be cutaneous, ligamentous, periosteal, and fascial as well. These also characteristically refer pain remote from the location of the TP itself, although not in the predictable patterns found with myofascial TPs.

THEORETICAL CONSIDERATIONS

What is a Myofascial Trigger Point?

Although there remains some controversy as to the exact histopathologic nature of TPs, the following definition by Travell and Simons[2] seems appropriate for the practicing clinician. According to these investigators, a myofascial TP is "a hyperirritable focus, usually found within a taut band of skeletal muscle or in the muscle's fascia, that is painful on compression and that can give rise to characteristic referred pain, tenderness, and autonomic phenomena."

It should be remembered that normal muscles do not contain TPs, have no taut bands, are nontender to firm palpation, and do not refer pain, tenderness, or autonomic phenomena.

Trigger points may be found anywhere in any skeletal muscle. They are often palpable as small indurated areas (ie, nodules) or bits of disorganized fibrous tissue (adhesions). They are usually found in predictable locations in a given muscle, and certain muscles harbor TPs far more frequently than others. If one views the typical locations of TPs from an anatomic perspective, it can be shown that these places tend to be in areas that are prone to increased mechanical strain or impaired circulation, are associated with adhesions, or are subject to the development of any combination of these three.

Certain muscles have a far greater demand put on them than others and therefore tend to harbor a greater number of pain-producing TPs (eg, upper trapezius, levator scapulae, infraspinatus, quadratus lumborum, and gluteus minimus).

Increased Mechanical Strain

The following examples illustrate the development of TPs as a result of increased mechanical strain.

The lateral border of the iliocostalis lumborum will come under increased stress and shortening should there be any pelvic unleveling. This muscle not only extends the lumbar spine but also laterally bends the spine and helps compensate for a contralateral short leg. This chronic shortening may initiate the formation of TPs or may aggravate latent TPs, sending pain into the upper posterior ilium adjacent to the sacroiliac joint on the same side.

The medial gastrocnemius muscle (rather than its middle or lateral sections) may come under increased stress as a result of overpronation of the foot, which creates overload strain on the medial side of this muscle.

The anterior deltoid, especially its medial border (rather than the less frequently involved middle and posterior parts of this muscle), comes under increased stress because of the far more frequent need forcefully to flex the shoulder rather than to extend it.

Impaired Circulation

Impaired circulation often occurs at or near musculotendinous junctions and twists in muscles. Examples of this are the levator scapulae near the superior angle of the scapula at its insertion and in its midsection where it twists before it ascends into the neck and musculotendinous areas of the extensors of the forearm below their origin and of the supraspinatus muscle.

Trigger Points Associated with Adhesions

Trigger points also tend to be found in association with adhesions in the muscle and its fascia. Adhesion formation is the result of local dystrophic changes or injury repair.

What Makes a Trigger Point Hyperirritable?

Trigger points are by definition always tender when they are compressed, whether they are active or latent. This sensory hyperirritability appears to be due to sensitization of two major types of muscle-pain receptors: chemonociceptors and mechanonociceptors. Nociceptive impulses are mediated by muscle group III and group IV afferent nerve fibers, which also mediate the protopathic type, dull aching pain usually associated with TPs. Both types of nociceptors are easily sensitized by bradykinin, prostaglandins, potassium, histamine, serotonin, and perhaps substance P and the leukotrienes.[3,4] These small nerve fibers are unresponsive to phosphate and lactate,[5] both of which are metabolic end products once thought to be responsible for producing muscle pain.

Electron microscopy of biopsy specimens from tender spots in muscles (TPs) show the presence of degranulating mast cells (the source of histamine) and large clusters of platelets (the source of serotonin).[6] In the presence of these inflammatory substances and sensitizing agents mechanonociceptors are far more irritated by mechanical deformation, which may be caused by muscular contraction, stretch of a muscle, or direct digital compression at the site of the tender spot (TP). This deformation in turn causes pain that, if sufficiently intense, will produce the symptoms associated with myofascial pain and dysfunction syndromes.

A TP thus appears to be a small, discrete region that is inflamed. This inflammation, however, is so low grade that it is usually only noticed when it is irritated by compression, by needle penetration, or at times by high-intensity ultrasound.

There are no other overt signs of inflammation, although penetration by a needle thermocouple shows that the temperature of a TP is higher than that of the surrounding tissue.[7] Because the inflammatory process is of such a low-grade nature, treatment that addresses the inflammation itself tends to be unsuccessful. Ice, for example, will chill the underlying muscle and may aggravate symptoms by further impairing local circulation. Systemic anti-inflammatory medication is also of no use, probably because it cannot perfuse the area of the TP, again as a result of impaired local circulation.

How Are Trigger Points Associated with the Palpably Taut Bands of Skeletal Muscle in Which They Are Usually Found?

Trigger points are usually located in taut bands of skeletal muscle. These are usually easily palpable or may feel almost threadlike. The TP is the spot along the band where local tenderness reaches its maximum. One or more TPs may be found in any individual band. These palpable bands remain taut because of the sustained interaction between actin and myosin filaments, the contractile elements of muscle tissue. Normally actin and myosin filament interaction is the result of motor neuron action potentials. Because the taut bands associated with TPs are electrically quiescent, however, this shortening of skeletal muscle is not a centrally mediated contraction (ie, from the central nervous system) but rather a locally mediated response due to an energy crisis at the site of the TP (physiologic contracture).

Tearing of the sarcoplasmic reticulum (SR) around a muscle fibril as a result of acute or chronic overload strain releases ionic calcium. Release of calcium ions causes a strong interaction between actin and myosin filaments, resulting in contraction and sarcomere shortening. This produces a palpably taut band. Because the SR is torn the calcium pump cannot retrieve all the interstitial calcium. The continued presence of interstitial calcium ions therefore sustains the contraction and the presence of band tautness. This in turn leads to both runaway metabolism caused by the continued energy demand and impairment of local circulation caused by muscle shortening. This results in localized tissue ischemia. Adenosine triphosphate (ATP), a high-energy phosphate, becomes depleted in the SR compartment, which leads to the failure of the ATP-dependent calcium pump. Even after SR repair continued runaway metabolism and impaired local circulation, which lead to both depletion of ATP in the SR and local ischemia, allow calcium ions to remain interstitially. This sustains both the "locking" of myosin heads onto actin filaments and the continued presence of palpable muscle band tautness. It becomes evident, then, that treatment should be directed toward improved circulation (eg, heat) and release of the actin and myosin filaments (eg, stretching).

Concurrently, initial SR tearing causes localized inflammation and pain. This may account for the initial presence of sensitizing agents such as histamine and serotonin. The resulting reflex vasoconstriction together with impaired circulation due to muscle shortening leads to ischemia, further tissue damage, and the continued presence of sensitizing agents. Figure 11-1 summarizes the events described above and illustrates how these events can lead to the dystrophic changes reported by various investigators.[8-11]

The foregoing explanation as to how a tender TP is associated with a taut band helps explain the following clinical observations:

- Prolonged muscle shortening (eg, from poor sleep position at night) may cause tissue ischemia, resulting in stiffness and pain on waking. Poor sleeping postures may lead to or aggravate torticollis, lower back pain, shoulder joint pain, and the like. These painful syndromes may be acute or resolve after a short time as a result of improved circulation from movement (this usually takes about 30 minutes).
- Sustained voluntary contraction (eg, holding a telephone receiver between the shoulder and ear) will also increase tissue ischemia and may turn a latent TP into an active one.
- Frequent repetitive contractions with little or no rest time between contractions (eg, in meat packing and other assembly line–type operations) again result in ischemia and a possible increase in TP activity.
- Increased fatigability of the muscle may result from decreased tissue oxygenation.

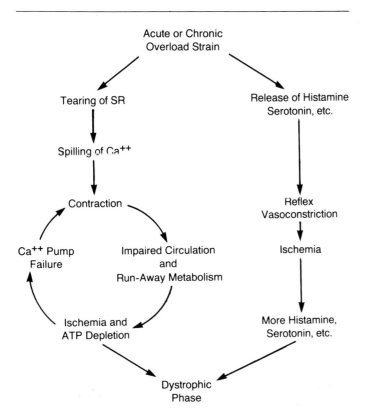

Figure 11-1 Acute or chronic overload strain.

- Shortened range of motion may be caused by muscle shortening.
- Reflex muscle weakening as the muscle "learns" to avoid potentially pain-producing contractions may develop.

Referred Pain

Trigger points can give rise to characteristic patterns of referred pain. These pain patterns are not dermatomal, myotomal, or sclerotomal, nor do they follow any peripheral nerve distribution. This seems to imply a centrally mediated neuroanatomic pathway that reproducibly relates the pattern of referred pain to its site of origin.

These pain patterns can be broken down into essential and spillover pain zones.[2] The essential pain zone is the region of referred pain that is found consistently in most patients when the TP is active. The spillover pain zone is the region where some patients experience pain beyond the essential pain zone because of greater activity of the TP. At times more than one muscle is referring pain into a particular region of the body. This results in a composite pain pattern, which is the total referred pain pattern of more than one muscle. For example, compression of trapezius TPs may cause neck, head, and tooth pain. The tooth pain is actually caused by temporalis muscle TPs that are activated by trapezius TPs.

Referred Tenderness

Trigger points may refer tenderness to the area to which pain is usually referred regardless of whether or not referred pain is present at the same time. This phenomenon is probably mediated by the sympathetic nervous system.

Referred tenderness is frequently present when it is looked for and easily leads to the conclusion that the area of tenderness is also the source of the tenderness. This quite often leads to misdiagnosis. For example, referred tenderness may be present over the dorsum of the wrist, which also makes the tendons there tender to palpation. This may lead to the conclusion that a tendinitis is present. This tenderness, however, is not infrequently referred to the wrist from TPs in the extensor muscles of the forearm. This referred tenderness disappears as soon as the causative TP is inactivated.

Referred Autonomic Phenomena

Trigger points may refer vascular, secretory, and pilomotor autonomic changes. These are mediated via the sympathetic nervous system. Referred autonomic phenomena include coryza, lacrimation, localized sweating, decreased skin resistance to an electric probe, skin temperature changes, and pilomotor activity.

Other Phenomena Associated with Trigger Points

Trigger points often cause increased motor unit activity, including the induction of satellite TPs in muscles located in the pain reference zone of another muscle. This results in muscular tics and twitches, muscle cramps, and composite pain patterns. TPs and their taut bands lead to decreased stretch range of motion, muscle weakness, and muscle fatigability.

Types of Trigger Points

Trigger points are classified as follows[2]:

- Active TPs are those that are symptomatic with respect to pain. They refer a pattern of pain at rest or during motion (or both) that is specific for that muscle. They are always tender, prevent full lengthening of a muscle, cause muscle weakness, and initiate a local twitch response when the taut band is snapped near the site of the TP.
- Latent TPs are clinically quiet with respect to pain but may have all the other clinical characteristics of active TPs. These represent the majority of TPs.
- Primary TPs are activated by acute or chronic overload strain and are not activated as a result of TP activity in another muscle.
- Associated TPs develop in response to compensatory overload, shortened range of motion, or referred phenomena caused by TP activity in another muscle. There are two kinds of such TPs:
  1. Satellite TPs are activated because the muscle in which the TP is located is in the zone of referral of another muscle.
  2. Secondary TPs are activated because the muscle was overloaded as a synergist or an antagonist of a muscle harboring a primary TP.

What Kinds of Stimuli Activate Trigger Points?

Trigger points are directly activated by acute or chronic overload strain, direct trauma to the muscle, and chilling. They are indirectly activated by other trigger points (ie, satellite or secondary TPs) or by being in the pain reference zone of a visceral organ (eg, angina pectoris may activate TPs in the pectoralis major). Arthritic joints put aberrant overload strain on muscles, which attempt to stabilize these joints. Finally, emotional distress leads to increased tone in many muscle groups. When this is prolonged, TPs are activated.

SUMMARY OF HISTORY AND PHYSICAL EXAMINATION FINDINGS

Patients may remember the mechanisms of injury if TPs are present as a result of acute overload strain (eg, head position during an automobile accident). This aids in locating the pain-causing TPs. In the case of chronic strain or indirectly activated TPs, patients will complain of an insidious onset with perhaps one or more previous episodes of acute pain.

Referred pain from TPs tends to wax and wane in intensity from hour to hour or day to day as more or less strain is incurred by the muscle.

Patients often complain of stiffness rather than pain, especially those in older age groups (older than 40 years). They may also complain of decreased range of motion.

Stretching the muscle may reproduce pain, particularly if the taut band harboring the TPs is specifically stretched. Muscle weakness may be found on resisted testing as the muscle "learns" to avoid reproduction of pain. Contraction of the muscle, especially in its fully shortened position, elicits pain. Examination may also reveal the presence of a taut palpable band of muscle, focal tenderness in a taut band (the TP), or a local twitch response on snapping across a taut band. The last of these is pathognomonic of the presence of a TP. A local twitch response is usually seen as a transient dimpling under the skin along the taut band near its musculotendinous region. This part of the muscle band has normal sarcomere length and therefore retains the ability to shorten, whereas sarcomeres are already in a state of contraction in the area of the TP, which is commonly located in the belly of the muscle.

The examiner may see a characteristic pattern of referred pain, usually deep and aching, that may be accompanied by dysesthesias. The painful complaint may be reproduced by compression of the TP. Finally, TP therapy will result in elimination of symptoms. (Although elimination of referred pain is highly suggestive of a TP, spray and stretch therapy of the pectoralis major may eliminate the precordial pain of myocardial ischemia.[2])

THERAPEUTIC CONSIDERATIONS

Treatment of myofascial pain and dysfunction syndromes centers on (1) inactivating the TP, (2) lengthening the taut band within which TPs are located, and (3) eliminating factors that tend to perpetuate these syndromes. Although directing treatment toward any one of these may eliminate the remaining two, all three should be considered if treatment is to be successful (ie, a polymodal approach to treatment).

Trigger Point Inactivation

Trigger points can be eliminated by hyperstimulation analgesia (also known as counterirritation), improving circulation at the site of the TP, and lengthening the taut band (discussed in the next section).

Hyperstimulation Analgesia

Hyperstimulation analgesia or counterirritation is one of the oldest methods used for the control of pain. It includes the application of mustard plasters, hot cups, hot wax, blistering agents, ischemic compression, and, more recently, dry needling, brief intense cold, electrical stimulation [eg, transcutaneous electrical nerve stimulation (TENS)], and high-velocity/low-amplitude manipulation of spinal facet joints. Although some of these methods are more effective than others, any one may relieve chronic pain for long periods of time (days or weeks) or even permanently.

Hyperstimulation analgesia is successful because it breaks the pain-spasm-pain cycle that so often perpetuates a painful condition. This is accomplished through controlled inhibition of pain, or "closing the gate" to noxious input from parts of the body (ie, TPs).[12] Stimulation of the reticular formation of the brainstem, which has large sensory receptive fields, inhibits the transmission of nerve impulses in dorsal horn cells, thereby "closing the gate" to the perception of pain. Noxious sensory input must first cross synapses in the dorsal horn before ascending the spinothalamic tracts. If this mechanism is blocked, the perception of pain may be decreased or eliminated.

Ischemic compression is often an effective way of inactivating a TP. Compression is applied with a thumb, knuckle, elbow, or rubber-tipped dowel (T bar). Because compression is by definition painful, the pain itself serves as the hyperstimulant. Pain is usually relieved within 20 to 60 seconds. Pressure is applied directly on the TP to within the patient's tolerance; excessive pain stimulation is counterproductive because this leads to reactive muscle contraction (guarding) as the patient seeks to avoid the pain. As the pain subsides, the operator slowly increases compression until, ideally, the painful stimulus is eliminated. At the same time, one can often feel a "release" or softening of the indurated area that is the trigger point. This is probably due to local "unlocking" of actin and myosin filaments; softening does not occur when the area of the trigger point is fibrosed, however. Reactive hyperemia after compression improves local circulation and aids in the elimination of sensitizing agents. Nimmo, an early clinical investigator of TP phenomena, has presented material in seminars that suggests serial, short duration (7 seconds) compression applied to several TPs in a muscle.

Dry needling of a TP may also be successful but may cause considerable pain because the needle is made to penetrate the heart of the TP. Acupuncture needles are more appropriate than the large-caliber needles used for intramuscular injections. Not only does the dry needling cause hyperstimulation analgesia, it may cause enough physical disruption of the TP to improve circulation.

Local anesthetic injection of a TP, as used by Travell and Simons,[2] is similar to dry needling except that the locally injected anesthetic agent eliminates most of the pain of needle penetration and probably also washes away some of the sensitizing agents that are present. Local anesthesia at the site of the TP also blocks pain and interrupts the pain-spasm-pain cycle.

Brief intense cold stimulation of the skin overlying the TP and its pain referral area is effective in releasing taut bands and inactivating TPs, particularly when done in combination with passive stretch (see below, Spray and Stretch Technique). Intense cold stimulates cold receptors in the skin, which tends to inhibit pain. The underlying muscles should not be cooled because chilling may lead to muscle contraction and result in further impairment of circulation, thereby increasing TP activity and referred pain. Vaporized coolant sprays such as ethyl chloride and the fluorinated hydrocarbons are most effective at providing a sufficiently intense stimulus. Ice used as a superficial coolant can also be effective, although it is not as cold.

Moderate- to high-intensity electrical stimulation will also effectively supply the required hyperstimulation. One study[13] examined the effects of brief, intense TENS at TP sites in cases of severe pain. Electrical stimulation was applied for 20 minutes, which frequently relieved pain for several hours and sometimes for days or weeks.

In another study[14] TENS and acupuncture were used to relieve lower back pain. Similar points were stimulated, again resulting in pain relief that usually lasted several hours. Interestingly, there was no statistical difference in the duration of pain relief when the two forms of treatment were compared.

Improving Circulation

Improving circulation at the site of a TP would decrease the concentration of agents that sensitize nociceptors, thereby decreasing tenderness and TP activity. It would also increase the supply of ATP, which may allow some degree of muscle filament unlocking by decreasing the concentration of interstitial ionic calcium. (ATP is needed to pump ionic calcium back into the SR.)

Circulation can be improved with the use of heat in the form of heating pads (dry), hydrocollator hot packs (moist, which are more effective than dry pads because moist heat is more penetrating than dry heat), low-intensity ultrasound, and short-wave diathermy. Heat should be applied at the site of the TP for 5 to 15 minutes, after which gentle stretching and range of motion exercises can be performed to enhance the effectiveness of this type of treatment. Generalized soft tissue massage in the area of the trigger point may also increase circulation but is not nearly as effective as localized ischemic compression at the TP.

The application of heat after ischemic compression, muscle stripping, spray and stretch techniques, and injection techniques not only enhances the effectiveness of these treatments by improving circulation but is also helpful in preventing so-called rebound pain. Rebound pain is sometimes experienced several hours after these types of treatments and may last from several hours to 1 or 2 days. This pain is felt after the initial treatment of a TP and appears to be similar to postexercise soreness both in quality and duration.

Lengthening the Taut Band

Lengthening of the taut band is perhaps the most effective type of treatment for several reasons. Lengthening disengages the actin and myosin filaments, allowing more normal muscle length and increased range of motion. This allows normal movement during everyday activities and results in normal, patterned proprioceptive input to the central nervous system, which may prevent the resumption of pain. This is why post-treatment range of motion exercises increase the chances of successful permanent elimination of these painful syndromes, particularly those that are longstanding. Lengthening of taut bands also improves circulation at the site of the TP.

Lengthening can be accomplished at home in the form of gentle unforced stretching of the involved muscles (preferably after the muscle has been warmed).

Spray and Stretch Technique

Lengthening of the taut band is effectively accomplished by the use of the spray and stretch technique, which was first introduced by Kraus[15] and later was popularized by Travell. This technique utilizes a vaporized coolant spray that blocks the pain experienced when the muscle is passively stretched. Pain is blocked through central inhibition (hyperstimulation analgesia). The key to this technique is the passive stretch of the taut band harboring the TPs. A nonspecific stretch of the muscle as a whole is not nearly as effective.

The patient is put into as comfortable a position as possible to enhance muscle relaxation. The part of the body affected is then positioned so that a mild stretch is exerted specifically on the taut band. One or two sweeps of coolant are then sprayed over the area of the involved muscle to reduce any pain that may be felt by this position. The spray is held approximately 18 in away from the skin to allow for sufficient cooling of the spray. As the taut band is passively stretched, successive parallel sweeps of the spray are applied over the skin from the TP to the area of referred pain. As much of the referred pain pattern as possible should be covered in order to block the pain and to decrease muscle ''spasm'' centrally. After each application of the spray and stretch technique, the muscle is selectively moved through as full a range of motion as possible to normalize proprioceptive input to the central nervous system. Several muscles of the myotactic unit as well as muscles harboring satellite TPs may need to be treated to eliminate the referred pain. After this treatment a moist hot pack is applied in the region of the TP. Several treatments may be needed to eliminate the pain syndrome. Good results should be seen after 4 to 6 treatments. If pain persists after 10 treatments or so, other factors may be perpetuating TP activity (see below).

If vaporized coolants are not available, ice may be used in their place. Care should be taken to prevent chilling of the underlying muscles, which is less likely with the use of vaporized coolants.

Muscle Stripping

Stripping the taut band of muscle with slow, firm pressure is as effective as the spray and stretch technique. It is, however, somewhat more painful for the patient and often cannot be accomplished if the painful symptoms are severe. Muscle stripping is accomplished by applying a lubricant to the skin and slowly sliding the thumb, knuckle, or elbow along the edge of a taut band with firm pressure while at the same time attempting to bow it out. This has the effect of applying brief ischemic compression as the thumb slowly slides over the TPs and of passively lengthening the taut band. Lengthening done in this fashion not only disengages the myofilaments but also stretches the fascial envelope around the taut band. Small adhesions that may have developed between layers of fascia and that restrict normal intermuscular and intramuscular glide may simultaneously be broken.

Muscle Stretching

Stretching techniques can also be used to lengthen taut muscle bands and to relieve pain. Regular stretching of the involved muscles at home is an important part of any myofascial treatment regimen (see Chapter 13).

Elimination of Perpetuating Factors

Elimination of perpetuating factors is often just as important as the actual treatment. Perpetuating factors may include the following: structural imbalances, occupation, persistence of associated TPs, nutrition deficiencies, hypometabolic disease, and psychologic distress.

Structural imbalances due, for example, to a short leg, Morton's foot, or scoliosis, often chronically overload muscles as they attempt to compensate for these imbalances. Occupationally related postural habits and movement patterns chronically overload muscles and lead to what have come to be known as chronic strain syndromes. These syndromes are distressingly common and at times difficult to correct short of changing occupations. Persistence of TPs in other muscles of a myotactic unit or of satellite TPs facilitates referred pain patterns unless the primary TPs are eliminated.

Nutrition deficiencies may require correction. Vitamins C, B_1, B_6, B_{12} and folic acid play an essential role in normal muscle metabolism. Iron deficiency anemia decreases oxygen perfusion of tissues and of TPs in particular (because of their poor circulation). The hypometabolic diseases hypoglycemia and hypothyroidism may be the underlying causes of TP perpetuation because of their resultant inadequate supply of nutrients to muscle tissues. Finally, psychologic distress will greatly increase the tone of many muscles, particularly those of the upper back and shoulders. This causes chronic shortening of these muscles and perpetuation of pain.

Summary of Therapeutic Techniques

The best treatment regimens are polymodal, meaning that they simultaneously address several factors contributing to the pain syndrome. For example, treatment by ischemic compression into TPs or the use of high-voltage probes should be followed by spray and stretch of the taut band to lengthen it.

Range of motion exercises need to be performed to establish more normal proprioceptive input. Heat application to the TP area should follow to enhance local circulation and to prevent postinjection soreness. Finally, patients need to be instructed about how to avoid poor postural mechanics and need to be given stretch exercises to be done at home.

PAIN SYNDROMES OF THE UPPER LIMBS

Shoulder Pain

Shoulder pain and dysfunction are most often of myofascial origin. The following muscles refer pain into the shoulder and are listed in decreasing order of importance: infraspinatus, deltoid, levator scapulae, scalenes, supraspinatus, subscapularis, and trapezius. The teres major and minor, pectoralis major and minor, and serratus posterior and superior may also contribute to shoulder pain.

Infraspinatus

The infraspinatus is by far the most frequent cause of shoulder pain (Fig. 11-2). TPs in this muscle refer pain deep into the shoulder joint that is often described by patients as arthritic pain because it is deep and can be severely aching and debilitating. Referred pain from this muscle is often misdiagnosed as subdeltoid bursitis, supraspinatus tendinitis, or arthritis (especially if joint changes are seen on radiographs). Pain is also felt in the anterior shoulder and down the anterior upper arm over the biceps. If TPs are very active pain may refer to the extensor area of the forearm and into the hand, setting off TPs in the extensor muscles and causing additional wrist and hand pain. Infraspinatus TPs often also activate deltoid TPs. Patients sometimes complain of a numbing in the

shoulder and arm that after further questioning is more accurately described as a numbing ache (like a "paralysis" with no objective sensory loss).

Range of motion is usually but not always limited on attempted internal rotation and adduction of the shoulder, as when the patient attempts to scratch the lower back or to fasten a bra strap. If pain is severe, reaching across to the opposite shoulder may be impossible. These TPs cause shoulder girdle fatigue and decreased grip strength (probably because of forearm extensor TP activity). Pain is elicited on resisted testing of the infraspinatus and middle and posterior deltoid muscles.

The infraspinatus is an important muscle in shoulder joint mechanics. During shoulder abduction, along with the subscapularis it resists the upward pull of the humeral head by the deltoid muscle and simultaneously externally rotates the humerus. If the infraspinatus is unable to carry out these functions subacromial impingement may result, leading to irritation of the subacromial bursa and supraspinatus tendon. Activities done above shoulder level, for example the military press over-arm pitching, tennis, etc., should be avoided because of possible subacromial impingement.

Patients with active TPs will find it difficult to sleep because of pressure on TPs if they are lying on the involved side or because of stretching of the muscle if they are lying on the uninvolved side. Supporting the involved arm on a pillow while sleeping on the uninvolved side is a significant help.

Infraspinatus TPs additionally refer tenderness to the anterior shoulder area. Treatment of these TPs often reduces or eliminates tenderness in the anterior deltoid muscles and the insertion of the supraspinatus tendon. Should friction massage of the supraspinatus tendon be necessary, treatment of these TPs may make this procedure less painful for the patient.

Anterior Deltoid

Anterior deltoid TPs refer pain and tenderness in the area of the muscle itself (Fig. 11-3). TPs in this muscle are often satellite TPs due to referral from the infraspinatus muscle or direct trauma to the muscle itself (because of its exposed position). Adhesions are sometimes found in this muscle from previous trauma.

Trigger points and their taut bands typically restrict external rotation and extension and will need to be cleared to restore

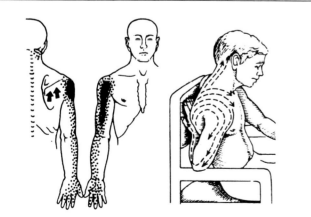

Figure 11-2 Infraspinatus TPs. Location of TPs (*short, straight black and white arrows*) and pain patterns (*stipples*), stretch positions and spray patterns (*dashed arrows*) for muscles that cause pain. The *dashed arrows* trace the impact of the stream of vapocoolant spray applied to release the muscular tension during stretch. *Source:* Reprinted from *Medical Rehabilitation* (p315) by JV Basmajian and RL Kirby with persmission of Williams & Wilkins Company, © 1984.

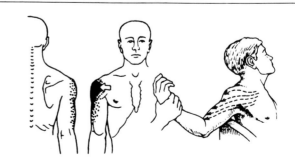

Figure 11-3 Anterior deltoid TPs. See Fig. 11-2 for explanation of patterns. *Source:* Reprinted from *Medical Rehabilitation* (p315) by JV Basmajian and RL Kirby with permission of Williams & Wilkins Company, © 1984.

range of motion once infraspinatus TPs have been cleared. Occasionally, taut tender bands in this muscle are mistaken for the biceps tendon and may lead to a misdiagnosis of bicipital tendinitis.

Posterior Deltoid

Trigger points in this muscle, along with those in the levator scapulae, are the most frequent cause of myogenic posterior shoulder pain (Fig. 11-4). TPs are usually located posterior to the humeral head and may be mistaken for tenderness in the musculotendinous portion of the infraspinatus. Pain is referred to the area of the muscle itself. Pain is elicited on resisted testing, reaching across to the opposite shoulder anteriorly, and near the end of external rotation while the arm is abducted at 90° because of the shortening reaction in the muscle.

Levator Scapulae

This muscle is one of the most frequent myofascial sources of pain (Fig. 11-5). Its primary referral area is the base of the neck, which causes painful limitation of neck rotation (torticollis). Pain may also be referred to the posterior shoulder joint over the area of the humeral head and along the medial scapular border; it is then often referred to as scapulocostal syndrome.

Levator scapulae TPs painfully restrict ipsilateral rotation of the neck because of a shortening reaction of the taut bands in

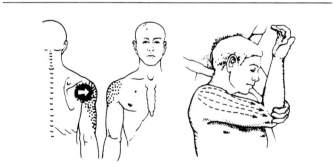

Figure 11-4 Posterior deltoid TPs. See Fig. 11-2 for explanation of patterns. *Source:* Reprinted from *Medical Rehabilitation* (p315) by JV Basmajian and RL Kirby with permission of Williams & Wilkins Company, © 1984.

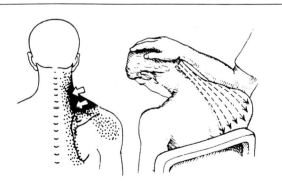

Figure 11-5 Levator scapulae TPs. See Fig. 11-2 for explanation of patterns. *Source:* Reprinted from *Medical Rehabilitation* (p315) by JV Basmajian and RL Kirby with permission of Williams & Wilkins Company, © 1984.

the muscle. If the TP is less active, Sperling's test (ipsilateral rotation and extension) will produce pain on the ipsilateral side of the neck. Full shoulder abduction is limited and accompanied by reproduction of posterior shoulder pain.

These TPs are activated by holding a telephone receiver between the shoulder and ear; sleeping on a sofa with the head on the armrest, which causes prolonged stretching deformation of the muscle; postural stress due to shoulder girdle asymmetry; and psychologic distress. Treatment with the spray and stretch technique is satisfying because there is often dramatic restoration of normal function.

Scalenes

The scalene muscles have a frequent incidence of TP activity (Fig. 11-6). In one study[16] nearly 50% of a group of asymptomatic students harbored latent TPs on at least one side. The pain pattern is similar for all three scalenes and includes the anterior chest, the upper arm both anterolaterally (as with the infraspinatus) and posteriorly, the thumb and index finger, and the medial scapular area (as with the levator scapulae). The entire pain pattern may be present or only parts of it. If pain is referred selectively, for example to the shoulder and upper arm, it may be confused with shoulder joint involvement. Pain may "migrate" from one part of the referral pattern to another, which should lead to the conclusion that there is a more centrally located cause (ie, scalene TPs). Tenderness is referred to the infraclavicular fossa and disappears immediately after inactivation of TPs.

Patients may exhibit restlessness of the neck and arm in an attempt to find relief. Satellite TPs in the extensors of the forearm may be activated, causing wrist and hand pain and stiffness (see below, Forearm Extensor Muscles and Brachioradialis). Functional testing of the shoulder will be uninformative.

Supraspinatus

Supraspinatus TPs are not nearly as frequent as those of the infraspinatus. They refer pain around the shoulder area,

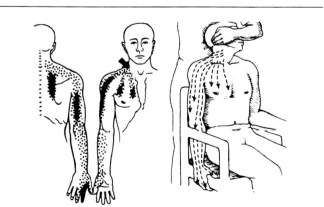

Figure 11-6 Scaleni TPs. See Fig. 11-2 for explanation of patterns. *Source:* Reprinted from *Medical Rehabilitation* (p315) by JV Basmajian and RL Kirby with permission of Williams & Wilkins Company, © 1984.

especially in the mid-deltoid region (Fig. 11-7). This shoulder pain is easily misdiagnosed as subdeltoid bursitis not only because of its pain referral pattern but also because the patient will feel pain during shoulder abduction and as a dull ache at rest. When the muscle is less severely involved, the patient will have difficulty fully abducting the shoulder while, for example, combing hair or shaving. Pain may also be felt strongly at the lateral epicondyle of the humerus, mimicking tennis elbow pain. Referred tenderness and chronic strain due to shortening may cause tenderness at the tendinous insertion.

The supraspinatus is seldom involved by itself; TPs usually occur in association with TPs in the infraspinatus or upper trapezius. Shortening of this muscle is often the cause of snapping or cracking sounds inside the glenohumeral joint, which are due to the resultant abnormal glide in the joint. Inactivation of TPs may eliminate these noises.

This muscle is also important for glenohumeral joint stability. Basmajian[17] described how the supraspinatus produces a "wedging" of the humeral head against the upturned glenoid fossa to prevent downward movement (Fig. 11-8). Should the glenoid fossa be tilted downward slightly, as it would be in a rounded shoulder posture, the supraspinatus would be overloaded and more likely to develop TPs or a tendinitis. Careful examination of scapular posture is important in the context of shoulder joint stability. Release of pectoral TPs may be necessary to release the scapula.

Travell and Simons[2] have observed radiographically that early calcific deposits at the insertion of this tendon may resolve with inactivation of TPs in this muscle. Even if a tendinitis is present, elimination of TPs is helpful because this decreases the chronic strain on the tendon.

Subscapularis (Fig. 11-9)

Pain is felt both at rest and on motion over the posterior shoulder and may extend over the scapula and posteromedial arm. Occasionally pain also refers in a strap-like area around

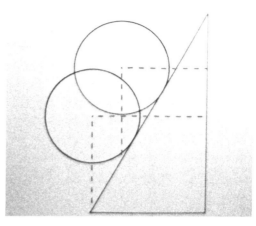

Figure 11-8 Supraspinatus produces "wedging" of the humeral head against the upturned glenoid fossa to prevent downward movement. *Source:* Reprinted from *Muscles Alive*, 5th ed, by JV Basmajian and CL DeLuca with permission of Williams & Wilkins Company, © 1985.

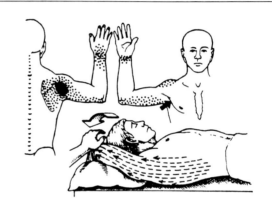

Figure 11-9 Subscapularis TPs. The *curved white arrow* identifies the direction(s) of pressure applied to stretch the muscle. See Fig. 11-2 for explanation of the other patterns. *Source:* Reprinted from *Medical Rehabilitation* (p316) by JV Basmajian and RL Kirby with permission of Williams & Wilkins Company, © 1984.

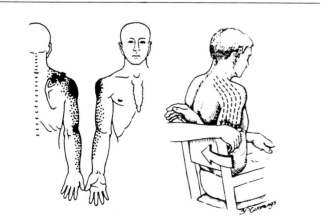

Figure 11-7 Supraspinatus TPs. The curved white arrow identifies the direction(s) of pressure applied to stretch the muscle. See Fig. 11-2 for explanation of patterns. *Source:* Reprinted from *Medical Rehabilitation* (p315) by JV Basmajian and RL Kirby with permission of Williams & Wilkins Company, © 1984.

the wrist. Shoulder abduction is painfully limited especially if external rotation of the arm is added to the movement. Resisted testing also elicits pain. If the examiner palpates the humeral head during passive horizontal flexion of the shoulder he or she will notice decreased posterior glide of the humeral head in the glenoid fossa. The subscapularis along with the infraspinatus counters the upward movement of the humeral head in the glenoid fossa during shoulder abduction. This prevents subacromial impingement. TPs in this muscle will tend to allow the humeral head to impinge on the inferior acromion due to the overpowering action of the deltoid muscle, possibly irritating the subdeltoid bursa and/or the supraspinatus tendon.

Travell and Simons[2] make a very strong case for the myogenic origin of "frozen shoulder" known also as adhesive capsulitis[18] or periarticular arthritis.[19,20]

"Frozen shoulder" begins with the activation of subscapularis TPs which lead to painful limitation of abduction and external rotation due to stretch-activation of pain. Continued limitation of motion overloads other muscles within the same myotactic unit (ie, infraspinatus, supraspinatus, teres major, deltoid, and pectoralis major and minor), which further increases pain and decreases ranges of motion. Eventually all the shoulder girdle muscles may become involved. Dystrophic connective tissue changes due to vasospasm combined with marked limitation of motion may lead to adhesive capsulitis and subacromial fibrosis.

The most common TPs are easily accessible because they lie along the axillary border of the subscapularis. These TPs should not be overexamined because they can easily be activated, leading to an acute episode of shoulder pain. TPs also may be activated by repetitive forceful internal rotation (eg, swimming the crawl and over-arm pitching), stopping a fall by reaching back to brace oneself, dislocation, and prolonged immobilization in a sling.

Spray and stretch technique for subscapularis TPs may require release of other muscles that block abduction and external rotation. These include the pectoralis major and anterior deltoid. These can be sprayed in a position similar to that for the subscapularis.

Trapezius

A TP in the upper trapezius (Fig. 11-10) near the distal clavicle and another in the lower border of the lower trapezius near the medial scapular border both refer pain and tenderness to the top of the shoulder over the acromion. These TPs may cause tenderness of the acromioclavicular joint ligaments even in the absence of pain. Stress testing of the acromioclavicular joint ligaments does not reproduce pain when it is referred from these TPs, however. The TP in the lower trapezius (Fig. 11-11) also refers pain into the ipsilateral posterior neck and suboccipital region.

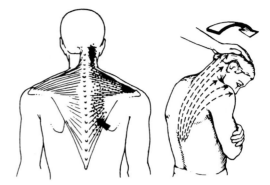

Figure 11-11 Lower trapezius TPs. The *curved white arrow* identifies the direction(s) of pressure applied to stretch the muscle. See Fig. 11-2 for explanation of the other patterns. *Source:* Reprinted from *Medical Rehabilitation* (p314) by JV Basmajian and RL Kirby with permission of Williams & Wilkins Company, © 1984.

Elbow Pain

Pain at the elbow, when not joint related, is most often due to microtearing of the common flexor or extensor tendons or referred into the elbow from myofascial sources. Even if tendinitis is present TPs will invariably also be present in the relevant muscles, which puts a chronic strain on that tendon. The most frequent sources of referred pain are the supinator and the forearm extensor muscles. Also involved may be the brachioradialis and triceps muscles.

Supinator

This muscle refers pain and tenderness primarily to the lateral epicondyle of the elbow and also to the dorsal web space between the thumb and index finger (Fig. 11-12). The lateral elbow referral is frequently the cause of so-called tennis elbow. It typically causes twinges of pain at the elbow, and tapping the lateral elbow elicits exquisite tenderness. The hand extensors may be involved secondarily and may also refer pain to the lateral elbow. According to Travell and Simons,[2] each one of Cyriax's[21] sites of tendinitis at the lateral elbow can be

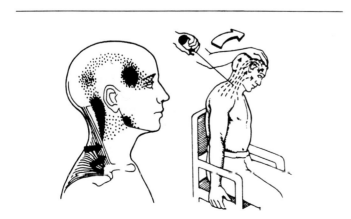

Figure 11-10 Upper trapezius TPs. The *curved white arrow* identifies the direction(s) of pressure applied to stretch the muscle. See Fig. 11-2 for explanation of the other patterns. *Source:* Reprinted from *Medical Rehabilitation* (p314) by JV Basmajian and RL Kirby with permission of Williams & Wilkins Company, © 1984.

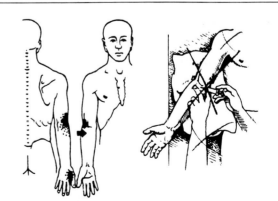

Figure 11-12 Supinator TPs. See Fig. 11-2 for explanation of the patterns. *Source:* Reprinted from *Medical Rehabilitation* (p316) by JV Basmajian and RL Kirby with permission of Williams & Wilkins Company, © 1984.

accounted for by TPs in the supinator, extensor carpi radialis longus, and triceps muscles.

Supinator pain referral is activated by playing tennis with an extended elbow, which does not allow the biceps brachii to take part in the supination required to control the head of the tennis racket. The supinator may also entrap the deep branch of the radial nerve, causing extensor weakness.

Ischemic compression and deep muscle stripping are more successful than spray and stretch because it is difficult to put an adequate stretch through this muscle.

Forearm Extensor Muscles and Brachioradialis

Many of these muscles refer pain to the lateral or posterior elbow, including the extensor carpi radialis brevis, brachioradialis, and extensor digitorum (see below, Wrist and Hand Pain), again leading to a diagnosis of tendinitis (Figs. 11-13 and 11-14). Muscle stripping is quite straightforward and usually successful.

Triceps Brachii

Referred pain to the elbow is caused especially by TPs in the medial head, which refer pain either to the lateral elbow from

the lateral side of this muscle or to the medial elbow from the medial side of this muscle, and in the anconeus, which refers pain to the lateral elbow (Fig. 11-15). Although TPs in the triceps occur less frequently than in the extensors or supinator muscles, the triceps TPs cause chronic elbow pain probably because these TPs are overlooked.

Patients show a tendency to carry the elbow slightly flexed out of the painful range of motion. Ischemic compression and muscle stripping are easily accomplished for this muscle, as is spray and stretch technique.

Wrist and Hand Pain

The most frequent cause of wrist and hand pain is myofascial referral from the forearm flexors and especially from the forearm extensors. Pain is referred variously to the wrist, hand, and fingers, depending on which TPs are active. Tenderness may also be referred to the wrist, leading to a misdiagnosis of tendinitis at the wrist. TPs in these muscles increase tendon tension and therefore relative compression of the carpal joints, which causes cracking and crepitus at the wrist due to abnormal joint glide. Patients often feel a sense of stiffness in the wrist and hand, making them believe that they have arthritis. Pain is elicited from extensor TPs when the wrist and fingers are flexed, which stretches these muscles, and on full wrist extension, which creates a shortening reaction in these muscles. Resisted testing reproduces pain, as does a firm grip (eg, a handshake). When pain is referred into the proximal interphalangeal joints by the digital flexors it is often accompanied by tenderness around the joints themselves, and patients describe the joint as feeling swollen even though there is no evidence of swelling. TPs in the forearm extensors are easily activated by TPs in the scalenes and infraspinatus.

Chronic strain in the extensor muscles is palpable as a ''nubbly'' feeling in the fascia surrounding the belly of these muscles. Muscle stripping should be applied to these muscles

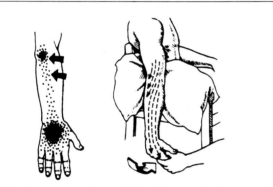

Figure 11-13 Extensores carpi radialis TPs. The *curved white arrow* identifies the direction(s) of pressure applied to stretch the muscle. See Fig. 11-2 for explanation of the other patterns. *Source:* Reprinted from *Medical Rehabilitation* (p316) by JV Basmajian and RL Kirby with permission of Williams & Wilkins Company, © 1984.

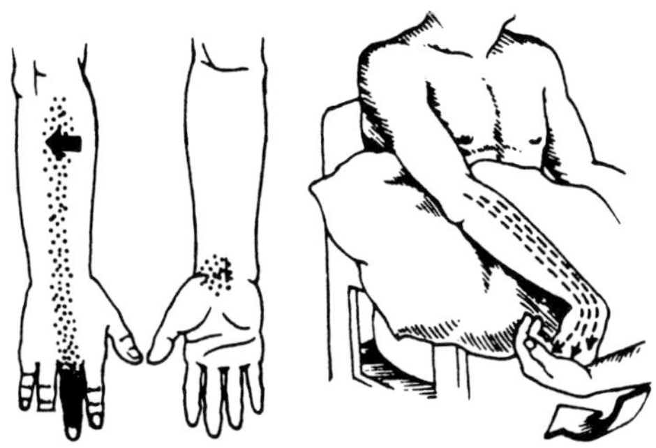

Figure 11-14 Middle finger extensor TPs. The *curved white arrow* identifies the direction(s) of pressure applied to stretch the muscle. See Fig. 11-2 for explanation of the other patterns. *Source:* Reprinted from *Medical Rehabilitation* (p316) by JV Basmajian and RL Kirby with permission of Williams & Wilkins Company, © 1984.

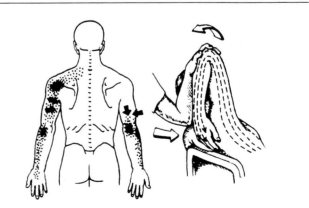

Figure 11-15 Triceps TPs. The *curved white arrow* identifies the direction(s) of pressure applied to stretch the muscle. See Fig. 11-2 for explanation of patterns. *Source:* Reprinted from *Medical Rehabilitation* (p316) by JV Basmajian and RL Kirby with permission of Williams & Wilkins Company, © 1984.

to help eliminate the many small adhesions that are present (Figs. 11-16 and 11-17).

PAIN SYNDROMES OF THE LOWER LIMBS

Hip Pain

Pain is referred into the hip from the following muscles: quadratus lumborum, piriformis, gluteus minimus, and adductor longus.

Quadratus Lumborum

This muscle is perhaps one of the most frequent causes of myofascial lower back, sacroiliac, and hip joint pain and also one of the most overlooked sources of pain (Fig. 11-18). TPs from the deeper parts of this muscle refer pain to the sacroiliac joint and deep into the lower buttock; the more superficial TPs refer pain to the lateral ilium and greater trochanter and may also refer pain into the groin in the region of the inguinal ligament. Attempted compression of the ipsilateral sacroiliac joint will elicit pain and/or tenderness.

Deep tenderness in the buttock and trochanteric region is sometimes misdiagnosed as trochanteric bursitis. Satellite TPs

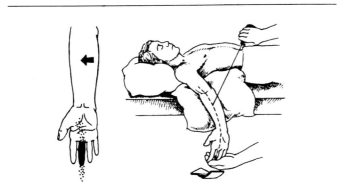

Figure 11-16 Middle finger flexor TPs. The *curved white arrow* identifies the direction(s) of pressure applied to stretch the muscle. See Fig. 11-2 for explanation of the other patterns. *Source:* Reprinted from *Medical Rehabilitation* (p317) by JV Basmajian and RL Kirby with permission of Williams & Wilkins Company, © 1984.

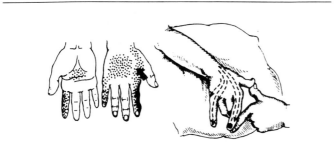

Figure 11-17 First dorsal interosseous TPs. See Fig. 11-2 for explanation of patterns. *Source:* Reprinted from *Medical Rehabilitation* (p317) by JV Basmajian and RL Kirby with permission of Williams & Wilkins Company, © 1984.

Figure 11-18 Quadratus lumborum TPs. The *curved white arrow* identifies the direction(s) of pressure applied to stretch the muscle. See Fig. 11-2 for explanation of the other patterns. *Source:* Reprinted from *Medical Rehabilitation* (p317) by JV Basmajian and RL Kirby with permission of Williams & Wilkins Company, © 1984.

in the posterior gluteus minimus may be activated secondarily and refer pain down the leg in a sciatic-like pattern. This produces a composite pain pattern that may confuse the diagnostician. Acute episodes of pain will produce a contralateral flexion antalgia and painfully restrict lumbar range of motion. Hip joint movements are restricted by lumbar spasm (eg, restricted SLR). Apart from the trochanteric and buttock tenderness, the hip itself is otherwise functionally normal. TPs in this muscle are activated by a contralateral short leg or small hemipelvis, or a flexed innominate which forces the ipsilateral muscle to pull the trunk to the same side to compensate. This chronic overload easily activates these TPs.

Palpation of the quadratus lumborum is best accomplished with the patient in the sidelying posture with the arm abducted overhead to open the space between the iliac crest and the 12th rib. Treatment is best accomplished by using the spray and stretch technique, particularly when the muscle is inaccessible because of obesity. A tilted pelvic girdle is easily corrected with lifts, or with release or strengthening of appropriate muscles (ie, iliopsoas, hamstrings, gluteals, etc.).

Piriformis

The piriformis muscle primarily refers pain to the lateral buttocks, greater trochanter, and lateral sacrum. Again, referred tenderness may lead one to think of trochanteric bursitis. Active TPs restrict a combination of adduction and internal rotation, and the figure-of-four test may cause posterior buttock pain due to a shortening reaction of the muscle. Occasionally, these TPs will cause dyspareunia when the woman is in the so-called missionary position because of the shortening reaction cited above. Taut bands in this muscle may also entrap the peroneal part or all of the sciatic nerve. This may result in neurologic symptoms in the posterior lower limb.

The piriformis is most often involved in the short-leg side of a tilted pelvis as it strains to stabilize a rotated and tilted sacrum. Abnormal sacroiliac or lumbar spine mechanics may therefore perpetuate TPs in this muscle. Ischemic compression and the spray and stretch technique are both easily applied to this muscle (Fig. 11-19).

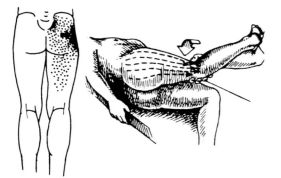

Figure 11-19 Piriformis TPs. The *curved white arrow* identifies the direction(s) of pressure applied to stretch the muscle. See Fig. 11-2 for explanation of the other patterns. *Source:* Reprinted from *Medical Rehabilitation* (p319) by JV Basmajian and RL Kirby with permission of Williams & Wilkins Company, © 1984.

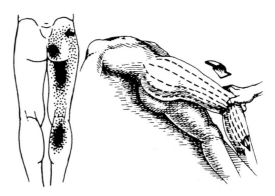

Figure 11-21 Gluteus minimus posterior TPs. The *curved white arrow* identifies the direction(s) of pressure applied to stretch the muscle. See Fig. 11-2 for explanation of the other patterns. *Source:* Reprinted from *Medical Rehabilitation* (p319) by JV Basmajian and RL Kirby with permission of Williams & Wilkins Company, © 1984.

Gluteus Minimus

Trigger points may be located in the posterior and anterior portions of this muscle (Figs. 11-20 and 11-21). Each TP has its own distinctive pain referral pattern. The posterior TP refers pain to the medial lower buttock and into the posterior thigh and calf. This is suggestive of an S-1 radiculopathy, which if present may perpetuate these TPs. These TPs also increase the tone in the hamstring and calf muscles, which shortens them. Stretching the gluteus minimus before hamstring and calf stretching allows these two muscles to lengthen much more readily.

The anterior TP refers strongly down the lateral thigh and may extend down to the lateral malleolus. It also refers to the lower buttock. This portion of the muscle strongly abducts the hip and elevates the contralateral pelvis during the swing phase of normal gait. A tilted pelvis that is lower on the contralateral side will therefore cause chronic overload strain on this muscle and perpetuate TP activity.

Adductor Longus

Trigger points in this muscle strongly refer to the anterior hip and proximal to the patella anteriorly. This pain pattern is strongly suggestive of hip joint arthritis, for which it may be mistaken. Pain is elicited on resisted strength testing and when the leg is put into the figure-of-four position (Fabere-Patrick test). There is marked restriction of hip abduction. Spray and stretch is the preferred treatment (Fig. 11-22). Muscle stripping in this muscle, although effective, is often too painful for the patient.

Knee Pain

The myofascial origins of knee pain are the vastus medialis and biceps femoris.

Vastus Medialis

This muscle refers pain deep to the patella; such pain is all too frequently misdiagnosed as chondromalacia patella. Pa-

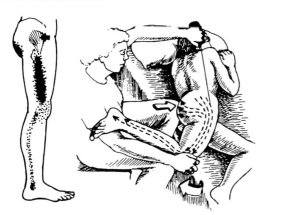

Figure 11-20 Gluteus minimus anterior TPs. The *curved white arrows* identify the direction(s) of pressure applied to stretch the muscle. See Fig. 11-2 for explanation of the other patterns. *Source:* Reprinted from *Medical Rehabilitation* (p319) by JV Basmajian and RL Kirby with permission of Williams & Wilkins Company, © 1984.

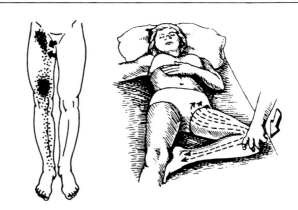

Figure 11-22 Adductor longus and brevis TPs. See Fig. 11-2 for explanation of patterns. *Source:* Reprinted from *Medical Rehabilitation* (p319) by JV Basmajian and RL Kirby with permission of Williams & Wilkins Company, © 1984.

tients complain of joint stiffness and loud cracking noises as the patella suddenly releases during knee flexion. The vastus medialis is an important stabilizer of the patella and by extension of the knee joint itself. It counters the lateral pull of the other three quadriceps muscles and ensures proper patellar tracking and therefore efficient use of the quadriceps during knee extension. Any valgus deviation of the knee, due for example to overpronation of the foot, will put additional strain on this muscle and perpetuate TP activity.

It is difficult to get adequate stretch on this muscle during spray and stretch technique unless the TPs are very active. Slow, deep stripping massage releases these TPs quite well (Fig. 11-23).

Biceps Femoris

Trigger points in this muscle refer pain and tenderness to the popliteal fossa. Pain is easily elicited on resisted testing and in fact may produce cramping. Unless the TP is very active, the stretch range of motion is not significantly reduced. Pain may be activated when the patient attempts to sit cross-legged as a result of compression of the TP. Patients may complain of hamstring cramping rather than referred pain.

The spray and stretch technique is an easy and effective method of deactivating these TPs (Fig. 11-24).

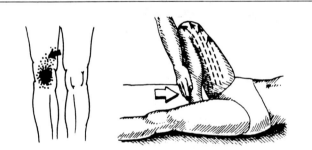

Figure 11-23 Vastus medialis TPs. See Fig. 11-2 for explanation of the patterns. *Source:* Reprinted from *Medical Rehabilitation* (p319) by JV Basmajian and RL Kirby with permission of Williams & Wilkins Company, © 1984.

Figure 11-24 Biceps femoris TPs. The *curved white arrow* identifies the direction(s) of pressure applied to stretch the muscle. See Fig. 11-2 for explanation of the patterns. *Source:* Reprinted from *Medical Rehabilitation* (p319) by JV Basmajian and RL Kirby with permission of Williams & Wilkins Company, © 1984.

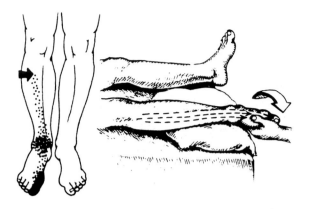

Figure 11-25 Tibialis anterior TPs. The *curved white arrow* identifies the direction(s) of pressure applied to stretch the muscle. See Fig. 11-2 for explanation of the other patterns. *Source:* Reprinted from *Medical Rehabilitation* (p320) by JV Basmajian and RL Kirby with permission of Williams & Wilkins Company, © 1984.

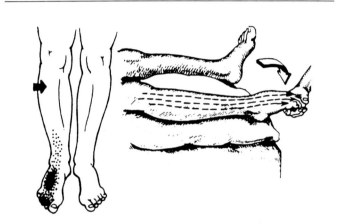

Figure 11-26 Extensors digitorum and hallucis longus TPs. The *curved white arrow* identifies the direction(s) of pressure applied to stretch the muscle. See Fig. 11-2 for explanation of the other patterns. *Source:* Reprinted from *Medical Rehabilitation* (p320) by JV Basmajian and RL Kirby with permission of Williams & Wilkins Company, © 1984.

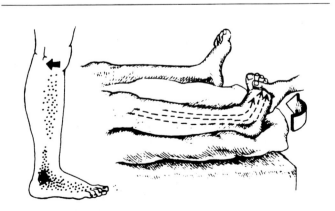

Figure 11-27 Peroneus longus and brevis TPs. The *curved white arrow* identifies the direction(s) of pressure applied to stretch the muscle. See Fig. 11-2 for explanation of the other patterns. *Source:* Reprinted from *Medical Rehabilitation* (p320) by JV Basmajian and RL Kirby with permission of Williams & Wilkins Company, © 1984.

Ankle and Foot Pain

When ankle or foot pain is the patient's complaint, TPs in the tibialis anterior, extensor digitorum, or peroneus longus muscle are the most likely causes. All three muscles are effectively treated by deep stripping massage.

Tibialis Anterior

Trigger points refer pain, tenderness, and stiffness deep into the anterior ankle and the great toe. These TPs are activated as a result of overpronation of the foot and excessive dorsiflexion, as when running uphill (Fig. 11-25).

Extensor Digitorum

Trigger points refer pain and tenderness over the dorsum of the foot and into the middle three toes. Tenderness in these areas will make an ill-fitting shoe uncomfortable, which is sometimes the patient's only complaint (Fig. 11-26).

Peroneus Longus

Peroneus longus TPs refer to just posterior to the lateral malleolus. This muscle is usually strained on inversion sprain injuries of the ankle and can therefore be the source of residual pain at the lateral ankle. TPs should be cleared promptly after an inversion sprain because this muscle is an important stabilizer of the ankle (Fig. 11-27).

TREATMENT-RESISTANT MYOFASCIAL PAIN SYNDROMES

John C. Lowe

Myofascial pain syndromes are quickly and dramatically relieved with myofascial therapy in most cases, even when the clinician is relatively inexperienced with this therapeutic approach. Some patients, however, respond poorly to the treatment regardless of the clinician's skill.

INCIDENCE OF TREATMENT-RESISTANT SYNDROMES

There are no statistics regarding the incidence of treatment-resistant myofascial pain cases. Prevalence studies in clinical populations have reported variable percentages of patients with myofascial pain. Wolfe[1] estimated that 6% to 15% of clinic patients had fibrositis, which can be interpreted as generalized myofascial pain syndromes with widespread and profound physiologic sequelae. Fricton[2] found that 55.4% of patients had myofascial pain of the masticatory muscles. He also reported that in a pain clinic 85% of patients had myofascial pain and in an internal medicine clinic nearly 30% of patients were reported to have myofascial pain.[2]

Fricton[2] also reported a prevalence study of a general, nonclinical population of people who had no obvious indications of joint or muscle problems. Examinations by palpation revealed that 26.7% of the total number of people had positive myofascial findings in the masticatory muscles. He estimated that possibly 50% of patients with myofascial pain have other conditions that may be involved in some interactive way with the myofascial pain syndromes.[2] Unless the other conditions or contributing factors are controlled or eliminated, they can render the patient resistant to specific myofascial therapy.

CONTRIBUTING FACTORS

Many factors can contribute to the patient's resistance to improvement. In some cases, there may be one significant factor. When it is controlled or eliminated, the patient will respond well to treatment. In other cases, multiple factors may interact to sustain the patient's pain syndromes. These may have to be pinpointed and defused one at a time before the pain will permanently cease.

Travell and Simons write, "In the absence of such factors, the muscle with fully inactivated trigger points (TPs) should be no more susceptile to TP activation than the normal muscle was originally."[3(p103)] In other words, by eliminating contributing factors and effectively treating the involved myofascia, the patient's pain syndrome should be no more likely to return than it would be to appear in someone who had never had the condition. The level of the patient's improvement is directly related to the potency of the inactivated contributing factors.

Travell and Simons[3(pp104–106)] and Lowe[4] have compiled lists of contributing factors. The following account is not all inclusive. It does, however, survey the conditions that this author has found to most commonly maintain resistance to myofascial therapy.

Chronic Muscle Overloading

Chronic or repetitive mild to moderate overloading of a myofascial tissue may induce sustained constrictions and TPs. Thus when treating a patient for a specific muscle syndrome, it is good strategy to explain the function of the involved muscle and to describe or demonstrate a few of the activities that might overload it. At that point, the patient may be able to identify an activity responsible for the syndrome. If not, the knowledge imparted about the role of the involved muscle may enable the patient to recognize the overloading activity when he or she performs it.

The targeted muscle may be sore after the first couple of treatments. This soreness is similar to what follows strenuous exercise and is a different quality from the pain of the myofascial syndrome. It can be diagnostically valuable. When the patient uses the sore muscle during day-to-day activities, his or her attention will be drawn to it. If the patient has been advised to look for activities that irritate the sore muscle, he or she will be likely to identify one or more actions that must be modified.

Gross Structural Distortions

Cailliet[5(p53)] writes that 75% of all postural low back pain can be attributed to an accentuated lumbar lordosis. Pain from a hyperlordosis can come from compression of the facet facings,[5(p56)] compression of the discs with increased intradisc pressure, or narrowing of the intervertebral foramina.[6(p500)] Hypertonicity of the lumbar paraspinal muscles can be induced by facet articular compression[5(p92)] or probably from any other spinal condition that generates noxious sensory bombardment of the spinal cord at that level. Hypertonicity can also develop from shortening of the myofascia to accommodate the abnormally close distance between the muscle's upper and lower attachments. When the muscle as a whole is chronically shortened, small foci of intense myofascial constrictions can develop in the muscle mass, and the constrictions can create or activate TPs.

Hyperkyphosis of the thoracic spine is likely to lead to myofascial pain syndromes of the thoracic erector spinae muscles. Thoracic hyperkyphosis can induce and maintain hypertonicity in the thoracic erectors in at least two ways and thereby bring about myofascial pain syndromes.

First, an accentuated thoracic kyphosis causes the head and neck to jut forward of the body's theoretic gravity line. This positions the patient's head out in front of the torso to some degree. The cervical and upper thoracic erectors are then required to "guy-wire" the head and neck in a position in space that allows at least minimally effective biomechanical and perceptual functions. This continual guy-wiring chronically overloads the thoracic myofascia. Such overloading can induce the pathophysiologic processes that create and sustain myofascial pain syndromes.

The second way in which a thoracic hyperkyphosis can cause troublesome hypertonicity is through the spinal degeneration that tends to accompany this accentuated curve. Lateral thoracic roentgenograms often show degenerative changes in the segments at or close to the apex of a thoracic hyperkyphosis. The biochemical or biomechanical changes involved in the spondylosis may reflexly generate hypertonicity of both the segmental and the longitudinal muscles. The myofascial constrictions function to minimize motions that might exacerbate the damage to the vulnerable degenerating segments. But these constrictions can become severe enough to critically impede blood flow, especially when compounded by the necessity of the myofascia to guy-wire the head and neck or when fatigue causes the patient to slouch into an even more severe thoracic hyperkyphosis.

Structural Imbalances

Many people have some degree of imbalanced body structure. Structural imbalance is an extremely common contributing factor to myofascial constrictions and TPs.[7(pp50-53)]

Evaluating posture and structural balance should be a part of the initial examination of a patient. Any errors in either should be corrected as soon as possible, preferably before starting specific myofascial therapy. This is especially important with myofascial pain syndromes of the neck, back, and lumbar muscles. Imbalanced axial structure tends to provoke chronic overloading of some of these muscles. This occurs in the patient's life both outside the clinician's office and inside it during treatment. If the patient is treated in a standing or sitting position, for example, the overloaded muscles may be unable to relax because of their activity in supporting the patient's erect posture. Most often the imbalance involves a short lower extremity, but it can involve what is variously called a small hemipelvis[3(p109)] or a unilaterally small innominate.[8(pp61-62)]

Vertebral Subluxations

Spinal joint fixations and their associated segmental neural alterations are directly related to hypertonicity of muscles innervated by the same spinal segments.[9] The hypertonicity can lead to such heightened intramuscular pressure in limited areas of the muscle that local circulation is impeded. TPs are likely to form or activate at these locations.

In patients with severe, chronic subluxations, the segmental muscles are likely to be engaged in myofascial pain syndromes with active TPs. The phenomenon, however, may also affect myofascial tissues as distant from the spine as the upper and lower extremities. Some pilot studies suggest that relieving cervical spinal joint fixations reduces TP sensitivity in the levator[10] and infraspinatus muscles.[11] This effect probably is based on the manipulative therapy altering spinal cord reflexes, thereby diminishing motor nerve output. This reduces excess tone in the muscle fibers that are a part of the motor unit derived from the manipulated segment of the spine.[12]

Spinal Pathology

A number of spinal pathologies can give rise to myofascial pain syndromes through somatosomatic reflexes. These reflexes can be generated by osteochondrosis, degenerative joint disease, osteoporosis, uncinate spurs, rheumatoid arthritis, discogenic spondylosis, and congenital block vertebra.[4]

According to principle, low levels of sensory input through the recurrent meningeal nerve[13] to the cord from lesioned spinal tissues generate hypertonicity of the anatomically related deep segmental muscles. As the duration or intensity of the sensory signals from the lesioned area increases, the more superficial longitudinal erector muscles are likely to become involved.[8(p58)]

When only the segmental muscles are involved, the spinal level to which they are responding can be rather precisely localized. Deep palpation immediately to the left or right of the spinous processes will elicit a deep tenderness or referred pain (or both). On the other hand, when the sensory output from the lesioned tissue is severe enough to stimulate the more superficial longitudinal erector spinae muscles, the segmental level may be less precisely related to the myofascial constrictions and TPs. TPs can be detected in these muscles through palpation, but the segmental relation to the spinal cord may be obscured. These larger erector muscles receive their motor nerve supply from various spinal cord segments both above and below the level where the sensory signals from the lesioned tissues enter the cord. The resulting hypertonicity may therefore span numerous spinal levels. Locating constrictions and TPs in these longitudinal muscles, then, may not direct the examiner precisely to the lesioned spinal level. Diagnostic methods other than palpation are necessary to show the relation of the myofascial involvement to the spinal pathology.

Postural Habits

Two other spinal conditions that are important as contributing factors are chronic cervical hyperextension and excess lumbosacral facet approximation.

The referral patterns for the suboccipital muscles are commonly reported by people who are shorter or taller than average, especially women. These people most often complain of pain in the area of the forehead. They typically attribute it to sinusitis and have taken sinus medication with no benefit except for a weak placebo effect. Many of them have submitted to useless allergy testing and desensitization shots. When the clinician palpates the supine patient's occipital and suboccipital muscles, extremely tender spots are easily found. Compression of these points for 10 to 15 seconds is likely to provoke pain over the forehead.

The contributing factor in many of these cases is hyperextension of the cervical spine and the occiput on the upper cervical spine. A short person tends to spend too much time looking up at most other people. He or she also tends to raise the eyes higher while driving by slightly hyperextending the neck and head and looking down the nose over the dashboard and hood of the car. All this keeps the posterior and upper cervical muscles shortened, and this creates and sustains heightened intramuscular pressure. The pressure may stay right on the threshold of collapsing the muscles' blood and lymph vessels. When these muscles tighten further for any reason, the pressure will cause ischemia and pain. Even emotional arousal, because it produces generalized muscular hypertonicity, may push the intramuscular pressure over the critical point and induce pain.

Tall people have a similar myofascial problem. In their case, though, it appears that they are attempting to shorten themselves by accentuating all their anteroposterior spinal curves (the cervical lordosis being one of these). Even though these people are exaggerating their spinal curves in the lumbar, thoracic, and cervical areas, the posterior cervical muscles are more likely to develop pain syndromes. These muscles are more susceptible because the neck and head muscles have smaller diameters and are therefore more sensitive to pressure and more prone to injury.[14]

Patients with referred pain from L5–S1 TPs are fairly common. Their main and often only complaint is pain across the low back close to the lumbosacral junction. The pain is often bilateral and severe enough to be debilitating. A neutral lateral lumbosacral roentgenogram usually shows excess lumbosacral facet approximation, or facet joint jamming. The L-5 disc may look severely wedged posteriorly. Many of these patients are large framed and poorly conditioned. They carry more torso weight than their spinal supporting tissues can tolerate. Some, for instance, are former football players who have put on weight from sedentary jobs. It appears that the patient's upper torso compresses the L5–S1 posterior articulations, and this gives rise to sustained, intense segmental hypermyotonia to protectively minimize movement of the compressed facet joint facings.[4] Oblique lumbosacral x-ray views may show early degenerative changes such as sclerosis of the facet articular surfaces.

Nutrition Insufficiencies

Even borderline inadequacies of certain nutrients create neural hyperexcitability that induces and sustains hypermyotonia. Some inadequacies impair the energy metabolism in muscle cells. Assuming that the patient is free from malabsorption syndromes, most of the neuromuscular effects of nutrition inadequacies and deficiencies can quickly be relieved with a vitamin B complex formulation.

Low vitamin C intake makes patients highly prone to bruising from soft tissue manipulation. Patients with myofascial pain syndromes should be encouraged to begin vitamin C supplementation immediately. Otherwise, they are likely to experience extreme soreness the day after being treated with soft tissue techniques.

Some patients' constricted myofascia quickly deteriorates into dystrophic tissue.[3(p35)] The author suggested that this occurs most readily in patients with inadequate intakes of antioxidant nutrients. Among other functions these nutrients stabilize muscle cell membranes, including lysosomal membranes. When these membranes are friable from inadequate antioxidant protection (resulting in membranous peroxidation), the pathophysiologic processes occurring in the constricted myofascia may easily disrupt the membranes so that the muscle's cells deteriorate and are replaced with fibrous or dystrophic tissue.

Once dystrophy has occurred, localized myofascial tension is more tenacious and can render the involved tissues highly resistant to treatment. After determining that the lesion is indeed muscular,[15] cross-friction techniques may then be necessary for therapeutic improvement.[16]

Hematologic Problems

Marginal anemia from deficiencies in vitamins B_{12} and B_6 and folic acid may increase susceptibility to TP irritability, along with other symptoms. A vitamin B_{12} inadequacy may leave a patient easily fatigued and depressed.[3(p128)] A vitamin B_6 inadequacy may cause weakness, insomnia, irritability, and nervousness.[3(p122)] A folic acid inadequacy, like a vitamin B_{12} inadequacy, may cause a patient to fatigue easily and to be depressed; in addition, a folic acid inadequacy may cause the patient to sleep poorly and to feel cold, as though he or she has hypothyroidism.[3(p132)]

All these effects, along with myofascial pain, may result from marginal anemia with a low hemoglobin or red blood cell count. When the red blood cell or hemoglobin count is low too little oxygen may be delivered to muscle cells, which can impair muscle energy metabolism. The impaired energy production can manifest as muscle weakness. This can lead to a slumping posture that strains paraspinal myofascia and activates its latent TPs. The patient is especially prone to this when the slumping posture is superimposed on biomechanical faults such as a thoracic hyperkyphosis. The relative lack of myofascial movement because of fatigue and weakness causes tissue fluids to stagnate, enabling metabolic wastes to excite types $A\delta$ and C sensory receptors. This can produce a noxious sensory assault on the central nervous system that is reflected as severely active TPs.

Anemia is especially likely to occur in patients who do not take a multivitamin and mineral supplement, in pregnant women, and in those who have heavy menstrual periods. Patients who take the anti-inflammatory drugs prednisone and naprosyn may also be anemic. Prednisone can induce peptic ulcers with resultant perforation and hemorrhage.[17(p1522)] As this process begins and proceeds, anemia may develop and become severe. Naprosyn can impair platelet aggregation and prolong bleeding time.[17(p2201)] This can cause significant blood loss through various routes in the body and leave the patient anemic.

Elderly patients are particularly at risk when under medical care. The physician may have the patient taking a drug that prolongs bleeding (eg, naprosyn) and an anticoagulant drug at the same time. These two may have a lethal net effect. At minimum, the combination may induce anemia and, in turn, secondary myofascial pain syndromes that are treatment resistant.

Metabolic and Endocrine Disorders

Hypothyroidism, even when marginal, can produce a generalized, severe neuromuscular hyperirritability and in doing so can severely amplify or perpetuate myofascial pain. T3 and T4, the two thyroid hormones, appear to affect directly the production of ATP inside the mitochondria. ATP is the primary source of energy for muscle contraction and relaxation. When the T3 or T4 levels rise, the mitochondria in most cells increase in size and number and produce significantly increased amounts of ATP.[18] When the T3 and T4 levels drop, the reverse may occur: decreased size and number of mitochondria and a decrease in their output of ATP. This can give rise to energy-deficient contractures and TPs that are violently

irritable and thoroughly recalcitrant to treatment. When the hypothyroidism is relieved, the TP irritability responds dramatically to specific myofascial treatment.

Hypoglycemia is particularly troublesome for patients with myofascial pain syndromes. During a hypoglycemic episode, specific myofascial therapy will barely decrease TP sensitivity, fail to affect it, or actually increase it. The pain may, however, completely subside within 20 minutes after the patient eats.

The two classifications of hypoglycemia are fasting and postprandial or reactive. The symptoms are the same. At first, the patient may tremble and shake, sweat, and experience tachycardia and anxiety. If the episode progresses and insufficient energy is available to the brain, the patient may experience restlessness, visual disturbances, impaired speech and thinking, and may pass out. Some patients will have no symptoms other than severe, debilitating myofascial pain, usually referred to the neck or head.

If hypoglycemia is suspected, the patient should be asked whether in the past similar pain or other unpleasant symptoms have been relieved shortly after eating. If the answer is yes, the patient should eat some bread, a banana, or some similar food. This may cause the pain to subside dramatically within 20 to 30 minutes. While the patient is waiting for the time to elapse, distracting stimulation such as a TENS unit or moist heat may make him or her more comfortable. Some patients, however, are unable to sit or lie still during the episode and may be more comfortable moving about.

Adverse Drug Reactions

The patient with asthma, emphysema, or asthmatic bronchitis who is taking xanthine drugs such as theophylline or aminophylline may find that persistent myofascial pain can be relieved by reducing the blood level of these drugs. Other xanthines include caffeine, which is contained in coffee, tea, soft drinks, and various drug preparations, and theobromine, which is an ingredient in chocolate. Travell and Simons[3(p90)] point out that a moderate amount of caffeine often reduces TP pain, possibly by causing vasodilation in the skeletal muscles, but that excess caffeine increases muscle tension and TP irritability. Caffeine and the other xanthines produce this effect by stimulating the adrenal glands to release epinephrine and norepinephrine.

The synthetic estrogen compound ethinyl estradiol can cause hypoglycemia.[17(p1974)] This compound is in some birth control pills and is prescribed in an extremely potent form called Estinyl to stimulate the build-up of the endometrium of the uterus. The drug can induce migraine headaches and severe myofascial pain, probably because of its hypoglycemic effect. Birth control pills have a lower content of ethinyl estradiol, but some women may be extremely sensitive to it and experience headaches referred from neck and head TPs.

Ephedrine and its isomer pseudoephedrine are drugs used in some over-the-counter medicines such as nasal vasoconstrictors or decongestants for hay fever and cold symptoms. Their effects are similar to those of epinephrine but less potent and more prolonged.[19(p90)] These agents do not act directly on effector cells. They do, however, stimulate the release of epineprine and norepinephrine and can intensify and prolong the effects of catecholamines previously released by the adrenal medulla.[19(p88)]

Phenylpropanolamine is also used in over-the-counter nasal decongestants as well as in sleep aids and appetite suppressants. Its effects are similar to those of ephedrine and pseudoephedrine. These agents are all sympathomimetics; that is, because these agents stimulate the release of epinephrine and norepinephrine and intensify and prolong their actions, the body is put in an emergency state. Anxiety, tremulousness, heart palpitation, and insomnia are common, depending on the amount taken and individual sensitivity. As part of the sympathomimetic effect of these agents, skeletal muscles are stimulated. Myotonia is increased, and this heightens intramuscular pressure. This can activate TPs at various locations in the body, depending on how close to threshold the TPs are.

Phenylpropanolamine and other similar drug agents are especially problematic because they are ingredients in decongestants. Many patients with myofascial pain referred to the forehead take sinus medications to control the imagined or misdiagnosed sinusitis. The drugs may only exacerbate the myofascial pain syndrome by heightening intramuscular pressure and speeding the rate of nerve conduction.

Benzodiazepines such as Valium, Atavan, and Xanax are often prescribed to help patients sleep. They do induce restful and restorative sleep, but when a patient tries to stop the drug he or she is likely to experience what is known as the rebound phenomenon: the patient will not be able to sleep well without the drug.[20] The patient may also experience anxiety and other symptoms, suggesting that the benzodiazepine has sensitized the sympathetic system. The sympathetic sensitization and the fatigue from insomnia may stimulate multiple myofascial pain syndromes through neuromuscular hyperirritability.

Adrenocortical steroids increase the vulnerability of myofascial tissues to acute and chronic overloading. These steroids are usually prescribed as prednisone and are listed by collagen investigators among agents that are known connective tissue disruptors. They block collagen cross-linking, interfere with collagen synthesis, and alter the ratio of constituents of connective tissue matrices. People who take these for various periods of time will have a watery, jellylike quality to their myofascial tissues, much like tissues of people deconditioned through inadequate resistance exercises. People who do not work out lack the thicker, stronger fascia of people who do. Thin, weak fascia is more vulnerable to injury from minor mechanical stresses. Weak muscles can be damaged easily and their SR ruptured. This may lead to prolonged contraction that sustains TP activity.

The person taking prednisone has the same predisposition. The relatively thin and weak fascia is poor protection for muscle cells, so the patient is more likely to experience treatment-resistant myofascial syndromes.

Impaired Sleep

Sympathomimetic drugs can create insomnia or light, nonrestorative sleep. This leaves the patient fatigued and too weak to resist gravitational pull on the body. The resulting slumping posture can impede circulation and irritate joints and their soft tissue supports. Both these consequences can create or worsen myofascial pain syndromes.

It is important to note also that myofascial pain is a powerful noxious stimulus and can cause as well as result from impaired sleep. Alleviating myofascial constrictions and pain, therefore, can have a profound sleep-inducing effect.

Psychologic Factors

Mental stress heightens the tone of skeletal muscles[21(p6-15)] and can activate TPs that are close to threshold. Overly conscientious people appear to be particularly susceptible to this effect.

CONCLUSION

One contributing factor or a combination of several can render a patient's myofascial pain syndromes resistant to treatment. Relieving the patient's pain and dysfunction depends on the clinician's skill at identifying these factors and helping the patient eliminate or control them.

REFERENCES

Myofascial Trigger Points

1. Travell J, Rinzler SH. The myofascial genesis of pain. *Postgrad Med.* 1952;11:425–434.

2. Travell J, Simons D. *Myofascial Pain and Dysfunction: The Trigger Point Manual.* Baltimore: Williams & Wilkins; 1983.

3. Mense S. Nervous outflow from skeletal muscle following chemical noxious stimulation. *J Physiol.* 1977;267:75–88.

4. Perl ER. Sensitization of nociceptors and its relation to sensation. *Adv Pain Res Ther.* 1976:1–29.

5. Kniffki K-D, Mense S, Schmidt RF. Responses of group IV afferent units from skeletal muscle to stretch, contraction and chemical stimulation. *Exp Brain Res.* 1978;31:511–522.

6. Awad EA. Interstitial myofibrositis: hypothesis of the mechanism. *Arch Phys Med.* 1979;54:449–453.

7. Travell J. Introductory comments. In: Ragan C, ed. *Connective Tissues: Transactions of the Fifth Conference.* New York: Josiah Macy, Jr Foundation; 1954:12–22.

8. Bengtsson A, Henriksson K-G, Larsson J. Reduced high-energy phosphate levels in painful muscle in patients with primary fibromyalgia. *Arthritis Rheum.* 1986;29:817–821.

9. Fassbender HG. *Pathology of Rheumatic Diseases.* New York: Springer-Verlag; 1975.

10. Kalyan-Raman UP, Kalyan-Raman K, Yurus MB, Masi AT. Muscle pathology in primary fibromyalgia syndrome: a light microscopic, histochemical and ultrastructural study. *J Rheumatol.* 1984;2:808–813.

11. Popelianskii L, Zaslavskii ES, Veselovskii VD. Medicosocial significance, etiology, pathogenesis, and diagnosis of nonarticular disease of soft tissues of the limbs and back [in Russian]. *Vopr Revm.* 1976;3:38–43.

12. Melzak R, Wall PD. Pain mechanics: new theory. *Science.* 1965;150:971–979.

13. Melzak R. Prolonged relief of pain by brief, intense transcutaneous somatic stimulation. *Pain.* 1975;1:357–373.

14. Fox EJ, Melzack R. Transcutaneous electrical stimulation and acupuncture: comparison of the treatment for low-back pain. *Pain.* 1976;2:141–148.

15. Kraus H. The use of surface anesthesia in the treatment of painful motion. *JAMA.* 1941;16:2582–2583.

16. Nielson AJ. As cited in Travell J, Simmons D. *Myofascial Pain and Dysfunction: The Trigger Point Manual.* Baltimore: Williams & Wilkins; 1983:349.

17. Basmajian JV. *Muscles Alive.* 4th ed. Baltimore: Williams & Wilkins; 1978.

18. Annexton M. Arthrography can help "frozen shoulder." *JAMA.* 1979;241:875.

19. Bateman JE. *The Shoulder and the Neck.* Philadelphia: WB Saunders; 1972:134.

20. Kopell HP, Thompson WAL. Pain and the frozen shoulder. *Surg Gynecol Obstet.* 1959;109:95–96.

21. Cyriax J. *Textbook of Orthopaedic Medicine.* Baltimore: Williams & Wilkins; 1969.

Treatment-Resistant Myofascial Pain Syndromes

1. Wolfe F. The clinical syndrome of fibrositis. *Am J Med.* 1986;81:7.

2. Fricton JR. Epidemiology of myofascial pain syndromes. Presented at the First International Symposium on Myofascial Pain and Fibromyalgia; May 8, 1989; Minneapolis, Minn.

3. Travell JG, Simons DG. *Myofascial Pain and Dysfunction: The Trigger Point Manual.* Baltimore: Williams & Wilkins; 1983.

4. Lowe JC. *The Purpose and Practice of Myofascial Therapy* [audio album and treatment room manual]. Houston: McDowell Publishing Co; 1989.

5. Cailliet R. *Low Back Pain Syndrome.* 3rd ed. Philadelphia: Davis; 1968.

6. Shafer RC. *Clinical Biomechanics.* 2nd ed. Baltimore: Williams & Wilkins; 1987.

7. Lowe JC. *Spasm.* Houston: McDowell Publishing Co; 1983.

8. Homewood AE. *Neurodynamics of the Vertebral Subluxation.* St Petersburg, Fla: Valkyrie; 1977.

9. Triano JJ. The use of instrumentation and laboratory procedures by the chiropractor. In: Haldeman S, ed. *Modern Developments in the Principles and Practice of Chiropractic.* New York: Appleton-Century-Crofts; 1980:246.

10. Vernon HT. Pressure pain threshold evaluation of the effect of spinal manipulation on chronic neck pain: a single case study. *J Can Chirop Assoc.* 1988;32:191–194.

11. Lowe JC. A pilot study of the effect of cervical spinal manipulation on the sensitivity of infraspinatus trigger points. Unpublished data.

12. Cole WV. Experimental evidence. In: Hoag JM, Cole WV, Bradford SG, eds. *Osteopathic Medicine.* New York: McGraw-Hill; 1969:112.

13. Lowe JC, Wirt N, Smith CY. The recurrent meningeal nerve: its anatomy and some of its clinical aspects. *TCC Rev.* 1979;5:13–16.

14. Schiffman E, Fricton J, Haley D, Tylka D. A pressure algometer for myofascial pain syndromes: reliability and validity testing. In: *Proceedings of the Fifth World Congress on Pain;* 1988:412.

15. Hammer W. Inert versus contractile. *Dyn Chirop.* 1989;7:14.

16. Hammer W. Tidbits on soft tissue. *Dyn Chirop.* 1989;7:34.

17. *Physician's Desk Reference.* Oradell, NJ: Medical Economics Company; 1982:1522, 1974, 2201.

18. Sterling K. Thyroid hormone action at the cell level. *N Engl J Med.* 1979;300:173–177.

19. Meyers FH, Jawetz E, Goldfein A. *Review of Medical Pharmacology.* 4th ed. Los Altos, Tex: Lange Medical; 1974.

20. Clark G, Fossgreen J, Moldofsky H, Merskey H. Panel discussion on etiologic mechanisms of muscular pain. Conducted at the First International Symposium on Myofascial Pain and Fibromyalgia; May 9, 1989; Minneapolis, Minn.

21. Jacobson E. *Progressive Relaxation.* Chicago: University of Chicago Press; 1974.

Chapter 12

Friction Massage

Warren I. Hammer

Perhaps the most valuable of all the modalities, electric and otherwise, for the treatment of pathology caused by chronic overuse soft tissue syndromes is friction massage. Although not yet demonstrated by any adequately controlled histologic studies,[1] friction massage represents another excellent empiric method of healing that has stood the test of time. This particular method of massage was discussed in the 1940s by Mennell[2] and was clinically described as Cyriax's deep massage and manipulation.[3,4]

Practitioners are often impressed with the latest "scientific breakthrough" modality, or they may regard friction massage as a simplistic, time-consuming method. The method is far from being simplistic because it requires a functional examination to find the location of the source of the pain. Again, as emphasized in the preceding chapters, a tender area is not necessarily the source of the pain. Practitioners who do not "touch all the bases" before determining where they should put their finger often become frustrated with poor results. Even after they "touch all the bases," their technique may be faulty or their knowlege of the exact location and direction of the tissue to be treated may be inadequate.

As explained in Chapter 2, which discusses the pathology of soft tissue, the biologic healing of soft tissue injury in muscle, tendon, and ligament is similar. When soft tissue is stressed beyond its biomechanical yield strength (for example, when a tendon is stretched more than 4% of its resting length[5]), microtearing must occur. The normal response to microtearing of collagen is inflammation. If the initial inflammation is rested and allowed to heal, a normal scar along the normal lines of stress will result. If excessive overuse or immobilization occurs increased fibrous scar tissue will result, which may spread and become tethered to surrounding normal tissue. Increased fibrous tissue results in a loss of mobility and extensibility of the tissue. Loss of extensibility means loss of function. Loss of function results in reaggravation of the tissue during normal use and a vicious cycle of microtearing-inflammation-scarring. The scar itself may become a source of nociceptive stimulation.[6]

Because friction massage involves pressure and movement directed across the scar tissue, most of the theories as to why friction works are based on theories concerning the effect of motion on healing tissue. It is well accepted today that early motion of injured tissue results in repair with reduced scar tissue formation.[7–9] In the early stages of healing, scar tissue is not as strong as in later stages, and it is thought that the remodeling phase of the inflammatory response depends on mechanical stimuli. Forrester et al[10] state that the tension required to create the preferential direction of the collagen molecules in the fibers is similar to the behavior of bone as explained by Wolff's law. Munro et al[11] state that synthesis of collagen and mucopolysaccharides is an interdependent process and that trauma to the tendon induces new collagen synthesis.

Cyriax[4] mentioned transverse motion across the involved tissue and the resultant traumatic hyperemia as the chief healing factors of friction massage. He held that moving across the fibers at a right angle would not injure the normal healing tissue but would prevent the formation of or break down abnormal scar tissue. He stated that transverse friction moved the involved tissue while longitudinal friction affected the transportation of blood and lymph. Traumatic hyperemia may add to the local damage with subsequent release of bradykinin and histamine, resulting in vasodilation and reduction in edema.

In the acute stage of an early lesion collagen is immature, and during the first 4 days fibroblasts are laying down a gel-like substance.[5] It takes up to 2 weeks for mature cross-links to form.[5,12] In the early stages of an acute lesion it is reasonable to use only a light friction pressure. In the chronic stages a deep, stronger friction is necessary. Light friction in the acute stage is primarily used to aid in the promotion of normal orientation of collagen, to maintain the mobility of the tissue, and thereby to prevent future adhesions. Cyriax[4] recommends immediate treatment of ligamentous lesions, for example lesions of the medial collateral ligament,[4] to prevent adhesions, which represent the most common side effect of ligamentous sprains. In such a lesion, because the knee is usually unable to move beneath the ligament, friction creates movement by moving the ligament on the bone.

Cyriax[4] states that muscle bellies should be frictioned in the relaxed position to create the same muscle broadening that occurs when a muscle contracts. Tendons may be frictioned with minimal tensile tension, and tendons with a sheath should be stretched during treatment to roll the sheath over the tendon.

Mennell[13] confirms that acute tendinitis is a clear entity that is diagnostically distinguishable from an irritable muscle trigger point. He states that a tendinitis will elicit a palpable tenderness that will be painful on resisted testing. A trigger point may elicit a "jump sign" and will usually refer pain in a specific pattern. Friction over a trigger point may create exquisite pain. Friction may be useful after the trigger point is reduced to eliminate the taut fascia that can be the underlying promoter of the trigger point.

FRICTION ANESTHESIA

One of the most interesting effects of friction massage is the creation of anesthesia. On the basis of the gate theory of pain,[14,15] stimulation of the large fiber mechanoreceptors will cause presynaptic inhibition at the spinal cord, preventing the small-diameter (slower) fibers from reaching consciousness. The possibility of pain inhibition from central neurotransmission also exists. Usually within 3 minutes of friction, anesthesia begins.

Friction anesthesia can be used as a noninvasive method of gaining information to determine the source of the pain. For example, if passive shoulder horizontal adduction creates pain at the acromioclavicular joint and at the infraspinatus, and if resisted testing of the infraspinatus causes minimal pain at the infraspinatus, frictioning the acromioclavicular joint until it becomes numb could help us determine whether the joint or the infraspinatus was the principal lesion site. Retesting horizontal adduction and retesting the infraspinatus may now result in diminished pain, thereby incriminating the joint, or it may result in the same pain, thereby incriminating the infraspinatus. Numbing an area of pain that was previously sensitive on isometric testing and is much less sensitive after friction on postisometric testing also provides good feedback to both the practitioner and the patient. It affirms that we are dealing with the probable source of the pain.

Friction anesthesia can also be used to help distinguish between a partial and a complete tear of a tendon. For example, if a patient cannot actively abduct the arm more than 35° and shows weakness on resisted abduction, after the application of friction to the supraspinatus and the creation of numbness the patient may be able to abduct the arm to 135°. This may be evidence that a partial rather than a complete tear exists.

It appears that, as patients respond to friction massage, on subsequent visits the time required for anesthesia to occur lessens. Moderate to severely inflamed tissues (bursae) will not anesthetize under friction. (See contraindications below.)

FRICTION TECHNIQUE

After the involved muscle, tendon, or ligament is located by functional testing, the practitioner should use a reinforced finger (ie, middle finger over forefinger) that is just large enough to friction completely across the tendon and not just on the periphery or center of the tendon. At times, for example with a plantar fasciitis, plica, or patellar ligament lesion, a T bar with a rubber tip may be used. The belly of a muscle is treated in a relaxed, flexed position. The practitioner grasps the tender area with the flexed fingers of one or both hands together and pulls the contacted muscle. The contact is held without sliding the fingers along the skin as the practitioner attempts to broaden the muscle.

The skin should be dry (creams should not be used), and it is extremely important that during friction the skin of the practitioner and the skin of the patient move as one. Otherwise, bruising will occur. The principal element in friction is to go across the tissue with as much pressure as the patient can tolerate.

By making use of friction anesthesia, the practitioner should be able to keep the patient comfortable during the procedure. Pressure without friction is not effective. If the tissue to be frictioned is extremely sensitive, we can make use of friction anesthesia to reach deeper tissue. Frictioning begins lightly until a level of anesthesia begins; then the pressure is increased until a deeper level of anesthesia is reached. With this method it should be possible to arrive at the deepest tissue level within a few visits.

POSTFRICTION EXERCISE

When dealing with muscle belly tears, friction is actually providing exercise to the tissue. Only painless active contraction or painless passive motion may be allowed. In the early stages, stretching may aggravate a lesion.

After friction, tendons should only be exercised (ie, passively stretched) if there is minimal discomfort and no pain. Active and passive full range of motion exercises should always follow friction treatment if the patient can carry out the movement with minimal pain. Later in the healing phase, isometric, rubber tubing, and isotonic exercises are important.

TREATMENT TIME

A minimum of 10 minutes is usually required. Depending on the thickness of the scar and the length of time for which the problem has existed, up to 20 minutes may (rarely) be required. It often helps to precede friction with 5 minutes of ultrasound.

NUMBER OF TREATMENTS

If frictioning aggravates the condition or if the patient does not numb within 3 to 5 minutes, it is possible that the tissue will not respond to this type of treatment. Three unsuccessful treatments are usually sufficient to contraindicate further use of friction (see below, Contraindications). The practitioner may have to suspend the friction technique until the inflammation subsides.

Most overuse conditions respond within 2 weeks to 2 months. Patients should be scheduled about 3 times per week with a day in between. If the lesion is found on resisted testing, patients are made to realize that they will be dismissed when they can perform resisted testing 10 times in a row without pain before a treatment.

CONTRAINDICATIONS

Acutely inflamed tissue, hematomas, calcifications, and peripheral nerves should not be directly frictioned. Contrary to current thought, satisfying results can be obtained in chronic bursitis of the shoulder and hip. Shoulder bursitis is usually secondary to chronic tendinitis and will respond. The bursa is usually fibrosed and minimally inflamed.

Patients with chronic bursitis should be told in advance that it is possible that they will feel slightly more irritation after the first three visits. This type of case does not always anesthetize in the early stages. Of course, friction must be combined with examination of all the static and dynamic factors related to the problem area as well as with rehabilitation (including flexibility and strengthening).

ILLUSTRATIONS AND PROCEDURES

Figures 12-1 through 12-44 attempt to depict the exact location where friction massage should be applied. The arrows express the direction of friction. It is absolutely necessary that the practitioner review anatomic palpation to perform accurate friction; the text by Hoppenfeld[16] is recommended. The treatment locations are the most common areas of involvement, but it must be remembered that asymmetry in the human body is normal. Origins and insertions of muscles and ligaments are not necessarily exactly where our anatomy textbooks say they are. Sometimes the resisted test may lead us to an area of tenderness slightly off the usual site of pain. Frictioning of these "unusual" areas may be required. Most of the typical muscle areas are shown, but it must be realized that friction can be applied to any muscle, ligament, or tendon that is subject to strain and microtrauma.

Most of the illustrations depict areas that have fibrous adhesions due to tendinitis or muscle belly adhesions, minor tears, ligaments, and chronic bursitis. Tendinitis and muscle strain are found on painful resisted muscle testing, painful passive stretching, and pain on use and palpation. It may be necessary to discover the problem in ranges of muscle testing other than the neutral position. For example, supraspinatus abduction in the scapular range may have to be tested at several levels of abduction. Before a patient can be declared cured, retesting should be done in a similar variety of ranges of motion.

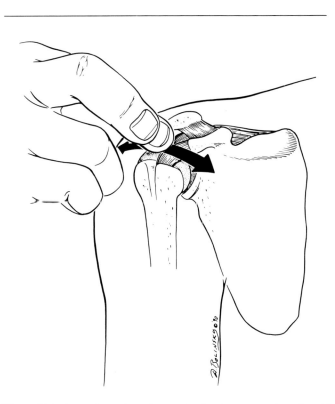

Figure 12-1 Supraspinatus insertion proximal to the greater tuberosity with the arm resting at the side. The usual location for frictioning is beneath the anterolateral acromion process. *Source:* Copyright © 1990 by David Bolinsky.

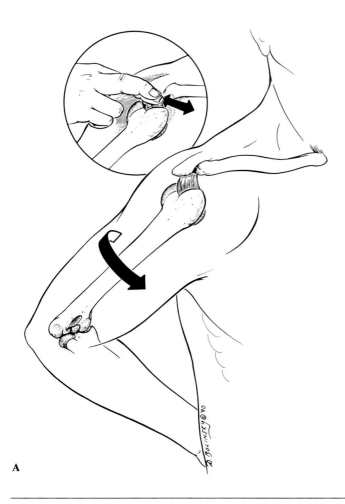

A

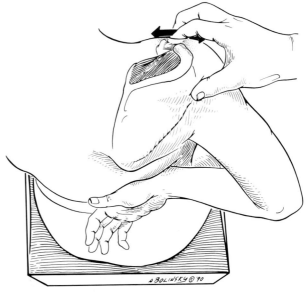

B

Figure 12-2 Supraspinatus insertion proximal to the greater tuberosity with the shoulder internally rotated. (**A**) The tendon is brought into a more sagittal position just below the anterior acromion. (**B**) Superior view of the supraspinatus tendon beneath the anterior acromion with the shoulder internally rotated. The forefinger should be between the anterior acromion and the greater tuberosity. *Source:* Copyright © 1990 David Bolinsky.

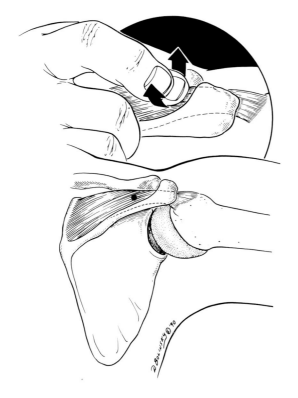

Figure 12-3 Supraspinatus. To friction the musculotendinous portion of the supraspinatus, the shoulder should be in a rested position of 90° abduction. This position allows the musculotendinous area to shift medially beneath the arch, where it can be treated. Deep pressure is required as the practitioner pronates and supinates the reinforced forefinger between the posterior clavicle and the anterior scapular spine. *Source:* Copyright © 1990 by David Bolinsky.

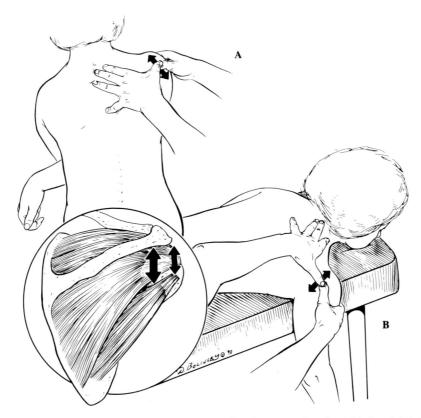

Figure 12-4 Infraspinatus. The most tender area, either the tendon body or the insertion into the greater tuberosity, is frictioned. (**A**) This position creates a minimal stretch. (**B**) This position allows better penetration by relaxing the deltoid. *Source:* Copyright © 1990 by David Bolinsky.

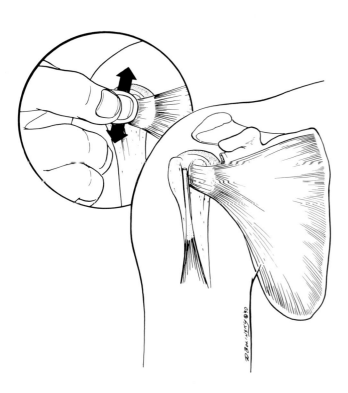

Figure 12-5 Subscapularis. Friction is applied at the most tender level of the bony lesser tuberosity. The overlying deltoid may have to be moved laterally to achieve better bony contact. *Source:* Copyright © 1990 by David Bolinsky.

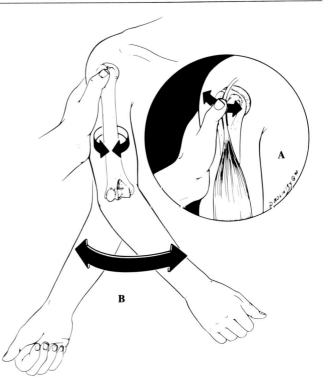

Figure 12-6 Biceps tendon at the bicipital groove. The long head of the biceps tendon may be frictioned directly. The elbow should be flexed with the shoulder externally rotated (**A**). Another method is to maintain contact on the tendon while the patient moves the forearm medially and laterally (**B**). *Source:* Copyright © 1990 by David Bolinsky.

Figure 12-7 Biceps muscle belly and musculotendinous portion. The muscle belly is held and pulled by the fingertips (**A**). The musculotendinous portion is pinched and pulled by the fingertips (**B**). The location of the lesion is determined by the location of pain during resisted biceps testing. *Source:* Copyright © 1990 by David Bolinsky.

Figure 12-8 Biceps tendon insertion. The practitioner contacts the tender radial tuberosity while fully supinating and pronating the forearm to 90°. *Source:* Copyright © 1990 by David Bolinsky.

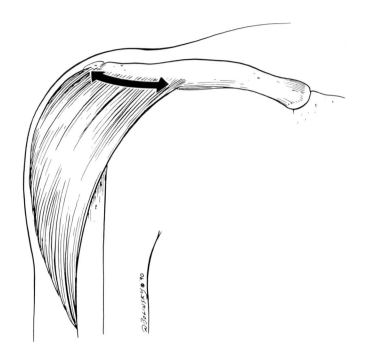

Figure 12-9 Anterior deltoid. The anterior deltoid may be traumatically strained, requiring friction at its clavicular origin. *Source:* Copyright © 1990 by David Bolinsky.

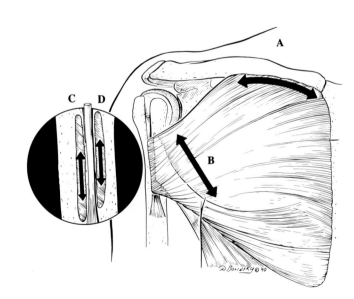

Figure 12-10 Pectoralis major and latissimus dorsi. The pectoralis major may require friction at its origin at the medial clavicle (**A**), at its belly toward the axillary area (**B**), or at its insertion lateral to the intertubercular (biceps) groove (**C**). The latissimus dorsi may require friction at its insertion medial to and at the inferior portion of the intertubercular groove (**D**). All friction contacts for the above muscles should be performed with the shoulder slightly abducted and externally rotated. *Source:* Copyright © 1990 by David Bolinsky.

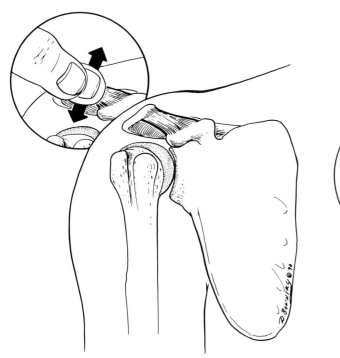

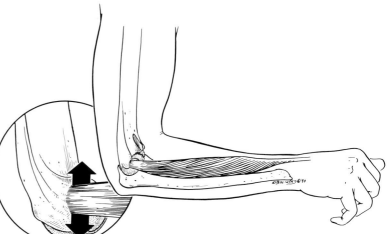

Figure 12-13 Extensor carpi radialis. The most frequent site for friction in lateral epicondylitis is just anterior to the lateral epicondyle. The elbow is flexed, and the forearm is pronated. *Source:* Copyright © 1990 by David Bolinsky.

Figure 12-11 Coracoacromial ligament. This ligament is not always palpable. Palpation should proceed from the superior lateral aspect of the coracoid tip. Frictioning should be considered when the ligament is tender to palpation or when the impingement test is positive with the shoulder flexed 90°, the elbow flexed 90°, and the forearm internally rotated (see Fig. 3-37). *Source:* Copyright © 1990 by David Bolinsky.

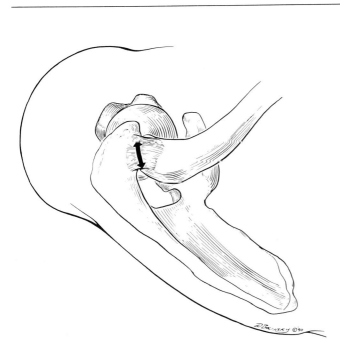

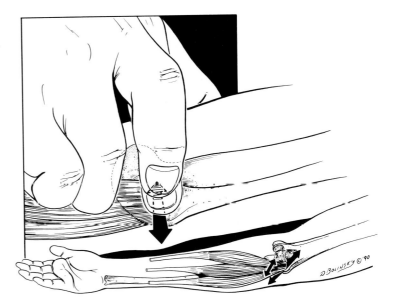

Figure 12-14 Common flexor tendon. The most frequent site for friction is on the anterior medial epicondyle or just inferior to the medial epicondyle. With the patient's arm in extension the friction is directed toward the line of the humerus. *Source:* Copyright © 1990 by David Bolinsky.

Figure 12-12 Acromioclavicular ligament (superior view). Friction should be applied with the forefinger along the joint line. The angle of the acromioclavicular joint is variable. *Source:* Copyright © 1990 by David Bolinsky.

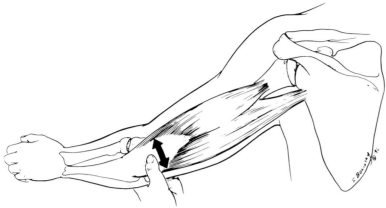

Figure 12-15 Triceps tendon. Friction is applied at the most tender posterior portion of the olecranon. *Source:* Copyright © 1990 by David Bolinsky.

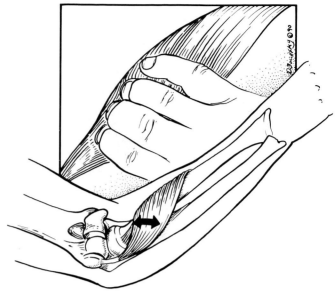

Figure 12-16 Supinator. The patient's arm is pronated to bring the muscle into a better position for friction. Either a muscle belly contact or localized finger friction is useful. *Source:* Copyright © 1990 by David Bolinsky.

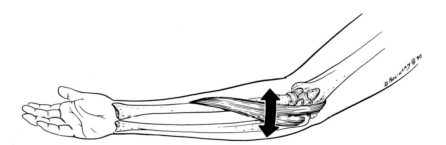

Figure 12-17 Pronator teres. The patient's arm is supinated. *Source:* Copyright © 1990 by David Bolinsky.

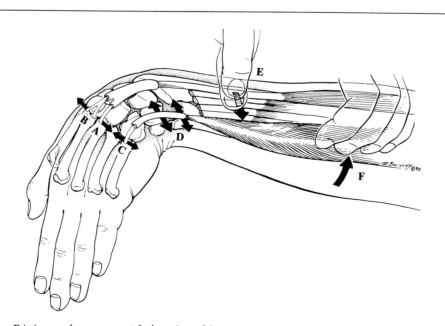

Figure 12-18 Wrist extensors. Friction may be necessary at the insertions of the extensor carpi radialis brevis (**A**), extensor carpi radialis longus (**B**), and extensor carpi ulnaris (**C**). The wrist is treated in flexion stretch if a sheath is involved (**D**). Resisted finger extension may create pain at the proximal tendons of the extensor digitorum (**E**). Muscle belly treatment may be necessary at the proximal location (**F**). *Source:* Copyright © 1990 by David Bolinsky.

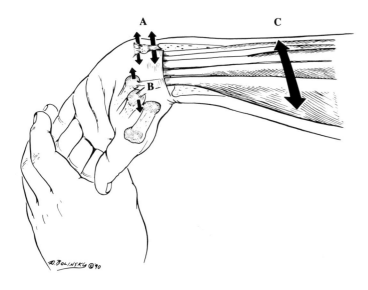

Figure 12-19 Wrist flexors. Friction may be necessary at the insertions of the flexor carpi ulnaris (**A**), the flexor carpi radialis (**B**), and tendons of the finger flexors (**C**). *Source:* Copyright © 1990 by David Bolinsky.

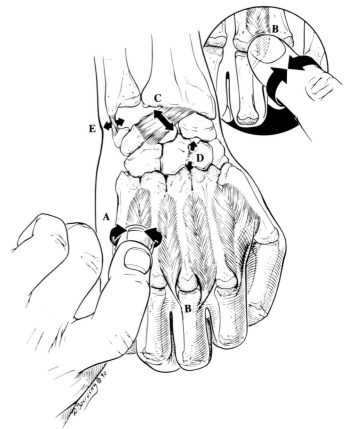

Figure 12-21 Dorsal interossei at the belly (**A**) and insertions (**B**). These muscles require pronation-supination friction. Wrist ligaments—intracapsular (**C**), carpal interosseous (**D**), and collateral (**E**)—may also require friction. *Source:* Copyright © 1990 by David Bolinsky.

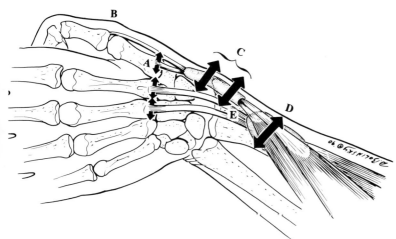

Figure 12-20 Abductor pollicis longus (**A**) and extensor pollicis brevis (**B**) at their insertions and their shared sheath (de Quervain's) (**C**). Friction may be necessary at the point (**D**) where the above muscles pass over the wrist extensors (intersection syndrome) (**E**). *Source:* Copyright © 1990 by David Bolinsky.

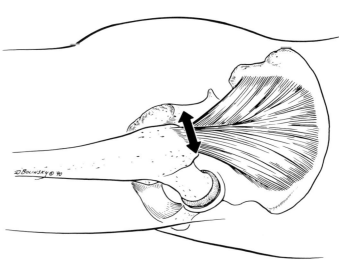

Figure 12-22 Gluteus medius at its insertion on the lateral surface of the greater trochanter. This is a possible area for chronic trochanteric bursitis. *Source:* Copyright © 1990 by David Bolinsky.

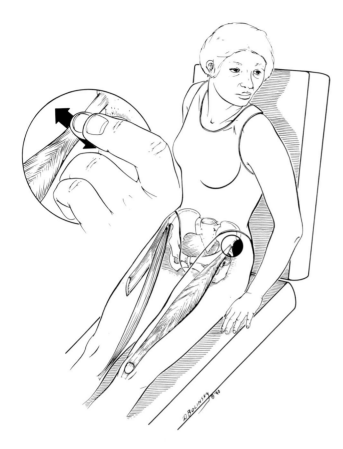

Figure 12-23 Rectus femoris tendon at its origin at the anterior-inferior iliac spine (approximately 3 in below the anterior-superior iliac spine). The patient is seated to relax the overlying sartorius muscle. *Source:* Copyright © 1990 by David Bolinsky.

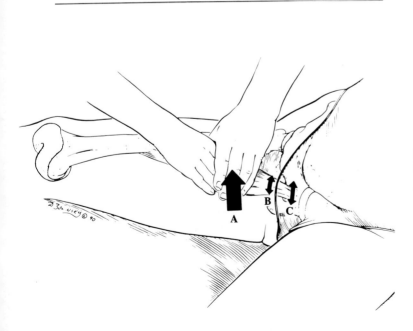

Figure 12-24 Adductor longus. This muscle may be frictioned at its belly (**A**), musculotendinous area (**B**), or pubic origin (**C**). *Source:* Copyright © 1990 by David Bolinsky.

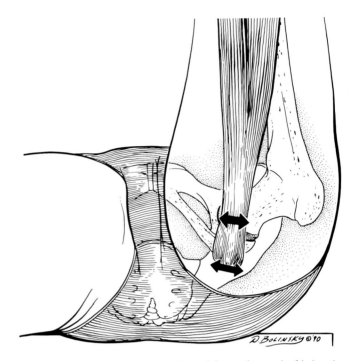

Figure 12-25 Hamstring. The hamstring origin may have to be frictioned at the ischial tuberosity or 2 in below. The knee should rest over a chair to stretch the muscle slightly. *Source:* Copyright © 1990 by David Bolinsky.

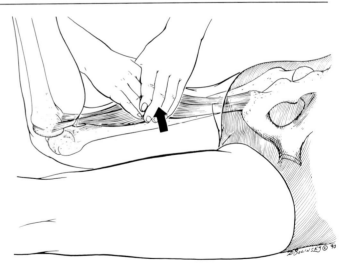

Figure 12-26 Hamstring belly. The knee is held flexed to relax the muscle. *Source:* Copyright © 1990 by David Bolinsky.

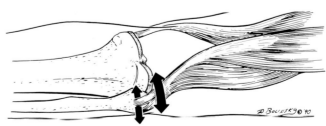

Figure 12-27 Biceps femoris insertion at the lateral side of the fibular head. Rarely, the semimembranosus insertion at the posterior medial tibial condyle may be involved (not shown). *Source:* Copyright © 1990 by David Bolinsky.

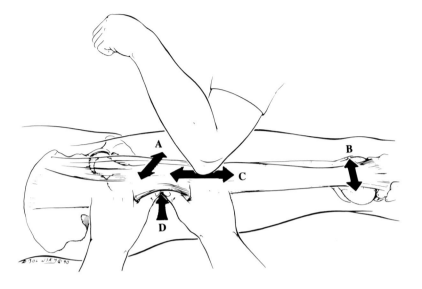

Figure 12-28 Iliotibial band. This muscle may be frictioned where the gluteus maximus and tensor fasciae latae meet (**A**), over the lateral epicondyle (**B**), or at its insertion on the proximal tibia (Gerdy's tubercle, not shown). Other treatments besides friction may include deep longitudinal pressure (**C**) or a tissue-lifting procedure (**D**). *Source:* Copyright © 1990 by David Bolinsky.

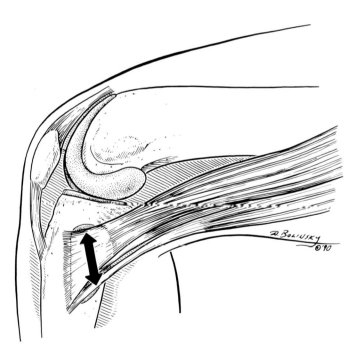

Figure 12-29 Pes anserinus. *Source:* Copyright © 1990 by David Bolinsky.

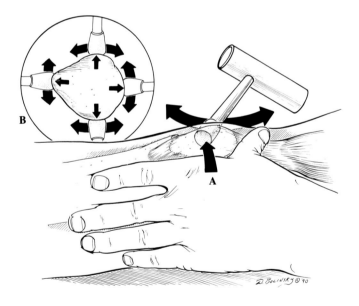

Figure 12-30 Friction beneath the patella for patellar tendinitis. (**A**) Tipping and pushing of the patella to open the opposite side to allow the T bar (or reinforced finger) to friction the tissue against the undersurface of the patellar bone. The knee is treated in extension. (**B**) Superior and inferior poles and medial and lateral retinacular areas. *Source:* Copyright © 1990 by David Bolinsky.

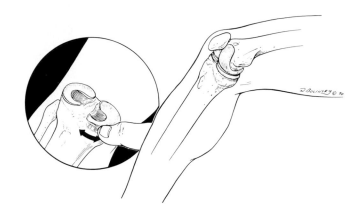

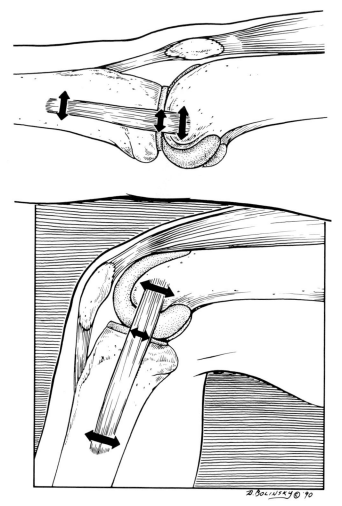

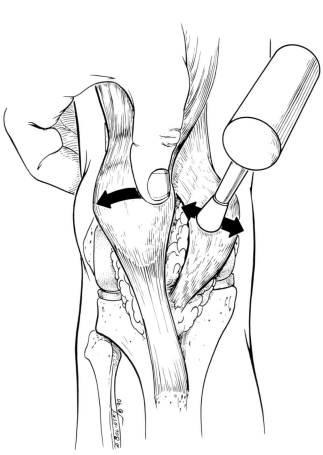

Figure 12-33 Meniscotibial (coronary) ligament. The knee is flexed about 90°, and the tibia is externally rotated to expose the medial side. The lateral side is rarely involved. It is important that the treating finger rest directly flat on the tibial plateau. *Source:* Copyright © 1990 by David Bolinsky.

Figure 12-31 Medial collateral ligament. A sprain of this ligament should be frictioned at the most tender site during maximum allowable extension and flexion. *Source:* Copyright © 1990 by David Bolinsky.

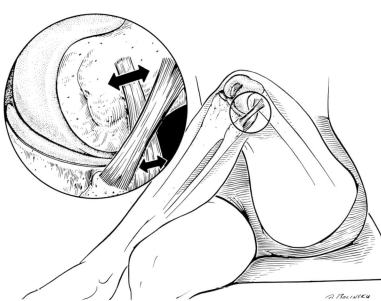

Figure 12-34 Plica syndrome. The plica is frictioned on the medial side with the knee extended and the patella held laterally. *Source:* Copyright © 1990 by David Bolinsky.

Figure 12-32 Popliteus. In popliteal tendinitis the popliteus may be palpated and frictioned either anterior or posterior to the fibular collateral ligament with the leg in the figure-of-four position. Rarely, the popliteus may have to be frictioned at its insertion on the proximal posterior tibia (not shown). *Source:* Copyright © 1990 by David Bolinsky.

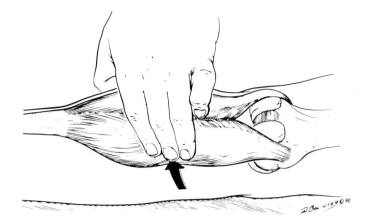

Figure 12-35 Gastrocnemius belly. The patient is prone with the foot plantar flexed. *Source:* Copyright © 1990 by David Bolinsky.

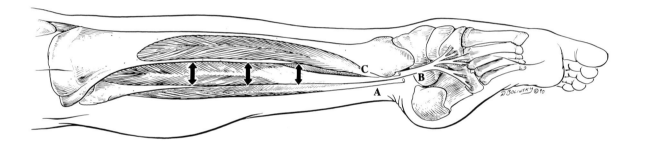

Figure 12-36 Posterior compartment muscles: flexor hallucis longus (**A**), tibialis posterior (**B**), and flexor digitorum longus (**C**). These muscles may be involved in posterior shin splints. *Source:* Copyright © 1990 by David Bolinsky.

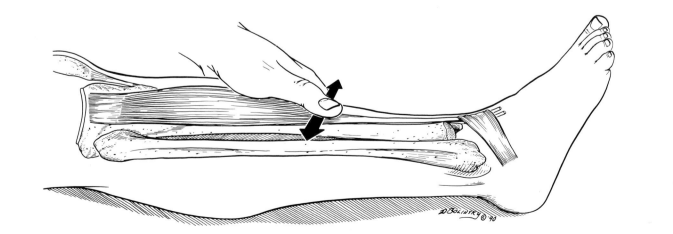

Figure 12-37 Tibialis anterior. This muscle is usually involved in anterior shin splints at its musculotendinous area. *Source:* Copyright © 1990 by David Bolinsky.

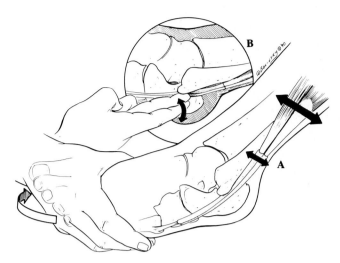

Figure 12-38 Peronei muscles. These are stretched in inversion and dorsiflexion (**A**) during friction. Friction at the level of the lateral malleolus requires a pronation-supination stroke (**B**). *Source:* Copyright © 1990 by David Bolinsky.

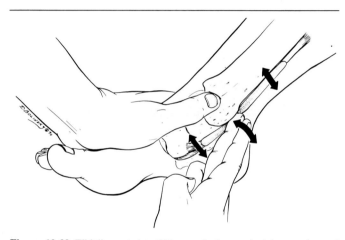

Figure 12-39 Tibialis posterior. This muscle is stretched in eversion and dorsiflexion during friction. Friction at the level of the medial malleolus requires a pronation-supination stroke. *Source:* Copyright © 1990 by David Bolinsky.

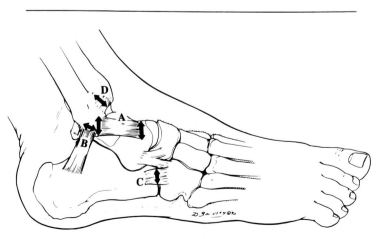

Figure 12-40 Lateral ankle ligaments often involved in ankle sprains: (**A**) anterior talofibular (most common sprain site), (**B**) calcaneofibular, (**C**) calcaneocuboid, and (**D**) anterior tibiofibular. *Source:* Copyright © 1990 by David Bolinsky.

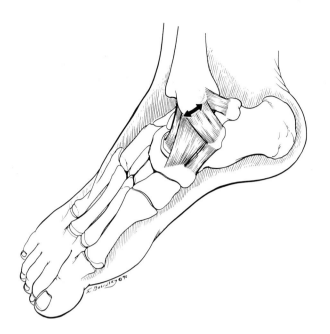

Figure 12-41 Medial ankle (deltoid) ligaments involved in ankle sprains. *Source:* Copyright © 1990 by David Bolinsky.

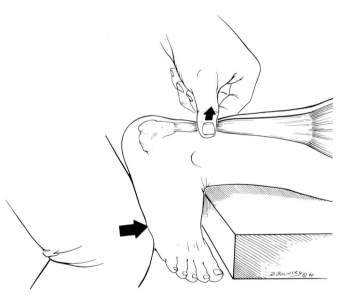

Figure 12-42 Achilles tendon. If the sides of the tendon are involved, the foot is held in dorsiflexion while the tendon is pinched and pulled. *Source:* Copyright © 1990 by David Bolinsky.

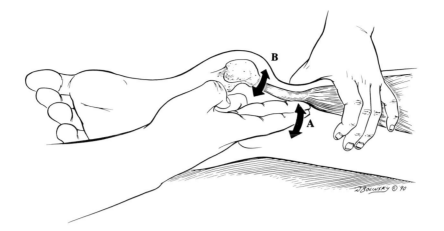

Figure 12-43 Achilles tendon (anterior portion). (**A**) The tendon is pushed over with the thumb so that the finger can friction in the pronation-supination direction. The insertion (**B**) receives friction in the normal cross-direction. The foot is plantar flexed. *Source:* Copyright © 1990 by David Bolinsky.

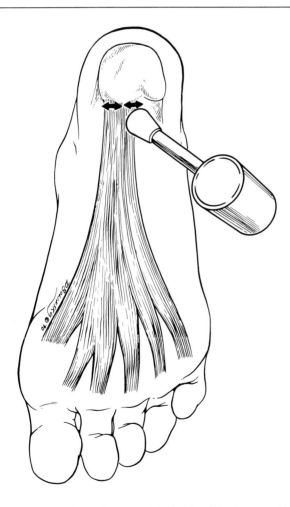

Figure 12-44 Plantar fascia. Because of the density of the tissue, a rubber-tipped T bar is necessary. It is difficult to sweep across the whole fascia, so that friction must be directed to one area at a time. *Source:* Copyright © 1990 by David Bolinsky.

REFERENCES

1. Walker JM. Deep transverse friction in ligament healing. *J Orthop Sports Phys Ther*. 1984;6:89–94.

2. Mennell JB. *Physical Treatment by Movement, Manipulation and Massage*. 5th ed. Philadelphia; Blakiston; 1947.

3. Chamberlain GJ. Cyriax's friction massage: a review. *J Orthop Sports Phys Ther*. 1982;4(1):16–22.

4. Cyriax J. *Textbook of Orthopaedic Medicine*. London: Bailliere-Tindall; 1984;2.

5. Teitz CC. *Scientific Foundations of Sports Medicine*. Toronto: Decker; 1989.

6. Palastanga N. The use of transverse frictions for soft tissue lesions. In: Grieve GP, ed. *Modern Manual Therapy of the Vertebral Column*. New York: Churchill Livingstone; 1986:819–826.

7. Hitchcock TF, Light TR, Bunch WH, et al. The effect of immediate controlled mobilization on the strength of flexor tendon repairs. *Trans Orthop Res Soc*. 1986;11:216.

8. Duran RJ, Houser RG. Controlled passive motion following flexor tendon repair in zones 2 and 3. In: *American Academy of Orthopaedic Surgeons Symposium on Tendon Surgery in the Hand*. St Louis, Mo: Mosby; 1975:105–114.

9. Salter RB, Simmonds DF, Malcolm BW, et al. The biological effect of continuous passive motion on the healing of full-thickness defects in articular cartilage: an experimental investigation in the rabbit. *J Bone Joint Surg Am*. 1980;62:1232–1251.

10. Forrester JC, Zederfeldt BH, Hayes TL, et al. Wolff's law in relation to the healing skin wound. *J Trauma*. 1970;10:770–779.

11. Munro IR, Lindsay WK, Jackson SH. A synchronous study of collagen and mucopolysaccharide in healing flexor tendons of chickens. *Plast Reconstr Surg*. 1970;45:493–501.

12. Ross R. The fibroblast and wound repair. *Biol Rev*. 1968;43:51–90.

13. Mennell JM. Therapeutic use of cold. *J Am Orthop Assoc*. 1975;74:1157.

14. Melzack R. *The Puzzle of Pain*. New York: Basic; 1973.

15. Melzack R, Wall P. *The Challenge of Pain*. New York: Penguin; 1982.

16. Hoppenfeld S. *Physical Examination of the Spine and Extremities*. Norwalk, Conn: Appleton-Century-Crofts; 1976.

Chapter 13

Therapeutic Muscle Stretching

Daniel Mühlemann and Joseph A. Cimino

INTRODUCTION: MUSCLE AND FASCIA ELONGATION WITH THE CONTRACT-RELAX-ANTAGONIST-CONTRACT TECHNIQUE

Stretching of muscles is a natural behavior of humans and many animals (eg, cats and dogs) that stretch their muscles after periods of inactivity. The reason for this is not fully understood unless we consider the fact that stretching "feels good."

Self-stretching exercises have gained wide popularity in most sports and are commonly advertised as, among other things, a nonspecific measure to decrease the risk of injury[1] and to prevent and improve postural problems. Often, these self-stretching exercises are performed with a lack of understanding of structure, biomechanics, and function of the loco-motor system. Stretching therefore may not stretch the desired tissues and may put stress on structures that do not need to be elongated. Dysfunction and pain from overstretched structures can result. Proper instruction in what, how, and when to stretch would certainly help reduce this risk but is not always readily available.

Therapeutic muscle stretching (TMS), specific muscle stretching performed, instructed, or supervised by a therapist in patients with dysfunctions of the musculoskeletal system, has been promoted by Janda[2] and by Evjenth and Hamberg.[3] The latter investigators have developed highly specific tech-

niques for stretching individual muscles that minimize the risk of injuring the surrounding soft tissues. As they state,[3(p7)]

> An understanding of why, when and how muscles or other structures should be stretched is prerequisite to stretching to benefit rather than degrade body function. The role of the therapist in stretching is then not just to understand and treat, but also to guide and teach patients self-stretching.

This chapter discusses TMS stretching, its background, performance guidelines, and selected techniques, based on the work of Evjenth and Hamberg.[3]

BACKGROUND

The Methods

In the late 19th century, Sherrington[4,5] observed that

- a muscle contraction is closely followed by a proportional relaxation of the same muscle
- the contraction of a given muscle inhibits the contraction of this muscle's antagonist(s).

Kabat[6] and Knott and Voss,[7] the developers of the proprioceptive neuromuscular facilitation (PNF) techniques, extensively used these mechanisms first in their work with children with cerebral palsy and later with paraplegics and patients with other disorders of the locomotor system. Their motion pattern–based PNF techniques are aimed at re-establishing normal motor control and function. The same observations made by Sherrington[4,5] serve as the basis for the contract-relax-antagonist-contract (CRAC) technique that this chapter

Note: The authors gratefully acknowledge the help of Fritz Zahnd and Dieter von Ow in the preparation of this chapter.

describes. The use of the term *PNF stretching* is discouraged, however, inasmuch as the use of postisometric relaxation and antagonist inhibition is the only similarity between PNF and TMS apart from the fact that both are therapeutic procedures.

The rationale behind static stretch (SS), contract-relax (CR), synonymously called hold-relax, and CRAC techniques has been well documented:

> The rationale of the SS method is founded upon minimizing the inevitable excitatory response of spindle afferents to stretch by avoiding rapid stretch. Spindle secondaries may also produce inhibition of physiological extensor muscles as a result of static muscle stretch. . . . [Bianconi et al. 1964, Hutton et al. 1973]. The rationale for the CR technique relies on the autogenic inhibitory influence of a stretched muscle following isometric contraction. The post contraction inhibition apparently results from the lingering influences of Ib fibres in response to tension on the Golgi tendon organ from muscle contraction. . . . [Smith et al. 1974]. This inhibition allows greater muscle lengthening to result from the continued static stretch. Reciprocal inhibition is the additional rationale for using the CRAC technique. The CRAC technique follows the same procedure as CR, but during the final stretch, the antagonist contraction augments the stretching force and produces greater inhibitory influences on the stretched muscle through reciprocal inhibition [Tanaka, 1976]. . . .[8]

Evaluations of the efficacy of different types of muscle stretching (SS, CR, and CRAC), however, have not shown uniformly that CRAC techniques are superior to SS and CR techniques in respect to increases in range of motion.[8,9] Nonetheless, clinical experience shows that CRAC techniques are effective and practical for the purpose of TMS. Therefore, CRAC techniques are widely accepted and used.

Muscle Shortening: Pathophysiology

Reasons for muscle shortening have been discussed extensively: Overuse, poor posture, lack of exercise or stretching, and reflex mechanisms are all considered contributing factors. Wyke[10] showed by electromyographic recordings that stimulation of mechanoceptors and nociceptors located in joint capsules can induce a significant reflex increase in activity in the segmental and peripheral muscles. These stimuli may activate the muscle until stimulation of the joint receptors ceases or adaptation occurs. Schmidt and colleagues[11,12] showed that nociceptive afferents from the muscle can significantly stimulate α and γ motor neurons. Acute or chronic algogenic stimuli can cause permanent increases of muscle tonus, which by itself may lead to muscle shortening, which again may stimulate nociceptors, which then may or may not lead to the perception of pain. Figure 13-1 shows this vicious circle.

Janda[2,13] created the term *muscular dysbalance* to describe muscle shortening of one or several muscles in conjunction

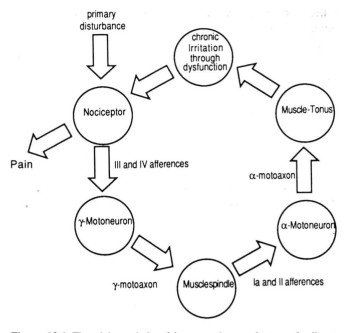

Figure 13-1 The vicious circle of increases in muscle tonus leading to stimulation of nociceptors. *Source:* Adapted with permission from *Zeitschrift für Physikalische Medizin* (1981;10:73–89), Copyright © 1981, Demeter-Verlag.

with weakening of the muscle's antagonist(s). In his experience with patients with posture-related problems, shortening is more likely to occur in tonic *postural muscles*, that is to say antigravity muscles that are primarily involved in maintaining posture. On the other hand, the *phasic muscles*, which are predominantly performing movements, show a tendency toward weakening (Table 13-1).

The distribution of slow-twitch and fast-twitch fibers is extremely variable[14,15] and depends on the individual muscle, favored activities (ie, long-distance running or weight lifting), and the individual tested. Investigations by Howald[16] show that vigorous training of the musculature can induce changes

Table 13-1 Examples of Postural and Phasic Muscles

Postural, Slow-Twitch	Phasic, Fast-Twitch
Hamstrings	Abdominal muscles
Iliopsoas	Vasti of quadriceps
Rectus femoris	Gluteus maximus, medius, and
Tensor fasciae latae	minimus
Adductors	Peronei
Piriformis	Tibialis anterior
Gastrocnemius	Pectoralis major (abdominal
Pectoralis major (clavicular and	portion)
sternal portions)	Rhomboids
Levator scapulae	Trapezius (lower or middle
Trapezius (upper portion)	horizontal portions)
Biceps brachii (short head)	Triceps brachii
Flexor carpi	Extensor carpi

Source: Adapted from *Muskelfunktionsdiagnostik* (p 244) by V Janda with permission of Uitgeveÿ Acco, Tienestraat 134–138, B-3000 Leuven (Belgium).

---

in the relation of slow-twitch to fast-twitch fibers in an individual muscle. Jowett and Fidler[17] demonstrated that prolonged hypomobility of a lumbar segment affects the distribution of the fiber ratio in favor of fast-twitch fibers in the multifidus muscle and that in idiopathic scoliosis slow-twitch fibers are predominant on the side of the convexity compared to the side of concavity.

Whether prolonged muscle shortening or muscular dysbalance can induce changes in the fiber ratio or whether the predominance of the fiber type in a muscle can induce muscular dysbalance or muscle shortening is not clear. Clinically, however, patients who demonstrate shortening of *phasic muscles* are frequently seen. Muscles, when worked hard or excessively and not fully elongated, run a high risk of shortening.[1] In accord with this observation, it has been demonstrated that under normal circumstances most of the skeletal muscles do not show a definite tendency in respect to the distribution of slow-twitch and fast-twitch fibers (Table 13-2). As Saltin and Gollnick state, "Human beings, in contrast to other species, have a more homogenous mixture of fibres in nearly all muscles. Thus the higher degree of specialization, with the result that a single fiber type is seen in a muscle or large area in some animals, rarely occurs in man.[18]

Specific populations of fibers (being part of selective motor units) may be primarily responsible for muscle shortening. They may even correspond with the localized, palpable bands in the shortened muscle. Whether or not the slow-twitch fibers, situated deep in the muscle belly[19] and therefore difficult to palpate, are responsible for the nociception-induced contractions, which may eventually lead to muscle shortening, has not, yet, been demonstrated.

REASONS FOR THERAPEUTIC MUSCLE STRETCHING

Decreased Range of Motion

Normal joint function is characterized by full and pain-free active, passive, or resisted range of motion with or without compression of the joint surfaces. Joint range of motion varies considerably and depends on the integrity of the joint and the surrounding soft tissues, the muscles that perform the movement, their controlling system (which in turn is responsible for important factors such as coordination), and such variables as age, constitution, exercise habits, and fitness.

Active movement depends on a contractile system including muscles, tendons, and fasciae as well as their osseous insertions.[20] Passive range of motion is controlled by various inert (ie, noncontractile) structures such as the articular surfaces of the joint, ligaments, joint capsules, intra-articular structures, fasciae, skin, and subcutaneous structures. The contractile system mentioned above may also limit range of motion passively when specific muscles are elongated fully in a direction that opposes their function(s). Full range of motion therefore depends also on the ability of the muscles to be fully elongated passively, and restricted range of motion may be due to muscles with an impaired ability to elongate fully.

Because one muscle can have one or several functions at one or several joints, muscle shortening can cause a variety of effects. They can be roughly categorized into three groups:

1. Shortened muscles with one single function at one single joint can restrict range of motion at a single joint and in the direction that opposes the direction of its contractile force only. *Example:* A shortened brachialis can restrict extension at the elbow only.
2. Shortened muscles with more than one function at a single joint can restrict range of motion at a single joint in all directions that oppose the directions of their contractile force. *Example:* A shortened adductor longus can restrict abduction, extension, and medial rotation at the hip.

The direction in which range of motion will be restricted depends on the position of the joint; if the

Table 13-2 Fiber Type Percentages in Normal Human Muscles

Muscle Type	Fiber Type (%)	
	Type I (Tonic), Slow-Twitch	Type II (Phasic), Fast-Twitch
Postural (tonic) muscles		
Hamstrings	56–78	22–44
Iliopsoas	40–49	41–61
Rectus femoris	22–52	49–78
Tensor fasciae latae	NA	NA
Adductors	42–76	35–58
Piriformis	NA	NA
Gastrocnemius	37–57	43–63
Pectoralis major (clavicular and sternal portions)	29–58	42–72
Levator scapulae	NA	NA
Trapezius (upper portion)	NA	NA
Biceps brachii (short head)	34–61	39–60
Flexor digitorum	27–68	32–73
Phasic muscles		
Abdominal muscles	35–57	43–65
Vasti of quadriceps	18–72	29–82
Gluteus maximus, medius, and minimus	36–67	33–62
Peronei	NA	NA
Tibialis anterior	63–84	16–37
Pectoralis major (abdominal portion)	NA	NA
Rhomboids	34–55	45–66
Trapezius (lower and middle portions)	NA	NA
Triceps brachii	8–58	42–92
Extensor digitorum	29–61	39–71

Source: Adapted from *Skeletal Muscle* (pp 196–197) by H Schmalbruch with permission of Springer-Verlag, © 1985.

shortened muscle is close to full elongation, further elongation will be limited or not tolerated. *Example:* A shortened adductor longus (functions: adduction, flexion, and lateral rotation at the hip) will not allow for abduction if the hip is already positioned in extension and medial rotation, extension if the hip is already positioned in medial rotation and abduction, or medial rotation if the hip is already positioned in extension and abduction.

3. Shortened muscles with one or more functions at two or more joints (multiarticular) can restrict range of motion in all directions that oppose the directions of their contractile force at any or all of the joints that are moved by these muscles. *Examples:* A shortened pronator teres will not allow for full elbow extension if the forearm is fully supinated or full supination if the forearm is fully extended. A shortened rectus femoris will not allow for full knee flexion if the hip is fully extended or full hip extension if the knee is fully flexed.

Therapeutic muscle stretching will restore the muscle's capacity for full elongation, which will then allow full range of motion.

Pain Originating from Contractile Structures

Pain originating from the muscle itself may be due to shortening of the muscle:

> The neuromuscular dysfunction appears clinically to start with injury by muscle overload that results in strong contracture (sarcomere shortening without propagated action potentials). This contracture would be localized and could be self-perpetuating as follows: the vigorously contracting fibers would produce local ischemia and hypoxia; they would also impose a high rate of energy consumption in a region of energy deficit, thereby contributing to an energy crisis. . . . Such severe local tissue distress would be expected to release nerve-sensitizing agents that could readily account for the local [trigger point] tenderness and for initiating referred pain, tenderness and autonomic phenomena.[21(p368)]

Prolonged muscle shortening may cause stimulation of nociceptive nerve endings. With time, muscle activity without intermittent periods of relaxation will hinder metabolic processes in the muscle and may initiate or contribute to the vicious circle of pain arising from hypoxia and vice versa.[12]

Pain originating from tendons, fasciae, and insertions may also be caused by prolonged periods or inadequate amounts of tension on these structures. Under normal circumstances (ie, as long as stress rates are mildly increased) the tissue's response to stresses is manifested as an increase in the rate of tissue production. Prolonged, abnormal stresses will therefore lead to tissue hypertrophy provided that nutrition of the tissue is normal and that the stress rate does not exceed the tissue's

ability to repair the microdamage. If this ability is overtaxed, prolonged or inadequate tensile loads exerted on tissues can lead to increased microdamage, inflammation, pain, and eventually atrophy. This occurs particularly in tissues with insufficient nutrition status or in poorly vascularized tissues such as tendons.[22] Chronic inflammation results in further reduced vascularization, which in turn will make the tissue more susceptible to microruptures. Pain, impaired healing capacity, and poor tissue repair will be the end result. TMS will relax and elongate the shortened muscle and thus allow for better circulation and metabolism, and pain will cease.

Reduced Healing Capacity and Insufficient Tissue Quality

The healing of traumatized soft tissues is a delicate matter. It depends on factors such as time, nutrition, and adequate intermittent tensile loads. The healing capacity is often reduced because stresses exerted on the tissues may exceed the tissue's capability for remodeling. Even though the amount of the newly formed tissue is normal or even excessive, its quality may be poor. The newly formed tissue may not be able to attenuate the energy of everyday tensile loads. Further damage and eventual fibrosis may result.

Repeated low-level stresses (ie, repeated, moderate tensile loads that do not cause microdamage or exceed the tissue's capacity to repair) are adequate stimuli for the production of properly aligned fibers—fibers that lie in the direction of normal forces. Carefully administered TMS will supply the adequate stimulus for the production of functional and healthy collagen fibers. In addition, the formation of interfiber bonds (microadhesions between properly aligned fibers) will be prevented, and already-formed bonds will be loosened.

Prevention of Atrophy

The effects of passive muscle stretching[23,24] on muscle tissue have been investigated in vitro. A substantial increase in metabolism and an anabolic state were observed. The prolonged prevention of full muscle elongation has been shown to cause muscle atrophy.[25] Normal mobility of the joint and full elongation of the muscle are necessary to prevent muscle atrophy.

INDICATIONS AND CONTRAINDICATIONS FOR THERAPEUTIC MUSCLE STRETCHING

Indications

Indications for TMS are to prevent atrophy and to treat dysfunctions of the musculoskeletal system:

- decreased range of motion due to muscle shortening
- pain from muscles and their appended structures
- reduced healing capacity and insufficient quality of tissue repair

Patients with such dysfunctions should be carefully examined, especially in respect to the function of the associated joints, muscles, tendons, fasciae, and insertions.

The most reliable clue to dysfunction caused by muscle shortening is an altered end feel.[20] A soft-elastic end feel is typically felt when limitation of movement is due to approximation or elongation of muscle tissue.[26] When this soft-elastic end feel is felt in a position that should under normal circumstances (eg, when compared with the other side) allow more movement, muscle shortening is a likely cause. Pain and restricted movement due to joint dysfunction must be treated before any attempt at using TMS.

Contraindications

Contraindications for TMS are as follows:

1. Lack of stability. TMS is contraindicated if integrity or stability is jeopardized or decreased by any (pathologic) process.
2. Endangered vascular integrity. Pathologic processes or drugs (eg, anticoagulants) can endanger vascular integrity or facilitate bleeding.
3. Inflammation or infection in and around the involved structures.
4. Acute injury to the soft tissues and muscles. If performed without sufficient time for healing to occur, TMS can cause new bleeding and delay healing. TMS must be postponed until scar formation is sufficient for moderate tensile loads to be tolerated.
5. Diseases of the soft tissues and muscles. Diseases of the soft tissues and the contractile system require careful evaluation before deciding whether TMS should be administered. Contraindications can be relative (ie, TMS can or cannot be administered depending on the actual condition of the tissue, the operator's skills, the patient's cooperation, and so forth) or absolute (as in conditions such as myositis ossificans).
6. Lack of patient compliance and excessive pain or reaction. Any therapeutic maneuver is contraindicated if the patient cannot or does not want to tolerate its application. If the pain during TMS is not tolerated even though TMS is administered skillfully and as painlessly as possible, then TMS maneuvers should not be used. Patients may be taught self-stretching exercises instead, the performance of which should be supervised and, later, controlled periodically.
7. When common sense says "No."

PREREQUISITES AND PERFORMANCE GUIDELINES

Prerequisites

Thorough Knowledge of Functional Anatomy

All the components of the muscle's action must be considered to make TMS effective.

Biomechanical Diagnosis

Once muscle shortening is considered causative for the dysfunction, an initial biomechanical diagnosis is established.[26] A trial treatment is performed, and on the next visit efficacy and benefits of the trial treatment are assessed. Depending on the outcome, the initial biomechanical diagnosis will be either confirmed or rejected. Rejection calls for a thorough re-evaluation of the patient's problem, and confirmation allows treatment to be continued.

Choice of Technique

Muscle stretching should be performed over the largest, least painful, and most stable joint that permits the elongating movement to occur.[3] For example, when stretching the rectus femoris the knee joint is used to produce elongation. If for any reason the knee joint will not tolerate the maneuver, the hip joint is used.

For simplicity's sake, it is preferable that the elongation movement involve one component of the stretching motion only. It can be extremely difficult, exhausting, and frustrating, as well as inefficient, to try to control and resist several movements simultaneously. For example, when stretching the long head of the biceps brachii the arm is extended, adducted, and externally rotated, the elbow is flexed, and the forearm is fully pronated. The muscle is now almost fully stretched. Full elongation can now be achieved by elbow extension alone.

Stimulation of the antagonists will help reduce their inhibition by the shortened muscle. Vibration or tapping of the muscle, any stimulation of the skin, or intermittent traction and compression of the joint are effective.

Knowledge of Outcome and Prognosis

Therapeutic muscle stretching is not a painless therapeutic maneuver, but only the muscles being stretched are permitted to hurt. TMS must be applied under full patient control. The informed consent of the patient will reduce fear and thus increase the patient's pain tolerance. Gains in range of motion and reduction of pain can be the result only of a consistent and adequately dosed application of TMS. Overstretching will rarely be tolerated and will cause inflammation and often severe pain immediately.

Performance Guidelines

The following sequence for TMS has consistently been shown to be effective:

1. Positioning
   - *Key points:*
     The positioning must not cause discomfort or pain. The end feel is soft-elastic, indicating a muscular restriction.
   - The patient should be in the most comfortable, secure, and biomechanically safe position possible. This may require the use of a stabilization belt (see below) to secure the patient to the table, making it easier to apply a controlled stretch to the shortened muscle. Once this has been accomplished, the extremity should be moved in the direction of restricted movement (which opposes all the components of the normal function of the shortened muscle) until a soft-elastic end feel is felt. Further movement in the restricted direction usually causes discomfort in the muscle being stretched. The position itself must not cause pain.
2. Isometric contraction (*Hold!**)
   - *Key points:*
     The position is held by active contraction of the shortened muscle for at least 7 seconds. No movement occurs.
   - As the operator holds the extremity in position, he or she then starts to apply gradually increasing force in the direction of restricted movement. The patient is instructed to resist this movement (by isometric contraction of the shortened muscle). Operator and patient now counterbalance their forces so that **no movement** occurs at the joint. The maneuver must be comfortable and painless. If painful the combination of force and time must be altered, with the force usually but not always being lowered and the time always being increased to up to 30 seconds. If pain free, this strong isometric contraction will tire the muscle(s) within 7 to 10 seconds.
3. Relaxation (*Relax!**)
   - *Key points:*
     The patient relaxes slowly. No movement occurs.
   - After the contraction, the patient is instructed to relax slowly. As the patient slowly relaxes, the force or resistance offered by the operator is released accordingly. Pain or any movement at all is undesirable now. It may take some time for the patient to relax fully. This time is well spent and necessary. TMS is effective only when the muscle to be elongated is given a chance to relax completely.

4. Antagonist contraction (*Move!**)
   - *Key point:*
     The patient moves actively in the direction of restricted movement.
   - The patient is now instructed to move actively in the direction of restricted movement by contracting the antagonist(s) of the shortened muscle. At this point, the operator may
     (1) gently assist the movement or
     (2) gently resist it (to make the movement less painful)
     Mild pain is permitted but only from the stretched muscle, and it must be felt there and only there. If pain is felt in areas other than the stretched muscle, the operator must identify and locate its origin. Joints and their surrounding tissues may be compromised.
   - If the pain is due to excessive joint compression, traction at the joint may eliminate the problem. If traction does not help, the following procedures may eliminate the problem:
     (1) careful repositioning
     (2) increased time of, or decreased resistance against, the isometric contraction
     (3) reassessment of the initial biomechanical diagnosis.
5. Once a new position of increased elongation is attained, it must be maintained for at least 10 seconds.
6. The sequence (2) to (5) is repeated a few times to improve range of motion progressively.

Note: The extremity is moved in a manner similar to that of a ratchet, in the direction that stretches the shortened muscle. Therefore, back slipping is never allowed once additional elongation (stretch) has been developed and taken up.

It is often useful and easier on the operator to use a stabilization belt to secure the patient on the table as well as to increase the efficacy of the stretching procedure. A belt is also useful to help the operator lift the patient's large and heavy lower limb when stretching muscles of the lower extremity. A belt can be bought through a physical therapy supply center or can be made from a 2-in wide, 10-ft long piece of flat webbing and a waist buckle (materials used to make backpackers' waist straps on their packs).

SELECTED TECHNIQUES

Note: In the following illustrations, *positioning* represents initial patient position prior to application of TMS. Following proper patient positioning, the sequence as outlined in the performance guidelines (isometric contraction, relaxation, antagonistic contraction) is performed until maximal elongation for that stretch sequence is completed. *Elongation* represents the final patient position following the application of TMS.

---

*Commands given by the practitioner.

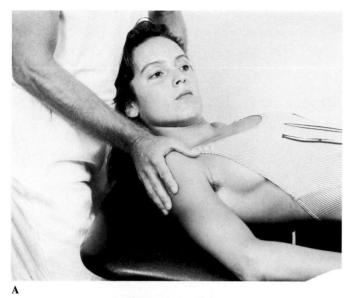

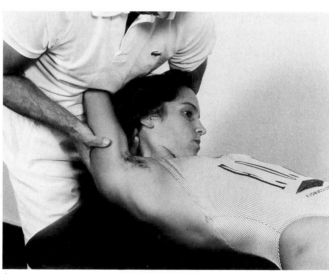

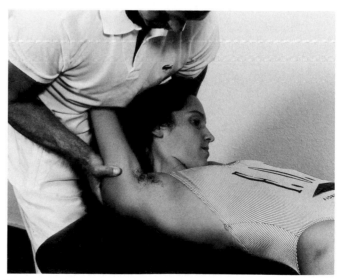

A

B

Figure 13-2 Trapezius, upper portion. (**A**) Starting position. (**B**) Full elongation.

Upper Extremity

Trapezius, Upper Portion (Fig. 13-2)

Origin: Superior nuchal line, nuchal ligament.

Insertion: Lateral third of clavicle, acromion.

Function: Shoulder fixed: ipsilateral sidebending, contralateral rotation, extension of neck and head; *head and neck fixed:* adduction, elevation, and protraction of scapula.

Relevance of shortening: Most disorders of the upper extremity because of alterations of scapulohumeral rhythm.

Positioning: Supine; head and neck in contralateral sidebending, ipsilateral rotation, and flexion; whole cervical spine and occiput fixed.

Elongation: Abduction, depression, and retraction of the scapula with simultaneous long-axis traction of cervical spine and occiput.

Levator Scapulae (Fig. 13-3)

Origin: Transverse process of atlas and cervical vertebrae 2, 3, and 4.

Insertion: Medial angle of scapula.

Function: Shoulder fixed: ipsilateral sidebending, ipsilateral rotation, extension of neck; *neck fixed:* adduction, elevation, and protraction of scapula.

Relevance of shortening: Most disorders of the upper extremity because of alterations of scapulohumeral rhythm.

Positioning: Supine; head and neck in contralateral sidebending, rotation, and flexion; whole cervical spine fixed.

A

B

Figure 13-3 Levator scapulae. (**A**) Starting position. (**B**) Full elongation.

Elongation: Abduction, retraction, and depression of the scapula via the flexed humerus with simultaneous long-axis traction of cervical spine to avoid compression.

Note: In the presence of shoulder pathology or pain, an alternative contact is used: thenar eminence on the superior angle of the scapula.

Pectoralis Major (Fig. 13-4)

Origin: Sternal half of clavicle, sternum to seventh rib, cartilages of true ribs, aponeurosis of obliquus abdominis externus.

Insertion: Lateral lip of bicipital groove of humerus.

Function: Adduction, flexion, and medial rotation of the arm.

Relevance of shortening: Tendinitis, disorders of the shoulder, increase in thoracic kyphosis.

Positioning: Supine; thorax fixated with stabilization belt securely strapped around patient and table.

Elongation: Depression (horizontal abduction) of arms with arms positioned in various amounts of flexion; simultaneous long-axis traction at the glenohumeral joints to avoid joint compression.

Biceps Brachii, Short Head (Fig. 13-5)

Origin: Tip of coracoid process of scapula.

Insertion: Radial tuberosity and by lacertus fibrosus to aponeurosis of forearm.

Function: Shoulder fixed: flexion and supination of the forearm; *forearm fixed:* flexion, adduction, and medial rotation of the arm.

Relevance of shortening: Tendinitis.

Positioning: Supine; extension, lateral rotation, and less than 90° abduction of the arm; flexion and pronation of the forearm. Thorax stabilized with stabilization belt.

Note: Operator uses medial hand to contact the distal humerus above the condyles.

Elongation: Extension of the forearm.

Biceps Brachii, Long Head (Fig. 13-6)

Origin: Supraglenoid tuberosity of scapula.

Insertion: Radial tuberosity and by lacertus fibrosus to aponeurosis of forearm.

Function: Shoulder fixed: flexion and supination of the forearm; *forearm fixed:* flexion, abduction, and medial rotation of the arm.

Relevance of shortening: Tendinitis.

Positioning: Side posture; extension, lateral rotation, and horizontal adduction of the arm; flexion and pronation of the forearm.

Note: Operator uses medial hand to fixate the distal humerus above the condyles to maintain lateral rotation, adduction, and extension.

Elongation: Extension of the forearm.

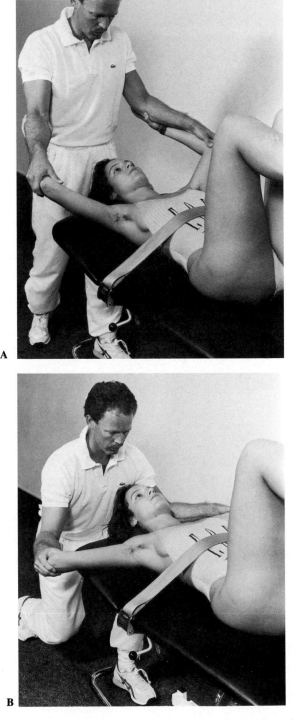

Figure 13-4 Pectoralis major. **(A)** Starting position. **(B)** Full elongation.

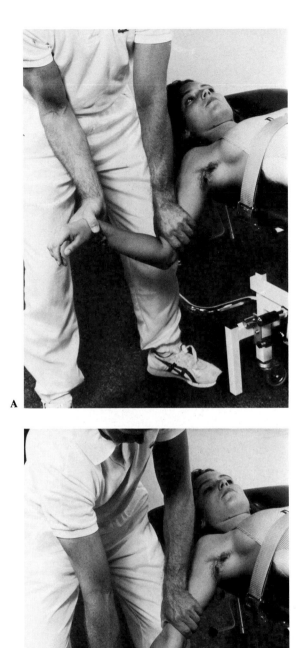

Figure 13-5 Biceps brachii, short head. (**A**) Starting position. (**B**) Full elongation.

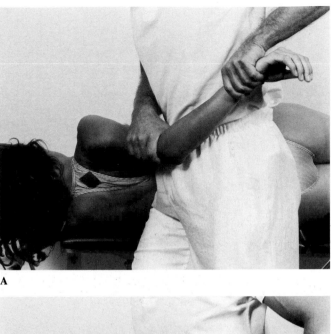

A

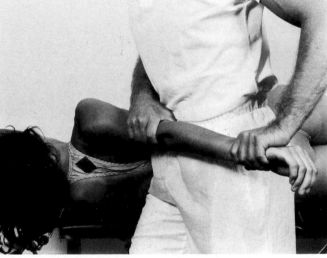

B

Figure 13-6 Biceps brachii, long head. (**A**) Starting position. (**B**) Full elongation.

Triceps Brachii (Fig. 13-7)

Origin: Medial head: lower posterior surface of humerus; *lateral head:* posterior and lateral surface of humerus; *long head:* infraglenoid tuberosity of scapula.

Insertion: Upper posterior surface of olecranon, deep fascia of forearm.

Function: Shoulder fixed: extension of the forearm; *forearm fixed:* extension, adduction, and medial rotation of the arm.

Positioning: Sitting; extension, lateral rotation, and horizontal adduction of the arm; pronation of the forearm.

Elongation: Flexion of the forearm.

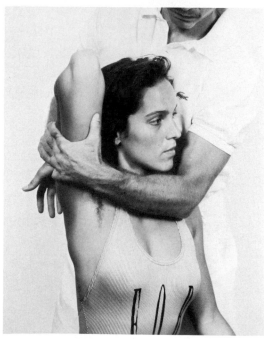

Figure 13-7 Triceps brachii. **(A)** Starting position. **(B)** Full elongation.

Supraspinatus (Fig. 13-8)

Origin: Supraspinous fossa of the scapula.

Insertion: Superior facet of greater tubercle of humerus and capsule of shoulder joint.

Function: Fixes head of humerus in glenoid fossa; assists deltoid in all phases of abduction; may slightly laterally rotate the humerus.

Relevance of shortening: Tendinitis.

Positioning: Side posture; operator's supinated forearm of stabilization hand acts as lever for glenohumeral joint separation. Patient is in position of slight sibebending of the upper body to allow increased adduction of the humerus.

Elongation: Adduction of the humerus.

Infraspinatus (Fig. 13-9)

Origin: Infraspinous fossa of the scapula.

Insertion: Middle facet of greater tubercle of humerus and capsule of shoulder joint.

Function: Laterally rotates the humerus together with teres minor.

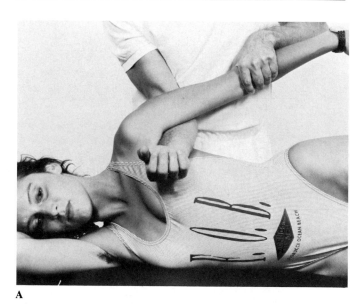

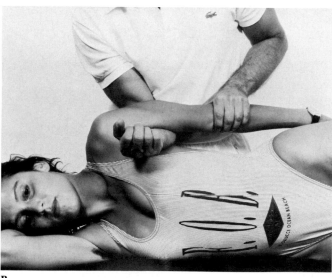

Figure 13-8 Supraspinatus. **(A)** Starting position. **(B)** Full elongation.

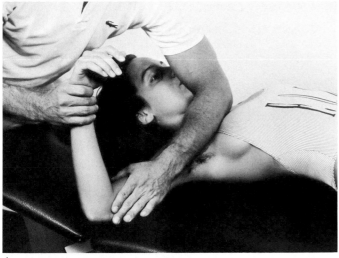

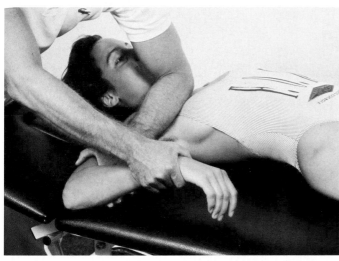

Figure 13-9 Infraspinatus. (**A**) Starting position. (**B**) Full elongation.

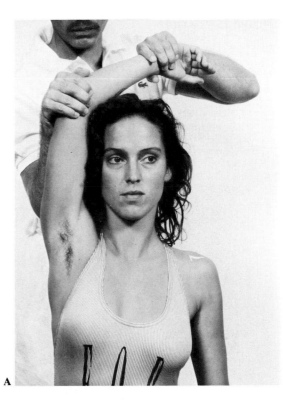

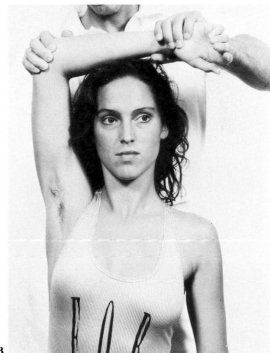

Figure 13-10 Teres minor. (**A**) Starting position. (**B**) Full elongation.

Relevance of shortening: Tendinitis.

Positioning: Supine; approximately 80° abduction of the humerus.

Elongation: Medial rotation of the humerus.

Teres Minor (Fig. 13-10)

Origin: Dorsal surface of axillary border of the scapula.

Insertion: Lowest facet of greater tuberosity of humerus and capsule of shoulder joint.

Function: Laterally rotates the humerus together with infraspinatus; extends and adducts the arm.

Relevance of shortening: Tendinitis.

Positioning: Close to full elevation and adduction of humerus.

Elongation: Medial rotation of the humerus.

Subscapularis (Fig. 13-11)

Origin: Subscapular fossa of the scapula.

Insertion: Lesser tuberosity of humerus and capsule of shoulder joint.

Function: Medially rotates the humerus; extends the humerus from an elevated position.

Relevance of shortening: Tendinitis.

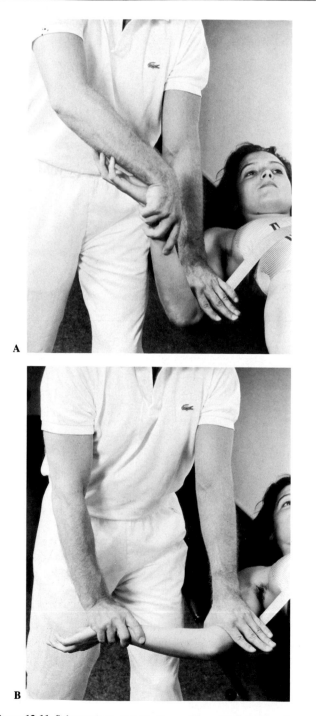

A

B

Figure 13-11 Subscapularis. (**A**) Starting position. (**B**) Full elongation.

Positioning: Approximately 45° abduction of the humerus.

Elongation: Lateral rotation of the humerus.

Pronator Teres (Fig. 13-12)

Origin: Humeral head: medial epicondylar ridge of humerus and common flexor tendon; ulnar head: medial side of coronoid process of ulna.

Insertion: Middle of lateral surface of radius.

Function: Pronates forearm; assists in flexion of the forearm.

Relevance of shortening: Tendinitis; entrapment of the median nerve (possible contribution to carpal tunnel symptoms).

Positioning: Supine; supination of the forearm.

Elongation: Extension of the forearm.

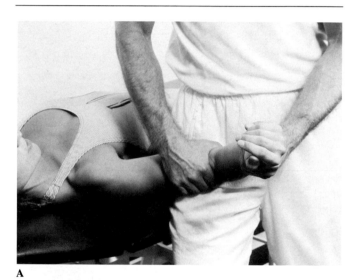

A

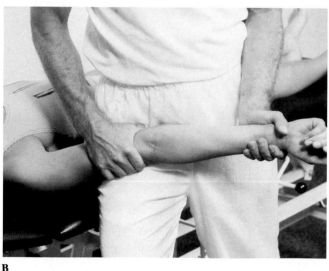

B

Figure 13-12 Pronator teres. (**A**) Starting position. (**B**) Full elongation.

Supinator (Fig. 13-13)

Origin: Lateral epicondyle of humerus, lateral collateral ligament of elbow, annular ligament, supinator crest, and fossa of the ulna.

Insertion: Lateral and anterior surface of the radius (upper third).

Function: Supination and flexion of the forearm.

Relevance of shortening: Tendinitis, entrapment of radial nerve.

Positioning: Supine; arm in 90° flexion, pronation of the forearm.

Elongation: Extension of the forearm.

Extensor Carpi Radialis Longus (Fig. 13-14)

Origin: Lower third of lateral supracondylar ridge of humerus, lateral intermuscular septum.

Insertion: Dorsal surface of base of second metacarpal.

Function: Flexes elbow, supinates forearm, extends wrist, and radially deviates the hand.

Relevance of shortening: Tendinitis, tenosynovitis; commonly seen in situations of repetitive overuse (repetitive use trauma).

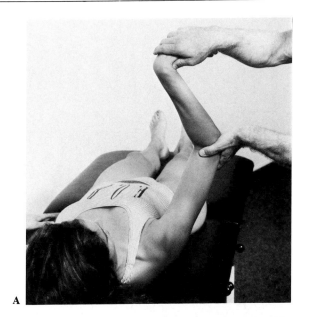

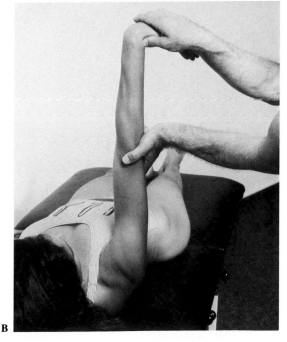

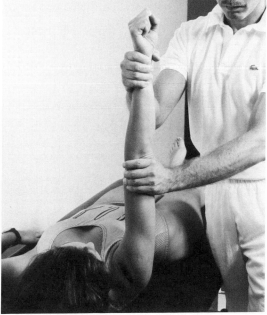

Figure 13-13 Supinator. (**A**) Starting position. (**B**) Full elongation.

Figure 13-14 Extensor carpi radialis longus. (**A**) Starting position. (**B**) Full elongation.

Positioning: Supine; arm in full medial rotation; some abduction, flexion, and pronation of forearm; wrist flexion and ulnar deviation.

Elongation: Extension of the forearm.

Extensor Carpi Radialis Brevis (Fig. 13-15)

Origin: Common extensor tendon from lateral epicondyle of the humerus, lateral intermuscular septum.

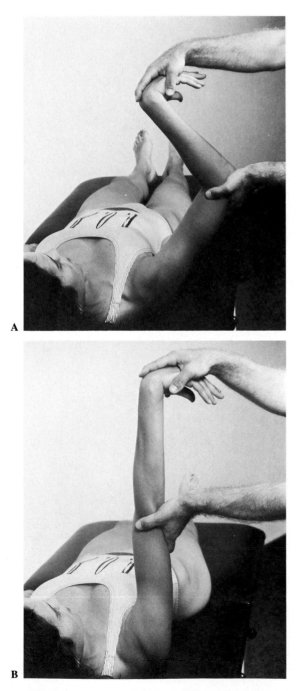

Figure 13-15 Extensor carpi radialis brevis. (**A**) Starting position. (**B**) Full elongation.

Insertion: Dorsal surface of the base of third metacarpal bone.

Function: Extends wrist, flexes elbow, supinates forearm.

Relevance of shortening: Lateral epicondylitis, tendinitis, tenosynovitis; commonly seen in situations of repetitive overuse.

Positioning: Supine; arm in medial rotation; some abduction, flexion, and pronation of forearm; wrist flexion.

Elongation: Extension of the forearm.

Extensor Digitorum Communis (Fig. 13-16)

Origin: Common extensor tendon from lateral epicondyle of the humerus, intermuscular septa.

Insertion: Dorsolateral surface of the distal phalanges of second to fifth fingers.

Function: Flexes elbow, pronates forearm, extends wrist and second to fifth fingers.

Relevance of shortening: Lateral epicondylitis, tendinitis, tenosynovitis.

Positioning: Supine; arm in medial rotation; some abduction, flexion, and pronation of forearm; wrist and finger flexion.

Elongation: Extension of the forearm.

Flexor Carpi Radialis (Fig. 13-17)

Origin: Common flexor tendon from medial epicondyle of humerus, fascia of forearm.

Insertion: Base of second and third metacarpal bones.

Function: Flexes the elbow, pronates the forearm, flexes and radially deviates wrist.

Relevance of shortening: Medial epicondylitis, tendinitis; commonly seen with golfers, raquetball players, tennis players.

Positioning: Supine; arm in lateral rotation, some abduction and flexion, and supination of forearm; extension and ulnar deviation of the wrist.

Elongation: Extension of the forearm.

Flexor Carpi Ulnaris (Fig. 13-18)

Origin: Humeral head: common flexor tendon from medial epicondyle of the humerus; ulnar head: olecranon and dorsal border of the ulna.

Insertion: Via pisiform bone to the base of fifth metacarpal and hamate bones.

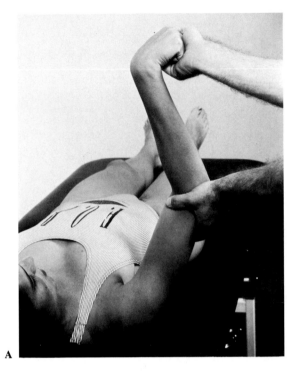

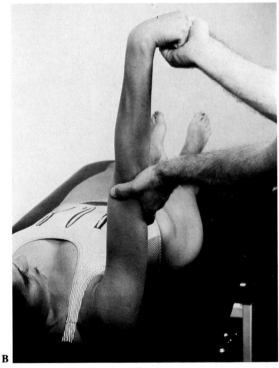

Figure 13-16 Extensor digitorum communis. (**A**) Starting position. (**B**) Full elongation.

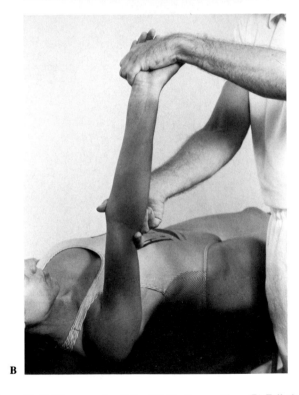

Figure 13-17 Flexor carpi radialis. (**A**) Starting position. (**B**) Full elongation.

Function: Flexes the elbow, pronates the forearm, flexes and ulnar deviates wrist.

Relevance of shortening: Medial epicondylitis, tendinitis.

Positioning: Supine; arm in lateral rotation, some abduction, flexion, and supination of forearm; extension and radial deviation of the wrist.

Elongation: Extension of the forearm.

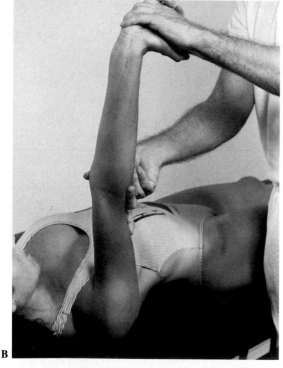

Figure 13-18 Flexor carpi ulnaris. **(A)** Starting position. **(B)** Full elongation.

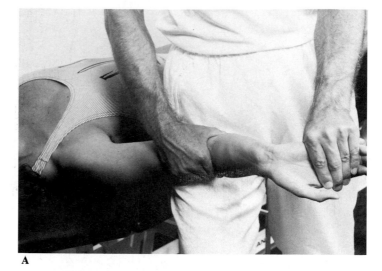

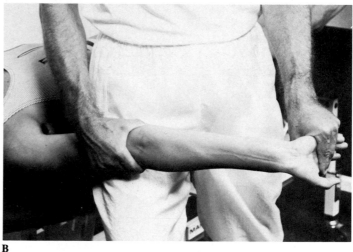

Figure 13-19 Flexor digitorum superficialis. **(A)** Starting position. **(B)** Full elongation.

Flexor Digitorum Superficialis (Fig. 13-19)

Origin: Humeral head: common flexor tendon from medial epicondyle of humerus; ulnar head: coronoid process of the ulna; radial head: oblique line of the radius.

Insertion: Margins of palmar surface of middle phalanges of second to fifth fingers.

Function: Flexes the elbow; pronates the forearm; flexes wrist and proximal and middle phalanges of second to fifth fingers.

Relevance of shortening: Medial epicondylitis, tendinitis.

Positioning: Supine; arm in lateral rotation; some abduction, flexion, and supination of forearm; extension of wrist and second to fifth fingers.

Elongation: Extension of the forearm.

Abductor Pollicis Longus (Fig. 13-20)

Origin: Upper third of the posterior surface of ulna, interosseous membrane, middle third of posterior surface of radius.

Insertion: Radial side of the base of the first metacarpal bone.

Function: Abduction of wrist and thumb.

Extensor Pollicis Brevis (Fig. 13-21)

Origin: Posterior surface of radius and ulna, interosseous membrane.

Insertion: Base of proximal phalanx of thumb.

Function: Extension and abduction of thumb and wrist.

Relevance of shortening: Tendinitis, tenosynovitis (de Quervain's disease).

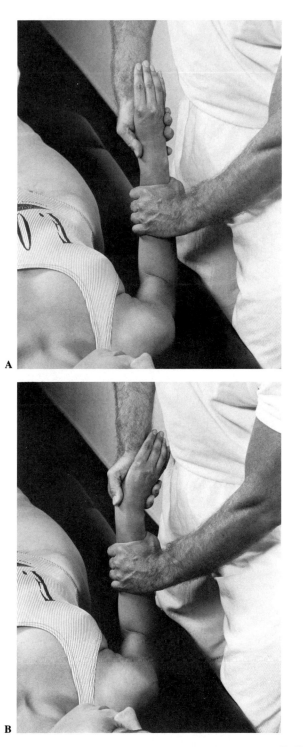

A

B

Figure 13-20 Abductor pollicis longus. (**A**) Starting position. (**B**) Full elongation.

Relevance of shortening: Tendinitis, tenosynovitis (de Quervain's disease).

Positioning: Supine or sitting; elbow flexion; full pronation of the forearm; wrist in neutral; first metacarpal bone in full flexion and adduction.

Elongation: Ulnar deviation of the wrist.

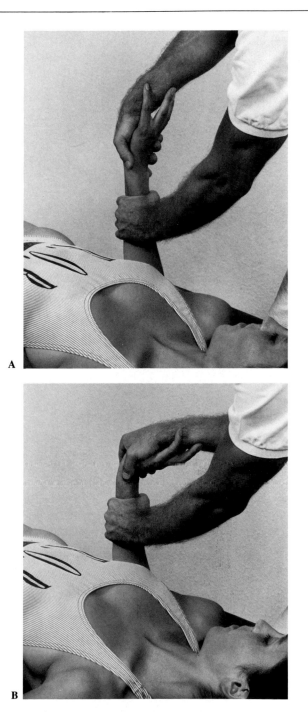

A

B

Figure 13-21 Extensor pollicis brevis. (**A**) Starting position. (**B**) Full elongation.

Positioning: Supine or sitting; elbow flexion; full pronation of the forearm, wrist in neutral; first metacarpal bone in full opposition and flexion.

Elongation: Extension and ulnar deviation of the wrist.

The Lower Extremity

Iliopsoas (Fig. 13-22)

Origin: Upper two-thirds of iliac fossa; iliac crest, anterior sacroiliac, lumbosacral, and iliolumbar ligaments; ala of the sacrum; anterior surface and the transverse processes and bodies of L1–5 and corresponding intervertebral discs.

Insertion: Lesser trochanter of femur, capsule of hip joint.

Function: Spine fixed: flexion, lateral rotation, and abduction-adduction (depending on position of the femur); *femur fixed:* flexion, ipsilateral sidebending, and contralateral rotation of the lumbar spine plus extension of the pelvis.

Relevance of shortening: Tendinitis, arthrosis of the hip, postural disturbances with increased lumbar lordosis, sacroiliac joint dysfunctions.

Positioning: Prone; flexion of the contralateral pelvis and thigh to flex slightly and to stabilize the lumbar spine; contralateral sidebending and ipsilateral rotation of the lumbar spine. Stabilization belt across the sacrum and the flexed hip, wrapping around the posterolateral thigh.

Elongation: Extension of femur.

Gluteus Medius (Fig. 13-23)

Origin: Outer surface of ilium from iliac crest and posterior gluteal line above to anterior gluteal line below.

Insertion: Lateral surface of greater trochanter.

Function: Abducts, externally rotates, and (depending on the position) flexes or extends the thigh.

Relevance of shortening: Tendinitis.

Positioning: Side posture; contralateral (superior) hip and knee in 90° flexion supported by pillow. Pelvis and lumbar spine fixated by belt. Firm pillow under the waist supports lumbar spine.

Elongation: Adduction of the thigh.

Rectus Femoris (Fig. 13-24)

Origin: Anterior inferior iliac spine.

Insertion: Upper border of the patella.

Function: Pelvis fixed: knee extension, hip flexion; *femur and leg fixed:* extension of the pelvis.

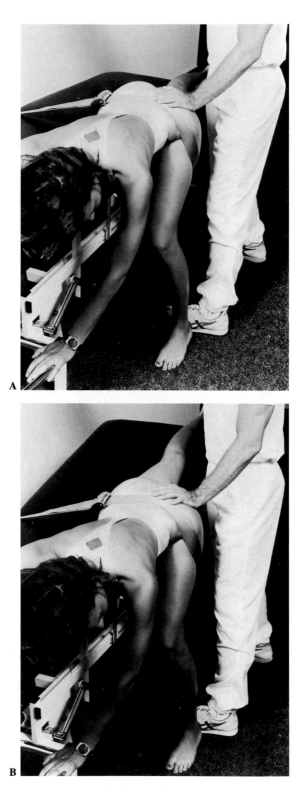

Figure 13-22 Iliopsoas. **(A)** Starting position. **(B)** Full elongation.

Relevance of shortening: Tendinitis, instability of the knee.

Positioning: Prone; flexion of the contralateral pelvis and femur to stabilize the lumbar spine; pelvis and hip flat on the

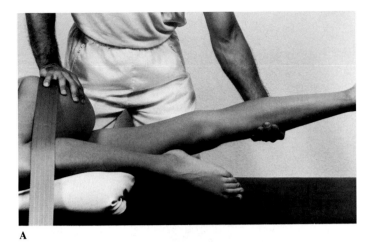

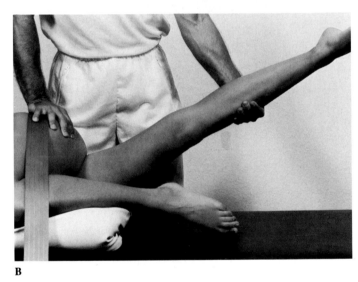

Figure 13-23 Gluteus medius. **(A)** Starting position. **(B)** Full elongation.

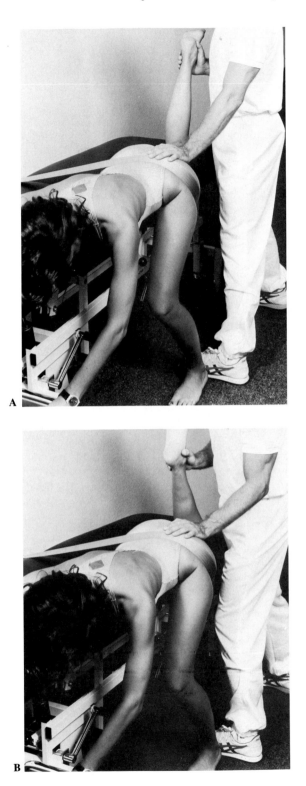

Figure 13-24 Rectus femoris. **(A)** Starting position. **(B)** Full elongation.

table. Stabilization belt across the sacrum and the flexed hip, wrapping around the posterolateral thigh.

Elongation: Flexion of the leg.

Hamstrings (Semimembranosus, Semitendinosus, and Biceps Femoris) (Fig. 13-25)

Origin: Biceps femoris, long head: ischial tuberosity and sacrotuberous ligament; biceps femoris, short head: lateral aspect of linea aspera; semitendinosus: superomedial facet of ischial tuberosity; semimembranosus: superolateral facet of ischial tuberosity.

Insertion: Biceps femoris: head of fibula and lateral condyle of tibia; semitendinosus: pes anserinus into superomedial tibia; semimembranosus: posteromedial surface of medial tibial condyle.

Function: Pelvis fixed: knee flexion and rotation (lateral hamstrings: lateral rotation; medial hamstrings: medial rotation), hip extension and rotation; femur and leg fixed: flexion of the pelvis.

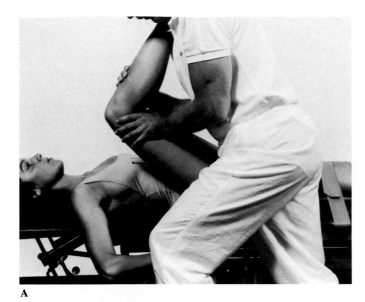

A

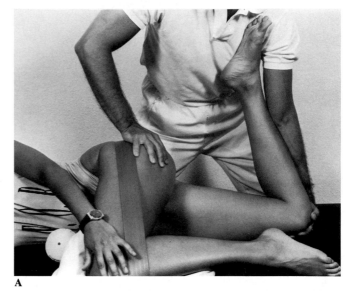

A

B

B

Figure 13-25 Hamstrings (semimembranosus, semitendinosus, and biceps femoris). (**A**) Starting position. (**B**) Full elongation.

Figure 13-26 Tensor fasciae latae. (**A**) Starting position. (**B**) Full elongation.

Relevance of shortening: Tendinitis, instability of the knee.

Positioning: Extension of the contralateral pelvis and femur to stabilize the lumbar spine; flexion of the femur. Stabilization belt across the opposite thigh and around the table.

Elongation: Extension of leg.

Tensor Fasciae Latae (Fig. 13-26)

Origin: Anterior part of outer lip of iliac crest, anterior border of ilium.

Insertion: Middle third of thigh along iliotibial tract, which inserts into lateral condyle of tibia.

Function: Abduction, medial rotation, and flexion of femur; counteracts backward pull of gluteus maximus on iliotibial tract.

Relevance of shortening: Tendinitis, iliotibial band friction syndrome.

Positioning: Sidelying; contralateral (superior) thigh flexed to stabilize lumbar spine and pelvis, supported by pillow; pelvis fixated with belt; ipsilateral (inferior) thigh in extension and lateral rotation.

Elongation: Adduction of the femur.

Adductors (Fig. 13-27)

Origin: Rami of os ischium and os pubis.

Insertion: Lesser trochanter to linea aspera, linea aspera, and medial supracondylar line.

Function: Adduction, flexion of thigh; rotational action depends on the muscle.

Relevance of shortening: Tendinitis; osteoarthritis of the hip.

Positioning: Flexion of the trunk (by having the patient curl the chest forward and rest on the elbows) to stabilize the lumbar spine and pelvis; thighs in 45° flexion (can be varied according to muscles that are shortened); stabilization belt across the pelvis.

Elongation: Abduction of the femur.

Gracilis (Fig. 13-28)

Origin: Lower half of pubic symphysis, upper half of pubic arch.

Insertion: Middle tendon of pes anserinus, medial surface of tibial condyle.

Function: Flexion, adduction, and medial rotation of thigh; flexion and lateral rotation of leg.

Relevance of shortening: Tendinitis, instability of knee.

Positioning: Supine; hips extended; stabilization belt across the pelvis, lumbar spine slightly kyphosed (by having the patient curl the chest forward and rest on the elbows); contralateral leg flexed over side of table.

Elongation: Abduction of the thigh.

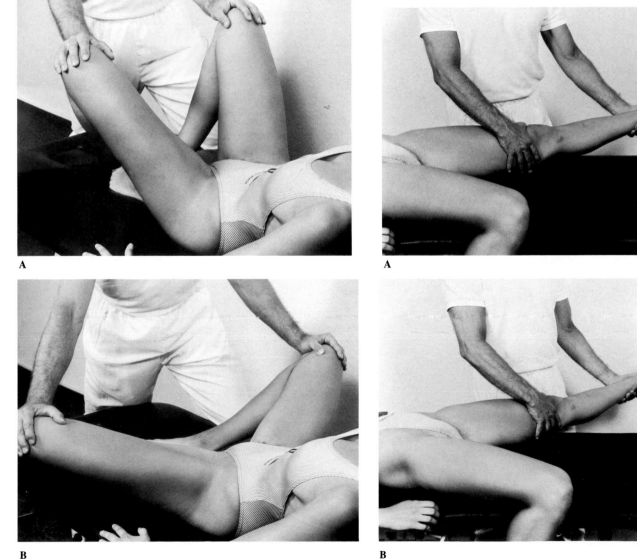

A

B

Figure 13-27 Adductors. (**A**) Starting position. (**B**) Full elongation.

Figure 13-28 Gracilis. (**A**) Starting position. (**B**) Full elongation.

Popliteus (Fig. 13-29)

Origin: Lateral condyle of the femur, oblique popliteal ligament of the knee.

Insertion: Posteromedial surface of tibia above soleal line.

Function: Flexion of leg, medial rotation of the tibia.

Relevance of shortening: Tendinitis, instability of the knee.

Positioning: Supine; knee in slight flexion (supported by pillow); leg in lateral rotation.

Elongation: Extension of the leg.

Gastrocnemius, Plantaris, and Soleus (Fig. 13-30)

Origin: Gastrocnemius, medial head: medial condyle of femur, capsule of the knee joint; gastrocnemius, lateral head: lateral condyle of femur, capsule of the knee joint; plantaris: lateral supracondylar line of femur, oblique popliteal ligament

A

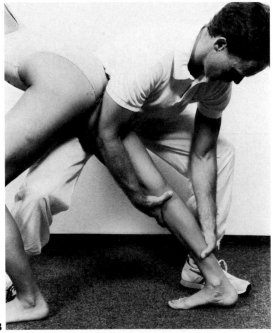

B

Figure 13-30 Gastrocnemius, plantaris, and soleus. (**A**) Starting position. (**B**) Full elongation.

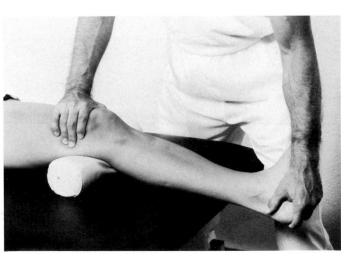

A

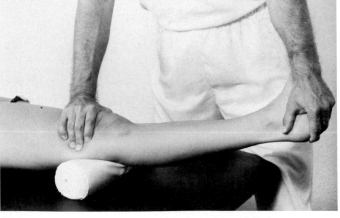

B

Figure 13-29 Popliteus. (**A**) Starting position. (**B**) Full elongation.

of the knee joint; soleus: posterior surface of head and upper shaft of fibula, medial border of tibia, interosseous membrane.

Insertion: Gastrocnemius and soleus: via Achilles tendon into posterior calcaneus; plantaris: posteromedial side of calcaneus.

Function: Plantarflexion of the foot.

Relevance of shortening: Tendinitis.

Positioning: Standing; contralateral thigh and leg in flexion; ipsilateral knee and hip extended to a position where heel does not contact the floor.

Elongation: Dorsiflexion of the foot by pushing heel to floor.

Tibialis Posterior (Fig. 13-31)

Origin: Lateral part of posterior surface of tibia, upper medial surface of fibula, interosseous membrane, deep transverse fascia and intermuscular septa.

Insertion: Tuberosity of navicular bone, plantar surface of cuneiform bones and base of second to fourth metacarpal bones, sustentaculum tali, cuboid bone.

Function: Plantar flexion and inversion of the foot.

Relevance of shortening: Tendinitis, shin splints, tenosynovitis.

Positioning: Prone; knee flexed 90°; foot in eversion (pronation); forefoot abducted.

Elongation: Dorsiflexion of the foot.

Peroneus Longus and Brevis (Fig. 13-32)

Origin: Peroneus longus: lateral condyle of tibia, upper two-thirds of lateral surface of fibula; peroneus brevis: lower two-thirds of lateral surface of fibula.

Insertion: Peroneus longus: lateral side of medial cuneiform and base of first metatarsal bone; peroneus brevis: tuberosity of fifth metatarsal bone.

Function: Plantar flexion and eversion of the foot.

Relevance of shortening: Tenosynovitis.

Positioning: Prone; knee flexed 90°; foot in inversion.

Elongation: Dorsiflexion of the foot.

Tibialis Anterior (Fig. 13-33)

Origin: Lateral condyle of tibia, upper two-thirds of lateral tibia, interosseous membrane.

Insertion: Medial and plantar side of medial cuneiform and base of first metatarsal bone.

Function: Dorsiflexion and inversion of the foot.

Relevance of shortening: Tendinitis, shin splints, tenosynovitis.

Positioning: Supine; knee supported, ankle over the end of the table, foot in full eversion.

Elongation: Plantar flexion of the foot.

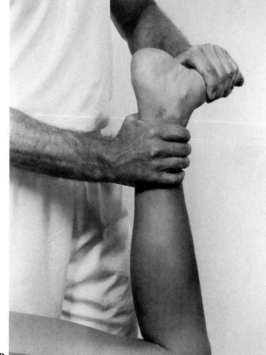

Figure 13-31 Tibialis posterior. (**A**) Starting position. (**B**) Full elongation.

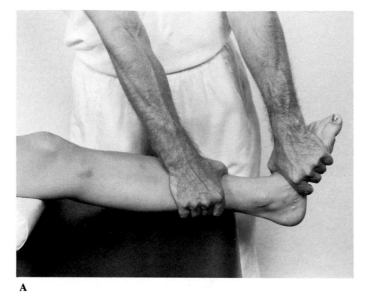

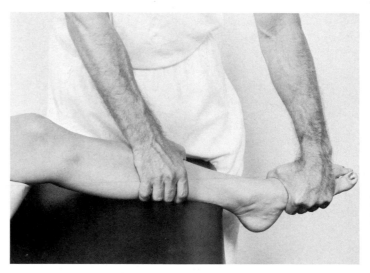

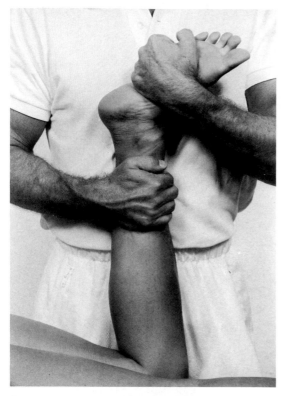

A

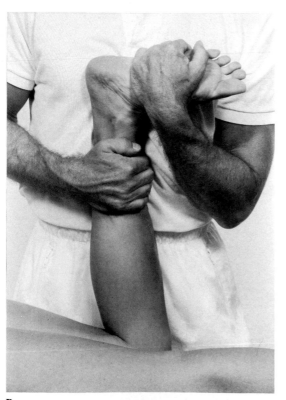

B

Figure 13-32 Peroneus longus and brevis. (**A**) Starting position. (**B**) Full elongation.

Figure 13-33 Tibialis anterior. (**A**) Starting position. (**B**) Full elongation.

Flexor Hallucis Longus (Fig. 13-34)

Origin: Lower two-thirds of posterior fibula, interosseous membrane.

Insertion: Base of distal phalanx of the great toe.

Function: Flexion of the great toe, plantar flexion of the foot.

Relevance of shortening: Tendinitis, tenosynovitis.

Positioning: Prone; knee flexed 90°; foot in plantar flexion; great toe in full dorsiflexion at metatarsophalangeal and interphalangeal joints.

Elongation: Dorsiflexion of the foot.

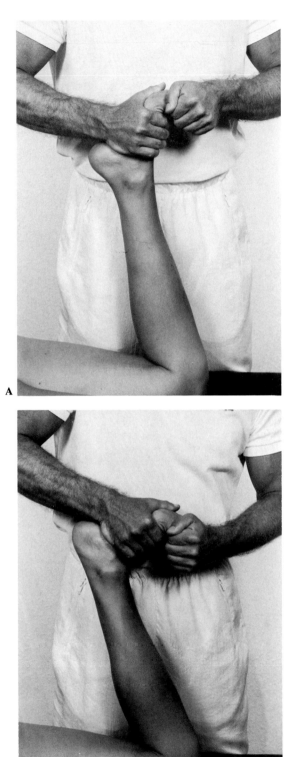

Figure 13-34 Flexor hallucis longus. (**A**) Starting position. (**B**) Full elongation.

REFERENCES

1. Ekstrand J. *Soccer Injuries and Their Prevention*. Linköping, Sweden; 1982.

2. Janda V. Die Bedeutung der muskulären Fehlhaltung als pathogenetischer Faktor vertebragener Störungen. *Arch Phys Ther*. 1968;20: 113–116.

3. Evjenth O, Hamberg J. *Muscle Stretching in Manual Therapy*. Alfta, Sweden: Alfta Rehab; 1985;1:7.

4. Sherrington CS. On plastic tonus and proprioceptive reflexes. *Q J Exp Physiol*. 1909;2:109–156.

5. Sherrington CS. *The Integrative Action of the Nervous System*. New Haven: Yale University Press; 1920.

6. Kabat H. Studies on neuromuscular dysfunction: XIII: new concepts and techniques of neuromuscular re-education for paralysis. *Permanente Found Med Bull*. 1950;8:21–143.

7. Knott M, Voss DE. *Proprioceptive Neuromuscular Facilitation*. New York: Hoeber; 1968.

8. Etnyre BR, Abraham LD. H-reflex changes during static stretching and two variations of proprioceptive neuromuscular facilitation techniques. *Electroencephalogr Clin Neurophysiol*. 1986;63:174–179.

9. Condon SM, Hutton RS. Soleus muscle electromyographic activity and ankle dorsiflexion range of motion during four stretching procedures. *Phys Ther*. 1987;67:24–30.

10. Wyke B. Neurology of the cervical spine joints. *Physiotherapy*. 1979;65:72–76.

11. Schmidt RF. Schmerzauslösende Substanzen. *Z Phys Med*. 1981;10:73–89.

12. Schmidt RF, Kniffki KD, Schomburg ED. Der Einfluss kleinkalibriger Muskelafferenzen auf den Muskeltonus. In: Bauer HJ, Koella WP, Struppler A, eds. *Therapie der Spastik*. Munich: Verlag für angewandte Wissenschaften; 1981.

13. Janda V. *Muskelfunktionsdiagnostik*. Leuven: Verlag für Medizin Dr Ewald Fischer; 1979.

14. Saltin B, Henriksson J, Nygard E, Anderson P, Jansson E. Fiber types and metabolic potentials of skeletal muscles in sedentary men and endurance runners. *Ann NY Acad Sci*. 1977;301:3–29.

15. Brooks GA, Fahey TD. *Exercise Physiology*. New York: Wiley; 1984.

16. Howald H. Training induced morphological and functional changes in skeletal muscle. *Int J Sports Med*. 1982;3:1–12.

17. Jowett RL, Fidler MW. Histochemical changes in the multifidus in mechanical derangements of the spine. *Orthop Clin North Am*. 1975;6: 145–161.

18. Saltin B, Gollnick PD. Skeletal muscle adaptability: significance for metabolism and performance. In: Peachey LD, Adrian RH, eds. *Handbook of Physiology*. Bethesda, Md: American Physiological Society; 1983;555–631.

19. Hoppeler H. Exercise induced structural changes in skeletal muscle. In: *ISI Atlas of Science*. Philadelphia: Institute for Scientific Information; 1988:248–255.

20. Cyriax J. *Textbook of Orthopaedic Medicine*. London: Hutchinson; 1969.

21. Simons DG, Travell JG. Myofascial pain syndromes. In: Wall PD, Melzack R, eds. *Textbook of Pain*. New York: Churchill Livingstone; 1989;368–385.

22. Kessler RM, Hertling D. *Management of Common Musculoskeletal Disorders*. Philadelphia: Harper & Row; 1983.

23. Senn E. Trophische Störungen im Bereiche des Bewegungsapparates, insbesondere der Muskulatur, 1. Teil: Ursachen. *Z Angew Bäder Klimaheilkd*. 1976;24:265–281.

24. Goldspink DF, Goldspink G. The role of passive stretch in retarding muscle atrophy. In: Nix WA, Vrbova G, eds. *Electrical Stimulation and Neuromuscular Disorders*. Berlin: Springer-Verlag; 1986;91–100.

25. Leivseth G, Tindall A, Myklebust R. Changes in guinea pig muscle histology in response to reduced mobility. *Muscle Nerve*. 1987;10:410–414.

26. Kaltenborn FM. *Manuelle Therapie der Extremitätengelenke*. Oslo: Olaf Norlis Bokhandel; 1985.

Chapter **14**

Rehabilitation of Soft Tissue Injuries

Mary Kay Campbell

The treatment of patients with soft tissue dysfunction is a challenge and involves the care of the whole patient, not only the injured and painful part. The treating health professional must evaluate the patient not only from a medical professional point of view but also from the patient's point of view by noting the patient's goal of returning to normal function. This is the ultimate goal of any rehabilitation process. The concept of normal function varies from patient to patient; therefore, the rehabilitation process does also.

This chapter discusses the evaluation of soft tissue injuries for rehabilitation and the importance of setting realistic goals for the patient, the components of a rehabilitation program, and options for treatment for selected diagnoses.

EVALUATION

The importance of a thorough evaluation of the patient is paramount and cannot be overstated. For each diagnosis or problem, specific goals must be set that are applicable to each patient. Hence two patients with the same diagnosis may not be treated in the same manner. Factors such as personality, personal interests, and overall health can be determining factors. Goals should be agreed on between the health professional and the patient, and there should be continual reevaluation with the introduction of each step of treatment.

General evaluation should include a thorough history of pain to determine the appropriate diagnosis; evaluation of the entire body, not just the injured part; palpation of affected joints; notation of atrophy, musculoskeletal noises, and locking of joints; tenderness on palpation of affected areas; and observation of noticeable muscle spasming. In this chapter evaluation for choice of rehabilitation treatment focuses specifically on posture, gait, and proprioception.

Posture Evaluation

Evaluation of posture can be helpful in determining the appropriate rehabilitation program for a patient. The malalignment of body parts can facilitate pathology at any joint. Correction of these abnormalities can facilitate the rehabilitation process and help avoid future or further injuries.

Sitting and standing postures in work and home environments are evaluated for the effects of muscle deconditioning. A postural syndrome can result from this deconditioning effect. Poor posture encourages loss of mobility and gradual development of adaptive muscle shortening on one side of the body with compensatory lengthening on the other side. The body adjusts itself to the position of the head to maintain the eyes and ears in a horizontal position. The musculoskeletal system below is affected by these changes, and this can eventually cause additional soft tissue dysfunction.

Treatments for postural deviations include but are not limited to proprioceptive training, strengthening of the trunk in diagonal patterns, strengthening of the limbs in diagonal patterns, and stretching and strengthening of antagonist muscle groups to balance posture.

277

Gait Evaluation

After injury, it is prudent to evaluate the gait of the patient. Abnormal gait patterns can cause back, hip, knee, ankle, and foot pain. Lack of correction of these abnormalities can predispose a person to future injury or inhibit return to normal function. The body must be considered the sum of its parts, with no part being ignored.

When walking, one foot is always in contact with the ground. Within one cycle of gait there are two periods of single limb support and two periods of double limb support. There are several components of gait: forward progression, which is a stepping movement with a wide range of comfortable and rapid walking speeds; alternate balancing of the body on one limb and then the other; and support of the upright body. Normal gait is traditionally divided into two phases: stance and swing. The stance phase consists of initial contact (heel strike), load response (foot flat), midstance (single leg stance), terminal stance (heel-off), and preswing (toe-off). The swing phase consists of initial swing (acceleration), midswing, and terminal swing (deceleration).

Evaluation of gait requires careful observation and attention to small deviations. The cause of the deviation must be determined. Causes of gait deviations may be spasticity, pain, altered body image, decreased balance, decreased proprioception, sensory loss, decreased strength, lack of stability, structural deformities, or past medical and surgical history. A gait evaluation may help determine what additional treatment goals are required. For example, genu recurvatum could be due to tight hamstrings, quadriceps, or gastrocnemius. Observation of gait in the clinic or by videotaping or footprinting on paper can measure velocity, cadence, ankle rotation, stride length, step length, weight-bearing distribution, and pressure areas. Other areas to observe are the lateral pelvic shift, vertical pelvic shift (pelvic tilt), pelvic rotation, center of gravity, normal cadence, patterns of shoe (sole) wear.

Treatments for gait deviations include but are not limited to resisted trunk movement in diagonal patterns, strengthening of the limbs in diagonal patterns, resisted gait activities, proprioceptive work with balancing activities, plyometrics, isokinetic exercises, and orthotics.

Proprioception

Proprioception is defined as the body's ability to vary the forces of muscles in immediate response to outside forces. This information is provided by muscles, tendons, and joint receptors and effects posture, muscle tone, kinesthetic awareness, and coordination. After an injury, this ability may be compromised. For this reason, stimulation of joint proprioceptors must be a component of the treatment plan. Proprioceptive neuromuscular facilitation (PNF) techniques and patterns are acceptable means to this end. As pain and effusion decrease, a patient may progress to more rigorous activities such as isokinetic exercise. Two-leg and single-leg balance activities are helpful for the lower extremities. Strengthening of the trunk musculature may also facilitate joint position sense.

TREATMENT OPTIONS

Once the diagnosis has been made, evaluation completed, and goals determined, the treatment process can begin. There are many options of treating the same injury; the method that suits the patient is usually the optimal treatment. Various treatment options are presented below.

Therapeutic Exercise

Active and passive exercises are used to increase range of motion, to increase strength, to decrease pain, and to decrease adhesions or scar tissue formation in undesirable locations. Most exercise for the selected diagnoses in this text involves active and active resisted exercise performed for stretching and strengthening. Therapeutic strengthening exercises involve movement of the joint, with speed and resistance being common variables. These exercises can be broken down into three categories: isometric, isotonic, and isokinetic.

Isometric exercise involves no joint movement and thus no joint irritation. It is usually recommended to maintain strength and to retard atrophy. There is no special equipment required for this type of exercise, and it can usually be performed in a short time period. An example of this type of exercise is a quadriceps set, which involves a tightening of the quadriceps muscles without movement of the knee joint. The disadvantages of this type of exercise are that there is no improvement in endurance and in eccentric muscle strength, and contraction is only observed in one specific range of the joint.

Isotonic exercise is movement of a fixed weight through the full range of motion with a fixed resistance and variable speed. This exercise is also known as progressive resistive exercise (PRE). The advantage of this exercise is that the affected muscles can be strengthened both concentrically and eccentrically. With these exercises the patient sees improvement in endurance, and this improvement can be objectively documented. There are some notable disadvantages. There is the same loading of the muscle through the entire range of motion, which can cause trauma or stress to the weaker part of the range of motion. There is also no noticeable development of muscle power.

With isokinetic exercise, the resistance to the muscle accommodates the force exerted (preset and fixed speed). Thus the resistance accommodates to the effort expended throughout the ranges. These exercises require specifically made equipment that is expensive. Often testing and treatment are time consuming, but with patients who are more active and who have goals that include athletic activities this type of exercise can be valuable.

Swimming and bicycling are considered important parts of some rehabilitation programs. These are supervised activities (exercises in a therapeutic pool and stationary bicycling) that can be continued in a patient's home program after discharge from treatment.

Proprioceptive Neuromuscular Facilitation

Movement components have been described in the literature as PNF patterns or spiral-diagonal combinations of movement. The philosophy of PNF contends that humans respond to the demands placed on the body and that body movements are specific and directed toward a specific goal. Activity is necessary for the development of coordination and endurance. In PNF, the stronger body parts are used to assist the weaker body parts to improve function; thus PNF is an excellent adjunct to the therapeutic strengthening program.

It has been observed that infant developmental sequences such as rolling from prone to supine, creeping, crawling, walking, running, and jumping are composed of spiral-diagonal combinations. Many motor skills, whether developmental, sport related, or activities of daily living, have common movement denominators that can be identified as diagonal patterns. These patterns can be used by patients to facilitate a specific motor behavior.

Proprioceptive neuromuscular facilitation is used clinically (1) to restore functional range of motion and the ability to initiate a motion into and through available range of motion (mobility), (2) to develop the ability to improve and maintain posture against resistance (stability), (3) to develop and improve unilateral weight-bearing ability (balance and coordination), and (4) to develop the ability to manipulate the environment (skill). The basic principles of PNF are summarized below:

1. *Tactile stimulation:* The manual contacts (hands over muscles, tendons, or joint) and the patient position act to facilitate the motor responses. The hands are in line with the direction of the desired diagonal movement.
2. *Visual input:* Visual feedback is given with the motor activity to reinforce movement. This is especially important when proprioceptive awareness is impaired.
3. *Verbal input:* Auditory stimulation must be timed with the proprioceptive input to allow the patient and therapist to work together. Commands are short, clear, concise, accurate, and positive.
4. *Joint receptor stimulation:* Traction (to promote motion) and approximation (to promote stability and posture maintenance) are applied to stimulate joint receptors.
5. *Appropriate resistance:* With isotonic movement, the amount of resistance should be the greatest amount applied to achieve an active contraction and to allow the patient to move slowly throughout the range of motion. With isometric movement, resistance is graded to match the patient's ability to hold a contraction.

6. *Stretch reflex:* This is a nonfatigable reflex that is facilitatory when accompanied by voluntary effort and followed by maximal resistance. Muscles must be taut, especially in rotation, to obtain a quick stretch.
7. *Normal timing:* This is a sequence of muscle contractions that allows smooth, coordinated movement. In a normal mature neuromuscular system this is distal to proximal movement.
8. *Patterns:* These are specific PNF patterns (synergistic muscle groups) that are diagonal and spiral and resemble movements in sports and work activities. The patterns are divided into upper and lower extremities.

The following techniques are offered as an adjunct to the treatment of selected tissue lesions as noted in subsequent sections of this chapter:

- Hold-relax is a technique generally used to increase range of motion and to decrease pain in painful joints. This method is based on an isometric contraction before the painful area.
- Contract-relax is used to increase range of motion when joints are not painful. This is based on an isotonic muscle contraction. A maximal contraction with subsequent relaxation causes an increase in range of motion.
- Slow reversal is a facilitation technique that utilizes the more powerful antagonist pattern to facilitate range of motion and strength of the weaker agonist. An isotonic muscle contraction is encouraged into the antagonist pattern.
- Repeated contraction encourages a unidirectional movement of an isotonic contraction in a desired range of motion.

To appreciate fully the philosophy, clinical application, and techniques of PNF, the reader is encouraged to consult the works of Knott and Voss,[1] Sullivan et al,[2] and Voss et al.[3]

Plyometrics

Plyometrics are exercises that store muscular energy via the force of gravity and are followed by an opposite and equal reaction. Patients who wish to participate in high-level athletic activities may wish to include plyometrics in the rehabilitation program. As the strength and coordination of the patient progress toward normal, these activities can be beneficial. Beginning activities include two-legged hopping in a straight line, two-legged hopping from side to side, one-legged hopping, and one-legged hopping from side to side. The plyometric progression may vary according to the discretion and imagination of the therapist, but the exercises usually progress from horizontal to vertical movements. A combination of these two movements is also possible. An example of a progression is squat jumps, two-legged hops, one-legged hops, triple jumps, and box drills (jumping over various box heights). Plyometrics are designed for the individual who has responded well to rehabilitation and should not be initiated before the patient has acquired good strength and co-ordination.

Modalities

Cryotherapy can be used to reduce effusion, pain, spasm, and spasticity. The effects are local anesthesia and va-soconstriction. Ice packs can be applied for 7 to 15 minutes to cool the injured area before exercising. Other cold treatments can be applied with ice cups, ice whirlpool (45° to 80°F), ice massage, and fluoromethane spray. Quick application of ice over the muscle belly can also be used to stimulate nerve fibers and to facilitate muscle contraction.

Heat can be used to improve blood supply, to increase metabolism, to encourage relaxation, and to increase the threshold of sensory nerve endings. Heat can be applied by conduction, convection, or conversion. Conduction is accomplished by hydrocollator packs, heating pads, and paraffin dip. This type of heat is beneficial to patients with arthritis. Convection is done with whirlpool baths (not exceeding 110°F), Hubbard tanks, and heated therapeutic pools. Conversion is accomplished by short-wave diathermy and ultrasound (US) (high-frequency acoustic vibration that penetrates tissues and joint spaces and converts to heat). US traditionally has been used for the production of deep heat. Because it is a high-frequency sound wave that produces a deep massage effect, it can be used for softening scar tissue as well as for decreasing muscle spasm. US can be used with 10% hydrocortisone cream as a coupling agent to intensify absorption of medication through the skin. This can be helpful in the treatment of tendinitis. There has been much research on this subject, with disputed results.

Electrical Stimulation

Electrical stimulation (ES) can be used to facilitate muscle contraction, to increase strength, to increase range of motion, to decrease swelling, and to decrease pain. An example of facilitation of a muscle contraction is ES to the quadriceps muscle. This treatment teaches the patient how to contract the quadriceps muscle with minimal or no pain. In this case, ES supplies the sensory input of what the contraction feels like. This is effective for patients who may need assistance in producing and controlling motor responses.

Patients who have been immobilized for long periods of time may benefit from ES to increase the bulk and strength of atrophied muscles. There is debate concerning the effectiveness of this type of treatment for normal muscle, but there seems to be an increased muscle response with stimulation.

Application of electrodes to soft tissue areas encourages muscular contraction at a rate that decreases effusion. This can

be a helpful modality when the patient is unable to move a joint or limb with enough effectiveness to discourage the accumulation of edema. The strength of the current depends on the condition being treated, machine type, sensitivity of the individual patient, and size of the electrode. In judging the sensitivity of the patient, temperament as well as placement of the electrodes must be considered. Treatment should be within the limits of a patient's physiologic and psychologic acceptance.

Manual Treatments

There are many manual treatment methods, including joint mobilization, stretching, PNF, trigger point techniques, and friction massage. These techniques are discussed in earlier chapters.

Home Exercise Program

An important component of rehabilitation is inclusion of the patient in a home exercise program. It is imperative that the patient take responsibility for personal health care and subsequent healing of medical problems. Encouragement is often warranted by the health professional; education of the patient is helpful in motivating a patient to perform exercises or to change daily habits to facilitate healing.

Cessation of Rehabilitation Treatment

Treatment should cease when (1) the patient has no further complaints and goals of treatment have been realized (abnormal functional tests are normal), (2) treatment has continued for a reasonable length of time and the patient has progressed to a permanent and stationary level (plateau) and is unable to improve further, or (3) the patient shows inconsistent signs of pain or discomfort and the health professional can document that the patient may be overstating his or her health complaints. (This type of patient is known as a malingerer. It is important to give this type of patient every available treatment and to document reactions to each treatment. Often, patients who seem to have malingering traits may have real soft tissue pain that has gone undiagnosed for a long period of time.)

TREATMENT PROTOCOLS FOR SELECTED SOFT TISSUE LESIONS

Treatment is initiated after a thorough evaluation, at which time goal setting and a treatment plan are determined. The treatment program should always be to the patient's tolerance, adjusting exercises and home programs as the patient's condition warrants. Treatment should be limited not only to the diagnosis but also to the other affected areas of the body.

Discomfort can be expected during a therapy session, but pain is an indication that the treatment is unsuccessful or that the patient is not ready for advanced activities. Stretching to warm up is recommended before strengthening activities are initiated. A home exercise program is imperative not only to improve joint integrity and to increase muscle strength and endurance but also to encourage patient motivation.

The following treatment recommendations and exercises that follow are presented as options, and each plan should be designed to suit the needs of the individual patient. Illustrations of the exercises for these diagnoses are presented following the treatment sections.

Shoulder

Acute and Chronic Bursitis

Modalities: Cryotherapy, ES, US.

Exercise: Isometric shoulder activities in all planes; scapular and shoulder PNF patterns to 90° flexion and abduction (pain free), increase range as pain decreases; PRE with weights as pain decreases.

Mobilization: Glenohumeral, scapular as indicated; friction massage if indicated.

Instruction: Shoulder stretching and strengthening exercises, ice massage.

Adhesive Capsulitis

Modalities: Cryotherapy, US, ES.

Exercise: Scapular and shoulder PNF patterns in available range of motion, PRE with weights as pain and effusion decrease, prolonged stretch.

Mobilization: Scapular and shoulder to increase joint play, distraction, friction massage at lesion site.

Instruction: Shoulder stretching and strengthening, ice.

Tendinitis: Supraspinatus, Infraspinatus, or Subscapularis

Modalities: Cryotherapy, ES, US.

Exercise: Pain-free range of motion exercises, scapular and shoulder PNF patterns, PRE with weights as pain and effusion decrease.

Mobilization: Friction massage over lesion site.

Instruction: Shoulder stretching and strengthening exercises, ice.

Tendinitis: Biceps (Long Head, Belly, Musculotendinous area, Insertion)

Modalities: Cryotherapy, US, ES.

Exercise: Scapular, shoulder, elbow, wrist PNF patterns; PRE with weights as pain decreases.

Mobilization: Friction massage over lesion site.

Instruction: Shoulder stretching and strengthening exercises, ice.

Brachialis Tendinitis

Modalities: Cryotherapy, US, ES.

Exercise: Scapular, shoulder, elbow, wrist PNF patterns; PRE with weights as pain decreases.

Mobilization: Friction massage over lesion site.

Instruction: Shoulder stretching and strengthening exercises, ice.

Triceps Tendinitis

Modalities: Cryotherapy, US, ES.

Exercise: Scapular, shoulder, elbow, wrist PNF patterns; PRE with weights as pain decreases.

Mobilization: Friction massage over lesion site.

Instruction: Shoulder stretching and strengthening exercises, ice.

Tendinitis: Pectoralis Major, Latissimus Dorsi, Teres Minor

Modalities: Cryotherapy, US, ES.

Exercise: Scapular and shoulder PNF patterns, stretching of antagonist muscle groups, PRE with weights as pain decreases.

Mobilization: Friction massage over lesion site.

Instruction: Shoulder stretching and strengthening exercises, ice.

Acromioclavicular or Sternoclavicular Sprain

Modalities: Cryotherapy, ES.

Exercise: Initial immobilization of shoulder (with exercises for wrist and hand), passive shoulder exercises in all planes to progress to active shoulder exercises, scapular and shoulder PNF patterns, PRE with weights as pain decreases.

Instruction: Isometric shoulder exercises to progress to active shoulder strengthening exercises.

Arthritis of Acromioclavicular Joint

Modalities: Heat, ES.

Exercises: Passive shoulder exercises in all planes to progress to active exercise in painfree areas, scapular and shoulder PNF for stretching.

Instruction: Active shoulder strengthening to maintain range.

Shoulder Instability

Exercises: Isometric exercises in all planes of motion, scapular and shoulder strengthening in PNF patterns for strengthening, trunk strengthening to encourage trunk stability.

Brace: Consider use of a brace or harness depending on the severity of the instability and the patient's activity level.

Instruction: Isometric shoulder activities to progress to active strengthening exercises.

Traumatic Arthritis

Modalities: Heat, ES.

Exercise: Passive shoulder exercises in all planes to progress to active exercises, scapular and shoulder PNF patterns.

Instruction: Shoulder stretching and strengthening exercises.

Elbow

Bursitis

Modalities: Cryotherapy, US, ES.

Exercise: Initial immobilization, active exercises to progress to elbow and wrist PNF patterns.

Brace: Consider use of a soft brace if indicated.

Instruction: Elbow exercises.

Tendinitis: Biceps, Triceps, Supinator, Pronator

Modalities: Cryotherapy, US, ES.

Exercise: Scapular, shoulder, elbow, wrist PNF patterns for stretching and strengthening; PRE with weights as pain and effusion decrease.

Mobilization: Friction massage over lesion site, mobilization to increase range of radioulnar joint.

Instruction: Elbow and wrist exercises.

Medial and Lateral Epicondylitis

Modalities: Cryotherapy, US, ES.

Exercise: Scapular, shoulder, elbow PNF patterns for stretching and strengthening; assessment of cervical-thoracic vertebral mobility and diagnosis of spinal pathology; PRE with weights as pain and effusion decrease.

Mobilization: Friction massage over lesion site, distraction.

Brace: If indicated to limit movement and to compress joint.

Instruction: Elbow and wrist stretching and strengthening.

Wrist

Arthritis

Modalities: Heat, paraffin bath, ES.

Exercise: Passive wrist exercises to progress to active exercises to maintain range of motion, wrist and hand PNF patterns.

Brace: Consider use of an orthosis for joint protection.

Instruction: Elbow and wrist stretching and strengthening.

Capitate Subluxation

Modalities: Cryotherapy.

Exercise: Isometric exercises to wrist and fingers, putty exercises; progress to elbow and wrist PNF patterns as strength increases.

Mobilization: Mobilization to improve joint movement around capitate.

Brace: If needed for stability.

Instruction: Elbow, wrist, finger stretching and strengthening.

Tendinitis: Extensor and Flexor Carpi Radialis

Modalities: Cryotherapy, ES, US.

Exercise: Massage to muscle belly, wrist and finger PNF patterns for stretching and strengthening, putty exercises, PRE with weights as pain decreases.

Mobilization: Friction massage over lesion site.

Instruction: Wrist and finger stretching and strengthening.

Tendinitis: Extensor and Flexor Carpi Radialis at Insertion

Modalities: Cryotherapy, ES, US.

Exercise: Wrist and finger PNF patterns for stretching and strengthening, putty exercises, PRE with weights as pain decreases.

Mobilization: Friction massage over lesion site.

Instruction: Wrist and finger stretching and strengthening.

Chronic Ligamentous Sprains

Modalities: Cryotherapy, ES, US.

Exercise: Isometric exercises for wrist stabilization, wrist and finger PNF patterns, PRE with weights as pain and effusion decrease, putty exercises.

Instruction: Wrist and finger exercises.

Hand

Tenosynovitis: Abductor Pollicis Longus and Extensor Pollicis Brevis (de Quervain's Disease)

Modalities: Cryotherapy, US, ES.

Exercise: Passive range of motion exercises to progress to active exercises and wrist and finger PNF patterns, putty and rubber band exercises, hand dexterity tasks, surgery if indicated.

Mobilization: Friction massage over lesion site, joint mobilization to decrease adhesion formation.

Instruction: Wrist and finger exercises, ice.

Tendinitis: Dorsal and Volar Interosseus, Extensor and Flexor Pollicis Longus and Brevis

Modalities: Cryotherapy, ES, US.

Exercise: Wrist and finger PNF patterns, putty and rubber band exercises, hand dexterity activities.

Mobilization: Friction massage over lesion site, carpal and metacarpal mobilization.

Instruction: Wrist and finger exercises, ice.

Carpal Tunnel Syndrome

Modalities: Cryotherapy, US.

Exercise: Initial immobilization (usually with orthosis), wrist and finger PNF patterns to progress to PRE with weights as pain decreases, putty exercises, hand dexterity activities, surgery if indicated.

Mobilization: Friction massage over lesion site, carpal and metacarpal mobilization.

Instruction: Wrist and finger exercises, ice.

Hip and Buttock

Osteoarthritis (Hip and Knee)

Modalities: Heat.

Exercise: Hydrotherapy (swimming), hip and knee PNF patterns, active exercises in all planes of motion.

Mobilization: Joint mobilization for capsular stretching, prolonged stretch.

Posture: Evaluation and treatment of deviations.

Gait: Evaluation and treatment of deviations.

Brace: Orthotics if needed to alleviate discomfort.

Instruction: Hip exercises, walking, swimming, bicycling.

Transient Synovitis

Modalities: Cryotherapy, ES.

Exercise: Hip and knee PNF patterns for stretching and strengthening, isometrics.

Mobilization: Joint mobilization for capsular stretching.

Brace: Orthotics to alleviate discomfort.

Instruction: Hip exercises, bicycling.

Capsulitis

Modalities: Cryotherapy, ES.

Exercise: Hip and knee PNF patterns for stretching and strengthening, active hip exercises.

Mobilization: Joint mobilization for capsular stretching.

Brace: Orthotics to alleviate discomfort.

Instruction: Hip exercises, swimming, bicycling.

Bursitis: Trochanter, Psoas, Ischium

Modalities: Cryotherapy, ES.

Exercise: Initial rest, gentle stretching of hip musculature, hip and knee PNF patterns.

Mobilization: Joint mobilization for capsular stretching, distraction.

Brace: Orthotics to alleviate discomfort.

Instruction: Initial rest; add gentle active exercises as pain decreases.

Tendinitis: Gluteus Medius, Psoas, Adductor

Modalities: Cryotherapy, US, ES.

Exercise: Bilateral hip, knee, ankle PNF patterns for stretching and strengthening; PRE with weights as pain decreases.

Mobilization: Friction massage over lesion site.

Posture: Evaluation and treatment of deviations.

Gait: Evaluation and treatment of deviations.

Instruction: Hip stretching and strengthening exercises, swimming, walking.

Tendinitis of Hamstring and Rectus Femoris Origin

Modalities: Cryotherapy, US, ES.

Exercise: Bilateral hip, knee, ankle PNF patterns for stretching and strengthening; PRE with weights as pain decreases.

Mobilization: Friction massage over lesion site.

Gait: Evaluation and treatment of deviations.

Instruction: Hip stretching and strengthening exercises, swimming, walking.

Iliotibial Band Friction Syndrome

Modalities: Cryotherapy, US, ES.

Exercise: Bilateral hip, knee, ankle PNF patterns for stretching and strengthening; PRE with weights as pain decreases.

Mobilization: Friction massage over lesion site.

Gait: Evaluation and treatment of deviations.

Brace: Orthotics for shoes for vigorous activities.

Instruction: Bilateral hip stretching and strengthening exercises, swimming, walking, bicycling.

Knee

Ligamentous Sprains: Acute and Chronic Medial and Lateral Collaterals

Modalities: Cryotherapy, US, ES.

Exercise: Hip, knee, ankle PNF patterns for stretching and strengthening; PRE with weights as pain decreases; proprioceptive training.

Brace: Knee brace for vigorous activities.

Instruction: Knee stretching and strengthening exercises, swimming, bicycling, walking.

Anterior Cruciate Sprain

Modalities: Cryotherapy, ES.

Exercise: Hip, knee, ankle PNF patterns (emphasis on hamstring strengthening); proprioceptive training; plyometrics (one- and two-legged hopping and jumping in a straight line, hopping from side to side, box jumping).

Gait: Evaluation and treatment of deviations.

Brace: Knee brace for vigorous activities.

Instruction: Hip and knee strengthening (emphasize hamstrings), swimming, bicycling, walking.

Posterior Cruciate Sprain

Modalities: Cryotherapy, ES.

Exercise: Hip, knee, ankle PNF patterns (emphasis on quadriceps strengthening); proprioceptive training; plyometrics (one- and two-legged hopping and jumping in a straight line, hopping from side to side, box jumping).

Gait: Evaluation and treatment of deviations.

Brace: Knee brace for vigorous activities.

Instruction: Hip and knee strengthening (emphasize quadriceps), swimming, walking, bicycling.

Pellegrini-Stieda Syndrome (Medial Collateral Ligament Calcification)

Modalities: Cryotherapy, ES.

Exercise: Hip, knee, ankle PNF patterns for stretching and strengthening; PRE with weights; surgery if indicated.

Posture: Evaluation and treatment of deviations.

Gait: Evaluation and treatment of deviations.

Brace: Orthotics to alleviate discomfort.

Instruction: Hip and knee exercises.

Osteoarthritis

Modalities: Heat, ES.

Exercise: Hydrotherapy (swimming), hip and knee PNF patterns, active exercises.

Posture: Evaluation and treatment of deviations.

Brace: Orthotics to decrease discomfort.

Instruction: Active knee exercises, swimming.

Tendinitis: Hamstrings (Belly and Insertions) and Popliteus

Modalities: Cryotherapy, US, ES.

Exercise: Hip and knee PNF patterns for stretching and strengthening, proprioceptive training, plyometrics (one- and two-legged hopping and jumping in a straight line, hopping from side to side, box jumping), wrapping or taping, massage to muscle belly.

Mobilization: Friction massage over lesion site.

Gait: Evaluation and treatment of deviations.

Instruction: Hamstring stretching and strengthening.

Tendinitis: Gastrocnemius Origin

Modalities: Cryotherapy, ES, US.

Exercise: Knee and ankle PNF patterns for stretching and strengthening, proprioceptive training, plyometrics (one- and two-legged hopping and jumping in a straight line, hopping from side to side, box jumping), wrapping or taping.

Mobilization: Friction massage over lesion site.

Gait: Evaluation and treatment of deviations.

Brace: Foot orthotics to decrease discomfort.

Instruction: Knee and ankle stretching and strengthening.

Tendinitis: Quadriceps Belly

Modalities: Cryotherapy, ES, US.

Exercise: Hip and knee PNF patterns for stretching and strengthening, PRE with weights as pain decreases, pressure wrap to quadriceps, massage to muscle belly.

Mobilization: Friction massage over lesion site.

Gait: Evaluation and treatment of deviations.

Instruction: Massage, ice, knee stretching and strengthening.

Tendinitis: Quadriceps Insertion (Patellar Tendinitis)

Modalities: Cryotherapy, US, ES.

Exercise: Hip and knee PNF patterns for stretching and strengthening, PRE with weights as pain decreases, proprioceptive training, plyometrics (one- and two-legged hopping and jumping in a straight line, hopping from side to side, box jumping).

Mobilization: Friction massage over lesion site.

Gait: Evaluation and treatment of deviations.

Brace: Patellar stabilization brace for vigorous activities.

Instruction: Ice, knee stretching and strengthening.

Meniscus Tears

Modalities: Cryotherapy, ES.

Exercise: Hip, knee, ankle PNF patterns for stretching and strengthening; PRE with weights as pain and effusion decrease; surgery if knee continues with pain, effusion, or locking in flexion or extension.

Mobilization: Joint mobilization to increase range of motion, distraction.

Instruction: Knee stretching and strengthening.

Knee Instability

Modalities: ES.

Exercise: Isometric exercises to hip and knee; hip, knee, ankle PNF patterns for strengthening; proprioceptive training.

Posture: Evaluation and treatment of deviations.

Gait: Evaluation and treatment of deviations.

Brace: For vigorous activities for joint protection.

Instruction: Hip and knee strengthening and isometrics.

Bursitis (Differentially Diagnosed from Tendinitis)

Modalities: Cryotherapy, ES.

Exercise: Isometrics; initiate hip and knee PNF patterns (straight-leg only) when pain and effusion decrease; proprioceptive training; plyometrics.

Posture: Evaluation and treatment of deviations.

Gait: Evaluation and treatment of deviations.

Brace: For vigorous activities.

Instruction: Hip and knee stretching and strengthening.

Plica Syndrome

Modalities: Cryotherapy, ES.

Exercise: Vastus medialis obliquus muscle re-education; hip, knee, ankle PNF patterns for stretching and strengthening; PRE with weights as pain decreases; proprioceptive training.

Mobilization: Friction massage over lesion site.

Posture: Evaluation and treatment of deviations.

Gait: Evaluation and treatment of deviations.

Brace: For vigorous activities.

Instruction: Quadriceps sets, knee stretching and strengthening, bicycling.

Lower Leg

Shin Splints (Tibialis Anterior and Posterior)

Modalities: Cryotherapy, ES, US.

Exercise: Knee and ankle PNF patterns for stretching and strengthening, proprioceptive training, plyometrics (one- and two-legged hopping and jumping in a straight line, hopping from side to side, box jumping).

Posture: Evaluation and treatment of deviations.

Gait: Evaluation and treatment of deviations.

Brace: Evaluation of shoes and need for orthotics.

Instruction: Ankle stretching and strengthening.

Gastrocnemius Tendinitis

Modalities: Cryotherapy, US, ES.

Exercise: Knee and ankle PNF patterns for stretching and strengthening, proprioceptive training.

Mobilization: Friction massage over lesion site.

Gait: Evaluation and treatment of deviations.

Brace: Evaluation of shoe and brace needs for vigorous activities.

Instruction: Ankle stretching and strengthening.

Foot and Ankle

Achilles Tendinitis

Modalities: Cryotherapy, US, ES.

Exercise: Knee, ankle, toe PNF patterns for stretching and strengthening; ankle taping; proprioceptive training.

Mobilization: Friction massage over lesion site.

Gait: Evaluation and treatment of deviations.

Brace: Ankle brace for vigorous activities, evaluation of shoes.

Instruction: Ankle and foot stretching and strengthening.

Tenosynovitis: Peroneus Brevis and Longus, Tibialis Posterior, Tibialis Anterior, and Flexor Hallucis Longus

Modalities: Cryotherapy, US, ES.

Exercise: Knee, ankle, toe PNF patterns for stretching and strengthening; ankle taping; proprioceptive training; plyometrics (one- and two-legged hopping and jumping in a straight line, hopping from side to side, box jumping).

Mobilization: Friction massage over lesion site.

Gait: Evaluation and treatment of deviations.

Brace: Evaluation of shoe and brace needs.

Instruction: Ankle and foot stretching and strengthening.

Ligament Sprain

Modalities: Cryotherapy, ES, US.

Exercise: Active range of motion exercises to progress to knee, ankle, toe PNF patterns for stretching and strengthening; ankle taping; proprioceptive training; plyometrics (one- and two-legged hopping and jumping in a straight line, hopping from side to side, box jumping).

Gait: Evaluation and treatment of deviations.

Brace: Ankle brace for vigorous activities.

Instruction: Ankle and foot stretching and strengthening.

Plantar Fasciitis

Modalities: Cryotherapy, ES, US.

Exercise: Active range of motion exercises to foot and ankle, ankle and toe PNF patterns for stretching and strengthening, proprioceptive training, taping.

Mobilization: Friction massage over lesion site, mobilization of ankle to increase range of motion.

Posture: Evaluation and treatment of deviations.

Gait: Evaluation and treatment of deviations.

Brace: Orthotics to decrease stress on fascia and to increase comfort during vigorous activities.

Instructions: Ankle stretching and strengthening.

Anterior Compartment Syndrome

Modalities: Cryotherapy, US, ES.

Exercise: Active range of motion exercises, knee and ankle PNF patterns, proprioceptive training, surgery if intracompartmental pressure increases.

Posture: Evaluation and treatment of deviations.

Gait: Evaluation and treatment of deviations.

Brace: Evaluation of shoe and possible brace needs.

Instruction: Ankle stretching and strengthening.

EXERCISES

The following exercises are examples of activities that may be used to supplement treatment protocol. Combinations of these exercises can be tailored to achieve the goals of the patient.

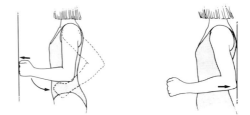

Figure 14-1 Shoulder isometrics. With elbow flexed to 90°, push fist into wall. Hold for 5 to 10 seconds. Do not move shoulder (isometric flexion). Relax and repeat. Then move to side with outside of elbow to wall. Push elbow out toward wall. Hold for 5 to 10 seconds. Do not move shoulder (isometric abduction). Relax and repeat. Then with back to wall push elbow backward toward wall. Hold for 5 to 10 seconds. Do not move shoulder (isometric extension). Relax and repeat. Repeat with other arm. *Source:* Copyright © 1990 by Rebecca Chamberlain.

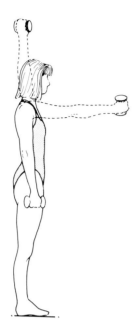

Figure 14-2 Shoulder flexion. Hold weights in each hand, arms at sides with elbows straight. Raise weight forward and straight up and over head. Keep elbows straight. Relax and repeat with other arm. Do not exercise both arms at same time. This exercise can also be done without weights. *Source:* Copyright © 1990 by Rebecca Chamberlain.

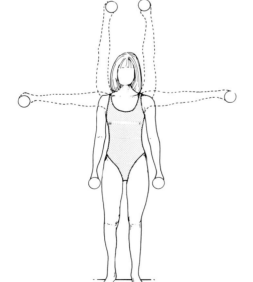

Figure 14-3 Shoulder abduction. Hold weights in each hand, arms at sides with elbows straight. Raise weights to side and over head. Rotate arms with palms up when shoulder position is reached. Return arms to side, bringing palms in as arms return to starting position. Exercise both arms at same time. This exercise can also be done without weights. *Source:* Copyright © 1990 by Rebecca Chamberlain.

Figure 14-4 Shoulder extension. Lean forward and bend trunk at waist, keeping knees flexed. Hold weight toward floor with palms facing each other and move weight back along body and up, keeping elbows straight. Return to starting position. Exercise one arm at a time. *Source:* Copyright © 1990 by Rebecca Chamberlain.

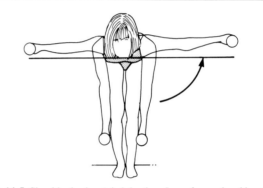

Figure 14-5 Shoulder horizontal abduction. Lean forward and bend trunk at waist, keeping knees flexed. Rest head on table. Raise both arms, lifting weights to side straight out and parallel to table. Relax. Exercise both arms at same time. This exercise can also be done without weights. *Source:* Copyright © 1990 by Rebecca Chamberlain.

Figure 14-6 Shoulder press. With arms up and elbows flexed, raise weight from shoulder level slowly up and down. Exercise one arm at a time. This exercise can be done without weights. *Source:* Copyright © 1990 by Rebecca Chamberlain.

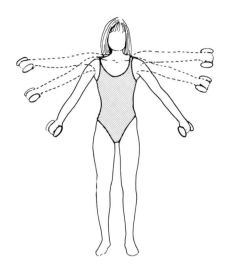

Figure 14-7 Supraspinatus strengthening. With thumbs pointed toward floor and shoulder in forward flexion (to 30°), raise arms to shoulder level, then lower slowly. Repeat. Exercise both arms at same time. This exercise can also be done without weights. *Source:* Copyright © 1990 by Rebecca Chamberlain.

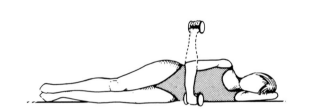

Figure 14-8 External rotation. Lie on left side with elbow flexed to 90°. Raise weight up as high as possible without moving upper arm. Lower slowly and repeat. Repeat on right side. This exercise can also be done without weights. *Source:* Copyright © 1990 by Rebecca Chamberlain.

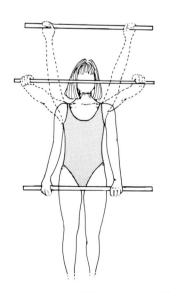

Figure 14-9 Wand exercise. Stand with back straight and feet shoulder-width apart. Hold wand with hands slightly wider than shoulder width. Slowly raise wand up over head. Return slowly to starting position. Relax and repeat. *Source:* Copyright © 1990 by Rebecca Chamberlain.

Figure 14-10 Triceps extension. From standing position, with left arm straight up over head and palm facing in, lower weight backward slowly until it touches back of shoulder. Return to straight-arm position, avoiding forward movement of shoulder. Repeat with right arm. Exercise one arm at a time. *Source:* Copyright © 1990 by Rebecca Chamberlain.

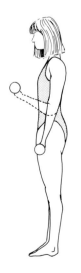

Figure 14-11 Biceps curls. Standing with arm straight, hold weight at side with palm facing forward. Bend elbow and bring weight to shoulder. Keep arm close to side of body. To return to starting position, turn palm down. Exercise one arm at a time. *Source:* Copyright © 1990 by Rebecca Chamberlain.

Figure 14-12 Supination-pronation. Support one arm on table. Hold weight and rotate it from side to side, keeping forearm stationary. Exercise one arm at a time. *Source:* Copyright © 1990 by Rebecca Chamberlain.

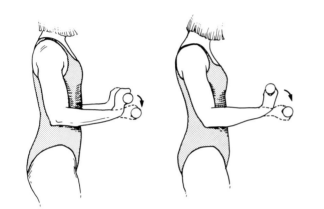

Figure 14-13 Wrist extension-flexion. Hold weight with palm facing down. Raise weight up and down, keeping forearm on table. Exercise one arm at a time. Then hold weight with palm facing up. Raise weight up and down, keeping forearm on table. Exercise one arm at a time. *Source:* Copyright © 1990 by Rebecca Chamberlain.

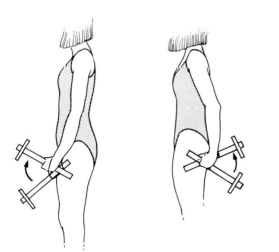

Figure 14-14 Radial wrist flexion and ulnar wrist flexion. In standing position, hold weight in handshake position. Flex wrist to move weight up and down, keeping elbow straight. Exercise one arm at a time. Then hold weight with palm facing back. Flex wrist to move weight up and away from body. Exercise one arm at a time. *Source:* Copyright © 1990 by Rebecca Chamberlain.

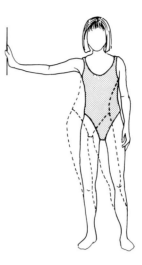

Figure 14-15 Iliotibial band stretch. Stand with right arm stretched to wall. Move right hip toward wall and keep elbow straight. Hold for 5 to 10 seconds. Relax. Repeat on other side. *Source:* Copyright © 1990 by Rebecca Chamberlain.

Figure 14-16 Groin stretch. In sitting position, place soles of feet together. Place elbows inside knees with hands at ankles. Push knees against elbows. Hold for 5 to 10 seconds. Relax. Push knees farther apart and repeat. *Source:* Copyright © 1990 by Rebecca Chamberlain.

Figure 14-17 Hamstring stretch. Lie on floor with hands held behind knees. Straighten knee to point of tightness and hold for 5 to 10 seconds. Relax. Repeat, bringing knee closer toward head. Repeat on other side. *Source:* Copyright © 1990 by Rebecca Chamberlain.

Figure 14-18 Hip flexor stretch. Lie on floor, face down, with one knee flexed. Raise flexed leg off floor until tightness is felt in front of thigh. Hold for 5 to 10 seconds. Return leg to floor, relax, and repeat with other leg. Avoid hyperextension of back. *Source:* Copyright © 1990 by Rebecca Chamberlain.

Figure 14-19 Quadriceps stretch. Lie on floor, face down, with left knee flexed. Hold outside of left ankle with left hand. Try to straighten leg, resisting with hand for 5 to 10 seconds. Relax. Bring knee closer to buttocks and repeat. Repeat with right leg. *Source:* Copyright © 1990 by Rebecca Chamberlain.

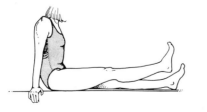

Figure 14-20 Quadriceps set. Sit on floor with knees straight. Pull toes and foot back and tighten quadriceps. Concentrate on inside muscle. Hold for 5 to 10 seconds. Rest for 5 seconds and repeat. *Source:* Copyright © 1990 by Rebecca Chamberlain.

Figure 14-21 Straight leg raise. Sit on floor with knees straight. Pull toes and foot back and tighten quadriceps. Raise leg about 6 in and hold in this position with quadriceps held tight for 5 to 10 seconds. Relax and repeat. Exercise one leg at a time. This exercise can also be done with weights. *Source:* Copyright © 1990 by Rebecca Chamberlain.

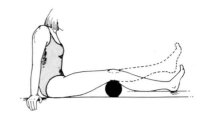

Figure 14-22 Short arc knee extension. Place towel roll under knee. Pull toes back and tighten quadriceps (straighten knee) and hold for 5 to 10 seconds. Lower foot slowly. Relax and repeat. Exercise one leg at a time. This exercise can also be done with weights. *Source:* Copyright © 1990 by Rebecca Chamberlain.

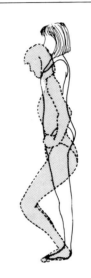

Figure 14-23 Quarter squats. Stand with feet shoulder-width apart and pointed straight ahead. Squat one-fourth of the way down. Return to standing position slowly and repeat. *Source:* Copyright © 1990 by Rebecca Chamberlain.

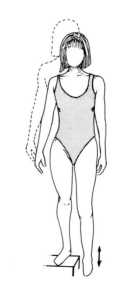

Figure 14-24 Step-ups. Stand next to 6- or 8-in step or stool. Step up with inside foot, then with outside foot. Step down with outside foot, then with inside foot. Relax and repeat. *Source:* Copyright © 1990 by Rebecca Chamberlain.

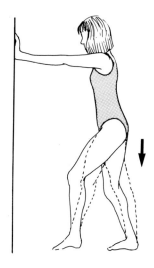

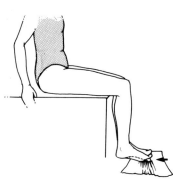

Figure 14-26 Toe flexion and extension. Place feet flat on floor about 8 in apart. Heels and knees should be in straight line. Place towel on floor. Repetitively curl toes, trying to pull towel toward arch of foot. Heels must be kept flat. When towel is completely under arch, push it away from heel by reversing action of toes. Keep heels flat on floor. *Source:* Copyright © 1990 by Rebecca Chamberlain.

Figure 14-25 Calf stretch. In standing position, support hands and body against wall or door. Place one leg behind the other with heel touching floor. Lean slowly forward by bending elbow and front leg until tightness is felt in rear leg. Hold for 10 to 15 seconds. Then bend same rear leg and hold for another 10 to 15 seconds. Alternate with other leg. Avoid bouncing movement. *Source:* Copyright © 1990 by Rebecca Chamberlain.

REFERENCES

1. Knott M, Voss D. *Proprioceptive Neuromuscular Facilitation.* 2nd ed. New York: Harper & Row; 1968.

2. Sullivan PE, Markos PD, Minor MA. *An Integrated Approach to Therapeutic Exercise.* Reston, Va: Reston Publishing Co; 1982.

3. Voss D, Ionta MK, Myers BJ. *Proprioceptive Neuromuscular Facilitation.* Philadelphia: Harper & Row; 1985.

Index